THE CAMBRIDGE HANDBOOK OF SMART CONTRACTS, BLOCKCHAIN TECHNOLOGY AND DIGITAL PLATFORMS

The product of a unique collaboration between academic scholars, legal practitioners and technology experts, this handbook is the first of its kind to analyze the ongoing evolution of smart contracts, based upon blockchain technology, from the perspective of existing legal frameworks – namely, contract law. The book's coverage ranges across many areas of smart contracts and electronic or digital platforms to illuminate the impact of new, and often disruptive, technologies on the law. With a mix of scholarly commentary and practical application, chapter authors provide expert insights into the core issues involving the use of smart contracts, concluding that smart contracts cannot supplant contract law and the courts, but leaving open the question of whether there is a need for specialized regulations to prevent abuse. This work should be read by anyone interested in the disruptive effects of new technologies on the law generally and contract law in particular.

Larry A. DiMatteo is Huber Hurst Professor of Contract Law at the University of Florida. He is the former Editor-in-Chief of the *American Business Law Journal*, a 2012 Fulbright Professor at the University of Sofia, and author or coauthor of 120 publications, including 12 books. His research interests are in the fields of contract law, international sales law, and legal theory.

Michel Cannarsa is Associate Professor and Dean at Lyon Catholic University Faculty of Law. His areas of research are international and European law, commercial law, comparative law, consumer law, law of obligations and legal translation.

Cristina Poncibò is Associate Professor of Comparative Private Law at the Department of Law of the University of Turin (Italy). Her research interests are in the fields of comparative law, comparative contract law, private law and market regulation.

T0381561

The Cambridge Handbook of Smart Contracts, Blockchain Technology and Digital Platforms

Edited by

Larry A. DiMatteo
University of Florida

Michel Cannarsa
Lyon Catholic University

Cristina Poncibò
University of Turin

CAMBRIDGE
UNIVERSITY PRESS

CAMBRIDGE
UNIVERSITY PRESS

Shaftesbury Road, Cambridge CB2 8EA, United Kingdom

One Liberty Plaza, 20th Floor, New York, NY 10006, USA

477 Williamstown Road, Port Melbourne, VIC 3207, Australia

314–321, 3rd Floor, Plot 3, Splendor Forum, Jasola District Centre, New Delhi – 110025, India

103 Penang Road, #05–06/07, Visioncrest Commercial, Singapore 238467

Cambridge University Press is part of Cambridge University Press & Assessment, a department of the University of Cambridge.

We share the University's mission to contribute to society through the pursuit of education, learning and research at the highest international levels of excellence.

www.cambridge.org
Information on this title: www.cambridge.org/9781009293167

DOI: 10.1017/9781108592239

© Cambridge University Press & Assessment 2020

First published 2020
First paperback edition 2023

A catalogue record for this publication is available from the British Library

ISBN   978-1-108-49256-0   Hardback
ISBN   978-1-009-29316-7   Paperback

To my mother, Rose DiMatteo, for her lifetime
of support, love and devotion
LAD

To Marie, Juliette and Alice
MC

To my father
CP

Summary of Contents

Contents

Contributors

Oscar Borgogno is a scholar-in-residence in the Department of Law at the University of Turin, Research Fellow at the University of Tilburg and MSc Candidate at the University of Oxford.

Roger Brownsword is Professor of Law at King's College London.

Michel Cannarsa is an associate professor and Dean of the Faculty of Law at Lyon Catholic University.

Lei Chen is Associate Professor of Law and Associate Dean at City University of Hong Kong.

Marc Clément is a judge on the Lyon Administrative Appeal Court.

Riccardo de Caria is a postdoctoral fellow at the University of Turin.

Claudio Demartini is a professor in the Department of Control and Computer Engineering at Politecnico di Torino, Italy.

Larry A. DiMatteo is the Huber Hurst Professor of Contract Law and Legal Studies at the Warrington College of Business at the University of Florida.

Mateja Durovic is Lecturer in Contract and Commercial Law at Kings College London.

Valentina Gatteschi is an assistant professor in the Department of Control and Computer Engineering at the Politecnico di Torino.

André Janssen is Chair Professor of Private Law at the University of Radboud, Nijmegen.

Fabrizio Lamberti is an associate professor in the Department of Control and Computer Engineering at Politecnico di Torino, Italy.

Mathieu Martin is an attorney of law in Lyon, France.

Eliza Mik is an assistant professor at Singapore University.

Lokke Moerel is Professor of ICT Law at Tilburg University.

Barbara Pasa is Professor of Comparative Private Law and Intellectual Property Law and Policy at the University of IUAV Venice.

Cristina Poncibò is Associate Professor of Comparative Law at the University of Turin.

Lauren Henry Scholz is an assistant professor at Florida State.

Eric Tjong Tjin Tai is Professor of Law at the University of Tilburg.

Piotr Tereszkiewicz is assistant professor of Law at Jagiellonian University.

Louis-Daniel Muka Tshibende is associate professor at Lyon Catholic University.

Sjef van Erp is a professor at Maastricht University.

Diana Wallis is the former president of the European Law Institute.

Angelia Wang is a teaching fellow at the Hong Kong Polytechnic University.

Preface

This book comprises the collected, revised and expanded papers from a conference on the impact of technology (smart contracts and blockchain technology) on contract law, held at the Lyon Catholic University in April 2018. The topics selected for the conference, and hence for the chapters of this book range across the areas of smart contracts and electronic or digital platforms, in order to illuminate the impact of new, often disruptive technologies on contract law. Alternatively, it addresses the issue of whether blockchain technology allows private parties to escape contract law, government regulation and the court system. The overwhelming conclusion of the contributing authors is in the negative. The second-order issue addressed in the book is: Does contract law need to be adjusted to address the contract law topics presented by this unique form of contracting? Furthermore, should governments intervene through new regulations targeted at smart contracts, blockchain technology and online platforms? Again, the consensus opinion is that contract law's flexibility will allow it to be applied to these types of technology or doing business without the need for substantial adjustments in the law. In the area of government intervention, the consensus sees little need to hastily rush to regulate smart contracts and blockchains since this relatively new technology is still in its infancy. However, targeted regulation of online platforms is needed for purposes of addressing data protection, privacy concerns and property rights.

As editors of this book, it has been our pleasure to work with leading contract scholars, practitioners and administrators of law, as well as technologists from a variety of countries from Asia, Australia, Europe and North America. We are in debt to all of the contributors to this volume, from whom we learned and have been enriched in this evolving area of law and technology.

We are also indebted to the Lyon Catholic University, University of Florida and the University of Turin (Torino) for their financial support, especially the Law School at Lyon Catholic University for hosting the conference. Special thanks go to Dean Cannarsa and Frédérique Genin for all their hard work. We have also been ably assisted in our work by the commissioning and editorial staff at Cambridge University Press, who had faith in the value of this project and who have been on hand to advise and help us as the book progressed from idea to finished work. In particular, we are grateful to John Berger, Matt Gallaway and Jackie Grant.

The value of any scholarly work such as the present one lies in the extent to which it advances knowledge in a given field. We trust that the readers of this work will find much to interest them, if not to enlighten, and that it will be of use to scholars in the civil and common law worlds who understand its importance to the advancement of the rule of law and as a modest contribution to the corpus of legal knowledge.

Larry A. DiMatteo, Michel Cannarsa and Cristina Poncibò

Part I

General Framework

Legal and Technological

1 Smart Contracts and Contract Law

Larry A. DiMatteo, Michel Cannarsa, and Cristina Poncibò

1.1 Introduction

Innovation is all pervasive in this day and age.[1] While new business development and innovative entrepreneurship are appreciated and encouraged, policy-makers foster innovation as well. The European Commission has declared: "We need to do much better at turning our research into new and better services and products if we are to remain competitive in the global marketplace and improve the quality of life in Europe."[2] Innovation is seen an economic driver and has led to political efforts to remove rules and regulations that limit or restrain its development. The economic perspective of the role of innovation in economic growth is also embraced at the firm level. As one commentator argues, "not to innovate is to die."[3]

While the concept of innovation originally concerned novelties in the broadest sense of the word – including imitation, invention, creative imagination, and social change – its current use is directed mainly at technological innovation.[4] The complexity of technological innovation poses a great challenge to the law. Catalina Goanta notes that disruption of the law is "a phenomenon through which law becomes decrepit in the face of modernity."[5]

Indeed, law mostly seems to be more reactive than proactive in dealing with fast technological and societal changes.[6] As the rapidity of innovation increases, academics and practitioners are persistently confronted with new technologies that may not align with existing legal frameworks, while governments are trying to address these challenges by determining how to best regulate or not regulate new technologies. In fact, stringent

---

[1] The word "innovation" has several meanings dependent upon context. "The introduction of something new" is the *Merriam-Webster* definition. In business, "innovation" is applying ideas to satisfy the needs and expectations of customers. Uber, Amazon, and Apple are three among numerous innovative companies that have disrupted industries during the past decade. Each has displaced dominant providers by expanding access, making purchasing easier and more transparent, providing customers more choice, reducing cost, and offering a platform for buyers and sellers to evaluate each other.

[2] European Commission, cited from http://ec.europa.eu/research/innovation-union/index_en. cfm?pg=why (last accessed October 15, 2018).

[3] C. Freeman, *The Economics of Industrial Innovation* (Cambridge, MA: MIT Press, 1982).

[4] B. Godin, "'Innovation Studies': The Invention of a Specialty" (2012) 50:4 *Minerva* 397–421. The author documents the origins and the scope of innovation studies.

[5] C. Goanta, "How Technology Disrupts Private Law: An Exploratory Study of California and Switzerland as Innovative Jurisdictions," TTLF Working Papers No. 38, Stanford-Vienna, *Transatlantic Technology Law Forum* (2018) at 1.

[6] See Professor Brownsword, "Smart Transactional Technologies, Legal Disruption, and the Case of Network Contracts," Chapter 17, in this book.

regulation of emerging industries can result in major setbacks for technological development. For this reason, governments often refrain from regulating innovative industries, like applications of blockchain technology, at early stages of development.[7]

Recently, there has been a profusion of articles and reports on blockchain technology. Some commentators argue that it could spark a revolution in many sectors of the economy, just as the Internet had done at an early time. It should be emphasized that the blockchain was developed as the result of a venture driven by libertarian ideas of eliminating the need for intermediaries, such as central banks, courts, and other governmental bodies. Central to this revolution is the idea of "contracting without the state" by entering smart contracts based on blockchain technology. This escape from the law is mere illusion, as law will continue to play a vital role in private transactions. This book provides a focused analysis of the place of blockchain technology, smart contracts, and digital platforms within the realm of contract law, as well as privacy and property law. It is the result of a broader research agenda aimed at exploring the impact of technological innovation on contract law in a comparative perspective.

The idea of smart contracts originated in the mid-1990s, when programmers and legal scholars published a series of papers explaining their potential.[8] Smart contracts are literally computer code that is placed on a blockchain, an open, distributed ledger that runs on the computers of thousands of users, and which has no central authority. "Smart" refers to the self-performing, self-enforcing quality of smart contracts. These so-called contracts are immutable, meaning that the code by default cannot be changed, thusly ensuring performance. However, for programmers, immutability presents a special challenge. Code contains bugs (coding errors), and code that cannot be altered needs to be written carefully to try to minimize the mistakes in the coding, since the bugs cannot be fixed after the fact.

Smart contracts also present a particular challenge to contract law and regulation in general. As automatization entails lack of human involvement, stringent questions relating to the validity of consent and intention to be legally bound arise. The genuineness of consent is also questionable in cases of fraudulent behavior. Moreover, recognizing smart contracts as legal contracts is not simply a policy objective to enable more innovation, but it is a policy objective that requires a lot of self-reflection about the nature and future of contractual relationships and business practice.

Smart contracts represent mechanisms for enforcing promises, allowing us to make credible commitments with each other on a blockchain. The fundamental question becomes whether we can trust the technology and the people using it without the support of the law and the courts. The answer is that law and government authorities will continue to remain relevant because market certainty demands an external mechanism to enforce promises and ensure that people can depend on the commitments of others. In the words of Hobbes, we tend to assume that the government's coercive power is the only way to create contracts.[9] This Hobbesian view has been labeled as "legal centralism," the

---

[7] While there is no precise definition, a regulatory sandbox is, broadly speaking, a framework within which innovators can test business ideas and products on a "live" market, under the relevant regulator's supervision, without fear of enforcement actions in case it is determined that their business model does not comply with existing regulations.

[8] One of the primary pieces is N. Szabo "Formalizing and Securing Relationships on Public Networks" *First Monday* (September 1, 1997), available at https://firstmonday.org/ojs/index.php/fm/article/view/548/469 (accessed January 5, 2018).

[9] T. Hobbes and J. C. A. Gaskin, *Leviathan* (Oxford: Oxford University Press, 1998).

assumption that "the legal system enforces promises in a knowledgeable, sophisticated, and low-cost way."[10] In many instances, the court system is costly and time-consuming. Moreover, people are often surprisingly able to enforce promises and maintain order in their own communities without government intervention.[11]

In this Hobbesian worldview, there is little trust, constant suspicion, and insecurity. In reality, although humans pursue their own self-interests and act opportunistically, most business relationships are heavily dependent on trust. For example, reputation is extremely important in small communities of traders characterized by repeat transactions. Negative reputational effects decrease the ability of a party to continue to transact business within that community.[12] In internet transactions, reputation is more difficult to foster because pseudonyms are often used instead of real names. When a person breaks a promise, she can simply erase her history by creating a new pseudonym with a clean reputation.[13] The power of blockchain technology is that it overcomes the shortage of trust in internet transactions between strangers. It also shows potential in overcoming transborder legal issues relating to applicable law and the ability to pursue a defendant in a foreign jurisdiction.

This book provides a focused analysis of the place of blockchain technology and smart contracts within the realm of contract law. The core questions asked include: (1) Are smart contracts legal contracts or a means to form and perform or enforce contracts? (2) If they are not "real" contracts, should they be regulated by contract law or otherwise? (3) If deemed to be a type of contract, how does contract law apply to this new form of contracting? (4) Can a form of contracting be truly autonomous, self-enforcing, and independent of the legal system? (5) Is general contract law sufficiently adaptable to regulate smart contracts or will specialized rules be needed? These questions are inherently overlapping because of the novelty of smart contracts, which are currently effective due to their narrow functional focus, but there are efforts to expand their applications to more and more types of use. The uncertainty of where the evolution of smart contracts may lead increases the uncertainty of how contract law will adapt to them. Contract law has proved to be sufficiently flexible and malleable in adapting to new technologies and transaction types. In the end, with advances in artificial intelligence (AI), a top-down regulatory framework may be needed. This book takes the initial step in discussing whether smart contracts fit into the existing framework of contract and regulatory law regimes.

The contracting world has entered an exciting period of innovation and research. In the diversity of presentation styles and author backgrounds, we hope this book will inspire

---

[10] O. E. Williamson, *The Mechanisms of Governance* (New York: Oxford University Press, 1996).

[11] For a more elaborate example, consider the New York diamond industry, as described in a classic article by Lisa Bernstein (Bernstein 1992, quoted by DiMatteo and Poncibò, Chapter 7). At one point, somewhat before the time she studied it, the industry had been mostly in the hands of orthodox Jews, forbidden by their religious beliefs from suing each other. They settled disputes instead by a system of trusted arbitrators and reputational sanctions. If one party to a dispute refused to accept the arbitrator's verdict, the information would be rapidly spread through the community, with the result that he would no longer be able to function in that industry.

[12] See Chapter 7, "Smart Contracts: Contractual and Noncontractual Remedies," on "Remedies."

[13] For a discussion of the term "whitewashing," see N. Nisan, T. Roughgarden, É. Tardos, V. V. Vazirani, and C. H. Papadimitriou, *Algorithmic Game Theory* (New York: Cambridge University Press, 2008) at 682. There are various ways to handle the problem of whitewashing. One is to distrust all newcomers, since they may have created a new identity to hide a bad reputation. Another possibility is to ensure that any pseudonym is tied to a real person or business, so that a bad reputation cannot be escaped.

greater understanding and collaboration between scholars and practitioners from different jurisdictions, as well as between the legal and tech communities, in approaching the intersection of law and technology.

1.2 Rush to Judgment: Is Additional Regulation Needed?

People are often enamored with new things; the shining new things today relate to the ever-growing menu of technological devices and services.[14] The new gadgets are often overhyped and their impact overestimated. One needs only to look back at the early stages of the internet age to see a tortured debate between those who believed the internet's freedom would be hindered by regulation and those who believed such innovation was subject to abuse and, thus, needed specialized rules to protect contracting parties. It turned out that both protagonists were correct. In the area of contract law, existing constructs were found to be easily adaptable to internet contracting, as well as long-standing torts such as trespass. However, more recently, the uses of social media as a weapon to breed hatred and misinformation in society suggest that greater regulation of such activities may be in order.

Smart contracts represent a much narrower domain than the creation of the Internet, but such technological innovations cause a great deal of uncertainty and panic, especially when coupled with prognostications about the capabilities of advanced AI in the future. The angst of futuristic surrender to an AI and robotically controlled world, alongside gene-edited humans, warrants caution at this early stage. But the current inquiry into the path to this future world is more of a philosophical inquiry, than the issues being posed by smart contracts and blockchain technology at the present state of development. This book looks at the role of contract law in the regulation of first-generation smart contracts and online platforms (using decentralized ledger technology) to determine if there is a sufficient fit to stave off the need for additional regulation. Max Raskin notes that "Innovative technology [often] does not necessitate innovative jurisprudence, and traditional legal analysis can help craft simple rules as a framework for this complex phenomenon."[15]

1.3 Formalism and Contextualism

There are two dynamics at work in contract law symbolized by the long-standing debate between formalists and contextualists. Formalists see the best form of law as consisting of fixed and hard rules. Contextualists see the best form of law as a blend of fixed rules and standards or open-textured rules. The formalists hope to make certainty and predictability the singular focus of law. The contextualists see the importance of tempering the written word with the context in which that word is used to ensure a degree of fairness or justice. The contextual approach to the interpretation of contracts and the application of contract law rules is considered to be mainstream view. In sum, firm or hard rules are needed to ensure certainty in law, but standards or principles are needed to provide flexibility to

[14] S. Ratcliffe (ed.) "Roy Amara 1925–2007, American Futurologist," *Oxford Essential Quotations* (4th edn. Oxford University Press 2016).
[15] M. Raskin, "Law and Legality of Smart Contracts" (2017) 1 *Georgetown Law Technology Review*. 305, 306, available at https://georgetownlawtechreview.org/wp-content/uploads/2017/05/Raskin-1-GEO.-L.-TECH.-REV.-305-.pdf.

allow rule adjustments in order to avoid injustice caused by the formulaic application of fixed rules.

In the area of contract law, rules pertaining to certain types of contracts are more formalistic in their constitution and application and others less so. In the areas of financial or banking transactions, as well as in letter of credit and secured transactions, fixed rules, with little discretion left to the courts, are dominant since they provide the needed security and trust required to make such transactions functional. However, in general contract and sales law, both certainty and flexibility are needed. In some areas of contract-sales law, such as in the area of contract formation where parties need to be able to rely on the enforceability of their contracts, the formulaic application of fixed offer-acceptance rules is essential. However, in other areas of contract law, such as in performance, breach, and remedies, more open-ended rules that allow context to be considered, such as trade usage and prior dealings, is required to moderate the words of the contract that lead to irrational or unjust outcomes. This is seen in policing doctrines, such as unconscionability and hardship. In remedies, the causal connection between breach and damages is moderated by the need to prove with certainty foreseeable damages and to determine whether the non-breaching party complied with its duty to mitigate.

The formalist-contextualist debate is replicated in the area of contract interpretation. This debate provides an analogy to the usefulness of smart contracts set within the complexity of contracts and contract law. Formalists possess absolute faith in the (potential) clarity in the written word. Their mantra is that freedom of contract dictates that meaning only resides in the four corners of an agreement. For them, real meaning informed by context has no place in the interpretation of contracts. In this world, contracts are pseudo self-enforcing. Despite the debacle of litigation, courts serve a merely perfunctory role of reiterating the plain meaning of the words of the contract. Some formalists have gone as far as to assume that businesspersons prefer the narrow objectivity of plain meaning interpretations of fully actuated written contracts.[16] There is no empirical evidence that this is true – that businesspersons prefer losing based on a formalist interpretation of their contracts when the true meaning of the contract is provable by using contextual evidence. In fact, contracts are never fully actuated or complete; thus, the ability of closing off the real world is limited due to the incompleteness of contracts. The formalist retort is that if a formalist approach to interpretation is accepted, parties will write clearer contracts that are susceptible to formal interpretation. This fails to recognize that such clarity is an illusion in complex contracts, strategic ambiguity provides the needed flexibility in such contracts, and some level of incompleteness will remain due to limited cognitive abilities, use of less than full information, and the prohibitive transaction costs of attempting to negotiate a complete contract.

Contextualists argue that there is no plain or singular meaning of words in that words in a contract can only be understood against the background of the words used. It is tempting to assert that the contextualists seek the intersubjective intent of the parties – what they assumed each other meant by a certain contract provision and not the purely objective interpretation of the plain meaning rule. But, a better understanding is that extrinsic evidence is no less objective than the written contract. The use of negotiations,

---

[16] A. Schwartz and R. Scott, "Contract Theory and the Limits of Contracts" (2003) *Yale Law Journal* 543. ("What contract law do business firms want the state to provide? A contract law for firms, we answer, would be narrower and more deferential to contracting parties than the contract we now have.")

prior dealings, course of performance, and trade usage evidence allows for the best objective interpretation of the meaning of the contract. When done properly it comes close to merging objective with subjective intent.

The importance of context to interpreting a contract or to understanding a contractual relationship varies among contract types and across different industries. Lisa Bernstein's majestic work on the American cotton industry showed that cotton contracts are completely ensconced in context.[17] Application of contract law is preempted by internal customs and dispute resolution structures. The premier remedy between cotton dealers is the nonlegal remedy of negative reputational harm. Under such a contract system, "vagueness and ambiguity likely have far more utility when transactors govern themselves by custom rather than law."[18] In such incidents, contracts separated from context are meaningless and therefore not subject to coding.

1.3.1 *Form and Context: Smart Contract*

The relevancy of the above discussion of the nature of contract law (rules-standards) and the different approaches to contract interpretation (formalism-contextualism) is to assess smart contracts ability to replace word contracts. The scope and recognition of smart contracts as contracts is mostly dependent on the formal nature of a specific type of contract and the contract law rules that apply to that specific type of contract. Thus, it is no surprise that the dawn of the smart contracts era has focused on simplistic payment, financial and transfer of title transactions. These are the most formalized areas of law populated by if-then rules that lend themselves to translation into computer code.[19] However, in more complex, long-term, relational, and ambiguous contract types coding is highly problematic. Such contracts generally allow some degree of party discretion by provisions that are vague and ambiguous. Such vague, standard-like contract provisions are necessary to provide the flexibility to manage such long-term commitments. For example, reopener or renegotiation clauses provide the parties future opportunities to adjust the contract to reflect real-world developments. Current technology is far from being able to convert complex contracts into code. To attempt to do so would be a disaster.

1.4 Enforceability of Smart Contracts

As with earlier internet contracting, is the smart contract simply a means to contract or a contract in and of itself? It may be both. In very simplistic contracts, such as the

---

[17] L. Bernstein, "Private Commercial Law in the Cotton Industry: Creating Cooperation through Rules, Norms, and Institutions" (2001) 99 *Michigan Law Review* 1724.

[18] Jeffery Lipshaw, "The Persistence of 'Dumb' Contracts," (2019) 2 *Stanford Journal of Blockchain Law & Policy*, https://stanford-jblp.pubpub.org/pub/persistence-dumb-contracts.

[19] "Legal automators tend to focus on … formalism (which defines 'the ideal if not necessary form of "law" [as] that of a "rule," conceived as a clear prescription that exists prior to its application and that determines appropriate conduct or legal outcomes')." F. Pasquale, "A Rule of Persons, Not Machines: The Limits of Legal Automation" (2019) 87 *George Washington Law Review* 1, 44, partially quoting Richard H. Fallon, Jr., "The Rule of Law as a Concept in Constitutional Discourse" (1997) 97 *Columbia Law Review* 1, 11 & 14. It should be noted that there are simple rules and more complicated ones and that coding currently is able to accommodate the former and not the latter: "The complicated structure of legal rules may prove an obstacle to formalization." Eric Tjong Tjin Tai, "Formalizing Contract Law for Smart Contracts," Tilburg Private Law Working Paper No. 06/2017, 8, www.ssrn.com/link/Tilburg-Private-Law.html.

execution of a payment for goods delivered or repayment on a loan, the parties can agree on the contract, but instead of going to a lawyer to write the contract they go to automators (lawyer or nonlawyer) to code the agreement. In this case, the coded contract is the equivalent to a written contract. In more complicated agreements, the smart contract is best described as a smart function of the contract.[20] In long-term contracts that include multiple payments over a prolonged period of time, it is unlikely that the paying party will encumber funds far in advance of future payments, thus diluting the self-enforcing nature of the smart contract.

Future AI-connected smart contracts will likely only result in smart contracts serving a supporting role than being an outright replacement of word contracts and the human management of contracts. Frank Pasquale has noted that AI relating to complex contracts is more likely to be reflected as "intelligence augmentation."[21] AI is unlikely to transplant human know-how and intuition, which is at the center of most business transactions. Further, law has been and will always be indeterminate (no single right answer). Law remains somewhere "between the crystalline clarity of rules and the chaos of unconstrained discretion." It is in this middle area that one finds "articulable standards that help us formulate convincing explanations and justifications of legal decisionmaking."[22] Contract law is inherently flexible in nature, which is its defining virtue and vice. Flexibility is open to various interpretations and applications, but it is also the genesis for innovation (creation of new types of contracts, methods of doing business, and so forth).

1.5 "Dumb, Smart Contracts" to "Smart, Smart Contracts": Issues of Completeness and Normativity

It is important to distinguish between different types of smart contracts. As some commentators have stated, smart contracts are actually "dumb contracts."[23] They are dumb because they are, at this point, only able to perform simplistic types of contracts involving financial transactions, such as transferring money or title to property. They are also dumb because of their lack of flexibility. Flexibility built into contracts through terms that are vague or standard-like, such as a duty to renegotiate due to a change of circumstances, cannot be replicated in code. The beauty of contract law is found in its malleability to respond to innovative contract types and still serve its facilitation and regulatory functions.

In the near future, the expanded use of smart contracts, beyond the simplest forms of transactions, is likely to come by way of the use of oracles and as part of or ancillary to

---

[20] Although, in long-term contracts, one commentator has noted that even the payment function may not be self-enforcing: "If the party owing amounts under the smart contract fails to fund the wallet on a timely basis, a smart contract looking to transfer money from that wallet upon a trigger event may find that the requisite funds are not available." S. Levi and A. Lipton, "An Introduction to Smart Contracts and Their Potential and Inherent Limitations" (May 26, 2018), https://corpgov.law.harvard.edu/2018/05/26/an-introduction-to-smart-contracts-and-their-potential-and-inherent-limitations (last accessed June 22, 2018).

[21] Note 19 above; Pasquale at 51.

[22] *Ibid.* at 56.

[23] Lipshaw, See note 18 above, *Stanford Journal of Blockchain Law & Policy*, 2019 (forthcoming), https://papers.ssrn.com/sol3/papers.cfm?abstract_id=3202484. https://papers.ssrn.com/sol3/papers.cfm?abstract_id=3202484 (last accessed November 18, 2018); K. Levy, "Book-Smart, Not Street-Smart: Blockchain-Based Smart Contracts and The Social Workings of Law" (2017) 3 *Engaging Science, Technology, and Society* 1.

word contracts. The simplest approach is to have specified oracles as definitive "sources of truth," though this may only be suitable for certain scenarios, such as the use of a market's official stock prices feed. Another approach is to have a number of oracles whereby the data are validated by consensus between them.

This book concludes that smart contracts are a means to the formation of a contract found in computer code. But, like other contracts, the courts are free to imply terms into the contract, such as the duty of good faith, and to void or adjust such contracts under policing doctrines such as duress, misrepresentation, mistake, unconscionability, and hardship. Additionally, courts and arbitral tribunals will continue to look at context outside of the computer code in the interpretation of smart contracts. Trade usage and business customs will continue to play a role in the interpretation and enforcement of smart contracts. The legal arbiters will also recognize changes in circumstances occurring subsequent to contract formation and not embedded in the computer code. The issue here is that if smart contracts are fully self-performing, then there cannot be a breach for which to apply the hardship principle or excuse doctrines. In response to automated performance, the courts may use hardship and excuse offensively to allow one of the parties to claw back certain unexpected costs incurred or profits bestowed on the other party (disgorgement or restitution damages). However, this response is more likely to occur in civil law rather than common law systems because the common law does not recognize hardship and the duty of good faith in some common law countries (England and Wales) is not an accepted principle. If the smart contract were of a longer-term nature involving multiple performances, the best way to adjust or terminate it would be through injunction. How a temporary restraining order or preliminary injunction would be enforced needs to be answered by the technologists.

From a descriptive perspective, smart contracts may or may not be enforceable legal contracts. This poses the normative question of whether they should or should not be recognized as legal contracts. One scholar has asserted: "A system of smart contracts is normatively suspect."[24] The answer, as with other types of contracts, is much more granulated than a yes or a no proposition. Smart contracts may meet the elements of a fully enforceable contract and others may not. As noted previously, a similar debate happened a few decades ago during the advent of internet contracting. First, there was the debate over whether the Internet should be unregulated or regulated. Second, should internet contracts be recognized as legally enforceable contracts? After much haranguing, it became clear that very little regulation, at least in the area of contract formation, or changes in contract law were needed. The Internet and other forms of electronic communications provided more efficient means to form contracts and the existing rules of contract law were easily applicable. The core changes that needed to be made related to contract formalities. Thus, national laws were amended to recognize electronic records as equivalent to written instruments and attribution replaced the need for a physical signature in countries with writing or statute of fraud requirements.[25] In the end, the creation of specialized contracts rules for internet contracts were deemed to be unnecessary; the old rules fit just fine!

---

[24] M. Verstraete, "The Stakes of Smart Contracts'" Ariz. Legal Studies Paper No. 18–20 (May 2018), https://ssrn.com/abstract=3178393, 6.

[25] See the U.S. Uniform Electronic Transactions Act (UETA), http://uniformlaws.org/Act.aspx?title=Electronic%20Transactions%20Act.

In the end, the efficiency of smart contracts is an illusion since their self-sufficiency requires the ability to code complete contracts. Since the ability of contracts to reach completeness is hampered by cognitive limitations, lack of full information, and the fact that information is often asymmetrically distributed between the parties, the ability of the parties to reach a complete contract is impossible as well as being cost prohibitive. Mark Verstraete describes the problem of incompleteness for smart contracts:

> Pure formalism and smart contracts both hinge their normative desirability on the belief that forming complete agreements is practicable. Empirically, this is not the case. Contracts are incomplete and the legal system provides implied terms to remedy this problem. In short, the costs of forming complete agreements would likely outweigh the supposed benefits from smart contracts.[26]

In sum, coding agreements to create smart contracts do not make them any less incomplete than language contracts. Furthermore, the self-performing nature of smart contracts becomes problematic due to the incompleteness of the contract, at least at the current stage of technological development.

1.6 Coverage

Advances in technology continue to transform the nature of international contracting. Inherently, changes in contracting practice pose questions for contract law and its application. Smart contracts, based on distributed ledger or blockchain technology, have been touted as able to convert law (contracts) into self-executing computer code, and, thus, these contracts can function outside of contract law and the court system. This book's broad view of the subject suggests otherwise. In fact, smarts contracts are not truly enforceable without contract law. The smartness of a contract may make it initially self-performing, but it is ultimately left to the courts to determine whether that performance should stand. The interesting challenge of smart contracts to contract law is that subsequent litigation or arbitration will be undertaken after performance and may not be based on a breach. Maybe contract law, just as it did in creating the principle of anticipatory repudiation or breach to proactively anticipate breach, will need to develop rules to retroactively deal with technically conforming performance. This type of structure is already in place through the retroactive nature of contract interpretation and through the application of contracts law's policing doctrines – duress or coercion, mistake, misrepresentation, and unconscionability or hardship. The book discusses the many related issues pertaining to smart contracts and legal regulation of this new phenomenon.

1.6.1 *Law and Technology*

The first part of the book provides a "General Framework: Legal and Technological," which discusses the legal meaning of smart contracts and the technology behind the evolution of smart contracting.[27] Dr. Riccardo de Caria describes a "smart contract" as a digital agreement written (or guided) by computer code, run on a blockchain or similar

---

[26] Verstraete at 42.
[27] This chapter review is partially based on the Conference Report written by and published in the ERPL, L. Tissaoui, J. Liu, and D. Marcotte Q. C. (2018) *European Review of Private Law* (ERPL).

distributed ledgers (decentralized), and automatically executed (or performed) without the need for an intermediary or human intervention. He concludes that there is no need to recognize smart contracts as a different type of contract in need of specialized rules. In sum, the smart contract is a technological development, not a legal one. Therefore, the existing general laws of contracts and sales law are applicable to them in the same way they apply to other types of contracts. In Chapter 3, "Technology of Smart Contracts," a number of technology and computer engineering experts provide a descriptive review of distributed ledger or technology using the blockchain, including an explanation of relevant technological terms such as "nodes," "mining," "wallets," "blocks," and "oracles," which provide the needed background to gain a basic understanding of smart contracts.[28]

1.6.2 *Smart Contracts and Contract Law*

The second part of the book, "Contract Law and Smart Contracts," examines the application of contract law to smart contracts. Mateja Durovic and André Janssen examine the rules of contract formation or conclusion of contract as they relate to smart contracts. They describe the process in which computer code is capable of monitoring, executing, and enforcing a legal agreement. Smart contracts can be seen as a vehicle for automating and enforcing legal rights. They examine the compatibility of smart contracts with existing contract law distinguishing purely self-enforcing smart contracts from the notional complete smart contracts. For the purely self-enforcing smart contract (where only the performance is smart), most issues would be governed by existing contract law. However, the application of certain areas of contract law, such as mistake, duress, or incapacity, will prove problematic. For example, there is a problem when a court voids a smart contract, but the performance of the contract, such as transferring of title, remains in existence on the blockchain due to its immutability.

Eric Tjong Tjin Tai further discusses the problematic relationship between smart contracts and certain areas of contract law, namely performance, force majeure, and excuse. He explains that the nature of the application of contract law rules will need to be adapted since the automated, self-performing nature of smart contracts shifts perspective from ex post assessment to ex ante programming. He emphasizes that memorialized contracts, whether in language or coded form, are greater than the written or coded form. In order to provide contextual support, contracts should not standalone; instead, it is best if they are situated within a larger contractual framework or agreement. Noting that, in the context of the law of excuse, causality (or at least attributability) is always contextual, Professor Tai stresses the complications and challenges that contract law application in these areas will present. In sum, some contract law rules will need to be adjusted because of the characteristics of smart contracts. The end result will likely include adjustments to how certain contract law rules are applied and the evolution of best practices in smart contracting to either provide greater insularity from contract law or make smart contracts more easily receptive to contract law's regularity function. In order to prevent injustices in performance, smart contracts will need to be made smarter, such as creating greater reliance on expert oracles in order to deal with change of circumstances. One rationale

---

[28] For example, the writers of Chapter 3 of this book work in the areas of computer engineering and technology.

for the recognition of smart contracts as contracts is that the contracting parties are willing to accept limited injustices for the security of performance. This is similar to the Scott-Schwartz thesis[29] that businesspersons prefer a formalistic approach to contract law where contextual evidence is excluded despite its probative value in showing the parties' real intent or meaning. However, they do not provide any evidence that shows that businesspersons abhor contextual interpretation. Does a businessperson really prefer to lose a dispute due to the literal meaning of a contract, instead of the intended meaning? This will also be the case for smart contract enforcement and interpretation.

Michel Cannarsa takes up the issue of "Contract Interpretation" in the context of smart contracts. Dr. Cannarsa refers to smart contracts as agreements based on code, able to enforce and execute themselves with no need for intermediaries or for reliance on trust, and well suited to machine-to-machine connections in the "internet of things." Because computer language is more reliable (assuming no errors or omissions in the code) than human language (which can be merely an expression of intent), interpretation can perhaps be easier, more systematic, and devoid of such presumptions as good faith. Dr. Cannarsa posited that smart contracts could conceivably contain interpretative rules coded within the smart contract that would leave less room for interpretative disputes.

Larry A. DiMatteo and Cristina Poncibò question whether smart contracts can be included within the traditional definition of contracts and its remedial structure given the limits of self-enforceability, the practical differences between self-enforcement, and traditionally conceived contract remedies due to their possible use of self-help remedies, and the immutability of coded contracts. Even though traditional contract remedies are (and will be) hard to apply to smart contracts, from a technological perspective and given that the blockchain is an ideologically driven technology committed to decentralization, traditional remedies may not be applicable. Instead, techno-legal measures are likely to fill the remedial gap. Remedies could be coded within the blockchain, and may include: community-based social repudiation and the use of consensus or voting as a means of dispute resolution.

1.6.3 *Electronic Platforms and Smart Contracts*

Piotr Tereszkiewicz discusses the economic notion of electronic platforms – describing them as two or more groups that need each other but which cannot capture the value of their mutual attraction on their own. He discusses the European Union's regulatory framework (E-Commerce Directive 2000/31 as an example) surrounding electronic platforms, a legal landscape that facilitates the commercial exchange and allows the operators to create, manage, regulate, and supervise the community through the Internet. The 2000/31 Directive qualifies a digital platform as a service provider, and the 2016 Discussion Draft on Online Intermediary Platforms deals with obligations and liabilities of intermediaries. Dr. Tereszkiewicz divides current regulation into two different approaches: general and sector specific. On the one hand, general provisions on platform liability are found in the Discussion Draft on Digital Platforms. On the other hand, sector-specific provisions that densely regulate platform-based business

---

[29] See Schwartz and Scott in note 16.

models are exemplified in the new EU Package Travel Directive. He concludes that sector-specific regulation ("a subject-matter approach"), guided by prior recognition of market failures, is a preferable approach for the immediate future.

Eliza Mik focuses on blockchain technology as an ideology with proponents viewing it as anarchical and "above the law." She poses the question of whether the technology will adapt to commercial needs or vice versa. She observes that there is a duality in blockchain technology – on the one hand, there is permissionless blockchain "public ledgers," which are open to everyone and, on the other, there are permissioned blockchain "private ledgers" with restricted access. Some attributes of a predefined processing transaction or unrestricted public blockchain are that ledgers are open, transparent, and visible. The downside is that privacy is not assured, and the required decentralization and resultant immutability means that no one is in control, responsible, or liable, and therefore, governance is difficult. By contrast, private blockchains, which are less ideologically oriented, can be designed for specific (usually commercial) purposes. The ledger becomes only as immutable and as confidential or transparent as its design allows.

Mik further discusses the shortcomings of public blockchains to illustrate that certain technological features that seem attractive from an ideological perspective may be detrimental to commercial transactions. She concludes that public blockchains and smart contracts have limited suitability for the needs of commerce and emphasizes that marketplaces, whether centralized or not, cannot rely on technology alone but require a solid, legal infrastructure that regulates their functioning. She expands the analysis to include the suitability of electronic platforms as contract substitutes. She asserts that there is more hope for the expanded use of platforms if they are secure, resilient, and adaptable – capable of continually and swiftly accommodating legal requirements.

1.6.4 *Smart Contracts as Legally Disruptive*

Roger Brownsword discusses how technology is disruptive to existing legal rules and the need for a balanced response to such disruption. He describes three approaches to the creation of rules to achieve a desired effect: coherent, regulatory, and technocratic. He suggests that a technocratic approach would more appropriately achieve a desired effect by the way technology is conceived and designed, not by the imposition of external rules (for example, through online specified conditions and terms). In this elegant chapter, Brownsword takes a broad "from the balcony" perspective of the relationship of technology and law as a general matter. He discusses the disruptive impact that technology has had on the traditional role of law – "the idea of law (and regulation) as an enterprise of rules (and standard setting)." New technologies challenge law's regulatory function involving the setting of rules – both facilitative and restrictive.

Brownsword asserts that lawyers, judges, and regulators will need to take a more technocratic approach to the regulation of new technologies – one that looks to the regulation of product design and the automation of processes. In short, law will need to achieve regulatory effects (such as protection of privacy) by requiring that the application of technology incorporate protections ex ante. He sees a future debate centering on the traditionalists seeking to maintain the coherency of legal doctrine and regulators seeking to co-opt new technologies as regulatory instruments. Thus, purity and coherency of law will often conflict with the eschewing of legal coherency in favor of the instrumental use of technological tools to prevent the abuse of technology by one party in relationship to another.

1.6.5 Technology in China

Angelia Wang and Lei Chen note that the blockchain and smart contracts are widely used in China in the areas of finance, banking, and industries within both the public and private sectors. This chapter acts as a case study of technology and law in one of the most important economies in the world. They provide examples in the form of copyright registration and the tracking of trademark usage. Wang and Chen highlight the challenges to smart contract implementation: understandability, rigidity of code, and rigidity by decentralization. They propose that the legal framework surrounding the technology should focus on monitoring rather than regulation – "the answer to the machine is in the machine."

They further examine the role of online intermediaries and assess the regulatory framework for the online platforms. They argue that despite the claim that intermediaries will be eliminated due to the decentralized architecture and the trustless relationship enabled by blockchain technologies, intermediaries will still exist and continue to play an important role socially and legally. In sum, Wang and Chen conclude that existing contract and regulatory law is sufficient to police smart contracts, but adjustments need to be made to the regulatory framework on platforms to deter platforms' rent-seeking behaviors by overlooking signals of infringements while ensuring that the regulation is not too excessive to stifle innovation.

1.6.6 Blockchain Technology: Privacy, Security, and Data Protection Issues

Lokke Moerel explores the issue of legal jurisdiction given that members of a blockchain are scattered throughout the world. She poses that if each node is considered a data controller, then they all must comply with the privacy protections required by the General Data Protection Regulation (GDPR). The alternative is to treat nodes simply as data subjects. This duality of controller-subject presents a dilemma for purposes of regulation. Sjef van Erp questions whether private law principles and concepts are adaptable to a digital environment or whether we need updated private law concepts or even a new type of private law. Louis-Daniel Muka Tshibende posits that the expression "smart contract" merely designates a corpus of automated modalities for the conclusion, performance, and termination of preexisting categories of contracts. Lauren Henry Scholz distinguishes algorithmic contracts from smart contracts. She asserts that algorithmic contracts present little problems for contract law, especially in business-to-business transactions. Scholz notes, however, that consumer privacy has not been protected under traditional contract law, and therefore, in the area of algorithmic contracts, the law needs to recognize nondisclaimable privacy rights.

Moerel discusses the unfitness of distributed ledger technology (DLT) for protecting personal data relative to the European Union's GDPR, which is designed and focused on the processor of data, who is required to ensure that data processing is set up to ensure that privacy requirements are met. DLT decentralizes data but it is not a data controller.

Lacking a better alternative, all nodes should be treated as controllers; independent from one another or that none of them are controllers (no-controller ecosystem). Considering all nodes are controllers implies the application of different national laws because the nodes are scattered around the world.

Alternatively, nodes could be considered as data subjects instead of data controllers, or as both? But then, is it possible for the nodes (as controllers) to control themselves (as subjects), and then how would we protect data subjects from themselves? A double-bind problem will arise, known as the Collingridge dilemma. When the technology erupts, the need for change is not apparent, whereas when the need for change does become apparent, the capabilities for it become limited by the complexity of the technology. It implies that if we don't know how to regulate, we should impose measures on companies to self-regulate until best practices are sorted out.

Van Erp notes that human beings "live in a world in which other people perceive us on the basis of the data thus assembled about us" and "because of this humans are in the process of losing their personhood and are becoming subjects of data instead of data subjects." The law needs to respond to this new digital reality – a hybrid world of the physical and data-based dimensions. Van Erp suggests that the law needs to reframe traditional property law and create a data property law system that transcends national legal regimes. He concludes that a differentiated property law approach will be required in today's digital reality.

Muka Tshibende focuses on the field of blockchain technologies and considers its impact on property and security rights. Law will need to focus on the interface between the virtual and transnational dimensions of transactions on the blockchain . He takes the perspective of a continental lawyer analyzing the validity of transactions – the validity and integrity of property title electronically created and transferred. In doing so, he relies not only on traditional legal tools but also on the most recent legislative initiatives, especially in France. He introduces a legal framework encompassing new ways of transferring property (based on blockchain technologies) and new types of titles (tokens in the context of initial coin offerings). Through this analysis, the core issue becomes whether these new transactions and these new property titles can be effective, in a national and an international context. Muka Tshibende raises concerns about the legal uncertainty and the best (local and global) regulatory responses to these technological challenges.

Scholz argues that algorithms should be understood as contractual agents, analogically to the lawyers working for a company. Her argument is permissive in that algorithms should not be perceived as contracts in and of themselves. It is important, she stresses, to preserve the term "contract" for legally enforceable matters. As long as the algorithm is a legally compliant agent, the algorithm should be enforceable as an "algorithm contract," with a self-enforcing feature. However, privacy concerns create a problematic definitional situation in consumer transactions. Even if we use specific elements (for example, social security numbers) to limit private data uses, the system will often still allow the collection of other data (metadata). She notes that remedial policy approaches differ. France and the United Kingdom have put in place privacy compliance checklists, whereas Germany put in place adopted general provisions to be followed by companies. If companies are given a checklist, they will try to check off the policing costs for themselves. When presented with general objectives, they will try to look into what they are doing and will seek to internalize the compliance processes. The later has the most promise as a regulatory approach.

1.6.7 Smart Contracts: Courts, Lawyers, and Consumers

Judge Marc Clément of the Lyon Administrative Appeals Court notes that an automatically self-performing smart contract can truly exist in a pure virtual world but becomes more complex when connecting to the real world – necessitating interfaces between the software and reality. This interface starts with "oracles" providing real-world parameters for coded self-performance and extending to other links to ensure contract content validation, contract legality, lawfulness of contract purpose, and measurement of contract results. This complexity will have two significant results. The first is more, not less, work for lawyers and judges. The second will be an enhanced reliance on burden of proof, enhanced advantage to party expertise, and an enhanced significance for party asymmetry. Judge Clément stresses the need for more "experimental law" within law schools using moot court cases to connect legal research to concrete cases.

Mathieu Martin, a practicing attorney discusses practical and ethical issues facing legal practitioners when confronting smart contracts. The issues addressed include the following: (1) How can one advise on a smart contract unless one is conversant with the underlying code? (2) How can code be created that can discern degrees of reasonableness? (3) Does the creation of smart contract templates render legal advice less important? Martin concludes that it is difficult to qualify smart contracts as legal contracts. Instead, they should be viewed as a tool and not as a replacement for language contracts. Nonetheless, smart contracts present opportunities for the lawyer in terms of contract solutions, where simplicity of management and self-enforceability are highly valued.

Oscar Borgogno notes that the tech community portrays smart contracts as infallible software able to carry out the entire contract cycle, from formation to enforcement. His chapter focuses on the potential areas, which could effectively benefit from smart contracts implementation. It argues that smart contracts can be a useable tool to effectively counteract consumers' inertia in triggering and enforcing their rights, which are standardized and easily verifiable. Smart contracts also have the potential to foster commercial relationships by lowering transaction costs arising from lack of trust. Thus, smart contracts are likely to provide better alternatives to traditional tools of business practice, such as letters of credit and escrow agreements. Lastly, the chapter notes that businesses already have commercial incentives to implement smart contracts. However, when it comes to consumer protection, regulators must take the lead by testing, through regulatory sandboxes, the potential of smart contracts for protecting consumer rights.

1.6.8 Observations and Visions of Technology and the Law: Smart Contracts, Blockchain, and Artificial Intelligence

Diana Wallis asserts that self-driving law, law informed by big data, and predictive technology can be seen as a flight from law and democracy. She emphasizes the importance of legislatures as guardians of law and democracy, of serving their oversight function in the face of rapid technological change. Advancement in technology has many positive effects (greater legal certainty, more precision and consistency, and more transparent and impartial decision-making), but it is the task of governments to monitor and regulate its negative ramifications. These negative effects include undercutting of party autonomy, moral atrophy, law as command rather than counsel, and the disappearance of the appearance of justice. In the end, the pure efficiency of technological advancement may prevent a normative assessment of its propriety.

1.7 Conclusion

It is important to note that the research in this book represents a moment in time. The interface between blockchain technologies and their future applications, as well as variations, continues to evolve at a rapid pace. Therefore, the interface between this technology and contract law, as well as government regulation, is fluid. This fluidity cautions against too quick of a response in adjusting contract law or enacting new regulations. However, given the tremendous economic potential of these new technologies or methods of doing business, regulators may feel compelled to intervene prematurely with new regulations. This would be a mistake unless certain types of abuses become evident. It is likely that the popularity of the notion of smart contracts means that blockchain technology is at an early phase of a hype cycle famously captured in Amara's law – "we tend to overestimate the effect of a technology in the short run and underestimate the effect in the long run."[30] This book attempts to make a first effort of presenting a detailed analysis of smart contracts not as a general phenomenon but in the light of the different faces of contract law and regulation in general.

---

[30] See note 14.

2 Definitions of Smart Contracts

Between Law and Code

Riccardo de Caria

2.1 Introduction: Definitions

Chapter 2 investigates the legal dimension of smart contracts.[1] It tries to examine to what extent this potentially breakthrough technology also implies a legal revolution: do smart contracts require new legal avenues to be developed, or is it instead appropriate to simply adapt existing legal categories to the new reality? In either case, how are and should they be regulated?

Before starting the actual analysis, though, I believe it is necessary to devote some space to defining the most relevant notions used in this work, i.e. blockchain and (decentralized) smart contracts. In fact, we can derive proper and (hopefully) sound legal consequences only from clear definitions.

Precision in these definitions is important, since it will inevitably have consequences for the legal analysis of smart contracts; at the same time, a definition that is too narrow would inevitably be inadequate for such a fast-moving field. Therefore, it is necessary to give a precise but elastic definition, one that can adapt to the next evolution of these technologies. I will now outline the relevant definitions, and then move on to outline the current legal framework (Section 2. 2), describe some relevant practical issues (Section 2.3), identify the main legal questions raised by the subject (Section 2.4), and offer some conclusive remarks (Section 2.5).

2.1.1 *Blockchain*

For the above reasons, it appears necessary to dedicate some words to defining blockchain[2] and distributed ledger technology (DLT) in general.[3] An arguably

---

[1] Parts of Chapter 2 have been published as articles in: R. de Caria, "A Digital Revolution in International Trade? The International Legal Framework for Blockchain Technologies, Virtual Currencies and Smart Contracts: Challenges and Opportunities," in VV.AA. "Modernizing International Trade Law to Support Innovation and Sustainable Development," Proceedings of the Congress of the United Nations Commission on International Trade Law, Vienna, 4–6 July 2017, Volume 4: "Papers presented at the Congress," United Nations, Vienna, 2017, p. 105, available at www.uncitral.org/pdf/english/congress/17–06783_ebook.pdf; and in R. de Caria, "Defining Smart Contracts: The Search for Workable Legal Categories," Oxford Business Law Blog, available at www.law.ox.ac.uk/business-law-blog/blog/2018/05/law-and-autonomous-systems-series-defining-smart-contracts-search; and in R. de Caria, "The Legal Meaning of Smart Contracts" (2018) 26 *ERPL*, 731. The title of the present book chapter contains a clear reference to the seminal work by L. Lessig, *Code and Other Laws of Cyberspace* (New York: Basic Books, New York, 1999).

[2] On the topic, one of the most important and recent works arguably is A. De Filippi & P. Wright, *Blockchain and the Law: The Rule of Code* (Cambridge, MA: Harvard University Press, 2018).

[3] A brief note on terminology is needed here: the terms "blockchain" (or block chain) and "distributed or shared ledger technology" are often used interchangeably.

appropriate definition, provided by the European Central Bank (ECB), describes the blockchain as "the ledger (book of records) of all transactions, grouped in blocks, made with a (decentralised) virtual currency scheme."[4]

According to an act recently passed in the State of Arizona, a blockchain is a "distributed ledger technology that uses a distributed, decentralized, shared and replicated ledger, which may be public or private, permissioned or permissionless, or driven by tokenized crypto economics or tokenless. The data on the ledger is protected with cryptography, is immutable and auditable and provides an uncensored truth."[5] The State of Vermont defined blockchain as "a mathematically secured, chronological, and decentralized consensus ledger or database, whether maintained via Internet interaction, peer-to-peer network, or otherwise."[6] The Malta Digital Innovation Authority Act, 2018, defined distributed ledger technology (or decentralized ledger technology; "DLT") as "a database system in which information is recorded, consensually shared, and synchronised across a network of multiple nodes, or any variations thereof."[7]

More generally, most virtual currencies are usually (and Bitcoin is the first example) based on the DLT,[8] i.e. a technology that, through computing and cryptography, has made it possible to keep and validate multiple copies of the same ledger (a sort of distributed database) across an IT network. Each ledger keeps a copy of the digital database of all the transactions that have ever occurred (a transactions record), which is formed by a number of blocks of encrypted electronic records, linked together and disseminated through a dense IT peer-to-peer network.

Anyone can check the database, but no one is able to modify it; thus, "this technology, in principle, enables a decentralised, rapid, resilient and rather secure means of recording any sort of transaction together with the history of previous transactions in a 'distributed ledger'." This scheme, which originated with Bitcoin[9] and is commonly known as "blockchain technology," is often based on open-source software, which is publicly available.

To sum up, "a block chain is a type of database that takes a number of records and puts them in a block (rather like collating them on to a single sheet of paper). Each block is then 'chained' to the next block, using a cryptographic signature. This allows block chains to be used like a ledger, which can be shared and corroborated by anyone with the appropriate permissions."[10]

[4] European Central Bank (ECB), "Virtual Currency Schemes – A Further Analysis," February 2015, at 33. Available at www.ecb.europa.eu/pub/pdf/other/virtualcurrencyschemesen.pdf (last accessed 28 November 2018).
[5] Arizona House, Bill No. 2417, available at www.azleg.gov/legtext/53leg/1R/laws/0097.htm and https://legiscan.com/AZ/text/HB2417/2017.
[6] Section I.1. 12 V.S.A. § 1913. Available at https://legislature.vermont.gov/assets/Documents/2016/Docs/ACTS/ACT157/ACT157%20As%20Enacted.pdf.
[7] The Malta Digital Innovation Authority Act, 2018, is available at http://justiceservices.gov.mt/DownloadDocument.aspx?app=lp&itemid=29080&l=1.
[8] Bank for International Settlements (BIS), "CPMI Report on Digital Currencies," November 2015, 5ff.; available at www.bis.org/cpmi/publ/d137.pdf.
[9] S. Nakamoto, "Bitcoin: A Peer-to-Peer Electronic Cash System" (2008). Available at https://bitcoin.org/bitcoin.pdf (last accessed 28 November 2018).
[10] UK Government Chief Scientific Adviser, "Distributed Ledger Technology: Beyond Block Chain," 2016, 17, at https://assets.publishing.service.gov.uk/government/uploads/system/uploads/attachment_data/file/492972/gs-16-1-distributed-ledger-technology.pdf (last accessed 28 November 2018).

The importance of blockchain technologies has also been noted by the International Monetary Fund (IMF), which, recognizing the possible benefits of virtual currencies (i.e. increasing speed and efficiency in making payments and transfers), stated: "the distributed ledger technology underlying some VC schemes offers benefits that go well beyond VCs themselves."[11] Therefore, if blockchain technology is applied to smart contracts, not only would they be self-executing and self-enforcing, without any need for intermediaries, but, in addition, every transaction would be automatically recorded in the distributed database. Thus, blockchain-based smart contracts[12] may be referred to as "decentralized smart contracts," given the absence of a central database/register.[13]

2.1.2 *(Decentralized) Smart Contracts*

The first thing to point out is that there is not a single and universal definition of smart contracts: as has been observed, "a search of the term smart contract uncovers a myriad of definitions,"[14] "a consensus definition [. . .] for smart contracts has yet to be reached,"[15] and "a generally accepted definition of smart contracts does not exist."[16]

And that is not because the term is new. In fact, already more than twenty years ago, Szabo famously defined smart contracts as "a computerized protocol that executes the terms of

---

[11] International Monetary Fund (IMF), "Virtual Currencies and Beyond: Initial considerations," 20 January 2016, 35, at www.imf.org/en/Publications/Staff-Discussion-Notes/Issues/2016/12/31/Virtual-Currencies-and-Beyond-Initial-Considerations-43618 (last accessed 28 November 2018).

[12] It is worth pointing out that the notion of "smart contracts" could encompass any automatically executed machine-based agreement (such as purchasing a snack from a vending machine), whereas blockchain-based smart contracts are a much narrower notion (some analogies between the two might still be usefully applied, as will be pointed out in Part 4.).

[13] M. L. Perugini & P. Dal Checco, "Smart Contracts: A Preliminary Evaluation," December 2015. Available at: https://ssrn.com/abstract=2729548; M. Raskin, "The Law and Legality of Smart Contracts," (2017) 1 *Geo. L. Tech. Rev.*, 304; A. Savelyev, "Contract Law 2.0: 'Smart' Contracts As the Beginning of the End of Classic Contract Law," Higher School of Economics Research Paper No. WP BRP 71/LAW/2016, 2016 and (2017) 26: 2 *Information & Communications Technology Law*, 116–134; L. H. Scholz, "Algorithmic Contracts," (2017) *Stan. Tech. L. Rev.* 128; J. Szczerbowski, "Place of Smart Contracts in Civil Law. A Few Comments on Form and Interpretation," Proceedings of the 12th Annual International Scientific Conference New Trends, 2017. Available at SSRN: https://ssrn.com/abstract=3095933; G. Jaccard, "Smart Contracts and the Role of Law" (10 January 2018). Available at SSRN: https://ssrn.com/abstract=3099885 or http://dx.doi.org/10.2139/ssrn.3099885; E. Tjong Tjin Tai, "Formalizing Contract Law for Smart Contracts" Tilburg Private Law Working Paper Series No. 6/2017 (18 September 2017). Available at SSRN: https://ssrn.com/abstract=3038800 or http://dx.doi.org/10.2139/ssrn.3038800; P. Catchlove, "Smart Contracts: A New Era of Contract Use" (1 December 2017). Available at SSRN: https://ssrn.com/abstract=3090226 or http://dx.doi.org/10.2139/ssrn.3090226; R. O'Shields, "Smart Contracts: Legal Agreements for the Blockchain," (2017) 21 N.C. *Banking Inst.* 177; L. Cong & Z. He, "Blockchain Disruption and Smart Contracts" (10 January 2018). Available at SSRN: https://ssrn.com/abstract=2985764 or http://dx.doi.org/10.2139/ssrn.2985764; T. Hingley, "A Smart New World: Blockchain and Smart Contracts," available at www.freshfields.com/en-gb/our-thinking/campaigns/digital/fintech/blockchain-and-smart-contracts/; R. Koulu, "Blockchains and Online Dispute Resolution: Smart Contracts as an Alternative to Enforcement," (2016) 13 SCRIPTed 40; K. Lauslahti, J. Mattila, & T. Seppälä, "Smart Contracts – How Will Blockchain Technology Affect Contractual Practices?", ETLA Reports No. 68 (9 January 2017). Available at: https://pub.etla.fi/ETLA-Raportit-Reports-68.pdf.

[14] Catchlove, "Smart Contracts: A New Era of Contract Use," note 13.

[15] Cong & He, "Blockchain Disruption and Smart Contracts," note 13.

[16] D. Linardatos, "Smart Contracts: Some Clarifying Remarks from a German Legal Point of View" (1 June 2018). Available at SSRN: https://ssrn.com/abstract=3193588 or http://dx.doi.org/10.2139/ssrn.3193588, p. 7.

a contract"[17] and argued that "the general objectives of smart contract design are to satisfy common contractual conditions (such as payment terms, liens, confidentiality, and even enforcement), minimize exceptions both malicious and accidental, and minimize the need for trusted intermediaries. Related economic goals include lowering fraud loss, arbitration and enforcement costs, and other transaction costs."[18] According to another definition by the same author, a smart contract is "a set of promises, including protocols within which the parties perform on the other promises. The protocols are usually implemented with programs on a computer network, or in other forms of digital electronics, thus these contracts are 'smarter' than their paper-based ancestors. No use of artificial intelligence is implied."[19]

More recently, other scholars and legal operators have defined smart contracts as:

- "self-executing electronic instructions drafted in computer code";[20]
- "a piece of computer code that is capable of monitoring, executing and enforcing an agreement";[21]
- "a software, [with] which computer code binds two, or a multitude, of parties in view of the execution of predefined effects, and that is stored on a distributed ledger";[22]
- "digital contracts allowing terms contingent on decentralized consensus that are self-enforcing and tamperproof through automated execution";[23]
- "an event-driven program that runs on a distributed, decentralized, shared and replicated ledger (blockchain) and that can take custody over and transfer assets on the ledger";[24]
- "contracts that are represented in code and executed by computers";[25]
- "a new generation of digital contracts";[26]
- "programs that perform part of the contractual obligations, and may contain and execute contractual conditions, as well as invoke physical remedies";[27]
- "smart legal contract is an agreement implemented in software."[28]

---

[17] N. Szabo, "Smart Contracts," 1994, unpublished, available at www.fon.hum.uva.nl/rob/Courses/ InformationInSpeech/CDROM/Literature/LOTwinterschool2006/szabo.best.vwh.net/smart.con tracts.html; N. Szabo, "Formalizing and Securing Relationships on Public Networks," First Monday, 1997, available at http://ojphi.org/ojs/index.php/fm/article/view/548/469; N. Szabo, "The Idea of Smart Contracts," 1997, available at http://szabo.best.vwh.net/idea.html; N. Szabo, "Secure Property Titles with Owner Authority," 1998; see also M. S. Miller, "Computer Security as the Future of Law," 1997, available at www.caplet.com/security/futurelaw.

[18] Szabo, "Smart Contracts," note 17.

[19] N. Szabo, "Smart Contract Glossary," 1995, unpublished. Available at www.fon.hum.uva.nl/rob/Courses/ InformationInSpeech/CDROM/Literature/LOTwinterschool2006/szabo.best.vwh.net/smart_contracts_ glossary.html, cited by R. Koulu, "Blockchains and Online Dispute Resolution," note 13.

[20] O'Shields, "Smart Contracts: Legal Agreements for the Blockchain," note 13, 179.

[21] Hingley, "A Smart New World: Blockchain and Smart Contracts," note 13.

[22] Jaccard, "Smart Contracts and the Role of Law," note 13, 4.

[23] Cong & He, "Blockchain Disruption and Smart Contracts," note 13.

[24] Szczerbowski, "Place of Smart Contracts in Civil Law," note 13, in the abstract and, similarly, in the introduction.

[25] E. Mik, "Smart Contracts: Terminology, Technical Limitations and Real World Complexity" (17 August 2017), 1. Available at SSRN: https://ssrn.com/abstract=3038406.

[26] De Filippi & Wright, "Blockchain and the Law," note 2, at 72.

[27] E. Tjong Tjin Tai, "Force Majeure and Excuses in Smart Contracts" (4 May 2018), Tilburg Private Law Working Paper Series No. 10/2018. Available at SSRN: https://ssrn.com/abstract=3183637 (last accessed 28 November 2018).

[28] M. Sokolov, "Smart Legal Contract as a Future of Contracts Enforcement" (25 May 2018). Available at SSRN: https://ssrn.com/abstract=3208292 or http://dx.doi.org/10.2139/ssrn.3208292, 14.

Recently, Arizona approved a bill which contains a legal definition of smart contract, very similar to some of the ones mentioned above: "an event-driven program that runs on a distributed, decentralized, shared and replicated ledger and that can take custody over and instruct transfer of assets on that ledger."[29]

Even more recently, Malta approved a bill (the above-mentioned Malta Digital Innovation Authority Act, 2018) that defined smart contract as "a form of innovative technology arrangement consisting of: (a) a computer protocol; and, or (b) an agreement concluded wholly or partly in an electronic form which is automatable and enforceable by execution of computer code, although some parts may require human input and control, and which may be also enforceable by ordinary legal methods or by a mixture of both."[30] Finally, the Joint Economic Committee of the Congress of the United States observed that "smart contracts might sound new, [but] the concept is rooted in basic contract law. Usually the judicial system adjudicates contractual disputes and enforces terms, but it is also common to have another arbitration method, especially for international transactions. With smart contracts, a program enforces the contract built into the code."[31]

In general, it may be said that there is a limited consensus on the core definition, according to which, apart from some nuances, smart contracts are words written in computer language which are automatically executed by a machine; some add to the definition the requirement that such contracts run on blockchain or similar distributed ledger technologies[32] (and, thus, may be called decentralized smart contracts).[33] Finally, another important aspect of the definition regards the possibility of adding the concept of artificial intelligence (AI) to smart contracts. In other words, may smart contracts be partially written or executed by AI?[34]

The word "smart," as nowadays understood, may seem to refer to the concept of AI.

However, as observed above, the original definition by Szabo explicitly provides that "no use of artificial intelligence is implied."[35]

Similarly, other authors have excluded the concept of AI from the idea and the definition of smart contracts, stating that "it is important to note that smart contracts are not merely digital contracts (many of which rely on trusted authority for reaching consensus and execution), nor are they entailing artificial intelligence (they are rather robotic, on the contrary)"[36] and that "a smart contract doesn't 'think', like a lawyer does or – who knows? – an artificial intelligence might one day be able to do so. Instead, smart contracts enforce the lines of computer code, which they have been

---

[29] Arizona House Bill No. 2417, note 5.
[30] The Malta Digital Innovation Authority Act, 2018, available at: http://justiceservices.gov.mt /DownloadDocument.aspx?app=lp&itemid=29080&l=1.
[31] "The 2018 Joint Economic Report," Report of the Joint Economic Committee Congress of the United States on the 2018 Economic Report of the President, Chapter 9: "Building a Secure Future, One Blockchain at a Time" (13 March 2018), at 210. Available at www.congress.gov/115/crpt/hrpt596/CRPT-115hrpt596.pdf.
[32] E. Tjong Tjin Tai, "Formalizing Contract Law for Smart Contracts," note 13, "While systems for smart contracts in the general meaning of the term can be and have been created without relying on bitcoin or blockchain technology, contemporary interest in the marketplace focuses on smart contracts that do rely on a virtual currency with blockchain technology."
[33] See de Caria, "A Digital Revolution in International Trade?," note 1, at 105.
[34] Even "Artificial Intelligence" has been defined in various ways, and a consensus upon a certain definition has not been reached yet. See e.g. B. J. Copeland, "Artificial intelligence," *Britannica* online, last accessed 14 November 2018 at www.britannica.com/technology/artificial-intelligence.
[35] Szabo, "Smart Contract Glossary," note 19, cited by R. Koulu, "Blockchains and Online Dispute Resolution."
[36] Cong & He, "Blockchain Disruption and Smart Contracts," note 13 at 11.

programmed for."[37] It has also been pointed out that "smart contracts do not need artificial intelligence to work, regardless of what their name may suggest"[38] and even that "the true intelligence of smart contracts can be questioned, as they do not contain artificial intelligence in themselves [...]. A smart contract should thus be perceived as an automated mechanism which performs its defined functions as certain preconditions are met. The established term 'smart contracts' is thus somewhat deceiving."[39]

In fact, it should be noted that smart contracts are based on the logic of "If this ... then that," where "this" and "that" are predetermined by the smart contract's author. Smart contracts are not particularly difficult to execute, but they may be extremely difficult to draft, since the standard difficulty in defining obligations for legal documents is even increased because it is necessary to express any given obligation with the formalist logic of "if this, then that."

However, some authors imply the possibility of including AI in the concept of smart contracts, probably envisioning a future in which AI-based smart contracts will be able to automatically translate human language and agreements into smart contract's formalistic logic.[40]

To sum up, it may be safe to assume that with the term "smart contract" many authors refer to what we call "decentralized smart contract," while normally AI is (at least nowadays) not necessarily considered as involved in the formation or execution of a smart contract.

Hence, we can define decentralized smart contract as any digital agreement which is (a) written in computer code (thus, a piece of software), (b) run on blockchain or similar DLTs (thus, decentralized), and (c) automatically executed without any need for human intervention (thus, smart).

2.2 Current and Evolving Legal Framework

To be sure, an international legal framework[41] specifically designed for blockchain technologies and smart contracts does not exist.[42] However, the topic is clearly under consideration at the legislative/regulatory level; as has been said, "today is all about blockchain brainstorming,"[43] and at national/regional level, particularly in the United States,[44] some regulations have been or are going to be enacted.

---

[37] Jaccard, "Smart Contracts and the Role of Law," note 13 at 3–4.

[38] Lauslahti, Mattila, & Seppälä, "Smart Contracts – How Will Blockchain Technology Affect Contractual Practices?," note 13.

[39] Lauslahti, Mattila, & Seppälä, "Smart Contracts – How will Blockchain Technology Affect Contractual Practices?," note 13, 17.

[40] See e.g. O'Shields, "Smart Contracts: Legal Agreements for the Blockchain," note 13 at 189; see also more generally Scholz, "Algorithmic Contracts," note 13, at 135–136.

[41] For an exhaustive picture of the current legal framework all over the world, see P. Tasca, "Digital Currencies: Principles, Trends, Opportunities, and Risks," Deutsche Bundesbank and ECUREX Research, ECUREX Research Working Paper, 7 September 2015 (version: October 2015), 43ff.

[42] See e.g. A. Mukherjee, "Smart Contracts – Another Feather in UNCITRAL's Cap," in *Cornell International Law Journal Online*, 8 February 2018. Available at: http://cornellilj.org/smart-contracts-another-feather-in-uncitrals-cap/.

[43] M. Hancock, Speech of the Minister for Cabinet Office, *Digital Transformation in Government and Blockchain Technology*, delivered at Digital Catapult, Kings Cross, London on 26 April 2016. Available at www.gov.uk/government/speeches/digital-transformation-in-government-and-blockchain-technology.

[44] Joint Economic Committee Congress of the United States, "The 2018 Joint Economic Report," Chapter 9: "Building a Secure Future, One Blockchain at a Time," Section "Regulatory Questions" (13 March 2018), 218 and ff., available at www.congress.gov/115/crpt/hrpt596/CRPT-115hrpt596.pdf.

As was observed, in fact, "the States of Delaware, Vermont, Nevada, Arizona, Hawaii, New Hampshire and Illinois in the United States all have sought legislation, or are seeking to pass legislation to recognise and capitalise upon the use of smart contracts and blockchain technology."[45]

In particular, the State of Arizona has drafted a detailed statute (Arizona House Bill 2417[46]), providing in particular that (a) "a signature that is secured through blockchain technology is considered to be in an electronic form and to be an electronic signature," (b) "a record or contract that is secured through blockchain technology is considered to be in an electronic form and to be an electronic record," and that (c) "smart contracts may exist in commerce. A contract relating to a transaction may not be denied legal effect, validity or enforceability solely because that contract contains a smart contract term."

The State of Vermont enacted a statute with detailed provisions on blockchain (§ 1913; Blockchain Enabling),[47] with regard to authentication, admissibility, and presumptions, providing, for example, that (a) "a fact or record verified through a valid application of blockchain technology is authentic," (b) "the date and time of the recordation of the fact or record established through such a blockchain is the date and time that the fact or record was added to the blockchain," (c) "the person established through such a blockchain as the person who made such recordation is the person who made the recordation," and, in any case, (d) "a presumption does not extend to the truthfulness, validity, or legal status of the contents of the fact or record."

In practice, "both States decided to recognize legal effects for the information that lies on a blockchain or a smart contract, hence incorporating it explicitly as part of the legal system. Furthermore, this approach is also consistent with the recent reaction of several market authorities, stating that security law may apply to the sales of token during an Initial Coin Offering (ICO), incorporating them de facto."[48]

More recently, Malta entered the field with its Malta Digital Innovation Authority Act 2018, in order to "provide for the establishment of an Authority to be known as the Malta Digital Innovation Authority, to support the development and implementation of the guiding principles described in this Act and to promote consistent principles for the development of visions, skills, and other qualities relating to technology innovation, including distributed or decentralised technology, and to exercise regulatory functions regarding innovative technology, arrangements and related services and to make provision with respect to matters ancillary thereto or connected therewith."

Nonetheless, most jurisdictions around the world still lack a specifically tailored regulation: this may be due in part to the complexity of these technologies, and mostly to the more general inability of modern states' legislative process to follow the rapid evolution of technology.

In addition, it must be said that, the blockchain being a (neutral) technology, it seems much more reasonable to wait and regulate the possible uses of it, rather than the technology itself, paying attention not to stifle innovation.

As regards the need for a specific regulation, it has been noticed that "the growing interest in blockchain technology, independent from a VC scheme, a priori raises fewer

---

[45] Catchlove, "Smart Contracts: A New Era of Contract Use," note 13, at 2.
[46] Arizona House, Bill No. 2417, note 5.
[47] Sec. I.1. 12 V.S.A. § 1913, note 6.
[48] Jaccard, "Smart Contracts and the Role of Law," note 13, at 10.

policy concerns, because the technology would be used in a closed system administered by regulated financial institutions."[49]

However, "[a]lthough the blockchain technology was initially meant to implement Bitcoin's currency business model, it now seems to be emerging as a promising means to achieve a number of other goals. Blockchain technology could find its way into the mainstream financial markets. The technology may be used in a variety of applications where data have to be transmitted without risk of corruption. The handicap for this technology might be that it first appeared in the particularly sensitive and highly regulated field of currencies, having attracted the regulators' attention while still at an immature stage, and with its potential not fully understood."[50]

Therefore, it is indeed possible that regulation of virtual currencies indirectly provides some rules related to blockchain technologies, and this may well have negative effects on the blockchain and, consequently, on decentralized smart contracts.[51]

Undoubtedly, these technologies are at the centre of the stage – for instance, Bank of America recently filed 15 blockchain-related patents,[52] while a research on Patentscope showed 449 results for the term "blockchain," 184 for the term "smart contract," and 63 for the term "smart contracts"[53].

To sum up, speaking of smart contracts, their legal status is still totally "unclear,"[54] and little has been written in this regard:[55] I will try to address some potential issues in the following paragraphs. However, as I will try to point out, the fact that there is no specific regulation on such issues clearly does not mean that current laws and general principles of law may not be applicable to them, or that they are unregulated at all: smart contracts are indeed pieces of software.[56] To be sure, In the absence of specific regulations, in my opinion, existing laws must regulate these technologies.[57]

2.3 Smart Contracts and Blockchain in Action

Business practice might be severely affected by such new technologies for a number of reasons: firstly, a lot of companies have started to accept payments in Bitcoin (and other virtual currencies) all over the world;[58] secondly, blockchain technologies may allow significant cost savings[59] and potential applications to everyday business are on their

---

[49] IMF, *Virtual Currencies and Beyond* 24.
[50] C. Scheinert, "Virtual Currencies, Challenges Following Their Introduction," EPRS | European Parliamentary Research Service, Members' Research Service, PE 579.110, 2016, 10.
[51] Scheinert, "Virtual Currencies, Challenges Following Their Introduction," note 50.
[52] Scheinert, "Virtual Currencies, Challenges Following Their Introduction," note 50.
[53] Patentscope (https://patentscope.wipo.int/search/en/search.jsf). Last accessed 15 March 2018.
[54] IMF, *Virtual Currencies and Beyond*, 23.
[55] See note 13.
[56] Savelyev, "Contract Law 2.0," note 13, at 20: "it is possible to argue that each Smart contract by its legal nature is also a computer program in a meaning of IP law."
[57] Tasca, "Digital Currencies: Principles, Trends, Opportunities, and Risks," note 41, at 26: "the general orientation is to adopt the current legislation already in place in order to deal with digital currencies in Europe."
[58] EY Switzerland, report available at www.ey.com/Publication/vwLUAssets/ey-news-release-switzerland-accepts-bitcoins-for-payment-of-its-services/$FILE/ey-news-release-switzerland-accepts-bitcoins-for-payment-of-its-services.pdf.
[59] Investigating the possible advantages of the technology goes far beyond the purposes of this chapter; I will just observe that businesses may consider adopting this technology for many different reasons (e.g. immutability, digitization, automation, paperless processes, rapidity, and absence of middle-man).

way;[60] lastly, what if instead of paper contracts, some businesses started to use smart contracts?[61] Moreover, what appears to be more appealing is that (at least in theory) smart contracts are automatically enforced without any need for a third party;[62] the reduction of transaction and litigation costs for undertakings may be massive.

In fact, smart contracts are self-executed pieces of software and, apparently, there is no need for a central third party (i.e., judges, arbitrators) to administer them: there is (once again, at least in theory[63]) no way of breaching them.[64]

We can imagine a scenario in which two enterprises, through a (decentralized) smart contract, define and regulate their business relations and payment obligations so that they are automatically executed via Bitcoin. Platforms to draft and use smart contracts in everyday life already exist; the best-known example is Ethereum, which, according to the definition provided by the company, is

> a decentralized platform that runs smart contracts: applications that run exactly as programmed without any possibility of downtime, censorship, fraud or third party interference. These apps run on a custom built blockchain, an enormously powerful shared global infrastructure that can move value around and represent the ownership of property. This enables developers to create markets, store registries of debts or promises, move funds in accordance with instructions given long in the past (like a will or a futures contract) and many other things that have not been invented yet, all without a middle man or counterparty risk.[65]

Going back to the opening point of this paragraph, and even considering the issues analysed in the following paragraphs, it seems rather likely that business practice will be affected by blockchain technologies and smart contracts. In any case, what is needed is at least a study-and-watch approach[66] to be ready when and if such innovations will come

---

60 The R3 project: "R3 is a financial innovation firm that leads a consortium partnership with over 50 of the world's leading financial institutions. We work together to design and deliver advanced distributed ledger technologies to the global financial markets" (www.r3cev.com/about/). In addition, as mentioned below in the chapter, the first blockchain-related patents are being filed.

61 The advantages and disadvantages of using smart contracts instead of a traditional paper contract should be evaluated on a case-by-case analysis, keeping in mind the objectives of each single agreement and the peculiarity of the situation. In any case, it has been observed that "it is quite possible to expect that at some moment of time Smart contracts will become routine technology, like Internet itself in 90s years of the last century" (Savelyev, "Contract Law 2.0," note 13, at 20).

62 Savelyev, "Contract Law 2.0," note 13, at 18: "there is no need to seek for enforcement of Smart contract by addressing the claims to third party – judiciary or other enforcement agency. And it is one of the main 'selling points' of this contractual form."

63 But, in practice, huge scandals have already made the deadlines, such as the "DAO case," speaking of which it has been said that "to date, the largest application of this kind of thinking has been the creation of a decentralized autonomous organization or DAO in 2016. The idea was to create an investing entity that would not be controlled by any one individual, but by shareholders voting based on their stakes on a blockchain. The entity was funded with $150 million. Soon after this money was raised, about $40 million of those funds were diverted from the organization, using part of the code that no one had anticipated" (Raskin, "The Law and Legality of Smart Contracts," note 13 at 36) and that "recent example with the hack attack on Ethereum DAO in June 2016 shows that certain mechanism of reaching a consensus between the parties to Smart contract on certain unexpected (non-programed) events is necessary" (Savelyev, "Contract Law 2.0," note 13, at 22–23).

64 Savelyev, "Contract Law 2.0," note 13, at 18: "Smart contract cannot be breached by a party to it."

65 The website is available at www.ethereum.org.

66 The same approach has been adopted by the ECB; see *Virtual Currency Schemes – A Further Analysis*, ECB, 2015, p. 33.

into the game of business practice. A similar position has been expressed, among the others,[67] by the Bank for International Settlements, which recognized that "digital currencies and distributed ledgers are an innovation that could have a range of impacts on many areas, especially on payment systems and services. These impacts could include the disruption of existing business models and systems, as well as the emergence of new financial, economic and social interactions and linkages."[68] Thus, the author concluded by saying that "central banks could consider – as a potential policy response to these developments – investigating the potential uses of distributed ledgers in payment systems or other types of FMIs."[69]

In any case, from the point of view of the law, it is necessary to start understanding smart contracts and to deal with the existence of such new tools. What are the legal issues raised by smart contracts?

2.4 Legal Questions

This section will briefly outline and address some legal questions that may arise using these technologies (in particular) with regard to private law, how such questions may be resolved on the basis of current legislation, and how they should be addressed by policy-makers. The greatest problem is related to the legal status of such technologies: in fact, as already mentioned, some countries have already legislated in this field, while others are evaluating if, when, and how to legislate.

As for the problems arising from their legal status, in the absence of specific regulation, authorities will likely (try to) apply current legislation.

Real troubles may come with "decentralized smart contracts" as defined above, i.e. smart contracts based on blockchain technologies, which automatically execute any given agreement, providing proof of that performance in the distributed ledger.

In this regard, the first thing to notice is that "using the blockchain functions imposes some technical limits: as a matter of fact, indirect e-commerce performances are not digitally executable. Therefore, the scheme is not covering any agreement regarding goods or services that, even though purchased on the Internet, have a material consistence or are to be performed in the real world, like a book delivery or a maintenance service."[70]

This is due to the dichotomy between real and virtual world: let us imagine that, through a smart contract, A sells an object to B (who regularly pays the agreed price), but thereafter C steals the real good from B; at this point, on the blockchain there is no way to change the status of owner of B, who may well sell his virtual "title" to D, who will never physically possess the good that he has bought but, at the same time, will never be able to stop the payment automatically executed by the smart contract. Therefore, it seems

---

[67] The Special Address of CFTC Commissioner J. Christopher Giancarlo Before the Depository Trust & Clearing Corporation 2016 Blockchain Symposium in which it was highlighted "The Need for a 'Do No Harm' Regulatory Approach to Distributed Ledger Technology."

[68] BIS, "CPMI Report on Digital Currencies," November 2015, 17, available at www.bis.org/cpmi/publ/d137 .pdf.

[69] Ibid at 18.

[70] Perugini & Dal Checco, "Smart Contracts: A Preliminary Evaluation," note 13, at 10.

possible to argue that smart contracts may function only with digital goods and digital inputs.[71] The dichotomy is extremely evident if one looks at how the events subsumed in smart contracts must be and are recorded in the blockchain: in order to be recorded in the virtual world, events must be translated in virtual inputs, while in the real world events happen independently from what is recorded in the blockchain. Thus, events happening in the physical world, which may be called off-chain events, must be somehow translated into virtual inputs in order to become on-chain events (i.e. events recorded on the blockchain).

As I will show later, a commonly proposed solution to this problem may be the adoption of oracles, i.e. "individuals or programs that store and transmit information from the outside world, thereby providing a means for blockchain-based systems to interact with real-world persons and potentially react to external events."[72]

Given the above-mentioned dichotomy, it has been observed that, since "discrepancies can occur between the two systems (legal/informatics) [...], [this] may result in unfair and unlawful smart contracts being enforced."[73] Nonetheless, even if such limitations had to be applied, smart contracts would still be applicable to a lot of goods in the modern era. Moreover, even considering oracles as not sufficient to overcome the issue, it is likely that a technological solution to this limitation will be developed and fully implemented.

Keeping in mind this important dichotomy, the first fundamental question is: what is the legal nature of smart contracts? Are they assets protected by intellectual property laws? A form of preemptive self-help? Ordinary agreements (which would raise the issues of jurisdiction and applicable law)? Once again, the possible reply depends on the chosen definition. According to the definition given above, we have to consider three main characteristics: the software, the distributed ledger (database), and the automatic execution. In any case, from a technical point of view, it seems that a smart contract is simply a piece of computer code or software. Thus, it seems appropriate to evaluate it firstly through the lens of intellectual property law.

2.4.1 *Assets Protected by Intellectual Property Laws?*

With regard to the traditional intellectual property categories, generally speaking, smart contracts (and blockchain) may and should fall within the sphere of protection of copyright given that, as observed above, they are indeed pieces of software.[74]

Moreover, the protection through patents, provided that such technologies are new, involve an inventive step, and are capable of industrial application, should also be considered as possible – as shown by the rising number of patent applications that may be found regarding these technologies[75] – at least in those countries that allow the

---

[71] Perugini & Dal Checco, "Smart Contracts: A Preliminary Evaluation," note 13, at 10ff.

[72] De Filippi & Wright, "Blockchain and the Law," note 2, at 75.

[73] Jaccard, "Smart Contracts and the Role of Law," note 13, at 8.

[74] Savelyev, "Contract Law 2.0," note 13, at 20: "it is possible to argue that each Smart contract by its legal nature is also a computer program in a meaning of IP law."

[75] A research on Patentscope showed 449 results for the term "blockchain," 184 for the term "smart contract," and 63 for the term "smart contracts." See Patentscope at https://patentscope.wipo.int/search/en/search.jsf (last accessed 15 November 2018).

patentability of software and those that recognize patentable inventions assisted by software.

In this regard, it has been noted that "some proponents also continue to advocate making blockchain technology accessible by offering the code under open source licenses or creating patent pools. And, as is the case with many promising new technologies, blockchain has also attracted patent trolls, as pointed out, among others, by the Chamber of Digital Commerce, a US advocacy group that promotes the emerging industry behind blockchain technology. It recently launched the Blockchain Intellectual Property Council (BIPC), which aims to create an industry-led defensive patent strategy to combat blockchain patent trolling."[76]

In addition, one may wonder if the blockchain per se may be protected as a database, either through copyright protection if "by reason of the selection or arrangement of their contents constitute intellectual creations"[77] or – in the EU – through a sui generis right granted by the Directive 96/9/EC on the legal protection of databases if "there has been qualitatively and/or quantitatively a substantial investment in either the obtaining, verification or presentation of the contents."[78] Considering that the distributed database is created automatically according to mathematical functions, it may be said that copyright protection should not be granted and the same reasoning should apply to the sui generis right given the lack of any substantial investment (unless one considers the energy necessary – sometimes called "gas"[79] – to run the blockchain as a substantial investment). In any case, it must be considered that the very purpose of the EU directive is to give incentives where needed:[80] thus, considering that blockchain-based applications are up and running without incentives, one may well argue that there is no need of protection at all, at least from the point of view of the Database Directive.

But does anybody own the blockchain? Given the above-mentioned considerations regarding copyright, patents and *sui generis right,* it is extremely difficult to answer the question, and there is uncertainty as to who – if anybody – owns the blockchain.[81] The answer may well be different if the focus is moved to the platform which allows the creation, management, and execution of smart contracts: in fact, while in most cases these platforms are currently either open source[82] or offered by nonprofit organizations,[83] it is indeed possible that (access to) such platforms may be sold as a service offered to customers willing to pay a subscription cost. In that case, either because the private blockchain at the core of the platform or the platform itself is patented, or because the software itself should be considered protected by copyright, the answer may be more clear, and this would open the door to a lot more questions and

[76] B. Clark, "Blockchain and IP Law: A Match Made in Crypto Heaven?", *Wipo Magazine*, February 2018, available at: www.wipo.int/wipo_magazine/en/2018/01/article_0005.html.
[77] TRIPs art. 10(2).
[78] Art. 7(1) of the Directive 96/9/EC on the Legal Protection of Databases.
[79] Ethereum, see at http://ethdocs.org/en/latest/contracts-and-transactions/account-types-gas-and-transactions.html?highlight=gas#what-is-gas.
[80] Recital 39 of the Database Directive: "this Directive seeks to safeguard the position of makers of databases against misappropriation of the results of the financial and professional investment made in obtaining and collection the contents by protecting the whole or substantial parts of a database against certain acts by a user or competitor."
[81] Clark, "Blockchain and IP Law: A Match Made in Crypto Heaven?", note 76.
[82] Such as Corda: www.corda.net/.
[83] Such as Ethereum: www.ethereum.org/.

problems regarding the relationship between the owner of the platform upon which smart contracts are run and its users.

As for the other two above-mentioned categories, some have recently argued, on the one hand, that "smart contracts are simply a new form of pre-emptive self-help"[84] and, on the other, that a "smart contract can be regarded as a legally-binding agreement."[85] I will move on to analyse both these suggestions.

2.4.2 *A Form of Preemptive Self-Help?*

Another interesting point found in the scholarship is the idea that smart contracts are simply a new form of self-help measures,[86] which parties to a contract adopt in order to ensure the performance of their agreements without the need of judicial enforcement.[87] This is consistent with what usually happens, at least now: two parties reach an agreement and thereafter translate (part of) it into a smart contract, and then leave the duty to perform it to the machine.

Some commentators have suggested that "if blockchain will allow financial transactions without banks, smart contracts may lead to contracts that no longer need courts to enforce them."[88] However, a possible solution to the dichotomy problem discussed above the use of oracles,[89] which would allow smart contracts to receive the necessary input from the outside world, however it must be noted that there would always be the need of a trusted third party (i.e. the oracles instead of the courts or arbitrators). It has been correctly observed that "the rule relies in the end on judgement by third parties of off-line events, which moves the computational aspect to the real world and lessens the claim of a self-contained environment."[90] Thus, one of the main advantages of smart contracts (the lack of a need for a third party to execute the agreement) would be missing.

Therefore – assuming one considers smart contracts as a form of preemptive self-help – if such contracts begin to be adopted in day-to-day business practice, there would appear to be a need for a general agreement (or at least an ad hoc provision to be included in the smart contract, even if it would clearly not be a self-enforceable provision) to be adopted between the parties. The provision should establish, in case of need of judicial enforcement related to the general agreement itself, or to the smart contracts depending upon it, what is the applicable law and which judge has the jurisdiction. In fact, as was observed, "given that smart contracts can only do what they are programmed to do, a separate but connected written contract would provide a place

---

[84] Raskin, "The Law and Legality of Smart Contracts," note 13, in the abstract the author concludes that "smart contracts are simply a new form of pre-emptive self-help."

[85] Savelyev, "Contract Law 2.0," note 13, at 10 and ff.

[86] Raskin, note 84.

[87] Raskin, "The Law and Legality of Smart Contracts," note 13, at 314ff. and also K. D. Werbach & N. Cornell, "Contracts Ex Machina" (2017) 67 *Duke Law Journal*, 313, 335.

[88] O'Shields, "Smart Contracts: Legal Agreements for the Blockchain," note 13, at 178 and note 5.

[89] See the project Oraclize at www.oraclize.it/. For a definition of "oracle," see for example https://blockchainhub.net/blockchain-oracles/: "an oracle, in the context of blockchains and smart contracts, is an agent that finds and verifies real-world occurrences and submits this information to a blockchain to be used by smart contracts"; see also: https://cointelegraph.com/explained/blockchain-oracles-explained.

[90] Tjong Tjin Tai, "Formalizing Contract Law for Smart Contracts," note 13, at 7.

to detail what will happen when unforeseen issues beyond the control of the parties occur."[91]

Similarly, it has been suggested "to couple [t]he use of smart contracts with a traditional written contract [...]. The complementary use of a written contract, alongside the novel smart contract will enable a safe and controlled transition into a new era of contract use."[92] Some scholars have concluded that this approach may give birth to hybrid agreements, partly written with traditional legal prose and partly written in computer code.[93] In this regard, it has also been said that using smart contracts "there is no need for conflict of laws provisions, since there are no collisions of various legal systems. Mathematics is universal human language. Thus, Smart contracts are truly transnational and executed uniformly regardless of the differences in national laws."[94] However, I do not agree with such a statement since, as I contend in this chapter, smart contracts should be subject to contract law, and it is clear that the applicable law will have a strong influence on them; for example, with regard to illegality and unconscionability, every country has its own particular rules, and a contract may well be valid in one place and null and void in another one.

2.4.3 *Issues of Jurisdiction and Applicable Law*

Finally, with regard to the idea that smart contracts "can be regarded as a legally-binding agreement,"[95] it has even been said that smart contracts do not create obligations in the true legal sense.[96] This conclusion, though, seems difficult to agree with. Firstly, smart contracts, as some scholars have concluded, are indeed an "agreement between the parties"[97] expressed in digital code and I believe that they should be considered as self-sufficient legally binding agreements. It has correctly been observed "at least some smart contracts may fall within the current contract law definition of contracts."[98] In fact, smart contracts can, at least in theory, meet all the requirements set forth under different national contract laws to be considered as contracts in the legal meaning of the term. For example, in Italy a contract is defined as the agreement between two or more parties to establish, regulate, or extinguish a legal relationship – with an economic dimension – among them, and its requirements are: (a) agreement between the parties, (b) *causa*, (c) object, and (d) form (only when prescribed under penalty of nullity). Such requirements, in practice, are quite easy to meet with traditional oral and/or paper-based contracts, and the same must be said with regard to digital agreements in the form of smart contracts.

Similarly, it has been observed that, under US law, "smart contracts memorializing legal agreements are likely to be deemed enforceable."[99]

---

[91] Catchlove, "Smart Contracts: A New Era of Contract Use," note 13, at 16.
[92] Ibid.
[93] De Filippi & Wright, "Blockchain and the Law," note 2, at 76ff.
[94] Savelyev, "Contract Law 2.0," 116–134.
[95] Ibid.
[96] Ibid.
[97] Werbach & Cornell, "Contracts Ex Machina," note 87, at 22.
[98] Sokolov, "Smart Legal Contract as a Future of Contracts Enforcement," note 28, at 25.
[99] De Filippi & Wright, "Blockchain and the Law," note 2, at 79.

Moreover, smart contracts do clearly create obligations which stand independently from the digital code of the smart contracts: if, for example, there is a bug in a smart contract between A and B, and A has undertaken to transfer her property in exchange for an agreed sum of money to B, she would still be obliged to transfer her property to B even if the smart contract does not work (similarly, if a vending machine does not deliver the chosen good after the insertion of the coin, it is clear that the owner of the machine is still obliged to perform and deliver the good). In this regard, I support the cautious conclusion already reached by other scholars: "even with reasonable precautions, though, smart contracts will sometimes contain mistakes."[100]

In any case, by entering into a smart contract, parties undertake to perform the obligation therein encapsulated. In addition, since – as was said – smart contracts will almost always be a translation of a precedent agreement already reached, the obligations of parties would nonetheless be, at the very least, to start the execution of the smart contract.

In general, in spite of the conceptual dissimilarities, there does not appear to be many differences between the functioning of a smart contract and that of a mechanical vending machine, or that of a software that suspends the supply of a service in case of missing payments (e.g. Netflix allows users to legally watch streaming videos in exchange for a monthly payment; in case of missing payments, the software will simply suspend the service, not allowing users to log in[101]). Whether humans perform the interruption by software, or by smart contracts with a record on the blockchain, does not in practice seem to make a relevant difference in legal terms.

I therefore agree with the scholars who concluded that "independently from being digitally expressed, every [smart] contract is ruled and guaranteed by the law and the parties will be free to file the Court for compensation in case a void agreement has been performed or execution has been spoiled by a malfunctioning due to a system bug"[102] and that "smart contracts do fall within existing contract law principles."[103] In other words, smart contracts "will not require any special set of new laws or regulations. Instead, existing legal principles [of contract law] will be adapted and perhaps modified, either statutorily or judicially, to deal explicitly with smart contracts and other emerging technologies – albeit most likely with a substantial lag time between adoption of the technology and adjustment of the law."[104] Smart contracts "provide many benefits and aids to efficiency, productivity and certainty, but they do not sit apart from the law. If a smart contract is operating illegally, then the contract would be rendered void or voidable. In this regard, smart contracts face the same issues as traditional contracts in determining legality."[105]

---

[100] A. J. Kolber, "Not-So-Smart Blockchain Contracts and Artificial Responsibility" (2018) 21 *Stanford Technology Law Review*, 198.

[101] See at https://help.netflix.com/legal/termsofuse?locale=en&country=IT: "if a payment is not successfully settled, due to expiration, insufficient funds, or otherwise, and you do not change your Payment Method or cancel your account, we may suspend your access to the service until we have obtained a valid Payment Method."

[102] Perugini & Dal Checco, "Smart Contracts: A Preliminary Evaluation," note 13, at 25.

[103] Catchlove, "Smart Contracts: A New Era of Contract Use," note 13, at 16.

[104] O'Shields, "Smart Contracts: Legal Agreements for the Blockchain," note 13, at 189.

[105] For similar conclusions, see also Catchlove, "Smart Contracts: A New Era of Contract Use," note 13, at 15–16.

To sum up, smart contracts will not "replace contract law."[106] The existing contract law framework appears more than adequate to accommodate even this revolutionary form of deal-making, without the need to create new legal categories that, contrary to a common belief among regulators and policy-makers, are not truly warranted in this case.[107] Having reached such a conclusion one might wonder: "what happens when the outcomes of the smart contract diverge from the outcomes that the law demands?"[108]

Once again, the answer depends on the applicable (contract) law. In relation to international trade, everything is different: it is self-evident that smart contracts may generate enormous problems if the applicable law and the competent jurisdiction are not clearly determined in the agreement. However, as observed above, smart contracts by their very nature cannot contain provisions not executable by software (such as the one regarding the applicable law), nor are they built with the intention to depend on a third-party judicial enforcement, and, therefore, it is still hard to imagine how they could include provisions on jurisdiction and applicable law.[109]

As observed above, it would therefore appear to be necessary, if such contracts are adopted in day-to-day trade practice, to establish a general agreement (or at least an ad hoc provision) that establishes, among other things, that in case of need of judicial enforcement related to the general agreement itself, or to the smart contracts depending upon it, what is the applicable law and which court has the jurisdiction.

In relation to international trade, this problem may otherwise be without solution; trying to establish the applicable law of a smart contract, in the absence of an explicit choice by the parties, would trigger the well-known problems amplified by the advent of the Internet. Should the applicable law be the *lex loci delicti*, *lex loci contractus*, *lex loci rei sitae* or *lex loci protectionis*? Or should we use other criteria?

Similar, if not worse, problems would arise regarding jurisdiction.

Therefore, there appears to be a great need for a solution to these uncertainties, or at least a model clause/provision/law that deals with applicable law and jurisdiction, if smart contracts are to become more common.

2.4.4 Probative Value

In any case, independently of the legal nature of such contracts, another issue to be faced is the probative value of blockchain technology. One possible solution may be to adopt legal presumptions, as the ones introduced by the State of Vermont discussed above. But, in the absence of such legal presumptions or any other legal disposition, it is fair to assume that every judge will proceed in different ways according to the procedural law of his country: he may appoint a court expert or he may consider the data in the blockchain

---

[106] Werbach & Cornell, "Contracts Ex Machina," note 87, at 4.

[107] For a similar position with regard to virtual currencies, see e.g. Tasca, "Digital Currencies: Principles, Trends, Opportunities, and Risks," note 41, at 26: "the general orientation is to adopt the current legislation already in place in order to deal with digital currencies in Europe."

[108] Raskin, "The Law and Legality of Smart Contracts," note 13, at 25ff.

[109] Savelyev, "Contract Law 2.0," note 13, at 20ff.

as written proof or just as a simple clue or not as proof at all. Once again, the applicable law will have the final answer.

2.4.5 *General Data Protection Regulation*

Finally, a few comments[110] regarding the relationship between blockchain and the EU Data Protection Regulation – Regulation (EU) 2016/679 of the European Parliament and of the Council of 27 April 2016 on the protection of natural persons with regard to the processing of personal data and on the free movement of such data, also known as General Data Protection Regulation (GDPR).

We have seen that smart contracts run on blockchain, which is a distributed database, and, as such, is made of data. Among such data it seems possible to store almost any type of data (even illegal),[111] including personal data.

In addition, following the approach adopted by the European Court of Justice (ECJ) in the well-known ruling in the case C-131/12 *Google* v. *Agencia Española de Protección de Datos* (AEPD), the GDPR introduced the so-called right to be forgotten (Art. 17 of the GDPR), which provides that data subjects have the right to obtain the deletion of their personal data. The problem is that once a piece of data is "chained" in the blockchain, it is almost impossible to delete it.

What then?

This problem seems both technical and legal at the same time: I believe it is necessary to find some technical ways to make the blockchain compliant with GDPR's requirements.

Considering that the GDRP has just become enforceable, it is probably too early for an assessment, but it would surely be wise to keep the topic under careful consideration in the coming months. In any case, privacy concerns regarding the nature of smart contracts have been raised even before the enforceability of the GDPR, considering the transparency inherent to the blockchain structure.[112] Some scholars have even affirmed that "innovation has to step back if main principles of law are at stake (e.g. the protection of privacy rights and personal data)."[113]

2.5 Conclusion

This chapter has tried to outline the legal landscape arising from blockchain technologies and particularly one of their foremost applications, decentralized smart contracts; it has tried to investigate if and to what extent such technologies may imply a legal revolution, or if it is sufficient to simply adapt the existing legal categories to them.

---

[110] For a preliminary evaluation, see Deloitte, "Blockchain from a Perspective of Data Protection Law: A Brief Introduction to Data Protection Ramifications," available at: www2.deloitte.com/dl/en/pages/legal/articles/blockchain-datenschutzrecht.html.

[111] M. Stockley, "Bitcoin's Blockchain Tainted with Links to Child Abuse Imagery" (21 March 2018), available at https://nakedsecurity.sophos.com/2018/03/21/bitcoins-blockchain-tainted-with-links-to-child-abuse-imagery/.

[112] De Filippi & Wright, "Blockchain and the Law," note 2, at 83–84.

[113] Linardatos, "Smart Contracts: Some Clarifying Remarks," note 16, at 16.

While I acknowledged that decentralized smart contracts and blockchain may become mainstream technologies, I believe that they are not going to prompt a legal revolution.[114]

This chapter focused on the issues related to private law. In this regard, the implementation of blockchain-based smart contracts creates problematic legal questions, particularly in relation to the applicable law and to jurisdiction. In fact, decentralized smart contracts are indeed designed with the purpose of avoiding the need of an intermediary to assure the exact performance of a contract, and to be self-sufficient and autonomous; however, sometimes, either due to a bug, or for other reasons related to the dichotomy between the real and virtual world, the intervention of a third party may be necessary to correct them and to reach the required lawful outcomes of the given contract.

Nonetheless, considering that smart contracts can arguably be deemed actual contracts in their legal meaning – or at the least some form of self-help technology chosen by parties to ensure compliance with contractual obligations – it seems that most of the legal questions arising with smart contracts can and should be dealt with under current contract law. However, it is necessary to identify which national contract law applies to decentralized smart contracts, and this may be resolved through an ad hoc provision in the agreement, or through the enactment of legal rules applicable to the most problematic aspects of smart contracts, i.e. applicable law and jurisdiction.

To conclude, smart contracts and the law are neither enemies nor incompatible, and they have a long road to go side by side.

---

[114] Similarly, even if not under a private law perspective, see De Filippi & Wright, "Blockchain and the Law," note 2, at 208: "in the end, however, blockchain technology does not spell the end of the rule of law as we know it."

3 Technology of Smart Contracts

Valentina Gatteschi, Fabrizio Lamberti, and Claudio Demartini

3.1 Introduction

Blockchain technology and smart contracts are receiving ever-growing attention from the industrial and research fields as well as wide coverage from the media. In fact, while at the beginning the core concepts of blockchain and smart contracts were only mastered by a small group of technology enthusiasts, recently a large number of people with different backgrounds have shown interest in this technology. Most of the discussion centers on the implications of its widespread adoption from different perspectives, such as the economic, legal, philosophical, and governmental ones.

The objective of this chapter is to provide the reader with a primer on blockchain and smart contracts. Specifically, the chapter will start by presenting the technological foundations that blockchain and smart contracts are built upon, by using examples which will illustrate how this technology works. Then, an overview of existing, soon to be developed, or potential applications of blockchain and smart contracts in different fields will be provided in order to help the reader understand how they could impact existing processes or, more in general, society. Finally, the chapter will focus on issues related to the widespread adoption of blockchain and smart contracts, mainly related to the legal and IT contexts.

In the last two years, blockchain and smart contracts have started to receive increasing attention from the wider public. In fact, this technology, which before was only known to a restricted group of technology enthusiasts or to researchers and innovators, started to be more and more frequently mentioned in the media as "The next big thing,"[1] "The philosopher's stone,"[2] or "The new Grail."[3] A blockchain is usually defined as a shared ledger, stored on and maintained by network nodes, which records transactions (in the form of messages sent from one node to another) executed among nodes.[4] Information stored on the blockchain can be inspected by anyone and cannot be modified or erased. Smart contracts are self-executing pieces of

---

[1] A. Ayvazyan, "Blockchain – The Next Big Thing," 2017, at www.catalysts.cc/en/big-data/blockchain-the-next-big-thing/ (last accessed December 29, 2017).
[2] M. Ramada, "For Insurers #Blockchain Is the New Black," 2016, at http://blog.willis.com/2016/12/for-insurers-blockchain-is-the-new-black/ (last accessed November 20, 2018).
[3] P. J. Duvivier, "Is the Blockchain the New Graal of the Financial Sector ?", 2016, www.linkedin.com/pulse/blockchain-new-graal-financial-sector-pierre-jean-duvivier (last accessed December 29, 2017).
[4] M. Swan, *Blockchain: Blueprint for a New Economy* (Newton, MA: O'Reilly Media, 2015).

code stored on the blockchain, which could act autonomously under given conditions.[5]

Even though blockchain technology was initially conceived for transferring money without the need to rely on intermediaries, recently a large number of actors have started to investigate whether it could be used in combination with smart contracts to reshape existing processes, by improving their efficiency and reducing costs.

As usually happens, the introduction of new breakthrough technologies in everyday activities has an impact not only on technology-related tasks but also on a variety of other different social, ethical, and legal spheres. In this view, before mainstream adoption, researchers should investigate the possible consequences of the everyday use of a technology to evaluate the impact on society and to foresee unexpected situations.

This is also the case for blockchain and smart contracts technology. In this context, it seems that a lot of research has been done to solve technical issues and to investigate new application scenarios, whereas repercussions on society and on existing regulations have started to be analyzed only recently. Furthermore, since the mechanism that blockchain and smart contracts are built upon is quite complex to grasp, as it exploits cryptography, networking, and game theory, people without a technical background could find it difficult to achieve a good level of mastery of this technology, which is a prerequisite for a subsequent investigation into how society could be reshaped to better embrace it.

The objective of this work is to address the above points, by providing the reader (without a technical background) with a primer on blockchain and smart contracts and by allowing him or her to reflect on consequences of their adoption. Specifically, the chapter aims to explain:

- *why* blockchain and smart contracts have been devised and *how* they work, by presenting in a simplified way the technical aspects behind this technology;
- *what* are the potential applications of blockchain and smart contracts and *who* can profit from them, by presenting an overview of existing, soon to be developed, or potential applications; and
- *which* issues could arise from the adoption of blockchain and smart contracts on a larger scale, by focusing on those issues which are related to the legal and IT contexts.

The rest of the chapter is organized as follows: Section 3.1.1 explains how a blockchain works, whereas Section 3.1.2 focuses on smart contracts. Section 3.2 provides an overview of blockchain and smart contract-based applications, by grouping them according to their application sector/scenario. Section 3.3 analyzes some key issues that should be addressed by researchers in the legal and IT fields before a mainstream adoption of this technology. Finally, conclusions are drawn in Section 3.4.

3.1.1 *How Does a Blockchain Work?*

The blockchain was first introduced in late 2008 by an unknown researcher acting under the pseudonym of Satoshi Nakamoto.[6] Nakamoto's objective was to create a framework

---

[5] N. Szabo, "Smart Contracts," 1994, paper published at https://archive.is/zQ1p8 (accessed October 16, 2018).

[6] S. Nakamoto, "Bitcoin: A Peer-to-Peer Electronic Cash System," Advance Access published 2008. Available at https://bitcoin.org/bitcoin.pdf (accessed October 16, 2018).

enabling people (and institutions) to exchange money without the need for intermediaries. In his vision, money transactions between parties would be recorded on a shared ledger, maintained by computers all over the world (the network "nodes").

As computer nodes could potentially modify and falsify transactions, Nakamoto devised a complex mechanism – based on cryptography rules and on majority consensus – for validating new transactions and writing them on the ledger. Thanks to this mechanism, only "valid" transactions could be inserted in the blockchain (i.e. transactions issued by a person entitled to spend the money). Moreover, once a transaction was recorded, it could not be modified or erased.

As the cryptographic mechanism made the validation process time consuming, he decided to perform this process periodically (e.g. every ten minutes), by grouping transactions into blocks (that's where the term "blockchain" comes from) and periodically validating the blocks (and, hence, the contained transactions). Each block was designed to contain not only information on the stored transactions but also a reference to the previous block, by making the whole blockchain assume a shape similar to a dynamic DNA chain, periodically increasing its size by adding new blocks at its end.

In order to better grasp the technological aspects underlying the blockchain, it could be worth considering the example illustrated in Figure 3.1. Alice wants to send some money to Bob. In order to enable the transfer, both Alice and Bob have a wallet, which is identified by a unique alphanumeric address (similar to the international bank account number (IBAN) address) and which stores their credentials. In order to trigger the transfer, Alice creates a message such as "Send 2 from my wallet address x1z to Bob's wallet address v4y" (for readability purposes, the message has been shortened in the figure). She then signs (locks) the message with her credentials (technically speaking, with her *private key*) and broadcasts the message to the other network nodes. As soon as the nodes receive the message, they perform two checks: first, they verify whether the message has truly been sent by Alice, by checking whether it was signed using the credentials linked to her address. In fact, only the owner of the credentials for address x1z (hence, Alice) would be able to correctly sign all the transactions coming from this address. Second, they verify if Alice's balance is sufficient. To perform this check, they scan all previous incoming and outgoing transactions from her address, which are stored on the blockchain. To this purpose, it must be recalled that each computer node stores a local copy of the blockchain. If Alice has sufficient money, they add her transaction, together with other transactions occurring in the same time frame, to a new block.

In order to add the block to the chain, computer nodes then start the so-called mining process, ideally similar to the extraction of gold from a mine (where no one knows where the gold is, and the one who finds it is rewarded). In this process they have to find a random number (i.e. randomly digging a hole in the mine), which, when combined with the summary of the previous block and the summary of transactions contained in the current block, produces a given result. When a (winning) node finds a suitable result, it broadcasts the result to other nodes, which check it. If they agree with the result, each node adds the new block to the chain and the winner receives a monetary reward (i.e. the gold). As a result, Bob sees in his wallet an incoming transaction from Alice's address.

The example above highlights some (admirable) technical choices, which guarantee decentralization and trust between parties. First of all, the cryptographic mechanism

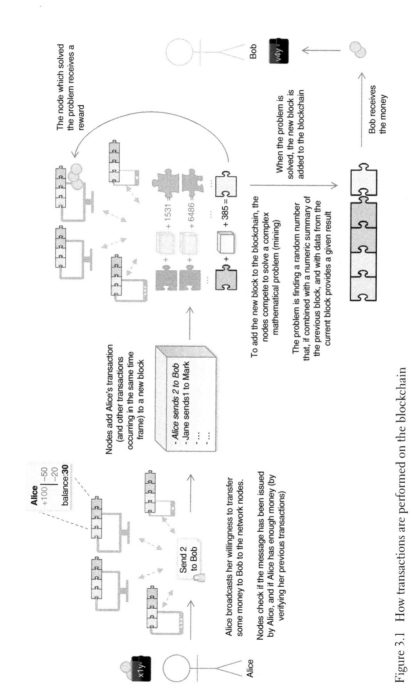

Figure 3.1 How transactions are performed on the blockchain

obliging users to sign a message with their credentials makes it nearly impossible to falsify the sender of a transaction (as only the owner of the credentials is able to create a valid message). Second, since each computer node has a local copy of the blockchain, shutting down or deleting the blockchain would require shutting down all the network nodes. To this purpose, it must be underlined that network nodes take decisions on a majority consensus basis (at least 51 percent of nodes should agree with a change to the blockchain). Hence, a malicious modification of the blockchain on a computer node would be discarded, as the resulting blockchain would differ from the one stored on remaining nodes. Third, the complex mathematical problem to be solved during mining reduces the probability that a single person or institution controls more than 51 percent of network nodes. In fact, solving the problem requires an incredibly high amount of computational power – and hence, computer hardware – which could hardly be possessed by a single person/institution. Moreover, as during this process (which could last several seconds or minutes depending on the underlying blockchain) the random number is combined with a summary of previous and current block data, falsifying a transaction in a previous blockchain block would require recomputing the random numbers for all the following blocks. This process, again, makes it nearly impossible to modify previously stored transactions. It must be underlined, though, that the whole mining process described above (which is generally referred to as *proof-of-work*) is quite inefficient, as the validation time and energy consumption by nodes are high. To reduce these inefficiencies, researchers are currently working on other validation mechanisms, such as the proof-of-stake, which delegate the validation to a selected portion of nodes. Such nodes are likely to be selected from among the ones having the highest amount of a given cryptocurrency, as it would be strongly in their interest to preserve a correct behavior of the blockchain, to increase the value of their holdings.

The framework devised by Nakamoto was initially conceived for the Bitcoin blockchain, the most famous blockchain of all, and was especially targeted to record financial transactions. Over the years, other blockchains were devised, which differ in terms of performance and stored data, such as Ethereum (probably the most famous Bitcoin competitor),[7] Ripple (a blockchain specially targeted to the banking sector),[8] Monero and Zcash (two blockchains focused on privacy),[9] and others. Depending on their needs, developers could choose the most suitable blockchain to rely upon.

From the architectural point of view, blockchains also differ in terms of write/read permissions. In particular, three types of blockchain exist, namely private, consortium, and public. Private blockchains are maintained by a limited number of network nodes belonging to an organization. Read rights could be limited to computers belonging to the network or could be granted to external computers. Consortium blockchains are generally used to share information among organizations. This type of blockchain is maintained by selected nodes belonging to the different institutions forming the consortium. In public blockchains, each computer can become

[7] Ethereum Team, "Ethereum White Paper – A Next-Generation Smart Contract and Decentralized Application Platform," 2010004, https://github.com/ethereum/wiki/wiki/White-Paper, 2014 (last accessed November 20, 2018).
[8] Ripple website, at https://ripple.com (last accessed November 20, 2018).
[9] Monero website, at https://getmonero.org (last accessed November 20, 2018); Zcash web page, at https://z.cash/ (last accessed April 19, 2018).

a network node and read/write the blockchain (as in the Bitcoin or Ethereum blockchains).

While public blockchains are capable of providing true decentralization and could be used when there is no trust between parties, private and consortium blockchains have the advantage of lowering validation time and costs, as network nodes are known and trusted. Furthermore, as read rights can be controlled, they provide greater privacy. Finally, it must be underlined that in cases of emergency (e.g. hacker attacks, bugs) these two latter types of blockchains could be easily modified or reverted to a previous state by making all network nodes agree on a previous version of the blockchain.

3.1.2 *How Does a Smart Contract Work?*

As previously mentioned, the blockchain was initially devised to store financial transactions between parties. As time passed, other assets started to be recorded, such as documents and certificates. In this context, the blockchain was used in the notarial context to store public records and attestations.[10] Due to its immutability, the blockchain was also used in the context of intellectual property rights.[11] In this case, an inventor could upload on the blockchain a document (or its *hash* – a numeric summary computed by applying a mathematical function to the document's content). The uploaded document/hash would then receive a time stamp, thus proving the existence of the document at a given time. In other cases, the blockchain has been used to record personal opinions, for example to avoid censorship.[12]

In recent years, researchers proposed to store more complex types of data on the blockchain, such as executable programs. It was the beginning of a second revolution (the first was Bitcoin transfers), which laid the foundation for new applications based on the blockchain. Such programs are referred to as *smart contracts* and are entities programmed to autonomously behave in a given manner when certain conditions are met. The idea of a smart contract is not new; in fact, it was introduced during the 1990s.[13] Nonetheless, it is only thanks to the blockchain that smart contracts have experienced a wide diffusion. The reason is quite simple: once a smart contract is stored on the blockchain, its code cannot be changed and can be inspected by anyone (even though some programming skills are required to understand it). Hence, everyone could know and foresee the behavior of the smart contract.

One of the metaphors frequently used to explain smart contracts is comparing them to vending machines. These are configured to take in money and to dispense food or other goods if the amount of money is sufficient and if the goods are available. Similarly, smart contracts take in some cryptocurrencies (in some cases, they do not even require a monetary input) and produce an output based on conditions specified in the code.

---

[10] M. Swan, note 4 before.
[11] J. L. de la Rosa, D. Gibovic, V. Torres, L. Maicher, F. Miralles, A. El-Fakdi, and A. Bikfalvi, "On Intellectual Property in Online Open Innovation for SME by Means of Blockchain and Smart Contracts," paper presented at the *3rd Annual World Open Innovation Conf. WOIC*, 2016.
[12] D. Lee, "Arachneum: Blockchain Meets Distributed Web," arXiv preprint arXiv:1609.02789, Advance Access published in 2016.
[13] N. Szabo, note 5 before.

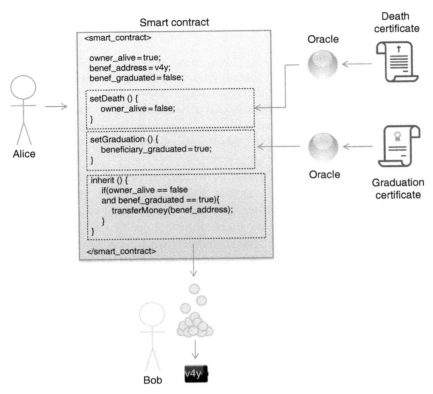

Figure 3.2 Example of a smart contract

To better understand the behavior of smart contracts, let us consider again the example of Alice and Bob. Alice is Bob's grandmother and is passionate about technology. Hence, she decides to code her last will in a smart contract (Figure 3.2). In her will, she specifies that all her money (in the form of cryptocurrency) should be transferred to Bob's wallet address when she passes away. Additionally, she can specify further conditions, for instance, that the money can be transferred only after Bob's graduation.

From a technical point of view, smart contracts could be seen as "evolved" wallet accounts. In fact, similarly to wallet accounts, they are characterized by a unique address and by a balance. In addition, they can store the *state* of some variables and their own *code* (in computer science, variables are containers used to store information). Hence, Alice could have shaped her smart contract to store three variables: owner_alive, initially set to true, to indicate whether she was alive or not; benef_address, to store the address of Bob's wallet (the beneficiary), which would be used to transfer the money to him after Alice's death; and benef_graduated, initially set to false, to indicate whether Bob graduated or not. The smart contract code would then contain some functions (i.e. portions of code with a given purpose), which could be used to modify the state (i.e. the value) of the variable. For example, the setDeath() function would be used to set the value of owner_alive to false in case of Alice's death, or the setGraduation() function would be used to set benef_graduated to true in case of Bob's graduation. Other functions, e.g. inherit(), would then be used to trigger the transfer of money to the beneficiary's address. In this case, the function would first check if the owner is dead (i.e. owner_alive is equal to false) and if the beneficiary graduated (i.e. benef_graduated is equal to true).

As smart contracts are not able to retrieve data from the real world, Alice's smart contract needs to rely on external services called *oracles*. Oracles take information from the real world (in this case, from death and graduation records) and inject it into the blockchain (e.g. by changing the value of the smart contract's variables). Hence, Alice could decide to rely on two oracles: the first one would periodically inspect death records, and if it finds a record related to Alice's death, it would trigger the setDeath() function. The second one would monitor graduation records and would eventually trigger the setGraduation() function, if Bob graduates.

Two different types of oracles exist, namely "software/hardware" and "inbound/outbound."[14] Software oracles generally extract information from web sources, whereas hardware oracles are used to gather data from the physical world through sensors. Inbound oracles are employed to insert information in the blockchain, whereas outbound oracles are used to reflect, in the real world, a blockchain state. For example, the oracles used by Alice are inbound software oracles, whereas, in other contexts, outbound hardware oracles could be used to let an intelligent locker automatically unlock as soon as a person pays for it (by issuing a transaction on the blockchain).

It is worth remarking that the role of oracles is extremely important, as their incorrect behavior could have negative consequences (e.g. the money could be transferred while Alice is still alive). Some companies exist, such as Oraclize,[15] which certify the authenticity of data (e.g. retrieved from web resources) for a small fee. Should Alice want to have an extra assurance, she could decide to rely on more than one oracle and let the smart contract trigger the transfer only when a variable state change is confirmed by the majority of oracles. In this way, a faulty oracle would be prevented by the others from injecting the wrong information on the blockchain.

For readability purposes, the smart contract example reported in Figure 3.2 has been intentionally kept simple. Nonetheless, it must be underlined that such a smart contract could contain several errors and bugs, which could lead to unexpected situations. In fact, in the example, functions setDeath() and setGraduation() could potentially be invoked by anyone (to invoke a function, one would need to know the address of the smart contract and send a particular transaction to it). Hence, Bob could invoke them in order to receive the money even if Alice is still alive, or he still has to graduate. The smart Alice could foresee this unexpected behavior and include, during the development of the smart contract, additional controls, such as letting the functions setDeath() and setGraduation() be invoked only by authorized addresses. In this way, each time the two functions are triggered, the smart contract would check the sender of the transaction invoking them and, if it does not belong to a white list of authorized addresses, would prevent the modification of the variables. From a coding perspective, such additional controls are usually included in the so-called modifiers, special functions which enable the execution of the smart contract only if certain conditions are verified. For the sake of readability, the modifier is not shown in Figure 3.2.

[14] J. Dourlens, "Oracles: Bringing Data to the Blockchain," paper published in 2017 at https://ethereumdev.io /oracles-getting-data-inside-blockchain.

[15] Oraclize. The company is described at www.oraclize.it (last accessed October 16, 2018).

The above example is quite simple. Nonetheless, it is worth remarking that more complex smart contracts could be written. For example, smart contracts are used in ICOs – initial coin offerings, the blockchain-based version of IPOs or initial public offerings. In ICOs, people aiming to invest in a company can send some cryptocurrency to a smart contract (by making a transaction to the smart contract's address). The smart contract would store in its variables the amount provided by each sender and would send back to the sender's wallet address a given amount of tokens. For example, by sending 1 Ether (the cryptocurrency of the Ethereum blockchain), a person could receive back 1000 "TOFU" tokens – the tokens created by a company aiming to use the blockchain to track the provenance of soy-based products – which he/she could keep as investment or trade for other cryptocurrencies as soon as the company's tokens get listed on trading platforms. ICOs' smart contracts, generally, are quite complex and contain additional variables, such as the start/end of the contribution time, a bonus percentage for early contributors, etc. In some cases, to increase security, additional functions are specified, for example, one to trigger a reimbursement to contributors if the minimum amount to be raised has not been reached, or to transfer the collected money (Ethers) to the company's address by exploiting the modifiers introduced above. Such functions are usually designed to be triggered only by a given address – e.g. the company's address – which could execute them by sending a particular transaction to the smart contract's address.

Apart from ICOs, smart contracts are the backbone of so-called DApps – decentralized applications. DApps could be seen as web applications where the code is run, instead of on a centralized server owned by a company, on the decentralized blockchain network. Whereas traditional web applications depend on a server's reachability, DApps can function even when a node is faulty/unreachable, as they are replicated on all blockchain nodes. Finally, in addition to ICOs and DApps, even more complex smart contracts are able to encode the rules to manage a group of people, the so-called DAOs – decentralized autonomous organizations. In DAOs, organizations can be run by relying on the rules written in the smart contract, without relying on external governance control entities.

3.2 Examples of Applications of Blockchain and Smart Contracts

Over the years, a number of applications of blockchain and smart contracts have been proposed in a variety of scenarios and sectors. Such applications use the blockchain to record different types of assets, ranging from financial to public (e.g. vehicle registries), semipublic (e.g. university degrees), and private (e.g. wills) as well as intangible (e.g. coupons) and tangible (e.g. electronic hotel room keys) assets.[16] In the following subsections, an overview of developed/devised applications is reported, grouping them according to their sector and context. The objective here is to provide the reader with a list of existing, soon to be developed, or potential applications of blockchain and smart contracts, in order to help him or her understand the huge impact this technology could have on society.

---

[16] L. Capital, *Bitcoin Series 24: The Mega-Master Blockchain List*, 2014, at http://ledracapital.com/blog/2014/3/11/bitcoin-series-24-the-mega-master-blockchain-list (last accessed October 15, 2018).

3.2.1 *Personal Data Management*

Applications in this area generally link to a user's wallet address with specific information related to his or her identity, interests, or credentials. By signing a transaction using credentials stored in his/her wallet, users can prove ownership of the address, and hence, can prove their identities. The advantage of having a blockchain-based proof of identity consists in the fact that there is no longer the need to rely on a centralized authority (whose databases could be vulnerable to attacks or modifications) and that individuals have full control of their credentials and, hence, of their associated identity data.[17]

A first example in this scenario is BitID, a prototype letting users log in to some websites using their Bitcoin wallet. In order to get authenticated, users have to scan a QR code (a code similar to a barcode) with their wallet's mobile application and sign a message with their credentials.[18]

Another field which is receiving increasing attention is KYC – know your customer – the process of determining the identity of a client, e.g. when he or she opens a bank account or undersigns an insurance policy. In this area, several companies are working on developing a blockchain-based KYC.[19] The underlying idea consists again in providing each person with a unique blockchain-based address. As a first step, the identity of the person would be verified by selected inspectors/institutions (which would physically check his or her ID card). Subsequently, for example while opening a bank account or undersigning a policy, the person would only need to sign a transaction with her credentials, in order to be verified.

More complex applications have also been devised whose final aim is protecting users' personal data.[20] Such applications mix on- and off-chain data. Each time a user wants to grant access to her data to an external application, the user can prove her identity on the blockchain and share the personal data linked to her address, which are stored off-chain and encrypted. In this way, the user can decide which data should be shared with the external application.

3.2.2 *Notary Services*

In the notarial context, several applications have been proposed. Apart from the example of Alice's last will shown above,[21] some researchers have proposed recording on the

---

[17] V. L. Lemieux, "In Blockchain We Trust? Blockchain Technology for Identity Management and Privacy Protection," paper presented at the *Conference for E-Democracy and Open Government*, 2017, at 57.

[18] BitID, see at http://bitid.bitcoin.blue/ (last accessed March 8, 2018).

[19] Civic, see at https://tokensale.civic.com/CivicTokenSaleWhitePaper.pdf (last accessed January 29, 2018); P. Dunphy and F. A. P. Petitcolas, A First Look at Identity Management Schemes on the Blockchain, paper, 2018, at http://arXiv preprint arXiv:1801.03294, Advance Access published 2018 KYC-CHAIN. 2016. *KYC-CHAIN* web page, at http://kyc-chain.com/# (last accessed December 29, 2017); also published in *IEEE Security and Privacy Magazine* special issue on "Blockchain Security and Privacy," 2018. V. L. Lemieux, before at 17.

[20] G. Zyskind, O. Nathan, et al., "Decentralizing Privacy: Using Blockchain to Protect Personal Data," in IEEEE Security and Privacy Workshops (SPW), 2015 IEEE, 180–184.

[21] P. Sreehari, M. Nandakishore, G. Krishna, J. Jacob, and V. S. Shibu, "Smart Will Be Converting the Legal Testament into a Smart Contract," in *Proceedings of the International Conference on Networks & Advances in Computational Technologies*, 2017, 203–207.

blockchain public records such as marriage certificates.[22] A more complex solution envisions the possibility of expressing the wish to get married by signing and sending a transaction to a marriage smart contract address.[23] The smart contract could also code additional conditions ruling family life. The couple could even decide to rely on the smart contract to manage their family budget.[24] In the case of divorce, the division of accumulated savings would be performed automatically, with a reduction of costs in notarial procedures.

Similarly to marriage certificates, records of property rentals and exchanges could also be stored on the blockchain. Recent studies have demonstrated the advantages of exploiting smart contracts in a real estate context.[25] First of all, relying on a unique shared ledger could reduce information fragmentation (e.g. homes for rent/sale are usually advertised on a variety of portals). Second, involved parties' identities can be easily verified, together with their previous history. Third, they could undersign a sell/lease agreement based on a smart contract. Finally, the required amount of money could be automatically transferred to the seller/lessor. It has been demonstrated that relying on a smart contract for property purchases can reduce the lead time from the signature of a sale contract to the registration of property ownership from four months to two days.[26]

Considerable research efforts have been devoted to intellectual property rights protection. In this view, several platforms have been developed to let authors prove the existence and authorship of a document.[27] By leveraging blockchain characteristics of immutability and public availability, such platforms store the hash (the summary) of the document together with a timestamp, thus proving the existence of the document at a given time. Other platforms take a step further, and rely on rules encoded in smart contracts to enable automatic licensing, by transferring crypto currencies to the author each time his or her content is viewed/listened to by the public.[28]

3.2.3 *Finance*

Finance and money transfers were the first application scenarios envisioned in the Bitcoin initiative. As Bitcoin transfers could require some time (on average 10 minutes), other blockchains have been devised, such as Ripple, which is intended to be the blockchain adopted by banks and guarantees a transaction time of a few

[22] R. Bova, "Four Weddings and a Funeral, Blockchain Style," 2014, at https://cointelegraph.com/news/david-and-joyces-wedding-demonstrates-how-easy-it-is-to-use-the-blockchain-technology-for-smart-contracts (last accessed March, 8, 2018).

[23] Q. DuPont and B. Maurer, "Ledgers and Law in the Blockchain," in *Kings Review*, 2015, at http://kingsreview.co.uk/magazine/blog/2015/06/23/ledgers-and-law-in-the-blockchain, Advance Access published 2015; S. Tual, *Mist Preview Discussion Thread*, 2014, at https://forum.ethereum.org/discussion/1576/mist-preview-discussion-thread (last accessed March 8, 2018).

[24] Wedding Chain, White Paper published at https://ukweddingunion.com/en/wedding-chain-white-paper.pdf (last accessed March 8, 2018).

[25] Deloitte, "Blockchain in Commercial Real Estate: The Future Is Here" 2017, www2.deloitte.com/content/dam/Deloitte/us/Documents/financial-services/us-fsi-rec-blockchain-in-commercial-real-estate.pdf (last accessed March 8, 2018).

[26] R. Beck, C. Becker, J. Lindman, and M. Rossi, "Opportunities and Risks of Blockchain Technologies" (Dagstuhl Seminar 17132), *Dagstuhl Reports*, 2017.

[27] POEX.IO, Proof of Existence web page, at "https://poex.io/" (last accessed March 8, 2018).

[28] Ascribe web page, at http://ascribe.io (last accessed March 8, 2018); Ujo Music web page, at https://ujomusic.com (last accessed March 8, 2018); Monegraph web page, at http://monegraph.com (last accessed March 8, 2018).

seconds.[29] Some interesting applications have been devised in the trading context as well. One of them is EtherDelta, a decentralized exchange which is managed by smart contracts.[30] The advantage of decentralization is that the user doesn't have to provide his or her funds to a trading platform owned by a company; instead, money is stored on a smart contract, which exchanges it for other tokens. Smart contracts have also been used in online lotteries[31] and pyramid-like rewarding systems.[32] Similarly, they have been used in sports betting, to provide a more transparent and cheap betting environment.[33] Prediction markets should be mentioned as well.[34] Such markets rely on the "Wisdom of the Crowd" assumption, according to which predictions made by groups of people are more likely to happen with respect to those made by a single individual. Users of these platforms can make a guess about a future occurrence, and, if their guess is correct, they can automatically receive a reward, triggered by a smart contract. To this purpose, it must be noted that these platforms strongly rely on oracles (usually several oracles gathering information from different sources and taking decisions on a majority basis) to verify the occurrence of an event in the real world.

A final application, which has been devised, is smart contract-based pension funds.[35] In this view, a working citizen could regularly send money to a smart contract, which would then, when the time comes, regularly give back retirement funds. The smart contract would be able to automatically produce forecasts, for example on the expected future monthly benefits, based on actual contributions.

3.2.4 *Industry*

This is one of the sectors where blockchain and smart contracts could provide wide benefits. Production and supply chains, for example, could profit from the fact that the blockchain is an unmodified ledger shared worldwide, by multiple organizations. In this view, the different actors involved in the production and supply of products could inspect or write on the blockchain data related to goods (hence, information would no longer be fragmented on multiple databases). As a consequence, for example, it would be possible to know, at any given time, the current and previous states of a product, by having the guarantee that inserted data have not been tampered with,[36] or to track the author of a document (e.g. for managing construction logbooks).[37] This could be particularly

---

[29] A. Jarrett, *Ripple and R3 Team up with 12 Banks to Trial XRP for Cross-Border Payments*, 2016, at https://ripple .com/insights/ripple-and-r3-team-up-with-12-banks-to-trial-xrp-for-cross-border-payments/ (last accessed March 8, 2018).

[30] EtherDelta web page, at https://etherdelta.com/ (last accessed March 8, 2018).

[31] Last is Me! web page, at http://lastis.me/ (last accessed March 8, 2018).

[32] EtherDice web page, at https://etherdice.io/ (last accessed March 8, 2018).

[33] FansUnite web page, at https://fansunite.io/ (last accessed March 8, 2018).

[34] Augur web page, at www.augur.net.

[35] R. Beck, C. Becker, J. Lindman, and M. Rossi, "Opportunities and Risks of Blockchain Technologies" (Dagstuhl Seminar 17132), in *Dagstuhl Reports*, 2017.

[36] R. Beck, C. Becker, J. Lindman, and M. Rossi, note before. IBM, "Adopting Blockchain for Enterprise Asset Management (EAM)," www.ibm.com/developerworks/cloud/library/cl-adopting-blockchain-for-enterprise-asset-management-eam/index.html (accessed October 16, 2018).

[37] Ž. Turk, and R. Klinc, "Potentials of Blockchain Technology for Construction Management" (2017) 196 *Procedia Engineering* 638–4.

useful in the aviation industry, where each aircraft component has to be carefully tracked and where the amount of paperwork to perform this task in a "traditional" way is huge.[38]

Not only industries but also customers could benefit from the exploitation of the blockchain to store information. In fact, several applications exist to record valuable goods in order to prevent counterfeiting. The most famous example is the provenance and ownership of diamonds,[39] authentication of parties,[40] but other goods such as sport/music tickets,[41] electronics[42] and pharmaceutical goods,[43] cars,[44] retail and other consumer products,[45] and timber have also been tracked.[46]

In this context, smart contracts are frequently used to manage the interaction between seller and buyer. Sheridan reports a simple example. In this example, a smart contract encodes the rules for a pizza delivery. If the food is delivered late, the smart contract automatically transfers back to the buyer half the price of the pizza.[47] Smart contracts could also be used to automatically convert money spent in shops, restaurants, etc. into loyalty points, which could then be exchanged for discounts.[48] In the e-commerce scenario, the solution presented by Monetha[49] relies on smart contracts to automatically change the reputation of parties involved in trades (on the basis of "how well" the trade was performed). An even more complex, visionary solution is represented by Prophet[50]: here smart contracts work in conjunction with artificial intelligence to support a demand-driven economy and the matching of supply and demand.

Finally, it is worth remarking that the blockchain could also simplify audit processes. In fact, should all the transactions between companies and individuals be recorded on the blockchain, such processes would be quicker and more efficient, with a dramatic reduction of bureaucracy.[51]

3.2.5 Insurance

In the insurance sector, the blockchain could bring tremendous changes.[52] It could be used, especially in combination with Internet of Things (IoT) sensors, to improve customer experience and reduce operating costs. In this view, smart contracts could

---

[38] S. Mansfield-Devine, "Beyond Bitcoin: Using Blockchain Technology to Provide Assurance in the Commercial World" (2017) 5 *Computer Fraud & Security*, 4–18.

[39] See Provenance, www.provenance.org, Everledger, www.everledger.io.

[40] Reply, Authentichain, www.reply.com/en/content/authentichain.date?

[41] Reply, Cloudchain, www.reply.com/en/content/blockchain-ticketing-solution-cloudchain.

[42] See Blockverify, www.blockverify.io.

[43] J. Thomason, "Blockchain: An Accelerator for Women and Children's Health?" (2017) 1 *Global Health*, 3.

[44] See Reply, "Best Practice: Safety First; Quality Assurance for Connected Cars," www.reply.com/en/industries/automotive.

[45] See Reply, "Automated Commerce: Recognise Me – But Don't Spy on Me," www.reply.com/en/industries/retail-and-consumer-products.

[46] B. Düdder & O. Ross, "Timber Tracking: Reducing Complexity of Due Diligence by Using Blockchain Technology," Advance Access published 2017.

[47] I. Sheridan, "MiFID II in the context of Financial Technology and Regulatory Technology" (2017) 12 (4) *Capital Markets Law Journal*, 417–427.

[48] Loyyal web page, at http://loyyal.com.

[49] Monetha web page, at www.monetha.io/ (last accessed March 8, 2018).

[50] Prophet web page, at http://profeth.org.

[51] S. Psaila, *Blockchain: A Game Changer for Audit Processes*, www2.deloitte.com/mt/en/pages/audit/articles/mt-blockchain-a-game-changer-for-audit.html.

[52] V. Gatteschi, F. Lamberti, C. Demartini, C. Pranteda, and V. Santamaría, "Blockchain and Smart Contracts for Insurance: Is the Technology Mature Enough?", (2018) 10 (2) *Future Internet*;

encode the rules for a damage reimbursement, which could be triggered as soon as an oracle detects a given situation such as a flight delay[53] or some dampness under the roof of a building.[54] Another use, aimed at reducing fraud, relies on a blockchain written by multiple parties (e.g. not only insurance companies, but also police officers, medical staff). Before paying a claim or acquiring a customer, insurance companies could check previous claims and infractions. In addition, smart contracts could be utilized to automatically compute a customer's risk and the related premium.

Smart contracts could also be exploited in a pay-per-use insurance scenario. Sensors could be used to automatically activate or deactivate a policy' coverage, while the record on the blockchain would be proof of the change.[55] Finally, smart contracts could be the key element to support peer-to-peer insurance. In fact, by leveraging their ability to rule DAOs, they could be used to hard-code the mechanism governing self-insured groups.[56]

3.2.6 Government, Healthcare and Education

Several applications for blockchain and smart contracts have been proposed in the government context. Estonia recently proposed adopting blockchain for e-Residency, in order to increase the security of identity management.[57] Other applications include exploitation of the blockchain to permanently record citizens' votes[58] (or politicians' programs, in order to check whether they have kept their promises). A blockchain-based voting system could be structured as follows: citizens able to vote could be provided with a token. In order to express their preference, they could send the token (i.e. make a transaction) to a politician's wallet address. The authenticity and nonchangeability of the vote would be guaranteed by the blockchain. A more complex solution would be to rely on smart contracts to create a DAO-based autonomous governance system,[59] where citizens could suggest modifications to existing laws and vote on them.

In healthcare, the blockchain could be used to store patients' medical data, with many advantages. First, the research community could profit from a wide database of medical data to perform analyses and studies on existing pathologies. Second, the medical history of each person would be recorded, improving medical treatments (e.g. in urgent cases, a doctor could be alerted about the patient's allergies to given treatments). Several companies are investigating these scenarios, in both the medical[60] and dental

---

V. Gatteschi, F. Lamberti, C. Demartini, C. Pranteda, and V. Santamaría, "To Blockchain or Not to Blockchain: That Is the Question" (2018) 20 (2), *IT Professional*, 62–74.

[53] T. Bertani, K. Butkute, and F. Canessa, *Smart Flight Insurance – InsurETH*, 2015, at http://mkvd .s3.amazonaws.com/apps/InsurEth.pdf (last accessed December 29, 2017).

[54] S. Davies, *Bitcoin: Possible Bane of the Diamond Thief*, 2015, at www.ft.com/content/f2b0b2ee-9012-11e4-a0e5-00144feabdc0 (last accessed June 30, 2016).

[55] F. Lamberti, V. Gatteschi, C. Demartini, M. Pelissier, A. Gómez, and V. Santamaria, "Blockchains Can Work for Car Insurance: Using Smart Contracts and Sensors to Provide On-Demand Coverage" (2018) 7:4 IEEE *Consumer Electronics Magazine*, 72–81.

[56] J. Davis, "Peer to Peer Insurance on an Ethereum Blockchain," 2016, at www.dynamisapp.com/whitepaper .pdf (last accessed December 29, 2017).

[57] C. Sullivan, and E. Burger, "E-Residency and Blockchain" (2017) 33:4 *Computer Law & Security Review*, 470–81.

[58] S. Ølnes, "Beyond Bitcoin Enabling Smart Government Using Blockchain Technology" (2016) *International Conference on Electronic Government and the Information Systems Perspective. Is there a publisher?* 253–64.

[59] S. Huckle M. White, "Socialism and the Blockchain" (2016) 8:4 *Future Internet*, 49.

[60] See MedicalChain White Paper, at https://medicalchain.com/Medicalchain-Whitepaper-EN.pdf.

contexts.[61] An interesting solution is presented by a Robomed White Paper.[62] In this case, the objective is to improve quality of healthcare systems. Here, a smart contract connects patients and healthcare service providers by automatically creating the most suitable treatment path and cutting down bureaucracy costs typical of the traditional process.

In the education scenario, the blockchain could be used to record competencies acquired by learners.[63] By having all their previous history stored on a single (shared) place, learners could more easily identify competencies they are lacking, and plan how to obtain them,[64] or to determine which jobs to apply for.[65] Similarly in the personal data management scenario, each learner could be provided with a wallet address, which could act as a container of competencies. In some cases, the hash of a certificate could also be stored. By relying on blockchain, job application fraud could be widely reduced, as human resources staff could easily access a person's previous training history. Another interesting application relies on smart contracts to compute rewards to be given to students (based on their marks), thus fostering learning.[66]

3.2.7 *Software and Internet*

In the context of the IoT, the blockchain could bring several benefits. For example, it could be used to store system logs, thus making it impossible for an attacker to delete or alter events history. In the Internet context, the blockchain has been used to store domain names, with the objective of replacing domain name systems (DNS) servers with blockchain-based ones.[67] Again, in the Internet context, smart contracts have been used in cloud storage.[68] In this scenario, users can rent out space on their hard drives, and a smart contract would automatically provide them with a reimbursement. Systems such as this one split portions of encrypted users' files among several computer nodes and, before

---

[61] Dentacoin White Paper, at https://dentacoin.com/web/white-paper/Whitepaper-en1.pdf.

[62] Robomed White Paper, at https://robomed.io/download/Robomed_whitepaper_eng_final.pdf.

[63] A. Grech, A. F. Camilleri et al., "Blockchain in Education, JRC for Policy Report" (2017), at http://publications.jrc.ec.europa.eu/repository/bitstream/JRC108255/jrc108255_blockchain_in_education%281%29.pdf (last accessed October 16, 2018). M. Turkanović, M. Hölbl, K. Košič, M. Heričko, and A. Kamišalić, "EduCTX: A Blockchain-Based Higher Education Credit Platform," IEEE Access, Advance Access published 2018.

[64] V. Gatteschi, F. Lamberti, F. Salassa, and C. Demartini, "An Automatic Tool Supporting Life-Long Learning Based on a Semantic-Oriented Approach for Comparing Qualifications," in *IADIS International Conference on Cognition and Exploratory Learning in Digital Age*, CELDA 2009; V. Gatteschi, F. Lamberti, A. Sanna, and C. Demartini, "Using Tag Clouds to Support the Comparison of Qualifications, Résumés and Job Profiles," in *ICETA 2011 – 9th IEEE International Conference on Emerging eLearning Technologies and Applications, Proceedings*, 2011; P. Montuschi, F. Lamberti, V. Gatteschi, and C. Demartini, "A Semantic Recommender System for Adaptive Learning" (2015) 17:5 *IT Professional*, 50–5.

[65] V. Gatteschi, F. Lamberti, and C. Demartini, "LO-MATCH: A Semantic Platform for Matching Migrants' Competences with Labour Market's Needs," *2012 IEEE Global Engineering Education Conference (EDUCON)*, 1–5. P. Montuschi, V. Gatteschi, F. Lamberti, A. Sanna, and C. Demartini, "Job Recruitment and Job Seeking Processes: How Technology Can Help" (2014) 16: 5 *IT Professional*.

[66] A. Aglietti, "Proof-of-Knowledge: Same Blockchain, Different Story," paper at https://log.growbit.xyz/proof-of-knowledge-efc138f2a17c (accessed October 18, 2018).

[67] H. Kalodner, M. Carlsten, P. Ellenbogen, J. Bonneau, and A. Narayanan, "An Empirical Study of Namecoin and Lessons for Decentralized Namespace Design," *Workshop on the Economics of Information Security (WEIS)*, 2015; Namecoin web page, at https://namecoin.org (accessed October 18, 2018).

[68] MaidSafe web page, at https://maidsafe.net; Storj web page, at https://storj.io (accessed October 18, 2018).

storing them, compute their hash to discover whether the same file has already been stored on the network (thus avoiding duplicates).

In the IoT scenario, blockchain and smart contracts provide the infrastructure for a secure and automatic interaction among devices.[69] For example, the cryptographic mechanism could be used during the authentication of IoT devices. More complex scenarios rely on smart contracts and oracles to let intelligent appliances interact with the real world.[70] In this view, an intelligent washing machine could automatically order (and pay for) spare parts in the case of malfunction. Another application is related to smart grids.[71] In this case, smart contracts can enable automatic energy trades between buildings, thus allowing neighbors to buy/sell electricity.

3.2.8 *Sharing Economy*

As previously mentioned, smart contracts can enable the creation of DAOs, which are one of the backbones of the sharing economy. Groups of individuals can cooperate to provide valuable tangible and intangible assets to the community. The community could then decide how to evaluate the asset and reward the creator/provider.[72] Existing sharing economy applications will soon be based on blockchain technology. For example, several companies are replicating services such as Airbnb,[73] Uber,[74] or Amazon's Mechanical Turk.[75] Finally, it must be mentioned that blockchain-based house sharing could benefit from intelligent lockers enabling access only after reservation.[76]

3.2.9 *Social Impact*

In the social field, several blockchain-based applications have been proposed to foster well-being and protect human rights in developing countries. For example, in order to increase financial inclusion, blockchain-based identification has been used successfully.[77] The blockchain also will allow people without bank accounts to be involved in money exchanges, as everyone can create a wallet address to receive/send money. In addition, the lower transaction fees lay the foundation for micro payments and

---

[69] K. Christidis and M. Devetsikiotis, "Blockchains and Smart Contracts for the Internet of Things," *IEEE Access*, vol. 4, 2292–2303, 2016; M. Conoscenti, A. Vetrò, and J. C. De Martin, "Blockchain for the Internet of Things: A Systematic Literature Review," pp. 1–6, in *IEEE/ACS 13th International Conference of Computer Systems and Applications (AICCSA)*, IEEE, 2016.

[70] S. Higgins, |*IBM Reveals Proof of Concept for Blockchain-Powered Internet of Things*, 2015, at www .coindesk.com/ibm-reveals-proof-concept-blockchain-powered-internet-things/ (last accessed December 29, 2017).

[71] See Lo3Energy web page, at https://lo3energy.com.

[72] A. Pazaitis, P. De Filippi, and V. Kostakis, "Blockchain and Value Systems in the Sharing Economy: The Illustrative Case of Backfeed" (2017): 125 *Technological Forecasting and Social Change*, 105–15.

[73] See BeeToken web page, at www.beetoken.com (last accessed July 11, 2018).

[74] See La'Zooz webpage, at http://lazooz.org.

[75] See Gems webpage, at https://gems.org.

[76] See Slock.it web Page, at https://slock.it.

[77] Banqu web page, at www.banquapp.com (last accessed July 6, 2018); G. Prisco, "Microsoft Building Open Blockchain-Based Identity System with Blockstack," ConsenSys, 2016, at https://bitcoinmagazine.com /articles/microsoft-building-open-blockchain-based-identity-system-with-blockstack-consensys -1464968713; S. Warden, "*Can Bitcoin Technology Solve the Migrant Crisis?*", 2016, paper at www.wsj.com /articles/can-bitcoin-technology-solve-the-migrant-crisis-1465395474.

more affordable money transfers.[78] Finally, smart contracts could be used to transparently track donors' funds, in order to ensure they reach the intended beneficiary.[79]

3.3 Mainstream Adoption of Blockchain and Smart Contracts: Open Issues

From the above overview, the blockchain and smart contracts, in the coming years, will become more and more part of the daily activities of people. The shift to a decentralized, (smart) code-based regulation of activities and agreements not only impacts the IT context, but also has numerous repercussions on existing processes and regulations.

Below, we report some key issues that should be addressed before a mainstream adoption of blockchain and smart contracts, focusing on those related to the legal and IT contexts. A first issue is related to *whether smart contracts are mature enough to complement/substitute legal contracts*. In the legal context, smart contracts have frequently been defined as "automatable and enforceable agreement[s]. Automatable by computer, although some parts may require human input and control. Enforceable either by legal enforcement of rights and obligations or via tamper-proof execution of computer code."[80] From this definition, it is clear that smart contracts should have some parts which are autonomously executed, and should be enforceable either by law or because transactions cannot be reversed.

Even though some legislatures, such as Arizona's, have started to consider smart contracts as legally effective as other contracts,[81] the research domain has expressed some concerns, such as: "The fact that a technological solution is innovative and elegant need not imply that it is commercially useful or legally viable."[82] In this view, one should distinguish between what is technologically viable and what is legally permissible. For example, a smart contract recording a money transfer could be legally invalid, because one of the parties lacks legal capacity or because the smart contract regulates the transaction of illegal goods.[83] Nonetheless, it must be recalled that when a transaction is issued on the blockchain, it cannot be reversed, thus making it impossible for a person to obtain a refund. Furthermore, wallet addresses are pseudo-anonymous. In fact, anyone could create a wallet address while still remaining anonymous. Only in some cases can the identity of a person be inferred by clustering together transfers from one address to another. This aspect makes it hard to identify the owner of a blockchain address and hence, prosecute him or her for committing illegal acts, such as fraud. A possible solution would be to develop a smart contract-based escrow system. Here a buyer could transfer

[78] J. Thomason, 2017, "Blockchain: An Accelerator for Women and Children's Health?" (2017) 1:1 *Global Health*, 3.

[79] Helperbit web page, at https://app.helperbit.com.

[80] C. D. Clack, V. A. Bakshi, and L. Braine, "Smart Contract Templates: Foundations, Design Landscape and Research Directions," 2016, also at *arXiv preprint arXiv:1608.00771*, Advance Access published 2016.

[81] "Arizona Gives Legal Status to Blockchain Based Smart Contracts," 2017, www.trustnodes.com/2017/04/03/arizona-gives-legal-status-blockchain-based-smart-contracts (last accessed March 23, 2018); D. A. Zetzsche, R. P. Buckley, and D. W. Arner, "The Distributed Liability of Distributed Ledgers: Legal Risks of Blockchain," Advance Access published 2017.

[82] E. Mik, "Smart Contracts: Terminology, Technical Limitations and Real World Complexity," *Law*, (2017) 9:2 *Innovation and Technology*, 269–300.

[83] M. Raskin, "The Law and Legality of Smart Contracts," (2017) 1 *Geo L. Tech. Rev.* 305–327.

money to a smart contract, which would freeze it until it can be confirmed that the seller's obligations have been fulfilled. In case of dispute, an escrow agent could intervene in the process, triggering a refund to the buyer or transferring money to the seller.[84] Even though this solution could be useful in some scenarios (e.g. in e-commerce), it should be noted that smart contracts have been devised to increase automation, and that needing to rely on a third party to validate a transaction could create a bottleneck in some contexts.

The fact that smart contracts are tamper-proof is a second critical issue. Even though this could be an advantage, in certain conditions, it implies that a faulty smart contract could continue to operate until its expires. Countermeasures would imply developing a smart contract whose code does not contain errors. Nonetheless, this is extremely hard, as demonstrated by recent hacker attacks on the Ethereum blockchain, especially to the DAO in June 2016 (resulting in a loss of around $60 million)[85] or to multisignature wallets in July 2017 (for a total of $30 million stolen).[86] Even though this kind of attack would be reduced in the future, due to an ever-growing community of "white hat" hackers,[87] there is still the risk that more complex smart contracts contain bugs. Furthermore, as smart contracts' code cannot be modified, during coding, developers have the impossible task of trying to foresee all the possible events that may occur during its lifetime and code the desired behaviour in advance. It unlikely that complex smart contracts would be able to cover all eventualities. One solution to this issue would be to allow the transfer of smart contracts to become effective only after a given amount of time (e.g. one day), by introducing a super party organism (similar to the use of an escrow agent) which could eventually delete (in the specified time frame) the money transfer in the case of a hacker's attack. Alternatively, one could rely on private or consortium blockchains, which could eventually reverse the transaction by agreeing on a previous version of the blockchain. Nonetheless, similar to the escrow agent example above, it must be recalled that needing to wait for a given amount of time before receiving a transaction, in some contexts, could be unacceptable. Likewise, in certain cases, deciding to rely on a private or consortium blockchain might not be a suitable choice, as in some contexts a full decentralization would be needed.

A third issue is related to the liability of DAOs. As in the context of DAOs, smart contracts enable the automatic governance of groups of people, and if the organization breaks the law, it could be difficult to determine who is responsible.[88] Should the developer of the smart contract be considered responsible if it fails to foresee the illegal behavior, and to block it? Or should the system or members of the system be considered responsible?

---

[84] EscrowMyEther web page, at http://escrowmyether.com/ (last accessed April 19, 2018).
[85] M. P. Gomez Gelvez, "Explaining the DAO Exploit for Beginners," in Solidity, 2016, at https://medium.com /@MyPaoG/explaining-the-dao-exploit-for-beginners-in-solidity-80ee84f0d47 (last accessed March 23, 2018).
[86] BlockCAT, 2017, *On the Parity Multi-Sig Wallet Attack*, at https://medium.com/blockcat/on-the-parity-multi-sig-wallet-attack-83fb5e7f4b8c (last accessed March 23, 2018).
[87] HACKEN – Tokenized Bug Bounty Marketplace Driven by White Hats. Accessed at https://hacken.io (October 18, 2018).
[88] J. A. Lee, A. Long, J. Steiner, S. G. Handler, and Z. Wood, "Blockchain Technology and Legal Implications of 'Crypto 2.0'," *Bloomberg BNA Banking Report*, 2015, vol. 3.

A fourth issue is related to the translation of legal contracts expressed in natural language to code.[89] It is very likely that the smart contract's code (the "dry code") will not completely reflect the legal contract's natural language (the "wet code"). From a technical point of view, this could happen because the programmer was not able to code all the information reported in the legal contract. Consequently, the smart contract would not self-enforce as intended and promised. Considering again the attack on the DAO, the "do no harm" imperative was only reported in terms of wet code, and was not hard-coded in the smart contract.[90] When the hacker exploited the bug in the DAO's smart contract, a long debate took place. Followers of the "code is law" principle claimed that the hacker should keep the stolen money, as the dry code has precedence over the wet one. Others claimed that, as the smart contract did not behave as expected, the hacker had no right to keep the money. This impasse was solved by the creation of a fork to the original Ethereum blockchain (i.e. a duplication), resulting in a new blockchain (Ethereum Classic). One blockchain contained the malicious transactions (Ethereum), whereas the other changed its behavior to neutralize them (Ethereum Classic). Apart from the technical aspects described above, it must be understood that sometimes the wet code cannot be fully converted into programmable code, as it purposely makes room for interpretation in case of dispute.[91] Being able to encode all the legal nuances in a smart contract is a hard task.[92]

In order to overcome this issue, researchers have proposed adopting different solutions. A first solution is to write smart contracts from the outset. This solution implies that lawyers work in conjunction with programmers and that both parties acquire some competencies, respectively, in programming and law.[93] A second solution foresees that lawyers draft the wet code having in mind the subsequent translation into dry code. This type of coding implies that the legal language adopted is logical, clear, and unambiguous.[94] Furthermore, common legal language should be shared among all the parties involved in the creation of the wet and dry codes. In the research domain, formalisms to represent wet code in a programmable-like way are currently under development. It is worth mentioning the experience reported by Frantz and Nowostawski,[95] where a system for semiautomatically creating smart contracts is

---

[89] S. Farrell, H. Machin, and R. Hinchliffe, "Lost and Found in Smart Contract Translation – Considerations in Transitioning to Automation in Legal Architecture," in (2017) *Proceedings of the Congress of the United Nations Commission on International Trade Law*, Wien, 95–104; P. De Filippi and S. Hassan, "Blockchain Technology as a Regulatory Technology: From Code Is Law to Law Is Code," *arXiv preprint arXiv:1801.02507*, Advance Access published 2018; D. Magazzeni, P. McBurney, and W. Nash, "Validation and Verification of Smart Contracts: A Research Agenda," (2017) 50:9 *Computer*, 50–57; S. Murphy, and C. Cooper, "Can Smart Contracts Be Legally Binding Contracts," An R3 and Norton Rose Fulbright White Paper published in 2016 at www.nortonrosefulbright.com/files/r3-and-norton-rose-fulbright-white-paper-full-report-144581.pdf

[90] L. Abegg, *Code Is Law? Not Quite Yet*, 2016, at "www.coindesk.com/code-is-law-not-quite-yet" (last accessed March 23, 2018).

[91] S. Farrell, H. Machin, at 88. See also P. De Filippi, S. Hassan at 88E. E. Mik, at 81.

[92] T. I. Kiviat, "Beyond Bitcoin: Issues in Regulating Blockchain Transactions" (2015) 65 *Duke LJ*, 569–608.

[93] M. Fenwick, W. A. Kaal, and E. P. M. Vermeulen, "Legal Education in the Blockchain Revolution," Advance Access published 2017.

[94] F. Al Khalil, M. Ceci, L. O'Brien, and T. Butler, "A Solution for the Problems of Translation and Transparency in Smart Contracts," Advance Access published 2017.

[95] C. K. Frantz, and M. Nowostawski, "From Institutions to Code: Towards Automated Generation of Smart Contracts, 210–15," in *Foundations and Applications of Self* Systems, IEEE International Workshops*, 2016.

proposed. In this work, wet code is formalized in terms of (a) Attributes (the characteristics of an actor), (b) Deontic (the nature of the statement, i.e. permission, obligation, or prohibition), (c) aIm (the action regulated by the statement), (d) Conditions (the conditions under which the statement holds), and (e) Or else (the consequences related to nonconformance). By using the proposed formalism (abbreviated as *ADICO*), natural language could be translated in the following form: "People (A) must (D) vote (I) every four years (C), or else they face a fine (O)".[96] The formalized wet code is then semiautomatically translated into dry code (e.g. aims are translated into smart contracts' functions, whereas deontic and conditions are reflected in smart contracts' modifiers). The advantage of this approach is that smart contracts could be created by people with limited coding competencies. Nonetheless, it must be noted that this approach is best suited only to simple (smart) contracts. In the case of complex ones modifications to the automatically produced code would be required.

Even though the above solutions – coding smart contracts from the outset, or defining wet code with the subsequent coding in mind – could be a first step toward a widespread use of smart contracts, it must be recalled that adopting this approach could imply losing the intrinsic ambiguity of legal rules.[97] Another aspect, which should be considered, is what could happen in case of oracle failures. In fact, even the most secure and well-developed smart contracts could behave in an unwanted manner, if a faulty oracle injects wrong information into the blockchain. This should be considered during the development of the smart contract, e.g. by defining the validation of a condition based on multiple oracles. Nonetheless, this approach is still prone to errors, as an ill-intentioned person could still perform a coordinated attack on multiple platforms inspected by the oracles. In this case, which one would be considered responsible? The developer of the smart contract? The oracle service used to gather the data? The web platform hosting the data?

Given the increasing attention by the wider public to smart contract-based startup funding, a side issue, which should also be considered, is the recent increase in phishing attempts during smart contract-based ICOs. As previously mentioned, in order to contribute to an ICO, a person has to send a transaction to a smart contract, which, based on the amount of the contribution, sends back tokens. Since companies usually raise millions of dollars, malicious individuals started to devise more and more sophisticated ways to steal money from inexperienced users, by publishing a fake copy of the website (e.g. on a different, similar-appearing domain, such as tofu.co instead of tofu.com), specifying their own wallet address instead of the smart contract's address. In some cases, they steal the startup's mailing list to send phishing e-mails (as happened recently during the Bee Token's ICO, when around $1 million was stolen).[98] In these cases, it is quite difficult to identify the culprits behind the phishing attempt, at least until they try to convert the stolen tokens using trading platforms (which could link the address of

---

[96] C. K. Frantz, M. Nowostawski, 94.

[97] P. De Filippi, and S. Hassan, "Blockchain Technology as a Regulatory Technology: From Code Is Law to Law Is Code," *arXiv preprint arXiv:1801.02507*, Advance Access published 2018.

[98] N. De, *Bee Token ICO Stung by $1 Million Phishing Scam*, 2018, at www.coindesk.com/bee-token-phishing-scam/ (last accessed April 19, 2018).

the phishing wallet to the identity of the guilty parties). A way to mitigate this drawback could be to train users to avoid these types of attacks. Furthermore, a blacklist of scam wallet addresses could be created. Such addresses could be prevented (e.g. by trading platforms) from converting stolen money into other tokens or currencies. Nonetheless, even though the thieves couldn't spend the stolen money, there is no guarantee that the original owner would be able to get it back, as only the thieves would be able to trigger a transfer from their wallet.

Similar to phishing attempts, another issue, which should be considered, is theft of a person's wallet credentials. Also in this case, token transfers cannot be reversed, and it is quite difficult to identify the thief. Usually, thieves search for users' credentials in e-mail accounts or documents stored in the cloud,[99] or obtain them by hacking trading platforms' databases.[100] As in phishing attempts, thieves' wallet accounts could be prevented from converting stolen tokens into other currencies.

A final issue is related to the life of a blockchain. Let us consider again the example of Alice's will. As network peers maintain blockchains, no one guarantees that a blockchain will live forever. For example, blockchains showing higher performance or rewards for network nodes could appear. In this case, the majority of nodes would dismiss the "old" blockchain. This could make it more vulnerable to attacks (as one could easily control most of the network). Furthermore, there is a high chance that the value of the related token will diminish (as the blockchain would be less appealing), having a considerable impact on Alice's inheritance. To this purpose, it is hard to define effective countermeasures. Thus it would be prudent to wait until blockchain and smart contract technology becomes more mature. In fact, as time passes, a few winning blockchains will remain on the market and will be adopted on a wide scale, thus also resulting in less-volatile prices of tokens.

3.4 Conclusion

In this chapter, a primer on blockchain and smart contracts technology has been provided. The chapter started by presenting the reader with an overview of how this technology works, together with a simple example to better illustrate its functioning. Next, an overview of existing, soon-to-be-developed, or potential applications of both blockchain and smart contracts has been provided, with the objective of showing the impact of this technology on a number of existing processes in various heterogeneous scenarios. Finally, some key issues, which should be addressed by researchers in the legal and IT domains, have been presented and discussed. The objective of this discussion was to highlight existing limitations of blockchain and smart contracts, as well as potential issues that could arise from their application, in order to allow legal and IT experts to reflect on how they could be preempted.

Potential issues identified are the adoption of smart contracts as (or in conjunction with) legal contracts, the translation from legal contracts to code, the liability of DAOs, as

[99] K. Parrish, *Hackers Stole Digital Coins While a YouTube Broadcaster Advised about ICOs*, www.digitaltrends.com/computing/ico-advisor-robbed-2m-during-youtube-livestream/ (last accessed April 19, 2018).

[100] Coincheck: World's biggest ever digital currency "theft," 2018, www.bbc.com/news/world-asia-42845505 (last accessed April 19, 2018).

well as the limitation of damages related to faulty smart contracts, the consequences of oracle failures, phishing attempts and theft of wallet credentials, and the life of a blockchain. Solutions identified involve the development of smart contract-based escrow systems, the creation of a super party organism which could neutralize the effects of a smart contract, the exploitation of private and consortium blockchains, the definition of approaches for automatic translation between traditional and code-based contracts, the usage of sets of oracles, the creation of address blacklists and the definition of suitable training initiatives for end users. Even though the above solutions could be viable in some scenarios, they still present some limitations. For example, by relying on escrow systems and on a super party organization, a key advantage of smart contracts – i.e. automation – would be lost, as the control process would become a bottleneck. Similarly, relying on private and consortium blockchains might not be feasible in those contexts in which a full decentralization is required. Replacing existing contracts with smart contracts, moreover, could be unworkable in some contexts where existing laws leave room for interpretation. Finally, relying on sets of oracles or on address blacklists might not provide a full guarantee that the correct information is inserted in the blockchain, or that stolen money is returned to the owner. Surely, a lot of research still needs to be done before a mainstream adoption of blockchain and smart contracts.[101] Nonetheless, it will be worth the effort, as this technology will bring tremendous changes to the world, as we know it.

---

[101] M. Peck, "The Blockchain Has a Dark Side," 53:6 (2016) *IEEE Spectrum*, pp. 12–13, 2016.

Part II

Contract Law and Smart Contracts

4 Formation of Smart Contracts under Contract Law

Mateja Durovic and André Janssen

4.1 Introduction

This contribution concentrates predominately on the formation of (blockchain-based) smart contracts. The crucial issue to be discussed here is whether the traditional legal concepts of contract formation are seriously challenged by the rise of smart contracts. Are smart contracts the end of contract formation as we know it or is it just much ado about nothing? And if contract law is in principle a good fit for the *formation* of smart contracts, do smart contracts have features which do challenge traditional contract law? And if yes what are those features? These are some of the questions this contribution will try to answer.

In this chapter, the blockchain-based smart contracts and the process of contract formation are discussed and exemplified. The chapter also deals with possible conflict areas between smart contracts and traditional contract law in general before ending with a short conclusion.

The main threads of argument regarding smart contracts in the legal scholarship seem to be whether or not they are contracts in the legal sense, whether they are a disruptive innovation in the legal system, and what are their benefits and potential threats. That being said, the *legal* scholarship on them is still rather scarce compared to the impact smart contracts might have in the future – even though the literature is quickly growing.[1] There is a multitude of information and documents on how smart

We would like to thank Jason Bond Lo for the revision of the final draft of this contribution.

[1] The following contributions are dealing exclusively or at least partly with the legal aspects of smart contracts: A. Börding, T. Jülicher, C. Röttgen, and M. von Schönfeld, 'Neue Herausforderungen der Digitalisierung für das deutsche Zivilrecht: Praxis und Rechtsdogmatik', (2017) *Computer und Recht (CR)*134; S. Bourque and S. Fung Ling Tsui, A *Lawyer's Introduction to Smart Contracts* (Lask: Scientia Nobilitat, 2014), pp. 4–23; C. Buchleitner and T. Rabl, 'Blockchain und Smart Contracts', (2017) *Ecolex* 4; A. J. Casey and A. Niblett, 'Self-Driving Contracts', (2017) 43 *Journal of Corporation Law* 1; P. Catchlove, 'Smart Contracts: A New Era of Contract Use', ssrn.com/abstract=3090226; A. Djazayeri, 'Rechtliche Herausforderungen durch Smart Contracts', (2016) *jurisPR-BKR*, 12/2016 no. 1; M. Finck, 'Blockchains: Regulating the Unknown', (2018) 19 *German Law Journal*, 665; N. Guggenheim, 'The Potential of Blockchain for the Conclusion of Contracts', in: R. Schulze, D. Staudenmeyer, and S. Lohse (eds.), *Contracts for the Supply of Digital Content: Regulatory Challenges and Gaps* (Baden-Baden: Nomos, 2017), p. 83–97; J. I-H Hsiao, 'Smart Contract on the Blockchain-Paradigm Shift for Contract Law', (2017) 14 *US-China Law Review* 2017, 685; C. Jacobs and C. Lange-Hausstein, 'Blockchain und Smart Contracts: Zivil-und aufsichtsrechtliche Bedingungen', (2017) *IT-Rechts-Berater (ITBR)* 10; M. Jünemann and A. Kast, 'Rechtsfragen beim Einsatz der Blockchain', (2017) *Kreditwesen* 531; M. Kaulartz and J. Heckmann, 'Smart Contracts – Anwendung der Blockchain-Technologie', (2016)

contracts work or what they are, especially on blockchain or bitcoin-devoted forums; however, they normally do not offer an in-depth analysis of related legal issues. Smart contracts definitely raise interesting questions about their legal nature. It is often said that existing smart contracts are neither particularly smart nor are they strictly speaking legally binding contracts.[2] Any discussion about smart contracts and their impact on today's contract law must begin with identifying a workable definition of the concept. Chapter 3 of this book[3] gives a detailed overview of the various blockchain technologies and their implementation. 'The general objectives of smart contract design are to satisfy common contractual conditions (such as payment terms, liens, confidentiality, and enforcement), minimize exceptions both malicious and accidental, and minimize the need for trusted intermediaries' like banks or other kinds of agents.'[4] Related economic goals of smart contracts include lowering fraud loss, enforcement costs, and other transaction costs, and they are thought to be able to provide full transparency of the transaction and to grant at the same time a high degree of privacy.[5] *Szabo's* definition can be simplified to a computer code that is created to automatically execute contractual duties upon the occurrence of a triggering event,[6] or agreements which execution is automated, usually by a computer programme.[7] A consensus definition can be distilled: a smart contract is a computer code which is operated by a computer and is

Computer und Recht (CR) 618; M. Kaulartz, 'Herausforderungen bei der Gestaltung von Smart Contracts', (2016) *Zeitschrift zum Innovations-und Technikrecht (InTeR)* 201; M. Kaulartz, 'Die Blockchain-Technologie: Hintergründe zur Distributed Ledger Technology und zu Blockchain', (2016) *Computer und Recht (CR)* 474; E. Mik, 'Smart Contracts: Terminology, Technical Limitations and Real World Complexity', (2017) *Journal of Law, Innovation and Technology (JLIT)* 269; R. O'Shields, 'Smart Contracts: Legal Agreements for the Blockchain', (2017) 21 *North Carolina Banking Institute* 177; P. Paech, 'The Governance of Blockchain Financial Networks', (2017) 80 *Modern Law Review* 1072; M. L. Perugini and P. Dal Checco, 'Smart Contracts: A Preliminary Evaluation', ssrn.com /abstract=2729548; M. Raskin, 'The Law and Legality of Smart Contracts', (2017) 1 *Georgetown Technology Review* 305; C.L. Reyes, 'Conceptualizing Cryptolaw', (2017) 96 *Nebraska L. Rev.* 384; P. Ryan, 'Smart Contract Relations in e-Commerce: Legal Implications of Exchanges Conducted on the Blockchain', (2017) 7 *Technology Innovation Management Review* 10; A. Savelyev, 'Contract Law 2.0: "Smart" Contracts As the Beginning of the End of Classic Contract Law', ssrn.com/abstract=2885241; J. Schrey and T. Thalhofer, 'Rechtliche Aspekte der Blockchain', (2017) *Neue Juristische Wochenschrift (NJW)* 1431; L.H. Scholz, 'Algorithmic Contracts', (2017) 20 *Stanford Technology Law Review* 101; J. M. Sklaroff, 'Smart Contracts and the Cost of Inflexibility', (2017) 166 *University Pennsylvania Law Review* 263; T. Söbbing, 'Smart Contracts und Blockchain: Definitionen, Arbeitsweise, Rechtsfragen', (2018) *IT-Rechts-Berater (ITBR)*43; T.F.E. Tjong Tjin Tai, 'Juridische aspecten van blockchain en smart contracts', (2017) 54 *Tijdschrift voor Privaatrecht* 563; T.F.E. Tjong Tjin Tai, 'Smart contracts en het recht', (2017) 93 *Nederlands Juristenblad* 176; K. Werbach and N. Cornell, 'Contracts Ex Machina', (2017) 67 *Duke Law Journal* 313; Werbach, "Trust, But Verify", : Why the Blockchain Needs the Law', *Berkley Technological Law Journal* (forthcoming, 2018), ssrn.com/sol3/papers.cfm?abstract_id=2844409.
2 Bourque and Fung Ling Tsui, A Lawyer's Introduction, p. 4; O'Shields, 'Smart Contracts: Legal Agreements for the Blockchain', 178.
3 'Technology of Smart Contracts', by Valentina Gatteschi, Fabrizio Lamberti, and Claudio Demartini.
4 N. Szabo, 'Smart Contracts', www.fon.hum.uva.nl/rob/Courses/InformationInSpeech/CDROM/ Literature/LOTwinterschool2006/szabo.best.vwh.net/smart.contracts.html
5 Buchleitner and Rabl, 'Blockchain und Smart Contracts', 5; Guggenheim, 'The Potentional of Blockchain', 94; Kaulartz, 'Herausforderungen bei der Gestaltung von Smart Contracts', 202; N. Szabo, 'Smart Contracts', www .fon.hum.uva.nl/rob/Courses/InformationInSpeech/CDROM/Literature/LOTwinterschool2006/szabo.best.vwh .net/smart.contracts.html
6 Paech, 'The Governance of Blockchain Financial Networks', 1082.
7 Raskin, 'The Law and Legality of Smart Contracts', 306; Söbbing, 'Smart Contracts und Blockchain', 44.

self-executing and self-enforcing,[8] the existence of some kind of artificial intelligence being not a requirement.[9]

As should become apparent, there is much debate and confusion around the definition of the concept of smart contracts. For blockchain-based smart contracts, a useful dichotomy can be drawn between the 'smart contract code' – that is, the computer code that is stored, verified, and executed on a blockchain – and the 'smart legal contract' – a complement (or maybe even a substitute) for a legal contract that applies that technology.[10] In essence, a 'smart legal contract' is a combination of the 'smart contract code' and traditional legal language.[11]

What became evident is that the term 'smart contract' is a misnomer.[12] A smart contract, as we know it right now, is, independently, from applicable law, is not a contract in the legal meaning of the word. The choice of such a name for the concept of a self-executing, computer-coded agreement is unfortunate as it exacerbates confusion around the topic. Some theoretical similarities however exist between smart contracts and legal contracts insofar as both 'are frameworks for regulating the interaction between different entities'.[13]

4.2 Evolution of Blockchain Technology and the Rise of Smart Contracts

There are smart contracts which function without blockchain technology – so smart contracts can exist without it.[14] However, there is little doubt that the main reason for the actual rise of smart contracts is the rapid evolution of the blockchain technology. This technology allows smart contracts to use their full potential for automation and this is why this chapter will focus on this kind of smart contracts. Bitcoin, which proliferated this technology, led to the establishing of *Ethereum*, which is a more sophisticated blockchain platform allowing for more complicated transactions (beyond transfers of currency, or bitcoins).[15] Ethereum developed its own coding language

[8] Börding, Jülicher, Röttgen, and Schönfeld, 'Neue Herausforderungen der Digitalisierung', 138; Kaulartz, 'Herausforderungen bei der Gestaltung von Smart Contracts', 203; Mik, 'Smart Contracts', 269; O'Shields, 'Smart Contracts: Legal Agreements for the Blockchain', 179. A slightly different definition offers Kaulartz, 'Herausforderungen bei der Gestaltung von Smart Contracts', 203.

[9] Jacobs and Lange-Hausstein, 'Blockchain und Smart Contracts', 13; Kaulartz and Heckmann, 'Smart Contracts – Anwendung der Blockchain-Technologie', 618; Söbbing, 'Smart Contracts und Blockchain', 44.

[10] J. Stark, 'Making Sense of Blockchain Smart Contracts', *Coindesk*, 4 June 2016, www.coindesk.com/making-sense-smart-contracts/

[11] Djazayeri, 'Rechtliche Herausforderungen'; Kaulartz, 'Herausforderungen bei der Gestaltung von Smart Contracts', 205.

[12] Buchleitner and Rabl, 'Blockchain und Smart Contracts', 6; Djazayeri, 'Rechtliche Herausforderungen'; Söbbing, 'Smart Contracts und Blockchain', 46.

[13] C. Lim, T. J. Saw and C. Sargeant, 'Smart Contracts: Bridging the Gap Between Expectation and Reality', 11 July 2016, *Oxford Business Law Blog*, www.law.ox.ac.uk/business-law-blog/blog/2016/07/smart-contracts-bridging-gap-between-expectation-and-reality.

[14] *Blockchain (technology)* is sometimes also referred to as *distributed ledger (technology)* or *shared ledger (technology)*. While these three notions still remain in flux (and some authors consider them to designate different forms of technology), we will refer to them interchangeably for the sake of simplicity. However, mainly the term 'blockchain' (technology) will be used in this contribution.

[15] See more detailed Scholz, 'Algorithmic Contracts', 120; Tjong Tjin Tai, 'Smart contracts en het recht', 177.

called *Solidity*.[16] Blockchain technology demonstrates how a network could be set up so that once a transaction is set in motion, the network can produce outputs autonomously, without the direct intervention of any party or any intermediaries.[17] Because of this feature, participants do not need to trust each other; they can rely on the system as a whole to carry out transactions – knowing that other parties cannot frustrate the intended outcome.[18] Blockchain not only allows verification of each transaction via nodes (the computers in the chain), but it also, by storing the contract in a 'block' and sending it to each node, makes the execution automatic and in principle *immutable* – thus allowing the 'digitization of trust through certainty of execution' and the 'creation of efficiency through removal of intermediaries and the costs they bring to the transactions'.[19] These characteristics are perhaps the greatest appeal of smart contracts which make use of blockchain technology.

There are various ideas discussed on how to make use of blockchain-based smart contracts in today's practice and in the future. One often-mentioned example is the distribution of compensation for damages resulting from the exercise of airline passenger rights[20] – for instance, under the Flight Compensation Regulation 261/2004.[21] These cases normally take place in a business-to-consumer relationship, which includes a large number of potential claimants for relatively small compensation sums. The criteria for the validity of the consumers' claims (delay or cancellation) are in principle purely objective and the conditions which trigger the compensation can be verified reliably by 'oracles' or external sources.[22] However, as mentioned correctly by *Guggenheim*, this simple example also shows that there is no claim simple enough to be determined only by simple objective criteria as an airline does not need to pay any compensation in case of force majeure (see Art. 5(3) of the Flight Compensation Regulation 261/2004), which is challenging to the automation of contracts.[23] Besides the well-known smart refrigerator example (the refrigerator automatically orders the food needed),[24] the 'pay as you drive' principle which is discussed in the insurance industry is another potential sphere of applicability of blockchain-based smart contracts.[25] Here the policyholder concludes a car insurance contract with the insurance company. The contract contains a 'pay as you drive,' provision, meaning the more risky one drives, the higher will be the premium the policyholder needs to pay. For the data collection function, the policyholder's car has

---

[16] See https://solidity.readthedocs.io/en/develop/.

[17] Clifford Chance, 'Smart Contracts. Legal Agreements for the Digital Age', November 2017, 2, www
.cliffordchance.com/briefings/2017/06/smart_contracts_-legalagreementsforth.html.

[18] This has led some authors to the conviction that only 'the code is the law' and that law is obsolete for smart
contracts (see L. Lessig, *Codes and Other Laws of Cyberspace* (New York: Basic Books, 1999), 24). However,
this opinion did not gain sufficient support as it is obvious that (contract) law remains to play an important
role for smart contracts. See, with more details on this aspect, Kaulartz and Heckmann, 'Smart Contracts –
Anwendung der Blockchain-Technologie', 618–623; Tjong Tjin Tai, 'Smart contracts en het recht', 179.

[19] Hsiao, 'Smart Contract on the Blockchain', 687.

[20] See e.g. Buchleitner and Rabl, 'Blockchain und Smart Contracts', 7.

[21] Regulation (EC) No 261/2004 of the European Parliament and of the Council of 11 February 2004
establishing common rules on compensation and assistance to passengers in the event of denied boarding
and of cancellation or long delay of flights, and repealing Regulation (EEC) No 295/91.

[22] See the detailed definition of 'oracles', in Chapter 3 of this book.

[23] Guggenheim, 'The Potential of Blockchain', 95.

[24] Djazayeri, 'Rechtliche Herausforderungen'.

[25] Buchleitner and Rabl, 'Blockchain und Smart Contracts', 7; Djazayeri, 'Rechtliche Herausforderungen';
Jacobs and Lange-Hausstein, 'Blockchain und Smart Contracts', 12; Kaulartz and Heckmann, 'Smart
Contracts – Anwendung der Blockchain-Technologie', 618.

a blockchain interface and the blockchain-based smart (insurance) contract adjusts the amount of the payable premium automatically according to the way the insured car is driven.[26]

4.3 Blockchain-Based Smart Contracts and the Process of Contract Formation

The way and method smart contracts are and will be created in the future can differ significantly – depending on three different aspects. These aspects are:

- the level of automation of the execution of the smart contract;
- the extent of separation between the actual agreed upon terms and the executed code; and
- the custodial rights and/or discretion of the smart contract and its execution from the parties.[27]

Considering the three mentioned axes, one can distinguish very roughly between two different kind of smart contracts.[28] The first category of smart contracts is concluded 'unsmart' and only their execution is 'smart' – so they are 'purely' self-enforcing smart contracts. They can be concluded either off-chain or on-chain, but even in the latter case the algorithms are exclusively employed as a mere tool in contract formation.[29] When describing the actual process of formation of *on-chain* smart contracts, the concept can be well explained through the Ethereum's process.[30] This process is as follows: The user first types out the contract in coding language, after downloading Ethereum software and becoming part of the network. The user 'proposes' a specific contract by making it available in the system. The contract has its own identification number and 'function[s] as an autonomous entity within the system, somewhat similar to how a website may operate on Internet'.[31] Another user may then 'accept the proposed contract' by communicating to it, for example, by making a payment.

The users and/or oracles may then communicate with the contract, for example, by informing that a physical package was delivered, after which the contract will automatically execute the payment.[32] Because a decentralized, permissionless (meaning anyone with the right hardware and software can get on it) platform needs to avoid spam, Ethereum will charge a user *gas* (their unit) as a fee for contracts, which will increase based on the complexity of the contract. Sometimes as mentioned previously, a smart contract will need information from the outside world to enable it to carry out the transaction (for example, if the smart contract is a stock option, it will need to know the

---

[26] For further examples, see Börding, Jülicher, Röttgen and von Schönfeld, 'Neue Herausforderungen der Digitalisierung', 137; Buchleitner and Rabl, 'Blockchain und Smart Contracts', 6; Kaulartz and Heckmann, 'Smart Contracts – Anwendung der Blockchain-Technologie', 619; Kaulartz, 'Herausforderungen bei der Gestaltung von Smart Contracts', 203; O'Shields, 'Smart Contracts: Legal Agreements for the Blockchain', 181; Raskin, 'The Law and Legality of Smart Contracts', 330; Tjong Tjin Tai, 'Smart contracts en het recht', 182.

[27] See Bourque and Fung Ling Tsui, A Lawyer's Introduction, p. 4ff.

[28] For the following differentiation, see Buchleitner and Rabl, 'Blockchain und Smart Contracts', 7; Scholz, 'Algorithmic Contracts', 108.

[29] Scholz, 'Algorithmic Contracts', 108.

[30] See https://ethereum.org/

[31] E. Tjong Tjin Tai, 'Force Majeure and Excuses in Smart Contracts', (2018) 10 *Tilburg Private Law Working Paper No. 4*, ssrn.com/abstract=3183637, p. 4.

[32] Tjong Tjin Tai, 'Force Majeure and Excuses in Smart Contracts', 4.

stock price). Blockchains are not connected to the Internet[33] and so the contract cannot by itself check the prices. It needs therefore an external source, an 'oracle'.[34] They thus allow more complexion for the contracts but at the same time they also undermine its decentralization. Furthermore, they introduce the requirement of trust for the third party that obtains the information from the outside source.

The blockchain technology and its applications are ways to developing quickly, and in the near future another category of smart contracts will probably see the daylight: Smart contracts which are not only executed 'smart', but also concluded 'smart' through the blockchain – so here contract formation *and* contract execution are smart. In opposite to the first-mentioned category of smart contracts, the blockchain technology will also be used for *finding* a (previously unknown) contracting party and *concluding the contract* which then will also be executed automatically.[35] Here the algorithms are not merely a tool, but they act as a sort of 'artificial agent' in the context of the formation of a contract between two or more contracting parties.[36] Here the legal questions can be quite different from the other category of smart contracts, especially, but not only, for the formation of contracts. For instance, can the provider of the blockchain platform legally be considered *de lege lata* as an agent? Or can the algorithm in itself be considered as an independent (electronic) agent? Or is it analogous to the concept of an electronic agent which is legally independent from its creator for this kind of technology *de lege ferenda*?[37] Because of the limited space available for this chapter, we can unfortunately only focus on the first category of smart contract and must leave the second one for later contributions.[38]

4.4 The Compatibility of Smart Contracts with the Requirements of Contract Formation

Leaving aside potential private international law problems in finding the applicable domestic law to determine the precise requirements for contract formation,[39] and knowing that numerous legal systems with different elements for a formatted contract exist (e.g. the respectively importance/unimportance of 'consideration' in (English) Common Law and (German) Civil Law, we have chosen the English legal system as the focal point for this contribution. Hence, we will discuss if a smart contract conforms with the Common Law requirements for formation of a valid and legally binding contract – however, we also take into consideration the Acquis Communautaire if necessary (e.g. for the inclusion and validity of standard contract terms). Each 'requirement' for the conclusion of a valid,

---

[33] The reason for that is that for blockchains to function, the result of an equation must be the same at each node. If, using our example of a stock price as a variable in an equation, the result at each node would be different, because they would be able to verify the price of the stock in real time, the blockchain would not be able to function.

[34] For example, a service called Oraclize is a bridge between Ethereum and the internet.

[35] Buchleitner and Rabl, 'Blockchain und Smart Contracts', 7.

[36] Scholz, 'Algorithmic Contracts', 108.

[37] For more details about the electronic agent discussion, see Börding, Jülicher, Röttgen, and von Schönfeld, 'Neue Herausforderungen der Digitalisierung', 139; Scholz, 'Algorithmic Contracts', 141.

[38] For more details, see Buchleitner and Rabl, 'Blockchain und Smart Contracts', 7; Scholz, 'Algorithmic Contracts', 101–147.

[39] See for the Private International Law aspects of smart contracts Bourque and Fung Ling Tsui, A Lawyer's Introduction, p. 13; Buchleitner and Rabl, 'Blockchain und Smart Contracts', 12; Djazayeri, 'Rechtliche Herausforderungen'.

legally enforceable contract will be discussed separately – offer and acceptance, consideration, intention to create legal relations, and capacity.[40]

4.4.1 *Offer and Acceptance*

The initial stage of a contractual agreement is not very different between smart contracts and traditional contracts because before any contract can operate, two parties must agree to some set of contractual terms.[41] The rules on offer and acceptance will in principle not pose an obstacle to smart contracts' recognition as legally binding. First of all, offer and acceptance, as well as the parties' conduct, are evaluated objectively.[42] This means that the fact that parties submit their cryptographic private keys to commit resources to a blockchain-based smart contract is proof of a commitment.[43] On platforms such as Ethereum one party must post its (on-chain smart) 'contract' on the blockchain, and it is then accepted by the cryptographic key of the other party. The posting of the on-chain smart 'contract' on the blockchain acts as an offer. Depending on the circumstances, you could also try to argue that it is conceptually not different from an advertisement and, therefore, only an invitation to treat.[44] However, as the 'offeror' posts his 'contract' on the blockchain in a binary computer code that specifies precisely the terms of the transaction, it will regularly be held to be exact enough to constitute an offer and not only an invitation to treat.[45]

Once the proposed smart contract is posted on the blockchain and fulfils the requirements for being an offer (especially the identification of the *essentialia negotii* of the contract), it is capable of acceptance by the offeree.[46] This acceptance can also be done by conduct, e.g. by performance. An example of acceptance by performance includes transferring control over a digital asset to the smart contract, that digital asset can be money, cryptocurrency, or a digital representation of an offline asset. The action of uploading the asset to the smart contract provides an unequivocal communication of acceptance.[47]

Therefore, the acceptance can occur either by performance or by the authorization of a transfer through the use of a special cryptographic key (password).[48] In either case there is

---

[40] The basic elements for a contract conclusion under German Law are (of course, with the important exception of consideration) quite similar. See for German Law in the context of smart contracts Kaulartz, 'Herausforderungen bei der Gestaltung von Smart Contracts', 201–204.

[41] Raskin, 'The Law and Legality of Smart Contracts', 322.

[42] *Smit* v *Hughes* (1871) LR 6 QB 597, 607 (Blackburn J). See also Kaulartz and Heckmann, 'Smart Contracts – Anwendung der Blockchain-Technologie', 621.

[43] Werbach and Cornell, 'Contracts Ex Machina', 368.

[44] Kaulartz and Heckmann, 'Smart Contracts – Anwendung der Blockchain-Technologie', 621.

[45] Regarding the conditions for a communication to qualify as an offer, cf *Partridge* v *Crittenden* [1968] 2 All ER 421; cf *Carlill* v *Carbolic Smoke Ball Co Ltd* [1892] 1 QB 296.

[46] Doubtful however, Söbbing, 'Smart Contracts und Blockchain', 46.

[47] Catchlove, 'Smart Contracts: A New Era', 11. One can write a smart contract saying that for 10 Ether (Ethereum's digital currency) I will transfer ownership of a car. I write the contract, including the terms I want it to contain, and upload it to blockchain, together with the digital token that represents the car, and 'gas' – payment for uploading the contract. That is the offer. Next, someone willing to accept will upload the 10 Ether to the smart contract – that is, acceptance. The smart contract will detect the upload of 10 Ether, and automatically transfer that to my wallet, while at the same time transferring the token to the person who uploaded the 10 Ether. I do not need to vouch that I received the 10 Ether; the token for car is transferred without my further verification or discretion.

[48] G. Jaccard, 'Smart Contracts and the Role of Law', (2017) *Jusletter IT* 22; J.J. Szczerbowski, 'Place of Smart Contracts in Civil Law. A Few Comments on Form and Interpretation', 9 November 2017. Proceedings of

a clear act of acceptance either by signature (personal cryptographic key) or by perfor-mance of the terms of a unilateral contract[49]. Another argument arises here, namely that on-chain smart contracts for now are unilateral contracts – promises that if X happens, I will give you Y, and thus capable of being accepted by performance. Overall, however, it is evident that the rules on offer and acceptance will not pose fundamental problems for the formation of smart contracts, as the procedure of the formation of such agreements accommodates elements of both, offer and acceptance.[50]

The adaptability of the contract law rules to smart contracts can again be illustrated by the vending machine example. Inserting the money creates a contract but not because of the technical functionality of the vending machine but because a 'wrapper contract' is created, as the law interprets the insertion of the money as valid acceptance of the offer which was made by the owner of the machine. Similarly, when the digital asset is uploaded to a smart contract, a contract is concluded between the two parties, because that act is an acceptance of the offer made by another user, no matter that the actual transfer of the assets will be done by the smart contract. Although the performance of the smart contract is automated, it still requires the contracting parties' exercising their will in order for it to become effective. Such intention is manifested at the moment when a party decides to enter into such an agreement on the terms specified by the offeror in advance.[51] The point of this section is to illustrate that the requirements of offer and acceptance demanded for a valid contract by contract law are satisfied in the common practice of formation of smart contracts.

The said assumption is consistent with traditional English contract law on forma-tion of contracts, and more precisely the approach based on will theory. The said theory once proposed by theorists such as *Pothier* or *von Savigny* is the underlying theoretical basis for contracts. Accordingly, a *consensus ad idem* – 'a meeting of the minds' – is required for the contract to be formed.[52] If this is true, why should such a consensus suddenly be unenforceable when expressed in a computer code rather than in a natural language? If both parties read and understand the terms written in computer code, which is also verifiable by a third-party adjudicator (courts or arbitral tribunals through the use of experts to distil the meaning of the computer code), then there is nothing preventing that meeting of the minds from being enforced and valid.[53] Freedom of contract as one of the pillars of contract law dictates that parties should be free to write down their bargains in whatever form and in whatever language they want.[54] The chosen language can even be a dead language as Latin

---

the 12th Annual Scientific Conference NEW TRENDS 2017, published by *Private College of Economic Studies Znojmo*, ssrn.com/sol3/papers.cfm?abstract_id=3095933, 336.

[49] *Carlill* v *Carbolic Smoke Ball Co Ltd*, 262 (Lindley LJ).

[50] This might, as outlined already before, be different for the other mentioned category of smart contract where the algorithms act as an 'artificial agent'.

[51] Savelyev, 'Contract Law 2.0', 11.

[52] See e.g. *Scriven Bros & Co v Hindley* [1919] 3 KB 564.

[53] However, problems arise if at least one of the contracting parties does not understand the computer code but nevertheless conclude the smart contract. In this scenario, the party that did not understand the computer code could try to advocate in hindsight for the existence of a 'mistake' and to rewind the smart contract. In German literature, this case has been discussed but has always been rejected so far as an 'Inhaltsirrtum', according to § 119(1) BGB. It is said that in principle it is the risk of the parties to conclude a contract not knowing the underlying computer code. See Jünemann and Kast, 'Rechtsfragen', *Kreditwesen*, 533; Kaulartz and Heckmann, 'Smart Contracts – Anwendung der Blockchain-Technologie', 622.

[54] J. J. Szczerbowski, 'Place of Smart Contracts in Civil Law', 335.

or a computer code[55] – as long as it is not a business-to-consumer relationship (which will be discussed separately later).[56] Moreover, given the past adaptability of English contract law to new modes of communications such as, letter[57] or telex and instantaneous communications like e-mails,[58] one can speculate that the same will extend to smart contracts when (or if) their use becomes widespread.[59] Lastly, one point should be made about contract law's treatment of 'automatic contracts'. It is clear from cases such as *Thornton v Shoe Lane Parking* (similar to *Szabo's* vending machine analogy) that a contract is formed at the second that coins are inserted into the machine, and the fact that later processes occur without human intervention does not preclude the formation of a contract.[60] In *R (Software Solutions Partners Ltd) v HM Customs & Excise*, it was held that an 'automatic medium for contract formation' can result in valid contracts.[61] Once the broker in that case put the criteria into a software, the software would seek and conclude contracts on the broker's behalf with no further requirement of human action, and it was found that a contract was completed. Hence, it is very likely that the formation of smart contracts on platforms such as Ethereum will be held and recognized in law as valid formation of a legally enforceable contract.

4.4.2 Consideration

One could make an argument that since consideration must only be legally sufficient but not adequate (equivalency of consideration) according to English contract law,[62] the consideration requirement is satisfied by smart contracts, since they, by definition, entail an exchange of digital assets – thus, in the example above 10 Ether for a car. While the argument is valid, and in fact courts have loosely applied (any consideration will do) the consideration requirement compared to the requirement of the intention to create legal relations and as illustrated by the 'practical benefit' doctrine,[63] that the requirement of consideration will not be a serious obstacle on the smart contracts' road to being legally valid.

Yet, *Werbach* and *Cornell* raise an interesting argument as they point out that smart contracts do not contain an *exchange of promises* as is usually the case in normal contracts and which is a requirement for a valid consideration. They illustrate their argument with an analogy, which is best cited in full:

---

[55] See, with more details, Jünemann and Kast, 'Rechtsfragen', 533; Kaulartz and Heckmann, 'Smart Contracts – Anwendung der Blockchain-Technologie', 622; Kaulartz, 'Herausforderungen bei der Gestaltung von Smart Contracts', 204.

[56] See Chapter 17, p. XXX

[57] *Adams v Lindsell* (1818) 1 B & Ald 681.

[58] *Entores v Miles Far East Corp* [1955] 2 QB 327; *Brinkibon Ltd v Stahag Stahl und Stahlwarenhandelsgesellschaft mbH* [1983] 2 AC 34.

[59] Norton Rose Fulbright, 'Can Smart Contracts Be Legally Binding Contracts', www .nortonrosefulbright.com/files/r3-and-norton-rose-fulbright-white-paper-full-report-144581.pdf, p. 22.

[60] *Thornton v Shoe Lane Parking* [1978] 2 QB 163 (Lord Denning MR).

[61] *R (Software Solutions Partners Ltd) v HM Customs & Excise* [2007] EWHC 971, para. 67.

[62] Illustration case: *Chappel & Co Ltd v Nestlé Co Ltd* [1959] AC 87.

[63] *Williams v Roffey Bros & Nicholls Contractors* [1989] 1 QB 1; *Rock Advertising Ltd v MWB Business Exchange Centres Ltd* [2016] EWCA Civ 553, the practical benefit point was not discussed by the Supreme Court in [2018] UKSC 24.

If someone balances a pail of water on top of a door, he does not promise to drop water on whoever next opens the door. Rather, he has merely set up the mechanical process by which that will happen. In a similar way, a contract to transfer one bitcoin upon such-and -such event occurring is not really a promise at all. It does not say 'I will pay you one bitcoin if such-and-such happens', but rather something like 'You will be paid one bitcoin if such-and-such happens' ... the so-called '[smart] *contract*' is not an exchange of promises or commitments. Creation of a smart contract – while setting certain events in motion – does not commit any party [to do] anything. There's nothing being prospectively promised.[64]

This certainly is a departure from the realm of traditional 'dumb' contracts. But that issue does not prevent the authors from reaching the conclusion that smart contracts are still nevertheless contracts. *Savelyev* asks himself whether a smart contract is not a contract because it does not contain any obligations, but he holds that such a conclusion would be too simplistic for several reasons. First, the parties still express their will when they enter into a contract and they are bound by the result of their actions. Secondly, contract law acknowledges certain types of agreements which are performed instantaneously at the moment of conclusion (executed contracts). *Savelyev* concludes that it is probably more correct to state that the main consequence of the conclusion of a smart contract is not an appearance of 'obligations' but the resulting self-limitation of certain rights by technical means.[65]

Werbach and *Cornell* argue that though such commitments might not constitute promises per se, smart contracts are agreements that purport to alter the parties' rights and obligations and that an agreement may still count as a contract even if it leaves nothing open to be done or performed.[66] For them, smart contracts constitute present agreements without further promises to perform. Hence, anyone who argues that these kind of contracts do not involve a 'promise' but more of a guarantee precludes it from being a contract and offers an unrealistically 'idealistic' view of contract law. Some consideration – benefit, right or detriment, loss or responsibility[67] – will be conveyed under smart contracts inducing a reciprocal promise,[68] and pragmatically there will almost always be sufficient consideration.

Lastly, another interesting point raised in relation to on-chain smart contracts is that they are unilateral contracts of the nature that 'if X then I will pay you', and thus the consideration for such contracts is in performance.[69] That does not prevent someone from committing a gift promise to the blockchain. Such a gift promise would be executed irrevocably in the same manner as other smart contracts.[70] Does this mean that smart contracts render gifts legally enforceable? It is submitted (though lack of authority on this issue should be noted) that the answer is no. Not every smart contract is a contract, and the fact that a gift executed via smart contract is irrevocable does not mean it is legally valid. A donor who changed his mind could potentially seek restitution under unjust

---

[64] Werbach and Cornell, 'Contracts Ex Machina', 340.
[65] Savelyev, 'Contract Law 2.0', 18.
[66] Werbach and Cornell, 'Contracts Ex Machina', 341.
[67] *Currie v Misa* (1876) LR 1 App Cas 554.
[68] Werbach and Cornell, 'Contracts Ex Machina', 370.
[69] *Carlill v Carbolic Smoke Ball Co Ltd* [1892] 1 QB 296, 265 (Lindley LJ).
[70] Werbach and Cornell, 'Contracts Ex Machina', 370.

enrichment, though the fact that the gift is a *fait accompli* would make it substantially harder to recover. All in all, both conceptually and pragmatically sufficient consideration will normally be present in smart contracts in order to render them legally enforceable.

4.4.3 *Intention to Create Legal Relations*

In commercial relationships, the intention to create legal relations is presumed in Common Law and will have to be disproved by the party alleging that there is no such intention.[71] Hence, smart contracts entered into in a business setting the intention to create legal relations will be presumed – regardless whether it is a business-to-business or a business-to-consumer transaction. Again a more nuanced view can be offered. *Savelyev* comes to the conclusion that by concluding a smart contract the contracting parties have the intention to use an alternative regulatory system and not traditional contract law and that therefore there might not be a true intent to create legal relations.[72] However, he also admits that if the result is factually the same in substance to the one regulated by 'usual contracts', it can (and must) be argued that the nature of the relations is the same.[73] The initial part of the argument is interesting – after all, the fact of eliminating lawyers and courts from the equation is an advantage[74] of smart contracts, so there is no intention of *legal* relations – but rightly rebutted. The parties do *not* wish to enforce their contracts in court, because they believe that such enforcement will be unnecessary, since the smart contract is guaranteed to be performed. That is not the same however as wishing that, should their contracts end up in court, they will not be upheld. In the conclusion of a smart contract, if the offer has been accepted, then it has also commenced being performed. Based upon this, it is very unlikely that a reasonable party would not see this as a binding and enforceable agreement'.[75] Hence, it is almost certain that the intention to create legal relations will be found in most smart contracts, especially in commercial settings. In any event, a precautious party which wants to ensure that there is an intention to create legal relations can do so by 'wrapping' the code up in a contract – a paper contract that acknowledges that the smart contract is a valid legal agreement.[76]

4.4.4 *Capacity*

Contractual relations require parties have the capacity to enter into contracts. Ethereum, and in fact most of the other available blockchain platforms, however do not check for full legal capacity. Instead, in principle, anyone can open an account without having sufficient legal capacity to do so. As smart contracts have no means to test for capacity, they can be entered into by minors, persons under the influence of alcohol or drugs, or any other incapacitated person. Therefore, people who in the real world would lack the capacity to enter into a contract could potentially do so on the blockchain platform.

---

[71] See e.g. *Esso Petroleum Limited* v *Commissioners of Customs and Excise* [1975] UKHL 4.
[72] Savelyev, 'Contract Law 2.0', 11.
[73] Ibid.
[74] Werbach, 'Trust, But Verify', 36.
[75] Catchlove, 'Smart Contracts: A New Era', 11.
[76] More details on legal 'wrappers' below.

However, if there was no capacity, then a party could invalidate the transfer of any assets *ex post* – through an action in unjust enrichment and technically through a reverse transaction.[77] The latter way of unwinding a transaction is problematic because in the realm of pseudonymous users with cryptographic strings of random letters and numbers, it is often difficult to identify who to sue. In addition, a reverse transaction can only factually rewind the contract but not legally as a void transaction might remain on the blockchain because the blocks are immutable.[78] More importantly, if someone possesses legal capacity, he will be free to enter into legally binding smart contracts.

Lastly, another small but interesting observation is that the contracting parties to a smart contract are, at a technical level, not people but only cryptographic private keys which represent individual persons.[79] Could a discussion of capacity be avoided if the parties are technically not human? Not really, as for autonomous smart contracts the private keys do not act by themselves; they are 'instructed' by humans.

In summary, the aim of the above section was to show that smart contracts are capable, by virtue of the flexibility and adaptability of English contract law and the very process of their formation, of being formed as legally valid contracts. However, the mainstream law firms are still advising their clients that for the sake of certainty, a legal 'wrapper' ought to be created.[80] The best approach will likely require an explicit process that incorporates the legal requirements for electronic execution of traditional, non-automated contracts – something like clicking an 'I agree' button before launching – rather than relying on speculative smart contract-friendly interpretations of Common Law rules.'[81]

Such 'code-and-contract' hybrids that entail both a smart contract and a paper contract acknowledging the smart one are perhaps the best intermediary solution. The drafting of the 'wrapping' may require more than just 'I accept that I am bound by the outcome of the smart contract', as such a clause could be unenforceable for incompleteness or uncertainty under Common Law. In the long run, given the efficiency-driven business world, the legal system should create legal certainty so that costly 'code-and-contract' hybrids can be avoided.

4.5 Conflict Areas between Smart Contracts and Traditional Contract Law

The above sections have shown that smart contracts can fulfil the requirements for the formation of contracts and that existing problems are not unbridgeable. This however does not mean that there are no conflict areas between smart contracts and traditional contract law outside the realm of contract conclusion. Some of them will be outlined in the following sections in order to provide a broader view of smart contracting.

---

[77] See also Jünemann and Kast, 'Rechtsfragen', 532; Schrey and Thalhofer, 'Rechtliche Aspekte der Blockchain', 1431.

[78] Schrey and Thalhofer, 'Rechtliche Aspekte der Blockchain', 1436.

[79] Werbach and Cornell, 'Contracts Ex Machina', 371.

[80] Clifford Chance, 'Are Smart Contracts Contracts? Talking Tech Looks at the Concepts and Realities of Smart Contracts' December 2017, Talking Tech, https://talkingtech.cliffordchance.com/en/tech/are-smart -contracts-contracts.html.

[81] Ibid.

4.5.1 *Flexible Enforceable Legal Contracts versus Firm Self-Enforcing Smart Contracts*

'A smart contract asks its parties to tie themselves to the mast like Ulysses and *ex ante* commit to abiding by the terms of the agreement.'[82] The main point about performance in smart contracts is as already been mentioned is that such contracts are fully automated and performed by computers with no intervention from human parties. Unlike the performance of traditional contracts, the performance of a smart contract cannot be stopped – neither voluntarily by the parties (they cannot breach or amend it), nor by a central entity, court, or any other supervisor.[83] So, traditional contract law is flexible while smart contracts are rigid or inflexible as they cannot be stopped or changed. Once the smart contract terms have been programmed into the code and executed onto blockchain, there is no longer a need for reliance on the willingness of the various parties to perform. Smart contracts are performance based and ensure a greater likelihood of performance than conventional contracts.[84] This 'self-enforceability' of the smart contracts is what primarily distinguishes them from traditional 'dumb' contracts. *Savelyev* describes it as being 'technically binding for all the parties ... [s]ubsequent change of circumstances or intent of the party to it is irrelevant'.[85] Therefore, he argues that smart contracts leave no room for opportunistic behavior or any efficient breach of contract and this creates tensions with classic contract law.[86] This is to an extent true. Contract law is neither adapted nor prepared to accommodate self-enforcing contracts; because of there self-enforcings nature, an action in court finding the terms of a smart contract unenforceable may have no practical effect because the contract will in most cases have already been performed.[87] Furthermore, due to the nature of blockchain technology, once a contract goes onto the blockchain it cannot be revoked or amended, meaning that any rescission, rectification, or variation is in principle impossible. One could imagine a blockchain where certain authorities have access to change the existing 'blocks', but that would of course undermine the very essence of blockchain technology.[88]

Not only are traditional enforcers like courts powerless in affecting the performance of smart contracts, the agreements cannot be amended or modified.[89] Smart contracts are not flexible and therefore unable to respond to changing circumstances or party' preferences.[90] This DNA of smart contracts puts them on a collision course with traditional contract law doctrines such as variation or frustration. An event that 'significantly chang[es] the nature [...] of the outstanding contractual rights and/or obligations from what the parties could reasonably have contemplated at the time of its execution that it would be unjust to hold them to the literal sense of its stipulation'[91] would render the parties discharged under the doctrine of frustration,

---

[82] Raskin, 'The Law and Legality of Smart Contracts', 309.
[83] Paech, 'The Governance of Blockchain Financial Networks', 1082.
[84] Catchlove, 'Smart Contracts: A New Era', 9.
[85] Savelyev, 'Contract Law 2.0', 15.
[86] Ibid.
[87] Werbach and Cornell, 'Contracts Ex Machina', 373.
[88] Savelyev, 'Contract Law 2.0', 19.
[89] O'Shields, 'Smart Contracts: Legal Agreements for the Blockchain', 178.
[90] Hsiao, 'Smart Contract on the Blockchain', 691.
[91] *National Carriers Ltd* v *Panalpina (Northern) Ltd* [1981] AC 675,700 (Lord Simon of Glaisdale).

but under a smart contract the parties will have to perform – or to be more exact, performance will follow no matter their choice or rights.

The term 'smart contracts' is a misnomer; they are in fact not smart at all – at least not in the way traditional contract law is smart. They are not smart enough to adjust as events unfold. Even beyond mistakes, parties may not anticipate the exact scenario that arises at the time of performance. Most contracts are incomplete, in the sense that they do not specify an outcome for every event possible. Courts can also fill in the blanks when the contractual expression of the parties' intent is ambiguous.[92] The self-enforceability and inability of courts to stop the performance of a smart contract could result in illegal contracts being performed[93] – exacerbating the already-anxious reservations about cryptocurrency and blockchain being used for illicit means. Computer code does not take into account possible legal nullity of the contract (unless taught to do so) and that discrepancies can occur between the legal and the automated systems, which then may result in unfair or unlawful smart contracts being enforced.[94] The described outcome is of course detrimental to the social welfare to the degree that computer codes are used to regulate and steer social behavior outside of existing regulatory frameworks.[95]

The only way possible to influence or to stop the execution of a smart contract is by programming it in such a way that it seeks external input from oracles on further execution at the occurrence of certain predefined events.[96] The external input can come from a human-controlled IT process into which the smart contract is embedded or from authorities or courts. Such a solution, where a smart contract has a clause stating that court decisions can be incorporated into a contract via an oracle, could sort out the problem of execution of illegal smart contracts. However, there is an important flaw in such an argument: it would require every party in every contract to agree to insert such a clause. However, since there can be no 'implied term' *ex post* in computer code, and assuming that in the near future there will be millions of such smart contracts executed every day, it would be impossible to police or determine if every contract has such a clause. Alternatively, 'multisig' technology could be implemented. In such a system contract performance requires two out of three keys: one is in the possession of each party and a third in possession of a mutually trusted third party (such as, an arbitrator). If two parties agree on performance, they both sign using their keys and the contract is executed. If there is disagreement, the trusted third party can choose to sign and thus activate the contract, or to withhold its signature, thus preventing the contract from being executed.[97]

Apart from problems of illegality, there is also the problem of variation within a smart contracts context. Once a smart contract is programmed and put onto the blockchain, it is supposed to run until its completion. A contract provision for modification of the smart contract in certain agreed circumstances would need to be programmed into the code from the outset, which is difficult given the current state of technology.[98] Therefore, it

---

[92] Werbach and Cornell, 'Contracts Ex Machina', 369.
[93] It goes of course without saying that the court can however declare the smart contract *ex post* as void. It then needs the law of unjust enrichment and a reverse transaction to rewind the original transaction.
[94] Jaccard, 'Smart Contracts and the Role of Law', 8.
[95] Ibid.
[96] Paech, 'The Governance of Blockchain Financial Networks', 1083.
[97] Werbach and Cornell, 'Contracts Ex Machina', 345.
[98] Catchlove, 'Smart Contracts: A New Era', 13.

may be required to programme broad allowance or variation in performance into the code. However, one has to understand that this would of course lessen the additional certainty otherwise gained through the use of smart contracts.[99]

4.5.2 *The Different Aims of Legal Contracts and Smart Contracts*

We have seen so far that while the formation of smart contracts does not challenge the traditional rules of contract law, their self-enforcing nature does because the traditional enforcers (courts and arbitral tribunals) might be helpless in providing an *ex post* solution.[100] This is the essential conflict between the immutability of smart contracts and the remedial function of contract law.[101] The problems arise from the underlying tension between the decentralized nature of the blockchains and centralized traditional enforcement procedures.

Smart contracts have been called the first real disruptive innovation in the legal profession, and it is said that the technology will eliminate (or at least drastically reduce) the need for lawyers, paralegals, judges, or arbitrators.[102] Others are convinced that lawyers are here to stay. In the words of *Raskin*:

> The creators of smart contracts have invited society to a party they are throwing. They say that this party has better food, booze, and music than the party being thrown down the street. But the other party has all of the people, even if the amenities are not as good. Whether society shows up to this new party is an open question. This is because legacy systems exist for a reason. By definition, they work. Both switching costs and uncertainty stand as barriers to the adoption of any new technology. Yet if the value of the new technology is overwhelming, such a change is more likely to occur. One way of reducing uncertainty is by situating the new in the old.[103]

The invitation to situate 'the new in the old' is ubiquitous across the literature. It shall be discussed further below. *Werbach* and *Cornell* conclude that smart contracts will not replace contract law. For them, even if smart contracts can meet the doctrinal requirements of traditional contract law, they serve a very different purpose.[104] Contract law is exclusively a remedial institution, and it does not aim to ensure performance *ex ante*, but to adjudicate the *ex post* grievances that may arise. Smart contracts instead eliminate the act of remediation by admitting no possibility of a breach of contract. However, the reasons that gave rise to contract law as such do not disappear. If the contracting parties cannot (or do not) represent *ex ante* all possible outcomes of a smart contract arrangement, the results may diverge from their mutual intent.[105] The smart contract might also lead to legally sanctioned results (e.g. in cases of duress, unconscionability or illegality). Hence, promise-oriented disputes and grievances will not disappear from the legal world, but only shift their complexion.

Whatever the future may hold, the discussion of smart contracts offers an opportunity to re-evaluate the existing norms of contract law. *Werbach* and *Cornell* reject, for

[99] Ibid.
[100] Raskin, 'The Law and Legality of Smart Contracts', 311.
[101] Ibid.
[102] See on this issue Tjong Tjin Tai, 'Smart contracts en het recht', 176.
[103] Raskin, 'The Law and Legality of Smart Contracts', 340.
[104] Werbach and Cornell, 'Contracts Ex Machina', 318.
[105] Ibid.

example, the argument that the function of contract law is to strengthen and affirm our moral obligations or to facilitate reliance through opting into predictable further consequences.[106] According to them, contract law exists to adjudicate the justice of a situation *ex post* and its basic function is to decide whether one party has failed to perform a contractual obligation. Therefore, contract law is primarily a remedial institution whose purpose is resolving disputes, taking the reasons as already given.[107] If that is the objective of contract law, then smart contracts do not even purport to do what contract law does as they have two very different objectives: Smart contracts want to ensure actions, while contract law functions to recognize and remedy grievances. So smart contracts cannot replace contract law – at best, smart contracting might be able to reduce the need for contract litigation and minimize transaction costs.

4.5.3 *Computer Code versus Natural Language*

Another thread often present in discussions of smart contracts is the language they are written in: the code. The code, being binary in nature, is said to be much less ambiguous and much more clear[108] and, thus, more certain, making transactions considerably less expensive due to the certainty of execution and the low risk of litigation.[109] The limitation of programming language still leaves some room for ambiguity, but this is significantly less than in plain English.[110] Several authors correctly argue that while programming language may in fact remove linguistic ambiguity, it will remain helpless in relation to changes of circumstances, lacunae, and questions of equity or good faith.[111]

Paech's proposal is to combine 'smart' and 'dumb' contracts – leaving parts of the agreement outside the blockchain record, as non-smart or modifiable, while other obligations are inserted into the blockchain as self-executory and immutable.[112] As already mentioned, others suggest that there should be a 'dumb' contract as a 'legal wrapper' which would set out the terms of the contract, incorporating the smart contract code by reference, as well as to insert a fail-safe in the smart contract that would allow the code to be terminated or amended in certain (agreed) scenarios.[113]

The more complicated and complex smart contracts have to be to ensure safety the lesser their appeal. However, not every smart contract needs in fact a bespoke human-negotiated contract alongside it. Standard contract forms will be widespread at least for business-to-consumer contracts and low-value agreements.[114] Still the reality today is such that the smart contract code and paper contracts coexist in individual transactions.

---

[106] Ibid, at 354.
[107] Ibid, at 361.
[108] Catchlove, 'Smart Contracts: A New Era' 10.
[109] Paech, 'The Governance of Blockchain Financial Networks', 1082.
[110] Catchlove, 'Smart Contracts: A New Era', 15. Sceptical, however, Tjong Tjin Tai, 'Smart contracts en het recht', 181. He is arguing that even computer experts have problems to understand the code.
[111] See e.g. Jacobs and Lange-Hausstein, 'Blockchain und Smart Contracts', 13; Guggenheim, 'The Potential of Blockchain', 96.
[112] Paech, 'The Governance of Blockchain Financial Networks', 1097.
[113] Lim, Saw and Sargeant, 'Smart Contracts: Bridging the Gap'; Ryan, 'Smart Contract Relations in e-Commerce', 15.
[114] Werbach, 'Trust, But Verify', 54. For possible legal implications see the following section on consumer law and smart contracting.

This can be imagined on a spectrum – contracts fully in natural language at one end and fully computer coded contracts at the other.

The uncertainty over the current position of smart contracts, combined with desired ambiguity,[115] means that for now high-value smart contracts will be in the middle of the spectrum – 'split' smart contracts including, a natural language contract with encoded performance clauses for automated aspects.[116] Commercial contracts contain numerous boilerplate clauses that protect the contracting parties from different edge-case liabilities. These clauses are not always suitable for representation and execution through a code. Having said that, it becomes clear that smart legal contracts will require, at least for the near future, a blend between code and natural language.[117]

This blend of computer code and natural language will continue to require solicitors for drafting purposes. Moreover, another development also secures their future – smart contracts will not eliminate commercial litigation. The self-executing nature of smart contracts means that a court order will have no practical effect on the performance.[118] This means smart contracts live to some extent outside traditional contractual remedies. Alternative causes of actions such as, unjustified enrichment and reverse transactions will play a more important role in smart contracts disputes.[119] Judges when confronted with injustice or injury will not 'throw up their hands and defer to a distributed ledger'.[120] Litigation will persist, but it will be shifted from claims of breach of contract to claims of restitution.[121]

4.5.4 *Consumer Protection Law and (Egalitarian) Smart Contracts*

Another element of conflict between smart contracts and traditional contract law is the protection of weaker parties – an idea that traditional contract law contains (at least to some extent) and which became of utmost importance with the rise of consumer protection law.[122] Business-to-consumer transactions are of particular interest for smart contracting as it is expected that this area will be the main sphere of applicability of smart contracts in the near future.[123] The question is now whether the general structure of

---

[115] Freshfields Bruckhaus Deringer, 'A Smart New World: Blockchain and Smart Contracts', www .freshfields.com/en-gb/our-thinking/campaigns/digital/fintech/blockchain-and-smart-contracts/
[116] Norton Rose Fulbright, 'Can Smart Contracts Be Legally Binding Contracts', 14.
[117] Stark, 'Making Sense'.
[118] Werbach and Cornell, 'Contracts Ex Machina', 373.
[119] Szczerbowski, 'Place of Smart Contracts in Civil Law', 335.
[120] Werbach, 'Trust, But Verify', 36.
[121] Werbach and Cornell, 'Contracts Ex Machina', 376.
[122] See in general about possible frictions between consumer law and artificial intelligence A. Jabłonowska; M. Kuziemski; A. M. Nowak, H.-W. Micklitz, P. Pałka and G. Sartor, Consumer Law and Artificial Intelligence Challenges to the EU Consumer Law and Policy Stemming from the Business' Use of Artificial Intelligence, EUI Working Paper LAW 2018/11, http://cadmus.eui.eu/bitstream/handle/ 1814/57484/WP_2018_01.pdf?sequence=1&isAllowed=y
[123] For the reasons, see Tjong Tjin Tai, 'Smart contracts en het recht', 182. Different, however, Savelyev, 'Contract Law 2.0', 20. He thinks that the main fields of applicability of smart contract are the business-to-business and consumer-to-consumer transactions. The exact impact of development of smart contracts on consumer law and policy is of course yet uncertain. It should also be pointed out that because to draft and enter smart contracts have high initial costs and require infrastructure and expert knowledge (coding), the access to it is not equal. Only those who can afford the powerful hardware and know how to computer-code or can afford to hire a programmer can (as of now) utilize the technology, though certain startups exist to allow 'laymen' to draft their own smart contracts.

smart contracts allows consumer protection at all or to what extent. It has been argued 'that the whole layer of legal provisions relating to consumer law [...] is non-applicable to smart contract', and, therefore, no conflict between consumer law and smart contracting exists.[124] However, this opinion does not give any reason for the non-applicability of consumer law in this scenario and should be rejected.[125] It almost goes without saying that EU consumer law (or the national law implementing EU directives on consumer protection) is in principle applicable to all B2C transactions, whether online or offline.

If we accept that consumer protection law is in principle applicable, numerous problems can arise in the smart contracts context. For instance, the right of the consumer to withdraw from the contract which is foreseen in several EU directives conflicts with the immutability of the blockchain and the self-enforcing nature of the smart contract. This conflict is not so clear given Art. 9(1) of the E-Commerce Directive 2000/31/EC[126] (equally applicable to business-to-consumers and business-to-business relations), which states that all Member States are bound to ensure that their legal systems allow contracts to be concluded by electronic means without undue obstacles, applies to smart contracts.[127]

Another highly problematic area is the application of the Unfair Terms Directive 93/13/EEC[128] to smart contracts – an area which is important for the determination of the content of a formatted contract. Some argue that the Unfair Terms Directive might not be applicable as it requires (see e.g. Art. 1(1) of the Unfair Terms Directive) an unfair contract *term* in a *textual* form – a requirement an algorithm may not fulfil.[129] This train of thought is however not very convincing as the Unfair Terms Directive does not per se require text form. In addition, it would be counter-productive if the protection of the Unfair Terms Directive grants could be circumvented by converting unfair terms into a smart contract code.

It is important to note that the content of smart contracts include terms that are individually negotiated.[130] However, Article 3(2) of the Unfair Terms Directive clearly states that the fact that certain terms have been individually negotiated shall not exclude the application of the Unfair Terms Directive to the rest of a contract (if an overall assessment of the contract indicates that it is nevertheless a pre-formulated standard contract). Hence, it can be concluded that the Unfair Terms Directive is in principle applicable to smart contracts.

This applicability of the Unfair Terms Directive triggers further legal discussions for smart contracting, especially Art. 5 of the Unfair Terms Directive, which requires that the

---

[124] Savelyev, 'Contract Law 2.0', 20.
[125] Numerous authors do not even discuss the problem of the applicability of consumer law for smart contracts and are assuming (naturally) its applicability in this context. See e.g. Buchleitner and Rabl, 'Blockchain und Smart Contracts', 12; Kaulartz, 'Herausforderungen bei der Gestaltung von Smart Contracts', 204; Kaulartz and Heckmann, 'Smart Contracts – Anwendung der Blockchain-Technologie', 618–621; Söbbing, 'Smart Contracts und Blockchain', 46; Tjong Tjin Tai, 'Smart contracts en het recht', 181.
[126] Directive 2000/31/EC of the European Parliament and of the Council of 8 June 2000 on certain legal aspects of information society services, in particular electronic commerce, in the Internal Market.
[127] Norton Rose Fulbright, 'Can Smart Contracts Be Legally Binding Contracts', 22. See also Tjong Tjin Tai, 'Smart contracts en het recht', 176, 181, 182.
[128] Council Directive 93/13/EEC of 5 April 1993 on unfair terms in consumer contracts.
[129] Söbbing, 'Smart Contracts und Blockchain', 46.
[130] Kaulartz and Heckmann, 'Smart Contracts – Anwendung der Blockchain-Technologie', 622, raise this question. However, they come to the conclusion that the (implemented) unfair terms directive is applicable in a smart contract scenario.

pre-formulated terms 'must always be drafted in plain, intelligible language'. But has been noted, parties are in principle free to choose any language for their contract they want, which includes 'computer language'. In a business-to-consumer context, this party autonomy is considerably limited due to the above-mentioned provisions – but it is very hard to defend the position that the underlying computer code of a smart contract is a plain, intelligible, language for the average consumers.[131] At the minimum, the Unfair Terms Directive obliges businesses to provide consumers with plain, intelligible translations of the computer code. Only through such presentation of terms can they become a valid part of the smart contract and give smart contracting for business-to-consumer transactions a future.[132]

4.6 Conclusion

Neither on-chain nor off-chain smart contracts challenge the classic elements of English Common Law on formation of contracts – offer and acceptance, consideration, intention to create legal relations, and capacity. That is at least true as long as the algorithms are exclusively employed as mere tools and not as 'artificial agents' which are not only executing but also concluding contracts.

However, we have identified other smart contracting features which do challenge the traditional contract law beyond the formation of contracts itself: The firm and self-enforcing nature of smart contracts is in conflict with the concept of flexible, enforceable legal contracts, and also the aims of legal contracts and smart contracts differ considerably. Furthermore, it is hard to bring the *ex ante* automated assessment of smart contracts in line with the traditional contract law concept of *ex post* authoritative judgments. Another challenge is that smart contracts 'think' in computer codes, while legal contracts are based on natural language. Finally, smart contracting also challenges some mandatory consumer protection law elements, such as the consumer's right of withdrawal from the contract. However, we should not be afraid of challenges and our contract law will 'survive' smart contracts. Smart contracts are neither the end of contract formation as we know it nor the end of contract law as such. We should see smart contracts as a litmus test for our contract law and as a welcomed opportunity to think whether it is still fit for the challenges of the twenty-first century.

---

[131] Similar Kaulartz and Heckmann, 'Smart Contracts – Anwendung der Blockchain-Technologie', 622; Kaulartz, 'Herausforderungen bei der Gestaltung von Smart Contracts', 204; Söbbing, 'Smart Contracts und Blockchain', 46.

[132] Similar Kaulartz and Heckmann, 'Smart Contracts – Anwendung der Blockchain-Technologie', 622; Kaulartz, 'Herausforderungen bei der Gestaltung von Smart Contracts', 204.

5 Challenges of Smart Contracts
Implementing Excuses

Eric Tjong Tjin Tai

5.1 Introduction

Smart contracts are an exciting development at the junction of computer programs and contracts, which has received new impetus through the rise of blockchain technology. Some adherents believe that they will completely supplant the existing practice of legal contracts, while other commentators are more critical about their actual use.[1] Either way smart contracts do provoke lawyers to reconsider the use of the traditional formalities and rules of contract law, and thereby may raise questions regarding the fundamentals contract law.[2]

If we wish to obtain a reliable view of what smart contracts may or may not do, in comparison with traditional contracting, it is essential to engage with actual legal practice and contract law. A large part of the existing legal literature regarding smart contracts unfortunately remains at a rather abstract level. This is understandable in that the first need is to make lawyers understand what smart contracts actually are; furthermore, the extant literature does raise important points to which I will return to later. However, a more detailed analysis of how contracts actually operate and what smart contracts can or cannot do may yield important results: this is relevant for advising clients about smart contract use, and may aid in improving smart contract practice.

In this contribution, I will try to advance the debate by focusing on an important part of contract law, namely the law of excuses. Smart contracts are supposed to secure actual

---

[1] The most relevant legal literature is: C.L. Reyes, 'Conceptualizing Cryptolaw', (2017) 96 *Nebraska L. Rev.* 384–445; K. Werbach and N. Cornell, 'Contracts Ex Machina', (2017) 67 *Duke L.J.* 313–382; M. Raskin, 'The Law and Legality of Smart Contracts', (2017) 1 *Georgetown Technology Review* 305–341; A. Savelyev, 'Contract Law 2.0: "Smart" Contracts As the Beginning of the End of Classic Contract Law', (2016) at ssrn .com/abstract=2885241; M.L. Perugini and P. Dal Checco, 'Smart Contracts: A Preliminary Evaluation', (2015) at ssrn.com/abstract=2729548; P. Paech, 'The Governance of Blockchain Financial Networks', (2017) 80 *Modern Law Review* 1072–1100; E. Mik, 'Smart Contracts: Terminology, Technical Limitations and Real World Complexity', (2017) 9 *Journal of Law, Innovation and Technology* 269–300, at SSRN: https://ssrn.com/abstract=3038406; J.M. Sklaroff, 'Smart Contracts and the Cost of Inflexibility', (2017) 166 *Univ. Pennsylvania L. Rev.* 263–303; A.J. Casey and A. Niblett, 'Self-Driving Contracts', (2017) 43 *Journal of Corporation Law* 1–33; R. O'Shields, 'Smart Contracts: Legal Agreements for the Blockchain', (2017) 21 *North Carolina Banking Institute* 177–194; M. Giancaspro, 'Is a "Smart Contract" Really a Smart Idea? Insights from a Legal Perspective', (2017) 33 *Computer Law & Security Review* 825–835; P. De Filippi and A. Wright, *Blockchain and the Law* (Cambridge, MA: Harvard University Press, 2018); T.F.E. Tjong Tjin Tai, 'Juridische aspecten van blockchain en smart contracts', (2017) 54 *Tijdschrift voor Privaatrecht* 563–608; T.F.E. Tjong Tjin Tai, 'Smart contracts en het recht', (2017) 93 *Nederlands Juristenblad* 176–182.

[2] T.F.E. Tjong Tjin Tai, 'Formalizing Contract Law for Smart Contracts', ICAIL 2017, https://ssrn.com /abstract=3038800 (July 2017).

performance, but to be able to do so appropriately they need to take into account the possibility that a contract party may raise a valid excuse for non-performance of his obligations. Smart contracts should be able to deal with the possibility of at least some excuses; hence, this analysis will test the suitability of smart contracts for actual contracting.

First, I will introduce smart contracts and highlight a few important aspects, in particular the use of oracles (Section 5.2). Next, I will provide a comparative overview of excuses and hardship, culminating in a 'common core' of the rules of various jurisdictions (Section 5.3), which will provide a generally accepted basis of how excuses function in contract law. Subsequently, I will investigate whether and how excuses can be dealt with in smart contracts (Section 5.4). This analysis will show some of the weaknesses of smart contracts, which lead to a more general discussion about possibilities and limitations of smart contracts (Section 5.5).

This preliminary analysis is made on the basis of contract law and not through empirical research, while I would submit that contract law itself is already a digest of contract practice, in that legal rules develop precisely through court cases where contractual issues cannot be resolved easily.[3] In the future, actual empirical research may provide further insights that are relevant for the current topic.

5.2 Characteristics of Smart Contracts

Smart contracts have by now been covered by a substantial number of articles. I will assume that the reader is familiar with the basic background and concepts, and will recapitulate only the main aspects insofar as relevant here.[4] As smart contracts are a development of the blockchain technology that lies at the basis of bitcoin, I will start with a brief summary of crucial aspects of bitcoin and blockchain.

5.2.1 *Bitcoin and Blockchain Technology*

Bitcoin is a decentralised, anonymous virtual currency that operates on a network of computers (often called nodes) which do not need to trust each other,[5] as consensus is obtained through an ingenious mechanism (proof of work) by which payment transactions are validated and accepted as part of the complete registry of payments, the blockchain.[6] The verification process is rewarded with new bitcoin: this process is therefore called 'mining', by analogy with actual mining of gold. Because of the decentralised nature of this process and the blockchain, it is practically impossible to hack the system in order to falsify the blockchain or to insert false transactions.

---

[3] Tjong Tjin Tai, 'Formalizing Contract Law'.
[4] An overview of technical literature (which does *not* take into account legal issues) is M. Alharby and A. van Moorsel, 'Blockchain-based Smart Contracts: A Systematic Mapping Study', (2017) 5 *Computer Science & Information Technology* 125–140.
[5] A copy of the blockchain is stored at each node.
[6] The literature on blockchain technology is massive. The reader may also consult the articles referenced in note 1, also S. J. Shackelford and S. Myers, 'Block-by-Block: Leveraging the Power of Blockchain Technology to Build Trust and Promote Cyber Peace', (2017) 19 *Yale J.L. & Tech.* 334–388.

Blockchain technology has been further developed outside the bitcoin system. Two characteristics are important, as they figure often in literature, even though they are not absolutely necessary for blockchain.

(1) The blockchain of the bitcoin system is public, as all participants [have] need access to it. Alternative implementations have led to the possibility of selecting participants. A 'permissioned' (instead of permissionless) blockchain only allows participants that have been accepted by the organisation controlling the specific blockchain. Such a blockchain may still be accessible for others, but only a selected participant node may verify and add new blocks. A step further is a 'private' blockchain, which is only accessible for the selected participants and not for the world at large.

(2) The blockchain is immutable: sets of transactions (blocks) that have been accepted cannot be changed retroactively; it is only possible to add new blocks that reverse earlier transactions (by return payments). However, it is theoretically possible to retroactively modify the blockchain and 'undo' undesirable transactions of blocks, if the majority of the participants in the system agree to do so. This is a 'hard fork', and an operation such as this has been executed to undo a 'hack' of the Ethereum blockchain.[7]

5.2.2 Smart Contracts

One of the extensions of blockchain technology that was suggested early on was the implementation of smart contracts. These are in essence programs that perform contractual obligations, and may contain and execute contractual conditions, as well as invoke physical remedies (such as providing or withholding access to a room, interrupting the starter of a car). Although discussed earlier,[8] smart contracts were only feasible in restricted environments (in particular the financial sector). With the advent of bitcoin, a cheap and secure way has become available for actually performing payments. A payment transaction is in essence a simple instruction. But, computers that are part of a blockchain network can also execute highly complex programs and instructions. Blockchain technology can thus be adapted fairly easy to process complex transactions. Thereby, it is possible to model complete contracts. This idea has become a reality with the Ethereum system,[9] which offers a fully capable computer language,[10] Solidity, in which to program contracts.

The paradigmatic way to use smart contracts where a user proposes a specific smart contract by making it available in the system. The contract has an identification number (id) and functions as an autonomous entity within the system, similar to how a website

---

[7] The DAO-hack, about which O'Shields, 'Smart Contracts: Legal Agreements', 184.
[8] For example, N. Szabo, 'Formalizing and Securing Relationships on Public Networks', (1997) 9 *First Monday*, at firstmonday.org/ojs/index.php/fm/article/view/548/469/; N. Szabo, 'The Idea of Smart Contracts', at szabo.best.vwh.net/smart_contracts_idea.html; S. Peyton Jones, J.-M. Eber and J. Seward, 'Composing Contracts: An Adventure in Financial Engineering', in: *ACM SIGPLAN International Conference on Functional Programming* (ICFP) 2000 (New York: ACM, 2000), 280–292; H. Surden, 'Computable Contracts', (2012) 46 *UC Davis Law Review* 629–700. See De Filippi and Wright, *Blockchain and the Law*, pp. 73–74; also discuss other examples.
[9] There are alternatives, but these appear at present not to have actual success in market acceptance and may in fact be inoperative.
[10] The language is Turing-complete, which (briefly put) means that it can do anything that any other sufficiently advanced computer language can do.

may operate on Internet. Another user may then 'accept' the contract by communicating to it on the blockchain, for example by making a nominal payment.[11] The users or parties to the contract can communicate with and by means of the contract, for example by signalling that a physical package has been received, after which the contract automatically executes the payment for the package.[12] These operations of the smart contract are executed by the nodes of the smart contract system, in a similar way as with mining bitcoin.[13]

The main advantage of smart contracts is the automatic performance of the obligations.[14] Performance is secured due to the automatic execution without possibility of human intervention once the contract is accepted and started. Further advantages are the impossibility of legal intervention (as the blockchain is not located in a single place and would be practically impossible to shut down) and the possibility to bypass the need for legal advice as the contract supposedly can be read without legal training (and only requires programming skills). In this chapter, I will not discuss whether these advantages actually hold up under close scrutiny.[15]

5.2.3 I/O Functions: Oracles

In order to provide the requisite functionality needed by contract practice, the smart contract system needs to be able to interact with the outside world; otherwise, it could only operate with conditional payments and signals of the users.

The smart contract environment needs to allow smart contracts to *send* signals to external entities or objects, such as computers or robots, whereby the smart contract can operate in the real world without human intervention. An example would be a hotel room that unlocks once you make the payment for the room.

Furthermore, the contract needs to be able to *receive* signals from the outside world. The facility to receive inputs are called 'oracles'. An 'oracle' is simply the entity or communication channel by which the smart contract system receives information about the external world.[16] I will distinguish three kinds of oracles: automated oracles, TTP oracles and expert oracles.

An example of an automated oracle is a self-driving car that sends a signal if it registers that it has been involved in an accident. Other examples are input/output devices, sensors *etcetera*, connections to websites or the Internet at large.

An oracle could also be connected to a human individual, who thereby functions as a trusted third party (TTP). An example is the courier who signals that he has delivered

---

[11] If the contract obliges one of the parties to pay a certain amount, the contract usually requires that party to pay the full amount up front, like a down payment or bank guarantee. The 'money' is for the duration of the contract locked within the contract. However, it is also possible that the contract involves periodic payments, and that it attempts to make a payment after each period, without requiring advance payment.

[12] See the example Safe Remote Purchase at solidity.readthedocs.io/en/develop/solidity-by-example.html #safe-remote-purchase.

[13] There are concerns that this may impose a too heavy computational burden on the nodes, see www .coindesk.com/turing-complete-smart-contracts/.

[14] De Filippi and Wright, *Blockchain and the Law*, p. 80: a decrease of monitoring costs (costs needed to monitor performance).

[15] See the references in footnotes 1 and 2 for a critical discussion.

[16] Mik, 'Smart Contracts: Terminology', 21–24 points out that smart contracts hereby require trust in these oracles.

the package to the address specified. This offers a means whereby the smart contract system can obtain information about a state of affairs that is fairly complex to determine.

An oracle may offer even more complex services, in particular by taking an evaluative role, such as assessment of damage or quality of delivered goods. This may amount to an expert evaluation, such as exist in international trade. These have varied names, such as surveyor, certification agency and conformity assessment body. It may also amount to providing judgement. The oracle thereby functions as an arbitrator or judge. Although at present such an oracle can only be fulfilled by a human expert, it is possible that in the future sufficiently advanced algorithms could fulfil a similar role. The smart contract may outsource specific balancing judgements that are hard, if not impossible, to program and in that way may be able to make the smart contract as a whole fairer or just.

5.2.4 *Programming Intentions and Legal Rules*

In order for smart contracts to fulfil a role similar to that of traditional contracts, the obvious approach seems to translate the normal contract rules in code. This involves both the actual intention of contracting parties[17] and the objective rules of contract law.[18] The rules of contract law have to be programmed in the smart contract, as these are the background of the agreement of the parties. Even if it could be assumed that parties do not want a specific legal system to be applicable and would instead opt for a '*lex cryptographica*', it seems reasonable to assume that non-lawyers would still believe that common doctrines like excuses would apply, even if they did not explicitly state so in their contract. Hence, a smart contract should have facilities for providing for such doctrines. In order to investigate the feasibility of doing so, the analysis should not rely only on a specific legal system. Instead, a better approach would be to adopt a comparative approach to determine the general outline of a certain doctrines that fits most jurisdictions and represent the background assumptions of most parties.

5.3 Law of Excuse for Non-performance

5.3.1 *Introduction*

When parties conclude a contract, we may presume that they do so with the expectation that the obligations from the contract are to be performed.[19] We may for the sake of the present analysis disregard the (in)famous statement that a contract is simply a promise to pay damages if it is not performed.[20] Indeed, it can be argued that smart contracts are useful precisely because they offer a means to ensure that the contract is going to be performed.[21] The right of the creditor to performance is, however, not absolute. Every legal system recognises that performance may be frustrated in various ways, without

---

[17] De Filippi and Wright, *Blockchain and the Law*, p. 84. Actually determining parties' intention is a complicated process which the smart contract literature seems to neglect.

[18] Reyes, 'Conceptualizing Cryptolaw', 415; Tjong Tjin Tai, 'Formalizing Contract Law'.

[19] See about this issue J.M. Smits, D. Haas and G. Hesen (eds.), *Specific Performance in Contract Law: National and Other Perspectives* (Antwerpen: Intersentia, 2008).

[20] As stated by Oliver Wendell Holmes, but currently not really accepted anymore, see J. Cartwright, *Contract Law*, 3rd edn. (Oxford: Bloomsbury, 2016), p. 273.

[21] Raskin, 'Law and Legality'.

thereby making the debtor liable for breach of contract. These possibilities can be discussed under the general heading of 'excuses'.

The law of excuses for non-performance is the result of a long and complicated history.[22] There used to be a variety of specific solutions in various jurisdictions, but scholarship and recent codifications have led to a closer approximation of the national rules.[23] In this chapter, I will argue that the differences can be disregarded for the purpose of implementation in smart contracts, and that we can assume an essential functional similarity. To do so, I will start with an introductory general analysis of the doctrine of excuses for non-performance, based primarily on the Draft Common Frame of Reference (DCFR), as a set of model rules drafted by European legal scholars on the basis of extensive comparative research amongst the legal systems of most European countries.[24] Subsequently, I will show that this analysis closely matches the outlines of several civil law systems. Then I will go into more detail about the English doctrine of frustration, to show that despite the different approach, this doctrine is essentially similar to civil law. I will take a broad perspective on excuses, by also analysing the related doctrines of withholding performance and hardship (unforeseen circumstances). My analysis concentrates on European legal systems, but it is relevant for other jurisdictions as well, given that the jurisdictions discussed here have influenced or been a model for most legal systems in the world.[25]

5.3.2 *Excuses and the DCFR*

One of the main principles of contract law is that the debtor has to perform the obligations that he has undertaken in the contract, and will be liable for non-performance. The creditor may obtain damages, or ask for an order for specific performance, or to terminate the contract. The liability of the debtor is, however, limited insofar as the non-performance has a cause for which he is not responsible and for which he should not be held accountable. This should not be assumed too quickly: while the debtor may not be accountable directly for theft by a third party, it may still be accountable for the loss of a good if it could have taken preventive measures against theft. Non-accountability is mostly assumed only in cases of overpowering circumstances, which are generally called force majeure.

However, even if the debtor is not accountable for the cause, the non-performance may still have consequences. This applies in particular if performance is temporarily or permanently impossible. In that case the creditor cannot obtain an order for specific performance of the obligation, but this does not block other remedies. The creditor may at the very least withhold performance and terminate the contract,[26] depending on the precise circumstances. Furthermore, impossibility itself does not rule out that the

---

[22] F. Ranieri, *Europäisches Obligationenrecht*, 3rd edn. (Vienna: Springer, 2009), Chapter 6.

[23] See the comparative work in H. Beale et al. (eds.), *Cases, Materials and Text on Contract Law*, 2nd edn. (Oxford: Oxford University Press, 2010), chapters 12, 19, 23–25; M. Schmidt-Kessel and K. Mayer, 'Supervening Events and Force Majeure', in: J.M. Smits (ed.), *Elgar Encyclopedia of Comparative Law*, 2nd edn. (Cheltenham: Elgar, 2012), p. 839; H. Kötz, *European Contract Law*, 2nd edn. (Oxford: Oxford University Press, 2017), chapters 12, 14 and 15.

[24] Ch. von Bar and E. Clive, *Draft Common Frame of Reference* (DCFR): Full Edition, 6 vols. (München: Sellier, 2009).

[25] See also section 3.6, where a few international developments are referenced.

[26] Kötz, *European Contract Law*, Ch. 13.

impossibility was due to a cause for which the debtor was accountable, and in that case damages may be awarded. Hence, the available remedies in case of impossibility may be quite like those for excuses in general, although not identical. The interplay between impossibility and excuses has in the past led to complicated rules and exceptions in this area of law.[27] Modern legal systems have fortunately managed to reach an appropriate solution by distinguishing clearly between the attributability of the cause of non-performance and the possible consequences of non-performance (liability, termination). Impossibility is thereby relegated to being a particular kind of cause of non-performance, a potential excuse, relative to certain remedies.

Part of the development of impossibility was the recognition of various kinds of impossibility.[28] Besides factual impossibility (such as delivery of a painting that was destroyed by fire) and practical impossibility (such as delivery of a ring that had sunk to the bottom of the ocean), the law discussed and sometimes recognises moral impossibility (for example, the actor who refuses to perform as he has to be with his dying wife). Closely related to these kinds of impossibility is the case that the obligation could only be performed by the debtor in violation of some legal prohibition (for example, prohibition against exporting currency); thereby, the doctrines of illegality and public policy (which may invalidate the whole contract) are related to moral impossibility.

Article III-3:104 DCFR captures the modern understanding of contractual excuses. It describes the general rule for excuses as impediments to performance which are beyond the debtor's control and could not reasonably be expected to have been avoided or overcome. The criteria of this article may be interpreted as a redefinition of the general requirement of attribution of impediments. The DCFR focus particularly on impossibility, as it only provides specific rules for temporary and permanent impediments.[29]

A relevant distinction has to be made between obligations of result and obligations of means (obligations to observe reasonable care and skill).[30] For the breach of the duty to exercise care or skill there is no valid excuse. The practical problem is rather how to prove the breach of the obligation. This chapter will therefore disregard obligations of means as not relevant for the present topic.[31]

Important in practice is that parties may contractually agree on which causes are or are not legally attributable to the debtor, by way of a force majeure clause.[32] Such a clause makes it easier to determine whether an impediment is a valid excuse, and allows parties to allocate contractual risks in a way they find appropriate.

In case of non-performance, the law generally requires the creditor to notify the debtor of the non-performance. On the one hand, this warns the debtor (who may not even know of the non-performance; for example if a package has not been delivered) and allows him to remedy the non-performance. On the other hand, notification allows the debtor to argue that the non-performance is due to an impediment that is outside its control, which constitutes force majeure. During this discussion, the creditor may withhold performance, which in essence means that he deliberately does not perform a counter-obligation to

---

[27] Ranieri, *Europäisches Obligationenrecht*, Ch. 6.
[28] Kötz, *European Contract Law*, pp. 206–207.
[29] Article III-3:104(3) and (4) DCFR.
[30] Kötz, European Contract Law, pp. 246–251; T.F.E. Tjong Tjin Tai, 'Professional diligence and the UCP Directive', (2016) 12 *European Review of Contract Law* 1–20.
[31] Mik, 'Smart Contracts: Terminology', 21 finds such obligations not suitable for programming in smart contracts.
[32] Explicated in the comments: DCFR, Vol. 1, p. 783 (Comments A. General).

enforce its right to the non-performed obligation (art. III-3:401 DCFR). Withholding performance can insofar be viewed as a justified reason for non-performance, and insofar is similar to an excuse.

Finally, a somewhat related doctrine is unforeseen circumstances or hardship.[33] This involves circumstances that were so unlikely that parties could not reasonably have been expected to include them in the contract. If such circumstances appear, they may have to renegotiate the contract, or the court may modify the contract. Actual applications of this doctrine in practice are comparatively rare; I will not discuss this in depth. Article III-1:110 DCFR provides a rule for this doctrine under the name of change of circumstances. The next few sections show that the outlines of the law as described by the DCFR can also be traced in modern codifications.

5.3.3 *German Law*

German contract law was modified extensively in 2002.[34] In the original Bürgerliches Gesetzbuch (BGB), the main category of excuses was impossibility, which was quickly found to be too limited for a fair distribution of contractual risks. The new BGB offers rules for excuses besides impossibility. The main rules are as follows:

- The creditor has no claim to performance if this is impossible for the debtor or for anyone to perform (§ 275(1) BGB).[35]
- The debtor may (even in case of impossibility)[36] have to pay damages for breach of obligation, except if he is not responsible (*nicht zu vertreten*) for the breach (§ 280(1) BGB, cf. § 286(4) BGB).
- The creditor may terminate (*Rücktritt*) the contract in case of breach, even if the debtor is not responsible (§ 323 BGB).
- The creditor may withhold performance of an obligation if the counter-obligation is not performed or is uncertain to be performed (§§ 320 and 321 BGB).

The liability for damages is therefore fault-dependent,[37] but termination is available regardless of responsibility for the breach.

As regards the responsibility of the debtor, this is determined according to §§ 276–278 BGB. The debtor is liable for intentional and negligent non-performance (§ 276 BGB), as well as for auxiliaries (§ 278 BGB). He is not liable for obstacles to performance that were not foreseeable and for which he has not taken on the risk.[38] Parties may, however, make differing contractual arrangements.[39]

---

[33] See comparatively H. Rösler, 'Hardship in German Codified Private Law: In Comparative Perspective to English, French and International Contract Law', (2007) 15 *European Review of Private Law* 483–513; E. H. Hondius and H.C. Grigoleit, *Unexpected Circumstances in European Contract Law* (Cambridge: Cambridge University Press, 2011); Kötz, *European Contract Law*, Ch. 15.

[34] B.S. Markesinis, H. Unberath, and A. Johnston, *The German Law of Contract: A Comparative Treatise* (Oxford: Hart, 2006); also S. Grundmann, 'Germany and the Schuldrechtsmodernisierung 2002', (2005) 1 *European Review of Contract Law* 129–148.

[35] Markesinis, *German Law*, p. 406.

[36] § 283 BGB, Markesinis, *German Law*, p. 456.

[37] Markesinis, *German Law*, p. 444.

[38] H. Unberath in: H.G. Bamberger and H. Roth, *Kommentar zum Bürgerlichen Gesetzbuch*, 3rd edn., vol. I (§§ 1–610) (München, C.H. Beck, 2012), comment on § 280 nr. 34, also comment on § 286, nr. 51–59.

[39] Unberath, in: Bamberger/Roth, Kommentar § 286, rndnr 52.

Finally, German law recognises unforeseen circumstances, what is called *Wegfall der Geschäftsgrundlage*, 'removal of the basis of the deal' (§ 313 BGB). This may lead to adaption of the contract.

5.3.4 *French Law*

French contract law has recently been recodified,[40] which has significantly clarified the doctrine of excuses. In case of non-performance, the creditor may invoke several remedies, including termination and damages (art. 1217 of *Code civil (Cc)*). However, damages are not due in case of force majeure,[41] when there is an event that impedes the performance of the obligation, which escapes the control of the debtor, which could not reasonably be foreseen at the time of conclusion of the contract, and of which the effects cannot be evaded through appropriate measures (art. 1218(1) Cc).[42] Force majeure includes impossibility, as is clear from art. 1282(2) Cc, where it is stated that temporary impossibility may lead to suspension of the contractual obligation, except if it is of such a nature that may justify termination. An exception to the duty to perform is withholding performance, *'refuser d'exécuter ou suspendre l'exécution de sa propre obligation'* (art. 1217 and art. 1219 Cc). Finally, since the recodification, French law does recognise the doctrine of hardship, in art. 1195 Cc: an unforeseeable change of circumstances which makes performance extremely onerous for one party may impose a duty to renegotiate the contract.

5.3.5 *English Law*

English contract law on excuses takes as its basis that liability for breach is strict.[43] The justification for strict liability in contract is that the debtor voluntarily accepted the obligation. However, not all contractual liability is strict. For example, in the case of a service involving an obligation of reasonable care, the debtor is only liable for breach if it is established that it was at fault.[44] This, in effect, is the distinction between obligations of result and obligations of means (Section 5.3.2).

The general doctrine of an exception to strict liability is called frustration.[45] In the leading case *Davis Contractors Ltd* v *Fareham Urban District Council* [1956] UKHL 3,[46] it is described as follows:

---

[40] 1 October 2016, see *Ordonnance* n° 2016–131 of 10 February 2016.
[41] Article 1231-1 Cc.
[42] '[L]orsqu'un événement échappant au contrôle du débiteur, qui ne pouvait être raisonnablement prévu lors de la conclusion du contrat et dont les effets ne peuvent être évités par des mesures appropriées, empêche l'exécution de son obligation par le débiteur.'
[43] N. Andrews, *Contract Rules: Decoding English law* (Antwerp: Intersentia, 2016), p. 266; S.A. Smith, *Atiyah's Introduction to the Law of Contract*, 6th edn. (Oxford: Clarendon, 2006), pp. 170–171; E. McKendrick, *Contract Law*, 7th edn. (Oxford: Oxford University Press, 2016), p. 749; Kötz, *European Contract Law*, pp. 252–254.
[44] McKendrick, *Contract Law*, p. 750; Smith, Atiyah's Introduction, pp. 170–171.
[45] Cartwright, *Contract Law*, 3rd edn. (Oxford: Bloomsbury, 2016), p. 261; Andrews, Contract rules, p. 266; Smith, *Atiyah's Introduction*, pp. 167–169, 182–192.
[46] AC 696 (HL).

frustration occurs whenever the law recognises that, without the default of either party, a contractual obligation has become incapable of being performed because the circumstance in which performance is called for would render it a thing radically different from that which was undertaken by the contract. *Non haec in foedera veni*. It was not this that I promised to do.[47]

This includes cases where the underlying purpose of the contract has been defeated.[48] However, the supervening event may not be self-induced.[49]

The literature shows various attempts at categorisation. Categories of frustration that are generally recognised are impossibility[50] (including moral[51] or practical impossibility[52]), frustration of purpose,[53] supervening illegality,[54] and hardship.[55] Because contractual liability is strict, it is not necessary to have a general doctrine of force majeure, in contrast to civil law systems where it has to be decided on a case-by-case basis whether a certain cause constitutes force majeure, in English law, everything is attributable except if it is covered by a specific force majeure clause, or is one of the (other) excuses discussed above.

A contract can contain a force majeure clause,[56] releasing a party from its obligations for certain rare events, whereby parties allocate the risk to a specific party.[57] Such a clause may be viewed as a species of frustration or a valid excuse,[58] or alternatively as not being part of frustration.[59] Force majeure clauses are interpreted narrowly, and in particular cannot be invoked when the event in the clause is caused by the negligence of the party relying upon the clause.[60]

There is no single factor which is decisive for frustration; courts use a 'multi-factorial' approach'.[61] The consequence of frustration is non-retroactive termination of the contract;[62] the contract is discharged immediately. This has been called Draconian,[63]

---

[47] Lord Radcliffe, [1956] AC 696, 728–9.

[48] Andrews, *Contract Rules*, p. 257. This is analogous with the German notion of *Wegfall der Geschäftsgrundlage*.

[49] *Maritime National Fish Ltd v Ocean Trawlers Ltd* [1935] UKPC 1; Cartwright, *Contract Law*, p. 265; Andrews, *Contract Rules*, p. 259; McKendrick, *Contract Law*, p. 708.

[50] Smith, *Atiyah's Introduction*, p. 183; McKendrick, *Contract Law*, p. 715. See *Taylor v Caldwell* [1863] EWHC QB J1.

[51] This may also be said to include illegality, cf. Andrews, *Contract Rules*, p. 252.

[52] Cf. Andrews, *Contract Rules*, p. 253.

[53] McKendrick, *Contract Law*, p. 716; Smith, Atiyah's Introduction, p. 184 speaks of frustration of the common venture.

[54] Considered as separate category by McKendrick, Contract Law, p. 715; Chitty/Beale, Chitty on Contracts, nr. 23–024.

[55] Smith, *Atiyah's Introduction*, p. 187. Hardship in the strict sense of unexpected circumstances in civil law systems is not strictly separated from other cases of frustration. An important difference is that such cases still only lead to termination; there is no remedy that leads to adaptation of the contract (Cartwright, *Contract Law*, pp. 268–269).

[56] For example see *Great Elephant v Trafigura Beheer BV and Others (Crudesky)* [2013] EWCA Civ 905.

[57] Andrews, *Contract Rules*, p. 248.

[58] Andrews, *Contract Rules*, p. 266; Smith, *Atiyah's Introduction*, pp. 188–189.

[59] Cartwright, *Contract Law*, pp. 264, 269.

[60] McKendrick, *Contract Law*, p. 714, referring to the leading case *J. Lauritzen A.S. v Wijsmuller B.V. (The Super Servant Two)* [1990] 1 Lloyd's Rep 1.

[61] McKendrick, *Contract Law*, p. 702, referring to *Edwinton Commercial Coproration v Tsavliris Russ* [2007] EWCA Civ 547.

[62] Cartwright, *Contract Law*, pp. 266–267; Andrews, *Contract Rules*, p. 252; Smith, *Atiyah's Introduction*, p. 192; McKendrick, *Contract Law*, p. 722.

[63] McKendrick, *Contract Law*, p. 703.

as termination may be contrary to the wishes of parties and may indeed hurt their interests needlessly.

English law does not recognise a general right of suspension of performance.[64] However, it may be possible that a party may postpone payment until performance is completed (the 'entire obligation' rule).[65]

5.3.6 *Analysis*

The civil law systems discussed above follow the broad outlines of the DCFR regarding excuses.[66] All recognize the notion of an impediment as a cause of the non-performance. German law uses a general notion of responsibility to delimit force majeure from impediments that come at the risk of the debtor, while French law uses a more material description of the notion of attribution, which is closer to the rule in the DCFR.

Although at first sight the common law approach in England seems to differ radically from the DCFR, after further consideration it mostly follows the structure of the DCFR. While common law does not recognise a general requirement that an impediment has to be attributable (instead opting for strict liability), the law does allow several exceptions to liability, such as impossibility and supervening illegality. Furthermore, in practice parties can contractually agree that certain causes or risks are not allocated to the debtor. In this way, a substantial number of causes of non-performance do not lead to liability, which effectively is the same result as in civil law systems.

The broad general agreement on the outline of the law of excuses finds confirmation in international developments such as art. 79 CISG and art. 6.2.2, 72.2 and 7.1.7. of the Unidroit Principles of International Commercial Contracts (PICC).[67] Similarly, US law has the doctrine of changed or unexpected circumstances.[68]

Hence, there is sufficient ground to assume a general consensus on the law of excuses. In case of non-performance, there are several ways in which the debtor may successfully excuse itself for the usual consequences of non-performance.[69] These excuses are categorised in various ways in different jurisdictions, but can for the purposes of the present chapter be lumped together as simply being causes for non-performance which may be excusable, or, in civil law terms, may be non-attributable. Valid excuses or non-attributable causes can be termed 'force majeure' or 'impossibility', depending on the cause. Even illegality or public order can be viewed as impediments (even though they may also lead to nullity of the contract). Most jurisdictions start from a presumption of attributability, in other words they have a fairly strict regime of contractual liability.

---

[64] Cartwright, *Contract Law*, p. 287.
[65] Andrews, *Contract Rules*, p. 307.
[66] Also Kötz, *European Contract Law*, p. 245.
[67] S. Vogenauer and J. Kleinheisterkamp, *Commentary on the Unidroit Principles of International Commercial Contracts (PICC)* (Oxford: Oxford University Press, 2009).
[68] L.L. Fuller and M.A. Eisenberg, *Basic Contract Law*, 8th concise edn. (St. Paul: Thomson West, 2006), p. 510; N.S. Kim, *The Fundamentals of Contract Law and Clauses* (Cheltenham: Elgar, 2016), p. 93; B. H. Bix, *Contract Law: Rules, Theory, and Context* (Cambridge: Cambridge University Press, 2012), pp. 81–83.
[69] Besides the requirement of default, which is part of the doctrinal discussion on remedies and will not be discussed here.

Withholding performance is recognised in most jurisdictions, even though the consequences can be complicated.

Similarly practical problems, with intricate rules in many jurisdictions, arise in case of multiple causes of non-performance, in particular if some causes can be attributed to the creditor as well, and in cases of temporary impossibility and/or repairable breach of an obligation. Unfortunately, space limitations does not allow an in-depth analysis of these topics.

A separate issue is hardship. This is allowed only rarely, in case of unforeseen circumstances. Most jurisdictions require prior negotiation by parties before termination, with the courts having a subsidiary role.[70] This characteristic means that the principle of hardship by necessity cannot be translated into clear rules. An appropriate solution requires respect for parties' wishes, but this is difficult to determine in the abstract.

5.4 Implementing Excuses in Smart Contracts

5.4.1 Introduction

The general outline of the law of excuses found in the aforegoing analysis is as follows:

- determine the cause of the non-performance, and
- whether the cause is attributable to the debtor.

I will focus on this two-step process. I will also briefly discuss impossibility, illegality and hardship, as these can be dealt with relatively quickly.

The question to answer is whether smart contracts can fully emulate the legal system and, if not, why and to what extent. Insofar as smart contracts can easily accommodate the legal rules, then there is no real tension between smart contracts and the law of excuse. Insofar as it may prove difficult to fully program legal rules, the choice can be made either to emulate the rules as far as possible (possibly by outsourcing the legal assessment through an expert oracle) or to deviate from the law by replacing the rules with simpler hard-and-fast rules. By taking the latter route, parties may lose some of the protection that the more complex or vague legal rules offer.

5.4.2 Determining the Cause of Non-performance

The first step in programming excuses in a smart contract is to determine the cause of non-performance. Certain causes may be easy to foresee and programmed into the contract, in particular where these causes are part of the smart contract environment. An example might be insufficient balance of cryptocurrency.[71] Other causes may be external and may be more difficult to assess. Detecting such causes would require the use of an oracle. The (non)delivery of a package could, for example, be ascertained by the courier, who then functions as an oracle. If the non-delivery is a cause of non-performance, the courier as oracle provides a simple way for determining whether this cause is present. But other causes

---

[70] M. Mekki and M. Kloepfer-Pelèse, 'Hardship and Modification (or "Revision") of the Contract', in: A. S. Hartkamp et al., *Towards a European Civil Code*, 4th edn. (Alphen a/d Rijn: Kluwer Law International, 2011), pp. 651–680. English law does not recognise hardship in the sense of circumstances that lead to revision of the contract.

[71] Although smart contracts usually require payment in advance which is only paid out to the other party when sufficient conditions are fulfilled, this is not always the case, such as in the example of periodic payment of a car lease.

may be rarer and harder to foresee, detect and code into the contract. Examples are strikes, bad weather, general power outage, seizure of goods by the police and illness.

While it is theoretically possible that in time best practices develop by which smart contracts can simply include lists of possible causes for excuse (Section 5.5), the determination of the actual cause is further complicated because dependent upon the kind of contract there may be different causes that are relevant, and different ways in which it can be ascertained that they occurred. For a contract of sale, there are different potential causes of non-performance than for a credit contract.

This problem may be evaded by allowing a general exception of 'force majeure', which may be invoked by the debtor, and is effectuated by calling an expert oracle. Thereby the contract enlists the aid of an outside expert or adjudicator. This in effect allowing Alternative Dispute Resolution (ADR) or Online Dispute Resolution (ODR) within the smart contract. The major disadvantage of this approach is that this effectively denies most of the benefits that smart contracts provide, namely, the automatic execution of the contract. For that reason I will not expand on this. Incidentally, invoking expert oracles also has the disadvantage that it may induce a disgruntled contract party to hold the oracle liable for a faulty opinion, or even threaten to do so, which could lead the oracle to delay its opinion.[72] This opens up a weakness in the supposed automatic enforcement of the contract.

A solution more in the spirit of smart contracts might be to operate similar to most legal systems and actual contracts, by starting from the presumption that breach is attributable, and only allowing a limited set of foreseeable relevant causes as an excuse. Any remaining, unforeseen causes would simply be at the risk of the debtor. This is not per se unfair, given the extensive attribution of causes in most jurisdictions. The debtor will usually be in the best position to identify possible causes of non-performance and to take precautionary measures. Also the debtor could insure against many common business risks. The debtor must consider for itself in advance whether it is willing to assume such uncertain risks. The contractual force majeure clause is not really different from this.

However, with a smart contract force majeure clause there still are three complications: (i) determining what is the relevant cause, (ii) separating causes (risks) allocated to the creditor and (iii) following proper procedure.

   (i) A cause may be the consequence of an underlying, earlier cause. The non-delivery of a package may or may not be attributable, depending upon the reason why the package was not delivered: was this due to a strike, the non-acceptance of the package by the debtor, a flood or a war which made delivery impossible? Hence, the non-delivery itself need not be the cause but only puts us on the trail for the actual cause! Indeed, there may be several factors which prima facie appear to be relevant causes: this may require sophisticated legal analysis to determine what the relevant causes that constitute excuse.

   (ii) A further complication arises if one cause is attributable to the creditor (such as non-acceptance of the package): in that case there may be a valid excuse, even if another contributing cause is attributable to the debtor. The non-acceptance in turn may be justified if, for example, the package clearly does not contain the item ordered (which might be visible such as in cases where the package is too small). This brief analysis shows that even if some facts are clear, a further investigation may be

---

[72] This is a well-known procedural tactic in traditional legal practice (which admittedly may have liability risks).

required to determine whether there are underlying facts that favor or disfavor a finding of excuse or not. This cannot be determined in the abstract. The determination of attributability is connected with determining the cause.

(iii) In actual legal practice, there usually is a discussion between parties to determine the cause of non-performance: this process is captured in the rules regarding notification of non-performance.[73] Although such a dialogue may be programmed to some extent in a smart contract (as it can code communication between parties), this is hard to do in a predictable rule-based manner.[74] In a court procedure, parties subsequently may take opposing positions regarding the relevant cause, and are required to provide proof, which allows the court to come to an informed decision on the identification of the actual cause. However, this whole process is *ex-post* and does not help to code how the smart contract should behave during execution. Legal rules tend to take the court's perspective (*ex post*), and not the perspective of parties during execution of the contract (*ex ante*).[75]

The above discussion shows that the developer of a smart contract would, if the contract involves significant monetary value, do well to make a thorough investigation of possibly relevant causes of breach and possibilities of interaction between causes. Case law and doctrine may provide many examples. For simpler contracts or contracts with little monetary value, such an exercise may be needlessly thorough as parties may be willing to take the unknown risks of unforeseen causes of breach. For more complicated cases, it is hard to code all relevant possibilities of interacting causes and deal with these in a satisfactory way. To do so, it would be necessary to program a large part of a hypothetical procedural discussion into the smart contract. This seems at present practically impossible.

At first blush it seems only feasible to program (a) a list of easily identifiable possible causes that can be identified through normal automatic oracles, or can non-contestably be verified through simple TTP oracles and (b) a presumption that such a cause, if present during a certain time frame, is the relevant cause of the non-performance. Multiple causality and impediments due to the creditor seem to be too difficult to deal with at present.

5.4.3 *Determining the Attributability of the Cause*

Assuming that the cause or causes of breach have been determined, the next step is to determine the attributability of the cause. Although the general rule of attributability in civil law systems is an open norm that requires judicial assessment and therefore is hard to program, in contractual practice the uncertainty of court discretion is partly bypassed by force majeure clauses, which spell out causes that count or do not count as force majeure. In principle, such a clause could be programmed as a rule in a smart contract. However, there are two complications.

Firstly, contract practice operates with fairly broad and open categories of causes.[76] In case of a dispute, parties and the court interpret the categories of causes and decide

---

[73] See also art. III-3:104(5) DCFR.
[74] Tjong Tjin Tai, 'Formalizing Contract Law'.
[75] As pointed out by Werbach and Cornell, 'Contracts Ex Machina', 361 and Mik, 'Smart Contracts: Terminology', 17.
[76] Sklaroff, 'Cost of Inflexibility', 279–286, describing the benefits of using general standards in contracts.

whether a specific state of affairs supports a claim of excuse or exemption. Smart contracts, on the contrary, require precisely programmable definitions of causes.[77] To operationalise a cause, it needs to be clearly defined. This may partly be solved by relying on a TTP oracle, but for more complicated cases an expert oracle would be required. This oracle would offer a binding decision as to whether there is force majeure. However, the effect is that the smart contract functions as a normal contract, where a dispute about attributability of a cause of non-performance is ultimately decided by an independent third party, typically a court or arbitration panel. This would be time consuming and would offer parties possibilities for inhibiting the execution of the smart contract, by invoking force majeure.

Secondly, attributability in practice is not only determined by looking at the specific cause in isolation: it may require taking into account other circumstances of the case. A strike may count as a force majeure event, but probably not if the strike is caused by clearly unacceptable and unnecessary behaviour by the debtor. The non-obtaining of a licence may seem force majeure, but not if the debtor received two licences for five boats and decided to allocate the licences to boats other than the boat which was subject to a contract.[78]

In sum, this and the preceding section shows for force majeure in relationship to smart contracts we are left with a choice between either:

– a simple default rule that lists a number of circumstances that count as force majeure and that are identified through automated or TTP oracles, where causality is presumed (given a relevant time frame), or
– a simple reference to an expert oracle.

Once it has been determined that there is in fact force majeure, the consequences can be programmed in a straightforward manner. Force majeure stands in the way of invoking a remedy for non-performance, as there is no breach. The creditor may, however, terminate the contract. Termination is also fairly easy to program (although it requires considerable legal acumen to correctly draft rules for post-termination arrangements, such as returning advance payments or valuation of partial performance).

5.4.4 Specific Categories of Excuses

The above analysis applies largely also to specific categories of excuses.

Impossibility can to a large extent be analysed similarly to force majeure. It is simply a specific kind of impediment. One difference between impossibility and force majeure, however, is that it is not common to find clauses that determine what counts as impossibility. This is insofar to be expected as absolute impossibility exists regardless of a contractual clause. However, for moral impossibility it could be feasible to add contractual rules. For a smart contract, it will be necessary to add rules to determine the presence of impossibility.

A complication is that impossibility may have specific consequences that differ from excuses in general. Impossibility may have to be recognised as a specific kind of impediment. This may, however, be difficult: as we already discussed, it is hard to explain in the

---

[77] Cf. Werbach and Cornell, 'Contracts Ex Machina', 367, on the difficulty to program force majeure.
[78] *Maritime National Fish Ltd* v *Ocean Trawlers Ltd* [1935] UKPC 1.

abstract how to determine what is the relevant cause of non-performance, and similarly it is difficult to determine whether such a cause forms an actual impediment which cannot be overcome, as this may involve knowledge of the world in general. That the courier has an accident may lead to 'impossibility' if the item is broken, or the event may be overcome if it is a general item that can be re-sent. A war may constitute an absolute obstacle, but this may not be so if there is no fighting in the specific area where the obligation is to be performed. Similarly determining whether impossibility is temporary or permanent requires a sophisticated analysis which seems infeasible for a procedural programming language. At present, such an analysis can only be realised through an expert oracle. This may be feasible only if the parties are content with significant delays when invoking such an oracle, as it will require complicated fact-finding and argumentation. It may be practically impossible to realise in typical smart contracts situations where parties wish to remain anonymous and/or are geographically remote.

A smart contract alternative would be not to fully model the legal rules, but rather to only allow those forms of impossibility that have been programmed in smart contracts. This effectively means that all other forms of impossibility are at the risk of the debtor. This may be fair in that the debtor consents to the contract: he may be the party that wrote the contract, and has better insight in the potential risks involved, while it may also decide to ask a higher price due to those risks. Conversely, the contract might simply add that the debtor can always invoke impossibility. However, such a clause can be easily abused as the debtor thereby can invoke it whenever it does not feel like performing. This amounts to a one-sided termination at will on the side of the debtor. Such a clause is generally considered to be unfair.[79]

Actually determining when there is a case of impossibility is complicated as well. Some kinds of causes could be implemented in theory fairly well, such as a general breakdown of the Internet, but others might require complicated assessments of data or factual situations. Such cases would probably have to rely on TTP oracles, except if technological advances make automated algorithmic oracles more powerful.[80]

For *illegality and public policy*, again a complicated analysis would be required.[81] Given the rapid changes in the regulatory landscape concerning cryptocurrencies, the possibility of mandatory law prohibiting the conclusion or performance of certain contracts is far from theoretical. Determining whether there is a public prohibition requires a legal analysis, not a factual analysis of causes. The only practical way to incorporate this possibility in a smart contract is again to have an expert oracle, which may be called when a party invokes the excuse of illegality. Incidentally, it is also possible that parties are fully aware about the illegal nature of their contract. As this is a separate problem of criminal enforcement, it will not be discussed this further.

5.4.5 *Hardship*

Hardship is a doctrine that has limited application.[82] By its very nature it may only be invoked successfully in rare circumstances. Indeed, one may argue that hardship is

---

[79] Cf. Annex 1 to the Unfair Terms Directive 93/13/EEC.
[80] Such algorithms would then still have to connect to relevant sensors and data inputs, which is not a self-evident problem.
[81] Cf. Werbach and Cornell, 'Contracts Ex Machina', 372–373.
[82] See also E. Janssen, 'Smart contracts en onvoorziene omstandigheden', in: H.N. Schelhaas, A.I. Schreuder and K.K.E.C.T. Swinnen (eds.), *Nieuwe technologieën, nieuw privaatrecht?* (Den Haag: Boom juridisch, 2017).

simply part of the deal (risk allocation). Even proponents of hardship recognise that a successful appeal to hardship is only to be allowed in extreme circumstances. For smart contracts, such an argument makes sense. It is well-nigh impossible to program for cases of hardship, except by having a general expert oracle determine when there is hardship. Subsequently, one would have to program facilities for determining an appropriate new contractual arrangement, which is very complicated to do and may make the smart contract unreadable, as it would require a program that allows for completely reprogramming its essential settings. At the very least it would mean a reassessment of contract price and/or delivery conditions.

It seems most likely that smart contract practice will simply decline to offer facilities for hardship. However, a party might start a court procedure to block execution of the contract because of hardship.

A further question relates to the German doctrine of *Wegfall der Geschäftsgrundlage*, frustration of purpose, because the assumption that formed the basis of the contract has fallen away. An example is a contract regarding sponsoring participation in a competition, which does not have any purpose if the competition is cancelled. A proper contract would of course have conditions about such presumptions, but it is possible that a certain presumption fails to be coded often due to the perceived unlikeness of such an occurrence. It is practically impossible to code for every eventuality. Even attempting to do so would lead to 'telephone dictionary' contracts that lawyers are infamous for.

A general approach to allow for these kinds of cases is to add a clause that allows parties to annul, terminate or modify the contract by mutual consent,[83] although it is unclear whether smart contracts actually can allow a complete renegotiation or modification if it has not been preprogrammed as a possibility.[84]

5.4.6 *Breach by the Other Party and Anticipatory Breach*

Breach by the other party should, according to the aims of smart contracts, be programmed correctly in a smart contract.[85] The major advantage of a smart contract of sale is in the certainty that the contract will be performed. For a contract of sale (to take the simplest example), the payment will only proceed or if the other party has performed or if the payment is not received,[86] the debtor may refuse performance (delivery of the object). The smart contract operates effectively like a bank guarantee, which temporarily stores the payment and releases it only upon confirmation that the conditions for payment have been fulfilled.[87] From this it follows that the smart contract cannot ignore the possibility that a party is justified in withholding performing, both when performance by

---

[83] Werbach and Cornell, 'Contracts Ex Machina', 367; O'Shields, 'Smart Contracts: Legal Agreements', 187.

[84] Sklaroff, 'Cost of Inflexibility', 291; B. Marino and A. Juels, 'Setting Standards for Altering and Undoing Smart Contracts', in: J.J. Alferes et al. (eds.), *Rule Technologies. Research, Tools, and Applications*, Proceedings 10th International Symposium, RuleML 2016, (Vienna: Springer, 2016), discuss possibilities for modification in Ethereum by turning on functions, but acknowledge that this requires functions to be preprogrammed. Also De Filippi and Wright, *Blockchain and the Law*, p. 85.

[85] Tjong Tjin Tai, 'Formalizing Contract Law'.

[86] Smart contracts, in their current implementation, require that a party who is obliged to pay a certain sum has to 'pay' it to the contract, which effectively holds it in escrow until it can pay it out to the other party.

[87] Tjong Tjin Tai, 'Smart contracts en het recht'. A somewhat similar financial instrument is a letter of credit, which smart contracts may also be compared to (S.M. McJohn and I. McJohn, 'The Commercial Law of Bitcoin and Blockchain Transactions', (2016) Suffolk University Law School Research Paper No. 16–13, at: https://ssrn.com/abstract=2874463).

the other party is due (breach by the other party) and when there is a reasonable expectation that the other party is not going to perform (anticipatory breach). However, to implement facilities for these occurrences entails all the above-mentioned complications: determining whether the other party is in fact to blame for the breach or whether the other party has a valid excuse.

Simply leaving out the possibility of breach by the other party as an excuse is not acceptable: if the smart contract is going to execute automatically, it should also automatically determine when it should not perform when the counter-performance is lacking.

Arguably a more sophisticated rule might be programmed by spelling out in detail under which circumstances the performance may proceed and when it should be withheld. However, as the case law on bank guarantees makes clear, it is difficult to state clearly, unambiguously and sufficiently when payment may proceed.[88] There may occur conditions where payment or withholding payment would be at odds with the actual intent of the contracting parties. An example is that payment may depend on the judgement of a specifically named independent arbitrator, who has died in the meantime. In general it would be possible to defer to the judgement of an outside expert or arbitrator to decide the issue (which in fact is not uncommon in cases of bank guarantees). But it would be more in line with the philosophy of smart contracts to accept that it is incumbent upon the parties to ensure that the conditions of the contract are sufficiently well elaborated to match the intentions of parties.

Without going into detail, we can at this point state that the issues involved for determining whether there is a right to withholding performance are similar to the complications that plague the determination of valid excuses.

5.4.7 Conclusion

From the aforegoing analysis, it follows that smart contracts, at least in their current implementation as a deterministic computer language, cannot fully emulate the way in which normal legal rules work out for excuses (impediments to performance). In particular problems of exhaustively coding causes, dealing with multiple causes, and attributing causes, are far more complicated than is feasible at present for straightforward coding. In case a party raises an excuse, the contract could either call the help of an expert oracle – which amounts to invoking arbitration, thereby acknowledging the failure to achieve the purpose of smart contracts – or refusing to provide for the nuances of excuses in practice, through hard-and-fast rules.

While it is certainly possible to approximate legal rules in computer code, there will be cases where the smart contract does not operate as a legal contract would. The effect is that one contract party loses some of the protection provided by a legal contract.

Indeed, it is likely that smart contracts will be more favourable to the party with the strongest bargaining power,[89] if the usual correctives of contract law (unfair terms, unconscionable terms) are found to be ineffective in regulating smart contracts (especially, because may not be cost-effective to obtain protection from traditional courts applying contract law).

---

[88] For example, *Rainy Sky SA and others v Kookmin Bank* [2011] UKSC 50.
[89] De Filippi and Wright, *Blockchain and the Law*, p. 85.

5.5 The Limits of Smart Contracts and the Evolution of Excuses

The above analysis is fairly pessimistic as to the possibility of fully capturing the complexities and protection that the doctrine of contractual excuses offers.[90] It is instructive to connect these findings with the more general discussion about the feasibility of smart contracts.[91]

5.5.1 Ex Ante *Regulation versus* Ex Post *Adjudication*

A fundamental problem with the approach of smart contracts is that programming involves *ex ante* regulation: a programmer must in advance consider all possibilities and make suitable arrangements in the program. Although traditional legal contracts do expect parties also to think about future possibilities and agree about the desirable outcome in such cases, in the end contract law acknowledges that it is impossible to arrange for every possibility. More specifically, contract law is effected through legal procedure, which essentially means that a court will adjudicate the issue *ex post*, when the facts are known.[92] This *ex post* characteristic of contract law is fundamentally at odds with smart contracts.[93] Another way to put this is that smart contracts shift the costs of contracting to the pre-contracting stage, as everything has to be drafted in the contract.[94]

As the above analysis makes clear, smart contracts are indeed unable to do a good job at dealing *ex post* with excuses arising during the performance of the contract. At the very least it seems that smart contracts should be modifiable, even though this would go against the general thrust of blockchain technology which prizes immutability.

Indeed, a more detailed analysis shows that contract law is not merely about simple if-then conditions, but also imposes upon parties complicated communication and negotiation processes, which may prove hard to program in procedural computer languages.[95]

5.5.2 *Vague Standards and Libraries of Conditions*

One way in which legal contracts allow parties to state in advance what they want is by allowing vague standards, which are applied to specific circumstances ex post (which is the job of the courts). Indeed, existing contractual practice benefits from vague standards,

---

[90] Similarly for an analysis of other contractual doctrines such as capacity and mistake: Giancaspro, 'Is a Smart Contract a Smart Idea?', s. 3.

[91] This ties in to the analysis of M. Verstraete, 'The Stakes of Smart Contracts', (2018) 50 *Loyola University Chicago Law Journal* (Forthcoming), on SSRN: https://ssrn.com/abstract=3178393, who points out that advocates of smart contracts tend to underestimate the role of the state in maintaining a private law regime.

[92] Incidentally, J. Goldenfein and A. Leiter, 'Legal Engineering on the Blockchain: "Smart Contracts" as Legal Conduct', (2018) 29 (2) *Law and Critique* 141–149, Available at SSRN: https://ssrn.com /abstract=3176363, argue that smart contract will have their own form of dispute resolution which may shape a new sector of law with as yet unknown actors.

[93] Section 4.2, footnote 68.

[94] Sklaroff, 'Cost of Inflexibility', 292, referring to D. Tapscott and A. Tapscott, *Blockchain Revolution* (London: Penguin UK, 2016), p. 103.

[95] Tjong Tjin Tai, 'Formalizing Contract Law'.

as they help to reduce costs.[96] It is unclear how smart contracts can be programmed to translate vague standards to deterministically programmable conditions. Some authors, such as Casey and Niblett, are optimistic and argue that smart contracts would not need to provide for excuses, as they would covered every eventuality.[97] However, they do not support this claim with a substantive analysis.

To be true, there are two possible lines of defence against an overly pessimistic standpoint. First of all, the practical problems described above may partly be resolved by experience over time. Arguably, contract law itself is the result of a long process in which practical problems were resolved and led to improvement of contract rules. Indeed, case law and doctrine already provide extensive lists of impediments and rules for attribution. Given sufficient time, it is possible that smart contract platforms would develop best practices,[98] which would provide functions[99] that contain standard provisions for most relevant and important kinds of impediments. This would amount to a very extensive force majeure clause. It should be noted that, as discussed in Section 4.2, some issues (in particular multiple causation and determining the actual cause) do not lend themselves to this kind of solution. However, it is conceivable that best practices will develop and lead to a fair approximation of the full detail of the law, covering most relevant and probable cases.

Nonetheless, this possibility would merit more discussion than is available presently. Actual computer practice (as any systems administrator and programmer knows) shows that the use of preprogrammed function libraries is not a simple task, as it brings with it problems about different versions of libraries being incompatible, and needs sophisticated knowledge about content and functionality to ensure an acceptable level of operability based upon user expectations. In contract law, there are similar issues, such as found in the 'battle of the forms', when conflicting sets of general conditions are declared to be applicable. It is not at all clear how smart contracts would work out, when confronted with such real-life problems.

Secondly, it may be argued that algorithmic prediction could offer solutions for complex cases.[100] This assessment seems overly optimistic: it ignores the current limitations of algorithms (mostly limited to pattern-recognition and qualification), the extent of variation in actual contract practice and the problem of multiple causality.

5.5.3 *Relational Contracts and the Use Cases for Smart Contracts*

Relational theory of contracting, which has been empirically validated as to how contractual relationships function in commercial practice, is at odds with the way in which proponents of smart contracts perceive contracts.[101] This more general argument cuts to

---

[96] Sklaroff, 'Cost of Inflexibility', 293–295; Mik, 'Smart Contracts: Terminology', 19–20; De Filippi and Wright, *Blockchain and the Law*, p. 77.

[97] Casey and Niblett, 'Self-Driving Contracts', p. 24. The translation of excuses to contractual conditions is, from the point of view of the present analysis, irrelevant.

[98] Werbach and Cornell, 'Contracts Ex Machina', 374–375; Paech, 'Governance of Blockchain', 1097.

[99] De Filippi and Wright, *Blockchain and the Law*, p. 82, envisage standard libraries similar to libraries of computer code.

[100] Casey and Niblett, 'Self-Driving Contracts', p. 24.

[101] Werbach and Cornell, 'Contracts Ex Machina', 367; K.E.C. Levy, 'Book-Smart, Not Street-Smart: Blockchain-Based Smart Contracts and the Social Workings of Law' (2017) 3 *Engaging Science, Technology, and Society* 1–15; De Filippi and Wright, *Blockchain and the Law*, p. 84.

the heart of the matter: complex business situations involve relations which are only partially captured in contracts, and such relations need a kind of flexibility that is fundamentally at odds with the rigidity of smart contracts. For such situations, the automatic execution of smart contracts is a bug, not a feature. Indeed, it appears that in business practice smart contracts tend to be used primarily for executing parts of broader framework contracts, such as financial securities and options. Under such restrictive conditions, smart contracts may operate quite well since they are supported by the safety net of contract law.

However, in specific situations the relational view of contracting may actually not hold, and may benefit from smart contracts. One example is a remote purchase of little monetary value.[102] Such cases involve one-off transactions where no long-term relation is involved, while there is no practical possibility to invoke the protection of the law (due to costs and distance). It seems likely that parties may in such circumstances prefer to limited enforceable remedies, instead of none at all. A hard-and-fast rule may therefore be acceptable here.

Another example is international trade. In that area there are similar problems of invoking legal protection for reasons of costs and time. Therefore, over time a sophisticated (or if one wishes, complicated) system of financial instruments[103] and long-distance agents[104] has developed. This system could at least to a certain degree be supplanted by smart contracts, as it already is based on 'automatic' payments when abstract conditions are fulfilled, to be determined by trusted third parties.

Nonetheless, present practice does not give clear indications how markets will develop. Take the example of long-distance consumer sales. The practice of online marketplaces or platforms such as eBay and Amazon and financial intermediaries such as PayPal gives contrary indications.[105] Such intermediaries[106] have their own conflict resolution rules, which require the buyer to file a substantiated complaint, and may return the buyer his payment without investigating the situation in detail. However, this practice only works because the intermediary is in command of the payment and may withhold it from the seller, and the intermediary may (in cases where neither party is clearly to blame) decide to pay the amount due out of its own pocket as part of its operating costs. This is feasible because the intermediary rely on reputation mechanisms (ratings) to filter out dubious market parties, and thereby its payments in a limited number of cases are offset by the profits of operating the intermediary business. In smart contract systems such mechanisms do not yet exist; it is for further research to see whether such mechanisms would improve smart contract reliability. Furthermore, the hard-and-fast rules lead to online complaints from sellers who find that they have to bear the risks of unjustified complaints by buyers and find that the intermediary offers insufficient protection. In effect, this means that the hard-and-fast rule offers insufficient protection for impediments to the creditor/buyer.

---

[102] Tjong Tjin Tai, 'Formalizing Contract Law'.
[103] Such as letters of credit and bank guarantees, mentioned above.
[104] Trade agents, distributors, but also auxiliaries such as independent assessors and surveyors (s. 2.3).
[105] These are preliminary findings, partly based on anecdotal evidence, of ongoing research in Tilburg. See further C. Busch and S. Reinhold, 'Standardisation of Online Resolution Services: Towards a More Technological Approach', (2015) 4 *European Journal of Consumer and Market Law* 50–58.
[106] For the sake of simplicity, I use this term to also cover marketplaces and platforms. See also the recent EU proposal for a regulation on promoting fairness and transparency for business users of online intermediation services of 26 April 2018, COM(2018) 238 final.

5.6 Conclusion

As the above analysis shows, smart contracts are not very well suited to deal with the nuances that are currently expected by non-lawyers and lawyers alike. This has been argued with respect to the doctrine of excuses for non-performance. Furthermore several more fundamental issues have been discussed, which should be taken into account when considering the suitability of smart contracts in actual practice. Two specific cases have been identified where the limitations of smart contracts may not be found to be prohibitive.

6 Contract Interpretation

Michel Cannarsa

6.1 Introduction

This chapter will focus on the issue of contract interpretation, trying to identify and deal with some of the questions at the intersection between law and technology. The current literature does not adequately address the issue of contract interpretation in the context of automated contracts. The current undertaking aims at providing a basic understanding for the legal community, through some commentary and modest proposals, relating to interpretative issues concerning the future widespread use of automated contracts.

The approach taken here, while assessing the role of interpretation in the context of automated contracts, will take a comparative orientation. 'Automation' of legal relations renews the relevance of comparing common and civil law theories, principles, rules, practices, and so forth. The author's view is that as far as contract interpretation is concerned, smart contracts are more 'compatible' with a common law framework than with a civil law one. This view may apply on a broader scale if one looks at the impact of technologies on legal systems (reliance of data, predictive justice, and automated rules, broadly speaking). The next two subsections will introduce issues at the intersection of law and technology, as well as the rise of smart contracts.

6.1.1 *Law and Technology*

It is not a bold assertion to say that our societies and economies are more and more data driven.[1] This applies progressively, but quite rapidly, to our legal orders. Indeed, laws, regulations, judicial decisions, contracts, and other legal products are information that can be translated from analog into digital data, from natural language to computer code. Once translated into digital data, legal information can be processed by various computer-based technologies.[2] The conjunction between digitalization of an enormous amount of data,[3] algorithmic techniques, and development of computer power is producing effects in the

---

[1] S. Abiteboul and G. Dowek, *Le temps des algorithmes* (Paris: Editions le Pommier, 2017); A. Basdevant and J.-P. Mignard, *L'empire des données, Essai sur la société, les algorithmes et la loi* (Paris: Don Quichotte éditions, 2018); Various authors, 'La datacratie', (2018) 164 *Pouvoirs*, p. 6.

[2] G. Berry, *L'hyperpuissance de l'informatique, Algorithmes, données, machines, réseaux* (Paris: Odile Jacob, 2017).

[3] The so-called Big Data phenomenon.

legal world, in the field of contract law among others, leaving much of what will happen in the coming years and decades quite unpredictable.[4]

A few things however seem clear: this stage of development is a stimulating challenge for lawyers, who have the responsibility to make sure that these evolutions comply with the founding principles of our legal orders. In order to do so, lawyers have to understand the technology and have to work hand in hand with experts from other disciplines, starting with computer scientists and developers. The same suggestion shall apply to experts from other disciplines that seek the help of lawyers in order to understand where technological development collides with legal rules.[5] At the moment though, the various analyses tend to focus on a first layer of the issue, consisting of understanding the technology. Lawyers are predisposed to try to place technological tools into legal boxes. After such placement, they compare these technological tools, and the way they operate, with traditional contract structure and frameworks.

This chapter views law and technology as a binary relationship that needs to be studied from both sides – from technology to law and law to technology. These reciprocal relationships will be superimposed: the legal one, with its traditional rules of contract interpretation and the technological one (smart contracts). This two-track analysis will allow us to determine whether smart contracts will modify contract interpretation as it is currently applied in practice. In doing so, the chapter will take a comparative perspective. In all likelihood, the interpretation of smart contracts will produce different effects in the common law and civil law worlds. Moreover, it is presumed here that the impact of smart contracts on civil law contract drafting and interpretation styles will be deeper. Indeed, the high level of precision required in the process of coding smart contracts seems incompatible with the traditional drafting approach found in civil law countries.

6.1.2 *The Smart Contracts Phenomenon*

Much interest has been devoted to smart contracts in recent years, especially and exponentially in the year, making it a 'hype cycle'.[6] Before going into further details

---

[4] And, at the same time, fascinating.

[5] The author's different experiences in this field tend to indicate a strong interest in the scientific community for a dialogue with lawyers. An approach based on hypothetical cases, anticipating future situations in order to test different scenarios, seems to be a pragmatic and efficient method to deal with technological developments from a legal perspective. This allows, among others, to gather empirical data and to be immune, at least to some extent, from paradigmatic bias. To this end, Lyon Catholic University Faculty of Law, together with Lyon Administrative Appeal Court, the Lyon Bar Council, INSA (school of engineers), and Transpolis (a company dedicated to innovation in the field of urban mobility and intelligent transportations systems), has created a 'Future of Digital Technologies Law Clinic' involving law and engineering students, practicing lawyers, judges, experts of intelligent systems and robotics, as well as representatives of the industry, in moot courts dedicated to future technologies (self-driving cars, domotics, medical robots, and so forth). The first two editions of moot courts were a big success (see description and summaries at http://lyon.cour-administrative-appel.fr/A-savoir/Communiques/29-juin-2018-Proces-fictifs-3-decisions-rendues-sur-vehicule-autonome-robot-compagnon-et-domotique). The 'Future of Digital Technologies Law Clinic' project is also included as a subgroup in the European Law Institute's Digital Law special interest group.

[6] The 'hype cycle' expression is taken from 'Quantum spring', *The Economist*, August 18, 2018, p. 49. Regarding the legal literature, see J. Bacon, J. D. Michels, C. Millard and J. Singh, 'Blockchain Demystified', (2017) 268 *Queen Mary University of London School of Law Legal Studies Research Paper*, available on SSRN at https://papers.ssrn.com/sol3/papers.cfm?abstract_id=3091218; L. W. Cong and Z. He,

about the technology in question, the starting point is that smart contracts are self-executing computer programs.[7] It is therefore doubtful that these computer programs fall into the traditional category of 'legal contracts'.[8] It is argued here that to recognize smart contracts as legal 'automated contracts' would entail the transplantation or modification of most contract law categories, theories, and rules to adapt to this new automated environment. First, this analysis would include testing the compatibility between an automated environment and traditional legal rules.[9] Subsequently, and if the answer is in the negative, several questions emerge and will need to be dealt with by lawyers and computer scientists in the near future.[10] The initial determination will need to be whether existing legal rules are rendered obsolete requiring the creation of new legal rules in order to preserve the integrity and consistency of our legal systems or if they are resilient enough to be adaptable to evolving transactional technologies. These are of course only some of the many questions arising out of the existing and forthcoming technological evolution. The answers will derive from the basic assumption that legal rules are needed, despite claims made by the blockchain community.[11] New and fast-evolving technologies challenge legal paradigms, and the objective of this chapter is to better understand some of these challenges.

'Blockchain Disruption and Smart Contracts', available on SSRN at https://papers.ssrn.com/sol3/papers .cfm?abstract_id=2985764; M. Finck, 'Blockchains: Regulating the Unknown', (2018) 19 *German Law Journal* 665; S. Grundmann and Ph. Hacker, 'Digital Technology as a Challenge to European Contract Law', (2017) 13 *European Review of Contract Law* 255; W. Kaal and C. Calcaterra, 'Crypto Transaction Dispute Resolution', available on SSRN at https://papers.ssrn.com/sol3/papers.cfm?abstract_id=2992962; E. Mik, 'Smart Contracts: Terminology, Technical Limitations and Real World Complexity', (2017) 9 *Law, Innovation and Technology*, 269; E. Tjong Tjin Tai, 'Formalizing Contract Law for Smart Contracts', (2017) 6 Tilburg Private Law Working Paper Series, available at: www.cs.bath.ac.uk/smartlaw2017/papers/ SmartLaw2017_paper_1.pdf; K. Werbach and N. Cornell, 'Contracts Ex Machina', (2017) 67 *Duke Law Journal* 313. Regarding literature in French see, T. Douville and T. Verbiest, 'Blockchain et tiers de confiance : incompatibilité ou complémentarité?', (2018) *Recueil Dalloz* 1144; L. Godefroy, 'Le code algorithmique au service du droit', (2018) *Recueil Dalloz* 734; F. G'sell and J. Deroulez, 'Nouvelles technologies – Projet d'ordonnance relative à l'utilisation de la technologie blockchain pour la transmission de certains titres financiers Une avancée réelle, des précisions attendues', (2017) 41 *La Semaine Juridique* 1797; B. Mallet-Bricout, 'Nouvelles déclinaisons de la dématérialisation des relations contractuelles : vers une équivalence des supports dans le secteur financier', (2018) Revue trimestrielle de Droit civil 233; M. Mekki, 'Les mystères de la blockchain', (2017) *Recueil Dalloz* 2160; J.-C. Roda, 'Smart Contracts, Dumb Contracts ?', (2018) *Dalloz IP/IT* 397; Special issue: 'Les smart contrats sur la blockchain', (2018) *Dalloz IP/IT*, 392; C. Zolynski, 'Fintech – Blockchain et smart contracts: premiers regards sur une technologie disruptive', (2017) 1 *Revue de Droit bancaire et financier*, dossier 4. The author has a legal background and is not a computer programmer or a computer scientist, but has used reasonable efforts to understand and explain automated contracts.

[7] These self-executing pieces of code, stored on the blockchain, could act autonomously in case given conditions occur (see N. Szabo, *Smart Contracts*, 1994, available at https://archive.is/zQ1p8).

[8] A significant part of the legal community rejects the idea that smart contracts are 'real' contracts. A quite clear description of self-executing computer programs and a distinction between 'smart contract code' and 'smart legal contracts' is provided by J. Stark in 'Making Sense of Blockchain Smart Contracts', available at www.coindesk.com/making-sense-smart-contracts; see also Mik, 'Smart Contracts', 284.

[9] The issue of compatibility between the legal and technological environments is a crucial one, especially regarding the acceptability of future technologies. The 'regulatory' approach of applying state's regulations to blockchains and to the broader technological environment, and the associated ethical concerns, are gaining momentum.

[10] See the above-mentioned transdisciplinary experience run by the Lyon Catholic University Faculty of Law (footnote 5).

[11] N. Szabo would not agree.

6.2 An Overview of Blockchain Technology and Smart Contracts

6.2.1 *Variety of Definitions*

As indicated above and before coming to the more specific topic of interpretation, a general presentation of smart contracts will be provided. Smart contracts are generally defined as computer programs, stored on a blockchain, which involves the use of shared ledgers, and stored on and maintained by network nodes that record transactions executed among nodes.[12] These programs are automated or self-executing. These types of blockchain transactions have been called 'crypto-contracts', 'smart contract code', or 'smart contract programs'.[13] There is an important distinction between the phrase 'smart contract code' and that of 'smart legal contract' (legally enforceable).[14] The first category consists of using blockchain technology to complement or replace existing legal contracts in the sense that computer code is used to *'articulate, verify, and enforce an agreement between the parties'*.[15] Some have described the blockchain as acting as a 'smart agent' or a 'software agent'.[16] This first category of smart contracts is a blockchain-based analogue of a legal agreement,[17] existence of which is limited to the 'on-chain' (virtual, dematerialized) world and which govern 'on-chain' assets. In theory, they are disconnected from the 'off-chain' world, and do not require formal recognition by the legal order, to be 'enforceable'.[18] These smart contracts are not clearly legally enforceable at the moment. Problems will however arise when a connection with the 'off-chain' world occurs or is needed. Indeed, this is where legal rules will generally be triggered and will most likely reject recognition and enforcement of these computer codes.

The second category consists of classical legal agreements that are coded,[19] fully or in part,[20] in order to perform automatically. These smart 'legal' contracts are legal agreements coded in order to perform automatically and to be self-executing, and are designed

---

[12] For a presentation of different applications of blockchain technology, see M. Swan, *Blockchain: Blueprint for a New Economy* (Sebastopol: O'Reilly Media, 2015).

[13] Stark, 'Making Sense'; Mik, 'Smart Contracts', 284: 'There are multiple options: the smart contract can be a translation of an existing agreement, it can be created in code from the outset or, lastly, a contract can be drafted in natural language with subsequent encoding in mind'.

[14] *Ibid.*

[15] *Ibid.*

[16] *Ibid.*; L. H. Scholz, 'Algorithmic Contracts', (2017) 20 *Stanford Technology Law Review* 128 at 135.

[17] This is called 'direct coding'. See Mik, 'Smart Contracts', 287: 'To avoid the difficulties of translating legal language into code, it is sometimes suggested that smart contracts be written in code from the outset. [...] The contract would be smart from its inception. To bypass the stage of drafting in legal prose, lawyers would, of course, have to learn how to program. Alternatively, programmers would have to learn the basic principles of contract law. Technical writings suggest that such direct coding of smart contracts would force lawyers to be more precise and structured in describing the rights and obligations of the parties.'

[18] This assumption remains at a quite theoretical level. As stressed by P. De Filippi and A. Wright: 'Even where smart contracts entirely replace formal legal agreements, these programs do not operate in a vacuum. While they can automate payment obligations and the transfer of valuable assets, smart contracts do not obviate the need for parties to agree to these agreements. Promises first need to be negotiated beforehand and then translated into code, and for a contractual relationship to emerge via a smart contract, parties still need to manifest consent to stipulated terms by using digital signature' in *Blockchain and the Law: The Rule of Code* (Cambridge: Harvard University Press, 2018), p. 78.

[19] Mik, 'Smart Contract', 287, who stresses, however, that 'assuming that the smart contract should mirror this document in all its nuances, there is potential for discrepancies between what was agreed and what was implemented. Such discrepancies are particularly unsettling given that once the smart contract commences self-enforcement, it cannot be stopped or amended'.

[20] The contract will be 'split', where just a portion of the contract is automated.

to be immutable or 'unstoppable'.[21] They constitute a connection between the virtual (on-chain) and the physical (off-chain) world and require a translation from natural (legal) language into computer code.[22] As discussed below, most issues and problems arise at the intersection between the virtual and the physical worlds.

It is important to note that there are deterministic smart contracts and non-deterministic smart contracts. Regarding the latter, the network has sufficient information to self-execute. Regarding non-deterministic smart contracts, the network needs outside information in order to determine an outcome, and therefore interacts with an 'oracle' (human agent or the smart devices of the Internet of things),[23] which provides the network with external feeds that are interpreted automatically. The 'oracle' establishes a connection between the virtual and physical environments. In any case, a connection between these two environments will occur in most circumstances, like, for example, when a smart contract controls physical movement of goods.[24] In this technological landscape, the need for intermediaries (like lawyers, courts, law enforcement, banks, and insurance companies) is limited.[25] The immutability of smart contracts is also a counterpoise to the importance of trust between parties, which is a central feature of contract law.

6.2.2 Language of Code

Coding legal agreements in order to make them self-executing means that contractual terms must be translated into computer code. This translation is most effective when contract language is phrased as 'if/then' propositions, such as 'if (when) the payment is confirmed, then ship product'. It is in this form of drafting that smart contracts can fit within the contract law paradigm from the formation process (program verifying that certain 'conditions' are present in order to activate the acceptance of an offer)[26] to enforcement (program triggers transfer of property, payment, and so forth provided certain 'conditions' are met, such as performance by the other party). It is in this simplistic form of drafting that smart contract technology may be used to replace language contracts and achieve the status of an autonomous or semiautonomous process.

The current debate surrounding smart contracts centers on whether smart contracts can be made to replicate language contracts and, if so, for what types of contracts? The problem with the translatability of language to code is that computers use 'dry codes' in the sense that computer language is clear and cannot have several meanings at the same time,[27] whereas natural language often has multiple connotations. On the positive side,

---

[21] Stark, 'Making sense'.
[22] *Ibid.*
[23] Like sensors transmitting weather's conditions, autonomous devices can convey complex information about such things as the political situation in a given country, business trends, the geopolitical environment and so forth.
[24] These assets are far from being all 'virtual' or incorporeal.
[25] Making professional intermediaries useless is central to blockchain 'philosophy'.
[26] Even if negotiation is likely to take place beforehand (De Filippi and Wright, *Blockchain and the Law*, p. 74).
[27] Computers work in 'bits', binary information and instructions, made of 0s and 1s. P. Catchlove, 'A New Era of Contract Use', available on SSRN at https://papers.ssrn.com/sol3/papers.cfm?abstract_id=3090226, p. 8: 'Smart contracts are codified using Boolean logic. Boolean logic involves a computation that resolves in a value as either true or false. Simply put, the computer coding does not permit ambiguity, something either

the singular meaning feature of smart contracts confer an objective dimension to contracting by limiting or excluding vague and subjective aspects of contract law. Subjectivity leads at times to arbitrary interpretations, actions, and decisions. Thus, one of the lens through which coded contracts may be viewed is the subjective-objective dialectic, between the intent of the parties and the code as written. If smart contracting continues to grow, the divergence between subjective and objective meanings will likely narrow as the common intent of the parties is merged into the literal meaning of coded terms.

6.2.3 *Physical and Virtual Environments*

Whether smart contracts can be used in a great variety of contractual relationships remains to be seen.[28] The fact is that complicated or long-term contracts may not be effectively translatable into code. Currently, with the advent of the 'Internet of things' or smart devices, smart contracts have become an efficient means to effectuate some types of transactions.[29] For example, machine-to-machine contracts are fully entrenched in an automated and computerized world. This can be seen at work in spare parts management found in the automotive industry where the process of producing and supplying parts has been almost fully automated.[30] This represents a new kind of ecosystem of smart devices that can effectuate machine-to-machine transactions. This leads of course to further questions, such as the legal personality of robots, which is outside the scope of this chapter's coverage.[31]

Smart contracts raise a number of legal and regulatory issues including, the questions of applicable law, consumer protection, taxation, and the criminal use of blockchain technology.[32] Another question still unanswered is the liability of a party

---

does or does not happen, is or is not triggered, as a result of the code'. Another computer language, 'Qubits' and other programming languages are being built in the area of quantum computing: 'Qubits are capable of superposition, meaning they can be in both states [0 or 1] at the same time. [. . .] Qubits can be connected, so that operating on one has an impact on the entangled ones, allowing their processing power to be harnessed in parallel'. in 'Quantum Spring', *The Economist*, 18 August 2018, p. 49. In interviewing computer scientists, they agree that quantum computing has tremendous potential (even though its realization may be many years in the future); it is reasonable to foresee that it will have a significant impact on the way the legal order works.

[28] Werbach and Cornell, 'Contracts Ex Machina', 322: 'Although there are significant challenges in accurately representing and interpreting contractual semantics computationally, computable contracts are being employed widely in fields such as finance'.

[29] J. Szczerbowski, 'Place of smart contracts in civil law. A few comments on form and interpretation', available on SSRN at https://papers.ssrn.com/sol3/papers.cfm?abstract_id=3095933: 'This practice [of relying on computer language] is commonly used in Internet commerce, so why should there be any difference if the complex (or even obfuscated) natural language of contracts is substituted by the machine-readable code'.

[30] The placement of sales orders, prepayment actions, spare parts transfers, pricing policy creation for customers, and spare part sales agreement have been automated.

[31] For reflections about 'robots personhood' see, European Parliament, Committee on Legal Affairs, Report with recommendations to the Commission on Civil Law Rules on Robotics, 27 January 2017, available at: www.europarl.europa.eu/sides/getDoc.do?pubRef=-//EP//TEXT+REPORT+A8-2017–0005+0+DOC +XML+V0//EN

[32] It is fair to say that technological developments also help in fighting against crime. There is software that can identify firms that are controlled by organized crime or involved in criminal activities. Automation makes the scrutinizing process of transactions and of firms much more efficient. See e.g., Crime & tech's software mentioned in 'Seeking the devil in the details', *The Economist*, August 18, 2018, p. 60).

for coding errors (code is defectively created or code is infected with a bug).[33] It is not clear whether current laws and principles (such as good faith) apply or if specialized legal rules are needed. On the theoretical and conceptual dimensions, an assessment is needed of the impact of the above-described technology on current legal rules and also on the structure of legal systems. The next section will focus on the impact of blockchain technology on contract interpretation – conceptually and in practice.

6.3 Traditional Interpretation of Smart Contracts

6.3.1 Traditional Interpretation

In the process of interpreting contracts, courts traditionally have taken it upon themselves to correct obvious mistakes, imbalances, or incompleteness in contract language by assessing the intent of the parties.[34] The first avenue for finding the parties' intent is in the natural language of the contract – natural or common meaning is considered as the expression of the intent of the parties. However, the (true) intent of the parties can be incompletely or ambiguously expressed in the form of the language of the contract.[35] The notions of incompleteness and ambiguity are themselves relative, especially when assessed by courts (and the distinction between interpretation and construction will not always be very clear).[36] The same contractual term could be clear in a given context and unclear in a different context or at a different period of time. It is worth adding that the more complex the contexts surrounding contracts, the more ambiguous or less precise

---

[33] '[T]he consequences of unsafe design choices for the programming languages for smart contracts can be fatal, as witnessed by the unfortunate epilogue of the DAO contract, a crowdfunding service plundered of 50M USD because of a programming error. Since then, many other vulnerabilities in smart contract have been reported'. And even without bugs, 'there are reasons to doubt smart contracts will always operate as desired. [... t]hey require reduction of human-readable language to machine-readable code. This limits their scope to those subjects and activities which can readily be specified precisely', Werbach and Cornell, 'Contracts Ex Machina', 351.

[34] Bacon et al., 'Blockchain Demystified', 34. The necessity to correct imbalances applies of course especially in B2C contracts. The interpretation in favor of consumers in B2C contracts is clearly stated in Directive EEC/1993/13 on unfair terms in consumer contracts:

> 'Whereas contracts should be drafted in plain, intelligible language, the consumer should actually be given an opportunity to examine all the terms and, if in doubt, the interpretation most favourable to the consumer should prevail' (recital 20); and 'In the case of contracts where all or certain terms offered to the consumer are in writing, these terms must always be drafted in plain, intelligible language. Where there is doubt about the meaning of a term, the interpretation most favourable to the consumer shall prevail'.   (art. 5)

[35] Ph. Simler, 'Interprétation du contrat', in *Répertoire civil*, Fascicule 10, Articles 1188 to 1192 (2017): '[natural] language is nothing but a rather imperfect way of expressing thoughts or intent. It is therefore possible that parties to a legal act expressed incompletely or imprecisely their intent, that they mistakenly used a term or even that their contract contains contradictory or incompatible terms'.

[36] As observed by Simler in 'Interprétation', 'objective interpretation is more than interpretation'; see also Tjong Tjin Tai, 'Formalizing contract law', (3.1): '[...] cases where a contract was later interpreted against the obvious or literal meaning of its wording quite often are based on various reasons having to do with reasonable expectations, fairness, protection of weaker parties, and other interests that appear to find social and political support (as can be deduced from similar statutory provisions adopted by democratically elected governments)'; and J. Sklaroff, 'Smart Contracts and the Cost of Inflexibility', (2017) 166 *University of Pennsylvania Law Review* 265, indicating that 'scholars criticize the unpredictable inconsistency in how courts interpret contract and provide remedies when they are breached'.

the contractual terms are likely to be.[37] In case of complicated transactions with thick contexts, computer-coded contracts will be much harder to create and natural language contracts will be much more efficient in phrasing and describing the intent of the parties and their respective obligations.

Traditional interpretation includes the subjective[38] and objective[39] approaches in which precedence is generally given to the first one in the civil legal tradition and to the second one in the common law tradition.[40] It should be noted that the admissibility of extrinsic or contextual evidence brings the approaches closer together (similar outcomes). Both approaches see the finding of the intent of the parties as the priority in the process of interpretation. Another part of the interpretive process is seeking interpretations that advance the objective consistency of the contract as a whole. One example encompassing these various approaches can be found in the French Civil Code.[41] French law gives courts extensive tools as regards interpretation of contracts. The *favor contractus* principle (presumption in favor of finding a contract in cases or ambiguity), allows courts to rely on objective criteria, such as usages, equity, and efficiency. Article 1194 of the French Civil Code states:

> If the common intent of the parties is hard to identify, courts will look for the hypothetical intent of the parties by referring to the subject matter of the contract, to the context, usages [;] ... these criteria are rather objective criteria on the basis of which courts give precedence to efficiency, opportunity, social and economic utility of the contract. [when interpreting a contract][42]

The idea of hypothetical intent gives a great deal of discretion to judges in the interpretation of contracts.

The use of contextual evidence outlined in the French Civil Code includes evidence that the negotiation context is assessed at the discretion of the court. The court's discretionary power is largely due to the vagueness and broadness of the interpretive criteria, which is not conducive to binary translation into computer code, which disdains discretionary aspects of interpretation in favor of clear and unambiguous terms.[43] Thus, as will

---

[37] 'The costs of complexity also extend to back end enforcement, where courts are often called upon to interpret a provision embedded within a complicated latticework of obligations.' M. Jennejohn, 'The Architecture of Contract Innovation', (2018) 59 *Boston College Law Review* 4.

[38] Simler, 'Interprétation', states: 'contract is a subjective norm, the expression of the intent of only the parties'.

[39] Werbach and Cornell, 'Contracts Ex Machina', 359, reminding that '[a] range of contract doctrines can then be explained as default rules, presumed to be what most parties would want unless they explicitly indicate otherwise'.

[40] Simler, 'Interprétation': 'courts look for the intent of the parties, rather than stopping at the literal meaning of its terms as prescribed in article 1188 of the French Civil Code'.

[41] 'A contract is to be interpreted according to the common intention of the parties rather than stopping at the literal meaning of its terms. Where this intention cannot be discerned, a contract is to be interpreted in the sense which a reasonable person placed in the same situation would give to it'. (art. 1188)
  'All the terms of a contract are to be interpreted in relation to each other, giving to each the meaning which respects the consistency of the contract as a whole. Where, according to the common intention of the parties, several contracts contribute to one and the same operation, they are to be interpreted by reference to this operation'. (art. 1189)
  'Clear and unambiguous terms are not subject to interpretation as doing so risks their distortion'. (art. 1192)
  'Contracts create obligations not merely in relation to what they expressly provide, but also to all the consequences which are given to them by equity, usage or legislation'. (art. 1194)

[42] See art. 1194 of the French Civil Code.

[43] See art. 1192 of the French Civil Code, in footnote 41.

be discussed below,[44] smart contracts rely on precisely coded terms aimed at excluding ambiguity and insulated from the contextual facts of the physical world. Simply put, the more you exclude natural language and facts, the more you exclude uncertainty and ambiguity. The inflexibility of smart contracts, by being limited to the coding of precisely fixed terms, is likely to limit a more expansive use of smart contracts.

In English common law, '[i]nterpretation is the ascertainment of the meaning which the document would convey to a reasonable person having all the background knowledge which would reasonably have been available to the parties in the situation in which they were at the time of the contract'.[45] In US common Law, maximizing the contracts' *ex ante* value is a guiding principle, which represents a mix of textualism and contextualism used by the courts in the interpretive process.[46] Objective interpretation prevails in the common law, where English courts approach contracts drafted by legal professionals as accurately reflecting the intent and meaning of the contracting parties. Thus, it is asserted that relying on a literal approach to interpretation best conforms to the parties' intent.[47] Beyond these examples from French law and English law, various international instruments follow the same paths.[48]

---

[44] See Section 6.3.2

[45] Lord Hoffmann, *Investors Compensation Scheme Ltd. c/ West Bromwich Building Society* [1998] 1 WLR 896, 912–913. For a comparative analysis of the new provisions on interpretation in the French Civil Code, see B. Fauvarque-Cosson, 'Les nouvelles règles du Code civil relatives à l'interprétation des contrats: Perspective comparatiste et internationale', (2017) *Revue des contrats* 2017, 363.

[46] E. A. Posner, 'The Parol Evidence Rule, the Plain Meaning Rule, and the Principles of Contract Interpretation', (1998) 146 *University of Pennsylvania Law Review* 533; R. J. Gilson, C. F. Sabel and R. E. Scott, 'Text and Context: Contract Interpretation as Contract Design', (2014) 100 *Cornell Law Review* 23.

[47] Fauvarque-Cosson, 'Les nouvelles règles', quoting E. McKendrick, Contract Law (London: Palgrave, 11th edn., 2015), § 9.7.

[48] Article 5:101 PECL – General Rules of Interpretation

'(1) A contract is to be interpreted according to the common intention of the parties even if this differs from the literal meaning of the words.
[...]
(3) If an intention cannot be established according to (1) or (2), the contract is to be interpreted according to the meaning that reasonable persons of the same kind as the parties would give to it in the same circumstances'.

Article 4.1 UNIDROIT Principles: (Intention of the parties)

'(1) A contract shall be interpreted according to the common intention of the parties.
(2) If such an intention cannot be established, the contract shall be interpreted according to the meaning that reasonable persons of the same kind as the parties would give to it in the same circumstances'.

Article 8 CISG

'(1) For the purposes of this Convention statements made by and other conduct of a party are to be interpreted according to his intent where the other party knew or could not have been unaware what that intent was.
[...]
(3) In determining the intent of a party or the understanding a reasonable person would have had, due consideration is to be given to all relevant circumstances of the case including the negotiations, any practices which the parties have established between themselves, usages and any subsequent conduct of the parties'.

6.3.2 *New Objects and Rules of Interpretation*

The rules of interpretation, as discussed above, developed to be applied to natural language contracts. That language, from the perspective of our topic, is described as 'wet code', whereas smart contracts are based on computer language known as 'dry code'. One of the main consequences stemming from this difference is that a smart contract is inherently inflexible and only interpretable as coded.[49] The dry computer code is the opposite of wet natural language. Smart contracts inflexibility can be seen as an advantage by providing transactional certainty in conformity with the *pact sunt servanda* principle. However, it is unable to adapt to changing circumstances[50] or the preferences of the parties in cases of modification or a mutual agreement to terminate the contract.[51] A positive aspect of computer code is that it is a universal language not vulnerable to the vagaries of national languages, thus, eliminating misunderstandings inherent in language and contractual relations. Some technologists predict that costs and risks of legal translation will be dramatically reduced and computer code will progressively replace legal English as a universal or common legal language.

It has been said that natural language always requires interpretation, at least much more than does computer code which leaves little room for interpretation.[52] Therefore, the fact of relying on a smart contract excludes judicial intervention, or at least reduces judicial powers, such as the judicial implication of terms.[53] Contract interpretation is generally required in cases of alleged breach resulting in a contractual dispute, while the self-executing and 'unstoppable' features of smart contracts make judicial intervention less likely.

As highlighted above, interpretation in the context of smart contracts further illustrates the civil law/common law divide. Contract drafting techniques in common law are partly based on preventing the need for courts to interpret or intervene into contracts. Common

DCFR II. – 8:101: General rules

'(1) A contract is to be interpreted according to the common intention of the parties even if this differs from the literal meaning of the words.

[...]

(3) The contract is, however, to be interpreted according to the meaning which a reasonable person would give to it: [...]'.

[49] 'Because smart contracts are nothing more than bits of logic executed in a deterministic manner, they can decrease the possibility of misinterpretation in instances where parties can reliably identify objectively verifiable performance obligations' (De Filippi and *Wright, Blockchain and the Law*, p. 82).

[50] It is worth mentioning that information feeds provided by oracles can allow smart contracts to respond to changing conditions in 'near real time' (De Filippi and Wright, *Blockchain and the Law*, p. 75).

[51] Unless a smart contract provides the possibility to reverse some of its parts, parties will be deprived from the capacity to renegotiate their agreement as is often done by commercial actors.

[52] The 'literal' meaning of code is central to the entire system of smart contracts with the intent of the parties being second in importance to the code itself.

[53] De Filippi and Wright, *Blockchain and the Law*, p. 78, are rather optimistic to this regard: 'If there is a dispute about whether a smart contract accurately memorializes the parties' intent or whether one party has breached the agreement, the contracting parties still retain the ability to bring legal proceedings or engage in private dispute resolution. Courts ultimately retain jurisdiction over the legal effects of a smart contract. They will construe the underlying code according to long-standing principles of contract law interpretation and, if necessary, the help of experts.' However, P. De Filippi and S. Hassan, in 'Blockchain Technology as a Regulatory Technology', available on SSRN at https://papers.ssrn.com/sol3/papers.cfm?abstract_id=3097430 warn about the fact that the 'inherent ambiguity of the legal system – necessary to ensure a proper application of the law on a case-by-case basis – ultimately gives software developers and engineers the power to embed their own interpretation of the law into the technical artifacts that they create'.

law contracts are therefore longer as drafters attempt to foresee all possible aspects of
contractual performance. The civil law approach generally results in shorter contracts
because drafters rely on more general legal concepts and assume that courts will play an
important role, through interpretation, in discovering the 'true meaning' of a contract.
Coding contracts can therefore have a significant impact on the civil law approach and
bring the two legal systems closer in the areas of contract drafting and contract interpretation. Coding contracts incentivizes the use of precise and comprehensive drafting
styles, on the basis of a 'if/then' writing style, which common lawyers are better equipped
to perform.[54] At the same time, the need for precise terminology and the avoidance of
vague standard-like terms should avoid the costs of drafting long and all-encompassing
contracts.[55]

However, if courts are in a position to interpret smart contracts, then the risk of
misinterpretation of computer code can be quite high considering the technical skills
required.[56] In order to avoid misinterpretation, the smart contract should incorporate
interpretive rules (possibly made to be self-executing). Thus, a plausible assumption is
that legal digitalized data can be efficiently processed for the purpose of interpretation.
Stefan Grundmann and Philipp Hacker identified three problems and avenues for
future research – whether special rules of interpretation should govern contracts
concluded by electronic means, the possibility of encoding interpretive rules into the
smart contract (to be discussed below), and the creation of a fully integrated contract
life cycle where the 'beginning, end and other stages tend to overlap and mutually
influence one another'.[57]

6.4 Smart Interpretation?

6.4.1 *Automated Interpretation*

Smart contract proponents often have a simplified view of the role of the law in transactions and assume that all dimensions of law can be automated.[58] In contract interpretation there is hope for the idea of automated interpretation. Despite the alleged
incompatibility between smart contracts techniques and traditional contract interpretation, the new technological tools can also be seen as consistent with the various features of
traditional interpretation, including the objective approach of the common law, as well as
advancing the principles of consistency of the contract as a whole and the enforcement of

---

[54] 'Yet, this drive towards an increasingly formalized language goes against the traditional conception of law,
perceived as an inherently flexible and ambiguous set of rules. Although the judicial system is subject to the
prerequisites of neutrality and impartiality, the quest for an objective rule of law has often been criticized on
the grounds that the meaning of the law must always (and necessarily) be construed according to the fact of
the case, following the interpretation of a judge', in De Filippi and Hassan, 'Blockchain Technology'.
[55] Business efficiency would be enhanced if computer programs allow identifying in advance the terms to use
and the possible inconsistencies and gaps in the contract.
[56] Mik, 'Smart Contracts', 285, stressing the fact that: '[d]espite consistent progress in the said areas, it is
presently impossible to automate the conversion of natural language into code – at least not without
a significant compromise in the quality of the output of such conversion. Machine learning enthusiast
might have been misled by the relative success of Google translate or the sensationalistic reports of AI-based
systems beating their human opponents at complex games'.
[57] Grundmann and Hacker, 'Digital Technology', 280.
[58] One of the risks of an over-hyped field like blockchains and smart contracts is the reproduction of the
communication tools and bias in the said field.

clear and unambiguous terms.[59] Smart contracts, correctly coded, eliminate the gap-filling role of the courts. In essence, smart contracts are a type of standard form contract[60] that tend to make interpretation easier and more systematic.[61] From this perspective, the idea of smart contracts as standard contracts is consistent with the phenomenon of 'regulated contracts' (contracts comprehensively regulated by codes or statutes).[62] The use of data and computer-based nature of smart contracts offer dramatic cost-savings compared to the cost of drafting traditional all-encompassing contracts.[63]

Automated tools offer the possibility of transplanting the field of 'traditional' contracts by fixing interpretive rules.[64] The automated rules would exclude the use of the suppletive or default rules of contract law.[65] Smart contracts are consistent with the practice of the written form as the entire agreement, four-corner analysis, and the enforceability of merger clauses.[66] Computer coding of contracts may develop as an efficient tool, as a substitute for completely integrated contracts, with reduced ambiguity, reduced inconsistency, and with less room for interpretive disputes.

The major obstacle to the efficiency of smart contracts is whether parties and their counsels possess the technical capacity to code their own interpretive rules. According to Kevin Werbach and Nicolas Cornell, '[i]n a well-functioning smart contract, interpretive questions are necessarily answered in determinative ways. In short, if you think that

---

[59] Werbach and Cornell, 'Contracts Ex Machina', 366: '[b]uilding a computerized system able to interpret smart contracts with similar levels of understanding to humans is effectively a challenge for artificial intelligence. And it is one unlikely to be solved any time soon'.

[60] 'Programmers or lawyers can create libraries of smart contract code specifically designed to implement certain functionalities that routinely appear in legal contracts' (De Filippi and Wright, *Blockchain and the Law*, p. 82); but Mik, 'Smart Contracts', notes that '[w]hile there are not obstacles to the creation of one-off, customized smart contracts, economies of scale dictate that smart contracts take the form of generic programs that can be used on a mass-scale. They could, for example, embody popular standard form agreements, such as car loans, mortgages or interest rate swaps. In such instance, only certain values would be customized for individual transactions'.

[61] Regarding this systematic approach, see O. Ben-Shahar and L. Strahilevitz, 'Interpreting Contracts via Surveys and Experiments', *University of Chicago Coase-Sandor Institute for Law & Economics Research Paper* No. 791 (2017), available on SSRN at https://papers.ssrn.com/sol3/papers.cfm?abstract_id=2905873, quoted in Grundmann and Hacker, 'Digital Technology'. In addition to the reduced ambiguity, the self-executing dimension of smart contracts and their systematic performance would be quite consistent with a process of standardization of contracts through the blockchain technology.

[62] This is the case in most civil law jurisdictions where contracts like sale or lease are regulated in the civil code by a set of suppletive and compulsory provisions.

[63] De Filippi and Wright, *Blockchain and the Law*, p. 74, quoting H. Surden ('Computable Contracts', (2012) 46 University of California-Davis Law Review, 629), who 'explored the concept of data-oriented contracts and investigated how the representation of contractual obligations as data can lead to the creation of "computable" contract terms'.

[64] We could, for example, imagine encoded terms providing for the interpretation in favor of debtor (formalizing, for example, the rule of art. 1190 of the French Civil Code: 'In case of ambiguity, a bespoke contract is interpreted against the creditor and in favour of the debtor, and a standard-form contract is interpreted against the person who put it forward.' Reinforcing the effectiveness of old legal principles through the technology is an interesting way to foster their acceptance. In the field of consumer law, making the *contra proferentem rule* more effective may be a desirable trend to explore in the current development of smart contract technology.

[65] Automated rules offer advantages and have similarities with existing trends in contract law (cost-saving and systematization).

[66] See e.g. art. 2.1.17 Unidroit Principles. Article 1189 of the French Civil Code (see above, footnote 41) as well relies on the idea of the contract as a whole, insisting on making sure that contractual terms are consistent with one another. This theme is also found in the common law through four corners or entire agreement clauses (Fauvarque-Cosson, 'Les nouvelles règles'). Encoded terms could ensure that contractual terms are consistent with one another.

contract law exists to facilitate reliance through opting into predictable future consequences, then smart contracts seem to serve this function even more seamlessly'.[67] But,
what would such coded interpretive rules look like? Computer scientists will have to
determine what can be done and what cannot within the current state of technology.[68] It
is implausible to believe that current technology is able to capture the broader aspects of
contracting (context) and the existence of unpredictable events that occur subsequent to
the coding of the contract.[69]

6.4.2 *The End of Interpretation by Courts?*

As stated by Primavera De Filippi and Samer Hassan:

> [the] modern approach to lawmaking presents a few benefits, especially as it reduces the
> ambiguities characteristics of traditional legal drafting. In the long run, the lack of textual
> ambiguity might reduce the need for canons of construction and other textual inter-
> pretation techniques – although factual ambiguity (i.e. did a real world event happen or
> not) will obviously remain.[70]

Besides this potential impact of smart contracts on the traditional interpretative tasks
performed by courts, new tools of decentralized dispute resolution, based on blockchain
technologies are emerging.[71] One of the objectives of these tools is to replicate existing
dispute resolution systems, with the intent of being more efficient, more transparent, and
cheaper than traditional litigation or arbitration. Numerous technological tools including smart contracts, escrow creation, and online dispute resolution structures combined
will continue to attract a growing number of technology-friendly parties.[72] The interest in
new technologies in the legal field, coupled with the interest of investors in LegalTech
startups (some funded by initial coin offerings, or ICOs), is a challenging and stimulating
evolution in the law.

At the same time, the fact that courts might be challenged in interpreting smart
contracts will inevitably create tensions between existing legal structures and emerging
technologies. Legal scholars have the responsibility to give current and future lawyers
a solid understanding of these various phenomena, including the multifaceted use of
computers, algorithms, and data analytics. Relying on technology to perform legal acts

---

[67] Werbach and Cornell, 'Contracts Ex Machina', 360.

[68] In order to know, for example, which items could be taken into account in the interpretive process in case of
nonnegotiated contracts, the rule contained in art. 1190 of the French Civil Code is useful – interpretation
is against the party that unilaterally drafted the contract (contra proferentem rule). In the case of smart
contracts, one of the drafters could be a computer programmer.

[69] See e.g. Kaal and Calcaterra, 'Crypto Transaction', confirming that: '[...] a temporary solution for the lack
of traditional jurisdictional means and legal control over smart contracts could be the programming of
existing legal rules, doctrines, precedent and their existing legal interpretation into smart contract code. In
essence, such existing rules that would pertain to a comparable and equivalent real-world transactions and
would be simply added as smart contract parameters'.

[70] 'Blockchain Technology as a Regulatory Technology'.

[71] See e.g. the JUR (Justice as a Service on the Blockchain) initiative: https://jur.io: it provides a 'consensus-
based dispute resolution structure that uses game theory and economic incentives to motivate voluntary
voting, and uses blockchain technology to record votes'.

[72] One interesting aspect will be the reaction of parties toward these new tools. Of course, for some parties,
going before an official (state) tribunal would remain the preferred option.

and functions will allow lawyers to dedicate more time to complex issues and invest more on human-based emotional or soft skills.[73]

6.5 Conclusion

If we think of interpreting smart contracts in a 'traditional' way, then a translation from code to natural language is required in order for judges to undertake the task of interpretation. If the smart contract is merely the computerized (coded) version of a regular legal agreement, such a translation should be a rudimentary undertaking or the court could simply be provided the language contract that had previously been translated into code. If there is no original and traditional 'legal' contract, the translation into natural language becomes much more difficult and tedious. This is of course a time-consuming and costly process. The technical response to translation costs would be the creation of computer programs, which translate natural language into code resulting in easy to 'code' and easily translatable contracts.[74]

However, it is quite likely that smart contracts, which represent a further step in formalizing contracts, will diminish the courts' ability to intervene through interpretation. In 'Smart Contracts and the Cost of Inflexibility', Jeremy Sklaroff argues that smart contracts could facilitate formalist interpretation of contracts based purely on the terms in the agreement as opposed to the parties' broader behavior,[75] favoring a hard parol evidence rule, and reducing how and when a court can imply contract terms through supplemental interpretation.[76] Given how smart contracts are built, doubts could emerge about the intent of the parties and the correspondence between their intent and the computer code. Did the parties understand properly and in its entirety the terms of the contract?[77] Can technology reshape the intended meaning of the parties, especially when the nuance of language may be an ill fit for the rigor associated with coding?[78]

In 'Formalizing contract law for smart contracts', T.F.E. Tjong Tjin Tai stresses the fact that 'interpreting the law is complicated by the fact that relevant rules may be found in other parts of the law.'[79] In a smart contract context, it is not obvious that the smart contract can go beyond the borders of the program to find relevant rules (off-chain elements and occurrences), limiting therefore the capacity to use blockchain technology

---

[73] However, lawyers and legislators must not delegate to technology the role provided by legal rules. Mik, in 'Smart Contracts' notes that software developers can hardly be expected to perform the task of fixing interpretive rules in a program from the outset, before the dispute arises. The deep knowledge of the principles governing contract interpretation and the importance of contractual context is outside the scope of the expertise and out of reach of program developers.

[74] The author's recent discussions with computer scientists and people involved in the development of blockchain-based smart contracts indicate that such tools already exist or are in the advanced stage of development.

[75] Sklaroff, 'Smart Contracts and the Cost of Inflexibility', 279.

[76] *Ibid.*, quoting Gilson et al., 'Text and Context' (noting that 'parties use written contracts to restrict attempts to add or modify obligations').

[77] It is fair to say that not all the parties (especially less-informed parties, like consumers) fully understand all the peculiarities of traditional contractual agreements written in natural language.

[78] In 'Contracts Ex Machina', 365, Werbach and Cornell wonder '[h]ow to reduce human-readable language to machine-readable code? Does it limit the scope of smart contracts to those subjects and activities which can readily be specified precisely? [...] On the other extreme, some contractual terms simply cannot be expressed through formal logic, because they imply human judgment. A machine has no precise way to assess whether a party used "best efforts," for example'.

[79] Tjong Tjin Tai, 'Formalizing Contract Law for Smart Contracts'.

in highly contextualized types of contracting. Courts generally come into play when complexity, doubts, and litigation around them arise.[80] Things become complicated when we move from the on-chain dimension to the off-chain one, and attempt to connect the two. When the connection with the physical world is made, things become legal; they assume a legal dimension and courts come into play. For the near future, automated contracts will be limited to effectuating parts of language contracts[81] and perform more simplistic and narrow types of contracts in specific areas, such as flight-delay insurance contracts.[82] Business players will continue to develop automated contracts based on private networks, availing themselves of the 'buzz' effect around smart contracts.[83] The development of 'private blockchains' is to a large extent a contradiction to the original idea of 'blockchain ideology'.[84] For lawyers, central issue remains how best to connect the virtual on-chain and the physical off-chain environments. In the field of contract interpretation, among others, it is still difficult to see how such a connection can be formally and systematically established.

In order to assure the smooth development of automated contracts, the courts must develop the expertise to interpret them and smart contracts need to provide for parties the ability to control real world consequences and be able to terminate the contracts if necessary during and after performance.[85] If traditional contract models and principles (reasonable efforts, good faith, commercial reasonableness) and complex or standard-like terms cannot be coded, there is greater risk of unfairness or injustice created by automated contracts working completely 'on-chain'.[86] This phenomenon could go hand in hand with the development of virtual assets, disconnected from the physical environment. These potential threats to the legal order provide incentives to shape new legal rules or adapt existing legal rules to the technological environment in order to bring automated contracts into the legal order.[87] For law professors, it also creates the responsibility to raise awareness among law students and to train them accordingly.[88] On the

---

[80] Issues of interpretation are even more frequent in international legal transactions and disputes (see Fauvarque-Cosson, 'Les nouvelles règles'). Using code may reduce the need for interpretation, since code is a universal language (see § 6.3.2).

[81] See the notion of 'hybrid agreements', used by De Filippi and Wright, *Blockchain and the Law*, p. 76: 'If smart contracts are used to model legal agreements, parties can create hybrid arrangements that blend natural-language contracts with smart contracts written in code'.

[82] Flight-delay insurance automated contracts are based on private networks and not on public blockchains.

[83] Flight-delay insurance automated contracts are again a good example.

[84] Regarding the original 'ideology', see Szabo, Smart Contracts.

[85] This seems however not to be taken for granted as stressed by De Filippi and Wright, *Blockchain and the Law*, p. 75, referring to Werbach and Cornell's 'Contracts Ex Machina': 'Once the wheels of a smart contract are put into motion, the terms embodied in the code will be executed, and they cannot be stopped unless the parties have incorporated logic in the smart contract to halt the program's execution'.

[86] Sklaroff, 'Smart Contracts and the Cost of Inflexibility', 265, stresses this risk, quoting R. E. Scott ('The Death of Contract Law', (2004) 54 *University of Toronto Law Journal* 369): 'The peril that public contract law faces is that many contracting parties have chosen to exit the public system of legal enforcement in favour of less costly alternatives over which they have more control. The result is that the law of contract is suffering from stagnation and . . . irrelevance'.

[87] See Grundmann and Hacker, 'Digital Technology', 270 confirming that new technologies 'engender novel market dynamics that, in many instances, necessitate regulatory responses'.

[88] If we take an actual law student, with the perspective of approximately fifty years of professional life in the legal field after completing her studies, the professional environment is likely to evolve in a way, which will be hard to imagine at the moment. Because new technologies generate gains of productivity, including in the legal field, it is prudent to invest in 'value-added' skills (emotional skills and coding ability) and to discard 'repetitive-type' tasks and skills.

technological side, adapting technology to the legal framework (rules and practice) is highly desirable, although the use of 'human oracles' is a way of bridging the gap between the on-chain and legal worlds.[89] Diana Wallis reminds us in Chapter 19 that preserving the legal order and the rule of law is the basis of democratic societies and requires various stakeholders, especially lawyers, to monitor the evolution of technologies in order to make sure that legal rules, adopted by democratically elected governments, remain effective.[90]

---

[89] Werbach and Cornell, 'Contracts Ex Machina', 365, according to whom incorporating arbitrators with the abilities to deal with 'non-machine-encodable terms' could be an option.

[90] See Chapter 19.

7 Smart Contracts

Contractual and Noncontractual Remedies

Cristina Poncibò and Larry A. DiMatteo

7.1 Introduction

This chapter will examine the impact of smart contracts' ability to self-perform, self-enforce, and self-remedy and the remaining applicability of contract law and contract remedies.[1] Smart contracts (coupled with blockchain technology)[2] have created visions of self-executing, self-enforcing, and self-remedying contracts that eliminate the need for courts or arbitral tribunals to apply contract law to disputes. The theory goes that since the possibility of breach is eliminated in such contracts, contract remedies become unnecessary.

It is best to start the current discussion with defining three important concepts – self-enforcement, self-help remedies, and "other remedies." Self-enforcement can be analogized to the remedy of specific performance (albeit with the extra step of obtaining a judicial order to perform). Self-help remedies may be analogized, in some cases, as a form of the remedy of injunction, such as the disablement of the time of use of the subject of the contract. Other remedies refer to the menu of remedies provided under contract law and their continued position as default law. The remaining importance of contract law remedies is premised on the view that no matter the degree of self-enforcement and the creation of self-help remedies in smart contracts, the parties will continue to have the ability to seek redress before courts and arbitral tribunals.

Just as the false argument that word contracts can be made to be clear and complete, the completeness of smart contracts is an illusion.[3] One commentator noted: "Terms of contracts, which are more complex than the immediate transfer of value and property are

---

[1] Portions of this chapter have become a shorter version of the analysis given in L. DiMatteo and C. Poncibò, "Quandary of Smart Contracts and Remedies: Role of Contract Law and Self-Help Remedies" (2019) *ERPL* (*European Review Private Law*) 805.

[2] A simple definition of smart contracts is stated as follows: "Smart contracts are self-executing electronic instructions drafted in computer code. This allows a computer to 'read' the contract and, in many cases, effectuate the instruction – hence the 'smartness' of the contract." R. O'Shields, "Smart Contracts: Legal Agreements for the Blockchain" (2017) 21 *N.C.B.I.* (*North Carolina Banking Institute*) 177 at 179. Smart contracts are different than ordinary electronic contracts in that the actual agreement is embodied in computer code, rather than English or another traditional language. See N. Szabo, "Smart Contracts: Building Blocks for Digital Markets" (1996), http://szabo.best.vwh.net/smart_contracts_2.html (coined the term "smart contracts").

[3] G. Cordero-Moss, "Interpretation of Contracts in International Commercial Arbitration: Diversity on More than One Level" (2014) 22 *ERPL* at 13 (sufficiently detailed and clear contracts can be interpreted internally "without them being influenced by any governing law. This impression has proven to be illusionary").

likely to not be efficiently encoded."[4] Thus, there remains a significant amount of "risk of *divergence* expressed in natural language between the meaning of the original contractual provision and its expression in code."[5] If word contracts are hopelessly incomplete, how can word contracts translated into code be any less incomplete? In the end, code is no different than the use of words since both are creations of human beings, meaning that perfect completeness will never by achievable. Also, contracts are always incomplete because parties cannot foresee all future events that may impact the parties' expectations related to their contract. Again, contract remedies will continue to play a role due to the unpredictability of future events.[6] The issue analyzed in this chapter is whether a complete set of remedies can be incorporated into smart contracts to preclude the need for contract law remedies in a default role. The chapter concludes that contract remedies will remain relevant, but recognizes that smart contracts may fill a void where enforcement of traditional remedies is not practical or too costly.

It is in the area of self-enforcement and remedies where the vision of smart contracts confronts the reality of contract law and business lawyering. Smart contracts need to be drafted by lawyers, focused on client interests and not technological prowess. In order for lawyers to best serve their clients, they would have to learn to write computable code, while judges would have to learn codes to interpret the contract or rely on an expert translation. Assuming that there is only a single interpretation of a computer code, does the issue over the correct or reasonable legal interpretation of contracts miraculously resolve itself? Put simply, is this a step too far in the advancement of the self-executing, self-enforcing smart contracts? Code will need to be converted into words, which reengages the same quandaries that have persisted in contract interpretation over the centuries.

Again, this chapter will provide some propositions relating to the role of remedies relating to the assertion that smart contracts are a self-enforcing legal regime. If smart contracts are completely self-enforcing, then there is no need for a remedial scheme. If smart contracts are not completely enforcing, can they provide a self-contained remedial system? Even if that is possible, the argument here is that self-enforcement or self-remedialization would still need to conform to the immutable rules of contract law. An unenforceable clause under contract law cannot be made enforceable simply by embedding it into a code; a contract term that is considered illegal or against public policy cannot be made legal in a smart contract. Finally, if a smart contract is too simple, then it may fail as to indefiniteness of terms.[7] In the end, the judicial remedies of adjustment (reformation) or voidance (rescission) will play the same roles in coded contracts as they

---

[4] S. Farrell, H. Machin, and R. Hinchliffe, "Lost and found in smart contract translation-considerations in transitioning to automation in legal architecture" (King & Wood Mallesons, Australia), 3, www.uncitral.org /pdf/english/congress/Papers_for_Programme/14-FARRELL_and_MACHIN_and_HINCHLIFFE-Smart _Contracts.pdf (last viewed April 22, 2018).

[5] Ibid.

[6] From a wider perspective of the public dimensions of private law, one scholar states that: "providing a private system of enforcement through code does not eliminate the state's role in contract." Mark Verstraete, "The Stakes of Smart Contracts" (2019) 50 (*Loyola University Chicago Law Journal*) 47 at 50.

[7] The indefiniteness of a contract may lead to its unenforceability (as a noncontract): "Certainty as to what constitutes the contractual terms (and whether they are comprehensive enough) is often a critical factor necessary to establish the formation of a legally binding contract in many jurisdictions. Smart contracts . . . may not satisfy such requirements." Norton Rose Fulbright White Paper, "Can Smart Contracts be Legally Binding Contracts: Key Findings" 4, www.nortonrosefulbright.com/files/norton-rose-fulbright–r3-smart-contracts-white-paper-key-findings-nov-2016–144554.pdf.

do in language contracts. Ultimately, courts will remain relevant in the enforcement and interpretation of smart contracts.

7.1.1 *Illusion of Self-Sufficiency*

The idea of a self-sufficient contract (fully comprehensive, perfect clear) is a cognitive impossibility. The claim that smart contracts can be fully self-executing belies the continuing role of contract law's interpretive and remedial functions in all types of contracts – whether smart or dumb. The fact that smart contracts may be self-executing does not mean that they overcome the problems of interpretation or prevent a party from seeking a remedy in court. Self-enforcement does not mean that human agents cannot move to block or prevent enforcement. While self-help remedies can be included in smart contracts, they do not block the use of the range of remedies that parties may seek under the general law of contracts.

If smart contracts are to claim the mantel of a fully self-contained, privatized legal system, then it will need to be fully self-enforcing and self-remedying. Can all issues of performance be converted into computer code? Is enforcement of a smart contract immune from the interpretive problems associated with ordinary contracts? These questions directly relate to the issue of contract remedies and their applicability to smart contracts. At the present, the conclusion is that contract law and judicially created remedies will continue to play a prominent role.

7.1.2 *Inflexibility of Smart Contracts*

Smart contracts are ultimately limited by their inflexibility. One of the great features of contract law is its inherent flexibility and malleability. It allows parties to improvise new types of contract terms that are customized to different types of contracts. In long-term, relational, and complex contracting, the contract is a combination of fixed terms, open-textured rules, and standards.[8] Smart contracts currently are only capable of replicating hard or bright line fixed terms or highly formalized rules. It is no surprise that smart contracts have first made their mark in financial transactions since banking and finance laws are based on highly formalized rules with very little room for adjustment or application of standards-like reasonableness.[9] It is these types of formal rules and terms that are more easily translatable to code.

The inflexibility of smart contracts versus word contracts provides a major obstacle to smart contracts expansion into the realm of more complex contracting where self-enforcement and self-remedying features may prove unattractive and inefficient.[10] Some contractual terms simply cannot be expressed through formal logic, because they

---

[8] Open-textured rules or terms are those that encourage the interpreter to look to the real world to find the correct interpretive meaning. The robust use of the reasonableness standard in Article 2 of American Uniform Commercial Code (UCC) is an example of an open-textured rule. Open-textured rules allow for the use of contextual input in the defining and application of the rule. See W. Twining *Llewellyn Papers* (University Chicago Law School Press 1968), 86.

[9] See UCC Article 3 (Negotiable Instruments) and Article 9 (Secured Transactions).

[10] Although one commentator notes that a degree of flexibility may be obtained by the use of a subsequent smart contract to amend or adjust an existing smart contract: "One possibility for achieving the effect of a reversal or change in terms is to create that result through the creation of a new smart contract which, when added to the existing contracts, has the effect of the desired reversal or change." H. Farrell,

imply human judgment. For example, a machine has no precise way to assess whether a party used "best efforts."[11] Word contracts help overcome the unpredictability of future events (change of circumstances) through provisions, which require a performance adjustment and the appropriate remedial response that smart contracts are unable to perform.

7.1.3 Smart Contracts and Remedies

Smart contracts may be outside the law, but they are not above the law.[12] The use of smart contracts to escape the legal system will not render traditional contractual defenses useless. Smart contracts' self-enforcement ability does not prevent self-enforcement from being subject to post hoc judicial review. In such cases, the remedies of restitution and disgorgement of profits may become more common since performance is not subject to breach.

The continuing importance of contract law remedies is supported by the role of such remedies in *ex post* adjudication. The *ex ante* view of contract law with its focus on the time of contract formation (consent of the parties), which is the domain of smart contracts, ignores contract law's ex post regulatory and remedial function.[13] In this regard, smart contracts cannot transplant contract law.[14]

An example of the irreplaceability of contractual remedies can be shown through a simple example. A transfer of an asset is executed by a smart contract, but is later invalidated in court due to fraud, duress, incapacity, illegality, and so forth. In the blockchain the asset remains the property of the transferee, but in the real world the law recognizes the title being held by the transferor. The only way to square this bifurcated ownership is for the court to issue an order of specific performance requiring the transferee to re-convey ownership through the blockchain.[15]

Finally, the problem of code writing and the possibility of contamination through a virus may lead to a breach of a smart contract: "The code embedding the contract terms can contain bugs or produce results that are not in accordance with the expectations of the parties."[16] Therefore, the self-enforcement can be viewed as a breach in cases where "its performance would not be as expected or intended by the parties."[17] Because of such possibilities, smart contracts may lead to the recognition of *ex contractu* legal remedies. The one that comes to mind is the tort of negligence. The divergence between a smart contract as intended and expectations of outcome could result in the emergence of torts

---

H. Machin, and R. Hinchliffe at 6. However, the speed of smart contract execution and the need of the parties to negotiate to any such changes may prevent a timely adjustment.

[11] D. Werbach and N. Cornell "Contracts Ex Machina" (2017) 67 *DLJ (Duke Law Journal)* 313–69, at 365.

[12] Farrell, Machin, and Hinchliffe at 2.

[13] Werbach and Cornell, note 11, at 361.

[14] "Smart contracting functions to ensure action. Contract law functions to recognize and remedy grievances. Smart contracts could not – even in theory – replace contract law." Ibid. at 363.

[15] A. Savelyev, "Contract Law 2.0: Smart Contracts As the Beginning of the End of Classic Contract Law" (2017) 26 *ICTL (Information & Communications Technology Law)* 1–19, available at https://papers .ssrn.com/sol3/papers.cfm?abstract_id=2885241.

[16] S. Hourani, "Cross-Border Smart Contracts: Boosting International Digital Trade Trough Trust and Remedies," www.uncitral.org/pdf/english/congress/Papers_for_Programme/11-HOURANI-Cross-Border _Smart_Contracts.pdf.

[17] Ibid.

"for negligent coding or negligent updating."[18] One could also imagine cases of intentional miscoding as the basis for an action of misrepresentation or fraud.

7.2 Trust as Remedy

Contracts allow parties to bind themselves to undertake some action in the future. Enforceable contracts are the legal vehicle that allows market economies to form and are the engine of capitalism. A market economy is impossible without the recognition of private property rights and the ability to transfer those rights through contracts. Contracts are a substitute for purely trusting the other party to perform. The ability to bring a claim for breach of contract through litigation or arbitration provides a party with a level of certainty that the other party will perform in the future. The strongest contracts, however, are those that are never enforced because they reflect a certain degree of trust between the parties.

According to Francis Fukuyama, trust is the single most important factor in creating a high-performing national economy. In his book *Trust: The Social Virtues and the Creation of Prosperity*,[19] Fukuyama argues that cooperative economic behavior rests upon a "culture of trust." Trust has traditionally been anchored in private contract or government intervention (regulation). Blockchain offers a third possibility often referred to as "trustless trust." The self-verifying, self-enforcing nature of smart contracts provides a level of certainty (some argue absolute certainty) beyond traditional trust structures. The next section examines the variety of trust structures or institutions and the idea of trustless trust offered by smart contracts.

7.2.1 Architecture of Trust for Smart Contracts

Until blockchain technology, there were two primary trust architectures: Leviathanian (deference to a central enforcement authority, generally a government regulatory agency) and peer-to-peer (reliance on social norms and other governance mechanisms in self-contained communities, such as the diamond[20] and cotton[21] industries). One commentator has also advanced the idea of creating a Leviathan for the blockchain by establishing a public "Superuser" (government authority) with the power to modify the content of Blockchain databases.[22]

Werbach argues that blockchain introduces a third kind of trust architecture, "trustless trust," which is a system that makes it "possible to trust the outputs of a system without

---

[18] M. Raskin, "The Law and Legality of Smart Contracts" (2017) 1 *GLTR* (*Georgetown Law Technology Review*) 305, at 328.

[19] F. Fukuyama, *Trust: The Social Virtues and the Creation of Prosperity* (New York: The Free Press 1995).

[20] Lisa Bernstein, "Opting Out of the Legal System: Extralegal Contractual Relations in the Diamond Industry" (1992) 21 *JLS* (*Journal of Legal Studies*) 115–57. See also B. D. Richman, "Community Enforcement of Informal Contracts: Jewish Diamond Merchants in New York," The Harvard John M. Olin Discussion Paper Series, Discussion paper No. 384 (9/2002), 1–55.

[21] L. Bernstein "Private Commercial Law in the Cotton Industry: Creating Cooperation through Rules, Norms, and Institutions" (2001) 99 *UMLR* (*University of Michigan Law Review*) 1724.

[22] Savelyev, above note 15. For a map of experiences, see M. Alharby, A. van Moorsel, Blockchain-based Smart Contracts: A Systematic Mapping Study, study presented at the Fourth International Conference on Computer Science and Information Technology (CSIT-2017), 125–40.

trusting any actor within it."[23] Yet, Werbach warns that blockchain's technical reliability should not be confused with trust. He says: "Trust is a manifestation of goodwill of the one being trusted – it involves a positive expectation about the other party and a willingness to be vulnerable."[24] Blockchain technology has neither of these attributes. In place of trust as a substantive virtue, the blockchain provides technical or procedural type of trust.

Secured through cryptography, implemented through distributed consensus, networks replace the personal trust found in most commercial contracts.[25] In Nick Szabo's words, "Trust-minimized code means you can trust the code without trusting the owners of any particular remote computer."[26] The nature of distributed ledgers makes certain activities trustworthy without the need to trust anyone in particular. Blockchain proponents argue that as a result, the costly mechanisms of intermediation and legal enforcement can be avoided. Instead of trusting banks, courts, and governments, blockchain proponents suggest, we can trust math and computation, in the form of open-source cryptographic protocols. If they are even slightly correct, the potential is extraordinary, due to the lower costs and greater efficiency of such a technological trust substitute.

For libertarians, these technologies represent economic activity outside the bounds of sovereign state control. Currently, the regulatory oversight over blockchain-based transactions is limited. Courts arguably will find it extremely difficult to determine jurisdiction over blockchain-based smart contracts due to party anonymity at the core blockchain transactions. Furthermore, the smart contract's performance is a fait accompli since the coded transaction is auto-executed on the blockchain, so, technically, there can be no claim for breach of contract.

This type of new trust architecture has powerful implications. The theory of governance of common-pool resources laid the groundwork for management of important resources as commons.[27] It has proven particularly significant in the digital economy, as an approach to both network infrastructure such as wireless spectrum and creative works such as software. "Trustless trust" has similar potential. But its implications are still unknown since the issues and consequences of the expanded use of the blockchain are undertheorized. Part of this lack of knowledge is due to the separation of the technological and legal elements of the technology. Thus, true acumen is only achievable by lawyers understanding the technological aspects of smart contracts and technicians understanding of the legal impact of the technology.

As noted above, the architecture of trustless trust provided by the blockchain is the basis for the argument that the technology can act as an alternative to the law. However, despite the expectation of the flawlessness of mathematically based systems, blockchains are systems designed, implemented, and used by humans. Subjective intent remains relevant

---

[23] K. D. Werbach, "Trust, But Verify: Why the Blockchain Needs the Law" (2016), Conference Paper, 1–74. Accessed October 23, 2018 at https://ssrn.com/abstract=2844409

[24] Ibid. 15.

[25] A. Walch, "In Code(rs) We Trust: Software Developers as Fiduciaries in Public Blockchains," G. Dimitropoulos, S. Eich, P. Hacker, and I. Lianos (eds.), *The Blockchain Revolution: Legal and Policy Challenges* (Oxford University Press 2018).

[26] N. Szabo, "The Dawn of Trustworthy Computing," Unenumerated Blog (December 11, 2014), http://unenumerated.blogspot.com/2014/12/the-dawn-of-trustworthycomputing.html (last accessed October 23, 2018).

[27] E. Ostrom, "Beyond Markets and States: Polycentric Governance of Complex Economic Systems," Nobel Prize Lecture (December 8, 2009), www.nobelprize.org/nobel_prizes/economicsciences/laureates/2009/ostrom_lecture.pdf Precisely, Ostrom uses the expression "governance of common-pool resources."

even when expressed through objective code. Blockchains are subject to selfish behavior, attacks, and manipulation. The scope of legitimate practices for blockchain-based systems is fundamentally a governance question, not a computer science one. Therefore, the efficiency of the blockchain in executing simply transactions (fund and information transfers) should not be seen as rendering law useless.

Scholars disagree on the relationship between code and law. Wright and de Filippi have predicted that blockchain will generate a new body of rules, "Lex Cryptographia," that is independent from state-created legal rules.[28] To the contrary, Werbach argues that, in most cases, economic agents will prefer to have the ability to enforce legal rights in court or by arbitration, as opposed to relying solely on the output of the blockchain. This recourse to legal institutions may, however, be limited if dispute resolution mechanisms are embedded in the underlying code.[29] However, this is unlikely to prevent a party from challenging the enforceability of that mechanism in an effort to seek legal remedies.

Due to its peculiar architecture smart contracts have been characterized as an independent "state of nature" outside the control of the state.[30] Such an outside law or private law system has been the subject of long-term inquiry by scholars, such as Anthony Kronman, Richard Posner, and Stuart Macaulay.[31] With respect to methods and contents, this is a diverse literature, but one with a common theme. Each of the writers is interested in the opportunities that individuals exploit, and the arrangements they invent, to enhance the security of their agreements where no legal remedies for breach exist or where those that do are plainly inadequate. Smart contracts seem to overcome these weaknesses in the traditional legal system.

7.3 Self-Help for Smart Contracts

This section analyzes smart contracts from the remedial perspective of contract law. Can smart contracts be a substitute for the remedies offered by contract law? This begs another question: Can there ever be a truly breach-less contract? The section concludes that the answers to these questions are in the negative. This conclusion rests on the commonsensical belief that at times smart contracts will diverge from party expectations and desired outcomes. Such divergence may occur due to mistakes or bugs (coding error), changes of circumstances, and cyber attacks (viruses). The fit of traditional contract law to the acceleration of technology is captured in the following statement: "Contract today increasingly links entrepreneurial innovations to the efforts and finance necessary to transform ideas into value."[32] The issue for contract law is that it is adaptable to technological innovation, such as in the case of the blockchain. The answer is likely

---

[28] See A. Wright and P. De Filippi, "Decentralized Blockchain Technology and the Rise of Lex, Cryptographia" (2015), 1–58. http://papers.ssrn.com/sol3/papers.cfm?abstractid=2580664 (last accessed November 10, 2018); M. Abramowicz, Cryptocurrency-Based Law (2018) 58 *ALR (Arizona Law Review)* 359.

[29] K. D. Werbach, "Trust, But Verify: Why the Blockchain Needs the Law" (2017), https://ssrn.com /abstract=2844409 (last accessed July 20, 2018).

[30] Kronman used the expression "state of nature" with respect to Contract Law. See the note below.

[31] S. Macaulay, "Non-Contractual Relations in Business" (1963) 28 *American Sociological Review* 55. A. Kronman, Contract Law and the State of Nature (1985) 1 *Journal of Law, Economics and Organization*, 5–32. R. Posner, *The Economics of Justice* (Cambridge: Harvard University Press 1981).

[32] R. J. Gilson, C. F. Sabel, and R. E. Scott, "Contract, Uncertainty, and Innovation" in S. Grundmann, F. Möslein, and K. Riesenhuber, *Contract Governance: Dimensions in Law and Interdisciplinary Research* (Oxford University Press, 2015) 156.

to be that the inherent flexibility of contract law, premised on freedom of contract and justice norms,[33] is adaptable to such change. A follow-up question is whether technological change results in a new transaction type? If so, does general contract law suffice or will a specialized rules regime be required?[34]

It is reasonable to expect that platform providers and tech developers will primarily rely on the blockchain ecosystem to solve any problems, such as mistake and change of circumstances arising out from a smart contract. The law will remain in the "shadows." But most contracts work within the shadow of the law. This is because most contracts are fully performed, performed enough to satisfy the other party, are readjusted through party negotiation, or simply "run out" because dispute resolution costs are prohibitive. In a small percentage of contracts, these mediating mechanisms fail and this is when the law comes out of the shadows. In the case of smart contracts, it must be recognized that no matter how self-enforcing the contract may be, self-enforceability does not prevent a party from seeking redress in a court of law.

With the lens of a comparative lawyer, one may say that blockchain technology, with its peculiarities (anonymity, decentralization), is equally "disrupting" the traditional civil and common law approaches to contracting, especially with respect to remedies. On the one hand, common law contract theorists have devoted particular attention to examining remedies for breach of contract. Part of the explanation for this attention is that remedies have played a crucial role in the development of the common law.[35] In the medieval writ system from which the modern common law evolved, causes of action were framed primarily in terms of remedies sought. The common law lawyer has thus traditionally approached contract issues through a remedial lens – a tradition kept alive in the practice of many common law faculties by starting contract courses with the subject of remedies. In addition, remedial issues are frequently of decisive importance in litigation and it is from litigation that the common law is developed. Because of this remedial perspective, the common law tends to prefer ex post enforcement, which is the opposite approach to smart contracts where all issues are viewed ex ante.[36]

The architecture of "trust" upon which smart contracts are based has two fundamental consequences for contract law. First, as noted above, smart contracts' automation shifts the focus on ex ante compliance instead of ex post contractual remedies. Currently, the most prevalent forms of security software methods include virus-scanning software, filtering firewalls, and detecting the traceroutes of attackers.[37] By using smart contracts, the parties are radically changing the paradigm of contract practice from ex post authoritative judgment to ex ante-automated assessments. Proponents of smart contracts believe that ex-ante automation results will only infrequently diverge from expected outcomes

---

[33] L. DiMatteo, "The Norms of Contracts: The Fairness Inquiry and the 'Law of Satisfaction' – A Nonunified Theory" (1995) *Hofstra Law Review* 349.

[34] Specialized rules can be developed within contract law or through statutory intervention. Examples are plentiful, including specialized rules for sales, negotiable instruments, letters of credit, consumer transactions, and so forth.

[35] See, P. Atiyah, *The Rise and Fall of Freedom of Contract* (Oxford: Clarendon Press 1979). G. Gilmore *The Death of Contract* (Columbus, OH: Ohio State University Press 1974).

[36] S. Issacharoff, "Regulating after the Fact" (2007) 56 *DePaul L. Rev.* 375.

[37] E. Mik, "Smart Contracts: Terminology, Technical Limitations and Real World Complexity" (2017) 9 (2) *Law, Innovation and Technology*, 269–300.

with the benefit of avoiding the costs of post hoc dispute resolution. Under this view the benefits of ex ante efficiency far outweigh bearing the costs of ex-post corrections.[38]

Second, the problem of avoiding injustice caused by error (improper coding) or changes in circumstances means that any such failures related to smart contracts, should be anticipated with coding that allows the triggering of self-help remedies or contractual adjustments. If such self-remedying provisions can be coded, then recourse to the courts to cure unjust outcomes will be lessened. This would require the loosening of the self-contained nature of blockchain technology to external triggers.

The central tenet of contract law is the freedom of parties to form and govern their own relationships. The creation and use of self-help remedies is within the scope of freedom of contract. Self-help enables the parties to keep their affairs private, out of the reach of interfering official bodies, thus creating a regulatory sandbox without supervision.[39] Also, platforms and developers have shown the desire to maintain individual control over the terms of the relationship, as well as a dislike or distrust for courts, which will incentivize them to create self-help remedies.

In contract law scholarship, the term "self-help" refers to private actions used to prevent or resolve disputes without assistance of a governmental official or disinterested third party.[40] The situations in which self-help may be invoked and the actions, which may be taken, are as varied as human imagination and creativity, such as in the case of the blockchain.

Indeed, self-help when used without challenge does not depend on formal invocation of the legal system. Our traditional approach toward contract doctrine is to consider actions occurring within a legal framework, an approach which precludes some forms of self-help. Because the law indirectly influences the decision to rely on self-help in the first instance, self-help remedies are likely to be underutilized in a system that focuses in large part on judicial actions.[41]

The current mainstream view treats self-help as an "extralegal" action rather than as an element of our legal framework. Although self-help is nonjudicial, it is not extralegal and does not lie outside the "shadow of the law." Self-help is a party's immediate reaction to a perceived problem. That reaction, however, does not occur in a vacuum. In most cases, parties, including platforms and developers, have "some understanding" of legal rights. That understanding guides the determination of how and when to use self-help. Thus, self-help is no different from many examples of social ordering that takes place under the "shadow of the law," influenced by but not explicitly invoking the legal regime. Thus, self-help remedies incorporated into smart contracts are within the scope of contract law analysis and not outside of it.[42]

---

[38] See J. H. Hsiao, "'Smart Contract' on the Blockchain – Paradigm Shift in Contract Law" (2017) 14 *US-China Law Review* 685–94.

[39] A regulatory sandbox is a framework set up by a financial sector regulator to allow small-scale, live testing of innovations by private firms in a controlled environment (operating under a special exemption, allowance, or other limited, time-bound exception) under the regulator's supervision. Therefore, in the case of smart contracts on blockchains, regulator's supervision is limited or absent. D. A. Zetzsche, R. P. Buckley, D. W. Arner, J-N. Barberis, "Regulating a Revolution: From Regulatory Sandboxes to Smart Regulation" (2017) 23 *Fordham Journal of Corporate and Financial Law* 31–103.

[40] M. P. Gergen, "Theory of Self-Help Remedies in Contract" (2009) 89 *B.U. L. Rev.* 1397–449.

[41] C.R. Taylor, "Self-Help in Contract Law: An Exploration and Proposal" (1988) 33 *Wake Forest Law Review* 839–907.

[42] Savelyev, above note 15.

A first type of self-help relevant for smart contract consists of the threat that one party will respond to its counterparty's failure to adjust by reducing or terminating future dealings. This strategy incentivizes parties to agree to exceptions to the immutability of smart contracts. Secondly, the morality of platforms and developers, their reliance on gossiping and reputation, rather than their calculations of individual gain, encourages proper behavior in approaching smart contracts. In other words, they act as members of the blockchain ecosystem and do not behave opportunistically even when it is in their economic interest to do so (even when they are not under threat of punishment or retaliation). Clearly, the Dao case that is described below in Section 7.5.5 has shown how platforms and their members are capable, in certain circumstances, of subordinating their own welfare to the community that serves them.

A third type of self-help is normative or dispositional informal sanctions, which can operate at the level of social groups rather than among individuals. In compact and homogenous communities, like blockchains, the community as a whole can sanction the breach of one member's obligation to another by ostracizing the malefactor, cutting off not just business ties but removing all the benefits of belonging to the group. The next section discusses some interesting examples of these types of mechanisms by distinguishing self-help remedies related to codifying, security, privacy, and performance, as well as blockchain-based self-help remedies.

7.4 Self-Help: Codifying, Security, Privacy, and Performance

Platforms and developers already rely on self-help based on blockchain technology.[43] Legal scholars have struggled in mapping and understanding approaches that are technical and not legal in a strict sense. Legal scholars emphasize the human side of transactions conducted via blockchain platforms, including the loss of a blockchain private key, receipt of a defective product, the ability to show ownership, to invoke state consumer protection rights, or the need to verify title to land before entering a transaction on the blockchain. Moreover, smart contracts cannot access outside information unless it is written into the blockchain. Werbach and Cornell state that:

> There is a Frankenstein dimension to a smart contract: An instrument that fuses something innately human (entering into and enforcing agreements) with something mechanical, derived from scientific experiments. Science fiction authors since Mary Shelley have warned of the consequences of such cyborgs. Perhaps the benefits of smart contracts will exceed the costs. Perhaps the benefits can be magnified or the costs minimized. We should, nonetheless, carefully assess the both sides of the ledger.[44]

For our purposes, we note that, contrary to the claims of promoters of blockchain technologies, the rule of the code cannot replace law and automation will not solve every risk with respect to smart contracts. Thus, contrary to the myth of code as law, the design of legally approved self-help remedies is inevitable.

[43] H. Eenmaa-Dimitrieva and J. Schmidt-Kessen, "Regulation through code as a safeguard for implementing smart contracts in no-trust environments" (2017) EUI Working Paper LAW 2017/13, 1–31.
[44] Werbach and Cornell, note 11 at 364.

7.4.1 *Codifying*

There are four issues that face developers in writing smart contracts, namely, the difficulty of writing correct contracts, legal training for coders, the inability to modify or terminate contracts, the lack of support to identify underoptimized contracts, and the complexity of programming languages.

7.4.1.1 Writing Correct Smart Contracts

The first issue is the difficulty of writing correct smart contracts. Correctness of smart contracts in this context means contracts that function as intended by their developers. The reason why it is important to have correct smart contracts is because they control valuable currency units. Thus, if smart contracts are not executed as intended, some of their currency units will disappear.

In an attempt to tackle this issue, a number of solutions are suggested. One solution is to semi-automate the creation of smart contracts to ease the process of writing them (translation of human-readable contract representations to smart contract rules).[45] By using smart contracts, the parties aim at changing the paradigm of contract practice to embrace automation where no breach of contract is admitted instead of the traditional ex post remedial perspective of breach. In this way, the parties deliberately try to preclude ex-post corrections by relying on blockchain technology. At the outset the use of smart contracts was characterized by high hopes in coding and technology, resulting in a failure to determine and analyze potential problems. Thus, incorporation of self-help into smart contracts was not properly vetted, which explains their underutilization in existing contracts.

Indeed, the most compelling reason for the use of smart contracts is their guarantee of performance (impossibility of breach). This is based upon the assumption that the electronic format and Boolean logic remove the need for nuance and interpretation by eradicating the ambiguity found in traditional contracts. This ignores the fact that in the real world it is both operationally and socially beneficial to leave some contract terms underspecified; vagueness preserves operational flexibility for parties to deal with unexpected circumstances and sets the stage for social stability in an ongoing relationship as advanced by relational contract theory.[46] Moreover, it is important to note that not all clauses in contracts are susceptible to automation and self-execution. Even where a clause might technically be capable of being automated, it might not always be desirable to automate it.

Another solution is to provide developers with guidelines to aid them in writing correct contracts. Smart contracts, for example, can be built from contract templates designed with input from legal experts. Some authors propose the use of smart contract templates, based on the idea of Ricardian contracts that is a digitally signed triple ⟨P, M, C⟩, where P is the legal prose (legal, business, and regulatory semantics) from which denotational

---

[45] C. K. Frantz and M. Nowostawski, "From Institutions to Code: Towards Automated Generation of Smart Contracts" *2016 IEEE 1st International Workshops on Foundations and Applications of Self* Systems (FAS*W)*, 210–15.

[46] I. MacNeil and D. Campbell, *The Relational Theory of Contract: Selected Works of Ian MacNeil* (Sweet & Maxwell 2001).

semantics are captured and represented; M is a map (key-value pairs) of parameters used in P and C, and C is the platform-specific code that expresses operational semantics.[47]

7.4.1.2 Training for Coders and Legal Engineering

After smart contracts are created, but before being placed on the blockchain, best practice would use lawyers in reviewing the contract terms to check their compliance with the law. Legal code audits could be implemented analogous to the security audits widely used by firms engaged in software development. This approach consists of a sort of legal engineering of smart contracts.[48]

Some experts have released online materials (such as tutorials) to help developers write correct smart contracts. The final solution offered here is the adoption of formal verification techniques to detect unintended behaviors or consequences of smart contracts.[49] This can help developers recognize those behaviors before posting their contracts to the blockchain. Some scholars have utilized formal methods to analyze and verify the correctness of smart contracts,[50] while others have combined formal methods with game theory techniques to validate smart contracts.[51]

7.4.1.3 Modifying Smart Contracts

The second issue to be addressed is the inability to modify or terminate smart contracts due to their immutability. In the real world, modification is a form of self-help – in that it permits parties to respond to problems arising in executory or partially executed contracts in order to preserve contracts and help avoid the need for official intervention that might otherwise be necessary. In particular, the law recognizes certain excuses that will absolve a party from performance or require some sort of modification.[52] In civil law, both impossibility and economic impracticability are bases for excuse. This poses a problem for the smart contract when the coders have not included in the coded text an ability to manage impossibility and impracticability.

In an attempt to tackle this issue, some scholars have presented a set of standards to allow smart contracts to be changed or terminated along the lines of traditional contract

---

[47] C. D. Clack, V. A. Bakshi, and L. Braine, "Smart Contract Templates: Essential Requirements and Design Options," arXiv:1612.04496 (December 16, 2016), https://arxiv.org/abs/1612.04496 (last accessed 20 November 2018).

[48] K. D. Werbach, "Trust, But Verify: Why the Blockchain Needs the Law" (2017), https://ssrn.com/abstract=2844409 (last accessed July 20, 2018).

[49] K. Delmolino, M. Arnett, A. Kosba, A. Miller, and E. Shi, "Step by Step towards Creating a Safe Smart Contract: Lessons and Insights from a Cryptocurrency Lab" in *International Conference on Financial Cryptography and Data Security* (Springer, 2016), 79–94.

[50] K. Bhargavan, A. Delignat-Lavaud, C. Fournet, A. Gollamudi, G. Gonthier, N. Kobeissi, N. Kulatova, A. Rastogi, T. Sibut-Pinote, N. Swamy, et al., "Formal Verification of Smart Contracts: Short Paper" in *Proceedings of the 2016 ACM Workshop on Programming Languages and Analysis for Security* (ACM, 2016) 91–96.

[51] G. Bigi, A. Bracciali, G. Meacci, and E. Tuosto, "Validation of Decentralised Smart Contracts through Game Theory and Formal Methods" in *Programming Languages with Applications to Biology and Security* (Springer, 2015) 142–61.

[52] In the common law, these circumstances are described primarily by the doctrines of duress, unconscionability, mistake, misrepresentation, frustration, and discharge for breach.

law.[53] Interestingly, such standards are taken from legal contracts and then defined to fit the context of smart contracts. For example, termination, rescission, modification, and reformation terms have been coded for smart contracts and tested on Ethereum. Another possibility, assuming the parties to a given smart contract are known (depending on the type of blockchain), the parties can create a new transaction to reverse undesirable outcomes of the previously coded and executed transaction in order to implement *post hoc* corrections of mistakes, bugs or any other problem that had occurred

7.4.1.4 Avoiding Underoptimized Smart Contracts

The third issue relates to the lack of support in identifying under-optimized smart contracts. To run a smart contract, each computational or storage operation in the contract costs money. An underoptimized smart contract is a contract that contains unnecessary or expensive operations. Such operations result in a high cost at the user's side. In an attempt to tackle this issue, scholars identified seven programming patterns (unnecessary and expensive operations in a loop) in smart contracts, which lead to additional costs. They have also proposed ways to enhance the optimization of such patterns to reduce the overall cost of executing smart contracts. For example, a tool was developed to detect contracts that suffer from those patterns. The tool was applied to current Ethereum smart contracts and found most of them suffer from such patterns.[54]

7.4.1.5 Complexity of Programming Languages

The last issue to be addressed is the complexity of smart contract programming languages.[55] Current smart contracts are based on procedural languages, such as Solidity. In a procedural language, the code is executed as a sequence of steps. Thus, programmers specify what should be done and how to do it. This makes the task of writing smart contracts in those languages cumbersome and error prone. For example, Pettersson and Edström attempted to prevent three kinds of common errors made by developers: failure to account for unexpected states, failure to use cryptography, and overflowing the Ethereum Virtual Machine's (EVM's) stack.[56] They proposed the use of a functional programming language called Idris to help mitigate these risks. Based on this scheme, they developed a code generator that transforms code produced by an Idris compiler to Serpent code (an Ethereum scripting language), which can be subsequently compiled into EVM bytecode. This process does not, however, solve the translation problem. In addition, in order to address this issue, others have proposed the utilization of logic-based languages instead of procedural languages. In logic-based languages, programmers do not necessarily have to specify the sequence of steps in creating a contract. This will ease the

---

[53] B. Marino and A. Juels, "Setting Standards for Altering and Undoing Smart Contracts" in *International Symposium on Rules and Rule Markup Languages for the Semantic Web* (Cham, Switzerland, Springer International Publishing, 2016), 151–66.

[54] Clack, et al., *supra* note 47.

[55] F. Idelberger, G. Governatori, R. Riveret, and G. Sartor, "Evaluation of Logic-Based Smart Contracts for Blockchain Systems" in *International Symposium on Rules and Rule Markup Languages for the Semantic Web* (Cham, Switzerland, Springer International Publishing, 2016), 167–83.

[56] J. Pettersson and R. Edström, "Safer Smart Contracts through Type-Driven Development" PhD thesis, Master's thesis, Dept. of CS&E, Chalmers University of Technology & University of Gothenburg, Sweden (2015).

complexity of writing smart contracts. However, algorithms for logic-based languages are expensive and may be inefficient.[57]

From a different perspective, Frantz and Nowostawski considered the issue of authoring smart contracts from the subject-matter expert's perspective by proposing a semi-automated method for the translation of human readable contracts to smart contracts on Ethereum. The authors developed a domain-specific language for contract modeling, where rules are expressed in plain English and then translated into the Solidity vocabulary.[58] However, this solution is anchored on Ethereum, and it is not clear how useable or adaptable it is on other platforms. In addition, it does not incorporate the semantics of the legal and business language a lawyer would use to draft denotational semantics.

7.4.2 Security Issues

Security and privacy measures protecting blockchain transaction are central in protecting the parties' rights and obligations. Marino and Juels note that "When promises are embedded in technology, one (perhaps the only) way to breach them is to disrupt that technology."[59] Most smart contracts include security measures aimed at deterring this type of breach. This presents a special challenge for programmers that in writing a smart contract, correctness matters a great deal since the consequences of bad code writing can be dire. "Bugs" are inherent in computer code so the effectiveness of smart contracts is dependent on the careful writing of code, since errors cannot be fixed after the fact.[60]

A review of the literature shows the existence of six security issues, namely, transaction-ordering dependency, timestamp dependency, mishandled exception, criminal activities, re-entrancy, and untrustworthy data feeds. In addition to these issues, several vulnerabilities have been found in Ethereum smart contracts.[61]

The first issue to be addressed is transaction-ordering dependency. This problem occurs when two dependent transactions that invoke the same contract are included in one block. The order of executing transactions relies on the miner. However, an adversary can successfully launch an attack if those transactions are not executed in the right order. For example, assume there is a puzzle contract that incentivizes the user who solves the puzzle. A malicious owner is monitoring the solutions provided by the users. Once a user submits a correct solution to the puzzle (Tu), the malicious owner immediately sends a transaction (To) to update the contract's reward (such as reducing the reward). Those two transactions (To and Tu) might be included in the same block by chance. If the miner executed To before Tu, the user would get a lower reward and the malicious owner would succeed in his attack. To prevent this type of manipulation, Natoli and Gramoli suggest the use of Ethereum-based functions to enforce the order of transactions.[62]

---

[57] Idelberger, et al., *supra* note 55, at 167.
[58] Frantz and Nowostawski, *supra* note 45, at 210–15.
[59] Marino and Juels, *supra* note 53, at 152.
[60] N. Szabo, "Formalizing and Securing Relationships on Public Networks" (1997) 2(9) *First Monday*.
[61] N. Atzei, M. Bartoletti, and T. Cimoli, "A Survey of Attacks on Ethereum Smart Contracts (sok)" in *International Conference on Principles of Security and Trust* (Springer, 2017), 164–86.
[62] C. Natoli and V. Gramoli, "The Blockchain Anomaly," in *15th International Symposium on Network Computing and Applications* (NCA), 310–17, IEEE, 2016.

Another suggested approach is using a guard condition such that a contract code either returns the expected output or fails.[63]

The second issue is timestamp dependency. This problem occurs when a contract uses the block timestamp as a condition to trigger and execute transactions (such as sending money). The block timestamp is usually set at the current local time by the miner who generated the block. The problem with the timestamp is that a dishonest miner could vary its value by about 15 minutes from the current time, while the block is still accepted by the blockchain system. As the timestamp of a block is not guaranteed to be accurate, contracts that rely on timestamp value are vulnerable to threats by dishonest miners. To avoid this problem, the block builder could use the block number as a random seed for contracts instead of using the block timestamp. This prevents manipulation because the value of the block number is fixed (miners cannot vary the block number value).[64]

The third issue is mishandled exception vulnerability. This problem occurs when a contract (caller) calls another contract (callee) without checking the value returned by the callee. In calling another contract, an exception (such as run out of gas) is sometimes requested by the callee. This exception, however, might or might not be reported to the caller depending on the construction of the call function. Not reporting an exception might lead to threats as in the KingOfTheEther (KoET) contract. In KoET, an adversary might send a transaction that results in an exception in order to buy the throne from the current king for free. With respect to this issue, some have highlighted the importance of checking the value returned by the callee. In the KoET example, the code can be improved to not release the throne till the payment from the adversary is completed successfully without any exception.[65]

The fourth issue is reentrancy vulnerability.[66] This problem occurs when an attacker utilizes a recursive call function to conduct multiple repetitive withdrawals, while their balances are only deduced once.

The fifth issue is the commission of criminal activities on the blockchain. An author highlighted the feasibility of constructing three different types of criminal activities in smart contract systems, namely sale of secret documents, theft of private keys and calling-card crimes, and a broad class of physical-world crimes.[67] These crimes can be implemented efficiently in the Ethereum blockchain by utilizing cryptographic techniques. There currently are no proposed solutions to the above two issues.

The last issue is the lack of trustworthy data feeds: oracles. An oracle is a party (or a technical source such as a database, or a person) who plays the role of "source of the truth" for a smart contract. The other parties of the smart contract trust that the oracle will provide the right information for the execution of the contract, because they cannot verify the information on chain. Putting it differently, using an oracle means receiving data from outside of a blockchain. An oracle provides a connection between real-world events

[63] L. Luu, D.-H. Chu, H. Olickel, P. Saxena, and A. Hobor, "Making Smart Contracts Smarter" in *Proceedings of the 2016 ACM SIGSAC Conference on Computer and Communications Security*, CCS '16 (ACM, 2016), 254–69.
[64] Ibid.
[65] *Supra* note, at 12.
[66] Ibid.
[67] A. Juels, A. Kosba, and E. Shi, "The Ring of Gyges: Investigating the Future of Criminal Smart Contracts," in *Proceedings of the 2016 ACM SIGSAC Conference on Computer and Communications Security*, CCS '16, (ACM, 2016), 283–95.

and a blockchain. In particular, some smart contracts require information (data feeds) from outside the blockchain.[68] The problem is that there is no guarantee that the information provided by an external source is trustworthy.

Zhang and other colleagues have proposed to develop a trusted third party between external sources and smart contracts to provide authenticated data feed for smart contracts.[69]

7.4.3 Privacy Issues

The two main privacy issues posed by smart contract are the lack of transactional privacy and the lack of data feeds privacy. An example of a lack of transactional privacy[70] in blockchain systems is when all transactions and users' balances are publicly available to be viewed. This lack of privacy could limit the adoption of smart contracts as many people consider financial transactions (such as stock trading) as confidential information.[71] Watanabe and colleagues have proposed to encrypt smart contracts before deploying them to the blockchain. Only participants who are involved in a contract can access the contract's content by using their decryption keys.[72]

A lack of data feed privacy occurs when a contract that requires a data feed sends a request to the party that provides those feeds. However, this request is exposed to the public as anyone in the blockchain can see it. Kosba and colleagues have proposed extending their Town Crier (TC) tool to support private requests.[73] Thus, a contract can encrypt the request using the TC's public key. Upon receiving the encrypted request, the TC can decrypt it using its private key. This guarantees that the content of the request is kept secret from other users and contracts in the blockchain.

7.4.4 Performance Issues

One possible performance problem relates to the sequential execution of smart contracts. In blockchain systems, smart contracts are executed sequentially (one contract at a time). However, this would affect the performance of the blockchain systems negatively as the number of contracts that can be executed per second is limited. With the growing number of smart contracts in the future, the blockchain systems will not be able to accommodate such a large scale of transactions. Zhang and colleagues suggest executing smart contracts in parallel as long as they are independent ("do not update the same

---

[68] J. I-H Hsiao, "'Smart' Contract on the Blockchain – Paradigm Shift for Contract Law?" (2017) *USCLR (US-China Law Review)* 685–94, 691.

[69] F. Zhang, E. Cecchetti, K. Croman, A. Juels, and E. Shi, "Town Crier: An Authenticated Data feed for Smart Contracts," in *Proceedings of the 2016 ACM SIGSAC Conference on Computer and Communications Security*, CCS '16 (ACM, 2016), 270–82.

[70] A. Kosba, A. Miller, E. Shi, Z. Wen, and C. Papamanthou, "Hawk: The Blockchain Model of Cryptography and Privacy-Preserving Smart Contracts" in *2016 IEEE Symposium on Security and Privacy (SP)* (IEEE, 2016), 839–58.

[71] Ibid.

[72] H. Watanabe, S. Fujimura, A. Nakadaira, Y. Miyazaki, A. Akutsu, and J. J. Kishigami, "Blockchain Contract: A Complete Consensus Using Blockchain," in *2015 IEEE 4th Global Conference on Consumer Electronics (GCCE)* (IEEE, 2015), 577–78.

[73] Zhang, et al., *supra* note 69.

variables").[74] By doing so, the performance of blockchain systems would be improved as more contracts could be executed per second. However, parallel execution of contracts faces a challenge in how to execute contracts that depend on each other at the same time. It is, therefore, essential to conduct research on identifying and tackling performance issues to ensure the ability of blockchains to handle larger scales of transactions.

7.5 Blockchain-Based Self-Help

Platforms and developers also represent interesting cases of cooperative self-help based on their ecosystems. Economists frequently refer to historical institutions in discussions of the institutional determinants of economic development and the economic role of social capital. Particular attention in recent years has been lavished on the Maghribi traders of the eleventh-century Mediterranean, following the work of Avner Greif.[75] In the absence of formal legal contract enforcement, the Maghribis developed an informal contract-enforcement mechanism based on multilateral relationships within a closely-knit "coalition." This mechanism exemplifies both the feasibility of private alternatives to the public legal system as a basis for economic transactions and the key role of social capital and informal institutions in developing economies. Furthermore, the Maghribis held "collectivist" Judaeo-Muslim beliefs and norms, which led them to develop different institutions from their "individualistic" Christian counterparts, and this is held to exemplify the pivotal role of cultural differences in explaining institutional and economic development. Economists have drawn far-reaching lessons from Greif's work.

Can understanding the Maghribis-like system help us to understand smart contact governance and management? For example, the use of self-help remedies for smart contracts is based on multilateral relationships within blockchain coalitions. Platforms and developers share a "collectivist" view of their roles because of their commitment to the world of the Code. Cox, Arnold and Villamayor-Tomás argue that the blockchain is an example of Commons 3.0 in that it provides a technical solution (cryptographic consensus) to the problem of cooperation in joint or group production at scale while still maintaining the benefits of commons-type (polycentric) institutional governance. A blockchain is a trustless commons in which effective rules are embedded in constitutional smart contracts that are cryptographically secure and crypto-economically implemented.[76]

This view of the blockchain as a collective or closely knit coalition is curious with respect to trustless smart contracts where the parties do not know each other, nor identify themselves in their communities. To be precise, blockchain networks can be private with restricted membership (permissioned blockchains), or they can be accessible to any person in the world (unpermissioned blockchains). There are also "consortium blockchains," where the process of validating transactions is controlled by a fixed set of nodes.

[74] M. Vukolić, "Rethinking Permissioned Blockchains" in *Proceedings of the ACM Workshop on Blockchain, Cryptocurrencies and Contracts*, BCC '17 (ACM, 2017), 3–7.

[75] A. Grief, "Reputation and Coalitions in Medieval Trade: Evidence on the Maghribi Traders" (1989) 49(4) *JEH (Journal of Economic History)* 857–82. The author referred to "informal contract-enforcement mechanism based on multilateral relationships within a closely-knit 'coalition'." See also A. Grief, *Institutions and the Path to the Modern Economy: Lessons from Medieval Trade* (Cambridge: Cambridge University Press 2006). For additional examples, see notes 20 and 21.

[76] M. Cox, G. Arnold, and S. Villamayor-Tomás "A Review of Design Principles for Community-Based Natural Resource Management" (2010) 15 *ES (Ecology and Society)* 38.

In addition, the parties are not identifiable in the case of crypt transactions. In these cases, they are anonymous. .

In our case, blockchains minimize the amount of trust required from any single actor in the system. They do this by distributing trust among different actors in the system via an economic game that incentivizes actors to cooperate with the rules defined by the protocol. In other words, the case considered here confirms that the social dimension of contracts matters in a technological age.[77]

This comes close to resembling the 1990s vision of cyberlaw experts that digital communities would define their own rules, free from state involvement. In fact, Wright and De Filippi draw a direct connection between the blockchain's "Lex Cryptographica" and the "Lex Informatica" of software code. They argue that the blockchain "could make it easier for citizens to create custom legal systems, where people are free to choose and to implement their own rules within their own techno-legal frameworks."[78]

The next sections review some examples of community self-help, such as mining, deposits, gossiping and, as last resort, social repudiation.

7.5.1 Mining

At the heart of bitcoin there is a set of protocols often called Nakamoto Consensus.[79]

Consensus means that participants in a network have confidence that what they see on their ledgers is accurate and consistent. Without a robust means of ensuring consensus, any bitcoin participant could, for example, spend the same bitcoins multiple times (known as the double-spend problem), or claim it had more currency than it really did. The trouble with most approaches to consensus on digital systems is that it is easy to create a nearly infinite number of fake network nodes (known as a Sybil attack). Even if most real users are honest, an attacker can create enough nodes to dominate the network and impose its own false consensus on the system (this challenge is well known in cryptography and is referred to as the "byzantine generals problem").

Until bitcoin, it had no scalable solutions. Nakamoto's answer cleverly combined cryptographic techniques with insight from game theory. The basic approach is called a byzantine fault tolerant protocol. Instead of trusting an individual actor, you trust a network of actors, who express themselves through voting. In Nakamoto's version, these actors engage in a process known as mining, through which they validate and establish consensus over chunks of bitcoin transactions. Every full node sees every transaction, and there is only one consensus ledger mirrored across every machine on

---

[77] K. Levy, Book-Smart, "Not Street-Smart: Blockchain-Based Smart Contracts and the Social Workings of Law" (2017) 3 *ESTS (Engaging Science, Technology, and Society)* 1–15.

[78] Wright and De Filippi, *supra* note 28, at 44–47. See generally J. Reidenberg, "Lex Informatica: The Formulation of Information Policy Rules through Technology" (1997) 76 *TLR (Texas Law Review)* 553 (developing the concept of Lex Informatica by analogy to the historical Lex Mercatoria).

[79] S. Nakamoto, "Bitcoin: A Peer-To-Peer Electronic Cash System" (2008) at https://bitcoin.org/bitcoin.pdf (Digital currencies such as Bitcoin that are based on encryption techniques are often referred to as cryptocurrencies.); Nick Szabo, "The Dawn of Trustworthy Computing," *Unenumerated Blog* (December 11, 2014), at http://unenumerated.blogspot.com/2014/12/the-dawn-of-trustworthycomputing.html.

the network. Even if some of the miners are untrustworthy, the system holds so long as the majority is honest.

The major limitation of such a protocol is the possibility of Sybil attacks[80]: if it is easy and rewarding to be untrustworthy, some participants will be. Hence, the second cryptographic technique in bitcoin is proof of work. Proof of work makes voting costly. Bitcoin's proof of work system requires miners to solve cryptographic puzzles involving one-way functions known as hashes. Votes require massive and growing computing power, which is sufficiently expensive to deter Sybil attacks. The benefits of cheating are less than the costs. Nakamoto Consensus affirms the integrity both sides of each individual transaction and of the ledger as a whole. It does so by aggregating together transactions into blocks. The proof of work system is tuned dynamically to generate a valid solution to the hashing puzzle for a block roughly once every ten minutes. Each block thus validated is cryptographically signed with the hash of the prior block, creating an immutable chain of sequential blocks. The longest chain of blocks represents the consensus state of the system.

Bitcoin is also designed to be censorship and tamper resistant. There is no central control point or network where a government could manipulate or block. Once a transaction is recorded, it cannot be changed. The final key piece of Nakamoto Consensus is the game-theoretic or psychological dimension: why will miners bother to mine? Proof of work is expensive, literally; it requires expensive computing hardware and even more use of electricity. Miners would not be incentivized sufficiently out of altruism. Nakamoto's solution was elegant. The miner who successfully validates a block receives a reward in a valuable currency.[81]

7.5.2 Deposits or Escrow Services

Deposits can be used to establish a level of trust between new and existing agents. This approach is akin to using agents to participate in an incentive-based protocol to provide correct (verifiable) computations.[82] This approach is adapted for a privacy-preserving computation protocol and for verifiable computations on Ethereum.[83] Each agent that wants to participate in these protocols is not trusted by default. This distrust results from the openness of the blockchain platform (no central authority gives access) and the direct accessibility of cryptocurrency. Assuming a rational agent, there is a motivation to break privacy or allow incorrect solutions if this optimizes the agent's own utility function. To deter this type of behavior, new agents have to deposit a certain cryptocurrency value for participation. In the aforementioned protocols, this deposit is returned when an agent decides to stop participating. However, dishonest or corrupt agents can be penalized by destroying their deposit or distributing it to honest agents.

[80] John R. Douceur, "The Sybil Attack," *Revised Papers from the First International Workshop on Peer-to-Peer Systems* 251 (2002), http://nakamotoinstitute.org/static/docs/the-sybil-attack.pdf
[81] "Bitcoin: The Magic of Mining" *Economist* (January 10, 2015), at 58, www.economist.com/node/2163812.
[82] R. K. and I. Bentov, "How to Use Bitcoin to Incentivize Correct Computations," in *Proceedings of the 2014 ACM SIGSAC Conference on Computer and Communications Security* (New York, USA: ACM Press, 2014), 30–41.
[83] G. Zyskind, O. Nathan, and A. S. Pentland, "Decentralizing Privacy: Using Blockchain to Protect Personal Data" *IEEE Security and Privacy Workshops* (May 2015) 180–84.

7.5.3 *Gossiping*

Gossiping can be used to communicate experiences with other agents in a P2P fashion and thereby establish trust or reputation scores. Indeed, when most people conduct business over the Internet, they are less interested in the legal consequences of their transactions than the interconnectedness that results from the exchange. This can be seen in the way that people rate their experiences on eBay, Uber, and TripAdvisor. Users of these service providers rate their experience with the vendor based on the quality and timeliness of the delivery of the service or product. These ratings create a reputation for the service provider and build relationships of trust in the network or community. Even though the nature of the marketplace means that participants will very likely never meet, their interactions give rise to exchanges where the parties to the transaction are relying on each other's status established through these conversations, rather than the strict legal rights expressed in terms and conditions

Clearly, it is an essential ingredient of any e-commerce reputation system to manage the integrity of feedback and to ensure that only genuine users provide it (and not, for example, by fake identities created by the person or persons who want to synthesize an improvement in their reputation). Anyone can browse eBay, but in order to join in the business of this community, buyers and sellers must first be registered with the platform. Exchanges are only possible when users are signed into the system with their unique identities. Even though users regularly use pseudonyms, those names are linked back to genuine pre-validated email addresses and credit cards. This system ensures that real people are the puppet masters of their avatars and that they must behave according to the rules of the marketplace. Under the rating system, the more stars received by a member, the more reliable and trustworthy they are, increasing their popularity with other members, and thereby resulting in significant economic advantages for those users.

Some cryptocurrency exchanges have designed trading platforms that provide information about the number of trades undertaken by each trader and the ratings provided by other users. The feedback is represented by color-coded dots and percentage rankings to reflect each trader's level of recent trading activity and the satisfaction of their customers. However, these apps are not built into the blockchain network and so suffer from a lack of decentralization since they depend upon the trustworthiness of those providing the feedback.[84]

Thus, the solutions available to prevent feedback abuse are generally reliable but centralized under the control of a trusted agent. However, by building a decentralized and distributed feedback management system on top of the blockchain, it is possible to provide reliable reputation ratings. A key feature of this system would be to attach more weight to the feedback of an established and trusted user on the network than new identities.[85]

---

[84] A. Schaub, R. Bazin, O. Hasan, and L. Brunie, "A Trustless Privacy-Preserving Reputation System," in J. H. Hoepman and S. Katzenbeisser (eds.), *ICT Systems Security and Privacy Protection* (SEC 2016); *IFIP Advances in Information and Communication Technology*, Vol. 471 (Cham, Switzerland, Springer International Publishing, 2016). See also D. Carboni, "Feedback based Reputation on top of the Bitcoin Blockchain," arXiv:1502.01504 (February 5, 2015) (last accessed November 20, 2018), https://arxiv.org/abs/1502.01504.

[85] Examples of proposed solutions are given in: A. Burak Can, B. Bhargava. "SORT: A Self-Organizing Trust Model for Peer-to-Peer Systems," *IEEE Transactions on Dependable and Secure Computing* 10.1 (January

7.5.4 *Reputation*

Reputation is invaluable in small communities with repeated transactions (like private blockchain environments). Parties not conforming to communal norms or that breach contracts suffer negative reputation consequences resulting in exclusion from future interactions. Thus, it is in parties' self-interest to build a reputation of reliability, honesty, and fair dealing.

However, integrity and reputation are of little importance in blockchain transactions. Misbehaving parties can simply erase their history by creating a new pseudonym.[86] In contrast, most people that conduct business over the Internet are more interested in interconnectedness. As discussed in the previous section, the rating of services create a reputation for the service provider and build relationships of trust in the network or community.[87]

In fact, participants use a variety of tools to promote their "reputations" in a decentralized blockchain. "Uprightly" is a platform that allows participants to enhance their reputations. It is independent of any other platform.[88] This way, users become market participants in order to safeguard their interests in the process. Further, Uprightly requires no third-party intervention; it is censorship-resistant; and decentralized.

7.5.5 *Social Repudiation*

The infamous Dao attack is the reason why Ethereum created a hard fork that split it into two platforms.[89] The Dao is the abbreviation for "The Decentralized Autonomous Organization" and is represented as a complex smart contract, which was considered to have revolutionized Ethereum forever. The Dao was not owned by anyone, and it previously worked as follows: a group of people developed the smart contract(s) that run the organization; followed by an initial funding period, where Dao Tokens were sold (namely: ICO11), which represent ownership (the right to vote). Once the funding was over, developers made smart contract proposals, and the users that owned tokens voted on approving and funding the proposals. Token holders had the option to opt-out from the organization and get back the money they invested, if for example, they did not endorse a smart contract that was getting funded. This was done through a split function in which the user would automatically opt out from the organization and get their money back. The user could also choose to create a child Dao and anyone else that did not agree on

2013), 14–27. H. Zhao and X. Li. "VectorTrust: Trust Vector Aggregation Scheme for Trust Management in Peer-to-Peer Networks" (2013) 64 *JS (The Journal of Supercomputing)* 805–29.

[86] N. Nisan, T. Roughgarden, É. Tardos, V.V. Vazirani and C. H. Papadimitriou, *Algorithmic Game Theory* (Cambridge: Cambridge University Press, 2008) at 682. Being able to cheaply create a new pseudonym in order to dodge a bad reputation is called whitewashing. One response is to distrust newcomers since their identities may mask a bad reputation or to require that pseudonyms be linked to a real person or business.

[87] W.L. Felstiner, R. L. Abel, and A. Sarat, "The Emergence and Transformation of Disputes: Naming, Blaming, Claiming . . ." (1980) 15 *LSR (Law & Society Review)* 631.

[88] "Uprightly" is discussed at https://bitcoinexchangeguide.com/uprightly-ico-upt-token/.

[89] The digital Decentralized Autonomous Organization ("DAO") had an objective to provide a new decentralized business model for organizing both commercial and nonprofit enterprises. It was instantiated on the Ethereum blockchain. The DAO raises funds and members write smart contracts to manage the investing of the funds. In the case mentioned here, a hacker managed to create a parallel DAO and stole 3.6 million units of Ether (i.e., a cryptocurrency).

funding (endorsing) a specific proposal, could join it. This design made it popular by offering flexibility, full control and complete transparency. However, this design allowed a hacker to exploit a re-entrancy vulnerability in the "split DAO" function. The attacker was able to steal one third of Dao's funds (3.6 million Ether), which was considered to be worth around $60 million at that time. The consequences of this attack had on Ethereum were unprecedented. The price of Ether dropped from $20 to $13 and the hack challenged the notion of immutability.

Interestingly, the incident ultimately led the Ethereum community to rescind (hard fork) the blockchain, by violating the underlying principle of distributed ledger technology.[90] The taking of Ether did not constitute a breach since the hacker followed Dao rules, but in a strategic and malicious manner. The ETH community's hard fork was a way to protect the agreement (crowd-sourced venture capital), but it did so via social repudiation (breach) of the "contract" itself. Thus, one may say that social repudiation provides an extreme, and inefficient, self-help mechanism to correct errors or manipulation of the blockchain. Clearly, the case also shows how platforms and their members establish guiding norms of behavior on the understanding that subordinating their own welfare to that of the community serves their own self-interests.

7.6 Conclusion

The chapter has explored the remedial perspective with respect to smart contracts. First of all, it noted the peculiar architecture of trust for smart contracts and its legal implications. In particular, it stresses the central role played by self-help remedies in blockchain environments, which is needed to keep the law in the background. Some different issues were identified with respect to self-help remedies, namely, coding, security, privacy and performance issues. Coding and security issues are the most commonly discussed issues. This is because smart contracts store valuable currency units and any security breach or coding error could result in the loss of money. The identified coding issues are the difficulty of writing correct codes, the inability to modify or terminate contracts, the lack of support to identify underoptimized contracts and the complexity of programming languages. The identified security issues are transaction-ordering dependency, time-stamp dependency, mishandled exception, reentrancy, untrustworthy data feeds, and criminal activities. The identified privacy issues are the lack of transactional privacy and the lack of data feeds privacy (oracles). The identified performance issue is the sequential execution of smart contracts. Although there are some proposed solutions to these problems, some of them are only abstract ideas lacking concrete evaluation. Presently, there is already a great deal of reliance on blockchain self-help, including the use of and forfeiture of deposits, gossiping, mining, and social repudiation. These remedies show that the social dimension of contracts remains relevant in the blockchain world.[91]

---

[90] A hard fork, or hardfork, as it relates to blockchain technology, is a radical change to the protocol that makes previously invalid blocks/transactions valid (or vice versa). This requires all nodes or users to upgrade to the latest version of the protocol software. Put differently, a hard fork is a permanent divergence from the previous version of the blockchain, and nodes running previous versions will no longer be accepted by the newest version, www.investopedia.com/terms/h/hard-fork.asp #ixzz5E3U9U2Pg (last accessed 10 November 2018).

[91] G. Sandstrom, "Who Would Live in a Blockchain Society? The Rise of Cryptographically Enabled Ledger Communities" (2017) 6 SERRC (Social Epistemology Review and Reply Collective) 27–41.

The key point made in the chapter is that the need for formal legal remedies is less frequent in smart contracts. It will be important to monitor the emergence of measures (proactive and reactive) aimed at preventing or (when necessary) respond to vitiating elements such as manipulation, errors in coding, breach, eavesdropping, and interference in smart contracts, as well as *ex contractu* or business responses, before resort is made to contract law and the legal system.

The continued implementation of self-help remedies may diminish the use of the formal legal system, but they cannot transplant the legal system or prevent the use of the legal system for parties to obtain contractual remedies. Smart contracts cannot avoid law as coded terms remain subject to judicial review, especially when highly scrutinized clauses (limitation of liability or limitation of remedy clauses) or unenforceable clauses (unconscionable terms, penalty clauses that are deemed to be excessive or avoidance of consumer protection law) are coded into the contracts. Smart contracts also remain subject to contract laws policing doctrines, such as mistake, duress or coercion, "surprising terms,"[92] misrepresentation or fraud, as well as implied terms, such as the duty of good faith and the duty of reasonable efforts in agency contracts.

---

[92] BGB §305c ("Provisions [that are] are so unusual that the contractual partner of the user could not be expected to have reckoned with them, do not form part of the contract").

Part III

Electronic Platforms and Networks

8 Digital Platforms

Regulation and Liability in EU Law

Piotr Tereszkiewicz

8.1 Introduction

The emergence of digital platforms over the last decade has become one of the most important challenges to contract and consumer law. Most digital platforms[1] operate through a web portal or a mobile application (app). They allow 'users' (buyers of services) to connect and transact with 'providers'.[2] Unlike two-party relationships between sellers or service providers on the one hand, and consumers on the other hand, digital platforms create three-party relationships between the platform (platform operator), provider (seller), and user. These relationships require a new architecture for liability and consumer protection. This chapter focuses on one of the more pertinent issues: whether digital platforms are intermediaries between suppliers of products and services; between buyers (end-users) of these products and services; or are parties to the contracts with the buyers. From the user perspective, it is not always clear who the counterparty is, the platform operator or a third party, whose services may be accessed through the platform. Most digital platforms fall somewhere along a spectrum between purely passive message boards and direct service providers.[3] A core legal issue relating to 'for business' digital platforms, such as *Uber* or *Airbnb*, is the platforms' legal status in relation to buyers of products and services marketed through their platforms. The variety of business models used in operating digital platforms makes the issue even more complicated.

The variety and complexity of digital platforms, and their legal status, is further made confusing since the European Union (EU) regulatory apparatus is not framed by a clear, consistent, or well-defined body of rules that can comprehensively be labelled as a 'law of platforms'.[4] The absence of a comprehensive legal framework on digital platforms does not mean that their structure, operation, activity, and liability are unregulated. Digital platforms are subject to existing general rules on electronic commerce, consumer

---

[1] The term 'digital platforms' is used as a synonym of terms 'electronic platforms' and 'online platforms'.

[2] V. Katz, 'Regulating the Sharing Economy' (2015) 30 *Berkeley Technology Law Journal*, 1067, 1071.

[3] Katz, 'Regulating the Sharing Economy', 1072.

[4] T. Rodriguez de las Heras Ballell, 'The Legal Anatomy of Electronic Platforms: A Prior Study to Assess the Need of a Law of Platforms in the EU' (2017) 3 *The Italian Law Journal*, 149, 151; C. Busch, H. Schulte-Nölke, A. Wiewiórowska-Domagalska, and F. Zoll, 'The Rise of the Platform Economy: A New Challenge for EU Consumer Law?' (2016) 5 *Journal of European Consumer and Market Law* 2016, 3, 4–5; O. Lobel, 'The Law of the Platform' (2016) 101 *Minnesota Law Review*, 87, 142–50; P. Rott and K. Tonner (eds.), *Online-Vermittlungsplattformen in der Rechtspraxis* (Baden-Baden: Nomos, 2018).

protection, data protection, intellectual property rights, and competition law.[5] Further, digital platforms operate under a contractual framework, created by a set of agreements between the operator and the platform users. This contractual framework, as will be shown below, contains provisions that aim to shape the relationship between the platform operator and the platform users (consumers), determining the rights and obligations of the parties, including the respective liabilities between the parties. This chapter will discuss legislative and scholarly attempts and proposals at regulating digital platform liability vis-à-vis the users of such platforms.

8.2 Legal Regime of the E-Commerce Directive

The major legal act applicable to digital platforms in the EU is 'Directive 2000/31/EC of 8 June 2000 on certain legal aspects of information society services, in particular electronic commerce, in the Internal Market' (E-Commerce Directive).[6] The E-Commerce Directive establishes the framework for service providers' liability, including liability towards consumers. Most importantly, Articles 12 through 15 of the E-Commerce Directive limit the liability of providers in respect of their assumed functions.[7] As a general principle, Article 15 of the Directive provides a safe harbour in which providers neither have any obligation 'to monitor the information which they transmit or store nor a general obligation actively to seek facts or circumstances indicating illegal activity'.[8] Members States are thus prohibited from imposing on service providers a general obligation to monitor the informational content passing through their platforms or to actively seek out illegal acts.

8.2.1 Liability under the E-Commerce Directive

The E-Commerce Directive distinguishes between different types of providers, such as 'access providers' and 'hosting providers'. The rationale underlying the E-Commerce Directive is that a platform-provider merely acts as a conduit. Therefore, the offering of technical services by providers should not give rise to secondary liability, such as being a contributory infringer in illegal activities transiting through the platform or website.[9] As such, access providers acting as a mere conduit are only liable for the improper transmission of data. As long as they do not intentionally collaborate with infringers, access providers are exempted under Article 12 of the E-Commerce Directive from both civil and criminal liability for content that is routed over their networks. Furthermore, hosting providers are excluded from liability for the content available on their websites as long as they do not have actual knowledge of the illegal activity or information. Once they obtain knowledge about illegal content or activities, they are obliged to remove the illegal

[5] Ballell, above note 4 at 151.
[6] Council Directive 2000/31/EC of 8 June 2000 on certain legal aspects of information society services, in particular electronic commerce, in the Internal Market ('Directive on electronic commerce'), OJ 2000 No. L178, 17 July 2000, p. 1.
[7] R. Weber, 'The Sharing Economy in the EU and the Law of Contracts' (2017) 85 George Washington Law Review, 1777, 1799.
[8] G. Spindler, 'Responsibility and Liability of Internet Intermediaries: Status Quo in the EU and Potential Reforms', in T.E. Synodinou, P. Jougleux, C. Markou, and T. Prastitou (eds.) EU Internet Law: Regulation and Enforcement (Cham: Springer International Publishing AG, 2017), pp. 289–90.
[9] See recitals 42–44 of the E-Commerce Directive; Spindler, 'Responsibility and Liability', p. 290.

content or block access to those engaging in illegal activities (Article 14 of the E-Commerce Directive).[10]

Although some of the concepts of the Directive are subject to interpretation, in particular the meaning of 'knowledge' of the provider,[11] the safe harbour privileges in the E-Commerce Directive are far-reaching. In sum, the legal position of digital platforms as providers of information services is relatively favourable, as risks of liability are moderate.[12] Nevertheless, it is unlikely that platform operators qualify as mere 'access providers' if they store the data of platform users (suppliers and buyers).[13] Accordingly, the liability exemption of Articles 12 and 13 would not apply. As Gerhard Spindler emphasizes, the safe harbour rules (privilege) apply only to providers who do not exercise any kind of control or monitoring of activities on their servers.[14] Further, Article 14 of the E-Commerce Directive does not provide for incentives for providers to take voluntary actions regarding legality of content; further, if they store or use the content, then they run the risk of being deemed to have constructive knowledge of illicit information.[15]

The narrow grounds of service provider liability under the E-Commerce Directive have framed the debate on the legal status of digital platforms with a view to their potential liabilities. Consequently, the starting point of the analysis is whether the conduct of digital platforms is 'merely technical, automatic and passive'. If the role of the service provider or platform is merely to act as technical intermediaries between parties supplying content and users of that content (consumers), then they are insulated from liability by the Directive.[16]

The importance of differentiating between 'active' and 'passive' platforms is of paramount importance under the E-Commerce Directive, as well as under most national laws. For example, the Dutch Supreme Court (Hoge Raad) characterized the relationship between the platform and the service supplier who uses the platform as a contract for intermediation (nl. *bemiddeling*) under Article 7:425 of the Dutch Civil Code.[17] The Court held that a passive platform is functionally equivalent to an 'electronic bulletin board' (nl. *elektronisch prikbord*). Such a platform does not prevent contracting parties from directly negotiating with themselves. By contrast, an *active* platform requires that the transaction between the interested parties be concluded exclusively through the platform. It follows that a distinction between 'active agents' (Active Accommodation Agent in case of Airbnb) and 'passive bulletin board' is recognized under Dutch law.[18] Typically, active agents will help service providers and service seekers to find each other,

---

[10] Spindler, above at p. 290. According to the CJEU Case 324/09, *L'Oréal* v. *eBay* [2011] ECR I-6011, para. 120: digital platform as a service provider may no longer benefit from the exclusion of liability when it has 'been aware of facts or circumstances on the basis of which a diligent economic operator should have identified the illegality in question and acted in accordance with Article 14 (1) (b) of Directive 2000/31'.

[11] See Spindler, above pp. 305–7.

[12] See also Weber, above note 7 at p. 1800; A. De Franceschi, '*Uber Spain* and the "Identity Crisis" of Online Platforms' (2018) 7 *Journal of European Consumer and Market Law*, 1, 2.

[13] R. Koolhoven, E.D.C. Neppelenbroek, O.E. Santamaria, and T.H.L Verdi, *Impulse Paper on Specific Liability Issues Raised by the Collaborative Economy in the Accommodation Sector* (European Commission, Brussels 2016), p. 49.

[14] See Spindler, above note 8 at p. 307.

[15] Koolhoven, above at p. 26.

[16] See the jurisprudence of the CJEU: Case 236/08, *Google France* v. *Louis Vuitton* [2010] ECR 1–0000, para. 120.

[17] Hoge Raad, judgement of 16 October 2015, Case 15/00688, ECLI:NL:HR:2015:3099.

[18] R. Koolhoven, et al., 'Impulse Paper', p. 26; R. Koolhoven, 'Het platform in de deeleconomie: elektronisch prikbord of bemiddelaar?' (2015) *Weekblad voor Privaatrecht, Notariaat en Registratie*, 991–92.

a service for which active agents are usually paid.[19] Since this help is more than just technical, automatic, and passive, the platform operators can not rely on the liability exemption under the E-Commerce Directive.

Platforms that act as 'passive bulletin boards' usually provide a communication medium in which the platform operator does not screen the content uploaded to its platform.[20] Specific websites, such as marktplaats.nl, have been characterized as 'a passive bulletin board' by Dutch courts.[21] In such cases, it may be assumed that platform providers act as neutral intermediaries under the E-Commerce Directive. Of course, some platforms are not fully passive or fully active, and, therefore, the distinction between 'active' and 'passive' providers may be difficult to determine. Hence, the uncertainty over whether a platform provider actually assumes an active or a passive role must be regarded as one of the core issues relating to the legal status of digital platforms.

In cases where a platform provides the underlying service (such as a transportation service offered via the platform), it follows that the E-Commerce Directive, including its safe harbour provisions, is not applicable. Thus, when a digital platform participates in the provision of an underlying service, the E-Commerce Directive does not apply to the platform. However, the E-Commerce Directive may still apply in cases where the platform plays an active role in determining the content of the underlying service (offered by a third-party supplier), but its liability exemption under the safe harbour provisions does not apply.[22] In light of the *Google Spain* judgement, digital platforms may bear liability to the consumers of e-services (clients of the platform) and to third parties.[23]

8.2.2 *Interplay of the E-Commerce Directive and Other Regulatory Regimes*

Under the E-Commerce Directive, it appears justified to distinguish between two categories of cases.[24] The first category includes cases where the service offered by a digital platform consists in providing the mechanism or infrastructure for users to interact with each other (digital intermediation). In these cases, digital platforms are deemed to provide an information society service, which according to Article 4 of the E-Commerce Directive requires no prior authorization or equivalent measures. This means that these digital platforms are free both to carry out their activities and to offer services in all Member States without being subject to nation-specific requirements (prior authorization or equivalent measures).[25]

The second category includes cases where digital platforms not only offer users the means to interact with each other, but also provide additional services, in particular providing payment facilities, screening services, or providing model contracts for the

---

[19] Details of how payments are made depend on business models of the different platforms.

[20] Koolhoven, above note 13 at p. 26.

[21] Ibid. at p. 76, referring to the judgement by the Court of Leeuwarden of 22 May 2012, ECLI: NL:GHLEE: 2012:BW6296 (Stokke/Marktplaats).

[22] V. Hatzopoulous and S. Roma, 'Caring for Sharing? The Collaborative Economy under EU Law' (2017) 54 *Common Market Law Review* 81, 99.

[23] CJEU Case 131/12, *Google Spain SL and Google Inc.* v. *Agencia Española de Protección de Datos (AEPD) and Mario Costeja González* [2014] 3 CMLR 50, paras. 97–99; Hatzopoulous and Roma, 'Caring for Sharing', 105.

[24] C. Cauffmann, 'The Commission's European Agenda for the Collaborative Economy – (Too) Platform and Service Provider Friendly?' (2016) 5 *Journal of European Consumer and Market Law* 235–36.

[25] See also Hatzopoulous and Roma, above note 22 at 99.

service provider and user.[26] In such cases, the question arises as to whether these digital platforms should be regarded as a provider of the underlying service (such as transportation, accommodation, and package travel services). Digital platforms characterized as providers of underlying services subject them to market access requirements applicable to providers of such services.

In *Asociación Profesional Élite Taxi* v. *Uber Systems Spain SL*, the Court of Justice of the European Union (CJEU)[27] proved an opportunity to consider this issue in detail. The CJEU held that an intermediation service, such as Uber, whose purpose is to connect, for remuneration, by means of a smartphone application, non-professional drivers using their own vehicles with persons needing transportation, must thus be regarded as forming an integral part of an overall transport service. Accordingly, it must be classified not as 'an information society service' within the meaning of Article 1(2) of Directive 98/34 (laying down a procedure for the provision of information in the field of technical standards and regulations), to which Article 2(a) of the E-Commerce Directive refers, but as 'a service in the field of transport' within the meaning of Article 2(2)(d) of Directive 2006/123.[28] The CJEU thus held that the E-Commerce Directive did not apply to Uber. In sum, the service provided by Uber is more than an intermediation service consisting of connecting a non-professional driver with a person seeking transport. Uber can best be characterized as an intermediation service that simultaneously offers transport services, through the use of software tools and by which it organizes transport. The CJUE concluded that such a service must be excluded from the scope of the freedom to provide services in general (safe harbour provisions) as well as from the scope of application of Directive 2006/123/EC on services in the internal market[29] and outside of the reach of the E-Commerce Directive. It follows that if Member States regulate the conditions under which such services are to be provided then Uber-like platforms are subject to Member State regulations and rules on liability.

The Uber judgement demonstrates that the CJEU takes an increasingly reluctant approach to shielding online intermediaries with the safe harbour provisions of the E-Commerce Directive.[30] The CJEU built its classification of Uber's services largely on an earlier decision. In *Grupo Itevelesa*, it held that the term 'services in the field of transport covers 'any physical act' of moving persons or goods from one place to another by means of a vehicle, aircraft or waterborne vessel, but also any service inherently linked to such an act'.[31] In the Uber case, the CJEU broadened the meaning of 'any physical act' to any platform that exercises 'decisive influence' over the conditions under which the service is provided. The CJEU considered several factors to be indicative in this respect, such as controlling 'the maximum fare by means of the eponymous application, participating in profits obtained from the client, controlling the quality of the vehicle, the drivers, and the conduct of the latter'.[32] This specific feature distinguishes Uber from online platforms offering hotel reservations or airline tickets that intermediate between

---

[26] Cauffmann, above note 24 at 236. On other typical services provided by digital platforms see Ballell, above note 4 at 167–68.

[27] CJEU Case 434/15, *Asociación Profesional Élite Taxi* v. *Uber Systems Spain SL*, EU:C:2017:981.

[28] CJEU Case 434/15. See also De Franceschi, above note 12 at p. 2.

[29] Council Directive 2006/123/EC of 12 December 2006 on services in the internal market, OJ 2006 No. L376, 27 December 2006, p. 36.

[30] D. Adamski, 'Lost on the Digital Platform: Europe's Legal Travails with the Digital Single Market' (2018) 55 *Common Market Law Review*, 719, 742.

[31] CJEU Case C-168/14, *Grupo Itevelesa and Others*, EU:C:2015:685, para 46.

[32] CJEU Case 434/15, para. 39.

traders (sellers) and clients (buyers). The high degree of control exerted by Uber over the terms of service is the key criterion for distinguishing between platforms that may be liable for the provisions of the underlying service and those that qualify as mere intermediaries and are not liable as a contracting party.

8.3 Position of the European Commission

As stated above, there is no specific set of rules currently tailored to regulate digital platforms at the EU level. Yet, digital platforms are well advised to take appropriate measures that enable users of these platforms to determine the party with whom they are concluding contracts.[33] By doing so, the platform buttresses its case that it is not directly liable since it acts only in an intermediary capacity. Also, failure to do so may violate the general prohibition of unfair commercial practices under Article 5 of Directive 2005/29/EC.[34] Under this Directive, traders have a duty of professional diligence not to mislead consumers by act or omission. Failing to inform the consumer about the identity of the other contracting party amounts to a misleading action. In 2016, the European Commission (EC) issued important documents aiming at clarifying its position regarding digital platforms.[35] In particular, the EC 'Communication on Online Platforms' establishes a framework for platform liability for the provision of underlying service towards end-users (consumers).

8.3.1 *Criteria for Establishing the Contractual Role of a Digital Platform*

The EC also issued the 'Communication on the Collaborative Economy', which provides criteria for establishing whether online platforms should be liable to a consumer as a contract party.[36] The level of *control or influence* that a platform exerts over the provider of such services will generally constitute the core test of liability. This level of control or influence can in particular be established in light of the following key factors:

a. Price: 'where the collaborative platform is only recommending a price or where the underlying services provider is otherwise free to adapt the price set by a collaborative platform' versus the platform acting as price setter.
b. Other key contractual terms: The question here is whether the platform sets terms and conditions (other than price) 'which determine the contractual relationship between the underlying services provider and the user'.
c. Ownership of key assets: does the platform or the service provider own the key assets used to provide the underlying service?

---

[33] European Commission, 'Guidance on the Implementation/application of Directive 2005/29/EC on unfair commercial practices', SWD (2016) 123 final, 122.
[34] Council Directive 2005/29/EC of 11 May 2005 concerning unfair business-to-consumer commercial practices in the internal market and amending Council Directive 84/450/EEC, Directives 97/7/EC, 98/27/EC and 2002/65/EC of the European Parliament and of the Council and Regulation (EC) No 2006/2004 of the European Parliament and of the Council ('Unfair Commercial Practices Directive'), OJ 2000 No. L149, 11 June 2005, p. 22.
[35] Commission Communication, *Online Platforms and the Digital Single Market Opportunities and Challenges for Europe*, COM (2016) 288. See Adamski, 'Lost on a Digital Platform', 719.
[36] Commission Communication, *A European Agenda for the Collaborative Economy*, 2 June 2016, COM (2016) 356, p. 6.

The Communication on the Collaborative Economy states: 'when these three criteria are all met [platform sets price, terms, and owns assets relating to the provided services], there are strong indications that the collaborative platform exercises significant influence or control over the provider of the underlying services,' which in turn indicates that the platform is the provider or co-provider of the underlying services.[37] Other factors to be considered include which party incurs the costs and risks related to the provision of the underlying services.

8.3.2 *Assessment*

Under the approach advanced by the above mentioned Commission Communications, the control that the digital platform exerts over the service provider is the major factor in determining the liability of the platform for services rendered. In the context of the collaborative economy, large platforms, such as Airbnb, exert substantial influence over small service providers that use the platforms to enter markets. Yet, it is questionable whether specific indicative factors of control, as proposed in the Communication on the Collaborative Economy, adequately capture the degree of control needed to hold the platform liable. Most importantly, the criterion relating to the ownership of key assets used to provide the underlying services appears to be derived from labour law, where it is used to determine whether a worker is an employee or an independent contractor.[38] As regards the platform economy, the question as to who owns key assets used to provide the underlying services might not be indicative of the actual influence or control exerted by the platform. This view gains support from the above-mentioned CJEU Uber judgement.[39]

In order to establish whether Uber exercises decisive influence over the conditions under which the service is provided to clients, the CJEU considered several factors,[40] but the ownership of the assets used to provide the service (motor vehicles) was not regarded as essential to establish decisive influence by the platform over persons actually providing the service.[41] It has been correctly claimed that in the Uber Spain judgement, the CJUE takes a step towards an enhanced liability level for digital platforms, given its focus on the actual control exercised by the platform and disregarding formal criteria, such as the platform-provider-user agreements.[42] While the criterion of control over the actual service provider may be appropriate in the case of collaborative platforms, it does not appear suitable for dealing with digital platforms serving larger traders that are strong market players in their own right. This consideration constitutes a major objection towards the criterion of 'control', as it may not be typical of all major business sectors.

---

[37] Commission Communication on the Collaborative Economy, p. 6.
[38] See for instance CJEU Case C-256/01, *Debra Allonby* v. *Accrington & Rossendale College and Others*, EU:C:2004:18; CJEU Case C-270/13, *Iraklis Haralambidis* v. *Calogero Casilli*, EU:C:2014:2185.
[39] CJEU Case 434/15, *Asociación Profesional Élite Taxi* v. *Uber Systems Spain SL*, EU:C:2017:981.
[40] Ibid. at para 39; note 22 above & accompanying text.
[41] Ibid. In para. 37, the CJEU emphasizes that 'passengers are transported by non-professional drivers using their own vehicles'. See also De Franceschi, above note 12 at p. 2.
[42] De Franceschi, above note 12 at p. 2.

8.4 Contract Law Approaches to Determining the Status of Digital Platforms

From the perspective of German private law, several criteria for establishing platform liability as a contract party have been proposed.[43] Under the criterion of the 'objective addressee perspective' (*objektiver Empfängerhorizont*), a platform may be deemed a contract party, where the platform appears as such in relations with users.[44] Therefore, it does not matter that a third party provides the actual service. This criterion has been established in respect of contracts for the carriage of passengers, where the liability of the carriage company falls on whoever assumes the appearance of a 'contract partner' towards passengers and not on whether a third party is charged with providing the carriage services.[45] Further, the 'objective addressee perspective' is also found in recent CJEU jurisprudence regarding consumer protection under the Consumer Sales Directive 1999/44/EC.[46] In the *Wathelet*[47] case, the consumer purchased a second-hand vehicle from a garage. Subsequently, the garage failed to make necessary repairs on the vehicle, claiming that the vehicle was not sold on its own account but individually by the owner of the garage as a third party. The garage insisted that it acted only in the capacity of an intermediary. The CJEU held that in circumstances in which the consumer can easily be misled in the light of the conditions in which the sale is carried out, the seller's liability, in accordance with Directive 1999/44, must be capable of being imposed on an intermediary. In this case, the garage created a likelihood of confusion that the garage was a party to the sale.[48] Thereby the CJEU took a purposive approach to the interpretation of the term 'seller' under the Directive.[49] The rationale being that it is essential for consumers to know the identity of the other contracting parties.[50]

The 'objective addressee perspective' approach justifies distinguishing between two types of digital platforms. On the one end of the scale, there are platforms the appearance of which justifies 'intermediary' status. The manner in which these digital platforms present different offers to potential clients signals to the clients the identity of the contract party as being someone other than the platform. Platforms such as eBay or Fly.com leave no doubt that they are acting as mere intermediaries, since different providers are prominently presented on their websites.[51] It is clear from the branding of such platforms that they provide products and services of other traders and that they are not themselves acting as a trader.[52] The non-platform service-product providers are tasked with the

---

[43] Cf. I. Domurath, 'Probleme bei der Einordnung von Plattformen als Vertragspartner', in P. Rott and K. Tonner (eds.), Online-Vermittlungsplattformen in der Rechtspraxis (Baden-Baden: Nomos, 2018), p. 44.

[44] See also Busch, et al., above note 4 at p. 5.

[45] Domurath, above at p. 58.

[46] Council Directive 1999/44/EC of the European Parliament and of the Council of 25 May 1999 on certain aspects of the sale of consumer goods and associated guarantees, OJ 1999 No. L171, 7 July 1999, p. 12. See also Domurath, 'Probleme bei der Einordnung', p. 58.

[47] CJUE Case 149/15, *Sabrina Wathelet* v. *Garage Bietheres & Fils SPRL*, EU:C:2016:840, on which see T. J. Dodsworth, 'Intermediaries as Sellers – A Commentary on Wathelet' (2017) 6 *Journal of European Consumer and Market Law*, 213.

[48] CJUE Case 149/15, para. 41.

[49] Dodsworth, above note 47 at p. 214.

[50] CJUE Case 434/15, *Asociación Profesional Élite Taxi* v. *Uber Systems Spain SL*, EU:C:2017:981.

[51] Domurath, above note 43 at p. 58.

[52] Dodsworth, above note 47 at p. 214.

execution of the transaction, including payment details.[53] On the other end of the scale, there are digital platforms, which do not contain individual offers of different providers and use a uniform image or a trademark, and thus appear as the contracting party. This dichotomy provides a useful starting point for analysing most business models based on digital platforms.

Admittedly, there are cases in which the legal status of a platform may be unclear according to the above classification scheme. For instance, some platforms may present themselves as simple hosts (mere intermediaries) in their general conditions, but in reality they assume an active role by assisting platform users in concluding contracts offered through the platform. Airbnb is an example of a platform seemingly acting as an intermediary but in fact plays an active role defining the roles of the contracting parties.[54] The Airbnb contract (pursuant to EU law) declares:

> As the provider of the Airbnb Platform, Airbnb does not own, create, sell, resell, provide, control, manage, offer, deliver, or supply any Listings or Host Services, nor is Airbnb an organiser or retailer of travel packages under Directive (EU) 2015/2302. Hosts alone are responsible for their Listings and Host Services. When Members make or accept a booking, they are entering into a contract directly with each other. Airbnb is not and does not become a party to or other participant in any contractual relationship between Members, nor is Airbnb a real estate broker or insurer. Airbnb is not acting as an agent in any capacity for any Member, except as specified in the Payments Terms.[55]

Similarly, Uber explicitly disclaims any status as a contract party under UK law:
> Uber UK is not a Transportation Provider and does not provide transportation services. Transportation services are provided to you under a contract (the Transportation Contract) between you and the Transportation Provider that is identified to you in the booking confirmation provided by Uber UK. [...] Uber UK is not a party to the Transportation Contract and acts as a disclosed agent for the Transportation Provider in communicating the Transportation Provider's agreement to enter into the Transportation Contract.[56]

Numerous digital platforms use similar language terms, regardless of the degree of their actual involvement into the provision of services, in order to avoid liability as a contracting party.[57]

Furthermore, unlike Uber and Amazon, Airbnb engages actively with dispute resolution between its users (hosts and guests).[58] It provides an informal negotiation service directly with Airbnb's customer service team, as well as binding arbitration administered by the American Arbitration Association (AAA) using its specially designed Consumer

---

[53] Platform operators sometimes provide model contract forms for agreements between providers and buyers. For instance, in the accommodation sector, the platforms 'Homeaway' and 'Rentalia' provide model contract forms, see Koolhoven, above note 13 at p. 136.

[54] V. Mak, 'Regulating Online Platforms – The Case of Airbnb' in S. Grundmann (ed.), *European Contract Law in the Digital Age* (Cambridge Antwerp Portland: Intersentia, 2018), p. 91.

[55] See www.airbnb.com/terms, pt. 1 (Scope of Airbnb Services).

[56] See www.uber.com/en-BE/legal/terms/gb.

[57] The 'Homeaway' platform: 'We are not a party to any rental or other agreement between users. This is true even if the Site allows you to book a rental or provides other ancillary products or services, as the Site may facilitate booking a rental or other tools, services or products, but we are not a party to any rental or other agreement between users', www.homeaway.com/info/legal/terms-conditions.

[58] Mak, 'Regulating Online Platforms', p. 98.

Arbitration Rules.[59] What is more, Airbnb provides 'Host Guarantee' coverage of US$1 million for damage caused by guests to a host's property. An additional service offered by Airbnb is 'Host Protection Insurance', which is designed to protect hosts against third-party claims of bodily injury or property damage and cover damages to common areas.[60] Providing the above-mentioned services makes Airbnb look closer to a contracting party and not merely as an intermediary. In particular, Airbnb conveys to users of its platform the impression that it takes care of safeguarding their interests in a comprehensive manner. This makes it difficult for guests to distinguish the respective roles of Airbnb and the hosts connected to the Airbnb platform.

8.5 Discussion Draft of Directive on Online Intermediary Platforms

A lack of a clear and comprehensive legal framework on digital platforms has inspired European scholars to elaborate a model law to guide future EU legislation. The Research Group on the Law of Digital Services has prepared a Discussion Draft of a Directive on Online Intermediary Platforms (Discussion Draft).[61] The Discussion Draft adopts an innovation-friendly perspective and follows a 'problem-driven approach' towards regulating digital platforms. The Discussion Draft rightly recognizes that platform business models involve three parties: the digital platform; suppliers who use platforms for marketing goods and services to customers; and customers who use platforms for obtaining goods or services. From a technical point of view, the scope of the Discussion Draft is currently limited to situations where the supplier provides goods, services, or digital content to a customer in return for payment.[62] The scope of the Discussion Draft is not intended to be comprehensive in covering all types of digital platforms. However, the Discussion Draft does provide a starting point for the legal analysis of platform business models in general.

8.5.1 *Content of Discussion Draft*

The Discussion Draft addresses the issue as to under what requirements a platform operator is liable for a non-performance by the supplier to the consumer. It is worth emphasizing that the Discussion Draft follows the liability approach adopted in the E-Commerce Directive but places it within the context of contract law.[63] According to Article 16 of the Discussion Draft, 'a platform operator who presents itself to customers and suppliers as intermediary in a prominent way is not liable for non-performance under supplier-customer contracts'.[64] This Discussion Draft provision will be analysed below. Furthermore, the Discussion Draft sets out two further instances for platform operator liability. First, a platform operator may be liable to customers for failure to remove misleading information given by suppliers (Article 17). Second, a platform operator

---

[59] See www.airbnb.com/terms, pt. 19. 2 (Dispute Resolution and Arbitration Agreement).
[60] See www.airbnb.com/host-protection-insurance.
[61] Research Group on the Law of Digital Services, 'Discussion Draft of a Directive on Online Intermediary Platforms' (2016) 5 *Journal of European Consumer and Market Law*, 164.
[62] Discussion Draft, Art. 2(e).
[63] Research Group, 'Discussion Draft', 165.
[64] Similarly Cauffmann, 'The Commission's European Agenda', 240.

may be liable to customers or suppliers for misleading statements about suppliers or their goods or services and about customers (Article 19).

The most notable provision in the Discussion Draft is Article 18, which states:

1. If the customer can reasonably rely on the platform operator having a predominant influence over the supplier, the platform operator is jointly liable with the supplier for non-performance of the supplier-customer contract.
2. When assessing whether the customer can reasonably rely on the platform operator's predominant influence over the supplier, the following criteria are to be considered in particular:

    (a) The supplier-customer contract is concluded exclusively through facilities provided on the platform;
    (b) The platform operator can withhold payments made by customers under supplier-customer contracts;
    (c) The terms of the supplier-customer contract are essentially determined by the platform operator;
    (d) The price to be paid by the customer is determined by the platform operator;
    (e) The platform operator provides a uniform image of suppliers or a trademark;
    (f) The marketing is focused on the platform operator and not on the suppliers; and
    (g) The platform operator promises to monitor the conduct of suppliers.

In sum, the Discussion Draft proposes a Directive based upon the precept of reliance liability in order to protect the customer by allowing the customer to 'reasonably rely on the predominant influence of the platform over the supplier'.[65] Effectively, the provision of Article 18 (2) of the Discussion Draft prohibits platform operators from shifting liability to third-party suppliers.[66] When the test of 'reasonable reliance on predominant influence' is met, the platform operator is jointly liable with service providers to the customer for non-performance of the supplier-customer contract.

8.5.2 Assessment

The major difficulty posed by the Discussion Draft is the open-ended catalogue of liability requirements, modelled after the 'flexible-system approach' put forward by the Austrian private law scholar Walter Wilburg. The legal idea of 'flexible system' (*bewegliches System*) of legal requirements has been advanced in Austrian and German private law scholarship for several decades.[67] Further, the Discussion Draft provision on platform

---

[65] The choice of 'reliance liability' is supported by reference to C-W. Canaris, *Die Vertrauenshaftung im deutschen Privatrecht* (Munich: C.H. Beck, 1971). It is fair to say that the theory of Canaris is not without controversy in the German private law scholarship. It is an open question whether this theory should be generalized and serve as the basis of a pan-European liability provision. Cf. for a concurring analysis of 'legitimate expectations' in contract law, including the impact of 'self-presentation' of an actor on his/her liability, see J. Köndgen, *Selbstbindung ohne Vertrag: zur Haftung aus geschäftsbezogenem Handeln* (Tübigen: Mohr, 1981).

[66] An indicative (non-exhaustive) list of sub-criteria that may be used to determine the 'reasonable reliance of the customer on the predominant influence of the platform operator on the supplier' is provided in Article 18 (2) of the Discussion Draft. See M. Storme, 'A Civilian Perspective on Network Contracts and Privity' (2017) 85 *George Washington Law Review*, 1739, 1749–50.

[67] The idea of 'flexible system' draws on W. Wilbrug, *Entwicklung eines beweglichen Systems im Bürgerlichen Recht. Rede, gehalten bei der Inauguration als Rector magnificus der Karl-Franzens-Universität in Graz am 22. November 1950* (Graz: Kienreich, 1950). S. Breidenbach, *Die Voraussetzungen von Informationspflichten*

liability (Article 18 (2)) follows the approach adopted in European model laws on contract law, such as in the Principles of European Contract Law[68] (Article 4:107) and in the Draft Common Frame of Reference[69] (Article II. – 7:205) relating to the requirements of fraudulent non-disclosure in contract law.[70]

Basic assumptions underlying the 'flexible-system' merit explanation. As originally proposed by Walter Wilburg in 1950, and subsequently developed further by Wilburg's disciple Franz Bydlinski,[71] the justification for 'the flexible-system approach' is derived from the tension between classical private law's emphasis on freedom of contract and the limits to freedom resulting from consumer protection legislation.[72]

The idea of the 'flexible system' assumes and recognizes a plurality of principles (values),[73] including private autonomy (freedom of contract), protection of commercial exchanges (reasonable reliance on the other contracting party's statements or conduct), equivalence of the performances, and responsibility and self-reliance.[74] These principles are applied concomitantly with each individual principle or value being weighted when applied in a given case. Legal consequences are derived from the interplay and comparative weight ascribed to each individual principle in the process of the application of law. Clearly, these values conflict with one another in a given case. Wilburg's point was that the 'flexible system' would lead to a freer and more perfect development of contract law.[75]

Applied to the specific case of platform liability for non-performance by a supplier, the major assumption of the 'flexible system' is that not all of the criteria of Article 18 (2) of the Discussion Draft are needed to justify imposing liability. However evidence relating to more than a single criterion is needed.[76] If several or all of the criteria are met in a given case, a presumption is justified that the platform operator is a party to the contract from the perspective of the client or consumer and is therefore exposed to 'secondary' liability. At the same time, it is possible that while some of the criteria are met in a given case, their comparative weight is not significant enough to justify platform liability.

---

beim Vertragsschluss (Munich: C.H. Beck, 1989), applies the idea of 'flexible system' as a tool to lay down the requirements of pre-contractual disclosure under general contract law. For a comparative account of Wilburg's concept, see L. Hawthorne, 'Walter Wilburg's "flexible-system approach" Projected onto the Law of Contract by Means of the European Draft Common Frame of Reference Principles' (2012) 45 Comparative and International Law Journal of Southern Africa, 189.

[68] O. Lando and H. Beale (eds.), *Principles of European Contract Law*, Parts I and II (Alphen aan den Rijn: Kluwer Law International, 1999).

[69] C. von Bar and E. Clive (eds.), *Principles, Definitions and Model Rules of European Private Law. Draft Common Frame of Reference (DCFR)* (Oxford: Oxford University Press, 2010).

[70] For a comparative survey, see P. Tereszkiewicz, *Obowiązki informacyjne w umowach o usługi finansowe (Information Duties in Financial Services Contracts)* (Warszawa: Wolters Kluwer, 2015), p. 187.

[71] For instance, F. Bydlinski, 'Das österreichische Irrtumsrecht als Ergebnis und Gegenstand beweglichen Systemdenkens', in G. Hochloch, R. Frank and P. Schlechtriem (eds.), *Festschrift für Hans Stoll* (Tübingen: Mohr Siebeck, 2018), pp. 113, 124; F. Bydlinski, *System und Prinzipien des Privatrechts* (Wien: Verlag Österreich, 1996), p. 147.

[72] Hawthorne, note 67 above at p. 195.

[73] Wilburg, 'Entwicklung', p. 12; F. Bydlinski, 'A "flexible system" Approach to Contract Law', in H. Hausmaninger, H. Koziol, A.M. Rabello and I. Gilead (eds.), *Developments in Austrian and Israeli Private Law* (Wein New York: Springer, 1999), pp. 10, 11.

[74] F. Bydlinski, 'A Flexible System Approach', p. 13.

[75] Hawthorne, above note 67 at p. 195.

[76] C. Busch, 'Europäische Modellregeln für Online-Vermittlungsplattformen', in P. Rott and K. Tonner (eds.), *Online-Vermittlungsplattformen in der Rechtspraxis* (Baden-Baden: Nomos, 2018), p. 162.

The justification for the use of a broad set of criteria in the 'pre-dominant influence' test rests on the fact that different types of digital platforms form a continuum that occupies the landscape between a 'firm', on the one hand, and a 'transaction', on the other hand.[77] In some cases suppliers may be fully dependent on platform operators and actually constitute a part of their business structure, being only formally a separate legal entity. In other cases, suppliers cooperate with multiple platform operators, regarding them as ordinary commercial partners. Another factor to be weighed is the relative bargaining power between suppliers and platforms, which vary significantly depending on the business sector.

One of the criticisms of the liability test of the Discussion Draft is that it is too difficult to apply in practice. This problem becomes more pronounced if incorporated in an EU directive on digital platforms, which would have to be applied by courts in all Members States. It is uncertain whether the liability test under the Draft Directive will prove practicable with respect to mass-markets transactions. Some of the criteria in Article 18 (1) of the Discussion Draft are relatively easy to examine, in particular (a) whether the contract is concluded exclusively through facilities provided on the platform and (e) whether the platform provides a uniform image of suppliers or a trademark. Other criteria, such as (c) who determines the terms of the supplier-customer contract and (d) who determines the price to be paid by the consumer, involve a deeper examination of the relationship between the platform and the supplier, and their respective business models. The constraints of commercial secrecy regarding platform-supplier relationships are likely to constitute an obstacle in litigation of individual claims. The liability test may be easier to apply in class action proceedings, given the expertise of counsel and the greater incentive for digital platforms to settle such claims.

Another issue to be determined is whether joint liability should attach to the supplier in cases where the platform is the dominant party or actual contractor.[78] The Commission Communication, as mentioned above, assumes that only the digital platform remains liable to the consumer, as the platform is considered the actual service provider. This approach is straightforward and would make litigation less complex. The 'predominant-liability' test is most familiar to jurists from Germanic legal systems (in particular legal scholars and higher court judges), but it is unclear as to what extent it would appeal to judges in other national legal systems.

From a market structure perspective, it is essential to note that the approach towards platform liability, as proposed in the Discussion Draft, and also as noted in the Commission Communication, attaches platform liability to the fact that the platform exerts significant (predominant) influence on the supplier (provider) of the underlying service. It must be underscored that this approach towards platform liability draws mainly from the business model represented by Airbnb.[79] However, there are sectors, in which the 'predominant influence' test may not capture business reality, such as in the travel industry. The travel services sector is characterized by the presence of large, professional service providers, on whom digital platforms exert little influence. Rather, digital

[77] Ibid. at p. 162.
[78] Sceptically as to this point, see Cauffmann, 'The Commission's European Agenda', 240.
[79] K. Tonner, 'Der Vertrieb von Reiseleistungen über Online-Reiseportale', in P. Rott and K. Tonner (eds.), *Online-Vermittlungsplattformen in der Rechtspraxis* (Baden-Baden: Nomos, 2018), p. 129.

platforms in the travel industry market products and services of large independent market players. Most importantly, travel services are characterized by linking services or arrangements at the stage of sales and distribution, which gives rise to the need for specific consumer protection measures.[80] The next part will explore an alternative approach to platform liability based upon an analysis of the Package Travel Directive.

8.6 'Retailer-Liability' Approach to Digital Platform Liability

The second major approach towards regulating digital platform liability draws inspiration from the regulation of travel services. As emphasized by the main proponent of that approach, the German scholar Klaus Tonner, package travel law has long confronted the challenge of distinguishing between the liabilities of a travel organizer as a contract party and a travel agency as an intermediary between the travel organizer and traveller.[81] The determination of digital platform liability in general may benefit from this previous work done in the area of package travel services.

8.6.1 New Package Travel Directive as Referent

A major point of reference is the regulatory approach of Directive 2015/2302 on package travel and linked travel arrangements (Package Travel Directive),[82] which aims to protect consumers of travel services.[83] This approach adopts the assumption that certain digital platforms should be subject to liability standards comparable to those imposed on travel organizers under the Package Travel Directive.[84] One of the major objectives of the new Package Travel Directive is to clarify which party is responsible for complying with statutory duties in relation to travellers. Important guidance on the distinction between 'the travel organiser' and 'the travel retailer' is provided in Consideration 22 of the Directive:

> The main characteristic of a package is that there is one trader responsible as an organiser for the proper performance of the package as a whole. Only in cases where another trader is acting as the organiser of a package should a trader, typically a high street or online travel agent, be able to act as a mere retailer or intermediary and not be liable as an organiser. Whether a trader is acting as an organiser for a given package should depend on that trader's involvement in the creation of the package, and not on how the trader describes his business. When considering whether a trader is an organiser or retailer, it should make no difference whether that trader is acting on the supply side or presents himself as an agent acting for the traveller.

---

[80] K. Tonner, 'Der Vertrieb von Reiseleistungen', p. 130.
[81] K. Tonner, A. Halfmeier, and M. Tamm, *EU-Verbraucherrecht auf dem Prüfstand* (Berlin: Verbraucherzentrale Bundesverband e.V., 2017), p. 27.
[82] Council Directive 2015/2302 of 25 November 2015 on package travel and linked travel arrangements, amending Regulation (EC) No 2006/2004 and Directive 2011/83/EU of the European Parliament and of the Council and repealing Council Directive 90/314/EEC, OJ 2015 No. L 326, 11 December 2015, p. 1.
[83] A. de Vries, 'Travel Intermediaries and Responsibility for Compliance with EU Travel Law: A Scattered Legal Picture' (2016) 5 *Journal of European Consumer and Market Law*, 119, 124. On business models of online platforms in the travel sector see M. Colangelo and V. Zeno-Zencovich, 'Online Platforms, Competition Rules and Consumer Protection in Travel Industry' (2016) 5 *Journal of European Consumer and Market Law*, 75.
[84] Tonner, above note 79 at p. 130.

The Package Travel Directive provides that an agent or intermediary will be liable as an organizer, where 'irrespective of whether separate contracts are concluded with individual travel service providers, those services are: (i) purchased from a single point of sale and those services have been selected before the traveller agrees to pay, (ii) offered, sold or charged at an inclusive or total price, and (iii) advertised or sold under the term "package" or under a similar term'.[85] Hence, the Directive lays down an objective test as to who is considered to be the seller of a travel package. Once the test is met, an agent or intermediary becomes liable to the consumer as a travel organizer.

Noteworthy provisions focus on the party with the responsibility 'for the performance of the package' towards the client. According to Articles 13(1)–(2) of the Package Travel Directive:

> Member States shall ensure that the organiser is responsible for the performance of the travel services included in the package travel contract, irrespective of whether those services are to be performed by the organiser or by other travel service providers. Member States may maintain or introduce in their national law provisions under which the retailer is also responsible for the performance of the package.

It follows that the Package Travel Directive recognizes that the travel retailer who purports to be a mere intermediary may be liable as the organizer of the package if it assumes the role of the travel organizer from the perspective of the client. Article 23 of the Package Travel Directive ensures that such liability cannot be waived by contract:

> a declaration by an organiser of a package or a trader facilitating a linked travel arrangement that he is acting exclusively as a travel service provider, as an intermediary or in any other capacity, or that a package or a linked travel arrangement does not constitute a package or a linked travel arrangement, shall not absolve that organiser or trader from the obligations imposed on them under this Directive.

This provision ensures that a simple waiver of liability used by platform operators will not be effective to exempt them from liability to their clients.

Moreover, in addition to the possibility that a travel agent will be subject to the liability of the travel organizer, the Package Travel Directive provides for *shared responsibility* of travel organizers and travel retailers as regards safeguarding key interests of travellers. According to Article 5(1) of the Package Travel Directive, both the travel organizer and the travel retailer are obliged to provide the traveller with standard pre-contractual information. It follows that if a travel retailer, acting as an intermediary, breaches this pre-contractual duty (such as failing to inform the traveller that a swimming pool is not accessible due to rebuilding), then the travel organizer is in breach of the package travel contract if the swimming pool is indeed inaccessible.

Under the Package Travel Directive, the integral parts of the travel contract may not be altered afterwards without consent of the traveller.[86] Moreover, the travel organizer cannot levy additional costs, fees, or charges, which have not been communicated in advance either by the organizer or by the retailer.[87] Article 15 of the Directive provides that the traveller may address messages, requests, or complaints in relation to the performance of the package directly to the retailer through which it was purchased.

---

[85] Council Directive 2015/2302, Article 3 (2) (b).
[86] Ibid. at Article 6 (1).
[87] Ibid. at Article 6 (2).

The retailer is then required to forward those messages, requests, or complaints to the organizer without undue delay. The limitation period for responding to the traveller's request commences upon receipt by the organizer.[88] Furthermore, the travel organizer bears the risk of the travel retailer failing to forward the communications from the travellers in a timely fashion.[89] Finally, travel retailers facilitating linked travel arrangements are obliged to provide security for the refund of all payments they receive from travellers to protect travellers in cases of the insolvency of the retailer.[90]

8.6.2 *Assessment*

The depth of consumer protection measures imposed by the Package Travel Directive on travel organizers and retailers appears remarkable from the perspective of general contract law. Consequently, it is best characterized as a 'retailer-liability' model. This approach reflects the fact that travel retailers are rarely 'passive facilitators' but act as 'engaged collaborators' that should be subject to the liability comparable to that of the travel organizer. The Package Travel Directive is profoundly different to the approach of the E-Commerce Directive as regards intermediary liability. Most importantly, digital platforms that qualify as 'travel retailers' under the new Package Travel Directive will be subject to liability under the Directive and its national implementations. Thus, it is important to recognize that certain digital platforms active in the field of travel services will be subject to more stringent liability rules than digital platforms active in other fields of business. It should be noted that the standard terms of major digital platforms, such as Airbnb or Homeaway, explicitly exclude the platforms' status as an organizer or retailer of travel packages under Directive (EU) 2015/2302. These exclusions prove that platform operators realize that the Directive provides a substantial measure of client protection. It is unlikely that the courts will uphold such standalone disclaimers.

Should the regulatory model of the new Package Travel Directive be considered a suitable referent for drafting of general rules on the liability of digital platforms? Applying the model of the Package Travel Directive to platform liability in general would entail the recognition of a digital platform as a 'retailer'. In such a case, the distinction between 'intermediary' and 'contract party' would be a blurred one. Undoubtedly, designing platform liability to service users (consumers) as 'retailer-liability' would have serious implications. To begin, the retailer-liability approach has the advantage of being easier to apply than the multi-factored 'predominant-influence' test under the Discussion Draft. As far as legal certainty is concerned, the retailer-liability model would diminish the need for complex investigations by courts as to whether a consumer could have reasonably relied on the platform having 'predominant influence' on the trader. Most importantly, the 'retailer-liability' solution is favourable to consumer's interests, as it raises the likelihood of liability of digital platforms that act as more than mere intermediaries. Nevertheless, the 'retailer-liability' approach is not suitable as a 'one-fits-all' solution to the challenge of regulating platform liability. Differences across various business sectors are too significant to justify bluntly extending the regulatory approach adopted in Package Travel Directive. Small platforms, acting merely as

---

[88] Ibid. at Article 15 (2).
[89] de Vries, 'Travel intermediaries', 124.
[90] Council Directive 2015/2302, Article 19 (1).

'bulletin boards', should not face the risks of far-reaching liability. For now, more in-depth empirical investigations will be required to establish which business sectors are most similar to travel services as far as market position and commercial practices.

8.7 Conclusion

This chapter has sought to analyse different approaches towards regulation and liability of digital platforms, focusing on the EU perspective. The *EU Electronic Commerce Directive on information society service providers* provides the current regulatory and scholarly perception of platform liability. A closer inquiry reveals that an approach to digital platform liability based on the E-Commerce Directive is not adequate. In light of the scholarly writings and regulatory developments, two main approaches to platform liability are identified and discussed. One approach is found in the general provisions of the Discussion Draft on Digital Platforms. The other approach focuses on sector-specific provisions that densely regulate platform-based business models, as exemplified by the new EU Package Travel Directive. It is submitted that sector-specific regulation ('subject-matter approach'), guided by recognition of prior market failures, is a preferable approach in the immediate future. This approach focuses on business sectors, such as financial services, labour regulation, and carriage of persons or goods. At the current stage, given the diversity of business models and differences between business sectors, it is premature to enact general provisions on platform liability at the EU level. However, a reform of the E-Commerce Directive could provide an opportunity to include some specific provisions on digital platform liability.

9 Blockchains

A Technology for Decentralized Marketplaces

Eliza Mik

9.1 Introduction

Departing from their original design as cryptocurrencies or alternative payment systems, blockchains are increasingly marketed as a generic technology that can be deployed for a wide range of use cases.[1] Although, from a technical perspective, blockchains are meant to serve as *records* of transactions, they are often portrayed as platforms or technologies *enabling* transactions. What started out as a crypto-anarchist dream is now poised to disrupt traditional commerce. More specifically, the decentralized character of blockchain technologies is meant to disintermediate commercial exchanges, lower transaction costs and empower sellers and buyers alike. Amazon and eBay have created efficient online marketplaces supported by complex technical infrastructures and an intricate web of legal agreements regulating their use. Despite their popularity, however, they are often criticized for being centralized, i.e. controlled by a single entity that manages their operation, restricts who can trade on them and prescribes what can be traded. For many, such centralization and intermediation contradict the spirit of the Internet – the latter was supposed to be an open, egalitarian network enabling novel economic structures and direct forms of cooperation. It is claimed that blockchains, enable the creation of more advanced, decentralized transacting platforms. Purportedly, their superior technology enables a total reliance on code, obviating the need for any centralized entity controlling their use and/or operation. Centralized entities, being operated by humans, are prone to error and political as well as commercial bias. In contrast, code is objective and impartial. While one cannot trust centralized entities or commercial intermediaries, one can trust the code. In the popular blockchain narrative, the ability to trust code is, somewhat confusingly, referred to as "trustlessness." From a technical perspective, however, the term denotes the ability to confirm the truth of an event without recourse to a trusted third party in an adversarial environment where no one can be trusted.[2] Purportedly, once it is possible to trust the code underlying a marketplace, it is no longer necessary to trust centralized operators or, in fact, rely on any traditional institutions. In parallel, a subset of blockchain technologies, the so-called smart contracts (self-enforcing programs that embody legal obligations) are promoted as methods of eliminating counterparty risk by

---

[1] Trevor I. Kiviat, "Beyond Bitcoin: Issues In Regulating Blockchain Transactions," (2015) 65 *Duke Law Journal* 569, at 575.

[2] The problem is commonly referred to as the "Byzantine Generals Problem," see: L. Lampert et al., "The Byzantine Generals Problem," (1982) 4 *ACM Transactions On Programming Languages And Systems* 382.

technologically guaranteeing performance. Claims as to the transformative potential of blockchain technologies are often embellished with ideological undertones that, at times, seem to contradict logical reasoning. "Decentralization" and "trustlessness" are presented as ultimate values that must be strived toward – even if their implementation leads to commercially undesirable results and may hinder the widespread adoption of blockchain technologies.

To evaluate the usability of blockchains as technologies underlying or enabling decentralized marketplaces, it is necessary to differentiate between different types of blockchains and to distinguish between lofty ideological claims as to what blockchains *will* do and what blockchains *can* actually do. It is also necessary to critically analyze the concept of decentralization. Purportedly, decentralization leads to equality, individual empowerment and a dispersal of power deriving from a detachment from traditional institutions such as banks, courts, etc. In many contexts, decentralization can thus be regarded as synonymous with disintermediation.

9.1.1 *Roadmap*

This chapter seeks to discredit the popular belief that blockchains will revolutionize or disrupt commerce. More specifically, it aims to clarify that blockchains *as such* cannot serve as a technology or ideology for the decentralization of online marketplaces. To this end, the chapter examines the interrelated concepts of decentralization, disintermediation, trustlessness and immutability. It is necessary to understand what those terms actually mean and how they affect actual, commercial practices.

The chapter commences with a broad description of blockchains and introduces the important division between public and private blockchains, to demonstrate that only the latter could potentially serve as a technology that could provide a user-friendly and secure transacting environment. It confronts the practical implications of decentralization, focusing on the fact that the absence of formalized control usually translates into an absence of formalized governance processes. This factor alone could be regarded as one of the main obstacles preventing blockchains from widespread commercial adoption. Next, countering a number of popular misunderstandings, the chapter describes the implications of blockchains (a) being databases and (b) being immutable. In order to demonstrate the practical difficulties of creating blockchain-based, decentralized marketplaces, the chapter concludes with the presentation of a use case: the peer-to-peer marketplace called OpenBazaar.

Two caveats are necessary. First, the sheer amount of technical terms and the complexity of the technology render it impossible to present an exhaustive analysis of the potential legal problems accompanying the commercial deployment of blockchains. Ironically, while this chapter criticizes generalizations and an undisciplined use of technical terminology, it can be accused of *some* generalizations and technological simplifications – if only due to space constraints. It is, for example, impossible to fully explore the legal implications of different types of distributed consensus or present the full range of smart contracts. Second, some arguments made in popular "blockchain discourse" can be accused of being incoherent or outright illogical. After all, they are often made by crypto-anarchists and/or coders with no background in law, economics and limited commercial experience.

9.2 What Are "Blockchains"?

There is no universal definition of *a* blockchain.[3] The original bitcoin blockchain is often described as a decentralized, peer-validated ledger providing a publicly visible, chronological and permanent record of all prior transactions. It bears emphasizing that the bitcoin blockchain was devised for a single purpose: the prevention of double spending of cryptocurrencies in a system without a centralized entity controlling the generation and/or transfer of such currencies.[4] It was not meant to support complex transactions or to serve as a technology-enabling marketplaces – only to disintermediate payments. The Ethereum blockchain, in contrast, was created to enable smart contracts, i.e. equip the blockchain with more complex business logic.[5] At the time of writing, there are hundreds of different blockchains.[6] They vary, amongst others, in their underlying consensus protocols, read-and-write permissions and block sizes.[7] Unsurprisingly, they also vary in their functionalities and thus in their ability to support specific commercial uses. Given that some blockchains do not have blocks,[8] in many instances it seems more appropriate to speak of distributed ledger technologies ("DLTs"), which denote a broader category of geographically dispersed, synchronized data stores.[9] Given the multitude of different types of blockchains and the number of configurations of various technological features, it is difficult to generalize. Technically, each statement regarding blockchains *as such* should be qualified with references to a specific blockchain. Consequently, each legal analysis must focus on the *type* of blockchain in question and on its intended use. Notwithstanding the foregoing, the bitcoin blockchain provides a useful point of reference for a discussion of other blockchains as its many of its core characteristics are in fact shared by other public blockchains. It also exemplifies the main tenets of "blockchain ideology." First and foremost, however, it is necessary to differentiate between public (permissionless) and private (permissioned) blockchains.[10] In most instances, the term "permissioned" is used interchangeably with "private" and "permissionless" with "public."[11] The main distinguishing criterion is whether the nodes processing

---

[3] See generally: Angela Walch, 'The Path of the Blockchain Lexicon (and the Law),' (2016) 36 *Review of Banking and Financial Law* 713.

[4] Satoshi Nakamoto, "Bitcoin: A Peer-to-Peer Electronic Cash System," https://bitcoin.org/bitcoin.pdf (2008), 1.

[5] Vitalik Buterin, "Ethereum White Paper: A Next Generation Smart Contract and Decentralized Application Platform," github.com/ethereum/wiki/wiki/White-Paper (2015).

[6] Melanie Swan, *Blockchain: Blueprint for a New Economy* (Sevastopol: O'Reilly, 2015), p. 9.

[7] See generally: Xiwei Xu *et al.*, "A Taxonomy of Blockchain-Based Systems for Architecture Design," *IEEE International Conference on Software Architecture (ICSA)*, Gothenburg, 2017, 243–252.

[8] Corda, a distributed ledger, developed by the R3 consortium, famously "abandoned" the concept of blocks; see generally: Richard Gendal Brown, James Carlyle, Ian Grigg, Mike Hearn Corda: An Introduction (2016), available at https://docs.corda.net/_static/corda-introductory-whitepaper.pdf

[9] *Distributed Ledger Technology: Beyond Blockchain*, UK Government, Office of Science (2016); R. Maull, Ph. Godsiff, C. Mulligan, A. Brown and B. Kewell, "Distributed Ledger Technology: Applications and Implications," (2017) 26(5) *Strategic Change* 481, at 483.

[10] A detailed explanation can be found in the White Paper published by the BitFury Group, *Public versus private blockchains Part 1: Permissioned blockchains*, https://bitfury.com/content/downloads/public-vs-private-pt1-1.pdf (2015), pp. 10–11; David Drescher, *Blockchain Basics: A Non-Technical Introduction in 25 Steps* (New York: Apress, 2017), p. 216.

[11] For example, Robert Lai and D. Lee Kuo Chuen, *Handbook of Blockchain, Digital Finance, and Inclusion, Volume 2* (London: Elsevier 2018), 147. Where a distinction is made, the difference between permissioned and permissionless blockchains seems to relate to the *authorization* of participating nodes to perform certain actions, and the difference between public and private blockchains seems to concern the *authentication* of the identity of participants.

transactions are predefined or unrestricted, i.e. whether anyone can become a node or whether operating a node requires permission. In this context, "node" refers to a computer running an instance of the relevant software that enables the participation in a given blockchain network;[12] "processing" denotes the ability to view, create, validate transactions and/or add transactions to the blockchain. The meaning of the term "transaction" may vary between different blockchains but, in principle, it denotes the transfer of crypto-currencies from one account to another or, more broadly, a change to the state of the blockchain.[13]

9.2.1 *Public Blockchains*

Public blockchains, such as bitcoin and Ethereum, allow anyone to join the network without disclosing their identity, subscribing to any form of system rules or agreeing on any terms of use. The only prerequisite of participation is downloading the relevant software. Public blockchains allow anyone to participate in the *consensus process*, the process for determining which transactions and which blocks are added to the chain. Public blockchains are generally decentralized: there is no single entity controlling what becomes a node or how the blockchain is operated or used. Public blockchains are not managed or maintained by anyone – they are managed and maintained by everyone. It is claimed that public blockchains replace centralized trust in a single entity controlling the system, with "cryptoeconomics – the combination of economic incentives and cryptographic verification using mechanisms such as proof-of-work or proof-of-stake, following a general principle that the degree to which someone can have an influence in the consensus process is proportional to the quantity of economic resources that they can bring to bear."[14] Consequently, public blockchains usually involve a native cryptocurrency, which constitutes an incentive mechanism for maintaining the ledger by expanding computational resources to mine consecutive blocks.[15] It is important to emphasize that in public blockchains the participants operating the nodes are anonymous (or pseudonymous). Consequently, it is difficult to hold them accountable, verify their trustworthiness or establish a reputational history. It is also claimed that in public blockchains it is not necessary to authenticate the participants operating individual nodes because there is, from a practical perspective, *no need to trust them*. The trust traditionally placed in people is "replaced" with trust in the code of the blockchain. Another feature of public blockchains bears mentioning: universal transparency. Their contents are visible to all – not just to participants, but to everybody in the world. This architecture was originally designed to prevent double-spending by making "everything visible to everybody." In many commercial situations this feature is, however, highly undesirable. This total transparency of the blockchain's contents contradicts such commercially and legally important requirements as confidentiality and privacy. Moreover,

---

[12] Andreas M. Antonopoulos, *Mastering Bitcoin*, 2nd edn. (Sevastopol: O'Reilly 2017), p. 50.

[13] Jim Gray, "The transaction concept: Virtues and limitations," in Proc. 7th Int. Conf. on Very Data Bases (1981), 144–154. 337; C. H. Papadimitriou, *The Theory of Concurrency Control* (New York: Computer Science Press, 1986), p. 401; J.D. Ullman, *Principles of Database and Knowledge Base Systems*, Vol.1 (New York: Computer Science Press, 1988), 300, 301, 337.

[14] Vitalik Buterin, "On Public and Private Blockchains," https://blog.ethereum.org/2015/08/07/on-public-and-private-blockchains/ (August 2015), 5.

[15] For a detailed description of this process, see: Antonopoulos, Mastering Bitcoin, 26.

the law or private agreements often prohibit certain information from being publicly visible or accessible.[16]

9.2.2 Private Blockchains

In contrast, private blockchains involve participants with known identities. One can become a node upon the satisfaction of certain requirements and/or upon approval by an administrator. As the identities of the participants are known, they can be held legally accountable. Consequently, private blockchains can rely on less computationally intensive consensus algorithms because the system itself needs not be "trustless." There is no need to trust the code if it is possible to trust the individual nodes. In principle, private blockchains can restrict transaction processing and visibility to a select group of participants who have clearly defined rights.[17] In other words, not all nodes are equal in what they can do and what they can see. Private blockchains can also restrict who can use or transact on the blockchain. Participants are required to subscribe to system rules and/or legal agreements that describe their respective rights and obligations. It is worth observing that Vitalik Buterin, the creator of the popular *public* blockchain Ethereum, admits that private blockchains enjoy multiple technical advantages, such as speed, scalability, the ability to change the rules or even reverse transactions. He also admits that when the participants are known, transactions are cheaper since they can be verified by a few trusted nodes. Moreover, given the ability to restrict who can see the contents of the blockchain and who is allowed to add transactions to it, private blockchains can provide both privacy and confidentiality.

9.2.3 Weighing the Risks and Benefits

Although Buterin acknowledges that private blockchains are better suited to support commercial dealings, he extols the "the philosophical virtues" of their public cousins: freedom, neutrality and openness. Purportedly, these features protect the participants of public blockchains from its core developers, who are often regarded as a source of centralization and thus a potential point of weakness. The reasoning seems to be that core developers could by coerced by governments or bribed by third parties to compromise the integrity of the blockchain. Consequently, limiting the range of actions that core developers are authorized to perform provides the so-called censorship resistance, i.e. it shields the blockchain from external and internal manipulation. Proponents of public blockchains want to preclude the possibility of any interference by eliminating all points of control or authority that could be potentially compromised – even if such points lie within the network and pertain to the very people who created it. This reasoning demonstrates the obsession with preserving the "purity" of public blockchains and ensuring their immunity from of centralized control. One could thus claim that private blockchains are constrained by their underlying ideology, i.e. they must display certain core characteristics irrespective of their commercial desirability or practical implications. In contrast, private blockchains seem more responsive to the practical needs of

---

[16] Chris Reed et al., "Beyond BitCoin – Legal Impurities and Off-Chain Assets," (2018) 26 *International Journal of Law and Information Technology* 160, at 170.

[17] David Yermack, "Corporate Governance and Blockchains," (2017) 21 *Review of Finance* 7, at 16.

commerce and can be equipped with different functionalities depending on their intended use. Unsurprisingly, most legal controversies and practical problems concern public blockchains because, as indicated, they can be characterized by a strict adherence to certain technical features, such as decentralization and anonymity, as well as the absence of legal terms regulating their use.

9.3 Dissecting Decentralization

Enthusiasts of public blockchains emphasize their decentralized character, i.e. the absence of a single entity operating and/or controlling the blockchain. As indicated, the blockchain narrative equates decentralization with disintermediation and user empowerment. It could be claimed that the effective decentralization of a system is predicated on it being trustless or, in other words, that decentralized marketplaces have only become possible with the advent of blockchains. The reasoning is that as all rules are enforced by distributed consensus there is no need to trust a central entity or one's counterparty because it is possible to trust the code of the blockchain itself. The code will infallibly execute the transaction. Interestingly, this reasoning ignores the fact that the ability to trust the code implies the need to trust the person(s) who created the code. The *trustlessness* of the blockchain depends on the *trustworthiness* of the coders. Blockchain enthusiasts seem to overlook the fact that blockchain-based market places (assuming for the time being that such are technically possible) replace traditional intermediaries, such as lawyers or banks, with a new type of intermediary: coders. Leaving aside these logical inconsistencies, it is necessary to examine certain theoretical, technical and practical aspects of decentralization.

9.3.1 *The Theory*

On a *theoretical* level, blockchain ideology seems to assume that there is a natural, technological progression toward decentralization. Technology-driven decentralization is associated with the empowerment of individual users. This idea revives earlier associations of equality and devolution of power with the beginnings of the Internet. The latter was supposed to constitute a universal, decentralized network infrastructure enabling a myriad of different activities and applications. Blockchain ideology reflects a general disappointment with the Internet in its present form – a conglomerate of centrally controlled silos, such as Amazon or eBay, that reinforce existing power structures and remain at the mercy of individual governments. Unsurprisingly, blockchain ideology abounds with anarchic-capitalistic and anti-authoritarian attitudes as well as a celebration of the individual.[18] It is generally overlooked, however, that technology-based user empowerment, implicit in the idea of peer-to-peer commerce, masks the consistent trend toward a technocratic society managed by an elite of tech-savvy individuals. As demonstrated below, only the latter can benefit from individual empowerment if such empowerment requires a high level of IT literacy. Claims that decentralization will result in the empowerment of all users must therefore be approached with caution.

---

[18] Ian Bogost, 'Cryptocurrency Might Be a Path to Authoritarianism,' (2017) *The Atlantic*, 30.

9.3.2 *The Technology*

On a *technical* level, decentralization guarantees the resilience of a system, which has no single point of control and thus no single point of failure. At times, however, *decentralization* (absence of a controlling entity) seems to be conflated with *distribution*, which denotes the geographical dispersal of infrastructure or, more broadly, a certain network architecture.[19] In the latter instance, decentralization is not necessarily related to the concept of control. One could have a decentralized network that is controlled by a single entity. Unsurprisingly, arguments promoting decentralization are often difficult to follow (and to attack!) because it may not be clear whether its primary value lies in its *technical* attributes or in its *ideological* underpinnings. There are many systems, which are both distributed *and* centralized. For example, Amazon Web Services is global cloud-based network supporting a range of services that is controlled by one entity, Amazon.[20] While it appears that in the context of public blockchains, the arguments seem less concerned with the infrastructure and focused on the lack of monopolized control, it is often difficult to differentiate between the *technological* advantages of decentralized public blockchains and their *philosophical* superiority. If one abstracts from a purely technical definition (i.e. one that is concerned with the architecture of a network), then it is possible to say that the main criterion in differentiating between decentralized and centralized systems lies in the concept of control. The latter can, in turn, be associated with decision-making.

Logically, people who make decisions about a system are in control of such system. In principle, in a centralized system one entity makes decisions. The popular blockchain narrative implies that in decentralized systems the ability to make decisions is granted to all or most participants of the system. While this latter feature seems *prima facie* attractive as it implies the devolution of power to individual users, it is frequently forgotten that in public blockchains the decentralized peer-to-peer decision-making refers to the automated and *deterministic* execution of a consensus algorithm. There is no room for discretion; there are no individual choices beyond what is prescribed *or permitted* by the algorithm. Each node in the system follows the same protocol – the choices are binary: accept blocks that fulfil the prescribed criteria and reject those that do not.

Contrary to what is implied by the blockchain ideology, the decentralization of control does not translate in the ability to make actual decisions about the system, how it operates, whether it requires improvement or whether certain users or transactions should be excluded or prohibited. Consequently, when speaking of consensus algorithms, one must not assume that such consensus derives from or reflects actual human agreement. Consensus in the technical sense is not consensus in the legal sense. As indicated below, in the context of public blockchains, distributed consensus is generally unrelated to any

---

[19] The concepts of "decentralization" and "distribution" can be analyzed from multiple angles, the point made herein that sometimes these terms are used interchangeably – even when they should not. In many instances, a decentralized system is a subset of distributed system. For a thorough explanation, see: Alexander R. Galloway, *Protocol: How Control Exists after Decentralization* (Cambridge: MIT Press, 2004); Paul Baran, *On distributed communications*, RAND Corp, 1964; www.rand.org/content/dam/rand/pubs/research_memoranda/2006/RM3420.pdf.

[20] Amazon Web Services (AWS) is a secure cloud services platform, offering compute power, database storage, content delivery and other functionality to help businesses scale and grow. It provides multiple infrastructure services that absolve e-commerce businesses from purchasing and maintaining such infrastructure themselves; see generally: aws.amazon.com.

formalized governance process, i.e. the setting and amending of rules governing how the system operates.

9.3.3 In Practice ...

On a *practical* level, in a decentralized marketplace, there is no single entity that controls access to and use of the marketplace but there is also no entity that is accountable for the maintenance of its underlying technology and no entity that is accountable for the manner the marketplace operates. Decentralization means that there is no one that can be held accountable in the event of transaction failure. A transaction failure can be attributable to a technical problem or to the fact that the other party fails to perform. In the event of a technical problem, there is no recourse against the platform operators because, theoretically, the platform is operated by all of its users. In the event the other party fails to perform, there is no dispute resolution mechanism prescribed by the platform operator and no protections commonly accompanying the online use of credit cards.[21] The problem is exacerbated by the fact that anyone can transact anonymously and, consequently, enforcing the contract in the event of breach poses practical problems. The practical disadvantages of decentralization become apparent when blockchains are to serve as a technology underlying or enabling decentralized marketplaces. At this stage, it is helpful to distinguish between *maintaining and controlling* the infrastructure underlying the marketplace and *transacting* on the marketplace.

Theoretically, in the case of the bitcoin blockchain (as in most public ledgers) nobody can control the infrastructure, but anybody can participate in maintaining the blockchain by becoming a miner or by running a full node for the purposes of block validation. Anybody can also use the system to transfer bitcoin, i.e. to transact. In both instances, the only prerequisites are technical, such as downloading certain software or, in the case of mining, controlling adequate computational resources. It is a question of individual choice whether one wants to maintain *and/or* transact on the network. In the case of traditional centralized platforms, such as Amazon or eBay, the said distinctions are unwarranted because the users are *technically incapable* to maintaining or controlling the technical infrastructure underlying the platform – they are only allowed to use it within the parameters prescribed by the respective terms of use. By definition, the marketplace is operated and controlled by the central entity, Amazon, eBay, google etc. As an aside, it seems doubtful whether the average Internet user opposes all centralized institutions and commercial intermediaries. Users generally do not analyze their relationships with Amazon or eBay in terms of trust or control but focus on the convenience of the shopping experience, the security of their payment information and the ability to seek recourse in the event of a transactional failure. Amazon and eBay guarantee (both technologically and contractually) that the platform will operate in a particular way and, to a large extent, protect the transacting parties from failed performance.[22] More importantly, they absolve the transacting parties from worrying about the intricacies of the underlying technology and make their services easy to use. Their centralized character notwithstanding, users can trust both Amazon and eBay – such trust being based on

---

[21] See below.

[22] In the case of Amazon, the company will generally resend the product if the consumer claims that it has not been delivered; eBay offers an insurance policy and a buyer refund policy as well as an elaborate and generally effective dispute resolution scheme.

the solid technological infrastructure operated by these companies and on their status of publicly listed companies. If one was to oppose such centralized marketplaces, it can be suspected that apart from purely ideological reasons, such opposition would derive from the very desire or need to stay anonymous or to trade in illegal or restricted goods.

9.4 Decentralization and Governance

The lack of centralized control translates into the broader problem of governance, that is, rule setting and amendment. It translates into the absence of any control or, alternatively, the emergence of informal or hidden control structures. The resulting problems are usually discussed under the label of blockchain governance. Public blockchains suffer from an inherent lack of governance because there is no one to create or modify the rules governing their operation. The rules embodied in the protocol of the blockchain are *enforced* by a distributed network of nodes in a deterministic and unbiased manner. It is unclear, however, who makes those rules and who has the authority to change them. It is often overlooked that the creation of rules is equally important as their enforcement.[23] To explain: decentralized consensus algorithms seem of limited value if there is no clear process how to improve them. It cannot be assumed that any blockchain can be perfect "at inception" and, unlike all other software, be immune to the need of subsequent modifications – be it to fix coding errors or to adapt the system to the evolving needs of its users. Setting certain rules in advance and making them immutable by encoding them in the blockchain does not imply that such rules are optimal. A formalized governance process must exist to maintain and improve the code. This seems of particular importance for a technology enabling commercial exchanges and transfers of value. Private ledgers are often equipped with governance processes and expressly assume that the system will undergo subsequent amendments.[24] In contrast, public ledgers place absolute reliance on the code (i.e. the ledger itself) and on the vague concept of community.

9.4.1 *Clarifying the Terms*

The popular blockchain narrative downplays the importance of a formalized governance process. Some clarifications are required to convey the argument.[25] *First*, governance *by* the network must be distinguished from governance *of* the network. The former concerns the rules governing the range of actions permitted by the underlying protocol or, more broadly, what can be done on a particular blockchain. The latter concerns the rules governing the blockchain itself, i.e. what rules are embodied in the code running the blockchain. While technical and legal writing usually focus on the former, the rules governing the network are equally important. After all, they determine what is enforced

---

[23] Vili Lehdonvirta and Ali Robleh, "Governance and Regulation," in: Mark Walport (ed.), *Distributed Ledger Technologies: Beyond Blockchain* (London: UK Government Office for Science, 2016), pp. 40–45.

[24] For example, the creators of Tezos, a blockchain-based smart contract platform, emphasize the need for constant innovation: the code must be subject to a controlled process of improvement to remain competitive and, in the case of blockchains supported by a native cryptocurrency, to maintain the value of such currency. Consequently, the Tezos protocol specifies a procedure to change the protocol, including amendments to the amendment procedure itself; see: L. H. Goodman, "Tezos: A Self-Amending Crypto Ledger," Position Paper tezos.com/static/papers/position_paper.pdf (2014) (accessed June 12, 2019).

[25] It must be conceded that while this discussion can be accused of some oversimplifications, it conveys the sheer complexity of issues involved.

by the consensus protocol and what consensus protocol is implemented in the first place. In other words, the rules comprising the governance *of* the network determine the governance *by* the network.

Generally, governance *of* the network can be equated with secondary, or meta-rules, while governance *by* the network can be equated with primary rules.[26] *Second*, certain rules exist on-chain, and are implemented in the code of the blockchain. Examples are the rules determining the validity of blocks or transactions. Other rules exist off-chain, in the real world, and are not part of its code. Examples are the rules embodied in the legal frameworks underlying private blockchains. Such rules establish, amongst others, who is allowed to amend, access and use the blockchain in question. Consequently, on-chain governance would refer to the implementation of secondary rules at the system level. There are numerous practical obstacles to on-chain governance. From a technical perspective, assuming that governance rules display some level of complexity (similar to that found in constitutions and master agreements regulating complex legal relationships), they would be difficult to implement in code. Complex legal and commercial relationships do not lend themselves to an easy translation into a series of binary, if-then statements. Moreover, on-chain governance would also require on-chain computation to ensure the unbiased, deterministic execution of the rules. The computational capabilities of blockchains are, however, extremely limited. Lastly, the rules comprised in on-chain governance would have to be perfect and comprehensive because once encoded they would become immutable, i.e. impossible to modify. The latter problem alone renders on-chain governance impracticable, at least in the context of public ledgers. The very purpose of governance is, after all, to regulate how changes are made – including changes to the governance process itself. Due to these constraints, only off-chain governance seems practicable. Consequently, secondary rules determining the functioning of the blockchain, including its potential modifications, must exist in the real world.

9.4.2 *The Importance of Off-Chain Governance*

It is noteworthy that public blockchains do not have an express, formalized off-chain governance system. The existence of such governance would imply that somebody *is* in control and thus, from an ideological perspective, contradict the ethos of decentralization and "trustlessness." The latter is tied to the immutability of the code and the impossibility of outside interference. The absence of formalized secondary rules determining how the primary rules are made and amended does not mean, however, that public blockchains have no off-chain governance at all. It only means that such governance structures are hidden and informal, often manifesting themselves by references to the vague concept of "community." Enthusiasts of public blockchains ignore the fact that a formalized process of off-chain governance would create transparency as to who can make changes and how. Indirectly, it would also establish checks on core developers and legitimize any actual changes made to the blockchain. For it must not be forgotten that even the two most prominent public blockchains, bitcoin and Ethereum, have been changed on multiple occasions. Examples are the

---

[26] Ugo Pagallo, 'The Legal Challenges of Big Data: Putting Secondary Rules First in the Field of EU Data Protection,' (2017) 3 *European Data Protection Law Review*, at 36.

bitcoin forks following the block size debate[27] and the controversial Ethereum hard fork.[28]

In each instance, the forking of the blockchain has raised doubts as to the immutable and trustless character of blockchains. In each instance, it revealed the existence of *hidden* control structures within the respective bitcoin and Ethereum communities. Unsurprisingly, it has been observed that the absence of off-chain governance rules potentially prevents the mainstream, commercial use of public blockchains. In sum, on-chain rules require off-chain rules.[29] There must be a framework for amending the code of the blockchain. Irrespective of their technological sophistication, blockchains that lack formalized off-chain governance promote opaque power structures and prevent block-chain-based systems from adopting to new regulations and to the demands of the market. The unconvinced reader is invited to imagine a situation where the technology underlying Amazon or eBay remained unchanged from the late 1990s or where either company was incapable to respond to the requests of regulators and law enforcement. It can be suspected that neither marketplace could have survived.

9.5 Blockchains Are . . . Databases

It is rarely appreciated that, at a technical level, blockchains are *databases* or, as commonly stated, cryptographically secured ledgers. Ledgers and databases are collections of data, reflections of transactions occurring *outside* of them. Logically, transactions do not happen "on the pages" of ledgers and, while ledgers can record transactions or contain information about transactions, they cannot enable or execute transactions. It must be conceded that unlike traditional ledgers that only *record* assets or events, some blockchains are capable of generating and transferring a limited range of crypto-tokens. They are, in some sense, capable of executing simple transactions – but only if the term "transaction" is interpreted extremely narrowly, as the ability to create changes to the state of the ledger. In principle, blockchains are "only" *databases* with extremely limited computational capabilities. Apart from a limited number of native scripts, no code executes *within* the blockchain. Blockchains, by definition, have very limited computational capabilities. To state that a blockchain *in itself* could support a decentralized marketplace is tantamount to stating that amazon could be run "on" an excel spreadsheet or that the eBay ecosystem is nothing but a giant database. In reality, even a simple e-commerce website consists of a multi-tiered system made of different types of servers, networking equipment and databases. Consequently, blockchains cannot be regarded as transactional platforms – just like a ledger or register cannot *by itself* transact and move assets. For blockchains to serve as the technology underlying decentralized marketplaces,

---

[27] The ongoing bitcoin block size debate concerns the fact that the size of each block in bitcoin is limited to 1mb, resulting in slow transaction processing times and high transaction costs. For over a year, the bitcoin "community" argued over the expansion of the block size. In 2017, the debate resulted in the creation of Bitcoin Cash and Bitcoin Gold in 2017, different versions of bitcoin with bigger block sizes.

[28] The so-called DAO hack, which concerned the exploitation of a vulnerability existing in the code of the decentralized, autonomous investment vehicle and resulted in the "theft" of over $50 million in Ether. After much informal debate, the Ethereum community decided to rewrite the Ethereum blockchain in order to restore the funds. The immutability of the blockchain became questionable. The decision process was opaque, and part of the community forked creating Ethereum Classic.

[29] The Tezos and EOS blockchains have attempted to implement on-chain secondary rules, but such rules logically require an external, off-chain, framework on which they are to be designed.

their functionalities must be extended. This, however, requires adding protocol layers *on top* of them.[30] Blockchains cannot be analyzed in isolation but must be seen as one of many components of a larger ecosystem. This is made clear, for example, by the hyperledger architecture, which provides the technical framework for private ledgers and distinguishes, amongst others, between the consensus layer (which confirms the correctness of transactions that constitute a block), the smart contract layer (which processes transaction requests and determines transaction validity), the data store abstraction (which allows different data stores to be used by other components) and application programming interfaces (APIs – which enable other modules to interface to the blockchain).[31] The fact that blockchains are "only" data structures that require additional components to support or enable commercial exchanges has important practical implications.

That the blockchain is trustless, secure, immutable etc. does not imply that the other components in the system share these characteristics. The features of the blockchain are not inherited by the technologies or processes that connect to or write data into the blockchain. To illustrate: a blockchain can be regarded as a perfect piece of bread – fresh, tasty and nutritious. We rarely, however, eat bread by itself. We eat sandwiches. Hence, we add butter, cheese, pickles or lettuce. If any of these additional ingredients is spoiled, the whole sandwich becomes inedible – quality of the bread notwithstanding. The point is simple: a database by itself cannot support or serve as a transactional platform – its technological sophistication notwithstanding. Moreover, the attributes of the database must be distinguished from the attributes of the other components of the ecosystem. Logically, this reduces the value of blockchain-based platforms. The attentive reader would have noticed that this observation also renders the title of this chapter questionable – blockchains cannot by themselves support marketplaces, whether decentralized or not.

9.6 Blockchains Are . . . Immutable

Another selling point of blockchains is their "immutability." The term can relate to three distinct situations: the transactions recorded in the blockchain, other contents recorded in the blockchain and the code of the blockchain itself. In the first instance, it is stated that once a transaction is accepted into a block and once a block is appended to the ledger, it cannot be changed or reversed. This feature is commonly associated with guaranteed performance, finality of payment or, in the context of smart contracts, self-enforcement. The second situation concerns the fact that once any data is inscribed into the blockchain, it cannot be changed. Unsurprisingly, although their original purpose was to disintermediate payments and create an independent payment mechanism, blockchains are often regarded as a perfect record-keeping technology.[32] The third instance concerns the fact that (in most public blockchains) it is impossible to change their underlying consensus algorithm. In this context, immutability may be regarded as a component or precursor of "trustlessness" and "censorship resistance."

---

[30] Antonopoulos, Mastering Bitcoin, 218.
[31] Andreas See: www.hyperledger.org/wp-content/uploads/2018/07/HL_Whitepaper_IntroductiontoHyperledger .pdf.
[32] Angela Walch, 'The Path of the Blockchain', 735–736.

Immutability, however, introduces numerous problems. Moreover, its practical implications are rarely understood. First, not all blockchains are immutable. Private blockchains may give certain participants the right to edit the contents of a block, reverse transactions or even alter the underlying code. Second, "immutability" implies that something cannot be changed. In practice, however, the code of the two most prominent public blockchains, Ethereum and bitcoin, have been altered by means of forks.[33] Moreover, public blockchains remain at the risk of 51 percent attacks, which create the theoretical possibility of reversing transactions, double-spending funds and/or interfering with whatever information was inscribed in them.[34] Third, when speaking of blockchains as a perfect record-keeping technology, the immutability of the recorded data is incorrectly associated with its veracity and authenticity. Phrases like "uncensored truth" or "single source of truth" ignore the fact that inscribing data in a block does not guarantee its accuracy or authenticity.[35]

At this point it is helpful to distinguish between on-chain and off-chain assets. Broadly speaking, on-chain assets refer to assets that exist solely on the blockchain. Examples are crypto-currencies, such as bitcoin, or crypto-tokens, as exemplified by the ERC-20 standard.[36] Both are regarded as *native* to their respective blockchains. Technically, blockchains are only capable of correctly recording the generation and/ or transfer of on-chain assets. Only the latter can be validated by the underlying consensus mechanism. Off-chain assets are physical objects or other intangible assets that exist in the real world, such as cars, shares or cows. There is no natural connection between such assets and blockchains. Consequently, when a blockchain must record or track the transfer or creation of off-chain assets, it becomes necessary to associate such asset with the blockchain, usually by tagging and mapping it onto the blockchain. It is also necessary to contractually agree that such mapping will be regarded as authoritative by all participants. Even then, however, the blockchain can only record who *should* own the asset or where it *should* be but it cannot control or guarantee its actual physical location or lawful possession. Contrary to popular belief, consensus protocols are technically incapable of validating any off-chain events or assets. They cannot confirm whether the record has been created by the rightful owner or whether the rightful owner registered the correct asset. The veracity of the record depends on the trustworthiness of third parties: those who tag, map and register off-chain assets. Blockchain records, like all records, are only as trustworthy as their creators. In the words of one author, "the idea of a 'trustless' system is misleading when it comes to blockchain applications beyond cryptocurrency."[37] The problem is popularly

---

[33] Moreover, at the time of writing Ethereum is transitioning from a proof-or-work to a proof-of-stake consensus algorithm.

[34] Bitcoin forked into two separate ledgers in March 2013, with one half of the network adding blocks to one version of the chain and the other half adding to the other. For the next six hours, there were effectively two bitcoin networks operating at the same time, each with its own version of the transaction history. Ethereum famously split into two as a result of the DAO hack to revert the ledger to its state before the hack.

[35] This popular misconception might be attributable to the lack of understanding as to what facts can be technically validated by consensus algorithms; for a detailed description of validation criteria, see Antonopoulos, Mastering Bitcoin, pp. 217–219.

[36] The ERC-20 token standard enables the so-called Initial Coin Offerings, or "ICOs." There are different types of tokens, some of which may classify as securities.

[37] Victoria Louise Lemieux, 'Trusting Records: Is Blockchain Technology the Answer?' (2016) 26 *Records Management Journal*.

referred to as "garbage in, equals garbage out"[38] – if the recorded data is incorrect, the record is incorrect. The quality of the record-keeping mechanism changes nothing in this regard. Moreover, even if a particular off-chain asset was initially recorded correctly, the record may become incorrect if, as a result of a real-world transaction, it is transferred to another party but neither the transferor nor the transferee register the change. It is noteworthy that in the case of on-chain asset, it is impossible to transfer it without changing the record. As a result, the popular claim that blockchains allow greater certainty regarding legal rights must be confined to on-chain assets. Otherwise, the blockchain cannot ensure that its contents are correct. Lastly, immutability is detrimental in the event the record requires reversal, amendment or deletion, as may be required by laws or regulations.[39] In sum, immutability seems of little value if the recorded data is incorrect and if it is impossible to correct the record.[40]

9.7 The Transactional Layer: "Smart Contracts"

Many technical descriptions describe smart contracts as an additional layer representing the business logic in a blockchain ecosystem or – extending blockchains "to a platform for decentralized execution of general-purpose applications."[41] Purportedly, smart contracts reduce transaction costs by simplifying enforcement and, most importantly, protect the transacting parties from breach by technologically guaranteeing performance.[42] Seemingly then, by reducing counterparty risk without reliance on intermediaries, smart contracts appear to be the perfect technology to enable decentralized marketplaces or, more specifically, to serve as a transactional layer on top of blockchain databases. Paradoxically, however, a closer analysis reveals that smart contracts increase certain transactional risks and thus the need for "traditional" contracts that would allocate such risks. Before proceeding, it is worth observing that legal analyses of smart contracts are impeded by a multiplicity of conflicting definitions and descriptions of the term. Smart contracts are described as "systems which automatically move digital assets according to arbitrary pre-specified rules,"[43] "full-fledged programs that run on blockchains and have their correct execution enforced by the consensus protocol,"[44] or the embedding of legal terms in hardware and software to prevent breach or to control assets digitally.[45] Some

---

[38] Avi Mizrahi, "Factom CEO: Blockchain-Based Transparent Mortgages Can Restore Trust in Markets," *Finance Magnates* (March 3, 2016), retrieved from www.financemagnates.com/cryptocurrency/interview-2/factom-ceo-blockchain-based-transparent-mortgages-can-restore-trust-in-markets/

[39] Notably, Art. 16 of Regulation (EU) 2016/679 of the European Parliament and of the Council of 27 April 2016, gives data subjects the right to rectification of personal data, while Art. 17 gives data subjects the right to obtain the erasure of their data if certain conditions are fulfilled.

[40] Reed et al., "Beyond BitCoin," 171

[41] Igor Nikolic et al., Cit., at https://arxiv.org/pdf/1802.06038.pdf (2018) (accessed June 12, 2019).

[42] Gavin J. Wood, "Ethereum: A Secure Decentralised Generalised Transaction Ledger," proclaiming the impartiality of autonomous enforcement by code, available at http://gavwood.com/paper.pdf (2015); for a broader review of smart contracts, see Eliza Mik, 'Smart Contracts: Terminology, Technical Limitations and Real-World Complexity,' (2017) 8 *Law, Innovation & Technology* 1.

[43] Vitalik Buterin, "Ethereum White Paper."

[44] Loi Luu et al., "Making Smart Contracts Smarter," in *CCS'16, October 24–28, 2016, Vienna, Austria*, 254.

[45] Nick Szabo, "Smart Contracts: Formalizing and Securing Relationships on Public Networks," (1997) 2 (9) *First Monday*.

descriptions imply that smart contracts have legal implications[46] or that even if seen in purely technical terms, smart contracts can replace traditional contracts. Other definitions refrain from any legal references and describe smart contracts as blockchain-specific computer programs. Consequently, any analysis of smart contracts requires an in-depth review of the *specific* use case and/or implementation. As in the case of blockchains, it is impossible to generalize and assume that all smart contracts share the same set of common features. Despite their glorification as technology-enabling decentralized exchanges, smart contracts are accompanied by numerous technological problems.

9.7.1 *Problems with the Code*

With the exception of the bitcoin blockchain, which effectively equates smart contracts with transactions (i.e. transfers of bitcoins between "accounts" when the conditions in locking scripts are fulfilled),[47] smart contracts usually "sit on top" of and remain independent from the underlying blockchain. Consequently, the quality or correctness of their code is not validated by the consensus algorithm that guarantees the trustless character of the blockchain itself. Despite their constant glorification as a source of legal and commercial certainty, smart contracts are susceptible to the same problems as any other computer program. More specifically, the smart contract code may contain programming errors, both accidental, which are statistically inevitable, and intentional. As smart contracts control value in the form of cryptocurrencies or crypto-tokens, there are non-trivial financial incentives to deliberately create and exploit such errors. The fact that the code of the smart contract is publicly visible is generally irrelevant because it is extremely difficult to establish how a smart contract will operate without actually running it. The ability to inspect the code does not guarantee its quality. To re-emphasize: the qualities of the blockchain – assuming for the sake of argument that a given blockchain is secure, reliable and immutable – are not automatically shared by a smart contract operating *on* the blockchain. In order to trust the code of the smart contract, it is necessary to trust the person who created it: the coder.

Blockchain enthusiasts overlook the fact that software used in banking and finance transactions is rigorously tested for years before deployment.[48] The fact that in public blockchains such as Ethereum anybody is allowed to create smart contracts and put them on the blockchain seems attractive from the perspective of openness as it exemplifies the spirit of democratized access and equality. Once it is realized, however, that this open code is supposed to support commercial transactions which include payment data, the attraction fades. It can be doubted that platforms such as amazon or eBay would have thrived (or even survived) if the programs supporting the transaction infrastructure could be created and implemented by random users. Unsurprisingly, technical literature openly recognizes that smart contracts present security challenges.[49] Apart from the problems concerning the code of the smart contract, additional concerns may derive

---

[46] See e.g. Fan Zhang et al., "Town Crier: An Authenticated Data Feed for Smart Contracts," (2016) *Proceedings of the 2016 ACM SIGSAC Conference on Computer and Communications Security* 270.

[47] Antonopoulos, Mastering Bitcoin, pp. 128, 129, 137.

[48] See generally: the Principles for Financial Services Infrastructure, issued by a subcommittee of the Bank for International Settlements, www.bis.org/cpmi/info_pfmi.htm

[49] Kevin Delmolino et al., "Step by Step towards Creating a Safe Smart Contract: Lessons and Insights from a Cryptocurrency Lab," (2015) Cryptology ePrint Archive, Report 2015/460.

from the underlying blockchain. It has been observed that the execution of smart contracts in Ethereum (and in bitcoin) is vulnerable to manipulations by arbitrary adversaries, predominantly with regard to the selection and order of transactions.[50] Additional problems may derive from the programming language(s). Smart contracts are written in a new ecosystem of languages and runtime environments, each of which may introduce its own security concerns.

9.7.2 Encoding Obligations

Another subset of problems derives from the fact that the smart contract may incorrectly express the agreement, a problem that pertains to the difficulty of translating natural language onto code or expressing contractual obligations as a sequence of binary if-then statements. Two possible scenarios can be envisaged. In the first, which seems less likely on a mass scale, the parties decide to embody their agreement in code and create their own smart contract. Assuming that the parties are not coders, they have to delegate development to a third party who may be incapable of correctly capturing the original agreement into smart contract code. The coder may not understand the nuances of legal language and fail to correctly translate the agreement into a computer-readable form. The parties themselves will, however, not be able to determine the correctness of the "translation," short of employing other coders for verification. Alternatively, in the event that a ready-made smart contract resides on the blockchain awaiting invocation, its coder may (intentionally or not) misrepresent its functionality. In both situations, the smart contract does not match the original agreement and will not function in the way the transacting parties intended it to function. In addition, the smart contract may be incomplete in the sense that the rules embodied therein may not cover all possible scenarios that might arise during its lifetime. It must be observed that once smart contracts are deployed, they cannot be upgraded to reflect changing circumstances or amended to fix errors which became apparent during their operation. This highlights the importance of having a clear governance process that specifically prescribes what to do in such instance.

9.7.3 Interfacing with the Real World

The last set of challenges concerns the fact that neither blockchains nor smart contracts can directly interface with events occurring off-chain, i.e. in the real world.[51] Technically, the "execution environment of a blockchain is self-contained as it can only access information in the blockchain. Information about external systems is not directly accessible."[52] This limitation is overcome by means of the so-called oracles, i.e. third-party service providers that provide information about the external world. And so, whenever payment is conditioned on contractual performance that occurs off-chain, such as the delivery of a physical object, the smart contract must contact an oracle to verify that the performance has in fact taken place. It is noteworthy that oracles do not feed such information directly into the blockchain but "only" sign the unlocking scripts

---

[50] Luu, "Making Smart Contracts Smarter," 2.
[51] Antonopoulos, Mastering Bitcoin, 125, 132.
[52] Xiwei Xu et al., "A Taxonomy of Blockchain-Based Systems."

with their private key when an off-chain event is established as true. Moreover, oracles do not create or verify the information about such events themselves but obtain it from external data sources. Consequently, the parties to a smart contract must agree on a trustworthy oracle and on a trustworthy source of information.[53] Most importantly, the parties must agree beforehand that they will accept the information provided by their chosen oracle (and its data source) as true. Needless to say, the necessity to rely on oracles and external data sources destroys the decentralized character of public blockchains. Each oracle must be regarded as a "pocket" of centralization.

9.8 A Case Study: OpenBazaar

The practical challenges of decentralized marketplaces, including the difficulties arising from the lack of clear governance mechanisms and the impossibility to rely on, or *trust*, technology itself, can be illustrated by a description of OpenBazaar ("OB"). OB is an open source project aiming to create a fully decentralized marketplace for peer-to-peer e-commerce that has no transactions fees and no restrictions as to *what* can be traded and *who* can trade on the platform.[54] While OB cannot be described as a pure blockchain-based platform, it relies on a number of blockchain-related technologies to enable transactions, store data and secure payments.[55] It also reflects the common ideological objectives of blockchain enthusiasts: decentralization, disintermediation and the (purported) empowerment of the individual. It must be noted that while OB is not a company or organization but only "free open source code," an entity called OB1 acts as the core developer leading the evolution of the marketplace. Although OB1 is incorporated like any other traditional company and has received substantial venture capital funding, it seeks to maintain a public image aligned with the mainstream "blockchain ideology" by claiming to be a "fully distributed company" with "eleven team members from around the world."[56] The exact role and hence liability of OB1 remains unclear.

9.8.1 A Broad Description

As emphasized on the OB website, present e-commerce is centralized by such companies as eBay or Amazon, which restrict who can transact in the marketplace, what products can be traded, impose transaction fees and limit payment types to credit cards or PayPal. It is also observed that eBay or Amazon harvest personal information, which is often used for commercial purposes. In contrast, OB "returns power to the users. Instead of buyers and sellers going through a centralized intermediary, OpenBazaar connects them directly and enables them to exchange any type of goods. There being no intermediating entity – there are no fees and no trading restrictions."[57] Moreover, anyone can use the platform, remain anonymous and only reveal the personal information one chooses. In effect, OB

---

[53] Examples of oracles are: Reality Keys and Oraclize.
[54] See at https://openbazaar.zendesk.com/hc/en-us/articles/208020193-What-is-OpenBazaar-
[55] Payments consist in cryptocurrencies; transactions use the so-called Ricardian contracts and are secured by a bitcoin-specific multi-signature script. Moreover, OB also relies on the so-called InterPlanetary File System, or IPFS, for distributed content delivery. IPFS is a protocol and network designed to create a content-addressable, peer-to-peer method of storing and sharing hypermedia in a distributed file system.
[56] Details at https://ob1.io/about.html
[57] Details at https://openbazaar.org/blog/The-Beginners-Guide-to-Buying-Goods-Services-and-Cryptocurrency-on-OpenBazaar/

claims to provide a virtually anonymous, unrestricted platform for peer-to-peer e-commerce, both for private users and for businesses.[58] To this end, OB departs from the classic client-server model deployed by virtually all e-commerce marketplaces, such as amazon or eBay. OB is not a website that can be accessed from a browser, but a peer-to-peer application run by a decentralized network of nodes operated by the individual users of the platform. To transact on the OB marketplace, users must visit its website to download an OB server (i.e. the back-end application allowing the network to function) and an OB client (i.e. the visual front-end application enabling users to communicate and control the server), both of which are installed locally on the user's machine.[59]

From a technical perspective, "all stores and listings are hosted on the vendor's own computers and 'reseeded' by other network users." Consequently, unlike amazon or eBay, which do not require the parties *using* their platform to *maintain* the infrastructure underlying the platform, OB associates the participation in the marketplace with its maintenance – one cannot transact on OB if one does not run an OB node. The main advantage of this set-up lies in the technical resilience of the network, which is extremely difficult to shut down or interfere with. This is guaranteed by the absence of centralized servers, which are potential points of failure or interference. Moreover, individual users are technically in control of their nodes, accounts and transaction information. The disadvantage of this structure, however, lies in the fact that sellers operating shopfronts must keep their computers online permanently. While there are technical solutions to this "problem," they do require a relatively high level of computer literacy. It is also worth noting that as OB's source code is available on public repository, individual users as well as third parties are able to participate in developing the technology underlying the marketplace, be it by fixing bugs or by creating applications (such as wallets or search engines) for potential integration into OB.[60] Given the absence of a central entity managing the system as well as a formalized governance process, it is not clear who decides which improvements or applications find its way into the actual code of the platform.[61] In other words, apart from operating the nodes maintaining the network underlying the decentralized marketplace, users can *at least theoretically* participate in its ongoing development.

Needless to say, none of the traditional e-commerce platforms enables its users to code for the platform or otherwise become technically involved. In the case of OB, the ability (and obligation!) to directly participate in the operation and development of the marketplace comes at a price – no-one is responsible or accountable for its technical functioning. This is confirmed in the OB's terms of use, which state, amongst others, that OB is a network "without any central organization controlling the platform. This means you are responsible for your own activity on the network." Given that there is no central entity

---

[58] At the time of writing, the author can confirm the ability to create an account under a fictitious name, from a fictitious location and to accept the bitcoin equivalent of virtually any currency in the world. It can also be confirmed that there are no restrictions as to what products can be traded on OB, which, unsurprisingly, results in a large number of listings of illicit drugs.

[59] Users can choose to run the server elsewhere. The *client* is run on the user's own computer to connect to their server, but the *server* doesn't need to be run on a user's own computer.

[60] See at https://openbazaar.org/applications/

[61] The fact that the code is open source, and that third parties are permitted to develop code for the OB marketplace, does not mean that everyone has commit access to the *actual* code running the platform. Commit access implies the ability to change or add to the code already in operation and is usually limited to a select group of individuals who are the original or main developers of the code, i.e. "core developers."

responsible for the functioning of the marketplace, it is not clear what would happen if one of the components of the system malfunctioned. The resilience of the decentralized network underlying the marketplace must not be mistaken for the resilience, reliability and adequacy of its other components, such as wallets, search engines or the graphical user interface. Theoretically, if any component of the system malfunctions or requires redevelopment to meet changing demands (e.g. a change in regulations), there is no formal process of addressing such issues. The terms also state that "the OpenBazaar community of developers has worked hard to deliver a free platform for trade to the world. But as with any software, bugs will be found. The developers are not responsible for any monetary loss associated with problems in the software."[62] As an aside, it can be observed that if OB itself is "only code" and OB1 is not "officially" in control of the marketplace, it is unclear who the parties to the contract, if any, governed by those terms of use. One can only assume that the relevant clause aims at protecting the individual developers of the code. In this context, it is also interesting to observe that when creating individual storefronts sellers are also encouraged to "equip" their individual storefronts with legal terms of use. The mere existence of such terms, both for the benefit of OB and for the benefit of individual sellers, seems to contradict the (purportedly) super-jurisdictional character of the marketplace. After all, blockchain ideology carries the notion that any blockchain-based system is global in nature and "transcends" the law. From this perspective, there is little point to rely on legal terms if such terms, by definition, require recourse to traditional, *real-world* legal institutions. Moreover, the enforceability of such terms requires the de-anonymization of the transacting parties – a point seemingly forgotten by whoever equipped the OB marketplace with the "terms of use."

9.8.2 *Payment and Dispute Resolution*

Returning to the main discussion, the most interesting aspect of the decentralized marketplace lies in its transacting mechanisms. At present, OB supports payment in three cryptocurrencies: bitcoin, bitcoin cash and Zcash. This embodies the popular bitcoin narrative of giving people "more control over their own money." The accompanying inconvenience and high transaction costs accompanying the use of many cryptocurrencies are conveniently disregarded. More importantly, users cannot benefit from the protections commonly accompanying credit card payments, such as liability limitations in the event of unauthorized use of payment information or chargebacks in the event of non-performance. From the buyers' perspective, the inability to seek protection from their issuing banks is aggravated by the fact that OB itself does not provide any form of buyer protection – apart from the questionable mechanism of "moderated payments."

OB's payment process reflects the popular ideology that contractual performance can be secured by technological means. OB enables two types of payments: direct and "moderated." In the case of direct payments, buyers send bitcoin directly to vendors. This method is described by OB as "risky" because once bitcoins are sent, the payment cannot be reversed and it may not be possible to seek recourse against dishonest vendors. After all, both parties are allowed to sign up under fictitious names and the discovery of the IP address may not suffice to track down the defaulting counter-party. Consequently, OB recommends this method only if the seller trusts the vendor and only if the

---

[62] The terms only become visible during the download and installation process.

transaction involves small amounts. OB also encourages buyers to leave reviews on vendors and advises users to contact the other party before the purchase "to confirm they are responsive, both within OpenBazaar and through other means, e.g. email."[63] In the case of moderated payments, buyers add a third party to the transaction, a so-called moderator, to assist in the event of disputes. In moderated payments, which are practically synonymous with OB's dispute resolution method, the price of the goods is paid into escrow. This mechanism of securing payment relies on the bitcoin-specific "multi-signature" address, which is jointly controlled by the buyer, the seller and the moderator.[64] For the funds to be released, any two of these three parties must agree and provide their signatures. If either the buyer or the seller commences a dispute, the moderator determines which party prevails and releases the funds accordingly.

Two points bear emphasizing. First, moderators receive a percentage of the transaction called a dispute fee. These fees are displayed when selecting a moderator. It is questionable, however, whether persons who are effectively adjudicating disputes should have *transaction-specific* financial incentives. This not only contradicts well-established principles of adjudication but may also result in the exclusion of disputes involving smaller amounts. More importantly, moderated payments reintroduce transactions costs into the marketplace – unless the parties trust each other or are willing to risk non-performance, they will logically opt for this payment method. In other words, OB does not eliminate transaction costs but shifts them to a different stage in the transaction. It also burdens buyers with repetitive decisions whether to opt for moderated or direct payments. To save on the costs of moderation, users may decide to invest resources into investigating the trustworthiness of the other party. Again, OB fails to recognize that such investigations *are* transaction costs. Second, the viability of moderated payments is predicated on the trustworthiness of the moderator. Technically, anyone can become a moderator or, given that anyone can create multiple pseudonymous accounts, pretend to be multiple moderators. The OB website advises that in choosing a moderator, the parties should "do their due diligence," including "asking around," gauging the responsiveness of potential moderators and monitoring them on Slack.[65] After all, if a chosen moderator is unresponsive, both parties and the funds may be indefinitely locked.

In practice, as admitted by OB1, sellers and moderators have often colluded (or were the same person) to initiate disputes after receiving orders. To remedy the situation, OB1 has introduced a "verified moderator" program. Verified moderators are users publicly endorsed by OB1 and "non-OB1 contributors and developers," to be trustworthy.[66] The verification requirements are complex and require candidates to be technology literate. To become "verified," moderators must associate their OB node to other verifiable

---

[63] More details at https://openbazaar.zendesk.com/hc/en-us/articles/115002763971-Who-protects-users-on-OpenBazaar-

[64] As described on the blog: "OpenBazaar manages the counter-party risks of online trade with Bitcoin (and soon other cryptocurrencies) using multisignature escrow transactions. The buyer, seller, and a third party 'moderator' create an address that requires 2-of-3 signatures to release funds. Once the address is created, the buyer transfers their funds to the multi-signature address. Normally, the funds are released to the seller if the buyer receives the good or service, or the seller can refund the transaction back to the buyer and cancel the order. If the buyer or seller have problems with the order, they can initiate the dispute resolution process. The moderator investigates the situation, and co-signs with the winning party to release the funds." See: Verified Moderators, Increasing trust in the OpenBazaar network, (date) https://medium.com/open bazaarproject/verified-moderators-c83ea2f2c7f3.

[65] See at www.openbazaar.org/blog/how-to-choose-a-good-moderator-on-openbazaar/

[66] All quotes refer to the blogpost above.

identities via Keybase, a publicly visible directory of cryptographic keys that maps social media identities to encryption keys and cryptocurrency wallets,[67] to "establish *provable* links to other social media account to signal trust and confidence to users on the network."[68] Moderators must also prepare a policy statement of their services, digitally signed with their Keybase account. According to OB1, this policy statement "will create a fraud-proof [sic] of the verified moderator's dispute resolution policy, availability, out-of-network communication channels etc."[69] Candidates must provide OB1 with their Keybase profile and moderation policy for review and approval. If approved, the moderator is added to the list of verified moderators and preferentially shown in the moderator selection page in the settings.[70] The concept of "verified moderators" further increases transaction costs as it can be anticipated that those moderators who expand resources on becoming "verified" will seek to "compensate" by means of higher dispute fees.

9.8.3 *Control and Choice*

The OB website states that nobody is in control and that "there's no big company behind the scenes that can act as a gatekeeper, collect data, or restrict transactions for anyone."[71] It must be observed, however, that OB1 is *the* company behind the scenes – even if it is incomparably smaller than eBay or Amazon. An analysis of the OB1 blog, which describes its various activities and plans for the future development of the marketplace, reveals its actual decision-making power. At the same time, to create an impression of impartiality, OB1 repeatedly emphasizes that it does not want to make decisions, such as by approving technical solutions suggested by third-party contributors.[72] Even if one abstracts from the fact that OB1 is a company with *de facto* control of the marketplace, it must also be remembered that it consists of the core developers of OB – and core developers are often regarded as gatekeepers. It is noteworthy that the concept of censorship resistance pertains to the protection of a system from outside interference or internal manipulations. While the former commonly relates to governments or law enforcement, the latter are generally associated with core developers. Core developers are often seen as a potential destabilizing force as they control the code running a system. Another quote seems pertinent in this context. In describing OB as the freest marketplace on the planet, the OB1 blog emphasizes that "freedom implies choice: the right to choose who to trade with, to choose how to protect your purchase, or to choose the visibility of your listings. That freedom should also extend to your choice of currency. For your choice to be independent of any one developer's motives, including OB1."[73] Two points arise. First,

---

[67] More details, https://keybase.io.
[68] All quotes refer to the blogpost above.
[69] See at https://medium.com/openbazaarproject/verified-moderators-c83ea2f2c7f3
[70] In addition, verified moderators have the option to create a surety bond, which will incentivize moderators to remain honest. The bond is fully refundable, provided the moderator's services are reputable, and covers the period of verification (six months minimum). The bond will be in the form of a two-of-three multi-sig address, with OB1 and a non-OB1 contributor/developer as co-signers. OB1 will publish a list of partners to be used as the third party for these surety bonds. The size of the surety bond will be used to rank verified moderators. [reinvent the wheel]
[71] More details at https://openbazaar.org.
[72] See at https://github.com/openbazaar.
[73] "Freedom to Trade Means Freedom to Choose Currencies: The OpenBazaar Multiwallet," (26 July 2018) at medium.com/openbazaarproject/freedom-to-trade-means-freedom-to-choose-currencies-the-openbazaar-multiwallet-e12ba31edb70.

the last statement seeks to downplay the role of OB1 as the entity representing core developers. This amplifies the problem resulting from the absence of any clear and formalized governance structures with regard to how OB operates, what powers are given to the core developers and who creates or amends the rules of the marketplace. OB1's *de facto* decision-making power can thus be regarded as an example of an informal, opaque governance structure that indirectly contradicts the decentralized character of the marketplace. Control is not absent – control is hidden. In the event of a malfunction of one of the components of OB's marketplace, it is unclear how such malfunction would be remedied and by whom. On the one hand, OB1 assumes no legal liability as it claims that it has no control over the system; on the other, given its VC-funded background it is reasonable to assume that it has a vested interest in OB's success. Hence, in practice it can be assumed that it would seek to remedy any failures and/or malfunctions. Unfortunately, users of the OB marketplace have no guarantee as to its reliable and continued operation – and given that they *technically* participate in maintaining the network – no legal recourse against anyone. The fact that each user runs a full node on his or her computer does not protect the user from bugs in the cryptocurrency wallets or from latent errors in the networking protocol.

Second, the statement that "freedom implies choice" is meant to reflect the empowerment of individual users. This lofty rhetoric conveniently masks the fact that providing choices to the users requires that such users possess a high level of computer literacy.[74] To benefit from the choices given by the OB marketplace, the *average* user must know, amongst others, how to create a node, select the optimal cryptocurrency wallet and moderator. The problem does not necessarily lie in precluding less sophisticated users from transacting on OB but in exposing such users to risks they do not understand. Arguably, actual user empowerment does not rely on providing users with the ability to make choices but with ensuring that users can make the correct choices or understand their technical, commercial and legal implications. Traditional online marketplaces such as Amazon and eBay "limit" choices to the selection of products, vendors and delivery options without requiring any knowledge of the underlying technologies. In fact, both platforms provide state-of-the-art technology enabling users to focus exclusively on the transacting process.

9.8.4 *"Pockets" of Centralization*

On a more general level, it must be observed that although the OB platform is decentralized in a technical sense, it indirectly relies on multiple "pockets" of centralization, i.e. single points of control or trust. The first such "pocket" is OB1 itself because it holds *de facto* control over the marketplace. OB1 also controls the process of verifying moderators. The second "pocket" are the moderators, both verified and un-verified, because they are able to unilaterally decide on the outcome of a dispute – the blockchain-based multi-signature process notwithstanding. The existence of such "pockets of centralization" also confirms that it is impossible to contain or resolve all transactional risks by means of code or – to place all trust in technology itself. Irrespective of the technological

---

[74] See generally: OB1 blog, "The Beginner's Guide to Buying Goods, Services and Cryptocurrency on OpenBazaar," medium.com/openbazaarproject/the-beginners-guide-to-buying-goods-services-and-cryptocurrency-on-openbazaar-153a8dbd0efc (August 11, 2018).

sophistication of the OB marketplace, including the trustless character of some of its blockchain-based components, the buyer must trust the vendor, the moderator or both. Ultimately, all transacting parties must trust OB1. As both buyers and sellers can remain anonymous and as no one can eliminate or sanction dishonest users, the OB marketplace *increases* counter-party risk. After all, reputation systems alone are hardly sufficient to ensure transactional security. Users must effectively rely on their own investigations of the potential counterparty and on the minimal technological protections inherent in "moderated payments." The decentralization of the underlying infrastructure and the use of cryptocurrencies change nothing in this regard.

9.9 Conclusion

This chapter sketched the shortcomings of public blockchains to illustrate that certain technological features that seem attractive from an ideological perspective may be detrimental to commercial transactions. In particular, it demonstrated the limited suitability of public blockchains for the needs of commerce and emphasized that marketplaces – whether centralized or not – cannot rely on technology alone but require a solid, legal infrastructure that regulates their functioning. Code, whether trustless or not, cannot replace the need to trust human entities. Neither blockchains nor smart contracts can prevent transaction failures attributable to malfunctions of the technology itself or non-performance by the other party.

Irrespective of the underlying technology and irrespective of the network architecture, once the marketplace involves actual human persons and physical off-chain assets – decentralization and trustlessness become practically impossible or, at least, highly impracticable. Decentralized marketplaces, such as OpenBazaar, will remain attractive to few technologically literate users who value their underlying ideology, know how to manage the risks inherent in its use and, more importantly, may want to avoid the legal sanctions accompanying the trade in illegal goods or services. Once the actual meaning of certain blockchain-related terms becomes apparent, the actual use cases of public blockchains seem limited. In particular, immutability, coupled with the absence of clear governance structures, seems detrimental for many commercial applications. Any electronic platform must be secure, resilient, adaptable, i.e. capable of continually and swiftly accommodating legal requirements. No organization or commercial relationship can be governed exclusively by code. Blockchains require an external governance process enabling the network participants to make decisions about the network. Even the most advanced technology cannot exist on its own but requires a solid legal framework that regulates its use and the interaction between its users – if only to allocate the risks of transaction failures and prescribe dispute resolution procedures.

10 Regulating Smart Contracts and Digital Platforms

A Chinese Perspective

Jia Wang and Lei Chen

10.1 Introduction

The advent of technologies like the blockchain brings changes and challenges to daily life as well as the commercial world. Blockchain technology facilitates groups of individuals to reach consensus without relying on a relationship of personal trust.[1] The technology has been applied to numerous ways, such as cryptocurrency, logistics, financial services, and smart contracts.[2] However, proponents of blockchain technology overestimate the power of private ordering and minimize the need for trusted intermediaries. The onslaught of technologies inevitably brings challenges that are fundamental to the commercial organizations and the legal system entrusted to regulate the market. The challenges presented by new technologies relate to individuals who trade through various means and the platforms that facilitate the trades. Therefore, a general question is whether innovative technology will result in innovative legal frameworks? This is a pressing question in China where blockchain technology and smart contracts are increasingly being applied as e-commerce continues to expand.

This chapter explores whether the legal landscape will need to be fundamentally changed in view of the emergence of smart contracts in China. It further examines the role of online intermediaries and assesses the regulatory framework relating to online platforms. The chapter acknowledges gaps in the existing regulatory framework, but argues that the current legal framework can accommodate or mitigate the legal risks presented by smart contracts. Innovative technology generally does not lead to a need for innovative jurisprudence. On the one hand, it is premature to change existing legal framework in response to a still-evolving technology (blockchain-based smart contracts). On the other hand, the regulatory framework for platform operators needs to be adjusted carefully to incentivize them to diligently check and verify the information of vendors who conduct business on their platforms.

---

[1] Stephen Knack, *Trust, Associational Life and Economic Performance*, OECD conference paper, www.oecd.org/education/innovation-education/1825662.pdf. The lack of trust has particular implications for economic development underpinned by a robust regime of contracts; as indicated by Douglas North: "The inability of societies to develop effective, low-cost enforcement of contracts is the most important source of both historical stagnation and contemporary underdevelopment in the Third World." See *Institutions, Institutional Change and Economic Performance*, Cambridge University Press (1990), p. 54.

[2] More examples can be found here: Smart Contracts Alliance in collaboration with Deloitte (2018), "Smart Contracts: 12 Use Cases for Business & Beyond – A Technology, Legal & Regulatory Introduction," https://digitalchamber.org/wp-content/uploads/2018/02/Smart-Contracts-12-Use-Cases-for-Business-and-Beyond_Chamber-of-Digital-Commerce.pdf.

This chapter is divided into five sections. Section 10.2 discusses blockchain technology-based smart contracts. This section explains the core functions of smart contracts and discusses the development of smart contracts in China. Section 10.3 discusses the advantages and limits of smart contracts, identifies the industries that tend to rely on smart contracts in China, and focuses on the uncertainties of smart contracts. In particular, China's contract law is examined to determine if there are legal ambiguities with regard to formation, performance, and modification of smart contracts and the problems relating to enforcement, remedies, and dispute resolution. Section 10.4 evaluates the effects of past regulation of new technologies and discusses the regulatory models proposed for platform operators. It argues that the government needs to restrain itself from habitually relying on imposing heavier penalties on platforms as a form of regulation; rather it should pursue a more balanced approach taking the interests of different stakeholders into consideration. Section 10.5 analyzes the importance and benefits of online platforms as intermediaries. Section 10.6 recommends possible solutions to make the current legal system more accommodating to smart contracts, online platforms, and evolving technologies.

10.2 Development of Smart Contracts

This section provides context to the deeper analysis of the challenges smart contracts and online platforms present to existing law. The first part reviews the emergence of smart contracts in general and then focuses on the evolution of smart contracts in China.

10.2.1 Emerging Smart Contracts

Smart contracts are computer protocols that can embed the terms and conditions of a contract.[3] The human readable terms (source code) of a contract are translated into executable computer code that can run on a network. Contractual clauses can thus be made partially or fully self-executing and self-enforcing. Smart contract enthusiasts see blockchain technology as facilitating contracting and diminishing the role of intermediaries.

The idea of smart contracts is not a new concept. The classic prototype of a smart contract is the vending machine. Once money is inserted into the machine, then a contract for sale is executed automatically. The term "smart contracts" was coined by computer scientist Nick Szabo in 1993 to emphasize the goal of bringing what he calls the "highly evolved" practices of contract law and related business practices to the design of electronic commerce protocols between strangers on the Internet.[4] A more modern definition of a blockchain-based smart contract is "a piece of code deployed [on a] shared, replicated ledger, which can maintain its own state, control its own assets and which responds to the arrival of external information or the receipt of assets."[5]

---

[3] Riccardo de Caria "A Digital Revolution in International Trade? The International Legal Framework for Blockchain Technologies, Virtual Currencies and Smart Contracts: Challenges and Opportunities," p. 4, at https://aperto.unito.it/handle/2318/1632525.

[4] Nick Szabo, "Formalizing and Securing Relationships on Public Networks." Vol. 2, no. 9. 1 September 1997. First Monday, http://firstmonday.org/ojs/index.php/fm/article/view/548.

[5] Rani Subassandran, *Blockchain and Smart Contracts: Today and Tomorrow* (2018) www.courtsofthefuture .org/wp-content/uploads/Blockchain-Smart-Contracts-Today-and-Tomorrow.pdf.

The use of smart contracts has become increasingly popular as they have become "smarter." For example, bitcoin protocol only permits monetary transactions and does not offer the possibility of storing smart contracts or transferring assets. More advanced smart contracts, consist of computer code that executes the terms and conditions of a contract between parties.[6] The more sophisticated the code, the more automated, self-executing, and "smarter" the contract is. The early adoption of smart contracts was facilitated by digital rights management (DRM) schemes.[7] Smart contracts have been used to create copyright licenses, as well as the use of cryptography schemes for financial contracts. Ultimately, smart contracts may be created by computerized agents, through the Internet of Things (IoT) and placed online.[8]

In 2017, more than half of the world's approximately 400 blockchain-related patent applications originated from China,[9] which quadrupled the number of filings in 2016.[10] The United States ranked second in 2017, with 91 filings compared to 21 in 2016. Through March 2018, there were 456 registered companies in China whose business model was based on blockchain technology.[11]

Smart contracts are advantageous in many respects. Smart contracts, among third parties unknown to each other, provide a secure trustless means of transacting since the blockchain cannot be tampered with, as data is secured in a decentralized registry.[12] The cost involved in entering into and enforcing smart contracts is lower than traditional contracts. Also, blockchain transactions can be cost-efficient as repetitive types of contracting can be streamlined and carried out by prescribed programme codes. Moreover, smart contracts are almost entirely fraud-proof because records of the transactions are permanently kept on the blockchain. For example, in the field of logistics, blockchain-based smart contracts can shorten the chain of third-party agents, speed up delivery, reduce the price to consumers, and reduce the possibility of theft.[13] Smart contracts can be – at least in theory – fully automated and self-enforcing. Once the terms and conditions are set in computer code, the contract will run its course and the terms will be executed by computer systems on the basis of the code and certain exogenous events embedded in the code. In many commercial relationships, in particular in financial services, these properties make smart contracts very attractive. Automation, combined with the blockchain's distributed nature, significantly decreases transaction costs.

---

[6] Sergey Grybniak, "Advantages and Disadvantages of Smart Contracts in Financial Blockchain Systems," https://hackernoon.com/advantages-and-disadvantages-of-smart-contracts-in-financial-blockchain-systems-3a443145ae1c.

[7] For example, see the introduction of DRM at American Library Association at www.ala.org/advocacy/copyright/digitalrights.

[8] See note 8, 313. Max Raskin, "The Law and Legality of Smart Contracts", (2017) 1:2 Georgetown Law Technology Review 305–341.

[9] Global Times, "China Led Global Blockchain Patent Applications in 2017: WIPO," published on March 26, 2018/, www.globaltimes.cn/content/1095289.shtml

[10] Echo Huang, "China's Blockchain Ambitions Are Revealed in the Sheer Number of Patent Applications," https://qz.com/1240364/chinas-blockchain-ambitions-revealed-in-sheer-number-of-patent-applications.

[11] Ministry of Industry and Information Technology, *White Paper on the Blockchain Industry of 2018*, published in May 2018, www.miit.gov.cn/n1146290/n1146402/n1146445/c6180238/part/6180297.pdf, p 1.

[12] Pierluigi Cuccuru, "Beyond Bitcoin: An Early Overview on Smart Contracts" (2017) *International Journal of Law and Information* (25), 179,186. See note 8, Max Raskin "The Law and Legality of Smart Contracts" 316.

[13] DHK Trend Research, "Blockchain in Logistics – Perspectives on the Upcoming Impact of Blockchain Technology and Use Cases for the Logistics Industry" (2018) pp. 12–18, www.logistics.dhl/content/dam/dhl/global/core/documents/pdf/glo-core-blockchain-trend-report.pdf.

Technological innovation, such as the evolution of smart contracts, has its own disadvantages. For example, consumers may question the rental terms for an apartment after execution. If the data is already registered in a smart contract, it will be technically difficult to adjust or make corrections.[14] So a mistake in the language contract or in the coding of the language contract cannot be corrected due to the self-performing nature of smart contracts. Clerical errors are common in language contracts, but can be immediately corrected; but once coded, they become immutable. Ironically, the need for lawyers experienced in IT will increase in the future because programmers of smart contracts will need to know about the requirements of law and the legality of certain contract terms. Because smart contracts are autonomous in nature, promises memorialized in a smart contract are – by default – harder to memorialize in a natural-language legal agreement. Once a smart contract is put into motion, the terms embodied in the code will be automatically executed, unless the parties have incorporated code that allows smart contracts to self-terminate based on data provided by a third-party oracle.[15]

To summarize, smart contracts face major obstacles before they can become commonplace. First, laypersons may find it difficult to acquire a comprehensive understanding of the terms of smart contract codes. Second, smart contracts can only be applied with very specific terms and cannot accommodate the flexibility provided by standard-like contract terms. Third, once distributed, a smart contract can be triggered and executed only when the decentralized nodes reach consensus with the same data input.

10.2.2 *Development of Smart Contracts in China*

The Chinese State Council, in 2017, embraced blockchain technology in its 13th Five-Year Plan, resulting in a 30-fold increase in cryptocurrency market capitalization. This governmental policy has made blockchain and cryptocurrencies a major topic of debate in China.[16] Chinese policymakers are eager to set frameworks and standards to accelerate industrial adoption of blockchain technology, while protecting and educating investors in the nascent and unregulated cryptocurrency ecosystem.[17]

Chinese policy, however, remains unsettled, as the government weighs the benefits and dangers of the blockchain. In 2017, Chinese officials lauded the World Economic Forum White Paper, "Realizing the Potential of Blockchain." But, less than three months later, the People's Bank of China (PBC) announced an immediate ban on initial coin offerings (ICOs) and shut down all domestic cryptocurrency exchanges. At the same time, Sun Guofeng, the director of the Institute of Finance at PBC, clarified that the ban "should not prevent relevant financial technology companies, industry bodies, and other technology firms from continuing their research into blockchain technology."[18] At the

---

[14] See note 12, Pierluigi Cuccuru, "Beyond Bitcoin" 188–190.
[15] Kevin D. Werbach and Nicolas Cornell "Contracts Ex Machina" (2017) *Duke Law Journal* 67, 313.
[16] World Economic Forum Report, *What's the Future of Blockchain in China?*, www.weforum.org/agenda/2018/01/what-s-the-future-of-blockchain-in-china.
[17] For example, China has moved to more closely regulate Bitcoin. See Mark Schaub and Molly Su (2017) "Prospective Opportunities & Risks for Bitcoin in China," www.chinalawinsight.com/2017/08/articles/corporate/prospective-opportunities-risks-for-bitcoin-in-china/. In 2017, People's Bank of China ordered a ban on domestic initial coin offering (Notice on Preventing Financial Risk of Issued Tokens). Back in 2013, it ordered the Notice on Preventing Financial Risk of Bitcoin.
[18] "China Bans Issuance of Long-Term Certificates of Deposit," www.xinhuanet.com/english/2017-08/31/c_136571679.htm.

same time, China's Ministry of Industry and Information Technology launched the Trusted Blockchain Open Lab.[19] The lab promotes the exploration of blockchain technology independent of cryptocurrencies, or the exchanges that trade them.

Public-private partnerships have increased and the judiciary has been supportive of the developing blockchain industry. Guizhou Far East Integrity Management Company initiated, in collaboration with local government authorities, a project known as "Identity Chain." Identity Chain provides privacy protection through real-name identity and facilitated cross-chain technology to achieve different applications of blockchain value transfer and business collaborations. With one ID, a person may engage in numerous activities, such as registering for a telephone number, setting up a corporation, buying a car, and engaging e-commerce platforms. Identity Chain can connect and match all the activities in different scenarios with digital records corresponding to a single ID.[20]

The judiciary has recognized the data stored on blockchain as evidence in legal disputes. In July 2018, a court in Hangzhou confirmed the legal validity of electronic data stored via the blockchain as evidence in an online copyright dispute, involving the infringement of online broadcasting rights. The plaintiff used a third-party evidence storage platform to prove that the defendant published the plaintiff's copyrighted content on a website without approval. The third-party platform captured the infringing web page and conducted source recognition, before compressing the web content along with the call date by means of a hash function and uploading it to Factom and bitcoin blockchains. Previously, the Guangzhou Arbitration Commission issued the industry's first ruling based on the "arbitration chain,"[21] which uses distributed data storage, encryption algorithms, and other technologies to input transaction data on to the chain. Once a dispute arises, the data stored in the chain can be uploaded to the arbitrator's electronic system as an authenticated document to expedite arbitration. The uploaded material of real-time preserved data provides a chain of evidence to meet the requirements for authenticity, legality, and relevance of the evidence.[22]

In the private sector, smart contracts are widely used in financial services, food industry, logistics, legal services, intellectual property industry, and many other sectors.[23] For example, ZhongAn Online, an insurance-technology firm, uses blockchain to track the life cycles of poultry, so consumers can be assured that they are eating organically farmed chickens.

The supply chain and retailing sectors are more inclined to rely on blockchain technology to enhance the transparency of supply and prevent counterfeit goods from entering circulation. Online retailer JD.com has applied the technology to track domestic and international beef products for shoppers. Green Hand is part of the Alibaba Group

---

[19] See www.theasset.com/china-today.

[20] "Blockchain Technology Based Innovative Identity Chain – Create a New Model for Personal Credibility," www.qxgcx.gov.cn/article/xinyongzixun/chengxinxinwen/1725.html.

[21] The ruling was developed by Weizhong Bank, Guangzhou Arbitration Commission, Hangzhou Yibi Science and Technology's "arbitration chain" based on blockchain technology.

[22] "Weizhong Bank and Guangzhou Arbitration Commission, the first ruling of 'blockchain + certificate' was born," at www.sangbe.com/article/372362.html.

[23] See note 11, Ministry of Industry and Information Technology, "White Paper on the Blockchain Industry of China" (2018), p. 41.

and specializes in generating e-passports for physical goods. By scanning a QR code, identity verification is enabled and this triggers the recording of the logistics, origin, and destination of the goods. The tracking data is sent to a "block" that provides a unique identifier enabling customers to see the status of the shipment. VeChain is another blockchain platform offering a transparent, immutable, and secure platform to store information with a private key. In addition, logistics service providers can now manage goods at the granularity of single units for the very first time.[24]

The financial sector has also adopted blockchain technology. Ant Financial utilizes a blockchain network to raise funds for charitable purposes. In 2016, it successfully launched its first project using blockchain to raise funds for children with hearing disabilities. In 2017, it collaborated with the China Social Assistance Foundation.[25] Each donation has a tracking record, and, thus, enhances donors' confidence in the fund-raising. Everbright Securities operates a credits and voting blockchain and is developing applications for the capital markets and financial institutions in China.[26]

The intellectual property industry, as mentioned earlier in this chapter embraced technological measures early on to protect the rights and interests of IP owners. The copyright sector employs DRM to secure copyright royalties by securing the copyright work and only allowing access to users that pay a fee in order to view the works. The next step was the development of a blockchain to register copyrights that establishes a public record of ownership and copyright transactions. In this way, copyright protection is conferred automatically when a work is complete regardless of whether it has been registered.[27] Currently, copyright registration can be performed instantaneously at the cost of RMB 40 cents (USD 5 cents) per registration.[28] A similar system allows the tracking of the distribution of trademarked goods prior to the registration of the trade-mark. As a result, the mark can continue to be used within the same scope of products or services without infringing on similar or identical trademarks that are registered at a later time.[29] Smart contracts are an improvement over DRM in combating online copyright infringements and facilitating the collection of royalty fees.[30]

10.3 Challenges to Smart Contracts

This section reviews the challenges smart contracts present to business and law, including its current use in certain industries, application to relational types of contracts that require flexibility, and the application of contract law in general to smart contracts.

---

[24] www.vechain.com/#/solution/logistics.

[25] www.sohu.com/a/167829002_402387.

[26] Irene Aldridge and Steven Krawciw, *Real-Time Risk: What Investors Should Know About FinTech, High-Frequency Trading, and Flash Crashes* (Wiley, 2017), pp. 33–34.

[27] Art. 2, Berne Convention for the Protection of Literary and Artistic Works.

[28] Jie Hua, "The Role of Blockchain Technology and Smart Contracts in the Establishment of Entitlements and Transaction and its Regulatory Framework" (2018) *Intellectual Property* (2) 13, 17; citing Wu Jian, Gao Li, and Zhu Jingning, 2016(7), Copyright Protection Based on Blockchain Technology, *Broadcasting and TV Information*, 61.

[29] PRC Trademark Law, enacted in 1993, amended in 2001 and 2013; see art. 59(3).

[30] Micro Film (Micro Video) Copyright Centre is one such platform that allows content creators to upload their works and receive payments through a blockchain network that distributes monies specified by the terms encoded into a smart contract. See www.wsp360.org.

10.3.1 *Understandability and Rigidity*

Contracts define rights and obligations for the contracting parties. Some rights and obligations are easily translatable into code – particularly those related to the exchange of value or the transfer of title to a digitally represented asset, which can be written as if-then propositions. These promises are often binary in nature and thus naturally translatable into software. Other contractual provisions, however, are not as easy to code.[31]

Legal agreements often include open-ended terms that outline performance obligations. For example, a contracting party may promise to act in "good faith" because it might be difficult to precisely define what constitutes appropriate performance, while another party may promise to use "best efforts" to fulfill his or her obligations, because the most cost-effective or efficient manner of performance might not yet be foreseeable. There is value in keeping contracts open-ended or ambiguous, because it provides flexibility to the parties and lowers the transaction costs of negotiations. In many cases, vagueness may in fact result in more efficient contracts.[32]

As mentioned earlier in this chapter, smart contracts face three major obstacles in their application. First, smart contracts trigger the issue of understandability of such technology; as laypersons do not entirely understand coded contract terms relative to natural language.[33] Second, the contractual terms being translated into code must be specific, definite, and not be subject to change. The theory of incomplete contracts indicates that it is impossibly complex and costly for parties to create a complete contract[34]; the law provides default rules to fill in the gaps found in contracts. Uncertainty or flexibility in contracts is useful in facilitating performance under conditions of uncertainty, such as changing circumstances. The rigidity of codes renders smart contracts inflexible when conditions deviate from the initial expectations of the parties. Third, smart contracts are restricted by the decentralization of the blockchain nodes. The entire contract becomes nonfunctional if the inputted data contain discrepancies. The following subsection examines how these three obstacles affect the current contract law system. The observation is conducted within the framework of China's contract law, and related laws and regulations.

10.3.2 *Revisiting the Law of Contracts*

This section reviews the three core areas of contract law – formation, performance, enforcement, and remedies – to determine their continuing role or fit to smart contracting.

10.3.2.1 Formation of Contract

A contract is an agreement between two or more parties creating obligations that are enforceable or otherwise recognizable at law. For an agreement to be enforceable,

---

[31] *Virtual Currencies and Beyond: Initial Considerations*, IMF Staff Discussion Note, SDN/16/03, January 2016, p. 23.
[32] Oliver Hart, "Incomplete Contracts and Control" (2017) *American Economic Review*, 107(7), 1731.
[33] See note 12, Pierluigi Cuccuru, Beyond Bitcoin, p. 188.
[34] Oliver Hart and John Moore, "Incomplete Contracts and Renegotiation" (1988) *Econometrica*, 56(4), pp. 755–785.

three elements must be present: an offer (expression of a willingness to enter into a binding agreement), acceptance of the proposed terms, and a mutual exchange of value (consideration). Article 14 of the *PRC Contract Law* (CCL)[35] defines an offer as a party's manifestation of intention to enter into a binding contract with another party. The terms of the offer must be specific and definite. Within the context of smart contracts, codes posted to a ledger can be considered an offer.[36] However, a problem emerges when it comes to acceptance. Article 30 of the CCL provides that: "[T]he content of an acceptance shall be consistent with the content of the offer." For smart contracts, it is uncertain whether an offeree is entirely in agreement with the contents of the offer.[37] A further question relates to the inability of the offeror to withdraw its offer due to the speedy transmission of data and the irrevocability of encoded data on the blockchain.[38] This seriously undermines freedom of contract, which is the cornerstone of contract laws.[39]

If a smart contract meets the legal requirements of contract formation, the validity of the contract or its terms is subject to further judicial scrutiny. Article 52 of the CCL provides that if a contract is used as a façade to commit unlawful financing activities, the contract is invalid. Articles 39 and 40 of the CCL provide that standard terms are generally valid if the party providing the standard terms sufficiently brings them to the attention of the other party. The CCL further renders unenforceable standard terms that exempt from the liability of the party supplying the terms, increases the liabilities of the other party, or deprives the other party of any of its material rights. Parties to a smart contract are exposed to greater risks related to such terms because of their self-executing nature. Also, they may be disadvantaged if they cannot discern the contractual terms embedded in code, which could expose themselves to unreasonably greater liabilities imposed by the supplier or creator of the smart contract.

Chinese scholars have suggested that contract terms in natural language should be provided to all parties before the language is coded into a smart contract.[40] The dilemma here is if every smart contract has to be accompanied by a translation in human-readable language, the low cost of smart contracts will be diluted. The existence of a complete natural language version of the smart contract will also cause problems relating to interpretation. In case of a dispute, the court has to interpret the disputable contractual terms. If the coded contract is the true contract, the courts may not be able to rely on the human-readable language translation in the interpretation process.[41]

---

[35] PRC Contract Law was enacted in 1999.

[36] See note 8, 322.

[37] Zhen Mei and Yali Kang, "The Application of Blockchain Technologies in Finance and Reflection on Legal Issues" (2017) *Journal of Shanghai Li Xin School of Accounting and Finance* (4). Jing Jin, The Power of Classical Contract Law in Digital Age – With the Perspective of European Single Digital Market Policy (2017) *European Studies* (6).

[38] Zhou Run and Lu Ying "Impact of Smart Contracts on Chinese Contract System and Solutions" (2018) *South China Finance* (05) 93–94.

[39] See note 37.

[40] See note 38, p. 95.

[41] Stefan Grundmann and Philipp Hacker, "Digital Technology as a Challenge to European Contract Law – From the Existing to the Future Architecture" (2017) *European Review of Contract Law* 13(3), 255, 279. Xiaojing Zhou, "Development of Smart Contracts Based on Blockchain and Their Restrictions through the Lens of Law" (2018) *Legality Vision* (5) (Fazhi Bolan) 4.

10.3.2.2 Performance and Modification

Likewise, inconsistencies between the practice of smart contracts and statutory provisions are found in the areas of performance and modification. Under the CCL, legally binding agreements have to identify the parties and subject matter with particularity, and include mutual promises, which may be absolute or subject to conditions. A legally binding agreement may be written on paper or in electronic form, or may be oral in limited circumstances.

Smart contracts are not well suited to accommodate legal arrangements that are complex or relational in nature.[42] In order to implement a smart contract, parties need to precisely define performance obligations. In many commercial transactions, however, obligations will likely prove unpredictable,[43] and smart contracts will not be able to provide parties with the flexibility to structure their ongoing contractual relationship. Knowledge necessary for completing contracts often hinges on specific circumstances that cannot be easily standardized or coded. Moreover, automatic execution is costly to the extent that it would preclude efficient breach.[44]

To determine whether a smart contract has been successfully performed, the parties have to take a take-it-or-leave-it approach. Technically, only full performance can be recognized and executed by code. However, according to Article 94 of the CCL, delayed or incomplete performance cannot be recognized. However, in practice, it is possible to have partial performance or even substantial performance even though the performance does not fully conform to the initial contractual terms.

A contract may not be fully performed due to a change of circumstances, which renders the performance impossible or too costly to be performed. CCL Articles 68 and 69 provide a link between the impact of "change of circumstances" and the modification of performance obligations. Article 68 provides that:

> [T]he party which ought to discharge its debts first may suspend the discharge if it obtains evidence that the following conditions relating to the other party exist: (1) business operations seriously deteriorating; (2) diverting properties and withdrawing capital to evade debts; (3) falling into business discredit; or (4) other situations showing inability or possible inability to meet liabilities. A party that suspends [performance] without truthful evidence shall bear the liability for breach of contract.

Article 69 further provides that:

> [W]here a party suspends the discharge of its debts in accordance with the provisions of Article 68, it shall promptly notify the other party of the suspension. The party shall resume the discharge when the other party provides a guarantee of performance. The party that has suspended the discharge may dissolve the contract if the other party has failed to regain the capability of meeting its liabilities and to provide a guarantee within a reasonable period of time.

All these provisions indicate that modification of a contract is possible when circumstances change. The CCL[45] and the General Provisions of Civil

---

[42] Karen E. C. Levy, "Book-Smart, Not Street-Smart: Blockchain-Based Smart Contracts and the Social Workings of Law" (2017) *Engaging Science, Technology, and Society* (3), 1–15

[43] Ter Kah Leng, "Non-Absolute Obligations: Their Interpretation and Effect in Business Contracts" (2015) *International Journal of Humanities and Social Science*, 5 (6) (1), 1.

[44] Robert Cooter and Thomas Ulen, *Law and Economics* (5th edn., Pearson, 2008), p. 266.

[45] Art. 54.

Law[46] provide that gross misunderstanding can render a contract voidable. If both parties are at fault, they shall bear liability in proportion to their fault. However, due to the problem of understandability and the rigidity of coded contracts, as previously stated, a bug (code error) in a smart contract becomes immutable when recorded on the blockchain. Some commentators suggest that courts should treat an error in a smart contract as a "change of circumstances." However, Article 26 of *Judicial Interpretation of Contract Law II* states that only an event which occurs after the formation of contract and which was unforeseeable when the parties formed the contract can be a legitimate reason to render a contract voidable or subject to modification. Therefore, the ground of "change of circumstances" cannot be applied to a smart contract containing coding errors.[47]

The expansion of smart contracting into other types of contracts, other than simple if-then contracts, is unlikely because of the inability to code standard-like or open-ended terms. For instance, legal agreements often include representations and warranties, which cannot be fulfilled solely by referencing data stored or managed within a blockchain. These representations and warranties run the gamut of legal agreements where contracting parties often affirm ownership interests, agree to keep information confidential, or warrant that they will comply with applicable laws. Smart contracts – at least for the immediate future – will not be able to account for these more open-ended rights and obligations, which are neither binary nor standardized.

10.3.2.3 Enforcement, Remedies, and Dispute Resolution

The legal system offers remedies for breach of contract, such as the payment of damages or, in certain circumstances, an order of specific performance or injunction. Smart contracts limit the application of traditional remedies because the contract has been programmed and distributed on the network, and cannot be altered due to a change of circumstances. However, with a conventional contract, parties have greater flexibility to adjust or modify the contractual terms in order optimize performance, mitigate losses, or maintain the contractual relationship.[48] Without the ability to exercise the seller's right to cure and the buyer's duty of adaptation or mitigation of loss, contract remedies are a poor fit for smart contracts.

Apart from the limited scope of remedies, dispute resolution raises another concern for smart contracts. Due to the anonymity of smart contracts, it may be impossible to identify the parties to a dispute.[49] Due to the constraints of territorial jurisdiction and state sovereignty, there is no comprehensive legal institution for regulating cross-border disputes, except through Online Dispute Resolution (ODR).[50] This means that the

---

[46] Art. 157 of General Provisions. Adopted at the 5th Session of the Twelfth National People's Congress on March 15, 2017; became effective on October 1, 2017.

[47] See Zhou Xiaojing, see note 41 above, at 3.

[48] See note 47, p. 4.

[49] Wulf Kaal and Craig Calcaterra, "Crypto Transaction Dispute Resolution" (2018) *Business Lawyer*, 73 (1) 8, 109–152.

[50] Online Dispute Resolution (ODR) uses alternative dispute resolution processes, including mediation, arbitration, and negotiation to resolve a dispute. The parties may use the Internet and web-based technology in a variety of ways. See NCSC/Pew Charitable Trusts ODR Project Announcement at http://odr.info/; also see "Online Dispute Resolution" *Hong Kong Lawyer November* (November 2017), at www.hk-lawyer.org/content/online-dispute-resolution.

choice of law or jurisdiction, or the recognition and enforcement of ODR decisions, are all determined based on national law. In response to these challenges, the EU has created a union-wide ODR platform with translation services through the ODR Regulation (524/2013) and ADR Directive (2013/11/EU).[51]

The uncertainty in the enforcement of judicial judgments in transborder disputes[52] increases the importance of an effective redress mechanism to force compliance with decisions reached in the ODR process.[53] Several solutions for enforcing ODR decisions have been suggested. One solution would be to enforce ODR decisions through the courts as arbitral awards. Other options range from user reviews to chargebacks and escrow services. A more intrusive solution is direct enforcement by an e-commerce site, which requires a close interface between the marketplace, the payment method, and the ODR service. In China, courts at the provincial level, such as the Hangzhou Intermediate Court, have launched an ODR platform for judiciary services including mediation, arbitration, and litigation. This is a positive development in bringing greater certainty to dispute resolution to smart contracts.

10.4 Responses to the Challenges

This section examines the notion of a paradigm shift to code as law, the need for new laws to regulate blockchain and platform transactions, and the continued role of the judiciary in the on-chain world.

---

[51] The Regulation establishes an EU-wide portal for consumers and traders, who can submit complaints through the platform. The platform then directs the complaint to the suitable national ADR entity, which helps the parties in reaching an out-of-court settlement in accordance with the entity's own procedural rules. Full text of the Regulation available at http://eurlex.europa.eu/LexUriServ/LexUriServ.do?uri=OJ:L:2013:165:0001:0012:EN:PDF. The platform, which was launched in January 2016, is available at https://webgate.ec.europa.eu/odr. Unfortunately, the United Nations Commission on International Trade Law (UNCITRAL) has attempted to draft uniform procedural rules for ODR but the work has come to a relative standstill. The objective of UNCITRAL's Working Group III has changed since it started working on ODR in 2010. The stumbling block has been the fundamental difference between different jurisdictions regarding the acceptance of binding pre-dispute arbitral clauses in consumer cases. In July 2015, the Commission further specified the Working Group's mandate to focus on the "elements of an ODR process, on which elements the Working Group had previously found consensus." The Working Group will continue for one year, until the summer of 2016, after which it will be terminated regardless of the outcome. See United Nations Commission On International Trade Law, Working Group III (Online Dispute Resolution), Thirty-second session, "Annotated Provisional Agenda" (30 July 2018), p. 4, https://documents-ddsny.un.org/doc/UNDOC/LTD/V15/066/23/PDF/V1506623.pdf? OpenElement.

[52] Enforcement is considered to be necessary for efficient access to justice. The case law of the European Court of Human Rights (ECtHR) highlights the importance of enforcement as a part of fair trial provided for in Article 6 of the European Convention on Human Rights. See ECtHR, "Guide on Article 6: Right to Fair Trial (civil limb)" (2013) at 23–24, available at www.echr.coe.int/Documents/Guide_Art_6_ENG .pdf. There is also a UNCITRAL debate, as to the question of whether the acceptance of binding arbitration clauses in consumer relationships is linked with the possibility of enforcing these arbitral awards in accordance with the provisions of the Convention on the Recognition and Enforcement of Foreign Arbitral Awards (New York, 1958). See further, R. Koulu, "One Click Too Much? – Thoughts on UNCITRAL's Work on ODR Draft Rules, Part II" (2015), available at www.cyberjustice.ca/actualites/2015/03/13/one-click-too-much-thoughts-on-uncitrals-work-on-odrdraft-rules-part-ii/.

[53] The term of enforcement refers to different mechanisms of providing compliance with decisions reached in different dispute resolution procedures.

10.4.1 *Paradigm Shift From "Code Is Law" to "Law Is Code"*

The ecosystem based on blockchain and other technologies of encryption differs from the existing systems of code-based rules implemented by today's online applications.[54] With the advancement of artificial intelligence (AI) and machine learning, a paradigmatic shift, sometime in the future, is likely. In this future world, code will be seen as having the effect of law ("code is law") and law will be defined as code ("law is code").[55] Lawrence Lessig famously stated: "Code is law."[56] He argues that coders and software programmers, by making a choice about the working and structure of IT networks and the applications that run on them, create the rules under which the systems are governed. The coders therefore act as "quasi-legislators." In other words, "code is law" is a form of private sector regulation whereby technology is used to enforce the governing rules.

Currently, most online services either act as an intermediary or rely on other intermediaries, such as cloud-computing providers, search engines, payment processors, domain name registrars, and social networks in providing their services. The intermediaries craft their own rules and impose and enforce those rules, and to the extent that they are easily identifiable and located in a particular jurisdiction, they also serve as central points of control for regulatory authorities.[57] Therefore, there are inevitably tensions between intermediaries and the legal system related to online economic activities.[58]

With the advent of blockchain and machine learning, technology is progressively preempting the use of existing legal rules.[59] In order to improve the efficiency of smart contracts, technologies are being developed to address the problem of the rigidity of decentralization and computer codes. Commentators point out that smart contracts may not be so "smart."[60] In particular, commercial or private exchanges are often very complicated. Contract lawyers will readily attest to the impossibility of drafting a complete contract that takes into account all possible contingencies. Incomplete contracts are the norm and ambiguities in contractual terms are common and are often desirable. They are desirable because they address the hold-up problem and enhance efficiency.[61] Therefore, enabling smart contracts to accommodate changes, while maintaining the advantages of low cost, trustless transactions, will allow them to be applied in more types of contracts.

Sophisticated commercial contracts not reducible to if-then propositions, dependent on objectively verifiable facts, requiring manual administration are susceptible to misapplication or inadvertent non-application problems when translated to code. Smart contracts can be said to be smart to the extent they offer the efficiency of automated contractual performance and reduce the prospects of a dispute. This is not to say that

---

[54] M. Swan and P. Filippi (2017). "Toward a Philosophy of Blockchain," *Wiley*, Vol. 48, Issue 5, https://doi.org/10.1111/meta.12270.

[55] P. De Filippi, X. Lavayssière, "Blockchain Technology: Toward a Decentralized Governance of Digital Platforms?" in D. Bollier and A. Grear, (eds.), *The Great Awakening (The Works of Jonathan Edwards Series, Volume 4*, 2015).

[56] L. Lessig, *Code and Other Laws of Cyberspace* (Basic Books, 1999).

[57] De Filippi, P. and A. Wright, *Blockchain and the Law: The Rule of Code* (Harvard Academic Press, 2018), p. 6.

[58] See note 57.

[59] Harry Surden, "Machine Learning and Law" (2018) *Washington Law Review* 89 (1), 29.

[60] Adam J Kolber, "Not-So-Smart Blockchain Contracts and Artificial Responsibility" (2018) *Stanford Technology Law Review*, 25.

[61] Oliver Hart, "Incomplete Contracts and Control" (2017) *American Economic Review*, 107(7): 1731–1752.

smart contracts are simple; indeed, a smart contract could encompass a range of complex outcomes based on multiple inputs. However, a computer cannot be programmed to accurately ascertain, for example, whether a party has exercised reasonable efforts in the performance of their obligations. Viewed through this prism, smart contracts are not very smart.

Compared with contracts in natural language that accommodate more flexibility to allow parties to make adjustments to the initial terms, smart contracts are inflexible, unable to adapt to changing circumstances and the parties' revised preferences. Therefore, smart contract designers need to develop channels to accommodate real-time changes, making smart contracts a bit less immutable. Software developers have developed application programming interface (API) to address the problem of the rigidity of decentralization. API connects to the Internet and sends data to a server. The server retrieves the data, interprets it, performs necessary actions, and sends it back to the sender's system.

At this stage, to address smart contracts' problems relating to the rigidity of decentralization, an extrinsic data source (oracles) has been connected to smart contracts that allows for the future verification of a "particular factual condition" that is "objectively ascertainable through programmatic reference" to oracles.[62] In a blockchain system, an oracle is an agent that finds and verifies real-world occurrences (weather-related information, price indexes, real-time stock prices, and so forth) and submits this information to a blockchain to be used by smart contracts.[63]

With oracles, smart contracts can respond to changing conditions in real time.[64] Smart contracts can be coded to reference an oracle to modify payment flows or alter encoded rights and obligations according to the newly received information. Oracles also make it possible to determine or update specific performance obligations based on the subjective and arbitrary judgment of individuals. In this way, parties can rely on the deterministic and guaranteed execution of smart contracts for objective promises that are readily translatable into code. At the same time, they can assign to a human-based oracle the task of assessing promises that cannot easily be encoded into a smart contract, either because they are too ambiguous or because they require a subjective assessment of real-world events.[65] Optimistically, with sufficient data provided by trusted external sources, it is possible for smart contracts to be made more flexible. Moreover, with data communication facilitated by API and the increasingly sophisticated analytical capabilities empowered by machine learning, AI may be trained to draft, manage, and enforce smart contracts in the future.

It is important to note that reliance on trusted intermediaries is contradictory to the ideology of smart contracts as self-contained, self-performing governance structures.[66] An alternative to the use of a single trusted oracle is the use of a blockchain-like system of untrusted or partially trusted parties in which performance changes are made based on

---

[62] David M Adlerstein, "Are Smart Contracts Smart? A Critical Look at Basic Blockchain Questions" at www .coindesk.com/when-is-a-smart-contract-actually-a-contract.

[63] https://blockchainhub.net/blockchain-oracles.

[64] M. Ethan Katsh, *Law in a Digital World* (Oxford: Oxford University Press, 1995), p. 120.

[65] Pietro Ortolani, "Self-Enforcing Online Dispute Resolution: Lessons from Bitcoin" (2016) *Oxford Journal of Legal Studies* 36 (3), 595–629.

[66] See note 12, pp. 185–186.

the consensus of multiple sources.[67] This type of system would act as a decentralized oracle system. Nevertheless, this approach is problematic since it requires a predefined standard on data format and is inherently inefficient.[68]

The solution developed by Oraclize is to demonstrate that the data retrieved from the original data-source is genuine and has not been corrupted.[69] This is accomplished by accompanying the returned data together with a document called authenticity proof. The authenticity proofs build upon different technologies such as auditable virtual machines and Trusted Execution Environments (TEE).[70] The developers of blockchain applications and the users of such applications do not have to trust Oraclize. Data providers do not have to modify their services in order to be compatible with blockchain protocols. Smart contracts can directly access data from websites or APIs. Nevertheless, it is suggested by scholars that it is best to leave the determination of the availability of a remedy in case of nonperformance to human judges because such a task is too complicated for a smart contract to evaluate.[71]

Evolving technologies can, to some extent, address the limitations of smart contracts. However, technologies are double-edged swords since the adoption of a new technology may solve problems of other technological applications and, at the same time, create new problems. However, disruptive technologies like AI and machine learning could cause a paradigm shift by making legal rules more specific and tailor-made through data feeds.[72] Nonetheless, new pose questions as trust-free smart contracts are undermined when third-party sources of information are introduced.[73] Technology optimists may take solace in Charles Clark's eloquent statement that "the answer to the machine is in the machine."[74] Today's disruptive technologies have resulted in significant advancements. However, their long-term impact is yet to be tested and may require future technological solutions to address issues such as privacy, data protection, and government regulation.

10.4.2 Regulatory Efforts

The legal system offers remedies for breach of contract, such as the requirement to pay damages. Smart contracts have limited remedies compared with the remedies available for conventional contracts. Also, in traditional contracting, prompt adjustment or

---

[67] See the explanation provided by the website of Oraclize at https://docs.oraclize.it. For more information, see https://medium.com/coinmonks/a-guide-to-perform-web-queries-in-dapp-35683a386044.

[68] Eliza Mik, "Smart Contracts: Terminology, Technical Limitations and Real World Complexity," *Law, Innovation & Technology* (2017) 9.2, available at https://ink.library.smu.edu.sg/cgi/viewcontent.cgi?article=4298&context=sol_research, p. 23.

[69] www.oraclize.it.

[70] TEE is a secured area of a main processor. It guarantees code and data loaded inside to be protected with respect to confidentiality and integrity because it is an isolated execution environment. See Poulpita, "Trusted Execution Environment, Millions of Users Have One, Do You Have Yours?" at https://poulpita.com/2014/02/18/trusted-execution-environment-do-you-have-yours/

[71] Eric Tjong Tjin Tai, "Force Majeure and Excuses in Smart Contracts" (2018) *European Review of Private Law* (6) 787.

[72] Omri Ben Shaharand Ariel Porat, "Personalizing Mandatory Rules in Contract Law" (2019) *University of Chicago Law Review* 86, 255.

[73] Weldon, "Building an 'Oracle' for an Ethereum Contract," Medium (October 11, 2016), https://medium.com/@mustwin/building-an-oracle-for-an-ethereum-contract-6096d3e39551#.f335uyw5a; B. Arruñada, "Blockchain's Struggle to Deliver Impersonal Exchange," Pompeu Fabra University Economics and Business Working Paper Series 1549 (2017), https://ssrn.com/abstract=2903857, at 31.

[74] Charles Clark "The Answer to the Machine Is in the Machine," in *The Future of Copyright in a Digital Environment* (Kluwer, 1996).

modification by the parties may prevent or mitigate losses. However, with a smart contract, parties are less likely to make changes to avoid loss.[75]

Commentators have very different views on the appropriate regulatory model for smart contracts, and disagree as to whether a proactive approach should be taken. Some argue that there does not appear to be many differences between the functioning of a smart contract and that of a mechanical vending machine.[76] Therefore, a wait-and-see approach is preferable at this early stage of blockchain development.[77]

Other scholars have proposed different regulatory models for smart contracts. For instance, a "Superuser," such as a government authority, could be empowered to modify or terminate smart contracts.[78] Admittedly, the problem with this solution is that it eliminates the primary advantage of smart contracts of being free from external manipulation. The idea of a Superuser may result in the blockchain being hardly more attractive than traditional databases and registers maintained by state authorities. Another solution is to enforce the law by state authorities with an "offline" mode by pursuing specific users and forcing them to include changes to the blockchain as well as using conventional claims like unjust enrichment and damages.[79] This solution raises the concern that the application of conventional remedies will stifle innovation in developing alternative dispute resolution methods. In sum, the current proposed solutions are hardly satisfactory; an optimal solution has yet to be devised.

In the United States, some states have been working on legislative initiatives relating to blockchain technology. For instance, blockchain-related legislation has been proposed in Nevada.[80] In March 2017, Arizona enacted legislation legalizing smart contracts, defined in the law as "an event-driven program, which runs on a distributed, decentralized, shared and replicated ledger and that can take custody over and instruct transfer of assets on that ledger."[81]

In China, under the Law of Electronic Signatures,[82] a contract, signature, or record is not considered unenforceable merely on the basis of being in an electronic format as long as the record is capable of being reproduced for later reference. It would seem that smart contracts would be treated in the same way. Innovative technology promises to have a far-reaching impact on how legal agreements are recorded, evidenced, and performed. Meanwhile, existing concepts of what constitutes a legally binding agreement will endure. While thoughtful legislative initiatives are welcome, existing legal frameworks are currently able to provide the basis for the enforcement of smart contracts.

10.4.3 *Judiciary as Last Resort*

As previously noted, fully automated and self-enforcing smart contracts may deal with straightforward matters but are less capable of dealing with commercial scenarios that are

---

[75] See note 47, p. 4.
[76] See note 3, p. 13.
[77] See note 8, p. 316.
[78] Alexander Savelyev, "Contract Law 2.0: 'Smart' Contracts as the Beginning of the End of Classic Contract Law," (2017) *Information and Communications Technology Law*, 26 (2), 116, 133.
[79] See note 78.
[80] David M. Adlerstein "Are Smart Contracts Smart? A Critique Look at Basic Blockchain Questions" (2017) www.coindesk.com/when-is-a-smart-contract-actually-a-contract/.
[81] See "A Blockchain Primer for Lawyers", available at http://frontierofthelaw.com/2019/01/08/a-blockchain-primer-for-lawyers/
[82] Art 3, Law of Electronic Signature, enacted August 28, 2004 and amended on April 24, 2015.

more complex and where performance is unpredictable. Smart contracts applied to complex private and commercial relationships will have to remain open-ended and rely on courts and arbitration to provide remedies. A portion of contract law is made of mandatory rules or immutable principles. They are so fundamental to the regulation of economic activity that courts will not enforce otherwise-valid contracts if they are not in compliance with these principles.

A key function of courts is to adjudicate in matters where circumstances have changed in a way not foreseen by the parties at the time of entering into the contract. Smart contract allocates the risk in typical binary fashion without room for deviation unless it incorporates some reference to an external arbiter to decide whether such deviation has occurred. The contracting parties can agree that the contract's enforcement should be made contingent upon its fairness. This would require coding that provides a measure of fairness that can be objectively determined. In the area of complex contracts, in cases where performance is ongoing it will be necessary to maintain safety valves for a court or an arbitrator to be able to override contract provisions coded in the blockchain.

Courts would likely intervene post-performance to provide remedies if the contract is deemed invalid in cases of fraud, duress, forgery, lack of legal capacity, and unconscionability. This should be expected, and it does not prevent smart contract from becoming widely adopted. In particular, sophisticated parties are assumed to be more capable of protecting themselves when entering smart contracts. This may be beneficial for start-ups to avert legal risks and enhance the certainty of their contracts.

10.5 Online Platforms as Intermediaries

This section reexamines gatekeeping theory as it relates to online platforms, reviews the legislative history of existing e-commerce laws, looks at current practice in China, and analyzes the current trend toward increased liability for e-platforms.

10.5.1 Gatekeeping Theory Revisited

Enthusiasts of blockchain and similar technologies argue that individuals can directly trade with each other without the use of intermediaries, hence drastically reducing transaction costs.[83] However, the reality differs from this imagined world. Despite being presented as a decentralized, non-governed blockchain system, more advanced applications, such as Ethereum Classic, continue to rely on third parties for enforcement in the "more conventional form of state intervention."[84]

The next wave of disruptive innovation will arise from technology-enabled, platform-driven ecosystems now taking shape across industries.[85] Technology companies like Amazon, Google, and Alibaba have long understood the power of digital technologies. It is noteworthy that many of these companies' innovations do not involve

---

[83] Ally Financial Buy stocks online without the need for a traditional broker (2017), www.ally.com/do-it-right/investing/trading-without-a-broker/.

[84] Avtar Sehra, Building a Decentralised Ecosystem, slide 9, www.slideshare.net/arcatomia/ethereum-classic-18-august-2016?qid=f687c929-6875-4c92-9f42-422ceaba64cc&v=&b=&from _search=7.

[85] Accenture Technology Vision 2016 People First: The Primacy of People in a Digital Age, p. 11. Available at www.accenture.com/t20160804T100550Z__w__/us-en/_acnmedia/Accenture/Omobono/TechnologyVision/pdf/Technology-Trends-Technology-Vision-2016.pdfla=en#zoom=50.

the production of new products or services as much as the development of new platforms and platform applications on which products and services are traded. Such platform-based business models fundamentally change the way that companies do business. The top 15 public "platform" companies represent $2.6 trillion in market capitalization worldwide and continue to attract capital investment through their platform ecosystems and digital assets, which are believed to be value-creating. Moreover, there are more than 140 "unicorns," driven by platform strategies, with a total valuation of more than $500 billion.[86] It is anticipated in the near future, a core component of corporate and capital market valuations will be their platform ecosystems and digital assets.[87]

In the digital age, platforms typically act as online matchmakers that connect suppliers and consumers. By far, the most common types of transaction platforms are essentially digital matchmakers. In China, transactional platforms include Alibaba in e-commerce, Tujia in flat renting, and Didi in car-hailing services.[88] Profit margins for platforms that provide matching services is much higher than the vertical model of e-commerce where product or service providers build their own platforms to directly sell to customers.[89] More than conventional platforms, Internet users are involved in e-commerce as both suppliers and consumers with the assistance of social media. For instance, one can register a personal account on WeChat with a function called "Moment," which creates a friends circle where all the viewers who are "friends" of the account holder can access the displayed content. Alternatively, WeChat users can opt to have their accounts accessible to the general public. The publicly accessible accounts are under much stricter regulations than are enforced by "friends" of the WeChat account.[90]

The positive externality produced by matchmaking platforms is that they increase the variety and quality of product and service offerings available to users.[91] These network externalities are enhanced as customer bases increase in size, and providers join and provide additional innovative products.[92] The current literature suggests how to maximize capabilities, pricing, strategic alliances, and ecosystem value co-creation. Little research has focused on appealing to the provider side of the market. The rest of this section, and the next, will consider the operation of platforms from a legal point of view, as well as the elements of a liability regime for platform operators.

---

[86] "The Unicorn List," CB Insights (2015), www.cbinsights.com/research-unicorn-companies.

[87] Marshall Van Alstyne, Boston University, and MIT Sloan's Initiative on the Digital Economy www .accenture.com/us-en/insight-digital-platform-economy; Accenture, People First: The Primacy of People in a Digital Age (2016); Xia Han, Veronica Martinez, and Andy Neely, "Service in the Platform Context: A Review of the State of the Art and Future Research," in Anssi Smedlund, Arto Lindblom, Lasse Mitronen (eds.), Collaborative Value Co-creation in the Platform Economy, (Springer, 2018), p. 2.

[88] Didi Chuxing (DiDi), www.didiglobal.com/about-didi/about-us.

[89] The Fatal Problem of Platform Businesses, http://finance.sina.com.cn/zl/management/2018-08-31/zl-ihinpmnq4586705.shtml

[90] WeChat Official Platform Operation Rules, https://mp.weixin.qq.com/cgi-bin/readtemplate?t=business/ faq_operation_tmpl&type=info&lang=en_US&token=

[91] John W. Boudreau, Strategic Industrial–Organizational Psychology Lies Beyond HR (2012), https://doi .org/10.1111/j.1754-9434.2011.01409.x

[92] T. Eisenmann and A. Hagiu, "Staging Two-Sided Platforms," (2007) Harvard Business School Working Paper, 808–904.

To regulate online platforms as gatekeepers has theoretical roots.[93] The origins of the concept of gatekeeper can be traced back to Kurt Lewin, who described gatekeeping as the process of food reaching the family table. To put food on the family table requires a series of decisions to purchase, transport, and process the food.[94] Lewin employed the term "channels" to refer to the sources of information and the ensuing decision processes. Each channel consists of several sections, one for each decision. It is the gatekeeper who determines whether a type of food enters a given channel or whether it should be moved from one section to another.[95] The entrances to the channel and its sections represent decisions or action points that are called gates. In a word, gatekeeping is a process of items entering into a channel guarded by gatekeepers.

In the digital age, platforms act like gatekeepers. Some platforms provide content, products, or services by themselves, while others simply provide a virtual space for users to upload user-generated content or where users can offer their own products or services for sale. A persistent question arising from the platform economy is whether platforms should be liable in providing hosting and matchmaking services, when users break the law, such as by committing copyright infringement. Needless to say, the primary infringer is subject to tort liability. However, the platform may also be subject to liability even though there is no evidence showing that the platform was directly involved in the infringement. Curiously, despite its importance, the topic of third-party liability has received only scant attention by legal academics.[96] The justification to expand liability to third parties, such as platforms, is that primary liability is not sufficient to deter potential infringers.[97] While the fundamental reason for expanding liability to third parties is well established, little has been settled about the appropriate scope of third-party liability. Specifically, legal scholarship has little to say about the standard of liability that should apply to third parties.[98]

In the last decade, gatekeeping theory has been continuously challenged and modified.[99] Gatekeeping theory has been traditionally adopted by the financial sector. Gatekeepers are intermediaries whose cooperation is essential for many financial transactions: bankers, accountants, lawyers, credit rating agencies, and other

[93] Jonathan Zittrain, "A History of Online Gatekeeping" (2006) *Harvard Journal of Law and Technology* (19) 253; OECD, (2011), *The Role of Internet Intermediaries in Advancing Public Policy Objectives* (2011), www .oecd.org/sti/ieconomy/theroleofinternetintermediariesinadvancingpublicpolicyobjectives.htm.

[94] Kurt Lewin, "Frontiers in Group Dynamics" (1947) *Human Relations*, 1 (2), 145.

[95] Abraham Z. Bass, "Refining the 'Gatekeeper' Concept: A UN Radio Case Study" (1969) *Journalism and Mass Communication Quarterly*, (1), 69–72.

[96] A notable exception is the seminal article by Reinier Kraakman offering important insights concerning gatekeeper liability. See Reinier Kraakman, "Gatekeepers: The Anatomy of a Third-Party Enforcement Strategy" (1986) *Journal of Law, Economics, & Organization*, 2 (1), 53; Assaf Hamdani, "Who's Liable for Cyberwrongs?" (2002), *Cornell Law Review*, 87 (901).

[97] See Reinier H. Kraakman, "Corporate Liability Strategies and the Costs of Legal Controls" (1984) *Yale Law Journal* (93) 857, 865–867.

[98] But see Neal Kumar Katyal, "Criminal Law in Cyberspace" (2001), *University of Pennsylvania Law Review*, 1003, 1095–1101 (exploring the optimal regime of ISP liability for user crimes); William Landes and Douglas Lichtman, "Indirect Liability for Copyright Infringement: Napster and Beyond" (2003) *Journal of Economic Perspectives* (17), p. 113 (providing a framework for evaluating indirect liability for copyright infringement).

[99] J. Wallace, "Modelling Contemporary Gatekeeping. The Rise of Individuals, Algorithms and Platforms in Digital News Dissemination" (2017) *Digital Journalism*, http://dx.doi.org/10.1080/21670811.2017.1343648, available at www.mediachange.ch/media/pdf/publications/Wallace2017_Digital_Gatekeeping.pdf.

professionals.[100] Financial laws impose an obligation on financial institutions to monitor and detect their clients' illegal behaviors or be subject to liability if they continue to provide services to such clients either knowingly or negligently.[101] In many instances, laws holding intermediaries liable for aiding criminal activity incentivizes gatekeepers to report bad conduct in order preserve their reputational capital. However, in reality, reputational incentives may not be strong enough and the high threshold to be held liable produces a perverse effect.[102] Intermediaries are very careful to ensure that they never reach the level of culpable knowledge or negligence, which prevents them from screening for signals of potential fraud .

Legal commentators have long recognized that gatekeeper liability may affect the market for gatekeeping services. Yet, little consensus has been reached about the precise nature of this effect. Some have argued that gatekeepers may choose not to contract with clients who are inclined to commit misconduct in order to minimize their exposure to liability.[103] Others have maintained that gatekeeper liability produces a chilling effect on the market as the intermediary becomes overly cautious.[104] As a response, immunity rules have been introduced to exempt intermediaries from liability under certain circumstances. Safe harbor provisions were adopted in the United States with the enactment of the 1998 Digital Millennium Copyright Act. It establishes a set of notice and "take-down" rules that allow platforms to avoid liability if they promptly delete or block access to a copyright infringing link after it receives notice from a copyright owner. The policy consideration for the safe harbor rule for copyright infringement is that it is too costly for platforms to monitor the content that passes through their platforms and platforms do not profit from the infringing activities. The safe harbor rule has been followed in later legislation, particularly laws relating to e-commerce, where the notice and take-down rule has been introduced into regulations.[105]

---

[100] Gatekeepers are defined as "private parties who are able to disrupt misconduct by withholding their cooperation from wrongdoers", see Reinier Kraakman, "Gatekeepers: The Anatomy of a Third-Party Enforcement Strategy" 1986(2) The Journal of Law, Economics, & Organization,p. 53.

[101] Stavros Gadinis and Colby Mangels, Collaborative Gatekeepers, https://corpgov.law.harvard.edu/2016/05/12/collaborative-gatekeepers.
    Posted by Stavros Gadinis and Colby Mangels, University of California, Berkeley Law School, on Thursday, May 12, 2016. Financial intermediaries became the target of regulation because it has informational advantage and operates on the model of reputational capital. John C. Coffee, Jr., "Gatekeeper Failure and Reform: The Challenge of Fashioning Relevant Reforms" (2004), *Boston University Law Review* (84) 301, 308.

[102] While Enron and Worldcom are the most famous examples of large-scale accounting irregularities, they were not the only ones. See Daniel J. H. Greenwood, "Enronitis: Why Good Corporations Go Bad" (2004) *Columbia Business Law Review*, 773, 786; Andrew Ross Sorkin, 2 Top Tyco Executives Charged with $600 Million Fraud Scheme, *New York Times*, September 13, 2002, at C1, available at www.nytimes.com/2002/09/13/business/2-top-tyco-executives-charged-with-600-million-fraud-scheme.html (discussing the Tyco International Ltd. Racketeering scheme).

[103] Bruce A. Lehman, US Department of Commerce, Intellectual Property and the National Information Infrastructure (1995), pp. 114–124 (advocating the adoption of strict liability to ISPs for copyright infringement by their subscriber).

[104] See note 104 above, p. 116 (noting the concern that imposing strict liability on ISPs would drive service providers out of business and result in the failure of the Internet); Joel Seligman, *The Transformation of Wall Street: A History of the Securities and Exchange Commission and Modern Corporate Finance* (2nd edn., Kluwer, 1995), p. 77 (reporting concerns that the imposition of liabilities on gatekeepers under the Securities Act of 1933 would dry up American capital markets); Michael P. Dooley, "The Effects of Civil Liability on Investment Banking and the New Issues Market" (1972) *Virginia Law Review* (58), 776, 776–777 (indicate that the expansion of liability to underwriters would "discourage practically all financing").

[105] Xianlong Zhao and Mo Zhang, "Analysis on the Intellectual Protection and the 'Safe Harbor Rule' in E-Commerce Law," www.chinalawinsight.com/2018/09/articles/e-commerce, p. 3.

To summarize, online platforms' gatekeeping role is not a one-off action but requires a continuous process of checking and verifying the information placed by users on their platforms.[106] In this vein, it is critical to develop a model for platform liability to ensure that the mechanism of liability is able to deter wrongs without creating an undue chilling effect on innovation. Rather than imposing liability for the failure of platforms to monitor the quality of the products and services marketed, it is more sensible to oblige them to assess and verify the information provided by the vendors on their platforms.[107] Simultaneously, to supplement the liability regime with carefully devised safe harbor rules would give stronger incentives for platforms to diligently monitor the authenticity of the information provided by vendors and deal with complaints promptly.

10.5.2 Legislative History

This section reviews the legislative history of regulations relating to the Internet in China, assesses the effects of the regulations, and discusses liability models imposed on platform operators. Scholars have divided the development of the Internet into four stages. In the Internet 1.0 era (1994–2001), regulation focused on anti-virus and web security issues. During the Internet 2.0 era (2001–2008), a better-rounded regulatory framework was put in place. The most important laws enacted include the *Electronic Signature Law* of 2004 and the *Regulation for the Protection of the Right of Information Network Communication* of 2006. The Internet 3.0 era (2009–2014) witnessed the rise of AI, connected data, and semiotic architecture to the Internet. Highly interactive applications like WeChat became a phenomenon. Since 2012, China entered an age of the "mobile Internet" where mobile communication services and the Internet were fully integrated.[108] The focus of the legislation during this period has been on data protection, regulation of activities related to e-commerce, and the protection of intellectual property. The Internet 4.0 era, starting in 2015, saw the increasing utilization of big data, IoT, and cloud computing, with new regulations extending to the commercial sector and state security. The *State Cyber Security Law* came into effect on June 1, 2017. More recently, the *Law of E-Commerce* became effective on January 1, 2019.

The landscape of e-commerce has evolved with disruptive technologies and innovative business methods in recent years. According to *Report on the Data of Online Retail Market in China 2017*, the amount of transactions involving online retailing totaled 7175 billion RMB.[109] A persistent legal question during the development of e-commerce in China is, to what extent can platforms be held liable for the misbehaviors committed by vendors using their platforms? Laws pertinent to platform liability lie in the areas of e-commerce, fin-tech, data privacy, intellectual property, and the sharing economy. Lawmakers face two challenges: first, to define precisely what qualifies as an online platform services provider, second, to devise an appropriate liability regime in which

[106] Richard L Vining, Jr., and Phil Marcin, "Explaining Intermedia Coverage of Supreme Court Decisions" in Richard Davis (ed.), *Covering the United States Supreme Court in the Digital Age* (Cambridge University Press, 2014), p. 94.
[107] Bertin Martens, "An Economic Policy Perspective on Online Platforms" (2016) Institute for Prospective Technological Studies Digital Economy Working Paper 2016/05. JRC101501.
[108] By December 2017, Internet surfers who accessed the Internet through mobile communication services reached 753 million, which amounts to 97.5 percent of the Internet users. See CNNIC, *41st Report on the Development of Internet in China*, available at www.cac.gov.cn/2018-01/31/c_1122346138.htm.
[109] See www.100ec.cn/zt/17wlls.

platforms can be held contributorily liable for IP infringement that transpire on their platforms.

In a report published in 2010, the OECD uses the term "Internet intermediary" to refer to a party that stores, links, or transfers content provided by third parties but does not produce its own content.[110] However, this definition falls short of the reality of virtual space where the boundary between content producer and service provider is often blurred. In China, different laws have used terms like "online trading platform"[111] and "third party e-commerce trading platform"[112] to refer to platforms, and "Internet services provider"(ISP)[113] and "Internet information services provider" to refer to services providers.[114] The diversity of existing laws calls for clarification and the adoption of consistent terminology in future legislation. The 2019 *Law of E-Commerce* attempts to deal with the issue of inconsistent terminology.

In the drafting of the *E-commerce Law*, the definition of "e-commerce platform operators" was continuously broadened and now encompasses almost all types of traders who use the Internet as a means to run a business. Article 2 of the *E-Commerce Law* defines "e-commerce" as trading activities involving the selling of goods or providing services through the Internet or other online information networks.[115] Article 9 provides definitions for "e-commerce business," "platform," and "in-platform business." E-commerce business means natural persons, legal persons, or organizations (without the status of legal person) that engage in the business activities of selling commodities, or providing services, through the Internet or any other information network, including self-built websites. E-commerce platform business means a legal person or an organization which provides virtual space to host information on which multiple parties would be replied on to independently conduct trading activities or provides match-making services between suppliers and consumers. Finally, in-platform business means a vendor who sells commodities or provides services through an e-commerce platform. This three-layered definition covers all online trading and is all-inclusive for business conducted through social media, self-built websites, as well as centralized platform.

10.5.3 *Practice in China*

China adopts the gatekeeping model that allocates liability between the primary infringer and the platform operator. On the one hand, platform operators may be liable for contributory tort liability for the infringement committed by the primary infringer. On the other hand, limited immunity is provided for platforms if they take prompt measures to deter or terminate the infringement.

The 2006 *Regulation on the Protection of the Right to Disseminate Works through Information Networks* (Information Networks Regulation) for the first time provided

---

[110] Perset, K, "The Economic and Social Role of Internet Intermediaries" (2010) OECD Digital Economy Papers, No. 171, (OECD Publishing, Paris), http://dx.doi.org/10.1787/5kmh79zzs8vb-en,. at p. 9.

[111] Art. 44 of Law on Protection of Consumer Rights and Interests.

[112] Art. 3.2 of Regulation on the Services Provided by Third Party E-Commerce Trading Platform.

[113] Art. 36 of Tort Liability Law.

[114] Art. 45 of Advertisement Law.

[115] Note that "certain products or services offered and distributed online are excluded from this definition as this Law shall not apply to financial products and services and news information, audio and video programs, publication, cultural products, and other content services provided via information networks"(art. 2).

detailed safe harbor-like rules for ISPs. Article 22 provides that the regulation imposes fault liability on ISPs. Second, following the *American Digital Millennium Copyright Act*, it contains a notice-and-take-down mechanism to exempt search, linking services, and information storage service providers from tort liability. Third, if a file-hosting service provider or a search and linking service provider knew or should have known that linked material was illegal and still continued to allow users to upload and distribute the material, it is subject to contributory liability. Article 23 holds Internet service providers jointly liable if they knowingly or negligently (should have known) that linked works were copyright infringing. The courts have subsequently applied the rules of the *Information Networks Regulation* to other types of intellectual property infringement.

The 2009 *Tort Liability Law* adopts similar liability rules to fields other than intellectual property law. According to Article 6, a person shall be subjected to tort liability under two circumstances: (1) the person is at fault for an infringement upon a civil right or interest of another and (2) the person who is presumed to be at fault by law. Article 6 provides two principles to assess liability: fault and the presumption of fault. Despite the lack of a clear definition, Chinese scholars generally agree that fault may occur either intentionally or negligently.[116] On the one hand, Chinese textbooks define fault as "knowing and willing,"[117] which can be interpreted as persons who foresaw the consequences of their conduct and continued the improper conduct.[118] On the other hand, negligence refers to the failure to foresee something that a reasonable and prudent person would have foreseen or by failing to implement preventive measures.

Article 36 of the *Tort Liability Law* further clarifies the fault principle in relation to platforms that provide services online. Two circumstances have been stipulated where a network service provider will be considered liable either on its own or jointly with the party that committed the wrong: (1) when a service provider receives a notification concerning copyright infringement from a copyright owner and fails to promptly delete or block access to the work and (2) when a service provider knows about the infringement and fails to take necessary measures to stop the infringement or prevent further harm. Joint liability aims to punish any entity assisting, abetting, facilitating or inducing the commission of infringing acts.

The 2019 *E-Commerce Law* also positions e-commerce platform operators as gatekeepers and provides them with a degree of immunity. Article 38 provides that if an e-commerce platform operator knows or should have known that the products or services provided by an in-platform business owner (vendor) may cause harm to consumers and fails to adopt necessary measures to prevent the harm, the e-commerce platform operator shall be subject to contributory liability. Moreover, if the e-commerce platform operator fails to diligently check the qualification and license of the vendors (whose products or services impact the life or health of consumers) and thereafter causes harm to the consumer, the operator will bear contributory liability in accordance with the degree of its fault. Clearly, platform operators have a duty of care to check and verify the information provided by vendors for particular products and services.

---

[116] Shengming Wang, *Explanations to the Tort Liability Law of the People's Republic of China* (China Law Press: Beijing, 2010), p. 41

[117] Liming Wang, *Course Book of the Tort Liability Law of China* (People's Court Press: Beijing, 2010), p. 207.

[118] Lixin Yang, *Detailed Explanations to the Tort Liability Law of the People's Republic of China* (Intellectual Property Rights Press: Beijing, 2010), pp. 59–60.

In addition to the liability incurred by quality problems of the products and services, platform operators again are liable for infringement of intellectual property.[119] Article 42 provides that the platform operator has to take necessary measures and simultaneously forward complaint notifications to vendors. The act of simply forwarding the notification to the vendor does not satisfy the requirement of "taking necessary measures" and therefore cannot be used as a defense by a platform operator. The platform operator must take measures to prevent the harm. Platforms are liable if they fail to notify vendors in a timely manner or fail to take prompt action to prevent loss. Article 44 is a "red flag" rule for platform operators to be imposed if the infringement is so obvious that it is almost impossible for any reasonable platform operator to fail to detect. The judicial decisions[120] in the past have provided criteria for satisfying the knowledge requirement[121] and have been codified in Article 45.

Article 45 provides that a platform operator shall bear tort liability contributorily with the in-platform vendor if it knows or should have known of the infringement of intellectual property by the vendor but fails to adopt necessary measures like deleting, blocking access, disconnecting the link or disabling the transaction. Moreover, noncompliance with the statutory requirements may result in a fine of two million RMB and suspension of platform operator's license.[122]

Article 42 develops the notice-and-take-down procedure for e-commerce platform operators. It provides that the e-commerce platform operator shall bear contributory liability for loss caused by delaying to taking action to prevent the infringement. This liability rule is similar to Article 36(2) of the *Tort Liability Law*. The provision also gives platform owners a right to bring a claim against IP owners that provide false notifications. This rule can effectively prevent the complainants from abusing the notice-and-take-down rule. Moreover, Article 43 gives in-platform vendors the right to send counter-notices to defend the wrongful complaint. Once receiving a counter-notice, the platform operator should forward it to the complaining party. If the complainant fails to substantiate its claim or bring a legal action, the platform operator must terminate the injunctive measures taken against the vendor within 15 days of the receipt of the counter-notice.

Numerous uncertainties remain over the meaning of some of the statutory provisions. As mentioned earlier, Article 38 provides that platform operators are obliged to check the qualifications and license of in-platform vendors who provide goods or services relating to the health of consumers. On the one hand, it is unclear whether the platform operator has a one-off duty to check the license when the in-platform vendor registers with the platform, or a continuous duty to check the validity of the license. Obviously, a continuous duty increases operational costs and exposes platform operators to a higher risk of liability. Thus, the extent or scope of the platforms' monitoring function is unclear. Unlike offline intermediaries, online platform operators do have the ability or opportunity to inspect real products or services. Therefore, it is difficult for the platform operators to fulfill the duty to monitor and assess the quality and safety of products and services.

---

[119] Arts. 41–45 of the E-Commerce Law.

[120] *Yinian (Shanghai) Fashion Ltd v. Taobao*, Shanghai No. 1 Intermediary People's Court, 2011, No. 40 (Hu Yi Zhong Min Wu (Zhi) Zhong No. 40). Taobao was held liable for trademark infringement by a vendor on the platform because Taobao should have been able to take more effective measures to deter the infringement but failed to do so.

[121] Ten Typical Intellectual Property Cases of 2011, published by the Supreme People's Court, www .chinanews.com/cul/2012/04-18/3827065.shtml

[122] Art. 83.

The trend of imposing a duty of care to verify the information of vendors can be observed from other pieces of legislation. Article 44 of the *Law on Protection of Consumer Rights and Interests*[123] provides that platform operators must check vendors' real names, addresses and contact information. Furthermore, it must provide the vendor's contact information to consumers who suffer a loss. Failure to provide the correct information to the consumer results in a shift of liability from the vendor to the platform operator. The *Food Safety Law* has a similar provision.[124] But, it further provides that the platform operator must verify whether vendors have valid licenses for providing food or catering services.[125] The failure to verify licenses subjects the platform operator to fines and the suspension of its license.[126]

As observed above, the laws impose a heavier duty on platforms to monitor and assess the information provided by vendors, while at the same time limits their liability through safe harbor provisions. Article 42 of the *E-Commerce Law* provides that the platform operator has to take "necessary measures" once it receives a notification from a right owner. The phrase necessary measures include taking down and blocking access, as well as taking further measures such as terminating the transaction.[127] Regulators have shown a strong inclination to impose heavier liability on platform operators than ever before.[128]

10.5.4 *Trend of Liability*

It is difficult for regulators to trace and identify infringers due to the voluminous size of online data and the small scale of many online transactions. The rising costs of enforcement and the marginalized effect of punishment render enforcement less effective. On the other hand, the cost for individual platforms to monitor and detect cases of infringement is lower than it is for state law enforcement bodies. Therefore, the regulators tend to rely on platforms to reduce its enforcement costs.

Nevertheless, this functionalist approach has its limits. Online and offline platforms play different roles and provide different services.[129] The data processed by many online platforms is mostly automated and impersonal. Compared with brick-and-mortar stores, the online platforms' strength is to match suppliers with consumers, without having direct contact with the products or services provided by the suppliers.

Against the backdrop of greater obligations of platforms to verify information and liability for failing to act as gatekeepers is the difficulty of setting penalties to achieve socially optimal outcomes. Thus, the government cannot simply rely on gatekeepers to

---

[123] English version available at www.law.hku.hk/cprivacy/archives/179.refel.
[124] Art. 131.
[125] Art. 35.
[126] Art. 131.
[127] See Advertisement Law enacted on 27 October, 1994, and amended on 24 April, 2015; Food Safety Law enacted on 28 February, 2009, and amended on 24 April, 2015; Methods of Monitoring and Administration of Food and Drugs circulated on the Internet enacted on 7 November, 2017.
[128] Shaoqing Guo and Jiaxi Chen, Legislation on the Internet in China in the Last Two Decades: Review, Achievements and Reflection(2017) *Social Science Front* (6), p. 221.
[129] Lixin Yang and Xu Han, "ISPs' Legal Status and their Civil Liability" (2014) *Jianghan Luntan* (5), 84.; Hongjin Han, "Trading Platform Services Providers' Legal Status" (2009) *Contemporary Law Review* 23 (2), 99.

police the marketplace.[130] Rather, regulation and other policies are needed for dealing with enforcement failures. Admittedly, government regulations suffer from flaws of its own, including the lack of information and the persistent tendency toward regulatory capture and rent-seeking. Yet, since gatekeeper liability is also an imperfect, costly legal mechanism, policymakers should weigh the costs of government regulation against the costs of gatekeeper liability.

In China, Internet giants like Tencent contend that placing excessive liability on platform operators for failing to monitor vendors that is beyond their capacity will bring chilling effects and stifle the Internet industry.[131] Academics also point out that the balance between platforms' rights and obligations is tilted against the operators.[132] The rapid growth of the Internet and the lack of regulation have created cases of abuse. In order to avoid being accused of over- or underregulation, government authorities have deferred monitoring functions to platforms as gatekeepers, and avoid the problem of informational asymmetry between regulators and the regulated.[133] A consensus of scholars suggests that the government adopt a nonintervening approach and incentivize the industry to come up with self-regulating norms.[134] It is also suggested that it will be difficult to calibrate the optimal level of liability for platforms hosting copyrighted content.[135]

In sum, gatekeeping is a continuous process of data collection and processing. Governments face the problem of identifying misconduct and locating the wrongdoers on the platforms, due to informational asymmetry. Therefore, the challenge for lawmakers is to adjust the liability regime for platforms to deter wrongs without causing a chilling effect on innovation. The balance is best struck by creating carefully devised safe harbor rules aimed at providing incentives to platform operators to diligently check the information provided by vendors.

10.6 The Way Forward

Blockchain and other emerging technologies have fostered innovative forms and organizations to conduct business in both real and virtual spaces. Blockchain technology proponents tend to overestimate the power of private ordering and minimize the importance of trusted intermediaries.[136] However, the reality is that a complex and changing world often entails a more nuanced application of legal rules involving the human

---

[130] Lucian Arye Bebchuk, "Property Rights and Liability Rules: The Ex Ante View of the Cathedral" (2001) *Michigan Law Review*, 100(3): 601–639 (showing that liability rules may fail to produce optimal incentives to make investment ex ante); Steven Shavell, "Liability for Harm Versus Regulation of Safety" (1984) *The Journal of Legal Studies* 13 (2), 357 (exploring conditions under which regulation is superior to liability for harm).

[131] Xiongshan Cai, "Transformation from Regulation of Internet to Governance of Internet" in *Legislating in the Internet Plus Era and Public Policy* (Law Press: Beijing, 2016), p. 145.

[132] Ibid. at 221.

[133] Hanhua Zhou, "International Experience in Legislating for the Internet" in Internet Society of China (ed.) *Law of the Internet* (Publishing House of Electronics Industry: Beijing, 2016), p. 7.

[134] Ping Zhang, "A Discussion on Several Issues in the Regulation of the Internet" (2012) *Intellectual Property* (8), 3. Also see note 133, p. 222.

[135] Ming Yang, "The Weakness of the Provision for Platform Liability in the E-Commerce Law" (2017) *China Policy Review* (5), 48.

[136] Benito Arruñada, "Blockchain's Struggle to Deliver Impersonal Exchange" (2017) *Minnesota Journal of Law, Science and Technology*, 19 (1), 56, 106–112.

element.[137] Smart contracts have mostly "escaped" the reaches of law because they have been used only in the simplest forms of transactions.[138]

In China, blockchain technology is booming. Both public and private sectors have adopted smart contracts that are run on blockchains. Contract law faces challenges in every aspect in regulating this new phenomenon, including formation of contract, performance and modification of contract, enforcement, remedies, and methods of dispute resolution. These challenges reflect the intrinsic limits of smart contracts that are understandably rigid due to the nature of code and decentralization.[139] This chapter proposes a twofold regulatory model: (1) state regulation consistently throughout the country involving enforcement issues and (2) encouragement of the private sector to reach consensus on standards for self-regulation.[140] The need for fundamental change in contract law is unlikely.

No matter how technology advances, many aspects of sophisticated commercial agreements are not subject to automation, including matters requiring human judgment, the rendition of sophisticated or human-intensive services, and the resolution of disputes. Courts will continue to play an important role in adjudicating contract disputes involving smart contracts.[141]

Platforms will continue to evolve in matching suppliers with consumers both online and offline.[142] Nevertheless, applications enabling business-to-business (B2B) transactions mostly rely on "private" or "permissioned" systems, which are open only to pre-approved users and in which consensus is established by a fixed set of nodes.[143] The inherent contradiction of permissioned or private blockchains is that the smaller the network, the fewer the benefits of decentralization, and the greater the risk of manipulating it.[144] The advantage of blockchain applications would be considerably enhanced if the technology fulfills its promise of enabling individual users to own and keep full control of their historical record of transactional data, which is now in the hands of third-party centralized data silos (such as Google, Facebook, and Tencent). However, most blockchains perform simple transactions, such as trading in bitcoin, and continue to rely

[137] What Is Ethereum Classic, Cryptocompare (August 3, 2016), www.cryptocompare.com/coins/guides/what-is-ethereum-classic. Also see note 143, 76.
[138] Allens, Blockchain Reaction: Understanding the opportunities and navigating the legal frameworks of distributed ledger technology and blockchain (2017) www.allens.com.au/data/blockchain/index.htm?sku=fsdah5e556eqweqwg, pp 14–15.
[139] See section 10.3.1.
[140] Harry Surden, "Computable Contracts" (2012) UC Davis Law Review, 46 (629), p. 72.
[141] It is still very early to conclude that smart contracts will be able to revolutionize the existing legal framework by introducing the so-called Lex Cryptographia. Aaron Wright and Primavera De Filippi, Decentralized Blockchain Technology and the Rise of Lex Cryptographia (2015), www.ssrn.com/abstract=2580664.
[142] Admittedly, specialized enforcement and intermediation will entail agency costs. See David S. Evans, Economic Aspects of Bitcoin and Other Decentralized Public-Ledger Currency Platforms, Coase-Sandor Institute for Law and Economics, Working Paper No. 685 (2014), http://chicagounbound.uchicago.edu/cgi/viewcontent.cgi?article=2349&context=law_and_economics. See David Driesen and Shubha Ghosh, "The Functions of Transaction Costs: Rethinking Transaction Cost Minimization in a World of Friction" (2005) Arizona Law Review (47), 61.
[143] Vitalik Buterin, On Public and Private Blockchains, Ethereum Blog (August 7, 2015), https://blog.ethereum.org/2015/08/07/on-public-and-private-blockchains/ (describing the comparative advantages of public and private blockchains).
[144] Arvind Narayanan, Joseph Bonneau, Edward Felten, Andrew Miller, and Steven Goldfeder (eds.), Bitcoin and Cryptocurrency Technologies: A Comprehensive Introduction (Princeton University Press, 2016), 88.

on intermediaries such as exchanges (digital marketplaces) and wallets (digital storage services).[145] Nonetheless, blockchain transactions are largely unregulated.

In contracts, regulation of digital platforms has expanded. Platform operators are required to monitor the quality of certain goods and perform due diligence to detect infringements of IP rights, and check and verify the licenses and qualifications of vendors that provide food products and catering services. The reason why the duty of care is placed on the platform operator is because it is an efficient form of regulation. However, it is unreasonable to expect platforms to ensure the quality of goods and services. It is recommended that regulation focus on the duty of authentication, maintenance, and regular verification of vendor information.

10.7 Conclusion

Blockchain and other technologies have posed challenges that are fundamental to commercial organizations and the legal system that regulates them. This chapter explored whether the legal landscape will need to fundamentally change in China in view of the emergence of smart contracts. The feature of decentralization supported by blockchain technologies will continue as a way of growing the economy. In transactions involving rights in persona, the blockchain is incapable of dealing with relatively complex relational contracts due to the rigidity arising from codes as well as the structure of decentralization. In transactions involving rights in rem, blockchain can serve best as a consolidator of data. Hence, despite the claim that intermediaries will be eliminated due to the decentralized architecture and trustless relationships enabled by blockchain technologies, intermediaries will continue to play an important role, socially and legally.

The chapter concludes that despite regulatory gaps, the current legal framework can accommodate or mitigate the legal risks brought about by smart contracts. Innovative technology does not necessarily lead to innovative jurisprudence. The time is not yet ripe to impose a new legal framework for blockchain-based smart contracts.

However, adjustments need be made to the existing regulatory framework relating to online platforms to deter platforms' rent-seeking behaviors by overlooking signals of infringement. The regulation must be targeted so as not to stifle innovation. In China, the legal risks are becoming higher for platform operators who are not directly involved in commercial activities of vendors using their platforms to provide various goods or services to consumers. On the one hand, the scope of the duty of care to screen for misconduct and to promptly respond to complaints has broadened. On the other hand, safe harbor rules are limited in application. Regulators need to stay alert to misconduct by platforms in their role of gatekeepers. Regulations should focus more on the duty of platforms to monitor and verify the information of their vendors.

---

[145] Michael Abramowicz, "Cryptocurrency-Based Law" (2016) *Arizona Law Review* (58) 359, 413.

Part IV

Privacy, Security and Data Protection

11 Blockchain and Data Protection

Lokke Moerel

The irreversibility and transparency of public blockchains mean that they are probably unsuitable for personal data.

Open Data Institute, 2016[1]

11.1 Introduction

Despite the fact that blockchain technology (blockchain)[2] is not yet widely deployed, we have already seen quite a number of publications about the data protection issues. Initially, these publications[3] touted the promise of blockchain increasing privacy protection by, for example, facilitating decentralized identity management, allowing the sharing of data with trusted third parties only and presenting a new solution for crossborder data transfers, potentially

---

[1] J. Smith, J. Tennison, P. Wells, J. Fawcett and S. Harrison, "Applying Blockchain Technology in Global Data Infrastructure" (2016), in Technical Report, *Open Data Institute*, 16, theodi.org /article/applying-blockchain-technology-in-global-data-infrastructure/; V. Lemieux, "In Blockchain We Trust? Blockchain Technology for Identity Management and Privacy Protection" (2017), *Conference for E-Democracy and Open Government*, 57–62, perma.cc/46D3-WKKK; R. Neisse, G. Steri and I. Nai-Fovino, "A Blockchain-based Approach for Data Accountability and Provenance Tracking" (2017) *European Commission Joint Research Centre* (JRC), arXiv:1706.04507; U. Roth, "Blockchain Ensures Transparency in Personal Data Usage: Being Ready for the New EU General Data Protection Regulation" (2017), in Special Theme: Blockchain Engineering, *ERCIM News 110*, 32.

[2] This chapter uses of the narrower term of blockchain rather than distributed ledger technology (DLT), for reasons of readability, acknowledging that there are other forms of DLT to which this chapter would equally apply.

[3] M. Mainelli, "Blockchain Will Help Us Prove Our Identities in a Digital World" (2017) *Harvard Business Review*, hbr.org/2017/03/blockchain-will-help-us-prove-our-identities-in-a-digital-world; G. Zyskind, O. Nathan and A. Pentland, "Decentralizing Privacy: Using Blockchain to Protect Personal Data" (2015), *IEEE CS Security and Privacy Workshops*, ieeexplore.ieee.org/stamp/stamp.jsp?tp=&arnumber=7163223. S. Sater, "Blockchain and the European Union's General Data Protection Regulation: A Chance to Harmonize International Data Flows" (2017), *Tulane University*, papers.ssrn.com/sol3/papers.cfm? abstract_id=3080987; D. Connor-Green, "Blockchain in Healthcare Data" (2017) 21 *Intellectual Property and Technology Law Journal* 93; A. Tobin and D. Reed, "The Inevitable Rise of Self-Sovereign Identity" (2016, updated in 2017), *Sovrin Foundation 1*, sovrin.org/wp-content/uploads/2017/06frhe-Inevitable-Rise-of-Self-Sovereign-Identity.pdf.

replacing current contractual solutions, such as the EC Standard Contractual Clauses. In a second wave of publications, we saw a more in-depth discussion of the data protection issues raised by this new technology, generally concluding that public blockchain[4] features are "on a collision course with EU privacy law,"[5] are "profoundly incompatible at a conceptual level"[6] with the privacy protection principles of the EU General Data Protection Regulation (GDPR),[7] or in any event "that it remains to be seen whether EU data protection laws can embrace this development."[8] One author even concludes that there is "the risk that data protection legislation renders the operation unlawful, hence asphyxiating the development of an innovative technology with much promise for the Digital Single Market."[9] Indeed, the current conception amongst industry stakeholders is that blockchain is not compatible with the GDPR, resulting in a call for urgent revision.[10] These concerns are fed by public statements of, for example, Jan-Philipp Albrecht (the MEP responsible for coordinating the Parliament's input for the GDPR) that the GDPR requires that individuals can delete their data and that "this is where blockchain applications will run into problems and will probably not be GDPR compliant," and that therefore blockchain "probably cannot be used for the processing of personal data."[11]

---

[4] There are broadly three categories of blockchain: private, consortium and public. *Private* block-chains are maintained by a limited number of network nodes belonging to an organization. Read rights can be granted to computers that belong to the network, or could also be granted to selected external computers. *Consortium* blockchain is generally used by a number of different organiza-tions belonging to a consortium, and involves nodes of the relevant organizations only; here, also, read rights can be controlled. Public blockchain may involve any computer that opts to be a network node and can read/write the blockchain. Examples of the latter are Bitcoin or Ethereum. Another distinction is between permissioned and permissionless blockchain: permis-sioned blockchain is open to predefined subjects only and permissionless blockchain allows all those with the necessary technical capacity to take part. Private and consortium blockchain are mostly (but not necessarily) permissioned blockchain, and public blockchain is mostly permissionless.

[5] D. Meyer, "Blockchain Technology Is on Collision Course with EU Privacy Law" (2018), *IAPP*, at iapp.org /news/a/blockchain-technology-is-on-a-collision-course-with-eu-privacy-law/.

[6] M. Finck, "Blockchains and Data Protection in the European Union" (2017), 18–01 *Max Planck Institute for Innovation and Competition Research Paper (MPI Paper)*, 1.

[7] Regulation (EU) 2016/679 of the European Parliament and of the Council of April 27, 2016, on the protection of natural persons with regard to the processing of personal data and on the free movement of such data and repealing Directive 95/46/EC (General Data Protection Regulation or GDPR)

[8] M. Berberich and M. Steiner, "Blockchain Technology and the GDPR – How to Reconcile Privacy and Distributed Ledgers?" (2016) 2 *European Data Protection Law Review*, 426.

[9] Finck, "Blockchains & Data Protection in the EU," 1–2.

[10] See Meyer, "Blockchain Technology Collision with EU Law," for a number of quotes from stake-holders voicing concerns that it is incompatible with the GDPR, that the GDPR is therefore already out of date and therefore already needs urgent revision; see in similar vein (and with similar quotes) also S. Ward, "Blockchain to Clash with New EU Privacy Law" (2018), www.bestvpn.com/privacy-news/blockchain-clash-new-eu-privacy-law; and O. Avan-Nomayo, "Parity Forced to Shut Down ICO Passport Service (Picops) Due to GDPR" (2018), bitcoinist.com/parity-forced-to-shut-down-picops-due-to-gdpr/.

[11] See for quotes Albrecht: Meyer, "Blockchain Technology Collision with EU Law."

11.2 Difficulty of Identifying the Controller

The main issue raised by the authors[12] is that the GDPR hinges on the notion of a "controller"[13] who (alone or jointly with others) is responsible for compliance with the GDPR, in particular for implementing privacy-by-design principles[14] in blockchain and being the addressee of the requests and claims of data subjects.[15] In the current platform economy (with large intermediaries such as Google, Amazon, Apple and Facebook centrally collecting and processing data),[16] it would often be possible to identify *the* entity that is the controller. With public blockchain there would often not be a central point of control:[17] indeed, it dispenses with the need for intermediaries, as these are developed as open peer-to-peer systems for everyone to participate in and to effectuate trusted transactions with unknown counterparties.[18] In such a set-up, it would be difficult to identify *the* controller. The authors subsequently focus on the role and function of the "nodes,"[19] mentioning that all nodes in a decentralized fashion operate a public blockchain. The conclusion of the authors is that for these systems, either no node would qualify as a controller (with the result that no controller could be identified at all, which cannot be the case, as the requirements of the GDPR would not apply at all) or every node would qualify as such.[20] The authors then conclude that, for lack of a better alternative, each node qualifies as a controller and that therefore data

---

[12] The authors all also discuss whether the data stored on the blockchain qualifies as personal data under the GDPR but generally conclude that the GDPR applies to the processing of personal data stored on the blockchain also if pseudonymized, encrypted or hashed. This is a correct conclusion, as these measures all mitigate the impact on the privacy of individuals rather than fully anonymize the personal data that would bring these data outside the scope of applicability of the GDPR; see Article 29 Data Protection Working Party, "Opinion 05/2014 on Anonymisation Techniques" (2014), ec.europa.eu/justice/article-29/documen tation/opinion-recommendation/files/2014/wp216_en.pdf, 20. For reasons of space, I will refrain from discussing these issues here. See for the conclusion that GDPR applies, Finck, "Blockchains & Data Protection in the EU," 16 and Berberich and Steiner, "Blockchain Technology and the GDPR," 424; and C. Wirth and M. Kolain, "Privacy by Blockchain Design: A Blockchain-Enabled GDPR-Compliant Approach for Handling Personal Data" (2018), *Reports of the European Society for Socially Embedded Technologies*, dx.doi.org/10.18420/blockchain2018_03, 4–5.

[13] The entity that, alone or jointly with others, determines the purposes and means of the data processing (Art. 4 GDPR).

[14] Art. 25 GDPR.

[15] See for rights of data subjects Arts. 12–22 GDPR.

[16] Finck, "Blockchains & Data Protection in the EU," 6 describes it as follows: "the GDPR was fashioned for a world where data is centrally collected, stored and processed, [while] blockchains decentralize each of these processes." Blockchain would offer a record keeping function that "dispenses with the need for an intermediary," which is "in sharp contrast with the current data economy, characterized by economic centralization in the form of 'platform power'," whereby "large intermediaries such as Google, Amazon, Apple and Facebook control how we search, shop and connect."

[17] See for description of the various categories, footnote 4.

[18] Finck, "Blockchains & Data Protection in the EU," 6 and Berberich and Steiner, "Blockchain Technology and the GDPR," 422.

[19] It is a distributed peer-to-peer ledger stored on every node of the system. If a new transaction is effected, the nodes verify the legitimacy of the effected transaction and, for some applications, provide decentralized storage for the blockchain's ledger. Any device with an internet connection can be used as a node but, due to the processing and storage requirements, mostly computers are used as nodes. The node willingly contributes (a part of) its processing or storage abilities to the network. Alternatively, some forms of malware transform the device of an unsuspecting user into a node, sapping its processing or storage abilities.

[20] Finck, "Blockchains & Data Protection in the EU," 16 and Berberich and Steiner, "Blockchain Technology and the GDPR," 423.

subjects can invoke claims against each node independently.[21] The authors indicate that this may be different in case of private or consortium blockchain (permissioned blockchain operated by one organization or a consortium of organizations, respectively),[22] as in those cases, it might well be possible to identify a central intermediary that can qualify as the controller, such as the systems operator.[23] Consideration is subsequently given to the question of whether all nodes together could qualify as joint controllers, but this is generally rejected as these nodes "do not jointly determine the purposes and means of the processing."[24] Also considered is whether individuals could qualify as controllers themselves when they decide to use blockchain for a certain transaction, whereby the individual would be both a data subject and a data controller. The latter issue is raised but not discussed by the authors "as it would turn the conceptual GDPR framework on its head."[25]

11.3 Overview Issues Posed by Blockchain under the GDPR

The publications subsequently discuss all the issues and complications raised under the GDPR if each and every node qualifies as a controller:

- Jurisdiction and enforcement. Enforcement for Data Protection Authorities (DPAs) and data subjects would be difficult, as it is challenging to determine the exact number, location and identity of the nodes.

  As one author describes it:[26]

  "For the Bitcoin blockchain, there are currently approximately 11,000 nodes around the planet, of which about 1,800 are in Germany and 800 in France. If one were to address each of these nodes, some of which may not be found in a single jurisdiction, this would create two sets of problems. First, a large amount of nodes would need to be contacted and compelled to comply, as opposed to a single controller in a data silo scenario. Second, this may lead to forcing all nodes to stop running the blockchain software, where GDPR rights cannot be achieved through alternative means."

- Rights of individuals of access, correction and deletion. Nodes often only see the encrypted or hashed form of the data and are unable to make changes thereto, and therefore they cannot respond to the tasks the GDPR requires of the controller, such as providing data

---

[21] See Finck, "Blockchains & Data Protection in the EU," 17 who explains why it is justified that each node qualifies as a controller: "nodes are indeed not subject to external instructions, autonomously decide whether to join the chain, and pursue their own objectives [...] it appears that the Regulation's legal obligations would rest on each node, meaning that data subjects can invoke claims via-à-vis each node independently"; see also Berberich and Steiner, "Blockchain Technology and the GDPR," 424; Wirth and Kolain, "Privacy by Blockchain Design," 5, under reference to M. Martini and Q. Weinzierl, "Die Blockchain-Technologie und das Recht auf Vergessenwerden" (2017) *Neue Zeitschrift für Verwaltungsrecht (NVwZ)* 1251–1259.

[22] See for description of distinctions between different categories, footnote 4.

[23] Finck, "Blockchains & Data Protection in the EU," 16 and Berberich and Steiner, "Blockchain Technology and the GDPR," 424.

[24] See Finck, "Blockchains & Data Protection in the EU," 17; Wirth and Kolain, "Privacy by Blockchain Design," 5, under reference to R. Böhme and P. Pesch, "Technische Grundlagen und datenschutzrechtliche Fragen der Blockchain-Technologie" (2017), *Datenschutz und Datensicherheit (DuD)*, 473–81.

[25] Finck, "Blockchains & Data Protection in the EU," 17. Other than how Finck represents this, it seems to me an old issue that has already been extensively raised and discussed in respect of, for instance, social media networks. See on this in detail para. 4.8.

[26] Finck, "Blockchains & Data Protection in the EU," 17.

subjects with access to their data and the ability to correct or delete their data where required. Because of its immutability, the blockchain is, by definition, unable to forget, as a result of which the right to be forgotten will be impossible to enforce.[27]

- Data accuracy and data minimization. The immutability runs further contrary to the principles of data minimization and storage limitation. These principles require that controllers keep data up-to-date and do not process more data than required to fulfill the relevant purpose and also not retain such data longer than required for such use.[28] This requires that data are deleted or corrected when no longer accurate, that retention periods are defined, and that the data are deleted once such retention periods expire.

- Confidentiality. Public blockchain is an open system in which all data on the blockchain are available to all nodes. This means that, by definition, the nature of public blockchain is at odds with the GDPR's principle of confidentiality, which requires that access to data is only provided on a "need to know" basis.[29]

11.4 A Different Perspective: Blockchain in Context

I do not agree with the analysis in these initial publications for a host of different reasons. Before I discuss the GDPR issues raised in respect of deployment of blockchain in more detail, I will first give a broader perspective on blockchain as a new technology and the potential governance issues relating thereto.

11.4.1 Blockchain is a General Purpose Technology

Blockchain, like the Internet, is a general purpose technology,[30] which is subsequently deployed by actors for a certain purpose in a specific context. The authors, however, consider its data processing implications as if the technology in itself constitutes a data processing activity for which a controller has to be identified. This is similar exercise as attempting to identify in general who the controller is with respect to the entirety of data processing via the Internet or via email functionality. This is not a useful exercise. Everybody understands intuitively that it is impossible to identify one controller in respect of the Internet or in respect of all emails sent via email functionality. Controllership is decided based on a specific use or deployment of a certain technology, not with regard to technologies in general. Applying the question of controllership to the Internet at large would result in a similar conundrum as when applied to public blockchain: either all technical building blocks of the Internet would qualify as a controller or none of them would, a result that would pose similar data protection

---

[27] Finck, "Blockchains & Data Protection in the EU," 20–4 and Berberich and Steiner, "Blockchain Technology and the GDPR," 426.

[28] Finck, "Blockchains & data protection in the EU," 20 and Berberich and Steiner, "Blockchain Technology and the GDPR," 424–5.

[29] Digital Asset Platform, *Non-technical White Paper* (2016), bit.ly/2mmwje7, 7; see also R. Ribitzki et al., "Pragmatic, Interdisciplinary Perspectives on Blockchain and Distributed Ledger Technology: Paving the Future for Healthcare" (2018), *Blockchain in Healthcare Today*, blockchainhealthcaretoday.com/index.php/journal/article/view/24/21, 3.

[30] D. Tapscott and A. Tapscott, "Realizing the Potential of Blockchain: A Multistakeholder Approach to the Stewardship of Blockchain and Cryptocurrencies" (2017), in White Paper, *World Economic Forum*, www3.weforum.org/docs/WEF_Realizing_Potential_Blockchain.pdf, 31. See also W. Drake, V. Cerf and W. Kleinwächter, "Internet Fragmentation: An Overview" (2016) Future of the Internet Initiative White Paper, *World Economic Forum*, 11.

issues under the GDPR as identified by the authors in respect of blockchain. None of these issues have, however, hampered the development of the Internet, for the simple reason that controllership is not decided based on the technical level of operation of the relevant technology, but on who deploys this technology for a certain purpose. For example, a website owner uses the Internet to offer its website. It is the website owner who qualifies as the controller in respect of the processing of any personal data via the website and not the operator of the technical infrastructure. Below, I will explain why application of EU data protection laws has not hampered the development of the Internet and is equally unlikely to pose issues for blockchain.

11.4.2 *Blockchain as a New Global Resource*

The character and potential of this technology is well described by the World Economic Forum Report 2017 on blockchain (WEF Report).[31] The WEF Report describes blockchain as a new global resource[32] like the Internet and that requires global stewardship:[33]

> The few last decades brought us the internet of information. We are now witnessing the rise of the internet of value. [...] We can send money and soon any form of digitized value – from stocks and bonds to intellectual property, art, music and even votes – directly and safely between us without going through a bank, a credit-card company, PayPal or Western Union, social network, government or other middleman.

As blockchain is about value rather than "just" information, it cuts to the core of legacy industries like banking and also other forms of value such as public land registers or trademark registers.[34] As blockchain is about whether someone has ownership of money, stocks, houses or not (as evidenced by the case), the participants will insist that their stakes will be safeguarded (also in the long term) before the blockchain will be trusted. The prediction is therefore that, whenever applications are built for evidence and transfer of value, there will always be a set of governance rules reflecting the terms agreed by the participants of the ecosystem to regulate their relationship, as well as a governance mechanism for agreeing on changes thereto going forward.[35] The result will be that if a party participates as a member in this ecosystem, the rules of the platform will apply.

11.4.3 *No More Middlemen?*

The authors discussing the data protection issues predict that, due to the decentralized character of blockchain, the traditional middlemen will become obsolete, such as the

---

[31] Tapscott and Tapscott, "Realizing the Potential of Blockchain."

[32] Tapscott and Tapscott, "Realizing the Potential of Blockchain," 7: "So important is this new resource that some have called the blockchain a public utility like the Internet, a utility that requires public support."

[33] Stewardship involves, according to the authors: "collaborating, identifying common interests and creating incentives to act on them. We do not mean *government*, which involves legislating and regulating behavior and punishing those who misbehave."

[34] Tapscott and Tapscott, "Realizing the Potential of Blockchain," 8.

[35] Tapscott and A. Tapscott, "Realizing the Potential of Blockchain," 9: "It illustrates the profound differences between managing information creation versus value creation activities. The latter require deep negotiation, contractual and jurisdictional understandings, and the ongoing stewardship of application-level ecosystems." This may well be in the form of "membership rules" governing the decentralized organization, see P. de Filippi and A. Wright, "Decentralized Blockchain and the Rise of Lex Cryptographia" (2015) *Socials Sciences Research Network*, 31.

authorities that run the public land and trademark registries.[36] However, I believe block-chain will not make intermediaries obsolete but will likely replace the current intermediaries.[37] As the Internet disrupted many business models and intermediaries, the blockchain will in turn likely disrupt and replace even these new intermediaries with yet new intermediaries. As new business models are just emerging, it is difficult to foretell exactly what these intermediaries will look like. The first examples,[38] however, show that new intermediaries are indeed materializing, either as a single entity or as a consortium of entities often comprising of or being funded by incumbents, such as financial institutions, in charge of the governance of the platform or the entities operating an *application* on top of the platform for specific ecosystems.[39] In fact, permissioned blockchain is developed in response to the shortcomings of the initial public blockchain.[40] As a consequence, many different types are being developed, some of which have been designed for specific purposes or industries, while others are more generic. These applications are permissioned private and consortium rather than permissionless public blockchain, both in order to meet business needs and to gain social acceptance.[41] The generalized discussion by the authors on, for example, the enforcement issues due to blockchain's decentralized character is therefore likely not a realistic reflection of how these issues will be encountered in practice.

As Mik said in her contribution notes:[42]

> [O]nce it is acknowledged that there are different types of blockchains, it becomes clear that in most instances it is impossible to generalize. More specifically, arguments made in the context of permissionless blockchains (such as Bitcoin or Ethereum) lose their validity in the context of permissioned blockchain.

---

[36] Finck, "Blockchains & data protection in the EU," 6; Berberich & Steiner, "Blockchain Technology and the GDPR," 422.

[37] Tapscott and Tapscott, "Realizing the Potential of Blockchain," 5: "Of course, this does not mean that middlemen will disappear. Rather the technology provides profound opportunities for innovative compa-nies and institutions in the middle to streamline processes, increase their metabolism, create new value and enter new markets" and De Filippi and Wright, "Decentralized Blockchain technology," 51: "Even in a world dominated by decentralized data and organizations, powerful intermediary will still remain."

[38] See for an overview of the top 10 cryptocurrencies and a discussion of the set-up and governance of a number of these as well as subsequent governance challenges, Tapscott and Tapscott, "Realizing the Potential of Blockchain," 10–17. See also at p. 25 where the challenge is discussed that "powerful incumbents will usurp domains" by being the largest investors in these ventures.

[39] Tapscott and Tapscott, "Realizing the Potential of Blockchain," 8–9, describe that as to blockchain roughly three levels can be identified where decisions are made. The first is the platform level, the protocols such as bitcoin, Ethereum, Ripple or Hyperledger. The second is the application level, the tools that run on platforms, tools such as smart contracts that require massive cooperation between stakeholders to work. The third is potentially the overall ecosystem, the ledger of ledgers connecting (or not) the various platforms, such as bitcoin, Ethereum, Ripple and Hyperledger.

[40] See E. Mik, "Smart Contracts: Terminology, Technical Limitations and Real World Complexity" (2017), Singapore Management University, 10 *Research Collection School of Law*, ink.library.smu.edu.sg/cgi/viewcontent. cgi?article=4298&context=sol_research, 6; M. Mik, "Electronic Platforms: Openness, Transparency& Privacy Issues": "Public blockchains suffer from numerous shortcomings that make them inherently unsuitable as transactional platforms. [...] Permissioned ledgers were developed in response to these shortcomings." See also the contribution of Borgogno: O. Borgogno, "Smart Contracts as the (new) power of the powerless? The stakes for consumers and businesses": "Permissioned ledgers have been structured as a response to public ones."

[41] See Tapscott and Tapscott, "Realizing the Potential of Blockchain," 21, indicating that governance is critical to the success of commercial applications: "For example, Ripple's global payments steering group, a blockchain bankers network with defined rules and governance, has been a major step forward in terms of adaption and industry acceptance."

[42] Mik, "Electronic Platforms."

11.4.4 *Decentralization in a Broader Context*

In this context it is good to remember that the Internet also started out as a fully decentralized network. According to the early pioneers, the Internet would upend the existing social order through the distribution of communication tools, thereby replacing the existing centralized organizations.[43] The Internet was proclaimed to be a free haven where you could remain anonymous and beyond territorial jurisdiction.[44]

These predictions have not materialized. In recent years, we have, in fact, seen a radical concentration and centralization of Internet services, whereby a few large organizations control important hubs on the Internet (the platform economy).[45] Even governments and companies have by now transformed the Internet into the ultimate apparatus for political and social control by monitoring speech, identifying dissidents, and disseminating propaganda.[46]

It is therefore not a given that the second wave of decentralization promised by this technology will thus result in the level of decentralization assumed by the authors. As governments and companies over time managed to recentralize and monitor the decentralized Internet, they may well also succeed in again recentralizing and monitoring it. It is quite possible (and in my view very likely) that blockchain will ultimately be used to further increase control over transactions and behaviour of individuals, due to blockchain being used for central identity management and the permanent recording of every online activity.[47]

---

[43] De Filippi and Wright, "Decentralized Blockchain Technology," 19–20, under reference to: J. Barlow's "A Declaration of the Independence of Cyberspace" (1996), *Electronic Frontier Foundation*, projects.eff.org /~barlow/Declaration-Final.html.

[44] See Barlow, "A Declaration of the Independence of Cyberspace," declaring the Internet to be a "new home of [the] Mind" in which governments would have no jurisdiction. This paragraph draws on L. Moerel, "Big Data Protection, How to Make the Draft EU Regulation on Data Protection Future Proof" (2014), *Oratie Universiteit Tilburg*, www.mondaq.com/x/298416/data+protection/Big+Data+Protection+How+To +Make +The+Draft+EU+Regulation+On+Data+Protection+Future+Proof, 18.

[45] De Filippi and Wright, "Decentralized Blockchain Technology," 19–20, under reference to: "While the Internet has liberated information, and contributed to the democratization of markets, it has done little to transform many of the centralized organizations that existed before the dawn of the digital age. Governments and large corporations have in fact grown, as they leveraged the raw distributive power of the Internet," under reference to J. Goldsmith and T. Wu, *Who Controls the Internet: Illusions of a Borderless World* (Oxford: Oxford University Press 2006), pp. 142–161. See further Zyskind et al., "Decentralizing Privacy," 1.

[46] L. Moerel, "Big Data Protection," 18, under reference to N. Carr, "The Big Switch, Rewiring the World From Edison to Google" (2013), 242. N. Richards and J. King, "Three Paradoxes of Big Data" (2013) *Stanford Law Review Online* 66, www.stanfordlawreview.org/online/privacy-and-big-data/three-paradoxes-big-data, call this the "power paradox" and give the following example: "Many Arab Spring protesters and commentators credited social media for helping protesters to organize. But big data sensors and big data pools are predominantly in the hands of powerful intermediary institutions, not ordinary people. Seeming to learn from Arab Spring organizers, the Syrian regime feigned the removal of restrictions on its citizens' Facebook, Twitter, and YouTube usage only to secretly profile, track, and round up dissidents." Zyskind et al., "Decentralizing Privacy," 1.

[47] See in the same vein: De Filippi and Wright, "Decentralized Blockchain technology," 53: "The blockchain could be used, for instance, to manage identity, making it easier to monitor, surveil, or simply keep track of various online activities. Every transfer, vote, purchase can be recorded on the blockchain, creating a permanent record that will potentially push the boundaries of privacy law." In any event, as with the Internet, governments may well find intermediaries to "hook" on to (such as ISPs), to keep control over the ecosystem. See at p. 51: "Yet, the blockchain is (and will fundamentally remain) a regulatable technology. While states initially had a hard time grasping how to regulate a global and decentralized network like the Internet, they eventually came to the understanding that, as long as there are centralized chokepoints, regulation can be achieved, through the indirect regulation of the various intermediaries and online

11.5 Cross-Border Enforcement and Jurisdiction Issues

In the introduction, we saw that the authors predict that, as it will be difficult to identify *one* controller, blockchain will likely present many cross-border enforcement and jurisdictional issues, which will make it difficult, if not impossible, for individuals to enforce their data protection rights. However, if new intermediaries are emerging in respect of permissioned private and consortium platforms, the issue of identifying the controller for such blockchain will also be solved.

Also, here it is well to remember that the early predictions in respect of the Internet foresaw similar enforcement and jurisdictional issues.[48] Every encounter of consumers in cyberspace would raise the possibility that diverse laws would apply and multiple courts would have jurisdiction, and a myriad of court cases was predicted.[49] Another early prediction about e-commerce was that search engines and the global reach of the Internet would eliminate the need for wholesalers and other intermediaries, which would again give rise to many disputes directly between businesses and consumers.[50]

Contrary to these early expectations, there have been only isolated court cases dealing with online cross-border consumer disputes.[51] One of the mechanisms that explain why so few court cases actually materialized is that stakeholders quickly found practical solutions in the form of contractual self-regulatory systems.[52] Examples are the use of credit cards for online payments that bring their own dispute resolution system[53] and the emergence of large intermediaries like eBay, which was at first just regulated by the ratings and review consumers could post, but later

---

operators that actually run the network [. . .]. An analogous situation will likely take place in the context of blockchain technology. Even in a world dominated by decentralized data and organizations, powerful intermediary will still remain. If threatened, states and governmental actors could adopt a series of draconian measures to regulate the emerging online ecosystem and to retain control over the blockchain ecosystem."

[48] This paragraph draws from one of my earlier publications, where I described online cross-border enforcement issues and how best to regulate these extensively in: L. Moerel, "Binding Corporate Rules, Corporate Self-Regulation of Global Data Transfers" (Oxford University Press 2012), paras. 4.3–4.4.

[49] P. Swire, "Elephants and Mice Revisited: Law and Choice of Law on the Internet" (2005) 153 *University of Pennsylvania Law Review*, 1991–1992.

[50] P. Swire, "Law and Choice of Law on the Internet," 1991–1992.

[51] P. Swire, "Law and Choice of Law on the Internet," notes that "Surprisingly, however, the number of actual cases addressing choice of law on the Internet is far, far lower than the initial analysis would suggest. Although there is the possibility of diverse national laws in every Internet encounter, some mysterious mechanisms are reducing the actual conflicts to a handful of cases."

[52] P. Swire, "Law and Choice of Law on the Internet," 1976.

[53] P. Swire, "Law and Choice of Law on the Internet," 1990, gives this as the main reason for the fact that there are so few court cases involving online consumer purchases: "[. . .] credit card purchases (and systems such as PayPal that are based on credit and debit card accounts) have become the dominant means of payment over the Internet." As a result, "[s]ellers and buyers are subject to the elaborate rules of the credit card payment system, and so there is relatively little recourse to national courts. Credit cards have two decisive consumer protections compared with e-cash systems. If there is unauthorized use of the credit or debit card, the individual's loss is limited by U.S. statute, usually to $50.47 In addition, the credit card brings with it an already-functioning dispute resolution system. If a merchant claims that a customer has spent $200 on software, and the customer disagrees, then the customer is not charged for the $200 while the dispute is in process. With these ready-made ways to protect customers against unauthorized use and to resolve disputes, the credit card system inspires trust in consumers, creates effective dispute resolution mechanisms, and avoids the need for recourse to national courts."

introduced full-fledged dispute resolution.[54] Also, here new intermediaries have replaced the old intermediaries (retailers) by generating again the trust required to do business.

It is therefore a justified expectation that, due to the lack of government regulated supervision, the stakeholders involved will implement their own contractual self-regulatory mechanisms to ensure adequate dispute resolution, as happened with the Internet.[55]

As explained above, we already see a similar development where private and consortium platforms implement membership rules, determining which parties have read or read/write authorization. By controlling read rights, access to the information can be limited to those parties that need to know this information. To avoid jurisdictional and enforcement disputes, these rules will also provide who the responsible entity is, as well as a choice of law and forum.[56] Again, this may well be different with public platforms, especially those in the business-to-consumer (B2C) context. This is exactly the reason why it is expected that public platforms will become regulated by public governments.[57] This seems also the take of Borgogno in his contribution, indicating that, for blockchain applications in the B2C context, "policy makers and regulators should take the lead in order to guarantee a trustworthy translation into code of consumer contracts."[58] However, public platform also in the B2B context may well require public regulation (if not outright prohibition), as we already see that these forms are inherently prone to abuse for criminal activity due to full decentralization and encryption.[59]

---

[54] As P. Swire, "Law and Choice of Law on the Internet," 1991–1992, explains it in respect of the emergence of e-commerce: "Consumers can feel that it is very risky, however, to buy from a website they have never heard of, in a country far away. One major cure for this problem has been the phenomenal growth of auction sites, especially the Internet intermediary eBay [. . .]. Initially, trust in eBay was supposed to result from feedback ratings that customers gave to each other. Over time, however, eBay has created an entire legal system that accompanies each sale. The system contains at least a dozen consumer protections, including fraud protection for the buyer, an escrow service so that buyers can examine an item before payment goes to the seller, a verified identity program, and a system for fraud enforcement including referrals if necessary for criminal activity. [. . .] Although eBay initially became famous for small purchases, such as hobbyist collectibles, today's eBay includes numerous auctions for valuable items such as diamonds. Even these large consumer transactions appear to be conducted without recourse to national courts, avoiding judicial pronouncements."

[55] In fact, there is very little happening on the Internet that is not governed by some form of contract. Websites have T&Cs applicable to their use; online purchases are governed by purchase terms; access to the Internet is governed by the T&Cs of the ISP; the App stores have their T&Cs; search functionality is governed by the T&Cs of the provider of the search engine, etc.

[56] P. Botsford, *International Bar Association* (2017): "Any blockchain-based application raises potential jurisdictional knots: each transaction could fall under the jurisdiction of the various locations of the network, but this seems unworkable. Instead, parties (or platforms?) in a transaction will establish governing law and jurisdiction clauses to provide greater certainty about what laws would apply."

[57] See also Tapscott and Tapscott, "Realizing the Potential of Blockchain," 8, where it is predicted that for the Internet of value, many societies will expect government to protect the public interest: "while governments and regulators alone lack the knowledge, resources and mandate to govern this technology effectively, government participation and even regulation will likely have a greater influence over blockchain technologies [*author: than the Internet*] to ensure that we preserve both the rights and powers of consumers and citizens."

[58] Borgogno, "Smart Contracts as the (New) Power of the Powerless?" In respect to the B2B scenario, Borgogno concludes that there "will *just* be the need for oversight by public bodies."

[59] See on the potential of abuse of blockchain for criminal activity: De Filippi and Wright, "Decentralized Blockchain technology," 20–24.

11.6 Broader Governance Issues

That there will be contractual self-regulatory rules governing an *individual* block-chain does not take away more general regulatory concerns. As a general purpose technology, blockchain would benefit, for example, from global standard setting to ensure the interoperability of its applications on the various platforms, as well as to ensure interoperability between the various platforms. Below, I will explain that public institutions have never centrally regulated the Internet, which poses broader *governance* issues. We will very likely encounter similar governance issues with blockchain. For these broader governance issues, lessons can be learned from the current (lack of) central governance of the Internet and the emergence of Internet governance institutions to fill the gaps in central public governance.[60] It is clear that many find that the lack of comprehensive governance institutions for the Internet as a whole has often led to inefficiencies and by now even threaten the open character of the Internet.[61] As blockchain is expected to have a disruptive effect of a magnitude that is at least similar to that of the Internet,[62] it is clear that efficiencies could be gained if we would learn from the many governance issues encountered in respect of the Internet, and would be able to leverage the governance institutes that by now have emerged to deal with these issues.[63]

Note, however, that the broader Internet governance issues do not make the Internet inherently incompatible with the GDPR just because there is no central controller to be identified for the Internet at large. A similar conclusion will apply to blockchain technology. We already see new forms of governance and decision-making emerge in relation to blockchain as a general purpose technology (maybe even too many), mostly in forms of multi-stakeholder governance groups.[64] It is clear, however, that any global governance is at the moment very impromptu and opaque, which has the inherent risk, that "informal and invisible power dynamics emerge, often more centralized than they appear."[65] The governance will therefore require further thinking and may ultimately possibly also require public regulation.[66]

---

[60] See on the development of governance of the Internet (and how to balance the demands for national sovereignty and transnational cyberspace) as well as recent governmental fragmentation of the Internet: Drake et al., "Internet Fragmentation," 31–45.

[61] See on the different levels of fragmentation, which now threaten the open character of the Internet: W. Drake et al., "Internet Fragmentation."

[62] Tapscott and Tapscott, "Realizing the Potential of Blockchain," 8.

[63] See on current governance institutions of the Internet, Tapscott and Tapscott, "Realizing the Potential of Blockchain," 7.

[64] See for overview of all governance networks that already emerged in respect of blockchain: Tapscott and Tapscott, "Realizing the Potential of Blockchain," at Appendix: Global Solutions Network (pp. 36–40).

[65] Quote of P. De Filippi in Tapscott and Tapscott, "Realizing the Potential of Blockchain," 8. See also at 13 and 32. Note that, for each blockchain, there is, in the end, always a small group of core developers who have developed and set up the platform and have technical authority to make changes to the code, and they do so when specific failures are identified. Example here can be the Ethereum incident, whereby hackers managed to steal 3.6 million of the cryptocurrency Ether (with a total value of about US$50 million), which led the Ethereum community to agree to a hard fork splitting up the blockchain. See on this incident Tapscott and Tapscott, "Realizing the Potential of Blockchain," 15–7.

[66] See for some initial thinking on the societal challenges posed by decentralization and encryption (which are not new but are more difficult to control with blockchain) and some initial thinking how best to regulated these: De Filippi and Wright, 18.

11.7 GDPR Does Not Impose Requirements on Designers of Technology

The GDPR includes an obligation for the controller to set up data processing functions on the basis of privacy-by-design.[67] This requires controllers to mitigate the privacy impact on individuals from the outset, ensuring that their rights are already safeguarded in the design of the product or service (ex-ante) rather than that individuals have to enforce their legal rights after the processing has already taken place (ex-post).[68] The GDPR does not require providers of software and infrastructure that are used to process personal data to ensure that their products and services are developed based on privacy-by-design. As a consequence, individual controllers need to expressly instruct each of their technology suppliers to provide software and infrastructure that incorporate privacy-by-design in order to meet the controller's obligations under the GDPR. In other words, the GDPR only indirectly regulates the design of technologies, as the controllers deploying the technology will have to ensure that the technology they choose to deploy is compliant with the privacy-by-design principle under the GDPR. At first blush, this seems an ineffective way of regulating. An obvious and simple solution would have been to require software manufacturers to directly design products that are based on privacy-by-design.[69] This provision, however, did not make it into the GDPR.[70]

Though this indirect manner of regulating seems inefficient, the reality is that for technology developers it is often difficult to foresee all possible deployments of their technology. As a consequence, it is difficult to implement all requirements into their product from the outset. It is often in the feedback loop of the users, customers or society at large when the technology is deployed in practice that the design issues become apparent and are addressed. Too-strict upfront design requirements (in the form of

---

[67] Art. 25 GDPR. Relevant here is that privacy by design implies that compliance with and enforcement of legal standards is incorporated from the outset into technical designs.

[68] This paragraph draws on L. Moerel and C. Prins, "Privacy for the Homo Digitalis: Proposal for a New Regulatory Framework for Data Protection in the Light of Big Data and the Internet of Things" (2016), available at ssrn.com/abstract=2784123 (translation into English of: "De Homo Digitalis – Proeve van een nieuw toetsingskader voor gegevensbescherming in het licht van Big Data en Internet of Things," published by Wolters Kluwer), at 10 and 93, under reference to H. Nissenbaum, "A Contextual Approach to Privacy Online" (2011), Dædalus, *the Journal of the American Academy of Arts & Sciences*, www.amacad.org/publications/daedalus/11_fall_nissenbaum.pdf, 32–48; and O. Tene and J. Polonetsky, "Privacy in the Age of Big Data: A Time for Big Decisions" (2012) 64 *Stanford Law Review*, para. 1, iapp.org /media/presentations/12Summit/S12_De-identification_HANDOUT_1.pdf: "In the context of online privacy, this implies emphasis should be placed less on notice and choice and more on implementing policy decisions with respect to the utility of given business practices and on organizational compliance with fair information principles (FIPs). In other words, the focal point for privacy should shift from users to: (a) policymakers or self-regulatory leaders to determine the contours of accepted practices; and (b) businesses to handle information fairly and responsibly." See further L. Bygrave, "Hardwiring Privacy" in R. Brownsword, E. Scotford and K. Yeung (eds.), *The Oxford Handbook of Law, Regulation and Technology* (Oxford: Oxford University Press, 2017), p. 755.

[69] This would enable enforcement against the supplier rather than against each and every one of its customers using the relevant software for their data-processing activities. Suppliers generally have no commercial interest in the data collection itself, which may result in a better implementation of the principles of privacy-by-design than if this is left to data controllers. See L. Moerel and C. Prins, "Privacy for the Homo Digitalis," 10.

[70] Recital 61 of the GDPR only contains a recommendation to Member States that producers should be "encouraged" to design their products on the basis of privacy-by-design. To date, we have not seen national governments of the EU take action on this point.

standards) may even hamper innovation, and may even lead to "widespread adoption of inferior technology."[71] In the words of Behlendorf (CEO of the Linux Foundation):[72]

"The space is still so young that the desire for standards, while well-placed, runs the risk of hardening projects that have just come out of the lab" and "we need to avoid making serious architectural decisions that first become legacy and then become a hindrance."

In a similar vein, the Internet has gained such global presence also because it was not subject to upfront regulation from the outset.[73] It is subsequently in each and every use case that the legal requirements have kicked in (whether data protection, e-commerce, consumer protection or other) which have had their impact on the design of many new technologies. This is also evidenced by the fact that by now many basic privacy-by-design requirements have found their way in, for example, standard software design principles.[74]

Over time, EU data protection laws have proved to be well able to cater for the development of Internet-related technologies. The GDPR (as was its predecessor the Data Protection Directive) is technology agnostic[75] in the sense that it provides for general data protection principles and requirements but does not prescribe any technology or technical manner by which these principles and requirements should be implemented. As blockchain is an emerging technology still in its infancy, the GDPR works exactly as it is intended, challenging developers to think of creative ways to develop the technology in such a manner that the impact on the privacy of individuals can be mitigated and basic principles of the GDPR can be complied with. That this may take some development cycles to be achieved is fully understood.

The conclusions of the authors that public blockchain is at odds with the principles of the GDPR, and that the GDPR is thus unable to embrace this new technology, misses the point that the GDPR is intended to provide guidance on how to develop new technology in the first place. Also, the conclusion of one author that "we must be willing to adapt the law to technologic change and accepting of greater techno-legal interoperability"[76] seems off the mark, where the GDPR and the EU data protection supervisory authorities actively stimulate technical-legal interoperability. This is exactly why the principle of privacy-by-design is now codified in the GDPR, as it is well understood that technologic innovations may be able to better effectuate material data protection than any legal rule would ever be able to effectuate in practice (whether due to lack of compliance or otherwise).[77]

---

[71] Tapscott and Tapscott, "Realizing the Potential of Blockchain," 19.
[72] Quote from Tapscott and Tapscott, "Realizing the Potential of Blockchain," 19:

The report also notes that having too many protocols out there competing for too long, will also hamper further development of the blockchain, as it will be difficult for other parties to build applications that have to run on top of the platform layer.

[73] Drake et al., "Internet Fragmentation," 31.
[74] See e.g., International Organization for Standardization, "ISO/IEC 29100:2011, Information technology – Security techniques – Privacy framework," iso.org/standard/45123.html, Federal Office for Information Security, "IT Grundschutz Catalogues," bsi.bund.de/EN/Topics/ITGrundschutz/ITGrundschutzCatalog ues /itgrundschutzcatalogues_node.html, and Commission Nationale Informatique & Libertés, "Security of Personal Data," cnil.fr/sites/default/files/atoms/files/cnil_guide_securite_personnelle_gb_web.pdf. See also note 72 above.
[75] Recital 15 of the GDPR.
[76] Finck, "Blockchains & data protection in the EU," 2.
[77] See on the enforcement issues in respect of the rights of individuals to data protection: L. Moerel, "Binding Corporate Rules," at para. 4.3. See on the benefits of privacy-by-design requirements: the literature listed in

11.8 Individuals as Data Subjects and as Controllers: Does This "Turn the Conceptual" GDPR Framework on Its Head?

One of the authors raises the issue of whether individuals could qualify as controllers when they decide to use a blockchain for a certain transaction, whereby the individual would be both a data subject and a data controller,[78] which would turn the conceptual framework of the GDPR on its head. Contrary to what the author seems to think, this is not a new issue. Also, here we see that the Internet (and social media networks in particular) already presented us with a similar "conundrum," which has already been adequately solved within the EU data protection framework. The underlying issue was at the time (2008) well phrased by the International Working Group on Data Protection in Telecommunications:[79]

> "With respect to privacy, one of the most fundamental challenges may be in the fact that most of the personal information published in social networks is being published at the initiative of the users and based on their consent. While 'traditional' privacy regulation is concerned with defining rules to protect citizens against processing of personal data by the public administration and businesses."

As data subjects themselves publish their personal data on social media, for example, the social media networks argued they were not responsible (i.e. did not qualify as the controller) for the processing of these personal data but rather the data subjects themselves. This posed the question of whether EU data protection laws were also meant to protect data subjects against themselves. Clarity was brought by the Working Party 29[80] in its 2009 opinion on how to apply EU data protection law to social networks:[81]

> "Social Network Service (SNS) providers are *data controllers* under the Data Protection Directive. They provide the means for the processing of user data and provide all the 'basic' services related to user management (e.g. registration and deletion of accounts)" and "SNS should ensure privacy-friendly and free of charge default settings."

Applying this reasoning to our case, it is the organization (whether alone or jointly with others) offering the blockchain that provides for the "means for processing the user data." It is this organization that therefore has the responsibility to ensure that these "means" are developed based on privacy-by-design requirements. Stakeholders can therefore not just launch new technologies and then not take responsibility for their use.[82] This is why it is unlikely that public platforms with no governance mechanism whatsoever will be acceptable to regulators if consumers intend these platforms for large-scale use.

---

footnote 67. See further B. Brownsword, Chapter 12 "Smart Transactional Technologies, Legal Disruption, and the Case of Network Contracts," in L. DiMatteo, M. Cannarsa and C. Poncibò (eds.), *Smart Contracts and Blockchain Technology: Role of Contract Law* (Cambridge: Cambridge University Press 2019) (forthcoming), pp. 2–3, describing as a development the growing interest in "co-opting new technologies (either alongside or in the place of rules) as regulatory instruments."

[78] Finck, "Blockchains & data protection in the EU," 17.

[79] International Working Group on Data Protection in Telecommunications, "Report and Guidance on Privacy in Social Network Services – Rome Memorandum," (2008), www.datenschutz-berlin.de/pdf/publikationen/working-paper/2008/2008-Rome_Memorandum-en.pdf, 1.

[80] The predecessor of the European Data Protection Board under GDPR.

[81] Article 29 Data Protection Working Party, "Opinion 5/2009 on Online Social Networking" (2009), ec.europa.eu/justice/article-29/documentation/opinion-recommendation/files/2009/wp163_en.pdf, 5.

[82] Wirth and Kolain, "Privacy by Blockchain Design," 5.

The foregoing does not mean that there are no issues remaining. From a data protection perspective, the fact that current blockchains (both public and private/consortium) are immutable and (to a certain extent) inherently transparent may make it impossible to respond to rights of individuals to have their data corrected or deleted and are by definition unable to forget, as a result of which the right to be forgotten will be impossible to enforce. Again, I want to put the issues first in a broader context.

11.9 Issues with Blockchain Are Not Limited to Data Protection

Both the transparency and immutability of current blockchain is not just an issue from the perspective of data protection. For example, transparency is equally an issue for companies[83] and may be further contrary to confidential requirements applicable to financial institutions and health care professionals.[84] Another example is that storing too many data (especially transaction data) on the blockchain takes too much energy both to run and to cool the machines[85] and hampers its efficiency from an operational perspective. Suggestions to address this are to save block space by separating (segregating) the signature ("witness") information from the transaction data (the "payload") so the network can increase the transactions processed.[86] These measures may well also, to a certain extent, mitigate transparency issues. Secondly, the immutability of blockchain does not sit well with (i) smart contracts in more complex transactions (as contracts often have to be amended for unforeseen circumstances),[87] (ii) with technological malfunction (including in case of interference by hackers)[88] and (iii) more in general with human messiness (people are known to lose their blockchain private key).[89] Solving these issues

---

[83] See on transparency: V. Buterin, "Privacy on the Blockchain," *Ethereum Blog* (2016): "As seductive as a blockchain's other advantages are, neither companies or individuals are particularly keen on publishing all of their information onto a public database that can be arbitrarily read without any restrictions by one's own government, foreign governments, family members, coworkers and business competitors."

[84] Digital Asset Platform, *Non-technical White Paper*, 7: "confidential data should never be stored by a party not entitled to view that information, even if obfuscated or encrypted. As such, any potential solution designed for financial institutions must physically segregate confidential data." See also Ribitzki et al., "Blockchain and Distributed Ledger Technology," 3: "in most healthcare blockchains, sensitive information will be stored on the blockchain and only authorized entities should be given access to this information, making private and permissioned blockchains more appropriate."

[85] Tapscott and Tapscott, "Realizing the Potential of Blockchain," 14.

[86] See on the "segregated witness" (SegWit) solution proposed for the bitcoin protocol: Tapscott and Tapscott, "Realizing the Potential of Blockchain," 11.

[87] T. Tjong Tjin Tai, "Formalizing contract law for smart contracts," *ICAIL* (2017), www.cs.bath.ac.uk /smartlaw2017/papers/SmartLaw2017_paper_1.pdf, ssrn.com/abstract=3038800, 4: "The immutability means that contracts cannot keep up with changing circumstances"; and T. Tjong Tjin Tai, in his contribution "Force Majeure and Excuses in Smart Contracts" (2018), 10 *Tilburg Private Law Working Paper Series*, papers.ssrn.com/sol3/papers.cfm?abstract_id=3183637: "smart contracts are not very well suited to deal with the finesses that are currently expected when it comes to excuses to performance."

[88] L. DiMatteo and C. Poncibò, "Quandary of smart contracts and remedies: The role of contract law and self-help remedies" (2018) 26 (6) *ERPL* 805–824. The authors describe the Ethereum incident, whereby hackers managed to steal 3.6 million of the cryptocurrency Ether (with a total value of about US$50 million), which led the Ethereum community to agree to a hard fork splitting up the blockchain (which shows that immutability of the platform is not a given). See for different forms of malfunctioning: Brownsword, "Smart Contracts and Blockchain Technology."

[89] The issue of human messiness is well described in more general terms by D. Tapscott and A. Tapscott, *Blockchain Revolution: How the Technology Behind Bitcoin and Other Cryptocurrencies Is Changing the World* (New York: Penguin, 2016), p. 24:

will require tackling the immutability of blockchain, which may well also solve the issue of being able to respond to requests for deletion (right to be forgotten).

11.10 Right to Be Forgotten Is Not Absolute

The fact that the immutability issue is not addressed does not automatically mean that blockchain is therefore not suitable for all applications. Illustrative here is the judgement of the European Court of Justice in the Manni case.[90] The plaintiff (Mr. Manni) requested deletion of his personal information from the Italian public company register where information on his prior bankruptcy was recorded. He argued that this record in the company register was widely reused by data brokers, as a result of which his reputation was prejudiced, having a detrimental effect on his new business. The ECJ balanced the public interest in the legal certainty in trade and transparency of business information in the company register with the fundamental right to data protection and concluded that, in this case, the interference with the rights to data protection was not disproportionate, taking into account the limited amount of personal information held in the company register.

In line with the above ruling, registering limited personal data in a blockchain for public registers landownership, trademark ownership, company registers etc. may therefore well be justified. The above case entails that a balancing of interests should be made for each application. For other use cases, the balancing test may well conclude that such as blockchain will not be suitable as the impact on data protection will be disproportionate compared to the interest served with using the technology. An example of the latter would be if blockchain were applied to provide air passengers with expedited access through the airport, meanwhile also recording all money spent in airport shops and restaurants, subsequent transport and accommodations on the blockchain for purposes of a loyalty program.[91] It will not require much imagination to see that also using blockchain for the commercial loyalty program would be disproportionate.[92]

11.11 Privacy-by-Design Options

The transparency and immutability issues associated with both public and private/consortium platform can, to a large extent, be addressed by implementing privacy-by-design measures.

In its most basic form, a blockchain can be used to store plain text information or encrypted text on the ledger, which information can be accessed by those who have read rights. Naturally, this is not desirable from a privacy perspective but also not desirable

---

"Today, many people count on their bank or credit-card company, even talking with a real person, when they make an accounting error, forget their passwords, or lose their wallets or chequebooks. Most people with bank accounts in developed economies aren't in the habit of backing up their money on a flash drive or a second device, securing their passwords so they needn't rely on a service provider's password reset function, or keeping these backups in separate locations so that, if they lose their computer and all other possessions in a house fire, they don't lose their money."

[90] Case C-398/15, *Camera di Commercio, Industria, Artigianato e Agricoltura di Lecce v Salvatore Manni* [2017], ECLI:EU:C:2017:197.

[91] See for a loyalty program based on blockchain: "Loyal Web Page," at loyyal.com/.

[92] Knowing that any such data relating to travel of individuals through airports will be prone to law enforcement access requests.

from an economic perspective. Storing all information on the blockchain takes up a large amount of space. This means that fewer transactions can be processed per block on the chain and that a large amount of storage capacity is required. Therefore, most applications store part of the transaction in hashed form to prevent that everyone can access the information and to increase the number of transactions that can be stored on a single block. For example, basic applications store a plain text header on the block (block header)[93] and a hashed part that includes the payload[94] of the transaction.[95]

The following privacy-by-design solutions can be used to create a more privacy-friendly application than the example described above that consists of a plain text header and a hashed payload:

- Limit ledger storage. The original Bitcoin blockchain stores the full ledger on every node. This makes it almost impossible to make changes to prior blocks and thus provides for an indisputable ledger for all prior transactions. However, this also means that the personal data included on the ledger is shared with a large number of nodes (Bitcoin has approximately 9,500 nodes). Storing so many instances of personal data is at odds with the confidentiality principle of the GDPR, which requires access to personal data to be limited to the fewest possible recipients.

  A privacy-by-design solution is to no longer store the entire ledger on all nodes. In most Bitcoin instances, the validity of a new block is verified by a consensus mechanism. This means that the creator of the block provides a unique hash of the information. The nodes make the same mathematical equations and, if the outcome of this hash is the same, the block is verified. This requires the nodes to have access to the information included on the block. However, the nodes would still be able to fulfill their verification function if they would delete the information after verification. This will increase the confidentiality of the personal data included on the block and, at the same time, has economic advantages. If each node has to store a full copy of the ledger, a large amount of storage capacity is required that, in turn, requires a large investment in data storage and uses a lot of energy. Therefore, storing the ledger in one or a few instances rather than on every node has both privacy and economic advantages.

- Pruning. Most blockchain applications store all transactions since the start of the chain, dating back to the "genesis block," which means that all transactions on this blockchain are stored infinitely (and, as set out above, are sometimes stored on all nodes). Storing data infinitely is, by definition, at odds with the GDPR's data minimization requirement but also brings ever-increasing storage requirements. For example, during a stress test, the size of the blockchain of an Ethereum client increased to 40 gigabytes in the first three months of the test.[96]

  A privacy-by-design solution to this storage issue is pruning. Pruning enables the node to verify a new block without processing historical transactions by having the node download as many block-headers as it can and determine which header is on the end of the longest chain. Starting from this header on the longest chain, the node goes

---

[93] The block header contains metadata about the block, such as the version of the blockchain, an identification number of the previous block on the chain and information on the creator of the block.

[94] The payload of a block contains the actual transactions (or other information for which the blockchain is used) included in a block.

[95] Finck, "Blockchains & data protection in the EU," 5.

[96] See note 94 above.

back 100 blocks to verify that the chain matches up. Because this verification process removes the need for retaining the entire chain history for verification purposes, it allows for the removal of unused blocks, which drastically lowers the required storage and implements data minimization into the blockchain.[97] To ensure that no data are lost, the unused blocks can be stored in one or more archive nodes, which store all data just in case the rest of the network needs them in the future, but the "active" nodes no longer have to process these archived blocks.

• Privacy-friendly consensus. As set out above, the standard verification mechanism of blockchain is a consensus mechanism where nodes redo the mathematical equations done by the creator of a block. If the result is the same hashed value, the block is verified and can be added to the blockchain. To enable nodes to verify the hashed value, most applications send the information on the block to all nodes. This is difficult to combine with the GDPR's confidentiality principle, which requires access to personal data to be limited to the fewest possible recipients.

A privacy-by-design solution for this issue is the concept of non-interactive zero-knowledge proof, which makes it possible to verify the correctness of a computation, e.g. a hash, without having to execute the computation or even learning what was executed. For example, the proposed currency Zerocoin[98] works as follows. When a coin is purchased, a serial number is attributed to the coin, which can only be revealed using a random number. Using these two numbers, a user can generate a zero-knowledge proof for the fact that the user knows both the serial number and the random number. The network can then verify this zero knowledge proof without having access to the coin's serial number or the random number.[99]

The potential use of zero-knowledge proof is not limited to the transfer of coins using blockchain but can be used to verify any computation without having access to the underlying information. This enables nodes to reach consensus on a new block, without accessing the information on that block, and thus without sharing the personal data included on that block with the nodes.

• Editable blockchain. A more radical approach that solves a number of data protection issues is the editable blockchain, for which Accenture has been awarded a patent.[100] The editable blockchain uses the "chameleon" hash function, which allows for changing the underlying information without changing the outcome of the hash function. This allows for changes to the underlying information of which the hash is already included on the platform, which makes it possible to correct (human) error or intentional (fraudulent) inaccuracies. This would allow for the execution of individuals' rights under the GDPR, e.g. to correction and to be forgotten.

Solving the immutability of blockchain comes at a price. To a large extent, trust in blockchain application relies on the network's consensus on the content of a block and the immutability of the content thereafter. When removing this immutability, other measures should be implemented to retain (or gain) sufficient trust in the blockchain application for individuals and organizations to use it as a record of

---

[97] See note 94 above.

[98] I. Miers, C. Garman, M. Greend and A.D. Rubin, "Zerocoin: Anonymous Distributed E-Cash from Bitcoin" (2013), *IEEE*, DOI 10.1109/SP.2013.34.

[99] Miers et al., "Zerocoin," 398.

[100] Accenture, "Editing the Uneditable Blockchain, Why Distributed Ledger Technology Must Adapt to An Imperfect World" (2016), newsroom.accenture.com/content/1101/files/Cross-FS blockchain.pdf.

their transactions. Trust in a blockchain application could be retained if, for example, only a single trusted entity could make these changes, similar to the fact that only governments could make certain changes to governmental public registries. A different solution could be to implement a very strict change management procedure, which could include a consensus mechanism that would verify the legitimacy of a change. In any event, changes will have to be strictly logged to ensure that they can always be reviewed and explained in the future.

- Blockchain identity management. A final, even more radical privacy-by-design solution is not to store personal data (whether in hashed form or otherwise) on-chain at all. Rather, the blockchain could be used for "self-sovereign" identity management.

In the offline world, an individual's identity is mostly established by verifying his or her driver's license or passport. The strength of this system follows from a trusted central governmental authority that provides these proofs of identity. However, because the online world does not follow the national boundaries of the offline world, it is difficult to appoint a trusted centralized authority for an online proof of identity.[101] By now, there are many initiatives to provide individuals with a digital identity.[102] An example of how blockchain can be deployed for online identity management is the initiative of Microsoft and Accenture providing a blockchain-based solution designed to allow individuals direct control over who has access to their personal data. Rather than all service providers each collecting and storing the personal data required for providing services to an individual, the personal data are stored off-chain and the system only calls on these data when the individual grants access, whereby access can be limited both in scope and in time.[103] For example, when an individual needs to prove his or her identity when renting a car, the access to the identifying information can be limited to what is necessary to provide this proof and for a short period of time only.

Decentralized identity management has a number of benefits. From a privacy point of view, it enables individuals to take back control over their digital identity, coined the "self-sovereign identity."[104] Currently, many individuals are, for example, not aware of the use of their digital identity and personal data, e.g. for advertising purposes. By using a decentralized identity system, individuals would be able to decide whom to give access to which information for what period of time. A single decentralized identity system also has economic benefits. Right now, a large number of companies are storing similar information about the same individuals. A decentralized identity management system makes this duplicated storage obsolete and ensures that companies have access to up-to-date information on an individual, insofar as the individual wants the company to have such access.

---

[101] See for an overview of identity management issues and publications relating to blockchain: the Blockchain Hub, "Identity as a Bottleneck for Blockchain, The Road to Self- Sovereign Identity" (2017), blockchain hub.net/blog/blog/decentralized-identity-blockchain/; J. Eberhardt and S. Tai, "On or Off the Blockchain? Insights on Off-Chaining Computation and Data, Information Systems Engineering (ISE)" (2017), *TU Berlin, Germany*, at www.ise.tu-berlin.de/fileadmin/fg308/publications/2017/2017-eberhardt-tai-offchaining-patterns.pdf; Buterin, "Privacy on the Blockchain"; P. De Filippi, "The Interplay Between Decentralization and Privacy: The Case of Blockchain Technologies" (2016), 9 Journal of Peer Production 1.

[102] Sater, "Blockchain and the EU's GDPR," 31.

[103] Accenture, "Microsoft Create Blockchain Solution to Support ID2020," *Accenture Newsroom* (2017), newsroom.accenture.com/news/accenture-microsoft-create-blockchain-solution-to-support-id2020.htm.

[104] Tobin and Reed, "The Inevitable Rise of Self-Sovereign Identity," 3.

The use of blockchain for decentralized identity management is a clear example of the variety of uses of blockchain. The well-known use cases of blockchain are mostly focused on administering transactions, but it can also be deployed for privacy enhancing purposes, which should not be forgotten.

11.12 Conclusion

The technology discussed above is still in its infancy and will require further development to overcome the shortcomings of the initial public (Bitcoin) blockchain, including implementation of privacy-by-design requirements under the GDPR. This is an expected life cycle of development of new technologies for new use cases, and already new applications show promising solutions and privacy-by-design features. The review of each of the potential data protection issues shows that these can likely be addressed to ensure compliance with the GDPR. The conclusion is that the GDPR is well able to regulate this new technology as well. This does, however, not mean that this technology will thus be suitable for all use and deployment cases or that no other governance issues remain. It is clear that it is set to disrupt existing business models and that further thinking is required on how best to regulate this new technology. Without many concrete deployment cases available yet, it is difficult to foretell all impacts that blockchain may have on society and, therefore, what exactly such regulation (if any) would look like. The call from industry stakeholders for specific guidance on privacy-by-design requirements for blockchain is therefore too premature and may even hamper new developments.

12   Data Protection in Hybrid Worlds

Sjef van Erp

12.1 Introduction

Fundamental property law questions arise wherever access to the world around us is made possible by technology. This concerns the deep seabed, outer space and, more and more, virtual reality.[1] When first confronted with what is happening in the world of data, it might seem that one is entering a world of science fiction, but in fact, it is science fiction becoming reality. In other words, it seems that data not only is becoming but, already has been recognised as the new challenge for traditional nineteenth-century-based private law. We need to think of data in broad terms including data that we give to social media, data, which we use as input when we drive a car for example the (navigation system which stores past destinations), and data found in our medical files. And, of course, data also refers to "software," which in its most advanced form includes "artificial intelligence." But it is not only information, which we provide ourselves, it is also information "harvested" about us, and that it is no longer under our control.

More and more we live in a world in which other people perceive us on the basis of the data assembled about us. Looking at it from that perspective, one could conclude that humans are in the process of losing their personhood and are becoming subjects of data instead of data subjects. In order to restore people as data subjects, it is, in my view, absolutely necessary that the traditional legal framework be rethought from the perspective of this new digital reality. This requires the recognition that we more and more live in a hybrid world where the physical and data realities are inextricably getting mixed up. Law will have to become the hybrid legal reflection of this state of affairs. The Internet of Things, the world of automated and autonomous trading systems, robotics (some built to deliberately look like human beings), self-executing computer programmes (smart contracts), and derivative reality (distributed ledger technology or blockchain) are converting human beings into datasets. Data has become an essential part of a person's patrimony, known as one's "digital assets." Data are traded, can be seized and also inherited. This hybrid world raises very fundamental questions on the role of traditional (classical) private law. The following brief examination will focus on what is traditionally called "property law," arguing that we need to develop a new

---

[1]   Cfr. Ch. E. Biblowit, 'Deep Seabed Mining: The United States and the United Nations Convention on the Law of the Sea' (1984) *St. John's Law Review*, Vol. 58, 267 ff.; W. Erlank, "Finding Property in New Places – Property in Cyber and Outer Space, 18 Potchefstroom" (2015) *Electronic Law Journal*, (5) Vol. 18 (5); W. Erlank, "Rethinking Terra Nullius and Property Law in Space" (2015) 18 *Potchefstroom Electronic Law Journal*, (7); Joshua Fairfield, "Virtual Property" (2005) 85 *Boston University Law Review*, 1047 ff.

property law system (data property law) parallel to traditional property law. For the current undertaking, property law is defined as the right, which a subject has against a considerable and relevant group of other subjects regarding an object. By viewing property law from this perspective, rather in a more general way, it will be possible to approach the following question: Can we accept data ownership from a broad perspective, not limited to a single legal tradition?

12.2 Traditional Approach

For most lawyers, today's world is still viewed from a rather classical (nineteenth-century) viewpoint. Existing thought patterns are hard to change, particularly when they have been laid down in centuries-old legal rules, systematised and laid down in case law, statutes and codes. Characteristic of this approach is the attempt to qualify new things in terms of predefined categories, which should be seen as separate from one another, representing the legal reflection of the world in which we live. In private law, we traditionally separate the law of obligations (contracts and torts) from property law. Contract is a legal relationship between two or more specific persons, whereas tort liability is based on breaking a general duty; property law is about a person's rights against everyone else. There have been endless doctrinal debates about where the line should be drawn between these areas. Are contractual obligations different from obligations arising from violation of a duty? What is the essential difference between breaking an obligation and violating a duty? Is this negative (passive) approach ignoring that any obligation or duty must be linked with a positive (active) right? Can you have a right "against the world" (absolute right) or are all rights relative? Is the essential difference between contract and property that the group of persons who is burdened by the right of someone else is strictly limited in the case of contract and unlimited in the case of property? Are not there numerous situations where these dogmatic distinctions do not fit well with reality? All of the above questions cannot be answered with absolute mathematical certainty, especially when these questions are viewed from a comparative law perspective. Given all these uncertainties and ambiguities, proposed answers will not satisfy all situations. This applies even more to the questions we are now facing by the rapid development of the data economy. The approach taken here will be more comparative-pragmatic than dogmatic, without ignoring the intrinsic value of dogmatic thinking: the need to be precise and clear is most important.

Following this comparative-pragmatic approach, several levels of private law thinking must be distinguished, such as the differences between political choices, policy (socio-economic) choices, leading principles, ground rules and technical rules. The political choices concern decisions about the type of economy and the distribution of wealth that society prefers. The policy choices are about the aims of the law within a given political framework, and because they are so close to the political choices governments make these policy choices are by no means value-free. Leading principles create the overall framework of a particular part of the law within the confines set by the earlier mentioned choices; they separate one area of the law from another (such as contract from property). Ground rules further develop the structure of the law by giving content to the framework created by the leading principles in a more elaborate and specific manner. The final element (for day-to-day legal practice usually the most important part) consists of the technical rules of law.

12.3 Political Choices, Policy Choices and Leading Principles

From the perspective of property law the political choice is to have a market economy with freedom of data.[2] That freedom is not unlimited, as the type of market economy found in the European Union is a social market economy (also a political choice), requiring protection of the interests of weaker parties (those without bargaining power), such as consumers and private citizens using the Internet. As a result, although data traffic is free, certain data are exempted from that freedom, because they are given a special status under privacy protection laws.[3] The data economy is, therefore, characterised by the political choice that we have a social market economy, where socio-economic inequities are corrected through rules of mandatory law in order to strike a fair balance between the interests of the different parties, resulting in policy choices as to who should be considered a "consumer," who is "acting in a professional or business capacity," who is a "data subject" whose "personal data" should be protected and be free from involuntary data transactions.

Before, we even can analyse the above policy questions we need to look at the underlying foundations of the data economy. What are data and how are the entitlements to data distributed? In order to answer this, "data" must be defined as a legal concept, which becomes problematic given the enormous diversity of data. A definition is provided by the International Organization for Standardization, which defines data as: "reinterpretable representation of information in a formalised manner suitable for communication, interpretation, or processing," which "can be processed by humans or automatic means."[4] Taking the ISO definition as a starting point, the focus of this contribution will be on entitlement to data and consequently on determining the persons who can conclude legally undertake binding transactions regarding the data.

Legal systems have shown a remarkable resilience in the face of technological change. In property law, legal systems generally accepted intangibles (such as monetary claims) as an object which can be owned and traded, and developed a parallel property law regime to deal with entitlements regarding objects resulting from human creativity (intellectual property law). In other words, legal systems have been able to incorporate into their structure new developments regarding (property) objects, which were not of a physical nature. Although legal systems have been careful in their acceptance of what can be an

---

[2] Cf. The (Draft) Regulation of the European Parliament and of the Council on a framework for the free flow of non-personal data in the European Union (Brussels, 17 October 2018), which aims, according to its article 1 "to ensure the free flow of data other than personal data within the Union by laying down rules relating to data localisation requirements, the availability of data to competent authorities and the porting of data for professional users." Article 4(1), first sentence, reads: "Data localisation requirements shall be prohibited, unless they are justified on grounds of public security in compliance with the principle of proportionality." See also article 4(1) General Data Protection Regulation (Regulation (EU) 2016/679): "'personal data' means any information relating to an identified or identifiable natural person ('data subject'); an identifiable natural person is one who can be identified, directly or indirectly, in particular by reference to an identifier such as a name, an identification number, location data, an online identifier or to one or more factors specific to the physical, physiological, genetic, mental, economic, cultural or social identity of that natural person."

[3] Regulation (EU) 2016/679 of the European Parliament and of the Council of 27 April 2016 on the protection of natural persons with regard to the processing of personal data and on the free movement of such data, and repealing Directive 95/46/EC (General Data Protection Regulation), OJ 2016, L 119/1.

[4] ISO/IEC 2382:2015(en), Information technology – Vocabulary, 2121272, Note 2 to entry: data: term and definition standardised by ISO/IEC [ISO/IEC 2382–1:1993], available at www.iso.org/obp/ui/#iso:std:iso-iec:2382:ed-1:v1:en.

object of a legal transaction (i.e. transactions to which the law attaches consequences), new objects are likely to be added, despite the limitations on the number of legal objects or property rights suggested by the principle of *numerus clausus*. The recognition of new objects, endowed with property rights, happens slowly, because the object itself, sometimes even explicitly, is an element in defining the property right and is a very important qualifier of that right. Rights and objects are mutually dependent. Ownership of land gives its owner different rights and imposes different duties than "ownership" of a claim, although they have common characteristics as objects that can be transferred to someone else and can be used as security for a loan. It is for this reason that in some legal systems the word ownership when referring to tangibles is replaced with the more general term "entitlement," with the term ownership being reserved to signify the fullest right over tangible property.[5] This can also be seen in intellectual property law where such terms as "copyright," "patent" and "trademark" are used based on the nature of the object. Why would this be different regarding data? It will be clear that the words "data ownership" cannot be equated to ownership of physical things, given the different nature of the object.

There are several reasons why data poses far more complicated questions regarding the recognition as property than intangibles and intellectual property. First, given the magnitude of existing data and the acceleration of data collection, recognising data as a property object is daunting. Second, there are various types of data. Software, raw data, personal data, processed data, public data, and metadata are just a few examples of different types of data. However, despite these complications the differences are not as substantial as they seem since much data is controlled by only a limited number of companies. This concentration of control is analogous to the feudal era, where only a few persons were entitled to and controlled the land, while all others living on the land only had a derivative right from feudal titleholders or were simply tolerated by the feudal owners, as long as they paid their dues.[6] A modern example is the case of software developers who "own" the copyright to their software (data), and by licensing that software to users acquire and retain control over the software copies, which are stored by users on data carriers.

Software developers (Google, Microsoft, Facebook and Yahoo) and platforms (such as Uber and Airbnb or smaller developers) further process the data created by users. They then compile the data of their users and claim an intellectual property right, in order to sell the data to others for further processing, marketing or targeting of specific individuals. Data, in other words, is such a complicated object that the traditional approach to dealing with legal objects from the perspective of property law is very difficult to maintain. The difficulty of classical property law to provide for the data economy can be shown by an analysis of the three leading property law principles: numerus clausus, transparency (specificity and publicity) and hierarchy. The numerus clausus of property rights principle implies that a legal system can only recognise a specific and well-defined number of property rights; both number and content of the property rights are limited. As noted earlier, part of the numerus clausus of property rights is the acceptance of only a limited number of legal objects. The second leading principle is transparency, meaning that it has to be clear as to which object a particular right is claimed. Arguing: "I own" is pointless. The more important question is: What do you own? And, as a follow-up

---

[5] See, e.g., articles 5:1 jo 3:1 Neth. C.C. and paragraphs 90 jo. 903 German C.C.
[6] Cf. Natalie M. Banta, "Property interests in digital assets: The rise of digital feudalism" (2017) 38 *Cardozo Law Review*, 1099 ff.

question, how can others know? How it can be justified that you claim a right against a person who did not conclude a contract with you or who did not cause you any damage? Property rights can only function if the object has been specified and there is some form of publicity that justifies the claim. Finally, because property is attached to a bundle of rights, conflicts arise as to the relative strength of each right. This is the principle of hierarchy: property rights are characterised by an orderly structure among themselves.

We already recognise data, when created as "software" or a "database," as an object of specific property entitlements under intellectual property and database law. But can data being not the object of specific property entitlements, still be an object of general property law? Or is this an area where property law has no role to play and, therefore, all legal rights are contractual in nature? A contractual rights system would reinforce a feudal-like power structure. What bargaining power does an individual consumer have against tech giants? How can a private person avoid their data from being "harvested" from various websites to be used for profiling and targeted advertising or to influence their political opinions? In my view – and this to me is the essential policy question – it is crucial for re-balancing the power structure between users and data collectors, in order to effectively protect individual interests, that data needs to be protected by specific property rights.

12.4 Data as an Object of Entitlement

The object qualifies the right, so data must first be seen as an object, before further analysis can be undertaken as to the degree and the nature of the entitlements to be attached to such an object. This requires starting with the principle of transparency: Can we describe data specifically enough to call it an object of property law? In order to do this a list of policy-weighing factors needs to be developed, otherwise it will prove to be impossible to make useful distinctions. In an earlier work, I listed the following factors as key to the transparency requirement: (1) is the carrier of the information human (genetic information, an implanted chip) or non-human (a cloud server, hard drive, USB stick), (2) who is the person creating the content (consumer, business), (3) what is the nature of the content (personal, non-personal) and (4) what is the purpose and use of the content (private message, public information).[7]

Another problem is presented by the publicity requirement. If data can be described with sufficient specificity, how can we justify that others should know about the rights claimed as to such an object? Traditionally, it has been argued that possession of a movable thing can be seen as information to the outside world that the person being in control claims an entitlement. Valuable things (immovables, but also valuable movables such as aircraft, ships and so forth) are registered and at least everyone having a legitimate interest can consult the registry and verify the holders of the right. So far, with regard to data not many public registration systems exist. Exceptions include

---

[7] See Sief van Erp, "Ownership of data and the numerus clausus of legal objects" in United Nations Commission on International Trade Law (UNCITRAL), Modernizing International Trade Law to Support Innovation and Sustainable Development, Proceedings of the Congress of the United Nations Commission on International Trade Law, Vienna, 4–6 July 2017, Volume 4: Papers presented at the Congress (Vienna: United Nations, 2017), 69 ff.

registries related to births, marriages and deaths, and also land registries. Most data, however, are held on servers where privacy protection prevents others from accessing the information. From the perspective of general property law, this lack of publication or access creates a serious problem, if data is to be recognised as an object of property law.

Once it has been decided if in a particular case the data is specific and public enough to become an object of property law, it must then be determined who is the subject that may claim any entitlement to the data. Natural persons and legal persons are considered legal subjects. It may be time to consider recognising robots as legal subjects in light of the developments in artificial intelligence. This issue relating to such recognition is whether a robot can have patrimony over an object? If fully automated trading systems are considered, such as stock exchanges, as "robots" the robots possess patrimony over the database(s), which they use for trading. The debate whether a robot can be accepted as a legal subject has only just begun and it will, no doubt, take considerable time to be settled, much like the acceptance of corporations, associations and foundations as legal persons took a considerable amount of time.[8] If robots are considered as persons then there is no reason why they should not be entitled to data ownership.

As soon as it is accepted that specific data can be an object of general property law and that the problems of specificity and publicity can be solved, the question of whether a data subject should be given an entitlement equal to ownership in the sense of the powers, privileges, rights and immunities given to owners of physical things can be answered. Again, this is not a question, which can be dealt with without distinguishing different policy factors. Legal systems already give different answers based on how they categorise data property in the following areas: (1) the legal area (private law, public law, privacy law and so forth), (2) the type of object (tangible, intangible, the creative legal mind, to which digital objects would be added) and (3) the purpose of the right (full control, security, management). In any case, it will be clear that if data ownership is accepted, it is not the same as ownership of land, an entitlement to an intangible or an intellectual property right. Ownership of data is about access, control, exclusion, transfer and the power to duplicate and delete.

12.5 Final Remarks

Whether data ownership will be accepted or not is more a public policy decision than a purely legal-dogmatic one. Any policy choice in this area will have to start with

---

[8] See "Report with recommendations to the Commission on Civil Law Rules on Robotics," 27 January 2017 (2015/2103(INL)), in which the Legal Affairs Committee "59. Calls on the Commission, when carrying out an impact assessment of its future legislative instrument, to explore, analyse and consider the implications of all possible legal solutions, such as: [. . .] f) creating a specific legal status for robots in the long run, so that at least the most sophisticated autonomous robots could be established as having the status of electronic persons responsible for making good any damage they may cause, and possibly applying electronic personality to cases where robots make autonomous decisions or otherwise interact with third parties independently[.]" But in an open letter by artificial intelligence and robotics experts, industry leaders, law, medical and ethics experts, this approach was vehemently rejected (interestingly enough explicitly rejecting a trust/fiducie/Treuhand-based type of legal personality which would still require a natural or legal person to be involved). See also Sheikh Solaiman, Legal personality of robots, corporations, idols and chimpanzees: A quest for legitimacy, *Artificial Intelligence and Law* (2017), 25(2) 155 ff.

answering the question of whether data can be specified enough to be qualified as a legal object and be inserted into the numerus clausus of legal objects. This is crucial, because without the qualification as a legal object policy makers will not be able to answer the question of who is entitled to such an object and what right a legal subject might have against a considerable and relevant group of other legal subjects regarding that object. This area of the law requires that we think less dogmatically and try to answer questions not by starting from predefined, inherited definitions, which prevent us from approaching the problems with an open mind. Traditionally, the English common law distinguishes between land, movables and claims, an approach not shared by the civil law which takes a more unified approach. A differentiated approach, based on policy-weighing factors might, however, work well in today's digital reality. Our world has become hybrid, as evidenced by the Internet of Things; so, consequently, our law will have to adopt a hybrid legal framework in which data property law develops next to traditional property law.

13 Smart Contracts

Issues of Property and Security Rights

Louis-Daniel Muka Tshibende

No one puts new wine into old wineskins.[1]

13.1 Introduction

On the basis of the various definitions provided by academics from both Civil and Common Law jurisdictions, smart contracts are considered as *'agreements existing in the form of software code implemented on the Blockchain platform, which ensures the autonomy and self-executing nature of smart contract terms based on a predetermined set of factors'*.[2] For the purpose of the present chapter, the 'smart contract' notion is considered broadly. Smart contracts relate to blockchain-based automated modalities for the conclusion, performance and termination of pre-existing categories of contracts.[3] This approach corresponds to what the smart contract 'creator', Nick Szabo, put forward in the 1990s: a computerised transaction protocol that executes the terms of a contract.[4]

On the basis of freedom of contract, contracting parties should be considered as *'free to code any conditions they desire [...] to secure funds for the smart contract to dispose of [...] to express virtually any contract as a code'*.[5] Nevertheless, this freedom is not absolute. Considering contracts at both national and international levels, some legal issues need to be addressed, such as the identification of the law which will govern the said contracts. In the light of private international law standards, contracts can be governed by an international legal instrument, a non-state body of rules or domestic law. In any case, however, even international contracts cannot escape from overriding mandatory provisions and public policy rules of national jurisdictions with which they are connected.[6] This will be

---

[1] St Matthew, Chapter 9: 16–17, in *The Bible* (King James Version).

[2] A. Savelyev, 'Contract Law 2.0: "Smart" contracts as the beginning of the end of classic contract law', Higher School of Economics, Research Paper No. WP BRP 71/LAW/2016, available on SSRN at https://papers .ssrn.com/sol3/papers.cfm?abstract_id=2885241, at 2.

[3] Such a broad approach is developed by J. D. Hansen, L. Rosini and C.L. Reyes, 'More Legal Aspects of Smart Contract Applications', (Perkins Coie LLP, March 2018), pp. 1–4.

[4] N. Szabo, 'Smart Contracts', https://archive.is/zQ1p8 (1994), and 'Smart Contracts: Building Blocks for Digital Markets', www.alamut.com/subj/economics/nick_szabo/smartContracts.html (1996).

[5] J. J. Szczerbowski, 'Place of Smart Contracts in Civil Law. A few Comments on Form and Interpretation', Proceedings of the 12th Annual International Scientific Conference NEW TRENDS 2017, Private College of Economics Studies Znojmo (2017) 26/2 *Information and Communications Technology Law* 116.

[6] L.A. DiMatteo, *International Business Law and the Legal Environment. A Transnational Approach* (3rd edn., New-York & London: Routledge, 2017), p. 116 *et seq.*

the case even when dealing with smart contracts and blockchain technologies. The present chapter analyses the way Civil Law legal orders (especially French law) address issues resulting from the coexistence of traditional legal rules and new smart contract mechanisms. It focuses mainly on property and security rights issues which are crucial aspects of the validity of contracts but also of their effectiveness. The two main parts of the chapter will address the interface between blockchain technologies and the property and security rights, especially in the context of new emerging items of property, and will make prospective proposals designed to ensure the viability of this interface.

13.2 Overview of Legal Issues Relating to Property and Security Rights

13.2.1 *New Items Captured by Property and Security Rights*

Smart contracts are supposed to bring a higher level of safety in transactions, among others by securing their performance. The positive role that blockchain technologies can play also consists of securing, in a very innovative way, not only existing ownership but also subsequent transfers of it. Regarding new ownership items, some recent French regulatory proposals can be highlighted. Indeed, even if there is no formal and full recognition of blockchain technologies in French law yet, some recent provisions relating to French financial markets regulation implicitly refer to these technologies, such as saving bonds and initial coin offerings (ICO). The reform relating to saving bonds was implemented gradually. The first step was Ordinance No. 2016–520 of 28 April 2016, introducing the new articles L. 223–12 and L. 223–13 into the Financial and Monetary Code. These articles provide that some financial securities – saving bonds – can be transmitted by means of a *'shared electronic registration device'.*[7] Technically speaking, this expression includes blockchain technology, in fact, the expression blockchain appears later in the legislative vocabulary (the French expression used is: 'chaîne de blocs').[8] In particular, article L. 223–13 of the Financial and Monetary Code states that ownership transfer may result from the registration of the financial securities assignment within a shared electronic registration device. The second step is the so-called *Blockchain Ordinance* No. 2017–1674 of 8 December 2017, which extends the list of financial securities that may be registered in the blockchain and asserts that rights and obligations resulting from such a registration are subject to French law whenever the company issuing the securities has its statutory seat in France or whenever the securities were issued under French law.[9] Thus French law actively seeks to make blockchain technology operational in some contractual related domains. However, the French approach is more sector-specific compared to that of other legal orders, such as in the United States where the validity of contracts *'processed, executed, or otherwise enforced via smart contract computer code'* is expressly recognised in some jurisdictions.[10]

---

[7] In French: *'dispositif d'enregistrement électronique partagé'.*
[8] See National Assembly, *Draft law relating to the action plan for enterprises' transformation and growth*, No. 1088, 19 June 2018 (as amended on 12 September 2018).
[9] Articles L. 211-3-1 and L. 211-3-2 of the Financial and Monetary Code.
[10] Hansen, Rosini and Reyes, 'More Legal Aspects of Smart Contract Applications', 6, mentioning the laws of Arizona, California, Florida, Nebraska, Nevada and New-York.

Following the saving bonds regulation, the new momentum is reflected in the strong interest that financial market operators have expressed regarding the use of blockchain and smart contracts in the framework of ICOs innovative methods of financing. In practice, they are already being used in the context of legal lacuna or vacuum.[11] Most often carried out by start-ups, an ICO consists of offering to investors and savers (with a view to financing investment projects) cryptographic 'tokens' in exchange for either cryptocurrencies (such as bitcoins) or future services, a connected with blockchain technologies. In this area of financial activities, it is conventional practice to issue an informative document ('white paper') describing the counterparty. Tokens, whose legal status is debated in comparative law, can be assimilated to cryptocurrencies tradable on secondary markets. They can also represent assets such as a right to an income or to dividends. As designed and practiced presently, ICOs are essentially based on a corpus of various best practices. In order to implement a much more securing legal framework and in the light of the major issues raised by ICOs (reliability and stability of financial markets, information and protection of investors and savers, etc.), the French Financial Markets Authority (FMA) has undertaken – in parallel to UNICORN ('Universal Node to ICO's Research and Network') me public consultations which highlighted a call from the vast majority of ICO sector operators for the implementation of a new legal environment.[12]

Discussions driven by the FMA are still ongoing among the above-mentioned operators. Nonetheless, a draft law relating to the action plan for enterprises' transformation and growth (PACTE Bill)[13] has been proposed and aims to introduce an FMA's label on ICOs to meet certain investors protection criteria. Article 26 of the PACTE bill provides defines a token and an offer of tokens to the public.[14] By so doing, the legislature intends to address the issue of the legal nature of tokens in categorising them as incorporeal assets. It has the advantage of settling underlying issues regarding the way ownership of such assets can be transferred and the type of securities to which they may give rise (a pledge).[15] However, it does not solve all the identified legal issues. Nor does it provide a definite answer to the numerous questions raised by ICO market operators regarding the variable characteristics of tokens and, consequently, the correlative

---

[11] See French National Assembly, *Draft law relating to the action plan for enterprises' transformation and growth*, No. 1088 of 19 June 2018 (as amended on 12 September 2018), stressing that 'there is no clear legal framework for ICOs in so far as, according to French legislation and to the European legal order, tokens issued within this framework can correspond to different legal definitions depending on their peculiarities' (Translated from French into English by the author).

[12] See FMA, *Synthèse des réponses apportées à la consultation publique sur les initial coin offerings (ICO) et point d'étape sur le programme 'UNICORN'* (22 February 2018) www.amf-france.org/Publications/ Consultations-publiques/Archives?docId=workspace%3A%2F%2FSpacesStore%2Fa9e0ae85-f015-4beb-92d2-ece78819d4da

[13] French National Assembly, *Draft law relating to the action plan for enterprises' transformation and growth*, No. 1088, 19 June 2018 (as amended on 12 September 2018).

[14] It asserts that: '[...] constitutes a token: any intangible asset representing, in digital format, one or several rights, that can be issued, registered, preserved or transferred by means of a shared electronic registration device allowing, directly or indirectly, the identification of the asset owner. [...] An offer of tokens to the public consists of proposing to the public, in whatever forms it takes, to subscribe to those tokens. Issuers shall draw up a document designed to provide the public with all useful information on the proposed offer and the issuer' (Translated from French into English by the author).

[15] For a critical approach see FMA, *Synthèse des réponses apportées à la consultation publique sur les initial coin offerings (ICO) et point d'étape sur le programme 'UNICORN'*, p. 9.

issue of the applicability or the exclusion of financial regulations. The reason is that the draft law refrains from deciding if tokens shall in all circumstances be considered and treated as financial titles.

If tokens are considered as financial titles, it would inevitably lead to the application of the law relating to the issuance of financial titles and to the use of the FMA's power to implement regulations and impose administrative sanctions. Public and private actors, at both international and national levels, all agree that it is difficult to identify a uniform position about the legal characterisation of tokens because there are multiple possible solutions. Indeed, depending on the rights that investors obtain (via the tokens) in return for funds, a token may alternatively represent a capital security (entitling to a participation in the shared capital and to dividends), a debt security (carrying the right to repayment and entitlement to interest) or a security representing the right to certain services provided by the issuer.[16] This latter category are known as 'utility tokens', while the two others are called 'security tokens'. In the end, should they be considered or not as cryptocurrencies or be a representation of assets (that can be transferred by means of a sale contract, for example), tokens will logically be the object of a property right or a security right eligible for legal protection with respect to their creation and their circulation. This prerequisite for the development and dynamism of ICO markets is what lawmakers need to address.

13.2.2 Old Constraints Relating to Property and Security Rights

Some reservations must however be taken into account. The validity of property and security rights are subject to formalities. Under French law, for example, a mortgage requires an authenticated deed to be drafted by a public officer.[17] In this particular domain of property and security rights, the notary plays a central role which is not limited to the authentication of legal acts.[18] In most Civil Law countries, such as, France, Germany and Netherlands, the notarial deed requires not only that a deed is drafted by the notary and signed by the parties, but also that the notary confirms that the parties intend to be bound after having been warned about the legal consequences of their action. When such a formal act is required, even freedom of contract will not allow the parties to derogate from these rules.

Obviously, what is questionable here is the validity and automatic nature of smart contracts for these types of agreements or instruments. Due to the formal requirements of this area of law (delivery of an authenticated deed), the use of blockchain technologies is limited. Contracting parties must go through the legal process 'in person'. Otherwise, as mentioned above, the contract is not valid. This point can also be illustrated in international and comparative law. In particular, while adhering to the United Nations Convention on the Use of Electronic Communications in International Contracts,[19] some signatory states made reservations. Singapore declared upon ratification that '[t]he Convention shall not apply to electronic communications relating to any contract for the

---

[16] In that sense, see FMA, *Synthèse des réponses apportées à la consultation publique sur les initial coin offerings (ICO) et point d'étape sur le programme 'UNICORN'*, pp. 3, 6–9.
[17] French Civil Code, art. 2417.
[18] J. M. Smits, *Contract Law: A Comparative Introduction* (2nd edn., Cheltenham, UK: Elgar, 2017), p. 104.
[19] CUECIC, New-York, 2005, entered into force on 1 March 2013.

sale or other disposition of immovable property, or any interest in such property', and the Russian Federation declared upon acceptance that '[it] will not apply the Convention to transactions for which a notarized form or State registration is required under Russian law or to transactions for the sale of goods whose transfer across the Customs Union border is either prohibited or restricted'.

Beyond the question of validity, the effectiveness of rights is also at stake. Security rights generally require obtaining an enforceable title from a relevant public authority (e.g. court) prior to any seizure and sale by auction of the immovable property, and 'no court is going to enforce an illegal or incomplete contract'.[20] Relying on blockchain technologies would not change the situation as an automatic enforcement would be in contradiction with the actual requirements in terms of enforcement of security rights. These various current requirements seem to be intrinsically in contradiction with blockchain philosophy which, to its extremes, precludes any kind of controls or outside interventions.

Despite the above-mentioned constraints, however, it seems conceivable to use blockchain technologies in the process of transfer of ownership through contracts for which the intervention of civil law notaries is required. In France, dematerialisation of formalities which notaries are responsible for is already a reality. Decree No. 2017–770 of 4 May 2017, for example, places a legal obligation on notaries to realise their deposition formalities to the public office in charge of publishing immovable property transactions by electronic means. There seems therefore to be a digital technologies-friendly environment which will pave the way for future evolutions, including the use of the blockchain to transfer property and security interests. The issue than becomes whether something should be done to limit the 'disruptive' effects of these technologies on the notary and other professions. This issue is discussed below.

13.3 Prospective Proposals

Bearing in mind the legal issues raised above, a number of proposals have been made in order to make property/security rights and blockchain compatible. Some of the proposals concern States and public authorities, while others are related to lawyers and contracting parties.

13.3.1 Proposals for States and Public Authorities

Blockchain technology and smart contract tools leave states' lawmakers in a 'wait-and-see' situation.[21] In France, especially in the context of the PACTE Bill dealing among others with ICOs, the legislature has failed to make a definite choice between two possible options. The first one consists in general principles, implying a reform of the Civil Code. The second one relies on the draft and implementation of specific rules whose scope of application will be restricted to some sectors such as ICOs. As for the first option and for the moment, there is no ambitious reform project aimed to extend the

---

[20] C. Preziosi, 'Smart Contracts: Are They a Viable Replacement to the Standard Civil Law Contract?', www.camilleripreziosi.com/en/news-resources/1/2489/smart-contracts-are-they-a-viable-replacement (21 December 2017).

[21] Such an attitude can be understood for some countries (France and Switzerland, for example) that wish to become or remain attractive in the use of new technologies for financial contracts (e.g. the ICO), the economic repercussions being potentially significant.

general principles of contract law to blockchain and smart contracts. I will therefore focus on the issue of the regulation of ICOs. It seems that as to the question of whether to regulate or not, the vast majority of ICO market players in France are in favor of regulation.[22] The FMA has offered three options to the market operators: (1) promotion of a guide of good practices without affecting existing legislation or regulation; (2) extension of the scope of existing substantive rules so that they cover the ICOs as well as the public offering of shares and titles in general; and (3) proposal for new a legal framework tailored ICOs' peculiarities. The third option was approved by two-third of the replies that the FMA received. As a comparison, countries whose public authorities have shown interest in ICOs may be grouped into three categories: those that have focused only on the implementation of rules of good practice (Germany, Japan, Singapore and Switzerland), those that tend to rely on a notion of financial titles broadly defined (United States)[23] and finally those in which such a modality of fundraising is totally forbidden (China and South Korea[24]).[25] The operators that have been consulted by the FMA justified their preference for the third option by the critical need for a specific, adapted and secure legal framework. They also recognized that the new legal framework must be coordinated with other legal regimes such as consumer protection law.[26]

An alternative to governmental regulation is self-regulation. In France, some operators have unsuccessfully promoted the idea of a self-regulation. The idea took the form of an ICO Charter originally proposed and signed by six major sectorial actors in October 2017. Defining the whole ICO process in terms of financial and technological transparency, the Charter is based on ten points.[27] Another issue regards the geographical

---

[22] A public consultation conducted by the FMA collected 82 answers in total from digital economy operators, individuals, financial markets experts and infrastructures, scholars and law firms. See AMF, *Synthèse des réponses apportées à la consultation publique sur les initial coin offerings (ICO) et point d'étape sur le programme 'UNICORN'*, pp. 19–20.

[23] The United States Securities Exchange Commission's (SEC) doctrine, as explained recently by its president, is that cryptocurrencies, that are linked to ICOs, do not fall within the SEC's scope of competences, but instead in that of the Commodity Futures Trading Commission (CFTC), in charge of the supervision and regulation of forward transactions on financial titles in United States markets. See A. Tabuteau, 'ICOs: le projet de loi PACTE, entre innovation et protection de l'épargne', www.efl.fr /actualites/patrimoine/placements-mobiliers/details.html?ref=r-50e9a471-62e6-46e8-a409-14bdc13e2165 (25 July 2018).

[24] In these countries, contracts concluded within the framework of an ICO are null and void.

[25] *Impact study of the PACTE bill*, 20 June 2018, www.legifrance.gouv.fr/affichLoiPreparation.do? idDocument=JORFDOLE000037080861&type=general&typeLoi=proj&legislature=15, p. 345.

[26] EU Directives No. 2000/31/EC of 8 June 2000 on certain legal aspects of information society services, in particular electronic commerce, in the Internal Market and No. 2011/83/EU of 25 October 2011 on consumer rights (and their requirements relating to unfair terms, the professional pre-contractual duty to inform and the consumer right of withdrawal), but also Regulation (EU) on the protection of natural persons with regard to the processing of personal data and on the free movement of such data No. 2016/679 of 27 April 2016.

[27] Information provided by the ICO/ITO project (1); independent legal review of the ICO/ITO token and its issuer (2); White Paper features (3); access to the code and technical specifications of the smart contract of the ICO/ITO (4); KYC, anti-money laundering and anti-terrorist process (5); token and cryptocurrency raising process (6); use of ICO/ITO proceeds (7); ICO/ITO safety and security (8); acceptance of a third-party audit to measure the risk of the project (9); post-ICO disclosure. An eleventh point, entitled 'Commitment on the laws of listed States', declares that 'ICOs complying with this Charter shall not: be carried out by an issuer incorporated under the law of a State listed as "non-compliant" (by the OECD) [...] be governed by the laws of a non-compliant State' (ICO Charter, *Proposition for Self-Regulation rules for the ICO ecosystem*, www.icocharter.eu (Paris: 18 October 2017).

scope of the regulation to be implemented: should it be international or national? The PACTE Bill states that: 'pending the adoption of international and European rules that are necessary for these subjects, due to their transnational nature'.[28] Considering that blockchain technologies and smart contracts cannot be confined within national borders, most states are cautious in their regulatory approach. At this early stage, none of them are ready to design a legal framework which could be considered as too restrictive by the operators, pushing them to invest and localise their ICO operations and related contracts in other jurisdictions.[29] This concern has been expressed by the French Council of State.[30]

Another alternative as far as regulation of blockchain technologies is concerned is between mandatory and optional regulation. In France, the legislature has decided to opt for an optional regime rather than a mandatory one. The objective, as stressed by financial and economic media, is to prevent a distortion of competition which could be detrimental to France.[31] According to the French Council of State,

> this regime, optional by nature, consists of proposing to the issuers to seek an ex-ante visa from the Financial Markets Authority, in order to ensure that their offering presents the necessary guarantees to protect investors and prevent any abuse; [. . .] this regime, that is not imposed by the law of the European Union nor by the international law [. . .] presents an optional character [and] is likely to evolve in the future depending on economic and technological evolutions as well as the European and international normative framework.[32]

The bottom line resulting from this optional regime, for the operators that would abide by it, is to establish a White Paper for the purpose of providing information to token purchasers (description of the project related to the ICO and its evolution, rights resulting from the tokens, accounting treatment of the funds raised in the frame of the ICO).[33] The regime would also need to develop a procedure for applying for a visa from the FMA, establish rules ensuring the escrow of the funds raised and put into place a system preventing money laundering and terrorism financing.[34] In any event, such

---

[28] National Assembly, *Draft law relating to the action plan for enterprises' transformation and growth*, No. 1088, 19 June 2018 (as amended on 12 September 2018), p. 29.

[29] In mid-May 2018, seven ICO have been launched in France for a total amount of 80 million euros. About forty projects were concerned for the entire year, for which the FMA has recorded approximately 350 million euros as a projection. In 2017 at a global level, it is estimated that 4 billion dollars were raised by means of ICO mechanisms. See *Impact study of the PACTE bill*, 20 June 2018, pp. 345, 347; AMF, *Synthèse des réponses apportées à la consultation publique sur les initial coin offerings (ICO) et point d'étape sur le programme 'UNICORN'*, p. 2.

[30] Council of State's opinions, 19 June 2018, No. 394.599 and No. 395.021 on the PACTE bill, www.conseil-etat.fr/content/download/137301/1389845/version/1/file/Avis%20394599%20-395021.pdf, p. 17 *et seq.*

[31] B. Grange, Spokesman of Crypto Asset France (formerly Bitcoin France), interviewed by L. Boisseau, 'Les ICO auront bientôt un cadre juridique', www.lesechos.fr/12/09/2018/lesechos.fr/0302244399565_les-ico-auront-bientot-un-cadre-juridique.htm (13 September 2018).

[32] See Council of state's opinions, 19 June 2018, No. 394.599 and No. 395.021 on the PACTE bill, www.conseil-etat.fr/content/download/137301/1389845/version/1/file/Avis%20394599%20-395021.pdf, p. 17.

[33] In the existing practices, the 'white paper' must be distinguished from the 'manifesto' which, according to the FMA, aims to disclose a protocol on the grounds of which certain types of technological projects such as, at the origins, the bitcoin, can be developed. AMF, *Synthèse des réponses apportées à la consultation publique sur les initial coin offerings (ICO)*, pp. 3–4.

[34] See AMF, *Synthèse des réponses apportées à la consultation publique sur les initial coin offerings (ICO)*.

modifications of the French legal framework will require the renewal of the interpretation of numerous legal and regulatory provisions related to financial titles and securities in general.[35]

In the light of the current trends, it seems that states are bound to play an essential role in blockchain and smart contracts regulation. What is less clear is to determine the appropriate nature of regulation. Some issues must be addressed and regulated by states, for example, who is liable for a blockchain bug (the software publisher, its owner, the oracle, the nodes, etc.? Indeed, civil and criminal liability issues can be highly sensitive. Despite the argument that smart contracts and blockchain technologies are an illustration of a 'demonopolization' of states' power by use of computers, states cannot remain ideologically neutral.[36] One has to determine how to align the powers and competences of governments with blockchain in a technological context lacking a central authority and relying only on distributed technologies?[37] The key choices to be made include determining the most realistic playing field (international or national) and the status of the regulatory body (private, public or mixed).

I Public regulation is preferable, ideally combining international and national levels. In French law for example, pursuant to the third paragraph of article 34 of the Constitution, 'Statutes shall determine the fundamental principles [of]: systems of ownership, property rights and civil and commercial obligations.' Therefore, regarding the blockchain technology in general and smart contracts in particular, in the area of property and security rights, a legislative intervention aimed at adapting the legal framework will be of crucial importance. From the perspective of a safe contractual and business environment, a coordinated international policy would be much better than isolated and divergent national initiatives. If we consider that blockchain technologies and cryptocurrencies are the core of smart contracts, an international coordination is certainly a better option and more business-friendly than the ongoing trend: restrictive national regulations on cryptocurrencies drafted or enacted by single countries.[38]

Coordination at the international level could result in an independent authority, based on an international treaty establishing a corpus of uniform rules. Then and on the basis of subsidiarity, each signatory state would have the opportunity to establish a national regulatory body and implement domestic rules complying with the international uniform regulation. In such a two-level system, regulatory authorities could be given a status of a *'super-user with extra-powers'* of blockchains, in such a manner that the state, as a final resort, could at any time activate a 'red button'.[39] Single states could also delegate a part of

---

[35] For a non-exhaustive list, see: the general regulations of the FMA; the Criminal Code (since some sorts of tokens may have the same characteristics as a currency, the fact of putting into circulation unauthorised currencies on French territory is subject to criminal sanctions); the Commercial Code (articles L. 228-1, L. 228-36 (A), L. 228-38, L. 228-45, L. 228-65, L. 228-72); and the Financial and Monetary Code (articles L. 211-1 et seq., L. 213-1 et seq., L. 213-8, L. 213-21-1 (A)).

[36] Especially if one considers, for example, that, in 2016, Ethereum was hacked and millions of Ethers were stolen, and that in 2018 child abuse imagery was discovered in bitcoin's blockchain (S. Gibbs, 'Child abuse imagery found within bitcoin's blockchain', www.theguardian.com/technology/2018/mar/20/child-abuse-imagery-bitcoin-blockchain-illegal-content (20 March 2018)).

[37] Savelyev, 'Contract Law 2.0: "Smart" Contracts as the Beginning of the End of Classic Contract Law', 2.

[38] E.g. the Chinese Central Bank Regulation of Sept. 2017 targeting the bitcoin technology, the upcoming or envisaged Regulations in the United States and South Korea.

[39] Savelyev, 'Contract Law 2.0: "Smart" Contracts as the Beginning of the End of Classic Contract Law', 2.

their authority to institutional actors, such as the judiciary acting as oracles.[40] This role could also be played by notaries in Civil Law jurisdictions,[41] but also by certain competent corporate bodies sale of company shares.[42] The same delegation may also be given to attorneys, to certified accountants and to other regulated professions. These institutional actors could be liable in the event of a defective contract, and would be subject to professional (fiduciary) duties such as the duty of care, duty of confidentiality, and so forth. The above-described framework would result in greater accountability and confidence in blockchain technologies for smart contracts' and their users.

At the European level, the European Parliament, through Resolution No. 2016/2007 of 26 May 2016 on virtual currencies, also expresses in very clear and explicit terms the crucial need for regulation.[43] The Resolution embraces a wide range of issues,[44] as well as summarises the most important reasons why a regulation on blockchain and smart contracts is vital.

---

[40] For a definition of "Oracles," see V. Gatteschi, F. Lamberti and C. Demartini, Technology of Smart Contracts, Chapter 3 of the present book; S. Drillon, 'La révolution Blockchain: la redéfinition des tiers de confiance', (2016) *Revue Trimestrielle de Droit Commercial* 893.

[41] This is particularly feasible because it is possible to switch from the actual system to a blockchain-based real estate and land registry system. See Hansen, Rosini and Reyes, "More Legal Aspects of Smart Contract Applications," 19.

[42] In company law, as a matter of fact, a distinction is legally made between companies in which shares cannot be transferred without prior approval from competent bodies and those which shares are freely transferable; but even in the last case, the transferability can be restricted by contractual clauses. The intervention of an oracle who certifies that the triggering event (e.g. the approval) leading to the transfer of shares' ownership really occurred, will be necessary (see the relevant provisions in the Commercial Code, articles L. 223–12 et seq., L. 225–1 et seq. and L. 227–12).

[43] The European Parliament, Resolution No. 2016/2007 (INI) of 26 May 2016, para. 2, 'notes that virtual currencies and distributed ledger technology schemes entail risks which need to be addressed appropriately so as to enhance their trustworthiness, including in the present circumstances, namely: (b) the high volatility of virtual currencies and potential for speculative bubbles, and the absence of traditional forms of regulatory supervision, safeguards and protection, issues which are challenging for consumers; (c) the sometimes limited capacity of regulators in the area of new technology, which may make it difficult to define appropriate safeguards in a timely manner in order to ensure the proper and reliable functioning of distributed ledger technology applications when or even before they grow so large as to become systemically relevant; (d) the legal uncertainty surrounding new applications of distributed ledger technology [...] (i) the potential for "black market" transactions, money laundering, terrorist financing, tax fraud and evasion and other criminal activities based on "pseudonymity" and "mixing services" that some such services offer and the decentralized nature of some virtual currencies, bearing in mind that the traceability of cash transactions tends to be much lower still [...]'. In the same vein, the European Parliament also 'calls for a proportionate regulatory approach at EU level so as not to stifle innovation or add superfluous costs to it at this early stage, while taking seriously the regulatory challenges that the widespread use of virtual currencies and distributed ledger technology might pose'. (para. 14) And finally, focusing on some contracts related matters, it 'stresses the importance of consumer awareness, transparency and trust when using virtual currencies; calls on the Commission to develop, in cooperation with the Member States and virtual currencies industry, guidelines with the aim of guaranteeing that correct, clear and complete information is provided for existing and future virtual currencies users, to allow them to make a fully informed choice and thus enhance the transparency of virtual currencies schemes in terms of how they are organized and operated and how they distinguish themselves from regulated and supervised payment systems in terms of consumer protection' (para. 23).

[44] Role of public authorities, regulation framework, business opportunities, criminal risks, governments and users exposure to economic and financial risks, some contracts-related issues such as pre-contractual information, payment and consumer protection.

13.3.2 Suggestions for Lawyers and Contracting Practices

The spread of smart contracts requires not only regulatory actions, but also the development of new skills and competences for lawyers, and for them to adapt or update their contractual practices. Indeed, quality and efficiency of smart contracts will certainly depend in large part by partnerships between lawyers and coders. This is dependent on the lawyer's the capacity to share legal concepts and vocabulary with programmers (and vice versa). Coming back to ICOs, a new market for legal expertise is emerging: lawyers will have to advise clients on issues like the legal qualification of tokens, the identification of the applicable legal regime, the drafting of White Papers, the compliance with the know-your-customer (KYC) procedure, and the risks of investing.[45] The ethical rules that govern lawyers professional activity and the legal value of their acts (e.g. contracts) make attorneys and notaries trustworthy intermediaries, even in the blockchain 'disintermediated' context.[46]

Thinking about smart contracts as isolated and self-sufficient tools can lead to significant difficulties and misunderstandings, if only because some obligations that the contracting parties have to perform cannot be automated. Contracting parties have a vested interest in making sure that at all the stages of their contractual relationship (formation, performance, termination) are compatible with applicable law. In the field of property rights and security rights, another set of unsettled questions are to be taken into consideration in order to anticipate eventual difficulties and to adapt practices. For instance, what if there is a divergence between the coded version and the terms previously agreed and which one prevail? The stakes are high in regard to property rights and security rights. Indeed, the qualification of rights in an agreement could be in question (there could be an alternative between a sale contract, leading to a transfer of ownership and a loan/lending contract, leading only to an obligation of restitution). The nature of property rights could also be blurred (with options and alternatives between *usus, fructus and abusus*).

13.4 Conclusion

The advent of smart contracts bring many opportunities in terms of contractual practices and, moreover, for the evolution of contract law and property law on a larger scale. It is

[45] C. Dubucq, Attorney at law (Aix-en-Provence Bar), interviewed by Marraud des Grottes, 'Risques et opportunités de la blockchain pour les avocats', www.actualitesdudroit.fr/browse/tech-droit/blockchain/12997/risques-et-opportunites-de-la-blockchain-pour-les-avocats.

[46] Regarding the legal value of professionals' acts, Statute No. 2011-331 of the 28 March 2011 relating to the modernisation of judicial and legal professions and some regulated professions. The statute covers acts for the establishment of which an authenticated deed (and consequently the involvement of a notary) is not required. The attorney, by countersigning the act, certifies that (s)he has examined it and informed the signatory client about the legal consequences of the commitment undertaken, and that the client has knowingly signed. To this regard, see articles 1372 and 1374 of the Civil Code, according to which '[a] signed instrument, acknowledged by the party against whom it is set up or deemed by law to have been so acknowledged, constitutes proof as between its signatories and as regards their heirs or successors' (art. 1372); and '[a] signed instrument countersigned by the legal counsel of each of the parties or by the legal counsel of all the parties provides proof both of the writing and of the signature of the parties, equally as regards themselves and as regards their heirs or successors. The rules on alleging the forgery of the instrument provided by the Code of Civil Procedure may apply to it. Such an instrument does not require any statement in its author's own hand otherwise required by legislation' (art. 1374) (translated into English by J. Cartwright, B. Fauvarque-Cosson and S. Whittaker).

nevertheless crucial to address the 'legal uncertainty surrounding [their] new applications'.[47] In a Civil Law context, for instance, it may be asked whether it is a good idea (or not) to integrate blockchain technologies into the civil code as previously done for electronic contracts. This could be a *sine qua non* requirement for the validity of such contracts with, if necessary, a series of derogations from common rules (e.g. for consumer protection purposes). It seems obvious that 'smart contracts are indeed a viable replacement for certain types of agreements but are not a viable replacement for all standard Civil Law contracts'.[48] In any case, a global regulatory approach will be necessary. But on the latter point, reflections and initiatives are still in an embryonic stage. The questions are numerous and reflection is still in its early stage in a context of legislative and case law vacuum. An initial impulse could be to think of an extension of traditional contract law principles to smart contracts and the blockchain. Nevertheless, in so doing, would we not then be pouring new wine into old wineskins?

[47] European Parliament, Resolution No. 2016/2007 (INI) of 26 May 2016, para. 2 (d).
[48] Preziosi, 'Smart Contracts: Are They a Viable Replacement to the Standard Civil Law Contract?'

14 Algorithmic Contracts and Consumer Privacy

Lauren Henry Scholz

14.1 Introduction

Contracts are everywhere. In a paperless world, contracts of great length and complexity can be costlessly associated with transactions of the utmost triviality. Each device a person uses, and each application on that device, comes with a contract. Every website a person goes to and each transaction that she makes comes with a contract. At any given time, a networked person in a developed economy could be party to tens or even hundreds of contracts. Consumers, from the most sophisticated to the least sophisticated, are rationally ignorant of the terms in these contracts, which are offered on a "take it or leave it basis" along with the associated service or product. Form contracts have been a feature of transactions for hundreds of years.[1] Form contracts have made up the vast majority of enforceable contracts for at least the past thirty years.

While form contracts are not new, contracts' extensiveness and ubiquity in the lives of the average consumer in the developed world is novel. More and more terms circumscribe the practical rights and responsibilities possessed by every person in the information society.

Form contract practices, machine learning, and ubiquitous contracting taken together can enable personalized law – terms customized to each consumer based on their characteristics based on opaque, proprietary algorithms. Not all possible applications of personalized law are necessarily threatening for individual liberties. In another recent article, Ariel Porat and Lior Strahilevitz persuasively argued that personalized default rules in contract law have the potential to fix problems with impersonal default rules and fix the problems associated with personalized default rules.[2] However, if the law is not careful to create incentives for the creation of consumer-friendly personalized default rules, the rise of personalized law could have the potential to create the very opposite of equal justice before the law, a key goal of modern liberal governance.[3] In the past, the

---

[1] I am grateful to Professor Tina L. Stark of Emory University School of Law for alerting me to the long history of form contracts at her lunch presentation at the 2018 Conference on Contracts at Barry University School of Law.

[2] A. Porat & L. J. Strahilevitz, "Personalizing Default Rules and Disclosure with Big Data" (2014) 112 *Michigan Law Review* 1417–1478.

[3] P. Hacker, "The Ambivalence of Algorithms. Gauging the Legitimacy of *Personalized* Law," in M. Bakhoum, B. Conde Gallego, M. Mackenrodt & G. Surblyte (eds.), *Personal Data in Competition, Consumer Protection and Intellectual Property Law* (New York: Springer Publishing Co., 2018). O. Ben-Shahar & A. Porat, "Personalizing Negligence Law" (2016) 91 *New York University Law Review* 627–688 at 668–674 (sketching normative implications of personalized negligence law).

phrase "equal justice under the law" brought to mind lawyers evaluating the equality of
the justice meted out by representatives of the state. Even if the same laws apply to every
person, if different people received systematically different applications of that law, it
would be unfair. The rise of personalized law potentially turns this concern on its head.
Even if the procedural and substantive justice meted out by representatives of the state is
equal, what is the result when the underlying law that applies to each person is systematically unequal due to private contracting practices? When there is a different law for
each citizen, based on a dense contractual environment based on form contracts that
each person rationally does not read or understand?

To place contract law in the position of determining a significant proportion of an
individual's rights and responsibilities is to give it a heavy and important burden. The
literature suggests that given the current realities of consumer contract law, it is not
appropriate that algorithmic consumer transactions bear that burden. It is a well-
established point in empirical contract law research that individuals do not read form
contracts, and that such behavior is rational.[4] To actually read form contracts would be
prohibitively time consuming and ineffective for understanding the terms even for
relatively intelligent individuals. What's more, a consumer cannot alter or reject terms
in a form contract in any case. As Tess Wilkinson-Ryan observes in her recent Iowa Law
Review article, "A Psychological Account of Consent to Fine Print," form contracting
occupies an unusual position in the American policy psyche.[5] As she writes:

> Contracts are understood to be serious moral obligations, and yet everyday commercial
> activity requires that consumers sign agreements that contain terms they have not read.
> Most people see consent to boilerplate as less meaningful than consent to negotiated
> terms, but nonetheless would hold consumers strictly liable for both. This is an area with
> unclear – if not bipolar – norms, and we do not know how individuals assimilate
> conflicting preferences and bodies of evidence into judgments of consumer consent.

Wilkinson-Ryan's study came to the troubling conclusion that disclosures in consumer contracts have the effect of normatively justifying finding against consumers in
cultural legalistic discourse, even though it is understood that such disclosures play no
function in actually informing consumers. Put another way, disclosures add the
veneer of fair transactional process while making no functional improvement on
that metric.

In a Georgetown Law Review article, James Gibson strikes directly at the underlying
concern motivating judges to ignore the strong case for finding nearly any and all
boilerplate terms enforceable against consumers. Judges and other stakeholders ignore
the overwhelming case against the enforceability of consumer boilerplate due to the
perception that the modern consumer economy relies upon boilerplate to function.
They propose the weak argument that boilerplate contracts amount to consent to
specific fine print, because, as Gibson puts it provocatively, "we would rather be
naked than dead." But Gibson shows that choosing between the modern consumer
economy and boilerplate terms a false dichotomy. In the article, he performed an

---

[4] E.g., I. Ayres & A. Schwartz, "The No-Reading Problem in Consumer Contract Law" (2014) 66 *Stanford
Law Review* 545–610 at 556–57.
[5] T. Wilkinson-Ryan, "A Psychological Account of Consent to Fine Print" (2014) 99 *Iowa Law Review*
1745–1784.

empirical study suggesting that mass consumer transactions based on default rules could enable a consumer economy that functions precisely like the current one, except free of boilerplate terms.[6]

Perhaps the best defense of the substantive legitimacy and fairness of form contracts is the "informed minority" hypothesis, which Wilkinson-Ryan and Gibson do not directly address. The hypothesis goes as follows: given that form contracts are widely available and standard, vocal and sophisticated consumers will call out bad terms and that will encourage businesses to change abusive terms that conflict with reasonable consumer intuitions.[7] This argument has been extensively critiqued on its logical and normative merits in the academic literature. But perhaps the most persuasive arguments against the position are empirical.

An influential recent empirical study by Yannis Bakos, Florencia Marotta-Wurgler, and David R. Trossen based on the web-browsing behavior of nearly 50,000 subjects found that the myth of the informed minority to be without merit.[8] They found that the fraction of consumers who read such contracts is so small that it is unlikely that an informed minority alone is shaping software license terms. This study shows that the informed minority hypothesis is without empirical support, so it should be rejected.

Personalized form contracts may remove even the possibility of an informed minority negotiating on behalf of all. The aforementioned study did not examine the specific case of consumer transactions with algorithms. However, there is an *a fortiori* argument to be made here. When a proprietary algorithm determines the terms of each deal, finding out what term is allocated to which consumers is logistically difficult, because the final deals may not be uniform. When not even the text is uniform it eliminates the already-vanishingly low probability that an informed minority could negotiate for the majority. For the rare sticklers, or even individuals likely to be sticklers, the algorithm could simply award different terms.

Consumers are operating in a densely contracted environment that substantially differs from previous social ordering, but the legal salience of contracts has remained static. In a recent draft paper, forthcoming in the *Harvard Law Review*, Professors Robin Kar and Margaret Jane Radin have referred to the phenomenon of finding "contracts" where there is clearly no shared understanding of terms as "pseudo-contract."[9] They refer to the shift from the phrase "contract law" from referring to mutual assent to terms to referring to the unilateral creation of rules by private actors for a broad cross-section of society in their capacity as consumers as a "paradigm slip." As they write:

> This shift has been transforming the meanings of central contract law concepts. We view the shift as an untheorized paradigm slip, inviting a generalized theory of contract as assumption of risk and allowing private obligations to be created unilaterally without actual agreement. This sort of obligation is still called "contract." But it is pseudo-contract. The recent paradigm slip into pseudo-contract raises a complex blend of

---

[6] J. Gibson, "Boilerplate's False Dichotomy" (2018) 106 *Georgetown Law Journal* 249–292.

[7] C. P. Gillette, "Rolling Contracts as an Agency Problem" (2004) 2004 *Wisconsin Law Review* 679–722.

[8] Y. Bakos, F. Marotta-Wurgler, & D. R. Trossen, "Does Anyone Read the Fine Print? Testing a Law and Economics Approach to Standard Form Contracts" (2014) 43 *Journal of Legal Studies* 1–35.

[9] R. B. Kar and M. J. Radin, "Pseudo-Contract & Shared Meaning Analysis" (2019) 132 *Harvard Law Review*, 3–68, available at https://ssrn.com/abstract=3124018.

linguistic, factual, conceptual, normative and doctrinal problems. Under the mantle of contract, the problems of pseudo-contract have been largely hidden.[10]

This chapter argues that privacy is the canary in the coalmine with respect to the potential threat to civil liberties presented by personalized law by way of pseudo-contract regime. Without any deliberate choice on the part of consumers, or change in attitudes, contracts and practices have severely eroded consumer privacy over the past two decades. Thus, privacy terms provide an ideal case study to examine what limits on the ability of consumers to contract with businesses using algorithms to determine customized terms might look like. Personalized law, in the absence of proper fiduciary incentives or default rules, could be a major threat to the civil liberties necessary for a liberal society.

This article will proceed as follows. First, I will define the term "algorithmic contract," distinguishing it from the term "smart contract," and justifying the need for the term. Then, I will argue that business-to-consumer algorithmic contracts present issues distinct from business-to-business algorithmic contracts. After setting the stage in this way, I will introduce the information privacy issue. Section 14.4 will describe the privacy clauses and practices of e-commerce companies and their impact on individual rights. Finally, Section 14.5 will discuss the feasibility of limiting consumer algorithmic contracts on the specific matter of privacy, discussing the benefits and drawbacks of such an approach. Section 14.6 concludes.

14.2 Algorithmic Contracts versus Smart Contracts

In a recent Stanford Technology Law Review article, I coined the term "algorithmic contract."[11]Algorithmic contracts are contracts in which an algorithm determines the rights and responsibilities of a party by acting as either a gap-filler or a negotiator for the company in the process of contract formation. In gap-filler algorithmic contracts, parties agree that an algorithm, which operates at some time either before or after the contract is formed, will serve as a gap-filler, determining some term in the contract. An example of this is a company's purchase of a good on Amazon.com. Amazon has standard form of terms and conditions for all of its buyers, but sophisticated proprietary algorithms determine the good's exact price at any given time for each user.

In negotiator algorithmic contracts, one or more parties use algorithms as negotiators before contract formation. The algorithm chooses which terms to offer or accept, or which company to make the deal with. An example of this is high-frequency trading of financial products by investment banks and funds. They employ quantitative analysts who create or modify proprietary algorithms that, through machine learning, create real-

---

[10] The appropriation of the term "pseudo-contract" can be questioned. After all, aspects of contract law have altered over time, and the term "contract" has still applied. A loose comparison to the Ship of Thesus paradox may apply here: reasonable minds might differ as to precisely if and when, after a series of alterations, one thing becomes a different thing. See Plutarch, "Life of Thesus" XXIII in *Plutarch's Lives*; Andre Gallois, "Identity over Time" in *Stanford Encyclopedia of Philosophy* (2016), available at https:// plato.stanford.edu/entries/identity-time/. This terminological question is too dense to parse here. I adopt Kar and Radin's terminology in this article because the paradigm slip phenomenon they describe of the change in function of contract is accurate, and they make a strong argument for why pseudo-contract is categorically different from contract.

[11] L. H. Scholz, "Algorithmic Contracts" (2017) 20 *Stanford Technology Law Review*, 128–169, available at https://ssrn.com/abstract=2747701. The discussion in this paragraph and the next one is adapted from this article.

time strategies for buying and selling financial products. The point of using such algorithms is to efficiently bind the company to advantageous exchanges that a human analyst could not have thought of doing, including the individuals who wrote the program.

The algorithmic contracts that present the most significant problems for contract law are those that involve "black box" algorithmic agents. Black-box algorithms are computer programs that improve their performance over time by trying a certain solution, evaluating the outcome, and then modifying that solution accordingly to improve future outcomes. This trial-and error-process is done iteratively and automatically with the algorithm writing and altering its own code in the process. To illustrate the difficulty of determining why a black-box algorithm made a particular decision, Professor Price uses an illustrative example of Netflix suggestions:

> Netflix ... uses a technique called collaborative filtering. Collaborative filtering uses information groups of similar users to construct an underlying predictive model and makes recommendations based on that model. Using this approach, Netflix predicts which movies a user might like based on a customer's ratings of watched movies and by comparing that set of data to similar data from other customers. This allows predictions without any explicit knowledge; for instance, it might be true that the vast majority of people who liked *Notting Hill, Casino Royale*, and the television show *Dr. Who* turn out to like the cult foodie film *Tampopo*. Someone who likes the first three would be offered *Tampopo* as a recommendation, despite the lack of any clear or identified link. . . . Why? The model couldn't tell us[.] This lack of transparency is the "black-box" of black-box [algorithms].[12]

Black-box algorithmic contracts are formed by algorithms that have decision-making procedures that are not functionally human-intelligible before the program runs – and often cannot even be parsed after the program runs.[13] Human-intelligible means that a qualified human person can derive the logical process of the algorithm. The meaning and significance of human-human-intelligibility is discussed in detail in "Accountable Algorithms," a recent article written by Joshua A. Kroll, Joanna Huey, Solon Barocas, Edward W. Felten, Joel R. Reidenberg, David G. Robinson, and Harlan Yu.[14] While Europe has recently introduced a right to explanation to algorithmic decision-making in the General Data Protection Directive, the authors of "Accountable Algorithms" find that transparency and explanation are neither necessary nor sufficient for accountability for algorithmic action.[15] Their conclusions parallel Wilkinson-Ryan's study on form contracting discussed, *supra*: disclosure can often simply be used to help psychologically and culturally legitimate highly one-sided contractual terms without changing the functional context of the agreement. Merely adding more text to the wall that consumers are not reading does not make the reality of the transaction any closer to a meaningful meeting of the minds.

---

[12] W. N. Price II, "Black-Box Medicine" (2015) 28 *Harvard Journal of Law & Technology*, 419.

[13] For a further discussion of how artificial intelligence works and the discontents of the law's analysis of it, see M. Aikenhead, "The Uses and Abuses of Neural Networks in Law" (1996) 12 *Santa Clara Computer & High Technology Law Journal* 31–70.

[14] J. A. Kroll, J. Huey, S. Barocas, E. W. Felten, J. R. Reidenberg, D. G. Robinson, & H. Yu, "Accountable Algorithms" (2017) 165 *University of Pennsylvania Law Review* 633–706 at 639.

[15] For a description of the GDPR's right to explanation and its potential as a source of guidance for the American context, see M. Kaminski, "The Right to Explanation, Explained," University of Colorado Law School Legal Studies Research Chapter 1418–24 (2018), available at https://papers.ssrn.com/sol3/papers.cfm?abstract_id=3196985.

I have argued that in business-to-business transactions, algorithmic contracts are enforceable because the algorithm is acting as a constructive agent for the company using it. That means the acts are indicative of the company's intent. Professor Tom C. W. Lin has argued that high-frequency trading allows for the shielding of various well-established market manipulation practices merely because algorithms rather than humans are tasked with making the trades.[16] Ryan Calo has described more broadly the phenomenon of digital market manipulation.[17] The agency approach I propose provides a framework for allowing courts and policymakers to see the parallels between market manipulations by algorithmic traders versus human traders. The analogy makes clear that whether it is a human taking action deliberately or an algorithm (which by definition acts deliberately), either of them are the responsibility of a company if they constitute market manipulation. Both are agents of the company.

The term "algorithmic contract" enhances and clarifies the policy discussion about computer programs known as smart contracts. There is not a settled, universal definition of smart contract. However, definitions of the term from industry and academia agree on a few basic features. Commentators would agree to this simple definition: a smart contract is a piece of computer code that is capable of monitoring, executing, and enforcing an agreement.[18]

Smart contracts are simply computer code that helps to procedurally carry out agreements. However, smart contracts are not necessarily legally binding. Not all code is enforceable in contract law, just like not every expression of human language forms a contract. The term "smart contract" is unfortunate because it is misleading. The word "contract" implies a binding legal, or at least moral, obligation. But a smart contract is computer code that helps individuals to execute their agreements. Perhaps the term "contracting software" would have been more indicative, but "smart contract" is already the term of choice in society. The futurists and businesspeople who use smart contracts are indifferent to whether smart contracts are legally binding. Even the question of whether it is morally wrong to hack a smart contract to receive payouts under conditions the stakeholders and coders did not intend is up for debate in this community.[19] When the term "smart contract" is used outside of the community that created and originated uses of it, without a term to contrast it with, it could readily be conflated with morally or legally binding agreements. This creates the need for the term "algorithmic contract" to describe agreements made by algorithms that are legally binding. "Smart contract" refers to the software, whereas "algorithmic contract" refers to the agreement. An algorithmic contract is a legally enforceable contract formed by an algorithm. Not every smart contract is necessarily legally enforceable.

To summarize, the term "algorithmic contract" describes binding legal agreements that could be enforced in a court of law that are formed by algorithms.[20] "Smart contracts"

---

[16] T. C. W. Lin, "The New Market Manipulation" (2017) 66 *Emory Law Journal* 1253 at 1259–1270.

[17] R. Calo, "Digital Market Manipulation" (2014) 82 *George Washington Law Review* 995–1051 at 996.

[18] R. de Caria, "Law and Autonomous Systems Series: Defining Smart Contracts – The Search for Workable Legal Categories" *Oxford Business Law Blog*, available at www.law.ox.ac.uk/business-law-blog/blog/2018/05/law-and-autonomous-systems-series-defining-smart-contracts-search

[19] "DAO Hack, Attacker Sends Open Letter to Ethereum Community" *NewsBTC* (June 18, 2016) www.newsbtc.com/2016/06/18/dao-hack-attacker-sends-open-letter-to-ethereum-community/.

[20] In the most famous instance of use of decentralized smart contracts, when a hacker stole $50 million of virtual currency, the hacker clearly did it to make a point and start a conversation about what smart contracts mean. As contemporary reporting from WIRED indicated: "Stephan Tual, the COO of Slock.it,

describe code that is supportive of executing agreements regardless of whether the underlying agreements are legally enforceable or not.

14.3 Consumer Contracts versus Business-to-Business Contracts

My approach toward the enforceability of algorithmic contracts between businesses is a permissive one. Contract law should be reflective of contemporary business practices.[21] The notion of what constitutes agreement or even a contract can and should be sensitive to business norms. The Uniform Commercial Code (UCC) and the cases and jurisprudence arising from it are reflective of these principles.[22] In the case of business-to-business algorithmic contracts, the doctrinal argument is supported by several policy considerations. If businesses are strictly liable for the acts of an algorithm in contract formation, they will be faced with potential adversaries with the financial incentive and ability to pursue litigation. This would create accountability in algorithm usage, and an incentive to allocate risk of loss to the least cost avoider in advance. Arguments for enforceability based on the assumption of risk and economic efficiency are highly persuasive here.

Consumer algorithmic contracts present different considerations. Businesses in a given industry tend to operate within specialty norms. Even when businesses do not have actual knowledge of the content of forms they use, these forms are often coded to serve the general interests of repeat players in the industry. And, at least for the sale of goods, the norms for exchange of forms do not allow one party to unilaterally pick terms where neither party is rationally expected to read the forms, given an exchange of terms.[23] By contrast, the terms in consumer contracts are not generally shaped to the individual consumer's advantage, and what's more, consumers have less collective knowledge of terms and no ability to control terms.[24] Furthermore, much more is at stake when it comes to the algorithmic assignment of rights to human persons, as opposed to artificial persons by algorithmic contracts. Human persons have rights and responsibilities that companies do not. Some of these rights are nondisclaimable. In a liberal democracy, we should be concerned with individuals being autonomous and not subject to undue control by others.

---

the company that built the DAO, says the thief probably never expected to be able to spend the ether. Each unit of ether is unique and traceable. If the hacker tries to sell any of the stolen ether in a cryptocurrency market, the system will flag it. 'It's like stealing the Mona Lisa,'" he says. "Great, congratulations, but what do you do with it? You can't sell it, it's too big to be sold." K. Finley, "A $50 Million Hack Just Showed That the DAO Was All Too Human" in *Wired* (June 18, 2016) available at www.wired.com/2016/06/50-million-hack-just-showed-dao-human/.

21 This point is reflective of the rationale for the Uniform Commercial Code and how it should be interpreted in Uniform Commercial Code §1–103. "The Uniform Commercial Code must be liberally construed and applied to promote its underlying purposes and policies, which are: (1) to simplify, clarify, and modernize the law governing commercial transactions; (2) to permit the continued expansion of commercial practices through custom, usage, and agreement of the parties; and (3) to make uniform the law among the various jurisdictions."

22 A. R. Kamp, "Between-the-Wars Social Thought: Karl Llewellyn, Legal Realism, and the Uniform Commercial Code in Context" (1995) 59 *Albany Law Review* 325–398 at 338.

23 See Uniform Commercial Code 2–207. R. C. Bern, "'Terms Later' Contracting: Bad Economics, Bad Morals, and a Bad Idea for a Uniform Law, Judge Easterbrook Notwithstanding" (2004) 12 *Journal of Law and Policy* 641–796 at 649.

24 See discussion of Wilkinson-Ryan and Gibson above.

There is precedent for having different standards for consumer-to-business transactions versus business-to-business transactions. Because of the distinct concerns presented by consumer-to-business transactions, the common law has traditionally held consumers to different standards of reasonable behavior than companies. For example, in the United States, the UCC has a variety of rules that apply only to merchants.[25] As an influential treatise on the UCC put it, "If one is a merchant, he supposedly has a special skill or a particular knowledge; and for this reason he is held to a completely different set of rules which are generally stricter than the rules that apply to non-merchants."[26] The idea of merchant-specific, and even industry-specific, rules has had currency far beyond the UCC. This is based on a typical American philosophy of trusting in the skill of individual guilds and tradespeople in society and providing deference where practical and ethical.[27] Stakeholders have been applying this analysis to the digital context for two decades.[28] They have been somewhat hamstrung in this process by two influential and incorrectly reasoned opinions about consumer form contracting.[29] The poor reasoning in these opinions by an otherwise-brilliant jurist suggests that the judge saw no other way to have a broad digital consumer economy without companies determining the terms via boilerplate. However, the dense environment of default rules available in consumer

---

[25] L. D. Sparks, Esq., "The Regression of 'Good Faith' in Maryland Commercial Law" (2016) 47 *University of Baltimore Law Forum* 17–26 at 18; TA follows Article 2's methodology in drawing distinctions between rules for merchants and nonmerchants.

[26] S. Vanmeveren, "The Uniform Commercial Code-Sales-Special Treatment for Merchants" (1970) 7 *American Business Law Journal* 219–225 at 220.

[27] A. R. Kamp, "Between-the-Wars Social Thought: Karl Llewellyn, Legal Realism, and the Uniform Commercial Code in Context" (1995) 59 *Albany Law Review* 325–397 at 338.

[28] For a discussion of the merchant distinctions in the Uniform Computer Information Transactions Act, see M. L. Rustad, "Making UCITA More Consumer-Friendly" (1999) 18 *John Marshall Journal of Computer & Information Law* 547–590 at 557. UCITA has been unsuccessful in making state legislation for unrelated reasons.

[29] Bern, "'Terms Later' Contracting," 665–667:

> [Judge Frank] Easterbrook's cavalier treatment of both the statute and precedent has been roundly and rightly criticized. [Mark] Gergen states, "[t]here is one real howler in [ProCD and Hill] – they say that 2–207 applies only when there are two forms. This is just dead wrong." [Robert] Hillman is unequivocal in his condemnation of Easterbrook's treatment of section 2-207, noting, "[he] was plainly wrong about section 2-207's applicability. Nothing in the text of the section limits it to transactions involving more than one form." Likewise, [Jean] Braucher concurs that "[n]othing in the language of section 2–207 limits its application to two-form situations or even to forms at all," further noting that "[t]he Pro-CD analysis also is contrary to Comment 1 to Section 2–207, which refers to one-form transactions."

> Judge Easterbrook displays the same intellectual dishonesty when "distinguishing" away relevant case authority that applied section 2–207 to preclude enforcement of terms a seller first disclosed after the buyer made the purchase. Although none involved a purchase off a retail shelf, two of the three, *Step-Saver Data Systems, Inc. v. Wyse Technology* and *Arizona Retail Systems, Inc. v. Software Link, Inc.*, presented the very issue that was before the court in ProCD. In each the issue was whether a seller of software could bind the buyer to terms not disclosed to the buyer until after purchase by stating in those belatedly disclosed terms that opening the shrink-wrap package and using the software constituted agreement by the buyer. In each case, the respective court held that such terms were not enforceable, expressly relying upon the provisions of section 2–207. Only *Vault Corp. v. Quaid Software Ltd.* did not directly address the matter of enforce-ability of "terms later." It did not need to address the issue because it found that the Copyright Act preempted the Louisiana statute that made shrink-wrap licenses enforceable, upon which the software seller premised its contract claim. (Internal footnotes omitted)

transactions suggests otherwise.[30] Contract law is pluralist, encompassing awareness of ethical and pragmatic concerns.[31]

The carefully crafted business ethics enshrined in the common law of contracts and the UCC should be transferred to the algorithmic age. Laws developed based on out-moded notions of algorithmic capabilities such as the Uniform Electronic Transactions Act should also be clarified to encompass an agent-based approach to algorithmic involvement in contract formation. It would be incorrect as a matter of legal principle and imprudent as a matter of policy to have a contract law, given its underlying policy goals in promoting individual agency and consensual market transactions,[32] that serves to legitimate algorithmic exploitation.

Algorithmic exploitation comes in several forms.[33] First, unaccountable algorithms operate in the background of society, determining the terms of our access to many resources.[34] This enables an unseen form of social control by the corporate and government controllers of the relevant algorithms. Furthermore, big data processing techniques have been shown to be vulnerable to choosing strategies that perpetuate wrongful discrimination against socially and economically vulnerable groups. In addi-tion to raising serious moral concerns about the scope of free choice in a liberal democracy, allowing algorithmic contracts to enable perfect market discrimination by powerful actors would result in major market failure. Given these very real concerns, doctrinal limits on the enforceability of consumer algorithmic contracts should be explored.

Contract law doctrine offers multiple potential avenues for limiting the enforceabil-ity of consumer algorithmic contracts. For example, the doctrine of undue influence, an affirmative defense to contractual enforcement, may be relevant to this issue. Undue influence finds contracts unenforceable when the improper use of power or trust deprives a person of free will and substitutes another's objectives in its place. It is the exercise of enough control over another person such that the pertinent action by that other person would not have otherwise been performed.[35] The Second Restatement rule is: "Undue influence is unfair persuasion of a party who is under the domination of the person exercising the persuasion or who by virtue of the relation between them is justified in assuming that that person will not act in a manner inconsistent with his

---

[30] See discussion of Gibson above.

[31] "Pluralist [contract] theories attempt to respond to the difficulty that unitary normative theories ['such as autonomy or efficiency'] pose by urging courts to pursue efficiency, fairness, good faith, and the protection of individual autonomy." A. Schwartz & R. E. Scott, "Contract Theory and the Limits of Contract Law" (2003) 113 *Yale Law Journal* 541–619 at 543.

[32] See discussion of Uniform Commercial Code above.

[33] While the term "algorithmic exploitation" is my own, several scholars have described the phenomenon in detail. F. Pasquale, *The Black Box Society: The Secret Algorithms That Control Money and Information* (Cambridge: Harvard University Press, 2015); D. Keats Citron & F. Pasquale, "The Scored Society: Due Process for Automated Predictions" (2014) 89 *Washington Law Review* 1–33 at 3. The effects of this exploitation may also disproportionally impact marginalized groups. S. Barocas & A. D. Selbst, "Big Data's Disparate Impact" (2016) 104 *California Law Review* 671–732 at 674; P. T. Kim, "Auditing Algorithms for Discrimination" (2017) 166 *University of Pennsylvania Law Review Online* 189–203.

[34] Barocas and Selbst, "Big Data's Disparate Impact," 671.

[35] For a through discussion of recent undue influence, cases, see J. L. Harrison, "Defects in Consent and Dividing the Benefit of the Bargain: Recent Developments" (2015) 53 *University of Louisville Law Review* 193–228 at 218–26.

welfare."[36] Undue influence is often employed when there is a disparate capacity between parties.[37]

Other contract doctrine relevant to the question of whether the enforceability of consumer algorithmic transactions should be limited contracts is doctrines of capacity, duress, and procedural unconscionability.[38] I plan to explore these avenues of analyzing consent in consumer algorithmic transactions in more detail in an article forthcoming in 2019 entitled "Consumer Algorithmic Transactions."[39]

For the purposes of this chapter, it is sufficient to observe that in the case of consumer algorithmic contracts, a consumer potentially finds herself confronted with forming agreements with machine-learning algorithms armed with superior processing capacity and comprehensive knowledge of both general attendant circumstances and particular data about that person. Several scholars have sounded concerns about consumer contracting in the information era.[40] In contract formation, the diminished capacity of consumers relative to companies employing algorithmic decision-making, paired with knowledge about each individual consumer's vulnerabilities, at the very least sits uncomfortably with the reason why liberal society sees fit to enforce contracts between individuals.[41]

---

[36] Restatement (Second) of Contracts, § 177.
[37] Harrison, "Defects in Consent" at 220.
[38] Both capacity and duress could be useful to the case for some limits on the substance of what consumers may be able to agree to with black box, machine-learning algorithms. Humans have low capacity for reasoning relative to such algorithms (see the replacement of incredibly well-trained humans in favor of algorithms in the financial industry). "Duress," while the term sounds quite dire, is interested in most jurisdictions as operating quite similarly as the undue influence defense discussed in text. The capacity defense to contractual enforcement finds contracts to be voidable when one party is "unable to understand in a reasonable manner the nature and consequences of the transaction, or he is unable to act in a reasonable manner in relation to the transaction and the other party has reason to know of his condition." Restatement 115. The Second Restatement defines duress as "If a party's manifestation of assent is induced by an improper threat by the other party that leaves the victim no reasonable alternative, the contract is voidable by the victim." Restatement 175. However, the Restatement definition of improper threat is very broad. The Second Restatement provides, in pertinent part:

(1) A threat is improper if
  (a) what is threatened is a crime or a tort, or the threat itself would be a crime or a tort if it resulted in obtaining property,
  (b) what is threatened is a criminal prosecution,
  (c) what is threatened is the use of civil process and the threat is made in bad faith, or
  (d) the threat is a breach of the duty of good faith and fair dealing under a contract with the recipient.

(2) A threat is improper if the resulting exchange is not on fair terms, and
  (a) the threatened act would harm the recipient and would not significantly benefit the party making the threat,
  (b) the effectiveness of the threat in inducing the manifestation of assent is significantly increased by prior unfair dealing by the party making the threat, or
  (c) what is threatened is otherwise a use of power for illegitimate ends.
  Restatement Second of Contracts § 176.

[39] Restatement (Second) at § 15.
[40] E.g., M. Hu, "Algorithmic Jim Crow" (2017) 96 *Fordham Law Review* 633–696.
[41] There are few cases that directly address these issues because of the issue of arbitration. If there is an arbitration term in a contract, that term can fairly readily take the contract out of consideration of the courts. But the analysis in this section, and throughout the chapter, should influence self-regulation, state legislation, and Federal Trade Commission enforcement under its authority to regulate "unfair and deceptive trade practices." 15 USC § 45(a) (2012).

14.4 Privacy Clauses and Individual Rights

Contract law determines many of the rights consumers possess in their personal information. Companies routinely expressly promise more with respect to privacy and data protection than they deliver. In consumer contract law, the important keystone to begin with is browsewrap and clickwrap agreements because most consumer agreements with merchants are of this type. Clickwrap agreements are agreements in which consumers must click an "I agree" icon in order to proceed with a transaction.[42] Many courts have found clickwrap agreements to be enforceable contracts, at least when the clickwrap terms are not overreaching or abusive.[43] Browsewrap agreements are agreements in which terms available on a webpage purport to hold consumers who browse the website to have agreed to terms.[44] In these policies, most companies make representations about information privacy and data use.[45] Most courts which have considered the issue have held that in order to state a plausible claim for relief based upon a browsewrap agreement, the website user must have actual or constructive knowledge of the site's terms and conditions and have manifested assent to them.[46]

There is a widespread view among privacy advocates and commentators that consumers cannot rely on contract law to bring privacy claims. In their influential article, "The FTC and the New Common Law of Privacy," Professors Daniel Solove and Woodrow Harzog make the typical argument for the irrelevance of contract law to privacy.[47] They cite two cases addressing information privacy in the infancy of the consumer interest, the earlier of which occurred in the mid-1990s, and denied the coverage of particular privacy policies as binding contracts. Solove and Hartzog, among other scholars, have pointed to these same two cases as evidence, more than two decades later, that courts and company practices deny the applicability of contract law to privacy policies. This is empirically inaccurate. A recent article by Professors Omri Ben-Shahar and Lior Jacob Strahilevitz shows, through an empirical study of cases over the past decade, that most courts actually find privacy policies to contain binding promises from policies to consumers.[48] Ben-Shahar and Strahilevitz expressly bemoan the myopia of many privacy scholars in effectively extrapolating the law's approach to privacy from two rather idiosyncratic, lower-court cases, *Jet Blue Airways*

---

[42] *Nguyen v. Barnes & Noble Inc.*, 763 F 3d 1171, 1175–76 (9th Cir. 2014).

[43] E.g., *Omstead v. Dell, Inc.*, 594 F 3d 1081 (9th Cir. 2010) (refusing to find enforceable a clickwrap agreement that required consumers to bring all claims in Texas and also required consumers to relinquish their right to bring a class action suit against Dell for any reason whatsoever).

[44] *Nguyen v. Barnes & Noble Inc.*, 763 F 3d 1171, 1175–76 (9th Cir. 2014).

[45] A. McDonald et al., "A Comparative Study of Online Privacy Policies and Formats" (2009) International Symposium on Privacy Enhancing Technologies 35–55, available at www.robreeder.com/pubs/PETS2009.pdf

[46] *Cvent, Inc. v. Eventbrite, Inc.*, 739 F Supp 2d 927 (E.D. Va. 2010).

[47] E.g., D. J. Solove & W. Hartzog, "The FTC and the New Common Law of Privacy" (2014) 114 *Columbia Law Review* 583–676 at 595.

[48] O. Ben-Shahar & L. J. Strahilevitz, "Contracting over Privacy: Introduction" (2016) 45 *Journal of Legal Studies* S1–12 (on the centrality of consumer contract law in privacy regulation). Several other articles from this volume of the *Journal of Legal Studies*, entitled "Contracting over Privacy," deepen this point. F. Marotta-Wurgler, "Self-Regulation and Competition" (2016) 45 *Journal of Legal Studies* S13–40, L. J. Strahilivitz, "Is Privacy Policy Language Irrelevant to Consumers?" (2016) 45 *Journal of Legal Studies* S69-96, J. R. Reidenberg et al., "Ambiguity in Privacy Polices and the Impact of Regulation" (2016) 45 *Journal of Legal Studies* S163–90.

Corp. Privacy Litig. & Dwyer v. Am. Express Co.[49] Why aren't these words spelled out in full? It looks strange to me. A failure to look beyond these two cases leads to a broader myopia: missing that contract law and related interests may be the primary source of consumer privacy rights in the status quo.

Even where representation by a company is not binding in contract, a showing of reliance on a promise provides grounds for an individual to seek relief in promissory estoppel.[50] Promissory estoppel lies where a party relies upon another's promise, the defendant knew the party would rely on the promise, and injury results.[51] While the doctrine of promissory estoppel is not true contract law, relying as it does on reliance as opposed to bargained-for exchange, it is a frequent fellow traveler of contract law, as evinced by its presence in the Restatements of Contract.[52] That is to say, promissory estoppel tends to arise in a context where a contract could have or should have been formed, but for some reason, was not properly formed.[53] So, whether it is contract law proper or promissory estoppel, it is a mistake to cast contract law aside as a source of guidance for social ordering regarding privacy.

At the turn of the twenty-first century, a rash of articles pointed hopefully at the possibility of considering privacy as a type of property interest.[54] This was intended to give privacy violations the status of property infringements, which would include powerful equitable remedies such as injunctive relief. This would appear to be the long-awaited movement the field needed to take privacy remedies seriously. Several scholars argued that liability rules simply were not strong enough to protect the privacy interest.[55]

---

[49] In re *Jet Blue Airways Corp. Privacy Litig.*, 379 F Supp 2d 299, 327 (E.D.N.Y. 2005) (rejecting a hypothetical claim for damages based on "the loss of the economic value of their information" because "[plaintiffs] had no reason to expect that they would be compensated for the 'value' of their personal information ... [and there is] no support for the proposition that an individual passenger's personal information has or had any compensable value in the economy at large."); *Dwyer v. Am. Express Co.*, 652 N E 2d 1351, 1356 (Ill. App. Ct. 1995) (holding that the use of consumer data to target third parties did not violate the intrusion upon seclusion or appropriation privacy torts because the defendants were not disclosing particular cardholders' financial information, and finding that "a single, random cardholder's name has little or no intrinsic value to defendants").

[50] Restatement Second of Torts § 90.

[51] *Id.*

[52] Restatement Second of Contracts § 90.

[53] For a detailed discussion of how courts apply promissory estoppel, see M. J. Jimenez, "The Many Faces of Promissory Estoppel: An Empirical Analysis Under the Restatement (Second) of Contracts" (2010) 57 *UCLA Law Review* 669 at 672 ("My research suggests, first, that promissory estoppel is a much more significant theory of promissory recovery than has been previously thought, and seems positioned to continue to grow in importance in the coming decades. Second, and contrary to the claims made by some scholars writing in this area, the data reveal that promissory estoppel cannot be simply understood in terms of 'promise' or 'reliance'. Rather, most judges require the existence of both promise and reliance before allowing a promissory estoppel claim to proceed, although surprisingly few judges speak in terms of 'equity' or 'justice'. And last, but most significantly for purposes of explaining how judges tend to conceptualize the promissory estoppel cause of action, the data reveal that courts tend to treat promissory estoppel actions as traditional breach of contract actions, in that courts often award the (usually) more generous expectation measure of damages, which is typical in ordinary breach of contract actions, over the (usually) less generous reliance measure of damages, which is often awarded where non-contractual obligations have been breached (for example, in tort law).").

[54] For a comprehensive summary of this debate, see my discussion elsewhere. L. H. Scholz, "Privacy as Quasi-Property" (2016) 101 *Iowa Law Review* 1113, 1120–1124 (2016).

[55] L. Lessig, *Code and Other Laws of Cyberspace* (New York: Basic Books, 1999) 142–163 (advocating the use of property rights to protect privacy on the Internet); P. Mell, "Seeking Shade in a Land of Perpetual Sunlight: Privacy as Property in the Electronic Wilderness" (1996) 11 *Berkeley Technology Law Journal*

However, property interests can be alienated via contract. The worry is that people will contract away any property interest they have in their privacy.[56]

This debate was steeped in the classic framework distinguishing between liability rules and property rules as described by Guido Calabresi and A. Douglas Melamed in their seminal article "Property Rules, Liability Rules, and Inalienability: One View of the Cathedral."[57] In an article empirically describing the nature of that article's influence on American legal academia, Professors James Krier and Steward Schwab pointed out a key critique of the article:

> The cornerstone of [Calabresi and Melamed's article] was, of course, what Posner and many others have noted: the distinction between property rights and liability rules. The point of property rights, as Calabresi and Melamed explained, is to compel voluntary transacting where transaction costs are low.

In the context considered by Calabresi and Melamed – the context, particularly, of litigation – transaction costs are hardly ever low; they are high either because there are many parties to a lawsuit (high coordination costs) or high because there are few (high costs of strategic bargaining). Given this, Posner's statement implies that property rights and property rules are seldom the best approach to disputes over resources; liability rules and centralized judicial decision-making should be relied upon instead. The trouble is that liability rules and centralized judicial decision-making are themselves costly to employ. The issue in choosing between property rules and liability rules – between, that is, the decentralized means of the market and the centralized means of the state – is not whether transaction costs are low or high, but rather whether they are lower or higher than the assessment costs that must otherwise be expended. This is a very difficult question to resolve, which perhaps is why virtually the entire scholarly community reads Calabresi and Melamed in the convenient way that Posner suggests. Whatever the cause, the consequence is plain: Conventional thinkers opt for liability rules when voluntary exchange in the market would be costly, notwithstanding that involuntary exchange in the courts might be more costly yet. In short, the Cathedral's congregation takes on faith a proposition that the article's reasoning cannot support.[58]

In other words, the traditional narrative places a level of emphasis between property rules and liability rules that is unsustainable. In the context of privacy, there is more to a discussion of remedies than whether privacy – or any other interest – falls into the broad category of property or liability. The scholars who advocated a property approach did so because they presumed different and superior remedies would be available for the infringement of a privacy interest. However, they also constructed highly conditional

1–92 at 26–41; R. S. Murphy, "Property Rights in Personal Information: An Economic Defense of Privacy" (1996) 84 *Georgetown Law Journal* 2381–2418 at 2385.

[56] E.g., P. Samuelson, "Privacy as Intellectual Property?" (2000) 52 *Stanford Law Review* 1125–1173 at 1129; J. Litman, "Information Privacy/information Property" (2000) 52 *Stanford Law Review* 1283–1313 at 1284–1285 (outlining skeptical perspectives on privacy as property).

[57] G. Calabresi & A. D. Melamed, "Property Rules, Liability Rules, and Inalienability: One View of the Cathedral" (1972) 85 *Harvard Law Review* 1089. A concise summary of the meaning of property rules and liability rules and the implications Calabresi and Melamed lent to them can be found in an influential article by Professors James E. Krier and Stewart J. Schwab. James E. Krier & Stewart J. Schwab, "Property Rules and Liability Rules: The Cathedral in another Light" (1995) 70 *New York University Law Review* 440, 442.

[58] J. E. Krier & S. J. Schwab, "The Cathedral at Twenty-Five: Citations and Impressions" (1997) 106 *Yale Law Journal* 2121–2147, at 2134–2135.

and difficult to alienate property rights for privacy as property.[59] For property rights that stray from the ideal of real property, the law's approach is still difficult and developing,[60] so it is not clear that courts would award remedies similar to the remedies for real property right even if the privacy interest was not disclaimed via contract.

Several scholars have described the special status of the privacy right in a liberal democracy. Professor Anita Allen, in her book Unpopular Privacy, argued that governments should force individuals to maintain certain privacy rights and make them unable to contract them away because of the unique role privacy plays in human flourishing.[61] In his book *Intellectual Privacy*, Professor Neil Richards stopped short of arguing for mandatory privacy for all, but argued expansively for the critical role of privacy in enabling individuals to exercise critical civil liberties for a liberal democracy.[62] Taken together, Allen and Richards' work makes a strong argument for the necessity of preventing privacy from falling by the wayside incidentally by upholding pseudo-contractual obligations tailored to individual consumers. In the context of contract law, these arguments may suggest some limits on the ability of consumers to contract away privacy interests, or at the very least some very strong default rules. The feasibility of such limits will be discussed in the next part.

14.5 Limitations on Freedom to Contract Away Privacy Rights

The previous section argued that contract law doctrine offers multiple potential avenues for limiting the enforceability of consumer algorithmic contracts. This section discusses the potential for subject matter-specific contractual limits in the area of privacy.

In the case of consumer algorithmic contracts, a consumer potentially finds herself confronted with forming agreements with machine-learning algorithms armed with superior processing capacity and comprehensive knowledge of both general attendant circumstances and particular data about that person. In contract formation, the diminished capacity of consumers relative to companies employing algorithmic decision-making, paired with knowledge about each individual consumer's vulnerabilities, could amount to undue influence resulting in a voidable contract. Similar arguments limiting the enforceability of consumer contracts can be made from the doctrines of mental capacity and procedural unconscionability.

Another potential way of framing the legal protections consumers are entitled to when contracting with algorithmic agents of businesses is as a fiduciary duty. Perhaps, given the power contracts have to create personalized law, businesses that use algorithmic agents might have fiduciary duties toward consumers to have particular policies in place to protect their interests. *Black's Law Dictionary* defines a fiduciary duty as follows:

---

[59] *E.g.*, P. M. Schwartz, "Property, Privacy, and Personal Data" (2004) 117 *Harvard Law Review* 2055–2128; E. J. Janger, "Privacy Property, Information Costs, and the Anticommons" (2003) 54 *Hastings Law Journal* 899.

[60] J. E. Cohen, "Property as Institutions for Resources: Lessons from and for IP" (2015) 94 *Texas Law Review* 1–57 at 4; C. Mulligan, "The Story of Land" (2017) 95 *Texas Law Review See also* 12–17.

[61] A. L. Allen, *Unpopular Privacy: What Must We Hide* (Oxford: Oxford University Press, 2011).

[62] N. Richards, *Intellectual Privacy: Rethinking Civil Liberties in the Digital Age* (Oxford: Oxford University Press, 2015).

A duty of utmost good faith, trust, confidence, and candor owed by a fiduciary (such as an agent or a trustee) to the beneficiary (such as the agent's principal or the beneficiaries of the trust); a duty of utmost good faith, trust, confidence, and candor owed by a fiduciary (such as a lawyer or corporate officer) to the beneficiary (such as a lawyer's client or a shareholder); a duty to act with the highest degree of honesty and loyalty toward another person and in the best interests of the other person (such as the duty that one partner owes to another). For example, directors have a duty not to engage in self-dealing to further their own personal interests rather than the interests of the corporation.[63]

In the context of algorithmic contracts, one might imply a fiduciary duty not to include unreasonably one-sided terms on the basis of the different contracting abilities of a human versus an algorithm with access to superior processing capacity and extensive information about that particular human. Fiduciary duties have evolved and changed over time based on social and economic context.[64] In a recent article, Professor Jack Balkin has described a concept of "information fiduciaries" in the context of the First Amendment. As he writes:

> Because of their special power over others and their special relationships to others, information fiduciaries have special duties to act in ways that do not harm the interests of the people whose information they collect, analyze, use, sell, and distribute. These duties place them in a different position from other businesses and people who obtain and use digital information. And because of their different position, the First Amendment permits somewhat greater regulation of information fiduciaries than it does for other people and entities.[65]

Balkin argues that the fiduciary duty arises from the amount or type of information that an actor has about a human. While I think that Balkin is correct to trace the duty to control to information about consumers, I add to that argument for fiduciary duty in the particular context of algorithmic contracts the categorical difference in processing capability between a consumer and an algorithmic agent acting on behalf of a business. Furthermore my argument considers fiduciary duties outside the First Amendment context. Contract and fiduciary law are not usually understood as a forum where the First Amendment is relevant. Contracts are considered legal acts, rather than speech.[66] And fiduciary law is part of the broader context of business law, where enforcing a thin notion of "good faith" in transactions has been a traditional part of regulation, and this is considered regulation of conduct.[67]

One could potentially construct the fiduciary obligations of the company contracting to determine many or most terms in algorithmic contracts, or only a specific subcategory

---

[63] Duty, Black's Law Dictionary (10th edn., 2014).

[64] See, e.g., T. Frankel, "Fiduciary Law" (1983) 71 California Law Review 795–836 at 795–796. (discussing the rise of new forms of fiduciary obligation in the eighteenth and twentieth centuries); D. J. Seipp, "Trust and Fiduciary Duty in the Early Common Law" (2011) 91 Baylor University Law Review 1011 (describing the development of fiduciary obligations in the English common law).

[65] J. M. Balkin, "Information Fiduciaries and the First Amendment" (2016) 49 U.C. Davis Law Review 1183–1234 at 1186.

[66] F. Ghodoosi, "The Concept of Public Policy in Law: Revisiting the Role of the Public Policy Doctrine in the Enforcement of Private Legal Arrangements" (2016) 94 Nebraska Law Review 685–736 at 687; B. Arruñada, "Institutional Support of the Firm: A Theory of Business Registries" (2010) 2 Journal of Legal Analysis 525–576 at 537.

[67] G. Abend, The Moral Background: An Inquiry into the History of Business Ethics (Princeton: Princeton University Press, 2014).

of terms. The purpose of this section is to examine the rationale and sketch the potential implementation of limiting the ability of individuals to contract away their privacy with algorithms.

The reason to focus on privacy entitlements is that they have unique value with respect to enhancing individual capabilities and enabling individuals to contribute to a liberal democracy.[68] This may justify special protections. The capabilities approach to assessing regulation, as described by Professors Martha Nussbaum and Amartya Sen, was ably summarized in a recent article by Professor Gregory S. Alexander, who notes:

> A capabilities approach to human flourishing] approach measures a person's well-being not by looking at what they have, but by looking at what they are able to do. The well-lived life is a life that conforms to certain objectively valuable patterns of human existence and interaction, or what Sen calls "functionings," rather than a life character-ized merely by the possession of particular goods, the satisfaction of particular (subjec-tive) preferences, or even, without more, the possession of particular negative liberties. Social structures, including distributions of property rights and the definition of the rights that go along with the ownership of property, should be judged, at least in part, by the degree to which they foster the participation by human beings in these objectively valuable patterns of existence and interaction.[69]

Importantly, Nussbaum and Sen distinguish between the first-order patterns that constitute well-lived human lives ("functionings") and the second-order freedom or power to choose to function in particular ways, which they call "capabilities." As Sen explains, "A person's 'capability' refers to the alternative combinations of functionings that are feasible for her to achieve." Among the functionings that are necessary for a well-lived life are life, including certain subsidiary values such as health; freedom, understood as including the freedom to make deliberate choices among alternative life horizons; practical reasoning; and sociality. Although the actual achievement of these and other functionings is a necessary component of any plausible conception of the well-lived life, the experience of choosing among a number of possible valuable functionings (perhaps even including the choice not to function in certain ways) is itself an important function-ing. Accordingly, a proper concern for human autonomy requires looking beyond mere functionings to include the capabilities that various social matrices generate for their members.

This framework is instructive for understanding how private law should operate in the information era. As Professor Adam Werbach observed, the capabilities approach "applies anywhere there is an inequitable allocation of capabilities, including communications."[70]

Another reason why the idea of limiting the ability to contract away privacy, rather than a more general limit on the ability of humans to contract with algorithms, is the American tradition of subject matter and sector specific regulation. This approach has been employed extensively in the context of privacy law in particular, with specific federal legislation employed to regulate children, financial privacy, and even video rentals.[71]

---

[68] See discussion of Allen and Richards above.
[69] G. S. Alexander, "The Social-Obligation Norm in American Property Law" (2009) 94 *Cornell Law Review* 745–820 at 781.
[70] K. Werbach, "A Capabilities Approach to Communications Equity" (2017) 16 *Colorado Technology Law Journal* 11–32 at 24.
[71] B. J. Ard, "The Limits of Industry-Specific Privacy Law" (2015) 51 *Idaho Law Review* 607–621 at 611.

Privacy is particularly challenging as a subject of self-regulation because the terms of data disclosure are largely invisible to consumers. This creates a "market for lemons" along the lines of the famous George Akerlof paper.[72] Professors Edward J. Janger and Paul Schwartz applied the market for lemons metaphor to the case of privacy, specifically a federal statute on financial privacy. They cite Professor Richard Craswell's influential analysis of market failure for nonprice terms and apply it to the case of privacy in the information of economy in the following passage:

> Because terms that are good for buyers are generally more expensive for sellers, any seller that offers better terms will charge a higher price to make the same level of profits she could make by offering less favorable terms at a lower price. However, if most buyers have good information about prices but only poor information about non-price terms, they may not notice an improvement in non-price terms, while they will definitely notice the higher price.[73]

As a result, many buyers may stop purchasing from this seller. Once a sufficiently large number of buyers cease purchasing, the seller will lose money as a result of her decision to offer more favorable terms at a higher price. Craswell concludes, "In that case, no seller has an incentive to offer the more favorable terms, and the result is an equilibrium in which only bad contract terms (or 'lemons') can be obtained."[9] Craswell's parenthetical allusion to lemons suggests an unfortunate consequence when buyers and sellers are unable to signal the presence of a good product. In a lemons equilibrium, either bad products ("lemons") are offered for sale or bad contract terms are presented.

Consumers state that they care about privacy, yet most form contracts they enter into do not provide it.[74] This is a market-for-lemons situation. Consumers consistently indicate they desire privacy, through both their direct expressions and their consistent altering of privacy settings, where possible, to provide more privacy for themselves. The best evidence that consumers do not care about privacy is the fact that many of them agree to boilerplate contracts. But the overwhelming major of contracts literature, even the literature that finds that boilerplate consumer contracts are enforceable, do not make the claim that consumers assent to the substance of boilerplate agreements.

The disadvantage of singling out privacy entitlements for nondisclaimability via consumer algorithmic contract is that it would raise a consistent issue of when, in a consumer algorithmic contract, privacy entitlements are disclaimed to a sufficient extent to animate this rule. Furthermore, consumer algorithmic contracts operate in a context where trade secrets are king. Regulators will be unable to provide specific guidelines as to how to prevent consumer abuse, given that the underlying algorithms are necessarily hidden. This makes it incredibly important that regulation in this area ends up creating incentives for companies to prevent consumer-exploitative outcomes regardless of internal processes. Work by Professors Kenneth Bamberger and Deidre Mulligan has established that most successful privacy policy globally creates incentives for companies to reach general privacy objectives rather than directing companies to reach certain compliance

---

[72] G. Aklerlof, "The Market for Lemons: Quality Uncertainty and the Market Mechanism" (1970) 84 *The Quarterly Journal of Economics* 488–500.

[73] H. Beales, R. Craswell, & S. C. Salop, "The Efficient Regulation of Consumer Information" (1981) 24 *Journal of Law & Economics* 491–539.

[74] J. Cohen, "What Privacy Is For" (2013) 126 *Harvard Law Review* 1904–1933.

standards.[75] In the latter case, there is a race to the bottom, and companies ask themselves how they can do the least and still be in compliance. With more flexible rules that provide incentives and measure outcomes more holistically, companies have the incentive to seek to attain privacy goals. The risk of these more general approaches is that, if the incentives and punishments are too weak, they could yield results little different from industry self-regulation, which has proven inadequate in the privacy case. As Professor Ard put it in an article entitled "The Limits of Industry-Specific Privacy Law": "The industry-specific approach to privacy lawmaking is a poor fit for Internet surveillance. We can bolster many existing laws by translating them into industry-neutral, transaction-centered terms."[76]

14.6 Conclusion

This chapter recognizes the specter of an unaccountable, private personalized law crafted by entities agnostic to the public interest. It further recognizes the unique dangers presented by the loss of privacy, a core dignitary right, through contractual clauses that few read and fewer understand.

Mass loss of privacy is a particularly striking consequence of the slouch into a pseudo-contract regime from a true contract regime in consumer contract law. Privacy is just one of a genus of dignitary rights that individuals have that are at risk when they contract with algorithms armed with sophisticated methods of analysis and specific information about that individual consumer. Identifying and removing certain nondisclaimable rights from the scope of contract law in the case of consumer algorithmic contracts is one way to protect these essential rights. Another way may be to imply protective terms into contracts. The pitfall associated with either approach is the potential for the protective interest to be defined very narrowly, providing individuals with little practical protection of dignitary interests. More work is needed to determine the form these sector or right-specific exceptions or implied terms should take.

A privacy-specific approach to consumer algorithmic transactions can be justified due to privacy's role in fostering the capabilities necessary for the type of population that is necessary for a republic. However, preserving specific dignitary rights – of which privacy is merely one – is only a partial solution to the problem identified by this chapter. Contract law itself must be modernized to attend to the modern contracting environment.

---

[75] K. A. Bamberger and D. K. Mulligan, *Privacy on the Ground: Driving Corporate Behavior in the United States and Europe* (Cambridge: The MIT Press, 2015).
[76] Ard, "The Limits of Industry-Specific Privacy Law," at 620–621.

Part V

Smart Contracts

Courts and the Legal Profession

15 Smart Contracts and the Courts

Marc Clément

15.1 Introduction

In the world of smart contracts, machines execute automatically through a piece of software, which was agreed upon between parties. Execution of the contract is only dependent on the machine, i.e. it provides a guarantee that no human interference would prevent agreed resolutions from taking place. This new approach of contractual relationships is based on the assumption that machine coldness in the evaluation of commitments would lead to greater security and certainty for parties. It is clear that this approach is also developed under the assumption that court cases are uncertain and could lead to unforeseen results as regard the execution of contracts. Judges as human beings, as the argument goes, are unreliable and their affects create legal uncertainty. More generally, in a libertarian approach, legal rules could be supplanted by direct agreements for the benefit of the contractors.

The above assumptions that smart contracts as self-executing contracts that modify significantly the role of judges or lawyers should be rejected. It is submitted that smart contracts could create new legal difficulties and that, beyond the appearance of simplicity, they would lead to the creation of new legal concepts that would create more legal complexity not expected by smart contracts' proponents. To perform this analysis, it is necessary to understand in detail the functioning of smart contracts and to start from the technical point of view. The difficulty is that the definition of 'smart contract' is not stable and depends on technological choices: smart contracts are not abstract concepts but present themselves as technical solutions in a very empirical way. As a consequence, each solution may differ in its implementation and may lead to totally different legal questions.

This chapter aims to derive from the technological approach proposed by Ethereum and Solidity language[1] some general technical features of smart contracts. On the basis of this abstract 'smart contract' model, we will be able surmise how smart contracts my disrupt the existing legal environment. The potential legal benefits or associated risks of this technological approach will not be addressed. In other words, before questioning the quality of cheese made from unicorn milk, one should first question the mere existence of unicorns and their capacity to produce milk. Therefore, we will not take for granted that there exists a possibility to create a 'contractual space' that would escape from the influence of lawyers and the legal system.

The analysis will demonstrate that the smart contract environment is not a 'lawyer-free environment' due to the fact that smart contracts necessarily interfere with real-world

---

[1] See Ethereum at www.ethereum.org.

persons or institutions that would by the nature of our societies lead to legal issues. We do not investigate in detail the exact nature of these legal problems. The main reason is that the objective is not to find solutions to these legal questions but more modestly to acknowledge the mere existence of these questions. In addition, no uniform legal interpretation is available for each problem presented. For instance, the differences between common and civil law approaches of contract theory lead to different ways to take into consideration the intentions of parties or even the definition of a contract. It is clear that legal solutions would differ considerably depending on the jurisdiction.[2] However, despite these substantial practical differences in the effects and interpretation of contracts, these legal issues will not affect the analysis since the intent here is not to give a uniform legal interpretation of the effects of smart contracts but simply to identify the existence of pertinent legal questions. It does not matter that these legal questions could find different solutions in different jurisdiction contexts.

15.2 Concept of Interfaces

This chapter examines the environment of smart contracts. It introduce the concept of interfaces to designate the relationships between the computer code of a smart contract and other external elements. According to the analysis, these interfaces are the exact locations of the legal connections between a specific piece of software and the real world.

The first element to take into consideration is the fact that interfaces between the real world and software transactions' world are still governed by traditional laws. It is always possible to design an autonomous world of trading using a software platform. This would operate in the same way as a game: rules and sanctions could be designed completely independently from existing real-world rules. As long as this virtual world has no direct link with the real world, there is no need to take into consideration the legal rules that govern our societies. For instance, one can play with virtual drug trafficking as a character in a videogame and it does not matter if in the real world theses activities are prohibited. It is different when there is a connection between the virtual world and the real one. It is very important to note that the development of software is always driven by the capacity to propose a completely autonomous representation of the world. This is, for instance, true for scientific simulation of physics: a set of equations aims at representing reality; however, this representation is not reality and needs to connect to reality by certain parameters. Physics knows that although calculators and modelling of the universe can be extremely powerful, the most difficult part of a modelling exercise lies in the identification of the key values provided by the experiments, which makes the difference between pure intellectual speculation and a representation close to reality.

The second element, which needs to be stressed, is the fact that technology could create a fascination that prevents us from fully understanding how it is dependant on more traditional economic and legal issues. For instance, the development of platforms for buying traditional goods implies a parallel development of logistics. It is as important to have a good piece of software as to be able to deliver in time the physical goods or to allow return of goods in an efficient manner. It would be misleading to confine

---

[2] H. Beale, B. Fauvarque-Cosson, J. Rutgers, D. Tallon and S. Vogenauer, *Cases, Materials and Text on Contract Law* (Oxford: Hart 2010).

e-commerce to the exchange of music or software where the main part of it delivers physical goods. The reality of the e-economy is that it is deeply dependent on classic techniques and even emphasizes the role of them – like, for instance, the development of transportation means. This example shows that not all sectors of the classic economy are threatened by the e-economy: some are on the contrary boosted by it. E-economy relies on infrastructure from energy supply, telecommunication cables and logistic routes.[3]

15.2.1 Closed World of Software Engineers

It should also be taken into consideration the fact that software engineers and lawyers develop their activities in completely different worlds. This means that each profession has created a specific set of concepts, which feed a technical language. For instance, the term 'transaction' has clearly a specific meaning in law related to contractual relationships, while it has a totally different meaning in computer science and relates to the exchange of data between two pieces of software. The difference between the terminologies of two different domains is a well-known source of misunderstanding. However, the situation is particularly at risk in the domain of computer science for specific reasons.

Software designers use words in a close world. For instance, in Solidity, the language used by Ethereum, the basic brick is call a 'contract' but this term does not at all refer to any legal theory. A 'contract' in Solidity is a class, which is nothing else than a well-known computer language element being the core structure of object-oriented languages.[4] One should take into consideration that development of the software needs to manipulate words, but the meaning of the words is limited to their usage in the software. For instance, one can decide to call an Integer variable 'unicorn' and set this variable to a given value. This would lead to writing a line in the source code, which would read:

set integer unicorn = 1;

Nobody would deduce from this line of code that one has created a unicorn in the real world. We have simply set an Integer variable that has an initial value of 1. It may happen that in this IT world setting this variable to 1 is equivalent to the creation of an IT object which is defined as a 'unicorn'. This could, for instance, lead to the visualization of the image of a unicorn on a screen. But all these effects are circumscribed by the internal interactions of the software. If another piece of software wanted to communicate with this piece of software, it would need to define a common understanding of the variables and translate these into its own world. It could well be that reading *unicorn = 1* would lead this second software to animate a picture of a dragon on the screen.

Software engineers could be compared to Humpty Dumpty: 'When I use a word', Humpty Dumpty in rather a scornful tone, 'it means just what I choose it to mean – neither more nor less'.[5] Indeed, it should be clear that the choice of words constituting a piece of software is totally arbitrary and the only limit to the exercise is the strong internal coherence of these choices: if one has decided to call a variable *unicorn* with an

---

[3] J. Tirole, *Economy for the Common Good* (Princeton: Princeton University Press 2017). See, in particular, Chapters 14 and 15 on the impacts of digital economy.

[4] The tutorial proposed by Ethereum shows the use of the class 'contract': www.ethereum.org/token, and the Solidity 0.4.24 documentation explains in details the languages features: see in particular the *Introduction to Smart Contracts*: http://solidity.readthedocs.io/en/v0.4.24/introduction-to-smart-contracts.html.

[5] L. Caroll, *Through the Looking Glass* (UK: Macmillan 1871).

Integer type, it is expected that the use of this variable is in conformity with the grammar of the IT programming language and is, for instance, an integer number between −32 768 and 32 768 for a signed integer coded on 2 bytes. Many bugs in software developments are the consequence of expressions not respecting these expectations. The role of the computer programmer is to create a completely closed space of logical links. The distinction between signs and signification as highlighted in semiotics is crucial.[6] Words used by software engineers are merely signs which do not match with the meaning adopted in other domains and do not even match the meaning adopted in another piece of software.

This totally arbitrary approach to words' meaning is mitigated by an important factor that plays a crucial role in our analysis. This factor lies in the temptation for the programmer to use terms with a strong association in the real world. Instead of calling a variable *unicorn*, one could have chosen *obj130*, which would refer to the same variable with the same IT properties. However it is often preferred to adopt words, which are not neutral as regard to their potential meaning. This could be motivated by the need to develop an easy way to identify and to remember the variables in the programme. It could also be just a way to use funny names in software with no explicit intention to create confusion and to blur the boundaries between the real and software worlds. It has also to do with the intrinsic power of computer science, which aims at manipulating symbols and, therefore, provides a temptation to recreate the real world in an abstract manner.

However, as the example of the term contracts in Solidity language demonstrates, some choices are more clearly driven by an ambition that goes beyond the programming universe. But even in this context, a naming space for a piece of software remains an IT naming space. Nevertheless, one should not underestimate the power of imagination that the use of certain terms in IT has on readers, who will implicitly make links between the names chosen for coding and their other meanings. To illustrate this general trend, one can think of the term 'artificial intelligence': no clear content is given to the term in computer science, which develops algorithms and techniques without needing to stamp them with a brand. But 'intelligence' is a term known by every person as referring to the highest intellectual capacities of human beings. The porosity of the semantic fields – computer science versus human studies – creates potential confusion.

This point should be kept in mind in order to avoid misunderstandings: it is often said that smart contracts are not contracts in the legal meaning of the term. It is clear that the term 'contract' as an element of Solidity language has necessarily nothing to do with the term 'contract' as understood by lawyers. There is little to gain in trying to emphasize this point or to stress differences. It is much more fruitful to understand that the starting point of the debate is the usage of a single term to address very different concepts. On this basis, we acknowledge that contract in legal terms necessarily means something else than in computing, and we are interested in discovering the legal consequences of the design of software, which aims at executing commercial transactions.

---

[6] F. de Saussure, C. Bally, A. Sechehaye and A. Riedlinger, *Course in General Linguistics* (London: G. Duckworth, 1983).

15.2.2 *Do Blockchain Technologies Modify the Picture?*

The analysis will consider the development of pieces of software, which correspond to automatic exchange of values regardless of the technology supporting the development. The role of blockchain will be analysed as a means to guarantee execution of the software. It is however probably not by chance that smart contracts have developed in the context of blockchain technology. It is submitted that the protection of the code, either in public or in private centralized or distributed ledgers, plays a minor role as regards the legal challenges that smart contracts face. The assumption is that the issue is less to describe or even understand the functioning of the software than to analyse the interfaces between the software and the external world. If this assumption is true, then it is of minor importance to know how the software is actually coded and implemented, including the encryption techniques used.

At this point, it should be noted that there are two different aspects in the impact of blockchain technology on smart contracts. The one highlighted above refers to the security and inviolability of the software. This could be achieved using blockchain or other techniques. The intangibility of contract, which has been presented as a positive feature in favour of smart contracts technology, it is however not clear what type of advantages this intangibility gives to parties. It is clear that blockchain technology provides a safe repository for the agreement between contractors. However, most of the disputes related to contracts is not related to the mere existence of contractual clauses. Parties in the vast majority of contract disputes refer to disagreements on the correct interpretation of contract clauses or on incorrect execution of contractual obligations. The fact that the text is set in stone provides very few advantages. On the contrary, its a substantial problem in case where parties agree that there is a need to amend the contract. The need for flexibility in contractual relationships is to be stressed: parties adapt to the economic environment, and commercial relationships should allow the possibility to upgrade terms and conditions as time passes.

The argument of inviolability of software is often presented in a different perspective: the fact that software masters the contractual terms is a guarantee of proper execution that does not depend on parties' action. It is also difficult to identify precisely the advantage of building a complete new software environment based on crypto-transactions to achieve automated or self-executing contracts. For instance, automatic insurance payments could be performed without using blockchain technology. The limit in the development of fully automatic transactions is not the lack of proper technical tools – as high-frequency trading on financial markets demonstrates – but the need to perform some verification of data. In addition, e-commerce platforms already provide automatic execution through software: from payment to delivery (all steps of contract execution are totally automated). One can argue that these different pieces of software are totally unknown to consumers and that it makes a big difference. But the issue of the degree of transparency of code is not related to blockchain technology. It depends primarily on the open-source nature of the software and more crucially on the capacity of users to understand the complexity of the code!

The other aspect that is independent from the first one is the combination of smart contracts with cryptocurrencies. Since smart contracts have developed in the environment of cryptocurrencies, they play an important role in the transactions associated with smart contracts. However, smart contract approaches cannot be reduced to transactions in cryptocurrencies which would limit their scope dramatically. In the example of the

Axa flight insurance contract,[7] the contract materialized in a hybrid environment combining the Ethereum platform for registration of contracts and keeping track of flight status with payments in Euros.[8] No payments in Ether are performed.

In the context of pure cryptocurrency transactions, a piece of software could be completely autonomous and independent from any legal system. For instance, the Fomo3D lottery game[9] based on Ethereum represents a purely crypto-transaction world. However, this is only the case if it remains a pure game without expectations of real-life gains. If this is the case, there is little to analyse or to say about such an activity, since absolutely no effects are expected in the real world and gains or losses are of the same nature as gains and losses in a video game.

It should acknowledge that the expectation of Ether gains in Fomo3D are not pure virtual gains and could be converted into real-world gains that would necessarily raise legal issues. For instance, how will these gains be taxed? Would the participation in the game be legal for any physical person? What happens if it is proven that the game is not fair and that some privileged players harvest most of the gains? These potential legal issues may not necessarily materialize, depending on the behaviour of the participants in the game, who may choose to keep the virtual nature of their gains.

This is certainly not true for all smart contracts, with their potential use as substitutes for existing contracts, or to develop new contractual relationships. The concept of interface will be used to capture the link between the real world and software.

15.2.3 Coding Contractual Commitments

Given the specific role of words in the development of software, it is clear that it would not be enough to draft a variable 'force-majeure' as an equivalent of a contractual clause in a piece of software. The difficulty of defining precisely the scope of many concepts used in contract law poses a substantial problem for software developers if they want to introduce these legal concepts into smart contracts.

There is little possibility to really find a deterministic way to define a concept such as 'force majeure'. It refers loosely to a set of situations where a third party to a contract would identify an exceptional situation which would require special treatment preventing the contract not being executed in its normal way. One way to deal with this absence of explicit definitions would be to use machine-learning techniques on the basis of case law. It would be possible to select cases where force majeure has been recognized or not recognized by courts to implicitly create a software function which would use inputs and lead to a conclusion based on the case examples. This is obviously not an easy task: the inputs which are essential parameters used by case law are not easy to select; what would be the relevant elements used to trigger a 'force majeure' event? It would also pose a problem of adaptation over time in order to take into account new

---

[7] Fizzy contract for flight delay insurance proposed by Axa: https://fizzy.axa/en-gb/.
[8] See general conditions of the Fizzy contract: https://fizzy.axa/en-gb/static/media/conditions-generales.38af84e2.pdf.
[9] See explanations on Fomo3D here: https://powh3d.hostedwiki.co/pages/Fomo3D%20Explained, and it should be noted that it does not take too long to identify ways to exploit backdoors or bugs for draining the gains of the lottery. In addition, the lottery is clearly a Ponzi pyramid.

case law. In practice, approximation of legal concepts by machine learning is still a research domain. Moreover, it would be a paradox for smart contracts: reintroducing case law and more generally a specific legal environment into smart contracts implies that they are no longer self-referencial commitments but on the contrary belong to a legal tradition.

One could argue that smart contracts' coding could be more efficient in the description of deterministic behaviour, which could be captured perfectly by syllogisms. As syllogisms are often presented as the basic level of reasoning in law, it is tempting to conclude that legal reasoning could be perfectly represented by logic. A series of 'if . . . then . . . else' expressions would be the perfect candidate for this type of software. It should however be stressed that even if these logical structures seem simple and readable when a simple example is provided, the complexity could easily reach a level of expertise which is beyond the capacity of most people. For instance, combining a set of ten nested 'if . . . then' would constitute a substantial challenge for most brains! In addition, the evaluation of logical expressions in the premise of the 'if . . . then' structure may rapidly require some solid mastering of logic. For instance, a simple expression like *((delay > 2 hours) and not ((bad-weather) or (strike)))* requires a minimum knowledge of Boolean logic to be accurately assessed. Suppose that the variable *bad-weather* is determined by another Boolean expression like *((rain-fall > 5 mm/hour) and (wind-speed > 20 ms/s)) or (snow > 50 cm/day))*, then difficulty rapidly increases in interpretating of its logical value. In practice, a combination of several very basic instructions quickly becomes a challenge even for experts.

Coding contractual relationships directly in software is certainly not a task making contracts more readable for users. On the contrary, the result of coding operations is a very technical document that would only be accessible to IT experts. Introduction of machine learning or any statistical approach would need to make available the data sets used for these tasks and require an additional level of expertise.

15.3 Exploring Interfaces

It is in the links between the software and the real world that legal issues are found. We will therefore examine the different levels of connection between the software (smart contract) and the real world. These connections can be seen as interfaces between the code and real-world events or actions. This concept includes interfaces in the meaning of computer languages (communication of an object through methods or variables declared as public methods or variables) but also corresponds to more abstract interfaces like complex operations such as, the transformation of software specifications into computer code. The following analysis will review all the conditions that allow code either to be designed and implemented or to operate.

15.3.1 *First Interface: Legality of the Operation*

A first level of connection with real-world legal concepts is obviously the link with the lawfulness of the object of the smart contract. Smart contracts are not different from this point of view from any other type of contract. Contracting on illegal matters remains illegal whatever the contractual infrastructure.

This is a very abstract level of 'interface': if a piece of software has consequences in the real world, the performance of software meet legal requirements. At this stage, the idea is simply to clarify the difference between a pure virtual operation and an operation that has to cope with the standards of society. A virtual operation such as actions in video games could consist in selling drugs, contracting to kill a character or steal some goods. The only rules to obey are the ones decided by the game designer. This is completely different for software contracts having effects in concrete social environments.

The cryptocurrency ecosystems pretend to operate outside the rules of society in a self-governing space. This is not the case as long as they create concrete effects that go beyond the closed world of smart contracts. And it is difficult to imagine situations with no expected effects in the real world. Moreover, it is difficult to argue that smart contracts represent a new opportunity for businesses and consumers if they limit their role to a set of operations that does not have an effect in the real-world economy.

For instance, if delivering goods or services is at stake, then as long as these goods and services belong to the real world, the ordinary laws will apply. It is only in cases of pure exchange of cryptocurrencies that the link with the legal world could be limited, for instance if a loan of cryptocurrencies is formalized through a smart contract. However, even in these cases, the quality of the contracting person, such as age, legal capacity, sophistication, and so forth means that these on-chain transaction are still governed by law. In the same way, a betting contract may still be unlawful regardless of the fact that it is based on cryptocurrency and materialized in a piece of software. The mere fact that using IT networks and cryptology makes this activity difficult to track, but it does not mean that national and international laws do not govern them.

However, it should be acknowledged that in the absence of clear territoriality (jurisdiction) the question of lawfulness of the activity supported by the contract may be difficult to address. Let's take the example of a gambling contract based on cryptocurrencies: this could be perfectly well implemented with Ethereum and Solidity. It would benefit from blockchain implementation but it is not the block-chain technology by itself that would make the question of applicable law an issue. It is more the distributed nature of the contract implementation that matters and the possibility – or not – to identify clearly the parties to the contract. The exchanges of Ether are virtual actions. The legality of the gambling activity – which is highly regulated in most countries – would be difficult to assess in absence of reference to a specific state law. Nonetheless, virtual or not, a smart contract remains a contract between parties who are real persons. This means that the territorial link is not totally absent and could be established. This example shows that the question of legality of the activity covered by the contract is always at stake, even in cases when the extraterritoriality of the contract makes it difficult to determine the appropriate jurisdiction to file a claim.

15.3.2 *Three Additional Interfaces: Oracles, Subscription and Delivery*

More obvious interfaces correspond to the direct interactions between the code and external events. A smart contract needs three elements, as would any mechanical device. It needs a trigger: someone has to press the start button. It needs to collect information from external sources. It needs to deliver something.

Let us suppose that a company C offers a service S to a person P. This service would materialize in a smart contract, i.e. a self-executing computer programme, which would automatically trigger a payment of x Euros if conditions X and Y are fulfilled.

S(C, P) (*get* X;

get Y;

if (X *and* Y) *then return x* Euros;)

This very simple smart contract leads to a set of three interfaces with the outside world, which corresponds to the influence of the real-world environment on the software. These interfaces corresponds in this programme to (1) the subscription of the service by a customer (S(C, P)), (2) the acquisition of external conditions and data (get X, get Y) and (3) the action triggered by theses conditions (return x Euros).

15.3.2.1 Oracles

Oracles are inputs needed by the programme to operate. These are materialized in the example above by the 'get' functions. The software expects to receive or to actively seek some external values X and Y. For instance, a flight insurance contract would need to get the information on whether a flight has been delayed. This information can be retrieved from airport services or another source of information on flight arrivals. An interesting feature of the *oracles* is that they show the importance of the time factor in the execution of a contract. If a contract does not need any outside input, then it could be instantaneously executed on the basis of the inputs initially provided by parties. Such a contract would in practice be a simple calculation exercise based on these inputs and could be simulated by each contractor before contracting. It simply entails applying a formula to inputs provided by each contractor.

In most cases, contracting activities require the use of a substantial amount of information. In the example of incorporating a bad-weather parameter, the information is by itself a combination of multiple elements that needs to be transformed into a simple Boolean value. One can easily understand that the processing of this parameter is crucial for the performance of the contract and could be defined in many different ways. It would however be essential for the contractor to understand exactly what the insurance company requires to insure against a delay due to bad weather. The bad-weather parameter could range from a very exceptional meteorological situation to ordinary difficult weather conditions. Many aspects of the contract are therefore mastered in functions performed outside of the software.

A real contract would only emerge with a time dimension: the contract is in place to secure some possible futures. This means that external inputs are needed. These could come from contractors themselves, but this could pose a problem of potential bias. It is not totally excluded that contractors could be invited to report some events such as, in our example, the delay of a flight. However, it would be very unlikely that an insurance company would rely only on a subscriber's demand to pay compensation. The subscriber would equally hesitate to enter in a contract where the insurance company has the sole discretion to issue payment.

Oracles, therefore, act as trusted third-party inputs essential for the smart contract that depends on the verification of real-world developments. The importance of these inputs is that they provide crucial information in determining the outcome of the contract. For this reason, the question of trust in the quality and objectivity of these inputs is crucial. In the definitions or descriptions found in the parties' agreements, special attention should be paid to this sensitive aspect: mastering the quality of the oracles' data is of primary importance. Absence of conflict of interest and independence from parties is a key element. It could be achieved by linking the contract to external sources of information which none of the parties have any chance to influence. This could be, for instance, public meteorological services or timetables provided by airport services. However, it should be noted that the more tailored or specific the information needed by the contract, the more difficult it would be to rely on general public services. This means that the quality of the information will be more difficult to assess and that bias could be more easily introduced. For instance, automatic crop insurance will rely on very local weather conditions which are not necessary available at the level of the general public meteorological services.

Even in cases where no collusion between a contracting party and an 'oracle' is possible, the low quality of the service may require the need for another third party to verify or guarantee that the information provided is correct? It is not simple to combine various inputs to ensure better quality of information, as signal-processing techniques demonstrate.[10] Choosing to keep only the most likely measures or to compute an average of different inputs leads to very different results. Therefore, understanding the exact conditions at stake in a computer contract can be difficult.

A last element is also of highest importance in many pieces of software: what if the communication channel between the input (the oracle) and the software (the contract) modifies the input. This would be the case if there is an alteration of the message or a time delay in delivering the message. Let's, for instance, imagine that the service provided by the airport timetable publication software is not operating during a few hours that correspond to the time when a flight delay should be recorded. Then the contract would not be triggered automatically. The question is whether this means that no compensation is due.

All these aspects show that there is room for identifying potential conflicts of interpretation of smart contracts: by a bias introduced by one party in the selection of oracles or difficulties raised by the improper functioning of oracles.

15.3.2.2 Subscription of Contract

The subscription phase of the smart contract is the instantiation of the piece of software by the parties. This could take the form of tokens or the payment of an agreed amount in cryptocurrency. This action is the equivalent of a signature in traditional contracts: there is a point in time when it is considered that both contractors are mutually engaged. In this context, the identification of the contractors is still – as in traditional contracts – a crucial issue. Do parties have the right to engage themselves or money in this task? How can it be determined that the contracting parties have not violated identity rules? All these questions remain valid and are likely to become more complex and difficult to address in the

---

[10] This problem is known as 'multiple sensor fusion' where different sources of values are combined with different ranges of errors. The objective is to reduce the level of uncertainty of measures based on combination of different sensors using different measurement techniques.

IT world. IT security tools provide efficient means to ensure protection of transactions, but the bottleneck in security means it is often difficult to ensure that passwords are correctly secured and that only the relevant persons can access the system. As a consequence, legal issues attached to the subscription of a computer contract do not disappear in the smart contract world.

15.3.2.3 Delivery

A contract supposes that real world effect will occur if the contractual conditions are met. This means that general trade issues also govern delivery. Suppose that the vending machine returns a soda that is affected by a production problem such as the quality of the soda or the inability to be opened. Then, regardless of the media supporting the contract, the consumer would be entitled to consider that the contract was not correctly executed. Of course, examples given in the context of Ethereum refer often to return of an amount of Ethers or tokens, which is a straightforward transaction with no need for quality assurances. This is again the case as long as the exchanges in smart contracts remain based on cryptocurrency and no conversion in real-world outputs is required.

The boundaries of the contract's obligations are clearly an issue: suppose that the travel insurance company limits its obligations to deliver cryptocurrency payments, then the risks associated with conversion of the amounts received would be fully born by the consumer. This would be a serious limit for the potential market for smart insurance contracts, given the volatility of cryptocurrency markets and the lack of integration of cryptocurrencies in the financial system.

In the domain of business-to-business transactions, such as automatic contracting between machines for ensuring correct supply of goods for a factory, it would be difficult keep the outputs in the boundaries of the virtual world. The proper delivery and control of the correct execution of the contract are crucial, and one cannot expect that this dimension will be set aside if these automatic transactions are to take place.

15.3.2.4 From Intention to Software: A Fifth Interface

A fifth interface to be considered lies in the determination of the level of the agreement between contracting parties. The software represents the implementation of a service proposed by a company. We assume that the company is able to describe the functioning of the programme through specifications or terms of reference (ToR). These are natural languages texts, which are transformed in a piece of software.

ToR(C) -> S(C, P) (...)

There are two possibilities in this area: the company can propose the service by just giving potential customers a copy of the code S(C, P). It is however relatively unlikely that customers would read the code and be sufficiently confident in its logic to pay for the service. Needless to say, the market represented by these potential customers would be extremely limited. It is more probable that the company will propose the service on the basis of the terms of reference. In this case, a fifth interface is created as the customer expects a given functioning of the software based on the terms of reference.

As mentioned above, the act of contract subscription could be formalized by the payment of a sum in cryptocurrency. But it could be also done in a more traditional way, as is the case in the implementation of the flight insurance contract proposed by Axa that requires a payment in Euros with a credit card.[11] In all cases, there are some expectations, which are proposed to a consumer or a party in exchange for a specific behaviour. The interesting thing with smart contracts is that the expectations are likely to take place outside of the contract itself, since it would be difficult to just give a piece of software to a potential partner without any comment explanation. There is a need to describe in plain language the functioning of the contract. Contrary to normal contracts, it is hard to expect a layman to understand the computer language and to be able to analyse the logic behind it. It is even more difficult to identify potential customers with this approach. Of course, very few people analyse terms and conditions found in traditional language contracts. However, the signature of a piece of paper detailing clauses is considered to be the acknowledgement of a certain level of understanding and signifies a clear commitment. This could well be a fiction in many contracts that are signed daily; however, this fiction is far less plausible for a computer coded contract language, in particular when no obvious behaviour could be derived from the list of instructions related to the piece of software. This means that the subscription process is far more complicated than in traditional contracts. It is based on different steps, from general explanations of the advantages of the contract to a consumer to the final subscription act.

There is obviously an asymmetry of information between parties to a smart contract, because one party designs and proposes the contract before placing it on the blockchain. Therefore, this party has to convince the other that there are no traps in the functioning of the piece of software. The notion of confidence in smart contracts is more important that in other domains. Of course, one can imagine that a general practice of smart contracts may create this confidence progressively. The involvement of companies with a solid reputation is also a way to create this confidence. However, it is impossible to ignore that the subscription will need a plain text description of the functionalities of the programme and that this description by itself will necessarily create a representation of the software, which is unlikely to totally coincide with its object. This representation would not necessarily match with the terms of reference used by the developer of the software since its target is completely different: it is a document that aims at explaining in simple terms the purpose of the smart contract. The document is tailored for communication with customers.

A well-established practice in the blockchain and smart contracts world is to produce 'white papers' or concept papers. The most famous of these is the bitcoin concept paper issued by Nakamoto[12] or the Ethereum White Paper describing the functioning of the Ethereum system.[13] One can also refer for a more specific implementation of a smart contract to the decentralized autonomous organization (DAO) concept paper, which also provides a good example of a document aimed at describing the intentions of

---

[11] See the Fizzy contract proposed by Axa insurance company for automatic compensation in case of flights delays: https://fizzy.axa/fr/faq, payments and refund are made in Euros. It should be noted that the presentation of the contractual terms is far from relying on the code which can be consulted at the following address: https://etherscan.io/address/0xe083515d1541f2a9fd0ca03f189f5d321c73b872#code.

[12] S. Nakamoto (pseudonym), 'Bitcoin: A Peer-to-Peer Electronic Cash System', 2008, at https://bitcoin.org/bitcoin.pdf.

[13] V. Buterin, 'Ethereum: A Next-generation Smart Contracts and Decentralized Application Platform', 2013, at https://github.com/ethereum/wiki/wiki/White-Paper.

software developers and the methods they propose to implement.[14] The documents are highly technical and difficult to understand without solid knowledge of computer science and mathematics. They are similar to scientific papers which are addressed to peers. Their public diffusion is aimed at triggering reactions from specialists who will propose corrections or modifications. The link between the concepts as detailed in the White Papers and the actual implementation of the code may not be constantly maintained as updates and corrections are frequent in a domain where the development of a piece of software is continuously a 'work in progress'.

The conversion from terms of reference to software is also a very delicate operation; even for the service provider there is no obvious guarantee that this operation is done in a satisfactory way. In addition to the code itself, software engineers are use to including comments in the code itself: comments are elements making the code more readable and they would in some cases refer to the terms of reference. The exact contractual value of these comments is not clear and these elements increase the complexity of interpretation when, for instance, the comments do not correctly match the code they are supposed to explain.

Computer literature provides many technical solutions to address the numerous problems that can be identified in this field.[15] The literature would provide a service by offering or developing methodologies to reduce logical mistakes in the development of code by 'proving' software quality. However, code certification is still extremely rare, and it would be unlikely that certification would be a plausible solution in an open-source code environment, due to the fact that it is complex to rationalize the development process with a large evolving team of participants. In any case, one has to take into account that between the software developer's intentions described in the documents provided to the customers and the implementation of software, numerous unpredictable behaviours might occur. For example, hackers search for potential weaknesses in the code,[16] which may also lead to unforeseen results for the customer because a hack could lead to a divergence between the information received and the operation of the smart contract.

15.4 Ignoring Conflicts of Interpretation?

One could argue that some of the legal issues that have been identified could simply be ignored as risks that go to the very nature of a smart contract. In sum, if a party uses smart contracts then the party accepts the risks attached to them and, in particular, the party accepts the code and its environment 'as it is'. It needs to be stressed that the 'code as it is' option only work if the parties are willing to completely ignore the comments added to the code and documents describing its functioning. Otherwise, there will remain interpretation problems linked to the different potential meanings of code, comments and explanations. As stated above, even in the world of open-source software, code is rarely

---

[14] C. Jentzsch, 'Decentralized Autonomous Organization to Automate Governance', 2016 at https://github .com/slockit/DAO/blob/develop/paper/Paper.tex.

[15] J. A. Kroll, J. Huey, S. Barocas, E. W. Felten, J. R. Reidenberg, D. G. Robinson and H. Yu, 'Accountable Algorithms' Fordham Law Legal Studies Research Paper No. 2765268. Available at SSRN: https://ssrn.com /abstract=2765268.

[16] See, for instance, the description of hacks in Ethereum world highlighting that even code reviewed by experts could lead to severe bugs or backdoors exploited by hackers https://medium.com/solidified/the-biggest-smart-contract-hacks-in-history-or-how-to-endanger-up-to-us-2–2-billion-d5a72961d15d.

produced without associated plain text materials. It is possible draft a smart contract that only requires reference to its implementation in the code regardless of other indications. Nevertheless, such a clause would require the confidence of contracting parties in a mutual understanding of the code, and the notion of 'code as it is' itself is not necessarily understood by all parties in the same way. If we assume that it is possible to adopt such a radical view of the legal environment of smart contracts, it would nevertheless lead to additional difficulties.

Firstly, it would most likely reduce the interest in computer contracts in the case of the general public. There use would be limited to small value contracts because they are easier to implement and because the amount at risk due to faulty design is relatively small. Smart contracts would also continue to be used for highly specialized fields where both parties are sufficiently skilled to analyse in detail the technical aspects of the code. Needless to say, in the case of complex code, the results produced by the code may still be a mystery for experts.

Secondly, the notion of acceptance of 'code as it is' does not by itself rule out any interpretation: it would always be possible to argue that one party used misleading information to conclude the deal or that potential losses were not made clear at the time of concluding the smart contract. Consumer protection laws have been developed to protect citizens against these aspects of commercial relations, and they would not be discarded by the mere fact that the contract is implemented by software. On the contrary, it is more likely that these types of contracts would lead to specific information obligations and specific requirements as regards consumer protection.

The case of DAO demonstrates how difficult it is to accept 'code as it is' as a feasible option: in 2016, the DAO project proposed a platform for investments in projects based on Ethereum. It is reported that 3.6 million of Ether were stolen due to code deficiency, which corresponded to one-third the total investments made on the platform. The robbery, due to the design of the code, did not take place immediately but was frozen for twenty-eight days, which allowed the possibility to react to the attack. The community running the platform, therefore, faced a dilemma: shall the code be corrected and refunds issued to the investors or would the philosophy of the DAO prevail, which was to avoid any corrective action once the code is approved? The community was not able to find a consensus on this issue; however, the founders of the project issued a modification of the code (a 'fork' in the code) allowing investors to get their stolen Ether back. It should be noticed that this was an opportunity for the US Security and Exchange Commission to investigate the case and in particular to analyse if the DAO operations are covered by the US securities federal law. The SEC concluded that the securities laws did apply given the laws' broad definition of securities, which includes investments in cryptocurrencies, since these investments are made in expectation of profits.[17] Thus, US securities law governs an operation dealing with investments as in the context of the DAO, and the underlying infrastructure (tokens, Ether, etc.) is irrelevant to that coverage and enforcement of the law.

---

[17] See the 'Report of Investigation Pursuant to Section 21(a) of the Securities Exchange Act of 1934: The DAO' of 25 July 2017 and the press release on 25 July 2017 at www.sec.gov/news/press-release/2017–131 and the Investor Bulletin on Initial Coin Offering: www.investor.gov/additional-resources/news-alerts /alerts-bulletins/investor-bulletin-initial-coin-offerings.

15.5 Alternative Dispute Resolution Mechanisms and Effectiveness of Courts in a Utopian World

One proposed solution to the problems addressed above would be to integrate in the smart contracts alternative dispute resolution (ADR) mechanisms designed specifically for such contracts. This option looks promising in order to maintain the self-governing feature of smart contracts and could lead to innovative dispute resolution systems, such as the use of distributed juries. However, the selection and institution of panels in charge of arbitration and more generally the rules followed by these panels are difficult to create without reference to a legal system. It would not be very efficient to design a specific ADR reference book for each new contract. Moreover, to include in a contract its own arbitration rules would emphasize the problems already mentioned: what would be the level of information provided to contractors about the coded dispute resolution mechanism? The use of courts by plaintiffs relies on the fact that they trust the impartiality and independence of justice system. This trust would need to be created for each contract if specific ADR mechanisms are established.

Therefore, although arbitration mechanisms or mediation could be a useful way to address the need to find solutions for resolving disputes, any of these approaches would require defining the legal framework which governs smart contracts, and does not simplify the overall picture.

The Internet is often presented as a space with no territory, literally a utopian world. One argument often raised against the capacity of courts to address disputes related to smart contracts is the difficulty of identifying contractors and enforcing judgements due to the absence of a determinative territory. Judicial power is by definition one component of state institutions, and the state is defined in public international law by its territorial dimension. As a consequence, any legal system would require the possibility of referring a matter to another specific territory, and international law is basically a means to coordinate between these national legal systems.

These are clearly substantial problems but they are not specific to smart contracts and are not an issue for all smart contracts. It would, for instance, not be an issue in the context of Axa flight insurance contracts: the company is well known and each person obtaining its flight ticket insurance is identified. Moreover, the general contract conditions make it clear which law is applicable and the general liabilities of the company.[18] This example shows that companies providing a service to consumers are likely to prefer to maintain a clear link with classic legal instruments.

What if, despite solid arguments in favour of legal certainty, smart contracts are designed without clear indications on applicable jurisdiction? This is not an unknown situation for legal systems and international contract law would be able to find solutions.

Another issue is the difficulty of enforcing remedies in the context of the blockchain. The intangibility of blockchain is presented as an important feature in favour of the technology. As a consequence a contract recorded on the blockchain could not be erased or annulled. Therefore, it seems that a court decision would not have the capacity to be enforced. However this is not exactly the case. The first element is that not all contracts provide intangible effects. In the case of insurance for a specific flight delay, the contract

[18] See the general conditions of the Fizzy contract: https://fizzy.axa/fr/static/media/conditions-generales.38af84e2.pdf

is clearly limited in its objective. As a consequence, nothing prevents a judgement to order a compensation that would have the effect of annulling the contract.

In addition, one can imagine in the case of a recurring contract the creation of an 'anti-contract' which would mimic the functioning of the initial contract in order to annihilate its effects. For example, in the DAO case, the Ethereum blockchain was cut off by its members in order to block the effects of hacking.[19]

Finally, courts could provide compensation and this mechanism may be more efficient in collecting damages rather than just the cancellation of contracts.

It is true that obtaining these remedies is dependent on being able to identify the parties. This is certainly a substantial limit for enforcement of decisions requiring the power or authorization to modify an open-source piece of software deficiency. In the case of the development of smart contracts by a community, it is clear that the issue of liability of the group is difficult to engage as the group does not constitute a legal person and is not identifable. This issue is traceable to the origin of blockchain and cryptocurrencies, and most of the developments on the web do follow this model of decentralized open-source software. However, it is not clear that the potential development of smart contracts lies in these very specific environments. As long as some real-world effects of smart contracts are expected, then the abstract nature of a community of developers will fade. It is, for instance, the case in the Axa contract, which uses the Ethereum platform as an infra-structure but also relies on classic contractual mechanisms as regard to the relationships between the company and the customer. In this case, the smart contract platform is no more than a way to implement a contractual relationship, which is governed by normal legal rules.

15.6 Beyond Smart Contracts

Many of the issues that have been identified are not specific to smart contracts. For instance, the question of translation between specifications and software could be seen as a more general problem. Can we imagine and design tools to automatically convert natural language into legal language and then into computer code? Can we convert computer code into legal language? Such a possibility would provide opportunities to design contracts by expressing them in natural languages but would also – and probably with more immediate application – allow increasing transparency in current legal contracts.

Today, long and complex contracts are common even in simple types of transactions. Licences offered by phone operators or computer companies are long enough to dis-courage any customer from analysing them. It would be different if a tool could do the job of identification of main issues and indicate the potentially controversial or abusive terms in these contracts: reading a legal text such as a contract and transforming this text into plain natural language would be a tremendous advancement.

Exploring the five interfaces (presented in this chapter) between the real world and the smart contract leads to the conclusion that each of them raises substantial legal chal-lenges. Most of these challenges are not new to lawyers. They correspond to core contract law issues such as the exact content of the agreement or the liability of a third party in the execution of a contract. Taking into consideration these problems, it becomes obvious

---

[19] C. Jentzsch, above.

that instead of diminishing the role of lawyers and judges, legal professionals will be needed more than ever to secure the legal environment of smart contracts.

The example of smart contracts highlights a specific feature of legal systems. In liberal societies, legal rules are implemented when a specific need to regulate social behaviours is identified. This means that these rules will operate only in case of real-world effects. In contrast, the preservation of freedom of expression necessarily means that virtual experiences, stories, opinions and beliefs are protected and smart contracts could be part of this pure intellectual world. Regulation will, however, intervene if these virtual experiences lead to specific actions in the real world. This chapter has attempted to identify how smart contracts through their interfaces are in contact with the real world and have to comply with legal rules, and when regulation becomes necessary.

16 Usefulness and Dangers of Smart Contracts in Consumer Transactions

Oscar Borgogno

16.1 Introduction

The pace of technological innovation and the development of new solutions applied to problems in trade and commercial practice have increased exponentially in recent years.[1] The legal instruments which have traditionally been deployed in those areas, such as contracts, need to be duly investigated to assess whether they can be further enhanced or radically changed. In this respect, smart contracts, agreements executed automatically through a software run on a blockchain (or, more correctly, a distributed ledger), are currently among the most debated topics in the legal arena. A great part of the hype surrounding smart contracts is mainly due to the excitement of computer scientists who first presented them to the public.[2] At the opposite end of the debate, several legal scholars have questioned the potential and desirability of smart contracts, highlighting the difficulties in adapting their intrinsic technical constraints to the complexity of the real world.[3] Some have noted that the expression 'smart contracts' is misleading from a strictly legal perspective; they are not proper contracts, but act as a self-help remedy aimed at automating the performance of contractual obligations.[4]

The purpose of this chapter is to provide an overview of the cases where the use of smart contracts may be significantly beneficial in business-to-consumer (B2C) transactions. It illustrates the key aspects of smart contracts and the rise of distributed ledger technology (DLT). It also cautions against premature enthusiasm and exaggerated expectations

---

[1] See CB Insights, *The Global Fintech Report Q2*, 2017, www.cbinsights.com/research/report/fintech-trends-q2-2017/; M. Carney (Governor of the Bank of England), 'The promise of FinTech – Something New Under the Sun?', Speech at the Deutsche Bundesbank G20 Conference on 'Digitalising finance, financial inclusion and financial literacy' (Wiesbaden, DE), 25 January 2017, www.bankofengland.co.uk/-/media/boe/files/speech/2017/the-promise-of-fintech-something-new-under-the-sun.pdf?la=en&hash=0C2E1BBF1AA5CE5 10BD5DF40EB5D1711E4DC560F.

[2] For an overview about the rise of blockchain and its legal implications, see: M. Finck, 'Blockchain Regulation', (2017) 13 *Max Planck Institute for Innovation & Competition Research Paper*, DOI: http://10 .2139/ssrn.3014641; UK Government – Office of Science, *Distributed Ledger Technology: beyond block chain* 2016, https://assets.publishing.service.gov.uk/government/uploads/system/uploads/attachment_data/file/492972/gs-16–1-distributed-ledger-technology.pdf.

[3] See E. Mik, 'Smart Contracts: Terminology, Technical Limitations and Real World Complexity', (2017) 9 *Law Innovation and Technology* 269, DOI: http://10.1080/17579961.2017.1378468; E. Tjong Tjin Tai, 'Formalizing Contract Law for Smart Contracts', (2017) 6 *Tilburg Private Law Working Paper Series*, DOI http://10.2139/ssrn.3038800.

[4] A. Savelyev, 'Contract Law 2.0: "Smart" Contracts as the Beginning of the End of Classic Contract Law', (2017) 26 *Information and Communications Technology Law* 10.

288

about the the application and future of smart contracts. By building upon the extant legal literature on the topic, the chapter focuses on the capacity of smart contracts to mitigate some of the well-known problems affecting B2C and business-to-business (B2B) relationships. Unlike the efficiency-driven current developments in the business field, public policy intervention is crucial to unlock smart contracts potential in the consumer protection realm. In this respect, the adoption of regulatory sandboxes in the rail and air sectors will be discussed to assess the potential of smart contracts.

16.2 Setting the Scene

The debate around smart contracts is filled with ambiguities and misunderstandings. A great deal of this confusion stems from the fact that the expression was coined in the mid-1990s (pre-Internet era) dominated by the alluring rhetoric of the 'digital revolution'.[5] At the time, smart contracts were seen as a computerized protocol that could execute the terms of a contract.[6] Since then, technology has evolved at a rapid pace, opening the doors to e-commerce and online markets. It is worth pointing out that, according to the original definition, smart contracts do not necessarily need to be based on a blockchain. Interestingly, the business model of platforms such as Amazon, Netflix and iTunes, which automate contract formation and performance by digital means, fully meet the original definition of smart contracts. As the old-fashioned vending machine, they ensure that transactions occur as agreed upon by the parties. Moreover, their structure is specifically designed to follow a particular procedure in the event of non-performance by one party. For instance, in case of a non-payment, they react by suspending the supply of the digital content to the user. In this way, service providers avoid triggering the time-consuming remedies provided by contract law and civil procedure.[7] As commonly acknowledged by legal scholars, websites and vending machines do nothing more than but delivering goods, services or digital contents in response to a counter-performance (release of payment through a payment service provider such as PayPal). Thus, the original idea of smart contracts, when properly presented can be reduced to automated tools aimed at ensuring the performance of an agreement through either software or hardware.

Nevertheless, it would not be possible to understand the current new interest around smart contracts without referring to blockchain technology or, more appropriately, DLT.[8] In fact, it is more consistent to speak of DLT instead of blockchain because the former phrase is a broader category, which encompasses all the potential

---

[5] Mik, 'Smart Contracts', 273.

[6] N. Szabo, 'Smart Contracts: Formalizing and Securing Relationships on Public Networks', (1997) 2 (9) *First Monday*, http://ojphi.org/ojs/index.php/fm/article/view/548/469.

[7] See: M. Raskin, 'The Law and Legality of Smart Contracts', (2017) 1 *Georgetown Law Technology Review* 305, at 306, DOI http://10.2139/ssrn.2842258; P. Cuccuru, 'Beyond Bitcoin: An Early Overview on Smart Contracts', (2017) 25 *International Journal of Law and Information Technology* 179, at 185, DOI http://10.1093/ijlit/eax003. The Authors argue that smart contracts are simply a new form of self-help measures aimed at ensuring the performance of an agreement without the need of judicial enforcement.

[8] For an overview of technical and business literature on distributed ledger technology, see: J. Maupin, 'Mapping the Global Legal Landscape of Blockchain and Other Distributed Ledger Technologies', (2017) 149 *CIGI Papers*, www.cigionline.org/publications/mapping-global-legal-landscape-blockchain-and-other-distributed-ledger) technologies; G. Hileman and M. Rauchs, 'Global Blockchain Benchmarking Study', (2017) *Cambridge Centre for Alternative Finance Report*, ssrn.com/abstract=3040224; D. S. Evans, 'Economic Aspects of Bitcoin and Other Decentralized Public-Ledger Currency Platforms', (2014) 685

applications of smart contracts.[9] A distributed ledger is a decentralized, peer-validated crypto-ledger consisting of a network of nodes that provides a permanent chronological record of all prior changes.[10] DLT holds the promise of substituting commercial trust in intermediaries with trust in distributed technology and computer code.[11]

Further, depending on the type of DLT, records can be visible to the public or to a limited group of authorized users.[12] For the purpose of this chapter, it is worth highlighting the two main distinctions in the realm of DLT: unrestricted/restricted and public/private ledgers. Unrestricted (or permissionless) ledgers allow all those with the necessary technical capacity to take part in updating and validating new transactions. Restricted or permissioned ledgers are open only to predefined subjects. In sum, public and private ledgers differ in terms of access rights and visibility to third parties. Anyone can have access to the transactions in a public ledger, whereas a private ones can be read only by predetermined subjects (actual participants, third parties or supervisory authorities).

One can opt for a particular type of distributed ledger depending on preferences and aims. Fully decentralized ledgers are slow and deeply inefficient. This is due to the enormous shared computing activity carried out simultaneously by all the participants of the underlying peer-to-peer network. Cost-related and efficiency considerations aside, the choice of setting up an unrestricted versus a restricted blockchain needs to be evaluated considering many factors.[13] Firstly, identifying each user is only possible if the access to the distributed ledger is restricted. Secondly, assess the ways to design the consensus mechanism so as to provide incentives for the validation process of each transaction. Thirdly, the degree of transparency has to be articulated with the purpose of the distributed ledger – business confidentiality or data protection concerns are crucial to regulated markets and trade relationships. Fourthly, permissioned ledgers are likely to require a governance arrangement in order to define responsibilities and rules of functioning and access.[14]

Transacting parties can decide to make use of smart contracts by leaving the determination of performance to the software.[15] Clearly, the mere fact that certain

---

University of Chicago Coase-Sandor Institute for Law & Economics Research Paper, DOI http://10.2139/ssrn.2424516; F. Boucher, 'How Blockchain Technology Could Change Our Lives', (2017) *European Parlamentary Research Analysis*, DOI http://10.2861/926645.

[9] See: UK Government – Office of Science, *Distributed Ledger Technology: Beyond Block Chain* 2016; P. Athanassiou, 'Impact of Digital Innovation on the Processing of Electronic Payments and Contracting: An Overview of Legal Risks', (2017) 16 *ECB Legal Working Paper Series* 14, DOI http://10.2866/201593.

[10] For a comprehensive description, see Chapter 3 of this book.

[11] The expression of 'trust-less trust' has been advanced by K. D. Werbach, 'Trust, But Verify: Why the Blockchain Needs the Law', (2018) 33 *Berkeley Technology Law Journal* 487, DOI http://10.2139/ssrn.2844409.

[12] See: Athanassiou, 'Impact of Digital Innovation on the Processing of Electronic Payments and Contracting: An Overview of Legal Risks', 28.

[13] For an in-depth analysis, see: H. Eenmaa-Dimitrieva and M. J. Schmidt-Kessen, 'Regulation through Code as a Safeguard for Implementing Smart Contracts in No-Trust Environments', (2017) 3 *EUI Department of Law Research Paper* 10, DOI http://10.2139/ssrn.3100181.

[14] For a similar view, see: Athanassiou, 'Impact of Digital Innovation on the Processing of Electronic Payments and Contracting: An Overview of Legal Risks', 29.

[15] M. L. Perugini and P. Dal Checco, 'Smart Contracts: A Preliminary Evaluation', *SSRN Paper* 2015, p. 9, DOI http://10.2139/ssrn.2729548.

aspects of a contract are performed automatically does not mean that the transaction is 'free from the reach of regulation'.[16] The agreement still needs to be compatible with the relevant jurisdiction's legal framework.[17] According to the vast majority of legal systems, an essential element for the formation of a contract is the 'meeting of the minds' between the transacting parties.[18] In most cases, such a reciprocal intention can be expressed freely without any formal constraints. A contract can be formed by either spoken or written words and by the conduct of the parties. Thus, there are no legal obstacle preventing two parties from expressing their agreement in code or availing themselves of software running on a blockchain to execute their agreement.

The definition of smart contracts used in the present chapter lies at the intersection of the mid-1990s concept of a computerized protocol that execute the terms of a contract on one side and the opportunities arising from DLT on the other. In short, a smart contract is a piece of software run on a distributed ledger enabling automatic execution of an agreement – regardless of its lawful character – reached between two or more parties.[19] In this way, each asset transfer is timestamped and publicly recorded on the ledger. This chapter focuses on distributed ledger-based smart contracts.[20]

16.3 Features of Smart Contracts

16.3.1 *Strengths*

Smart contracts ensure ex ante the performance of a contract by eliminating the default risk at almost no cost without any external human intervention.[21] Thus, they allow the parties to set aside the enforcement-related costs related to breach. By definition, smart contracts render enforcement actions unnecessary since they mechanically execute the parties agreement. The use of smart contract becomes feasible when the expected costs of non-compliance (due to either potential litigation or search for alternatives) outweigh the

---

[16] A. Wright and P. De Filippi, 'Decentralized Blockchain Technology and the Rise of Lex Cryptographia', *SSRN Paper* 2015, p. 2, DOI http://10.2139/ssrn.2580664.

[17] As in the case of a vending machine selling prohibited drugs, the relevant law would still be applicable and enforceable. On this point, see: Eenmaa-Dimitrieva and Schmidt-Kessen, 'Regulation through Code', 42.

[18] See: J. M. Smits, *Contract Law: a Comparative Introduction*, (Cheltenham: Edward Elgar Publishing, 2017), p. 37.

[19] In this sense, for example, R. De Caria, 'A Digital Revolution in International Trade? The International Legal Framework for Blockchain Technologies, Virtual Currencies and Smart Contracts: Challenges and Opportunities', Vienna, 4–6 July 2017, hdl.handle.net/2318/1632525.

[20] Similarly, this chapter is *not* about the so-called algorithmic contracts (agreements in which an algorithm determine the rights and duties of one or both parties by acting indirectly as gap-filler or negotiator). It is possible that smart contracts are used in complementarity with algorithmic contracts. For an overview on this topic, see: L. H. Scholz, 'Algorithmic Contracts', (2017) 20 *Stanford Technology Law Review* 128; A. Ezrachi and M. E. Stucke, *Virtual Competition. The Promise and Perils of the Algorithm-Driven Economy* (Cambridge: Harvard University Press, 2016), pp. 56–81; See also: L. H. Scholz, 'Toward a Consumer Contract Law for an Algorithmic Age', *Oxford Business Law Blog – Law and Autonomous Systems Series* (17 April 2018), www.law.ox.ac.uk/business-law-blog/blog/2018/04/law-and-autonomous-systems-series-toward-consumer-contract-law.

[21] On the assumption that the software code does not contain bugs and it reflects truly the parties' intention. Similarly, the chapter does not consider environmental costs as well as the power-intensive nature of DLT. For a brief overview on the topic, see: N. Popper, 'There Is Nothing Virtual about Bitcoin's Energy Appetite', *The New York Times* 21 January 2018, www.nytimes.com/2018/01/21/technology/bitcoin-mining-energy-consumption.html.

expected value of the agreement. Furthermore, the activities performed through a smart contract, once recorded on the blockchain, cannot be reversed or cancelled. In short, the chief advantage of smart contracts is represented by the substantial reduction of the costs related to the exercise as well as the verification of rights. As a consequence, smart contracts have the potential to unlock trade in contexts where no exchanges have been carried out so far, in part due to the lack of trust.[22] Similarly, they can boost commercial exchanges by both reducing transaction costs and extending the level of trust between players. By ensuring an automatic performance, smart contracts remove the need to trust a another party's willingness and ability to perform. In addition, parties would not need to rely on the legal enforcement framework. Both consumers and merchants thus avoid the uncertainties of litigation.[23] By virtue of their tamper-proof, timestamped and immutable character, smart contracts offer a viable option to create and strengthen trade relationships. The transacting parties only need to rely on the correct functioning of the smart contract.[24] A new contractual crypto-proof environment based on automated contractual performance has thus the potential to boost commercial relations among unknown market players.

16.3.2 *Weaknesses*

Scholars have warned that the automatic character of smart contracts is incompatible with contract practice.[25] As demonstrated by the relational contractual theory, rights and obligation laid down in a written contract are just a part of the broader relationship between transacting parties.[26] Thus, these provisions are not always meant to be executed and performed according to their literal meaning. Performance of traditional contracts can be stopped voluntarily by the parties, whether in agreement or not. Parties quite often decide not to enforce certain contractual rights to further nurture business relationships. It is a common understanding in business practice that contracts are merely the formal side of an agreement, whilst the substantial side is the one arising from daily commercial relations. Accordingly, parties often amend and modify previous agreements so as to address new circumstances that arise after the conclusion of the contract. Smart contracts

---

[22] See: Eenmaa-Dimitrieva and Schmidt-Kessen, 'Regulation through Code', 35; K. D. Werbach and N. Cornell, 'Contracts Ex Machina', (2017) 67 *Duke Law Journal* 313, scholarship.law.duke.edu/cgi/viewcontent.cgi?article=3913&context=dlj.

[23] On the costs arising from litigation, see: R. Posner, 'The Costs of Enforcing Legal Rights', (1995) 4 *East European Constitutional Review* 71, chicagounbound.uchicago.edu/cgi/viewcontent.cgi?referer=www.google.nl/&httpsredir=1&article=3471&context=journal_articles; P. Hannaford-Agor, 'Measuring the Cost of Civil Litigation', (2013) 20 *Center for Jury Studies for the National Center for State Courts*, www.ncsc.org/~/media/Files/PDF/Services%20and%20Experts/Areas%20of%20expertise/Civil%20Justice/Measuring-cost-civil-litigation.ashx.

[24] Eenmaa-Dimitrieva and Schmidt-Kessen, 'Regulation through Code', 37, point out that with smart contracts, 'trusting a central authority is not necessary, because the technology will take care that the other party performs her obligation'.

[25] For a thorough analysis, see: Mik, 'Smart Contracts', 284.

[26] For an overview on the clash between smart contracts and relational contracts, see: K. E. C. Levy, 'Book-Smart, Not Street-Smart: Blockchain-Based Smart Contracts and The Social Workings of Law', (2017) 3 *Engaging Science, Technology, and Society* 1, DOI: http://10.17351/ests2017. For an in-depth analysis of the relational theory of contracts, see: A. Dixit, *Lawlessness and Economics: Alternative Modes of Governance* (Princeton: Princeton University Press, 2007); J. M. Feinman, 'Relational Contract Theory in Context', (2000) 94 *Northwestern University Law Review* 737, heinonline.org/HOL/Page?handle=hein.journals/illlr94&div=30&gsent=1&casa _token=&collection= journals#.

preclude these kinds of adjustments.[27] The rigidity of a preprogrammed software code excludes by definition the possibility to adapt an agreement to the mutability of business contracts.

As argued by law and economics scholars, in certain cases non-performance is an efficient outcome.[28] In fact, choosing not to provide a service and pay compensatory damages, because another party is willing to pay a higher price benefits society by creating a net surplus. In this way, resources can be allocated more efficiently. On the contrary, a smart contractual relationship would lock parties into performance, depriving them of rights of termination or to breach the contract. Smart contracts lack the capacity to adapt and prevent the transacting parties from adjusting their positions due to a change of circumstances. However, it must be said that a sophisticated smart contract could still leave the parties free to choose between various options: performing the primary obligation or opting for reimbursement of an agreed or statutory defined sum. In this respect, the law and economics justifications for non-performance would be preserved.

Admittedly, one of the major drawbacks in the use of smart contracts is the expression of contractual obligations in software code.[29] Only certain kinds of contracts can be coded as a series of 'running circumstances through conditional statements'.[30] Due to its inherent ambiguity, contractual language cannot always be reduced to binary algorithmic code. So far, legal terms have been drafted so as to be interpreted by humans, rather than translated into code.[31] Whilst the former is based on the principles of contract interpretation developed throughout centuries, the latter require a binary and mechanical logic. Also, smart contracts do not permit the presence of implied terms and contractual gaps. The parties are required to negotiate each term, which for other than the simplest of contract, is an expensive and time consuming process when the parties would prefer a degree of ambiguity.[32] Thus, in more complicated transactions smart contracts would increase the overall complexity of contract formation.[33] Furthermore, the parties would not be able to assess the code to determine if it accurately reflects the genuine the meeting of minds or, at least, the terms embedded within the original written text. A serious risk exists that the mechanism of a smart contract would generate

---

[27] J. Sklaroff, 'Smart Contracts and the Cost of Inflexibility', (2017) 166 *University of Pennsylvania Law Review* 263, at 265.

[28] For an in-depth analysis on this doctrine, see: R. Posner, *Economic Analysis of Law* (New York: Aspen Publishers, 8th edn., 2011), p. 151.

[29] For a first attempt of formalization of legal contractual language according to the needs of computer coding, see: Tjong Tjin Tai, 'Formalizing Contract Law for Smart Contracts'. For a general overview on the technical problems arising from the translation process from natural language to code, see: Mik, 'Smart Contracts', 287.

[30] See: Raskin, 'The Law and Legality of Smart Contracts', 313.

[31] For an in-depth overview on the topic, see: S. J. Burton, *Elements of Contract Interpretation* (Oxford: Oxford University Press: Scholarship Online 2009), p. 13, para. 1.2.2. DOI http://10.1093/acprof:oso/9780195337495.001.0001; S. Grammond, 'Reasonable Expectations and the Interpretation of Contracts across Legal Traditions', (2010) 48 *Canadian Business Law Journal* 345, ssrn.com/abstract=1474266.

[32] As highlighted by Sklaroff, 'Smart Contracts and the Cost of Inflexibility', 277, smart contracts shift the costs of contracting to the pre-contracting stage, as everything has to be drafted in the contract; Mik, 'Smart Contracts', 289 outlines that 'developers fail to recognize that in contract law, ambiguity is a feature, not a bug'.

[33] It is highly likely that in the following years lawyers will need to develop new skills in the field of computer sciences (such as coding) so as to be able to design and understand sophisticated smart contracts.

unintended consequences, especially for more complicated or sophisticated agreements. Thus, this new layer of complexity, if not properly addressed, could give rise to further litigation and enforcement costs.

16.3.3 *When Are Smart Contracts a Smart Choice?*

Both computing and legal reasoning can be reduced to a series of conditional statements. Legal reasoning often reflects 'if, then, else' logic. However, legal conditional statements are capable of reduction to code only in specific circumstances. For instance, encompassing theoretical concepts such as 'force majeure' and 'good faith' into an algorithmic code would be difficult.[34] It is quite clear then that only some kinds of agreements are eligible to be translated into smart contracts.

In the light of all the above, it is worth providing an early overview of the conditions under which smart contracts can prove useful and cost-efficient. First, the original agreement must consist of unambiguous and exact terms. This is the only way to easily reduce a natural language contract into programming language. Furthermore, when a variable depends on an event in the outside world, the coordination between the smart contract and offline oracles becomes crucial. Oracles are trusted data feeds that interface smart contracts with the external world, thus allowing a smart contract to be more flexible (adjustable between coded parameters).[35] Second, transacting parties must be willing to maintain the contractual provisions and effects immutably within the 'four corners' of the formal agreement. Third, in order to counterbalance the resources needed to draft and design effective smart contracts, their deployment is likely to be limited, at least at the beginning, to large-scale use (much like traditional standard form contracts). Of course, nothing prevents two transacting parties to set up a single-use smart contract.[36] Again, the perils arising from potential translation mistakes embedded into computer code suggests the use of standardized default templates for smart contracts which have undergone an in-depth monitoring process and have proved reliable.

Agreements used on a large scale and containing standardized terms and conditions is currently the best and most appropriate way to optimize smart contracts. Furthermore, when complex and large scope agreements are at stake, it is likely that only certain clauses and conditions are suitable for automatic performance on a distributed ledger. Accordingly, the following sections provide an overview of some of the most promising applications of smart contracts with reference to B2C and B2B relationships.

---

[34] For a similar view, see: M. Gianscaspro, 'Is a "Smart Contract" Really a Smart Idea? Insights from a Legal Perspective', (2017) 33 *Computer Law & Security Review* 825; Mik, 'Smart Contracts', 289; Raskin, 'The Law and Legality of Smart Contracts', 312.

[35] The trustworthiness of oracles and the related sources of information are crucial for the correct functioning of smart contracts. Since oracles are not part of the distributed ledger, they need to be designed and programmed in such a way to be sufficiently reliable. Even if the issue represents an important challenge to smart contracts functioning, I exclude it from my analysis since it is more about technology than law.

[36] It is possible that technological innovation will allow parties, in the immediate future, to easily design all the elements and features of a smart contract. However, at least for the moment, it is likely that smart contracts would consist in default templates of general terms and conditions, adaptable to the essential elements of each agreement (name of the parties, quantities of the goods transacted, consideration and so forth).

16.4 Stakes for Consumers

The debate around smart contracts and consumer protection is filled with alarms and high expectations. On the one hand, they have the potential to avoid consumer rights protection.[37] Wright and De Filippi have highlighted the potential negative effects of smart contracts on consumer protection.[38] Thus the question becomes how to ensure a sound implementation of consumer protection provisions by formalized and deterministic smart contracts? One solution would be to restrict their accessibility to more sophisticated parties (i.e. businesses). In fact, legal interpretation of contracts has traditionally aimed at restoring fairness between parties' respective obligations. It is not unusual for courts to make use of concepts such as good faith, protection of the weaker party and reasonable expectations, in order to interpret contracts against their literal meaning.[39] Because smart contracts run automatically on top of a distributed ledger and are immutable, the use of implied terms or creative interpretation becomes limited.

Policymakers, especially in the European Union (EU), have developed over the years a vast array of contractual rights to protect consumers in the light of their (economic) weaker position compared to businesses. However, it is worth pointing out that the mere automatization of contract performance on a tamper-proof distributed ledger does not hamper *per se* the implementation of consumer rights. Rather, the procedural terms and conditions embodied within a smart contract can be coded to include mandatory provisions of consumer protection. In this respect, smart contracts can prove to be a useful self-help remedy for those consumers who, so far and despite the rights granted to them, have been rather defenceless against the unilateral practices of businesses. Under the smart contract logic, businesses could not rely anymore on consumer inertia in enforcing their rights since those rights would be embedded into the code.

16.4.1 *Obstacles to Consumer Rights Enforcement*

As mentioned above, the EU has tried to protect consumers with a broad set of mandatory consumer rights.[40] These protections include the information duties of sellers, shifting the burden of proof related to remedies, withdrawal rights, and disclosure rules. Consumers are now empowered to protect themselves against abuses and unfair business practices. However, as already highlighted by many scholars and lawyers, consumers have not been able to effectively exercise all these legal rights and

---

[37] For instance, see: J. A. T. Fairfield, 'Smart Contracts, Bitcoin Bots, and Consumer Protection', (2014) 71 *Washington and Lee Law Review Online* 35, scholarlycommons.law.wlu.edu/wlulr-online/vol71/iss2/3, arguing that smart contracts have the potential to strengthen the bargaining position of consumers. However, the author confuses smart contracts with algorithmic contracts (see footnote 20).

[38] See, for instance: Wright and De Filippi, 'Decentralized Blockchain Technology', 26; Athanassiou, 'Impact of Digital Innovation on the Processing of Electronic Payments and Contracting: An Overview of Legal Risks', 47; Cuccuru, 'Beyond Bitcoin: An Early Overview on Smart Contracts', 191.

[39] On this point, see: Tjong Tjin Tai, 'Formalizing Contract Law for Smart Contracts', § 3.1.

[40] For an overview on this topic in the realm of European private law, see: E. Hondius, 'The Protection of the Weak Party in a Harmonised European Contract Law: A Synthesis', (2004) 27 *Journal of Consumer Policy* 245, DOI http://10.1023/B:COPO.0000040520.48379.60; European Parliamentary Research Service, *Consumer protection in the EU*, 2015, DOI http://10.2861/575862.

remedies.[41] Indeed, many consumers are not aware of the their legal rights or find it difficult to enforce them. Standardized contracts usually contain plenty of mandatory pro-consumer terms, which unfortunately often turn out to be ineffective. Enforcement cost are generally cost prohibitive and time consuming for individuals. As most of consumer contract claims are of negligible value, potential reimbursements for consumers are so insignificant to discourage costly legal procedures. In order to improve the situation, the EU introduced small claims procedures and has encouraged the adoption of collective redress mechanisms by the Member States.[42] However, with the view to avoid the disadvantages of class actions in the United States, the features of various collective redress mechanisms have diminished their effectiveness.[43] The outcome of such a lack of significant legal threats for businesses is an incentive not to take consumer rights seriously.

As noted above, the main obstacle to consumer protection lies in the very low thresholds of cost tolerance which consumers are willing to bear. In many cases, even when free of charge enforcement mechanisms are in place, consumers are discouraged by the efforts required to find out whether they are entitled make a claim.[44] Against this background, an automated self-performing process could improve the systematic functioning of consumer rights protection apparatus if those rights are accurately coded.

16.4.2 Facilitating Enforcement of Rights through Smart Contracts

Smart contracts have the potential to be implemented in such a way which could finally unlock the power of consumer protection rights.[45] As we have seen, smart contracts allow rights enforcements at almost no cost. Since smart contracts are by definition self-executing, they significantly reduce the need to seek ex-post enforcement. If consumer protection mechanisms (such as statutory warranties, claims for compensation due to impaired performance, cancellation rights) are incorporated into the code of smart contracts, they will be automatically executed whenever the conditions for them are triggered. In this way, consumers would not need to spend resources to ascertain whether they are entitled to any compensation or have to sustain additional expenses arising from dispute resolution procedures.

---

[41] See, in this sense: I. Benöhrp, *EU Consumer Law and Human Rights* (Oxford: Oxford University Press: Scholarship Online, 2013), p. 44, DOI http://10.1093/acprof:oso/9780199651979.001.0001; O. Ben-Shahar, 'One-way Contracts: Consumer Protection without Law', (2009) 484 *John M. Olin Law & Economics Working Paper*, chicagounbound.uchicago.edu/cgi/viewcontent.cgi?article=5068&context=journal_articles.

[42] See, for instance: Commission Recommendation of 11 June 2013 on common principles for injunctive and compensatory collective redress mechanisms in the Member States concerning violations of rights granted under Union Law, OJ L 201, 26 July 2013, eur-lex.europa.eu/legalcontent/EN/TXT/?qid=1398263020823&uri=OJ:JOL_2013_201_R_NS0013.

[43] As pointed out by D. Geradin, 'Collective Redress for Antitrust Damages in the European Union: Is This a Reality Now?', (2015) 16 *George Mason Law & Economics Research Paper* 3, ssrn.com/abstract=2593746, EU antitrust authorities took the view that US class action mechanism risk to trigger unmeritorious litigation to the detriment of society as a whole.

[44] Reference is made to legal technology companies which collect consumer claims online and enforce them by benefitting from economies of scales.

[45] See also: M. Fries, 'Smart Consumer Contracts – The End of Civil Procedure?', *Oxford Business Law Blog – Law and Autonomous Systems Series* (29 March 2018), www.law.ox.ac.uk/business-law-blog/blog/2018/03/smart-consumer-contracts-end-civil-procedure.

It is implausible to expect smart contracts to embody a limitless series of variables and external real world events.[46] However, it is plausible to expect that smart contracts could be coded to take account of the most common breaches of contract or violations of consumer rights in order to condition the contract's self-performing mechanism. Therefore, whenever the conditions stated by law are fulfilled, the smart contract would automatically trigger the related rights and procedure in order to reimburse each entitled consumer. In such a case, any issue of enforceability would not arise as the smart contract would comprehensively reflect the agreement between the parties, including all the mandatory consumer protection rules. Under this scenario, consumers would not need to be aware of all their rights in order to be protected, since the code would trigger the appropriate rights and remedies on their behalf.

In order to determine which consumer rights can be properly optimized through smart contracts, a preliminary assessment would be needed to see the rights that are able to fulfill the three conditions listed in the previous section.[47] First, only consumer rights that do not rely on ambiguous or abstract terms can be translated into code. Second, the said consumer rights cannot be dependent on any relational expectations between the parties. Third, the rights must be implemented on a large scale and in an identical (or, at least, standardized) form. In addition, since the likelihood of a bugs and of discrepancies is serious, it would be necessary to perform an in-depth analysis of the proper functioning of the smart contract before making it available on the market.[48]

Against this background, a first overview of the most viable implementations of smart contracts with reference to consumer protection can be provided. Passenger rights is an interesting testing ground and the most readily viable model. Airline delays and cancellations can be easily checked and embedded through oracles into smart contracts. Theoretically the concept developed in the next section could be applied to the enforcement of a vast range of consumer rights and, more generally, to protect weaker parties' rights (digital and communication sector, payment and financial services market, and data protection, just to mention a few).[49]

16.4.3 *Case of Passenger Rights*

Over the years, the EU has set up a general framework for the protection of passengers moving within the Internal Market by rail, bus/coach, ferry or air transports.[50] They all provide for a reimbursement right in case of delay or cancellation. The current analysis

---

[46] K. Jacob, 'Smart Contracting Can Reduce Legal and Operating Costs', *Oxford Business Law Blog – Law and Autonomous Systems Series* (5 April 2018), www.law.ox.ac.uk/business-law-blog/blog/2018/04/law-and-autonomous-systems-series-smart-contracting-can-reduce-legal, highlights that ultimately smart contracts would require the digitalization of the world (in the so-called Internet of Things).

[47] See Section 16.3.3.

[48] Regulatory strategies to set up appropriate precautions are illustrated in Section 16.6.2.

[49] European Parliamentary Research Service, *Consumer protection in the EU*, 2015, p. 4, highlighting that there is not a consistent and uniform definition of consumer in EU law.

[50] See J. Luzak, 'Vulnerable Travellers in the Digital Age', (2016) 5 *Journal of European Consumer and Market Law* 130, www.kluwerlawonline.com/document.php?id=EuCML2016027, arguing that the notion of passenger falls within the scope of the *consumer acquis* as the Directive (EU) No. 2015/2302 refers to article 114 Treaty on the Functioning of the European Union.

will focus on developments related to rail, ship and air passenger rights.[51] In February 2005, the European Regulation (EC) No. 261/2004 on compensation and assistance to passengers in the event of denied boarding and of cancellation or long delay of flights came into force, entitling air passengers to compensation ranging from €125 to €600.[52] In December 2009, European Regulation (EC) No. 1371/2007 on rail passengers' rights and obligations entered into force providing for compensation rights ranging from 25 per cent to 50 per cent of the fare depending on the length of the delay.[53] In December 2012, the European Regulation (EC) No. 1177/2010 concerning the rights of passengers when travelling by sea and inland waterway came into force, giving a compensation right to sea and inland waterway travellers amounting to up to 25 per cent of the ticket price (based on the length of the delay and the length of the travel).[54]

In this respect, we can conceive a system of smart passenger contracts structured so as to reimburse all the entitled consumers whenever the relevant requirements of delay or cancellation are detected. According to the EU Consumer Centres Network, the transport sector is one of the main sources of cross-border complaints within the Internal Market.[55] In fact, even though many carrier companies decided to establish accessible and straightforward complaint procedures to handle passengers' claims, there is still room for improvement as consumer rights are not consistently enforced.[56]

A smart contract mechanism aimed at automatizing the reimbursement procedure would require a trustworthy and reliable environment of interfaces. Often, the need to integrate smart contracts with real world events is mentioned as one of the major obstacles to the rise of DLT-enabled contracting systems.[57] In fact, a trustless and incorruptible net of oracles is as important as a comprehensive code for the proper functioning of a smart contract.[58] Contrary to other industries, the travel sector has the potential to be

---

[51] For the sake of simplicity, coach passenger rights will not be considered. However, the proposal put forward in this article theoretically might be applied also to that sector: in March 2013, the European Regulation (EC) No. 181/2011 concerning the rights of passengers in bus and coach transport entered into force, entitling bus and coach passengers of long-distance routes to a compensation up to 50 per cent of the ticket price if the carrier failed to provide a choice between refund or rerouting (art. 19).

[52] Regulation (EC) No. 2004/261 of 11 February 2004 establishing common rules on compensation and assistance to passengers in the event of denied boarding and of cancellation or long delay of flights, eur-lex.europa.eu/legal-content/EN/ALL/?uri=CELEX%3A32004R0261, art. 7-8. On 10 June 2016, the European Commission published the 'Interpretative Guidelines on Regulation (EC) No. 261/2004 of the European Parliament and of the Council establishing common rules on compensation and assistance to passengers in the event of denied boarding and of cancellation or long delay of flights', ec.europa.eu/transport/sites/transport/files/themes/passengers/news/doc/2016-06-10-better-enforcement-pax-rights/c%282016%293502_en.pdf, aimed at providing EU National Enforcement Bodies of EU Member States with a blueprint document tackling issues most frequently raised by passengers, and in an attempt to give clarity to the enforcement of existing passenger rights legislation.

[53] Regulation (EC) No. 2007/1371 of 23 October 2007 on rail passengers' rights and obligations, art. 17.

[54] Regulation (EU) No. 2010/177 of 24 November 2010 concerning the rights of passengers when travelling by sea and inland waterway, art. 19.

[55] European Consumer Centres Network, 'Revision of EU air passengers' rights legislation', *Position paper*, p. 2.

[56] On this point, see: Fries, 'Smart Consumer Contracts', highlighting that whilst some companies, like the Spanish *Renfe*, voluntarily comply with the relevant legislation by adopting an effective customer service strategy, others, like the German *Deutsche Bahn*, set up troublesome procedures to discourage consumers from claiming reimbursements.

[57] See: Mik, 'Smart Contracts', 297.

[58] For the purposes of the present chapter, technical problems arising from the implementation of oracles are bracketed as they represent a technical issue.

complemented with automatization.[59] Air traffic is highly controlled through advanced computerized systems run by airport authorities. Similarly, the rail sector is already overseen throughout the Internal Market and, in any case, it is not unrealistic to imagine a network of oracles able to track departure and arrival times of trains. The same is true for the cruise and ferry transport sector.

Smart contract systems could automatically verify whether the legal requirements for compensation are met and, if so, carry out the payments set by the relevant legal framework. However, the structure of the law is not the most suitable for a smooth and effective translation into code.[60] Take, for example, the concept of 'extraordinary circumstances' in the air passengers' rights legislation. Pursuant to Article 5(3) of Regulation No. 261/2004, an air carrier shall be exempted from paying compensation in case of delay or cancellation upon proof that the delay or cancellation was caused by extraordinary circumstances which could not have been avoided even if all reasonable measures had been taken. In the light of its inherent qualitative nature, it is unlikely that this assessment can be made through an algorithmic process. However, the regulatory authorities or legislature could provide a non-exhaustive list of narrowly defined cases that are presumed to be considered extraordinary (such as, for instance, airport congestion due to bad weather conditions).[61] Therefore, it is feasible to incorporate within the smart contract, complemented a network of oracles, many of the exceptional circumstances that would preclude the triggering of automatic compensation. The traditional system based on traditional procedures (alternative dispute resolution and litigation) would remain as a last resort remedy in cases so unique to require an individual assessment.

16.5 Stakes for Businesses

Turning the attention now on business trading practices, it becomes apparent that other implementations of smart contract might prove useful in this context as well. Smart contracts have the inherent potential to reduce transaction costs and to enable trading where, before, no market would have flourished.[62] By virtue of their ability to generate trust between market players, in the immediate future they are most suited to be implemented in B2B relationships.[63] In this respect, international trade sectors offer an interesting playing field to test smart contracts potential. It is worth pointing out that these kinds of smart contract applications can be beneficial with reference to both one-shot

[59] The establishment of trans-European networks (TENs) in the areas of transport has always been one of the main goals of the EU policies. For instance, in the rail transport sector, the EU has developed the so-called European Railway Traffic Management System (ERTMS): a European standard for the Automatic Train Protection (ATP) that allows an interoperable railway system in Europe and enforces compliance by the train with speed restrictions and signalling status. See: https://ec.europa.eu/transport/modes/rail/ertms_en. Similarly, in the air sector the Single European Sky initiative has been established. See: https://ec .europa.eu/transport/modes/air/single_european_sky_en. For a general overview (comprehensive of the ship sector), see: www.europarl.europa.eu/atyourservice/en/displayFtu.html?ftuId=FTU_3.5.1.html.
[60] Tjong Tjin Tai, 'Formalizing Contract Law for Smart Contracts', § 4, argues that smart contracts give occasion to reconsider the formalities and rules of contract law.
[61] See: Interpretative Guidelines on Regulation (EC) No 261/2004.
[62] For an in-depth analysis of the potential of smart contracts to create markets in 'no-trust' environments, see: Eenmaa-Dimitrieva and Schmidt-Kessen, 'Regulation through Code'.
[63] Allen and Overy LLP, Smart Contracts for Finance Parties, 2017, www.allenovery.com /SiteCollectionDocuments/Smart_contracts_for_finance_parties.pdf.

transactions and more sophisticated ones. Whereas the former could be completely automatized through software, as it is likely with B2C contracts, the latter could be 'smarted up' only to a certain extent (such as an escrow device related to a broader supply contract).

According to the WTO Report 2017 insight, world exports of manufactured goods amount to more than US$11 trillion.[64] Despite the pace of technological innovation in finance, international business practice is still significantly paper-based and cumbersome. The need to provide trust between parties in long-distance sales contracts has been traditionally satisfied using instruments such as letters of credit and escrow agreements. However, a large set of inefficiencies and obstacles arise from the interaction between players who are in different jurisdictions. Further, documentary processes of banking verification are time consuming and prone to human errors throughout the supply chain.[65] Against this background, smart contracts can be deployed to alleviate the hardships and inefficiencies which affect the current state of international trade.

In a broad array of cases, smart contracts to fulfil the three conditions stated previously.[66] First, international sales contracts contain highly standardized terms and conditions based on variables that are verifiable (shipment, delivery, timing, etc.). Furthermore, by adopting a reliable network of oracles, verification activities can be digitalized (a process that is already under way). Second, a vast array of international sales contracts are reached between parties from different jurisdictions, cultural backgrounds and commercial trades. This is one of the reasons why common law and its four-corner rule are widespread in international business practice: they rely more on the literal meaning of the text than civil law systems, allowing a higher predictability of law.[67] Third, businesses tend to operate in an environment where contracting activities represent a frequent and repetitive task. This would enable the development of smart contract platforms providing templates with general terms and conditions already translated into code. Of course, big business could develop their own smart contracts which could be approved by independent certification bodies. Permissioned distributed ledgers offer new contracting ecosystems that can connect a network of contracting parties or independent third parties through a the running nodes of a distributed ledger, thus allowing smooth, tamper-proof and trustworthy trade among the businesses. The letter of credit is a good example of the optimization of international business practice through the use of smart contracts.[68] A smart sales contract would, upon fulfilment of certain requirements, authorize the release of the sum agreed upon directly to the vendor's account. The benefits of such a mechanism

---

[64] World Trade Organization Report 2017, www.wto.org/english/res_e/booksp_ e/world_trade_report17_e .pdf.

[65] See L. W. Cong and Z. He, 'Blockchain Disruption and Smart Contracts', *SSRN Paper* 2017, DOI http:// 10.2139/ssrn.2985764, highlighting that a deal could not be reached if the bank issuing a letter of credit is not trusted by the counter-party banks or is not part of the trustworthy banking network.

[66] See Section 16.3.3.

[67] The 'four corners rule' implies that a document's meaning should be excerpted from the textual content of the document itself, without any external reference. See, for instance, G. Cuniberti, 'The International Market for Contracts: The Most Attractive Contract Laws', (2014) 34 *Northwestern Journal of International Law & Business*, scholarlycommons.law.northwestern.edu/njilb/vol34/iss3/3; I. MacNeil, 'Uncertainty in Commercial Law', (2009) 13 *Edinburgh Law Review* 68, DOI: http://10.3366/ E1364980908000966 http:// scholarlycommons.law.northwestern.edu/njilb/vol34/iss3/3.

[68] For an overview on letter of credits, see: R. A. August, D. Mayer and M. Bixby, *International Business Law* (London: Pearson Education, 6th edn., 2012), p. 662.

are twofold. First, parties are better suited to keep track of the flow of goods without fear of fraud: shipment, storing and delivering activities would all be duly recorded and time-stamped on the distributed ledger. As stated above, oracles and integrated networks Internet of Things would play a key role in ensuring the reliability of the system.[69] By virtue of the tamper-proof character of the distributed ledger, the time for verification and authentication would be substantially reduced as all parties would have access to the shipping and transaction records. Second, the flow of money would be accelerated, enabling almost instant payments. Parties would no longer need to rely on banking intermediation, leading to a reduction in transaction costs. This mechanism promises to be useful especially for those business actors who trade on a large scale. It is no surprise that the first implementations of smart contracts have taken place in B2B relationships.[70]

Escrow agreements represent another optimal testing ground for smart contracts in B2B relationships. A smart contract can easily be deployed as an escrow account linked to an exchange between two parties. The buyer of commodities or services would transfer funds to the smart contract's account. The oracles (such as geo-tagging devices) connected to the smart contract would in turn monitor the performance, and upon delivery of the goods to the buyer, the contract would automatically authorize the funds to the seller. As shown above, smart contracts based on distributed ledgers have the potential to create new markets and expanding existing ones by reducing transaction costs and revolutionizing business practice.[71] They can be structured in platforms capable of managing sophisticated multiple operations, minimizing human errors and risk of fraud as well as cutting costs and processing time. Unlike the B2C scenario, businesses are naturally inclined to develop smart contract applications in order to reduce transaction costs and strengthen their trading activities.[72]

16.6 Looking Ahead

DLT has been around for more than a decade, but business implementations are still in their early stages. The aim of this section is twofold. First, it reviews a typology of distributed ledger to determine which ones best fit smart contracts features. Second, it investigates which regulatory strategy policymakers and regulators should adopt in order to facilitate a safe experimentation of smart contracts in the B2C environment, as well as, in the B2B one.

[69] Even now, the process of verification and authentication need to be delegated to third parties.

[70] In 2016 *Barclays* and the FinTech start-up *Wave* declared to have executed a global trade transaction using a smart letter of credit run on a distribute ledger (www.barclayscorporate.com/insight-and-research/trading-and-exporting/blockchain-revolution-in-trade-finance.html). Further, *Bank of America Merrill Lynch*, in partnership with *Microsoft Treasury*, recently received industry praise for their blockchain-powered trade finance application which optimizes the standby letter of credit process, reducing issuance time from several weeks to potentially just several hours (news.microsoft.com/2016/09/27/microsoft-and-bank-of-america-merrill-lynch-collaborate-to-transform-trade-finance-transacting-with-azure-blockchain-as-a-service/).

[71] For the sake of brevity, the chapter focuses only on two examples in order to provide an overview of smart contracts potential benefits and on the main difference with the B2C relationships.

[72] Currently, R3 Corda consortium represents one of the most far-reaching and advanced implementation of a distributed ledger. It gathers more than forty top banks around the world and it is aimed at developing a standardized, private, global blockchain for the managing of financial services. For an in-depth analysis of its structure, see: R. G. Brown, 'Introducing R3 Corda: A Distributed Ledger Designed for Financial Services', *Blog Post*, 5 April 2017, www.r3cev.com/blog/2016/4/4/introducing-r3-corda-a-distributed-ledger-designed-for-financial-services.

16.6.1 *What Degree of Decentralization?*

Distributed ledgers can take a wide range of forms, depending on their degree of decentralization.[73] Thus, smart contracts therein embedded can be characterized by different levels of rigidity, accountability and stability. Even though they are often celebrated as innovative and disruptive, permissionless ledgers are not a good fit to thoroughly meet the needs of business practice.[74] Permissioned ledgers have been structured as a response to the shortcomings of the public ones. The main reason for this phenomenon is the irreversibility implied by permissionless ledgers, making any kind of external intervention almost impossible, no matter if legally compulsory, desirable or sought by the transacting parties. Also, public and fully decentralized ledgers are inherently costly as they require energy-intensive activities from a large network of computing nodes.[75]

In the light of the above, the evidence would seem to suggest that only a mitigated form of decentralization is desirable, irrespective of B2C and B2B environments. In order to be widely adopted by market players, smart contracts need to grant access to public policy enforcement mechanisms and traditional private law remedies. It comes as no surprise that the major technology companies are currently developing smart contracts platform prototypes based on permissioned ledgers so as to overcome the shortcomings deriving from the rigidity of public and permissionless blockchains,[76] while preserving the intrinsic features of smart contracts, such as incorruptibility and trust-worthiness. A proper balance needs to be stricken between decentralization and regulatory concerns (such as legal compliance, data protection, financial stability, and so forth).

In sum, the advantages and benefits of smart contracts vary depending on the needs of the transacting parties. Therefore, features such as automatization, immutability or incorruptibility should be refined according to the specific nature of each type of transaction. For instance, a platform running thousands of B2C smart contracts needs to ensure automatic exercise of consumer rights on a large scale. Long distance B2B sales contracts need to be run on tamper-proof ledgers, with an underlying community of nodes that are incapable of being biased or hacked.

16.6.2 *Which Regulatory Strategy?*

It is useful to assess regulatory strategies that policymakers should pursue based upon the above review of B2B and B2C smart contracts. As already pointed out by the legal scholarship, the range of possible approaches available is quite wide and goes from a 'wait-and-see' tactic to the issuance of guidelines or new laws to prevent potential problems.[77] As a preliminary remark, it should be clear that the burden of shaping new rules rest not only on government

---

[73] See Section 16.2.
[74] Cuccuru, 'Beyond Bitcoin: An Early Overview on Smart Contracts', 192.
[75] Athanassiou, 'Impact of Digital Innovation on the Processing of Electronic Payments and Contracting: An Overview of Legal Risks', 28.
[76] See, for instance: S. Mery and D. Selman, 'Make Your Blockchain Smart Contracts Smarter with Business Rules', IBM Developer Works, www.ibm.com/developerworks/library/mw-1708-mery-blockchain/1708-mery.html; M. Gray, 'Enterprise Smart Contracts: Resolving the Truth for Blockchains', Microsoft Azure Blog, 30 October 2017.
[77] For a first overview of the possible regulatory approaches for DLT-enabled activities, see: Werbach, 'Trust but Verify'; Finck, 'Blockchain Regulation', 11; G. A. Gabison, 'Policy Considerations for the Blockchain Public and Private Applications', (2016) 19 *SMU Science and Technology Law Review*, scholar.smu.edu/scitech/vol19/iss3/4.

bodies, but also on market players and public interest groups of stakeholders.[78] It is crucial that policymakers seek interaction and dialogue with companies in order to target the actual problems without stifling innovation. Furthermore, the appropriate strategy will depend on the different balances of interests at stake in B2C versus B2B scenarios.

Experimentation on smart contract applications in B2B relationships has been on going for some years through the joint efforts of software developers and merchants. Since the economic benefits arising from smart contracts in international trade and finance are clear, at this time there is no need for state intervention.[79] On the contrary, the success of smart contracts as a tool to enable consumer rights enforcement will depend on the approach that policymakers adopt to support their implementation. It would not be realistic to imagine that businesses will voluntarily avail themselves of using smart contracts as an instrument for consumer protection. As noted previously, consumer rights are largely neglected as consumers often elect not to pursue their small money claims. Thus, businesses will need to be required to code consumer protection rights into their smart contracts. In this respect, two main questions arise: which typologies of merchants should be forced to implement such mechanisms into their smart contracts? And how can public bodies ensure the soundness of such mechanisms?

Since both DLT and smart consumer contracts are still in their infancy, it would not be realistic to require all merchants to implement a new regulatory system.[80] As analysed above, passengers' rights offer a model to assess the functioning of smart contracts. Furthermore, rail and air sectors are already highly digitalized, which allows an easy coordination with a smart contract platform. Nonetheless, many complexities remain to be faced in order to ensure the implementation of consumer protections in smart contracts. Therefore, a wise first move may be the adoption of regulatory sandboxes.[81] They can be defined as legal tools that allow companies to test specific services, products or business practices under a legal framework which is different from the one they would otherwise need to comply with under normal circumstances.

This technique permits businesses and regulators to test different forms of regulations and assess which ones are most effective. Similarly, businesses are given the possibility to develop new activities without the risks arising from legal uncertainty. In this respect, there would be room to carefully develop a permissioned distributed ledger with a consumer contract embedded therein. The contract should be structured in a way to allow the triggering of reimbursement rights to the benefit of consumers (passengers) whenever the relevant legal conditions are met. Besides, the distributed ledger underlying the mechanism should be a permissioned one, formed by consumer organizations, rail service providers and governmental authorities. In this way, the reliability of the system would be ensured by the presence of regulators and consumer associations. Finally, from this early experimentation, public authorities and businesses would have the chance to learn how to further improve the effectiveness of consumers' rights optimized through smart contracts.

[78] Finck, 'Blockchain Regulation', 20.
[79] Public authorities would still need to oversee the process in order to ensure public policy objectives such as financial stability, data protection and so forth. However, the public intervention would not be essential to nudge or give incentives for the adoption of smart contracts. On this point, see: Financial Conduct Authority, Distributed Ledger Technology Feedback Statement on Discussion Paper, 2017, www.fca.org.uk/publication/feedback/fs17-04.pdf.
[80] See also, Fries, 'Smart Consumer Contracts'.
[81] Finck, 'Blockchain Regulation', 14, argues for the need of a process of polycentric co-regulation based on a continuous dialogue between policymakers and stakeholders instead of a top-down approach.

Regulatory experimentation aside, the theme of the neutrality of computer code is likely to play a key role in the world of smart contracts. While rights enforcements would be ensured, parties would still remain concerned, in B2B and in B2C relationships, about verifying the correctness of the translation into code and whether the algorithms will generate significant problems of reliability. In most cases, the stronger party will be the only one having the necessary resources to set up the smart contract and check its code. What can be done to ensure then the integrity of the mechanism? The answer is twofold. First of all, a private regulation system based on monitoring and marks of conformity granted by certification bodies could flourish. Thus, transacting parties would have the opportunity to decide whether the smart contract mechanism is appropriate for their needs.[82] Moreover, with reference to B2C relationships, government authorities could introduce a notification procedure under which smart consumer contracts whould undergo a monitoring process supervised by public bodies. Further, setting underlying distributed ledgers to be open to government authorities would ensure the possibility of intervention in cases of abuse or fraud.[83]

16.7 Conclusion

The present chapter has provided an early overview of the areas where smart contracts could successfully optimize current contract practices. After having clarified that smart contracts are a tamper-proof tool aimed at ensuring contract performance, the chapter carried out an analysis of their main characteristics. The inherent features of smart contracts, such as the impossibility to adapt the agreement to new situations and the complexities arising from the translation national language agreements into code, suggest that smart contracting is currently suited for a narrow set of contract transactions. In particular, rights and obligations embodied in smart contracts need to be standardized and replicable on a large scale. Furthermore, smart contracts exclude by definition any relational remedy found in day-by-day commercial practice. Therefore, current applications of smart contract need to be carefully identified.

On the positive side, smart contracts can be a vehicle for substantially reducing enforcement costs, which would allow the widespread and systematic exercise of consumer rights, particularly when involving small claims. Businesses would no longer benefit from consumer inertia and would be incentivized to comply with consumer protection rules. In this respect, the case of passengers' rights has been taken as an example to demonstrate how new technology can be used to restore a fairer balance of powers between merchants and consumers. Also, smart contracts have the capacity to enable trade exchanges in environments affected by lack of trust among potential transacting parties (no-trust contracting).[84] Indeed, by their tamper-proof and self-performing character, smart contracts can prove incomparably more effective than traditional tools used so far in international trade, such as letters of credit and escrow

---

[82] Depending on the importance of the matter, the state could decide to intervene by issuing specific form of regulation so as to ensure the reliability of the network of the certification bodies. It seems however too early to assess whether such an initiative will be necessary or not. It is worth highlighting that any attempt of fraud and abusive conduct would still be prohibited under the current law.

[83] As a corollary, we should wonder whether a potential liability for inadequate controls on smart contracts could arise towards market players. This requires further research.

[84] See: Eenmaa-Dimitrieva and Schmidt-Kessen, 'Regulation through Code', 27.

agreements. Barriers to trade could be substantially decreased, enabling the rise of new markets.

Nevertheless, the integration of smart contracts with the complexities of real world transactions will is not be an easy task. By definition, they require the drafting and the related encoding of comprehensive agreements capable of foreseeing a vast array of conditional events. Given the high investments required to implement a trustworthy smart contracting system, only certain players will avail themselves of such a mechanism. Joint initiatives among software developers and financial institutions have already been launched in B2B environments. Thus, it is just a matter of time before they will be deployed on a large scale to automatize less complex operations, such as letters of credit and escrow agreements. Smart contracts deployment as tools to improve the enforcement of consumer rights will require the joint effort of policymakers, regulators, consumer associations and proactive businesses. In such respect, policymakers and regulators should take the lead in order to guarantee a trustworthy translation into code of consumer rights be used on smart contracting platforms able to manage thousands of consumer contracts. The adoption of regulatory sandboxes on specific sectors (such as air, ferry and rail transports) may be a viable route to test the promises of smart contracts and to see how to make consumer protection laws more effective.

16.8 Postscript: Smart Contracts and Lawyers (Mathieu Martin)

16.8.1 *The Lawyer and "the Code Is Law"*

Smart contracts and lawyers are inextricably linked. After all, the lawyer is entitled to draft them. The smart contract, whether described as a contract or simple algorithm, challenges the lawyer by its philosophy ('code is law') and by its writers who are not jurists but developers. The issue is whether this technology will diminish the need for the legal profession. Before overhastily assuming the apocalyptic demise of the lawyer, we should note the lawyer's role and the status as trusted advisor and defender of client interests, and consider whether IT can be a substitute for the lawyer instead of being or simply a new legal tool.

Lawyers assist in the operation of justice and derive their power from law. For example, in France, Law no. 71–1130 of 31 December 1971 relating to the reform of certain judicial and legal professions states that 'No-one may, directly or through an intermediary, on a habitual and remunerated basis, provide legal consultations or write private deeds, for others' unless he/she carries on a regulated professional activity and is qualified to do so.' The lawyer, together with a few other legal professions, enjoys a monopoly in the field of legal assistance and advice, and therefore in the writing of legal instruments, and is a defender of the law, but his role is also to criticize it in the context of his role as defender of litigants.

If we agree that the 'code is law', we may well wonder what is this 'technological law' and who has the right to write a code with legal force. Indeed, and based on a strict interpretation of the above law, the author of a smart contract can only be a law professional. But what is this law that seems to prevail via the code? And what legitimacy must the lawyer give it? Far from imposing itself like the Matrix on Morpheus, 'Code is Law' can only be understood in the contractual context as the creation of a law by private parties. Thus, the parties create 'law' with the help of a lawyer. This is nothing new. For example, Art. 1102 of the French Civil code provides: 'Everyone is free to enter into a contract or not to enter into a contract, to choose the other party to the contract and to determine the content and the form of the contract within the limits set by law'.

Moreover, if the code is simply the translation of a legal document it is the merely an application of contract law, which has existed for over 200 years, where, in accordance with Art. 1103: 'Agreements lawfully entered into have the force of law for those who have made them'. Understood in this way, the smart contract is simply a new writing tool, thus, preserving the contractual autonomy of the parties. The principle of 'code is law' arising from the smart contract therefore does not at this stage call into question the role of the lawyer.

16.8.2 *Lawyer and Code*

The principle of 'code is law' is only valid if the parties and jurists can read and understand the code. Article 7.2 of the 'National Lawyers' Regulations states: 'The lawyer writing a legal instrument ensures the validity and full effectiveness of the instrument in accordance with the parties' expectations'. Smart contracts written in computer code will make it more difficult to achieve these legal objectives. This presents problems for both the lawyer, who needs the expertise to 'encode' law, and the parties, who need to be ensured that the smart contract is written to meet their expectations.

In order for the lawyer to work in this new technological environment, she will need to become a techno-lawyer or to surround herself with third parties that can read, write and translate code. Prior to smart contracts, technology contracts were written in natural language that formalized in legal terms, technical or IT actions and their consequences, possibly with the help of consulting technicians. Thus, regardless of the subject of the obligation or the service to be dealt with by the smart contract, whether or not relating to IT, the legal obligations need to be translated from language to code and from code to language. Smart contracts must therefore remain under the control of legal profession.

16.8.2.1 Lawyer as Smart Contract Publisher

The lawyer is, as a matter of practice, is a writer of documents. By virtue of this mission, the lawyer provides a service which must be in accordance with the applicable law. The written contract, coded or not, must conform to party and specifications and the rule of law. Lawyers may find themselves, especially in cases where coding is done in the law office, in the position of being software publishers.

However, the concept of software development necessarily brings with it the risk of the occurrence of anomalies or bugs in the very functioning of the smart contract. There are two kinds of such anomalies. One is the bad encoding of legal rules and terms; this is the parallel of a badly written traditional contract. The other type of anomaly is bad functioning of the contract (the smart contract does not work technically); this is also a risk that is attributable to the drafter or for writer. To assure himself that the a smart contract complies, the lawyer would need to 'test' as is the case for software solutions.[85] Only in

---

[85] We intentionally do not address the issue of smart contract negotiation in this article. It is hard to imagine a negotiation between two lawyers, their clients and their respective developers discussing, line-by-line, the writing of the code.

this way can the lawyer ensure that it is written appropriately and that the algorithm will work as intended. The 'robustness testing' of the contract occurs where one of the parties requests its enforcement: the contract clauses and mechanisms are used and/or work with a greater or lesser degree of success. The test should also forecast, in case of a dispute, whether jurists would hold a contract or specific contract terms legally valid.

Cleary, in the case considered here, in addition to the legal perfection of the instrument, comes the technical perfection of the code. In this regard, the formalization of the agreement by a lawyer may lead to the recognition of the lawyer as a developer and editor of smart contract software solutions. Following this logic, the lawyer may then offer various types of contracts, including standard smart contracts like standard software packages and customized smart contracts.

16.8.2.2 Lawyer's Ethical Obligations

Evidently, one of the greatest guarantees lawyers offer their clients is that of confidentiality. In this respect, Art. 66–5 of French Law no. 71–1130 of 31 December 1971 states:

> In all matters, whether in the domain of advice or that of defence, the consultations by a lawyer to his client or intended for his client, the correspondence exchanged between the client and his lawyer, between the lawyer and his colleagues and counterparts with the exception for the latter of those bearing the word 'official', interview notes and, more generally, all the documents in a file are covered by professional secrecy.

The above-mentioned principle of professional secrecy is absolute and is not limited in time, and covers all subjects (advice, defence etc.), as well as covering all mediums (paper, fax, electronic etc.). It will therefore also cover any exchange associated with or via the blockchain. However, in the context of a public blockchain, anyone can consult and see the various operations carried out. Accordingly, lawyers will have to choose the right blockchain and thus determine what can be visible on it, in order to uphold thier duty of confidentiality.

16.8.3 *Smart Contract as Universal Tool*

The following questions arise in drafting contracts: First, what is the legal system and law applicable to the contract? Second, in what language is the contract to be written in order that it can be read or translated by the parties? Third, the choice of medium: digital or paper?

The benefit of using new technology, such as machine-readable algorithm, is that it is written in a universal language and on a universal medium. However, given the blockchain's ubiquitous nature lawyer's may seek to limit applicable law by setting territorial limits on the smart contract. However, the blockchain technology associated with such a contract is not universal at this time. In fact, there are different blockchains and thus different codes/formats/languages at present. This question of format or medium has not arisen before as the hard copy and/or soft copy (word, pdf, etc.) have been the common means of contracting.

The benefit of smart contracts, subject to any translation into the language of one of the parties, is that they are accessible to all the parties to the contract and to third parties (read, copy, print). The decision to work within a public or private blockchain and the choice of the format/language to be used in the smart contract will be made on the basis of the nature and objectives of the contract. This choice, which may appear minor, may however prove to be extremely important in the event of a chain of smart contracts that are not all compatible with each other.

Finally, a remaining issue relates to the longevity of the smart contract for the lawyer, given that at some point the blockchain may cease to exist. A traditional contract is not limited by the longevity or lack of longevity of a technology. On the contrary, many questions remain open with respect to the storage of smart contracts over time: will there be an expiration date or validity limit for smart contracts relative to technical limitations?

16.8.4 *Lawyer's Intellectual Impoverishment*

The smart contract is used for its simplicity and its automatic implementation, without third-party intervention, since it is based on a succession of prerequisites and consequences following the 'if (...) then (...)' logic. However, we know that in the area of contracts, certain obligations do not work in a binary fashion, and that the lawyer is thus asked to suggest various nuances in the writing of the contract, or to propose some pragmatic solutions, such as the use of flexible concepts like 'good faith', 'reasonable character' and 'earliest opportunity'. As these concepts are neither measurable nor quantifiable with certainty, they are near impossible to code in a smart contract. This inability to code standard-like terms will limit lawyers use of smart contracts to simple types of transactions where the intended obligations do not require interpretation or nuance.

16.8.5 *Smart Contract and the Lawyer 2.0*

The principle feature of the smart contract is its immutable character: if coded the conditions are met, it is automatically implemented. In application of the principle of 'code is law' results in self-sufficient contracts. This idea of self-sufficiency or escape from the formal litigation system is not new to traditional contract law. Lawyers have long written contracts that provide for 'automatic' remedies (liquidated or penalty clauses) and express avoidance of the legal system (mediation and arbitration clauses). What changes, however, is the smart contract is not subject to human intervention and cannot be stopped if its implementation conditions are poorly written or formalized in code. The forced implementation of its terms is thus irremediable. This feature essentially means that smart contracts contain their own law.

Imposing 'code is law' irrevocably without any possible remedy brings us closer to Morpheus in the Matrix. Being 'imprisoned' by a code, which is valid as law without the possibility of recourse to a lawyer or a judge is closer to a dictatorship than a democratic institution. However, this an over dramatization of the actual facts; the next section will show that lawyers will continue to play the role of the legal gatekeeper.

16.8.6 *What Is Left for the Lawyer?*

An initial response is that law hates a vacuum and, therefore lawyers and politicians will eventually push for additional regulations targeting blockchain technology and smart contracts–regulations that will look to lawyers to understand, interpret, and provide counsel. Ultimately, the smart contract may be viewed as a purely conventional technical mechanism, in particular as a convention of proof where the lawyer can organize the conditions and define rules, which could question the performance of a smart contract. It is not the smart contract itself which will be challenged, but the conditions of its implementation or its effects.

In other words, the smart contract is similar to other technical and non-technical mechanisms, which have existed for many years. For example, with debit cards used to withdraw money from an ATM is a type of smart contract or is smart contract-like in its implementation. Here, the input of the code together with the insertion of a debit card (conditions met) results automatically and irrevocably in the dispensing of money if the account has sufficient funds (second condition met). However, while this is carried out automatically, there is no assurance that the party withdrawing the money is the true holder of the credit/debit card. Where there is any challenge to this payment, it is not the smart contract (the automatic payment instruction) that is questioned but the legitimacy of the third party (usurpation of identity). This still allows the lawyer certain latitude in contesting the performance of such agreements.

In particular, the concept of a third partyis already recognized in smart contracts and the blockchain through the use of oracles. Lawyers or arbitrators may be the professions used as trusted oracles in certain cases. However, the use of lawyers to serve as oracles comes with risk–potential liability if the lawyer makes a bad decision or provides faulty information.

Thus, in view of the need to write clear agreements that can plausibly be coded, the likelihood of the enactment of targeted (blockchain) regulations, and the continued application of contract law to smart contracts, this new technology will not transplant the role currently played by lawyers. Furthermore, without further technological advancement, lawyers will still be needed in the context of the drafting of complex contracts. Moreover, agreements will still need to be drafted, whether or not they are to be implemented through the blockchain. The smart contract is thus not a competitor to the lawyer who drafts contracts. On the contrary, it reinforces the enforceability of the contract.

A final question is how to determine the economic model for the lawyer offering services relating to smart contracts. Indeed, in a relatively classic way, the lawyer is selling an intellectual service on a time basis. However, the point is whether the value of the smart contract will be based on the time spent in writing it, or on the service that it provides. This brings us back to something mentioned earlier, namely whether the lawyer needs to develop new skills as a software solution editor, in which case he will then no longer bill the work of producing and drafting a contract, but, instead, in accordance with a licence model, will bill for his work on the basis of the use which is made of them. I smart contracts are considered not to be legal contracts (but merely as an algorithms), then the service rendered by the lawyer is not within the core duties of lawyering (to provide legal advice) Instead if the services rendered involves the creation of a code, then payment to the lawyer could be based upon intrinsic value, since the smart contract would be 'an asset per se'. Here the value is not the contract but the algorithm that is qualified as a contract.

The smart contract presents opportunities for lawyers in terms of contract solutions, which are relatively simple to manage. It is however difficult to qualify it as a contract, as such, and at this stage, to recognize it as a tool which will come to replace the lawyer, if only due to the complexity of individual national laws. Such technology does not herald the demise of the lawyer, as more than 200 years have been spent modifying the law regarding obligations within the French Civil Code. However, the status of the lawyer may change with the introduction of advanced artificial intelligence in the drafting and implementation of contracts.

Part VI

Future of Smart Contracts, Blockchain and Artificial
Intelligence

17 Smart Transactional Technologies, Legal Disruption, and the Case of Network Contracts

Roger Brownsword[*]

17.1 Introduction

Writing in 1920, John Maynard Keynes remarked that

> [t]he inhabitant of London could order by telephone, sipping his morning tea in bed, the various products of the whole earth, in such quantity as he might see fit, and reasonably expect their early delivery upon his door-step; he could at the same moment and by the same means adventure his wealth in the natural resources and new enterprises of any quarter of the world ... without exertion or even trouble.[1]

Had he been writing in 2020, Keynes would no doubt have marvelled at the development of information and communication technologies that have facilitated the 24/7 ordering and speedy delivery of the various products of the earth – all without significant exertion or trouble; and he would have been intrigued by the prospect of the so-called smart contracts (running on networks of distributed machines) that automate transactions and take humans out of the loop.[2]

Prompted by these latest technologies and their transactional applications, in this chapter, I pose and respond to two questions. First, how might contract lawyers, judges, legislators, and regulators engage with a world in which contracts are self-enforcing and where commerce is, so to speak, largely conducted by means of a 'conversation conducted entirely among machines'?[3] Second, and much more specifically, if smart contracts are utilised in business 'networks' (such as franchising or carriage or

[*] I am grateful to Eliza Mik, who provided some particularly helpful comments on an earlier draft of this chapter. Needless to say, the usual disclaimers apply.

[1] John Maynard Keynes, *The Economic Consequences of the Peace* (New York: Harcourt, Brace, and Howe, 1920) 10–12, cited in Douglas W. Arner, Jànos Nathan Barberis, and Ross P. Buckley, 'The Evolution of Fintech: A New Post-Crisis Paradigm?' [2015] University of Hong Kong Faculty of Law Research Paper No 2015/047, University of New South Wales Law Research Series [2016] UNSWLRS 62: available at https://papers.ssrn.com/sol3/papers.cfm?abstract_id=2676553 (last accessed 9 December 2017).

[2] On which, see, e.g., Aaron Wright and Primavera De Filippi, 'Decentralized Blockchain Technology and the Rise of *Lex Cryptographia*', https://papers.ssrn.com/sol3/papers.cfm?abstract_id=2580664 (10 March 2015) (last accessed 27 January 2018); D. Tapscott and A. Tapscott, *Blockchain Revolution*, (London: Portfolio Penguin, 2016) 101–103; Eliza Mik, 'Smart Contracts: Terminology, Technical Limitations and Real World Complexity' (2017) 9 *Law Innovation and Technology* 269; Karen E. C. Levy, 'Book-Smart, Not Street-Smart: Blockchain-Based Smart Contracts and the Social Workings of Law' (2017) 3 *Engaging Science, Technology, and Society* 1; and Roger Brownsword, 'Smart Contracts: Coding the Transaction, Decoding the Legal Debates' in Philipp Hacker, Ioannis Lianos, Georgios Dimitropoulos, and Stefan Eich (eds) *Regulating Blockchain: Techno-Social and Legal Challenges* (Oxford: OUP, 2019) 311–326

[3] Per W. Brian Arthur, 'The Second Economy', *McKinsey Quarterly* (October 2011), quoted in Nicholas Carr, *The Glass Cage* (London: Vintage, 2015) at 197.

construction) – where the law of contract has been slow to recognise both third-party claims (even though the parties are 'economically connected') and the parties' expectations of heightened cooperative rights and responsibilities[4] – how will the same contract lawyers, judges, legislators and regulators respond? Might a transactional technology comprising networked machines or nodes be the answer to a set of questions presented by networked business relationships and in relation to which the law of contract is arguably unsatisfactory?[5]

The chapter is in three principal parts. After sketching the disruptive effect of technology on both the law and on the way that lawyers reason, I respond to the two focal questions that I have posed.

In the first part of the chapter, I describe how technological developments can disrupt both (i) the traditionally 'coherentist' way in which lawyers think and (ii) the idea of law (and regulation) as an enterprise of rules (and standard setting).[6] While the first of these disruptions serves to highlight the inadequacy of existing legal rules and to provoke not just changes to the rules but to the way that lawyers think (coherentism giving way to a more 'regulatory' approach), the second disruption challenges the assumption that the way in which regulatory effects are to be achieved is by laying down rules – instead, lawyers begin to take a more 'technocratic' approach, realising that regulatory effects can also be achieved by various technological measures (concerning, for example, the design of products or places, and the automation of processes).

In the second part of the chapter, responding directly to the first of my focal questions, I suggest that many contract lawyers and judges will continue to think in their traditional way, engaging with smart transactional technologies as 'coherentists' with their priority being to maintain the integrity of legal doctrine. However, at the same time, legislators (and others who are associated with the regulatory enterprise) will adopt a 'regulatory-instrumentalist' mind-set, where the priority is to enact laws that serve desired regulatory

---

[4] See, e.g., Marc Amstutz and Gunther Teubner (eds.), *Networks: Legal Issues of Multilateral Cooperation* (Oxford: Hart, 2009); Gunther Teubner, *Networks as Connected Contracts* (Oxford: Hart, 2011); Roger Brownsword, 'Contracts in a Networked World', in Larry DiMatteo, Qi Zhou, Severine Saintier, and Keith Rowley (eds.), *Commercial Contract Law: Transatlantic Perspectives* (Cambridge: Cambridge University Press, 2012) 116; Roger Brownsword, 'Contracts with Network Effects: Is the Time Now Right?' in Stefan Grundmann, Fabrizio Cafaggi, and Giuseppe Vettori (eds.), *The Organizational Contract: From Exchange to Long-Term Network Cooperation in European Contract Law* (Aldershot: Ashgate, 2013) 137; and the chapters on networks in Part Two of Roger Brownsword, Rob van Gestel, and Hans-W. Micklitz (eds.), *Contract and Regulation: A Handbook on New Methods of Law Making in Private Law* (Cheltenham: Edward Elgar, 2017).

[5] Specifically on smart contracts and networks, see Florian Idelberger, 'Connected Contracts Reloaded – Smart Contracts as Contractual Networks' in Stefan Grundmann (ed.), *European Contract Law in the Digital Age* (Cambridge: Intersentia, 2018) 205. But, nb, Stefan Grundmann and Philipp Hacker, 'The Digital Dimension as a Challenge to European Contract Law – The Architecture' in Stefan Grundmann (ed.) (n 5) 3, at 38 cautioning that we should take care in deriving 'lessons from arrangements in digital networks (typically highly formalised) for those in the analogue world'. For the question of whether the networked nodes might themselves form a contractual relationship (potentially leading to joint liability to third parties), see the excellent discussion in Dirk A. Zetzsche, Ross P. Buckley, and Douglas W. Arner, 'The Distributed Liability of Distributed Ledgers: Legal Risks of Blockchain' (European Banking Institute, EBI Working Paper Series 2017-No. 14) 26–27.

[6] Let me emphasise that technologies (as potential regulatory tools) do not necessarily disrupt the idea that 'law' is an enterprise of subjecting human conduct to the governance of rules. However, if jurists persist with the idea that 'regulation' is also exclusively a rule-based enterprise, we will miss an increasingly important articulation of the power to channel human behaviour. See, further, Roger Brownsword, 'Law as a Moral Judgment, the Domain of Jurisprudence, and Technological Management' in Patrick Capps and Shaun D. Pattinson (eds.), *Ethical Rationalism and the Law* (Oxford: Hart, 2016) 109.

purposes and where the conversation is typically about acceptable risk management. Where this mind-set operates in conjunction with a technocratic approach, we will find that there is a growing interest in co-opting new technologies (either alongside or in place of rules) as regulatory instruments. This plurality of coherentist, regulatory-instrumentalist, and technocratic perspectives might lead to some very different, confusing, and 'at cross-purposes' conversations about smart contracts.

In the third part of the chapter, I turn to the second of my focal questions, specifically concerning smart contracts and networks. Here, I sketch a number of coherentist responses to the use of smart contracts – whether in the setting of connected consumer contracts or in business networks – in the light of which it becomes clear that a central question concerns the compatibility of smart contract effects not just with the law of contract but with background public policy. To the extent that the most pressing questions are about public policy, I suggest that a regulatory-instrumentalist approach to the use of smart contracts (both generally and in networks) is a more direct and more adequate form of engagement than traditional coherentism. For example, regulatory instrumentalists will not waste time agonising about whether smart contracts are, so to speak, 'fiat' contracts in the sense recognised by the law of contract; if there are any doubts about this, and if these doubts interfere with regulatory purposes, they will simply be removed by legislative decree. However, regulatory-instrumentalist and technocratic thinking, guided by serving specified policy objectives, might fail to engage with the constitutive values of the particular community and, indeed, with the integrity of the preconditions for any form of human social existence. Accordingly, if we are to rectify these potentially fundamental shortcomings of regulatory-instrumentalist and technocratic thinking, we need to renew, revitalise, and reimagine our coherentist instincts.

My tentative conclusions are as follows. First, if smart contracts provide an answer to some problems in business and consumer networks but if there are traditional coherentist questions or reservations about this, then it might need a regulatory-instrumentalist intervention (rather than an *ad hoc* coherentist accommodation) to clear the way. Second, to the extent that the coherentist reservations raise questions of public policy, then they will need to be addressed in a regulatory-instrumentalist way. Third, although regulatory-instrumentalism (with a technocratic adjunct) might be a better way of responding to new transactional technologies, it suffers from some potentially serious shortcomings. If we are to remedy the situation, we need to act on two fronts. We need to articulate a renewed form of coherentist thinking in which new technologies (whether for transactions or interactions) are explicitly assessed for their compatibility with a community's fundamental values; and, we probably need to reform our legal and regulatory institutions, internationally and nationally, so that the new coherentist mission is firmly embedded in legal and regulatory practice.

17.2 Two Types of Disruption to the Law

It is trite that new technologies are economically and socially disruptive, impacting positively on some persons and groups but negatively on others.[7] Famously, for instance,

---

[7] Compare, e.g., Clayton M. Christensen, *The Innovator's Dilemma: When New Technologies Cause Great Firms to Fail* (Boston: Harvard Business Review Press, 1997); and Monroe E. Price, 'The Newness of New Technology' (2001) 22 *Cardozo Law Review* 1885.

Instagram, a small start-up in San Francisco, disrupted the photographic market in a way that benefitted millions but that wiped out Eastman Kodak, one of the biggest corporations in the world.[8] However, it is not just economies and social practices that are disrupted by the emergence of new technologies; the law and legal modes of thinking, too, are disrupted.[9] Revolutionary technologies disrupt, first, the substance of legal rules (we realise that the traditional rules are no longer fit for purpose) and, second, the idea that social ordering is to be achieved exclusively by the use of legal rules (we realise that regulatory effects can be achieved by technological measures).

17.2.1 First Disruption

The first disruptive wave impacts on legal doctrines that were expressed in smaller-scale non-industrialised communities. Here, the legal rules presuppose very straightforward ideas about holding those who engage intentionally in injurious or dishonest acts to account, about expecting others to act with reasonable care, and about holding others to their word. Once new technologies disrupt these ideas, we see the move to strict or absolute criminal liability without proof of intent,[10] to tortious liability without proof of fault,[11] and to contractual liability (or limitation of liability) without proof of actual intent, agreement, or consent. Even if the development in contract is less clear at this stage, in both criminal law and torts we can see the early signs of a risk management approach to liability. Moreover, we also see the early signs of doctrinal bifurcation, with some parts of criminal law, tort law, and contract law resting on traditional principles (and representing, so to speak, 'real' crime, tort, and contract) while others deviate from these principles – often holding enterprises to account more readily but also sometimes easing the burden on business for the sake of beneficial innovation[12] – in order to strike a more acceptable balance of the benefits and risks that technological development brings with it.

---

[8] Evidently, in its final years, Kodak closed 13 factories and 130 photolabs, and cut 47,000 jobs. See, Andrew Keen, *The Internet is not the Answer* (London: Atlantic Books, 2015) 87–88.

[9] See, e.g., Richard Susskind and Daniel Susskind, *The Future of the Professions* (Oxford: Oxford University Press, 2015).

[10] Seminally, see, F.B Sayre, 'Public Welfare Offences' (1933) 33 *Columbia Law Review* 55. As Sayre remarks, the world was changing: the 'invention and extensive use of high-powered automobiles require new forms of traffic regulation; … the growth of modern factories requires new forms of labor regulation; the development of modern building construction and the growth of skyscrapers require new forms of building regulation' and so on (at 68–69).

[11] See Miquel Martin-Casals (ed.), *The Development of Liability in Relation to Technological Change* (Cambridge: Cambridge University Press, 2010). In their Preface to the collection, John Bell and David Ibbetson suggest that, with the development of new technologies, we can see the beginnings of a movement from 'tort' to 'regulation'. Thus (at viii):

> We see the way in which regulatory law, private insurance and state-run compensation schemes developed to deal with the issues the law now confronted. Regulatory law and inspections by officials and private insurers and associations dealt with many of the issues of preventing accidents. Compensation systems outside tort offered remedies to many of the victims of accidents. In this matrix of legal interventions, we can see that the place of tort law and of fault in particular changes. We become aware of [tort law's] limitations.

[12] For example, in the United States, the interests of the farming community were subordinated to the greater good promised by the development of the railroad network: see Morton J. Horwitz, *The Transformation of American Law 1780–1860* (Cambridge, MA: Harvard University Press, 1977).

In the case of contract law, the technologies of the nineteenth century had a significant disruptive effect on 'transactionalist' doctrine. Notably, there was a shift from a 'subjective' consensual (purely transactional) model to an 'objective' approach. In the United States, as Morton Horwitz puts it, against the background of an 'increasingly national corporate economy, the goal of standardization of commercial transactions began to overwhelm the desire to conceive of contract law as expressing the subjective desires of individuals'.[13] At the same time, in English law, in addition to the general shift to an objective approach, there was a particularly significant shift to a reasonable notice model in relation to the incorporation of the terms and conditions on which carriers (of both goods and persons) purported to contract. In the jurisprudence, this latter shift is symbolised by Mellish LJ's direction to the jury in *Parker v South Eastern Railway Co*,[14] where the legal test was said to be not so much whether a customer actually was aware of the terms and had agreed to them but whether the railway company had given reasonable notice. In effect, this introduced an objective test; but, as Stephen Waddams has pointed out, there was an even more radical view, this being expressed in Bramwell LJ's judgement, the emphasis of which is 'entirely on the reasonableness of the railway's conduct of its business and on the unreasonableness of the customers' claims; there is no concession whatever to the notion that they could only be bound by their actual consent'.[15] With this embrace of objectivism and reasonableness, contract law was able to shield the carriers of the nineteenth century against otherwise crippling claims for compensation (when valuable packages were lost or when there were accidents on the railways); and when, in the middle years of the last century, a mass consumer market for new technological products (cars, televisions, kitchen appliances, and so on) developed, it was able to make a fundamental correction to the traditional values of 'freedom of contract' and 'sanctity of contract' in order to protect consumers against the small print of suppliers' standard terms and conditions. Today, at any rate in the English law of consumer contracts, the abandonment of transactionalist thinking is complete. Following the Consumer Rights Act 2015, we can say that consumers engage, not so much in contracts, but in regulated transactions.

So, while intentionality and fault were set aside in the regulatory parts of criminal law and torts, classical transactionalist ideas of consent and agreement were marginalised in the *mainstream* of contract law, being replaced by 'objective' tests and standards set by reasonable business practice. In short, again to quote Horwitz, with the disruption of legal rules, there was a dawning sense that 'all law was a reflection of collective determination, and thus inherently regulatory and coercive'.[16]

17.2.2 Second Disruption

The second legally disruptive wave happens when, in already-industrialised societies, the technologies that are developed present themselves as tools that can be applied for

---

[13] Morton J. Horwitz, *The Transformation of American Law 1870–1960* (Oxford: Oxford University Press, 1992) at 37. At 48–49, Horwitz notes a parallel transformation in relation to both corporate forms and agency.

[14] (1877) 2 C.P.D. 416.

[15] Stephen Waddams, *Principle and Policy in Contract Law* (Cambridge: Cambridge University Press, 2011) at 39.

[16] Horwitz (note 13) at 50.

regulatory purposes. Arguably, this second disruption (manifesting itself in the turn to architecture, design, coding, and the like as regulatory tools) is as old as the (defensive) architecture of the pyramids and the target-hardening use of locks. However, the variety and sophistication of the instruments of technological management that are available to regulators today is strikingly different to the position in both preindustrial and early industrial societies. Whether or not this amounts to a difference of kind or merely one of degree scarcely seems important; we live in different times, with significantly different regulatory technologies. In particular, there is much more to 'technological management',[17] as I would term it, than traditional target-hardening: the management involved might – by designing products and places, or by coding products and people – disable or exclude potential wrongdoers as much as harden targets or immunise potential victims; and there is now the prospect of widespread automation that takes humans altogether out of the regulatory equation. Crucially, with a risk management approach well established, regulators now find that they have the option of responding by employing various technological instruments rather than rules. This is the moment when, so to speak, we see a very clear contrast between the legal and the regulatory style of the East Coast (whether traditional or progressive) and the style of the West Coast.[18]

Two things are characteristic of technological management. First, as I have emphasised elsewhere, unlike rules, the focus of the regulatory intervention is on the practical (not the paper) options of regulatees.[19] Second, whereas legal rules back their prescriptions with *ex post* penal, compensatory, or restorative measures, the focus of technological management is entirely *ex ante*, aiming to anticipate and prevent wrongdoing rather than punish or compensate after the event. As Lee Bygrave puts it in the context of the design of information systems and the protection of both IPRs and privacy, the assumption is that, by embedding norms in the architecture, there is 'the promise of a significantly increased *ex ante* application of the norms and a corresponding reduction in relying on their application *ex post facto*'.[20]

This evolution in regulatory thinking is not surprising. Having recognised the limited fitness of traditional legal rules, and having taken a more regulatory approach, the next step surely is to think not just in terms of risk assessment and risk management but also to be mindful of the technological instruments that increasingly become available for use by regulators. In this way, the regulatory mind-set is focused not only on the risks to be managed but also on how best to manage those risks (including making use of technological tools).

For example, with the development of computers and then the Internet and World Wide Web supporting a myriad of applications, it is clear that, when individuals operate in online environments, they are at risk in relation to both their 'privacy' and the fair processing of their personal data. Initially, regulators assumed that 'transactionalism'

---

[17] See Roger Brownsword, 'Technological Management and the Rule of Law' (2016) 8 *Law, Innovation and Technology* 100.

[18] Seminally, see Lawrence Lessig, *Code and Other Laws of Cyberspace* (New York: Basic Books, 1999). See, too, Roger Brownsword, 'Code, Control, and Choice: Why East Is East and West Is West' (2005) 25 *Legal Studies* 1.

[19] See, e.g., Roger Brownsword, 'Whither the Law and the Law Books: From Prescription to Possibility' (2012) 39 *Journal of Law and Society* 296; and 'Law, Liberty and Technology' in Roger Brownsword, Eloise Scotford, and Karen Yeung (eds.), *The Oxford Handbook of Law, Regulation and Technology* (Oxford: Oxford University Press, 2017) 41.

[20] Lee A. Bygrave, 'Hardwiring Privacy' in Brownsword, Scotford, and Yeung (note 19) 754, at 755.

would suffice to protect individuals: in other words, it was assumed that, unless the relevant individuals agreed to, or consented to, the processing of their details, it would not be lawful. However, once it was evident that consumers in online environments routinely signalled their agreement or consent in a mechanical way, without doing so on a free and informed basis, a more robust risk-management approach invited consideration. As Eliza Mik, writing about the privacy policies of internet companies, puts the alternative:

> What could be done . . . is to cease treating privacy policies *as if* they were contracts and evaluate consent and disclosure requirements from a purely regulatory perspective. Enhanced, or express, consent requirements may constitute a good first step. It could, however, also be claimed that the only solution lies in an outright prohibition of certain technologies or practices. In this context, the difficulty lies in regulatory target setting. The first overriding question is what is it that we are trying to protect? It can hardly be assumed that the 'protection of autonomy' is sufficiently precise to provide regulatory guidance.[21]

We might, however, take this a step further. Once we are thinking about the protection of the autonomy of internet users or about the protection of their privacy, why not also consider the use of technological instruments in service of the regulatory objectives (provided that they can be specified in a sufficiently precise way)? Indeed, writing in the context of non-negotiable terms and conditions in online consumer contracts, Joshua Fairfield expresses just this thought when he remarks that 'if courts [or, we might say, the rules of contract law] will not protect consumers, robots will'.[22] Imagine, for example, that regulators or consumers (just like legal practitioners) were able to rely on smart machines to scan online terms and conditions to see which, if any, were arguably unfair;[23] or imagine that a supplier's standard terms and conditions had to be displayed in a format that would not permit anything other than clearly fair terms. While, in the former case, a technocratic intervention might support a transactionalist view, in the latter it might achieve a more acceptable regulatory balance of interests.

Having seen how the development of new technologies can shake up our thinking about the law, we now need to look more carefully at the way in which contract lawyers, judges, and legislators are likely to frame their thinking about smart transactional technologies.

17.3 Two Responses to Smart Transactional Technologies: Coherentist and Regulatory-Instrumentalist

I have suggested that technological developments have disrupted traditional legal thinking in two ways: first, by prompting lawyers to ask whether the traditional rules are fit for purpose and then by opening up the possibility of supporting, or even supplanting, rules with technological measures. I will say more about the turn to a technocratic approach in

---

[21] Eliza Mik, 'Persuasive Technologies – From Loss of Privacy to Loss of Autonomy' in Kit Barker, Karen Fairweather, and Ross Grantham (eds.), *Private Law in the 21st Century* (Oxford: Hart, 2017) 363, at 386.

[22] Joshua Fairfield, 'Smart Contracts, Bitcoin Bots, and Consumer Protection' (2014) 71 *Washington and Lee Law Review Online* 36, at 39.

[23] Compare Hans-W Micklitz, Przemyslaw Palka, and Yannis Panagis, 'The Empire Strikes Back: Digital Control of Unfair Terms of Online Services' (2017) 40 *Journal of Consumer Policy* 367.

due course. However, in this part of the chapter, I want to focus, first, on the contrast between a traditional coherentist mind-set and a regulatory-instrumentalist mind-set and then on the location of these mind-sets in courts, legislative bodies, and regulatory agencies.

17.3.1 Coherentism and Regulatory Instrumentalism

According to Edward Rubin, we live in the age of modern administrative states where the law is used 'as a means of implementing the policies that [each particular state] adopts. The rules that are declared, and the statutes that enact them, have no necessary relationship with one another; they are all individual and separate acts of will'.[24] In other words:

> Regulations enacted by administrative agencies that the legislature or elected chief executive has authorized are related to the authorizing statute, but have no necessary connection with each other or to regulations promulgated under a different exercise of legislative or executive authority.[25]

In the modern administrative state, the 'standard for judging the value of law is not whether it is coherent but rather whether it is effective, that is, effective in establishing and implementing the policy goals of the modern state'.[26] By contrast, the distinctive feature of 'coherentism' is the idea that law forms 'a coherent system, a set of rules that are connected by some sort of logical relationship to each other'[27] – or 'a system of rules that fit together in a consistent logically elaborated pattern'.[28]

Drawing on Rubin, we can construct two ideal-typical mind-sets. One ideal-type, 'regulatory-instrumentalism', views the rules of contract law as a means to implement whatever policy goals have been adopted by the state; the adequacy and utility of contract law is to be assessed by its effectiveness in delivering these goals. The other ideal-type is 'coherentism', according to which the adequacy of the law of contract is to be assessed by reference to the doctrinal consistency and integrity of its rules.

17.3.2 Three Strands of Coherentist Thinking

While coherentism is distinguished by its desire for the integrity of doctrine, it comprises several strands of thinking.[29] Here, three strands are highlighted: formal, substantive, and classificatory (or template) coherence.

17.3.2.1 Formal (Internal) Coherence of Contract Doctrine

Common lawyers expect there to be a consistency and internal coherence within the body of precedents, rules, and principles that comprise the law of contract. Clearly, there might be some transactional uncertainty and inefficiency if rules that are regularly relied

---

[24] Edward L. Rubin, 'From Coherence to Effectiveness' in Rob van Gestel, Hans-W Micklitz, and Edward L. Rubin (eds.), *Rethinking Legal Scholarship* (New York: Cambridge University Press, 2017) 310 at 311.
[25] Rubin (note 24) at 311.
[26] Rubin (note 24) at 328.
[27] Rubin (note 24) at 312.
[28] Rubin (note 24) at 313.
[29] See, further, Roger Brownsword, 'After Brexit: Regulatory-Instrumentalism, Coherentism, and the English Law of Contract' (2018) 35 *Journal of Contract Law* 139.

on seem to be contradictory or in tension. However, one of the golden threads of traditional contract law jurisprudence is that the formal coherence of the law is viewed as desirable in and of itself.[30] Little more needs to be said: lawyers tend to default to this mode of thinking; it is entirely familiar. Crucially, while formal coherence calls for doctrine to be checked upwards, downwards, sideways, and backwards, it never looks forwards.

17.3.2.2 Substantive Coherence

In Edward Rubin's account of coherentism, the law not only displays an internal consistency and integrity, it also expresses and concretises higher 'natural law' principles, all this being distilled by an intellectual elite applying their rational wisdom.[31] Although there might be residual traces of such top-down 'pre-modern' thinking (as Rubin puts it), modern coherentism takes a more bottom-up approach, articulating principles that are generally judged to be both reasonable and workable.

In an influential article, as well as in a string of judgements, Lord Steyn proclaimed that the law of contract should be guided by the simple ideal of fulfilling the expectations of honest and reasonable people.[32] If Lord Steyn had said this about the law of negligence (where the reasonable man standard is both settled and prominent), it would have been unremarkable. However, to say this about the law of contract, with its traditional rhetoric of giving effect to the parties' will or intentions, was a significant intervention – and, crucially, it captures the coherentist idea that the law of contract should reflect those few simple principles that inform the everyday practice of transactors, whether they are buying or selling in the consumer marketplace or dealing in commercial markets. These simple principles include that parties should be free to choose both their own contracting partners and their own terms and conditions; that contracts are made to be performed; and that basic standards of honesty, fair dealing, and reasonableness should apply.

17.3.2.3 Classificatory or Template Coherence

We can introduce a third strand of coherentism by imagining a bookshop that has operated for a long time with a particular classificatory scheme, one that has served it well. The scheme starts with fiction and non-fiction but then it employs various subclasses. When new books arrive at the shop, they are shelved in accordance with this scheme. Occasionally, there will need to be some discussion about the right place to

---

[30] To take just one example, see Arden LJ in *Stena Line v Merchant Navy Ratings Pension Fund Trustees Limited* [2011] EWCA Civ 543, at [36]:

> In *Belize*, the Privy Council analysed the case law on the implication of terms and decided that the implication of terms is, in essence, an exercise in interpretation. This development promotes the internal coherence of the law by emphasising the role played by the principles of interpretation not only in the context of the interpretation of documents *simpliciter* but also in the field of the implication of terms. Those principles are the unifying factor. The internal coherence of the law is important because it enables the courts to identify the aims and values that underpin the law and to pursue those values and aims so as to achieve consistency in the structure of the law.

[31] Rubin (note 24).

[32] Seminally, see Johan Steyn, 'Contract Law: Fulfilling the Reasonable Expectations of Honest Men' (1997) 113 *Law Quarterly Review* 433.

shelve a particular book but this is pretty exceptional. In general, booksellers and customers alike know where to find the titles in which they are interested. However, with an explosion of books about new technologies – about genetics and the Internet, about neuro-technologies and nanotechnologies, about artificial intelligence (AI) and machine learning, and about blockchain and 3D printing – the bookshop finds that it has no ready-made class for these titles. Some of these books might be shelved, albeit imperfectly, under 'science fiction' or 'popular science', some under 'current affairs', some under 'smart thinking', and so on. For a time, the bookshop persists with its historic classification scheme, but these new books are shelved in ways that stretch and distort their classificatory indicators. An external consultant (reasoning in a way that is analogous to that of regulatory-instrumentalists) would advise that the classificatory scheme is no longer fit for purpose that it needs to be revised. However, the bookshop soldiers on, determined to find a place for these new titles in its old and evidently outdated scheme.

So it is with coherentists in the law. The law, like the bookshop, has its traditional classificatory scheme, its traditional templates. Faced with new technologies, the coherentist tendency is to apply the existing legal framework (the traditional template) to innovations that bear on transactions, or to try to accommodate novel forms of contracting within the existing categories. We need only recall Lord Wilberforce's much-cited catalogue of the heroic efforts made by the courts – confronted by modern forms of transport, various kinds of automation, and novel business practices – to force 'the facts to fit uneasily into the marked slots of offer, acceptance and consideration'[33] or whatever other traditional categories of the law of contract might be applicable.

With the advent of twenty-first century transactional technologies, the story continues; coherentism persists. For example, coherentists will puzzle about whether e-mails should be classified as either instantaneous or non-instantaneous forms of communication (or transmission),[34] they will want to apply the standard formation template to online shopping sites, they will draw on traditional notions of agency in order to engage electronic agents and smart machines,[35] they will want to classify individual 'prosumers' and 'hobbyists' who buy and sell on new platforms (such as platforms that support trade in 3D printed goods) as either business sellers or consumers,[36] and they will be challenged by agreements for the supply of digital content being unsure whether to classify such contracts as being for the supply of goods or the supply of services.[37] As the infrastructure

---

[33] As Lord Wilberforce put it in *New Zealand Shipping Co Ltd v A.M. Satterthwaite and Co Ltd : The Eurymedon* [1975] AC 154, 167. For a somewhat similar view, see Nicolas Petit, 'Law and Regulation of Artificial Intelligence and Robots: Conceptual Framework and Normative Implications' at 6: available at https://papers.ssrn.com/sol3/papers.cfm?abstract_id=2931339 (last accessed 17 February 2018).

[34] See, e.g., Andrew Murray, 'Entering into Contracts Electronically: the Real WWW' in Lilian Edwards and Charlotte Waelde (eds.), *Law and the Internet: A Framework for Electronic Commerce* (Oxford: Hart, 2000) 17; and Eliza Mik, 'The Effectiveness of Acceptances Communicated by Electronic Means, Or – Does the Postal Acceptance Rule Apply to Email?' (2009) 26 *Journal of Contract Law* 68 (concluding that such classificatory attempts should be abandoned).

[35] Compare, e.g., Emily Weitzenboeck, 'Electronic Agents and the Formation of Contracts' (2001) 9 *International Journal of Law and Information Technology* 204.

[36] Compare e.g., Christian Twigg-Flesner, 'Conformity of 3D Prints – Can Current Sales Law Cope?' in R. Schulze and D. Staudenmayer (eds.), *Digital Revolution: Challenges for Contract Law in Practice* (Baden-Baden: Nomos, 2016) 35.

[37] As Christian Twigg-Flesner points out in 'Disruptive Technology – Disrupted Law?' in Alberto De Franceschi (ed.), *European Contract Law and the Digital Single Market* (Cambridge: Intersentia, 2016) 21 at 32, '[n]either [classification] seems to make particularly good sense'.

for transactions becomes ever more technological, the tension between this strand of coherentism and regulatory-instrumentalism becomes all the more apparent.

17.3.3 Courts, Legislatures, and Regulatory Agencies

There is no standard operating procedure for engaging with new technologies: legal and regulatory responses to emerging technologies vary from one technology to another, from one legal system to another, and from one time to another. Sometimes, there is extensive public engagement, sometimes not. On occasion, special commissions (such as the now defunct Human Genetics Commission in the UK) have been set up with a dedicated oversight remit; and there have been examples of standing technology foresight commissions (such as the, also defunct, US Office of Technology Assessment);[38] but, often, there is nothing of this kind. Most importantly, questions about new technologies sometimes surface, first, in litigation (leaving it to the courts to determine how to respond) and, at other times, they are presented to the legislature.

With regard to the question of which regulatory body engages with new technologies and how, there can of course be some local agency features that shape the answers. Where, as in the United States, there is a particular regulatory array with each agency having its own remit, a new technology might be considered in just one lead agency or it might be assessed in several agencies.[39] Once again, there is a degree of happenstance about this. Nevertheless, in a preliminary way, we can make three general points.

First, if the question (such as that posed by a compensatory claim made by a claimant who alleges harm caused by a new technology) is put to the courts, their responsibility for the integrity of the law will push them towards a coherentist assessment. Typically, courts are neither sufficiently resourced nor mandated to undertake a risk assessment let alone adopt a risk management strategy (unless the legislature has already put in place a scheme that delegates such a responsibility to the courts).[40]

Second, if the question finds its way into the legislative arena, it is much more likely that politicians will engage with it in a regulatory-instrumentalist way; and, once the possibility of technological measures gets onto the radar, it is much more likely that (as with institutions in the EU) we will see a more technocratic mind-set.

Third, in some regulatory agencies there might already be a mind-set that is focused on making use of new technologies to improve performance relative to the agency's particular objectives (such as those relating to consumer protection or competition). For example, the UK Financial Conduct Authority is conspicuously sensitised to 'reg tech' (in the sense of utilising information technologies to enhance regulatory processes with

---

[38] On which, see Bruce Bimber, *The Politics of Expertise in Congress* (Albany: State University of New York Press, 1996) charting the rise and fall of the Office and drawing out some important tensions between 'neutrality' and 'politicisation' in the work of such agencies.

[39] Compare, Albert C. Lin, 'Size Matters: Regulating Nanotechnology' (2007) 31 *Harvard Environmental Law Review* 349.

[40] Perhaps we should view Patent Offices in this light. In the 1980s, there were major decisions to be made about the patentability of biotechnological products and processes, models of which could not be brought into the office to demonstrate how they worked and which also raised complex moral issues. For extended discussion, see Alain Pottage and Brad Sherman, *Figures of Invention: A History of Modern Patent Law* (Oxford: Oxford University Press, 2010); and, on the moral dimension of these debates, see Deryck Beyleveld and Roger Brownsword, *Mice, Morality and Patents* (London: Common Law Institute of Intellectual Property, 1993).

a particular emphasis on monitoring, reporting, and compliance).[41] Thus, the Authority recently announced that it was seeking views on the use of technology to make it easier for firms to meet their regulatory reporting requirements and, with that, to improve the quality of the information available to the agency.[42] Elaborating on this, the Authority said:

> The FCA regularly explores how technology can make our regulations more efficient and reduce the regulatory burden on firms. One of the ways we do this is through 'TechSprints' that bring together financial services providers, technology companies and subject matter experts to develop solutions to regulatory challenges.
>
> In November 2017, the FCA and the Bank of England, held a two-week TechSprint to examine how technology can make the current system of regulatory reporting more accurate, efficient and consistent. All regulated firms submit data to the FCA based on their financial activities. The data received from these regulatory reports are critical to our ability to deliver effective supervision, monitor markets and detect financial crime.
>
> At the TechSprint, participants successfully developed a 'proof of concept' which could make regulatory reporting requirements machine-readable and executable. This means that firms could map the reporting requirements directly to the data that they hold, creating the potential for automated, straight-through processing of regulatory returns.
>
> This could benefit both firms and regulators. For example, the accuracy of data submissions could be improved and their costs reduced, changes to regulatory require-ments could be implemented more quickly, and a reduction in compliance costs could lower barriers to entry and promote competition.[43]

As this elaboration highlights, when a technocratic approach is applied to the regulatory enterprise, it can impact on thinking in all dimensions of that enterprise – on rule-making and standard setting (including whether a technological measure will perform better than a rule), on monitoring compliance, and on detecting and correcting non-compliance.

Summing up, the technological disruptions of the last couple of centuries have provoked a fractured legal and regulatory discourse which we can expect to be directed at smart transactional technologies. There are historic conventions about which institu-tions engage in which kinds of conversations (at any rate, explicitly so)[44] but whether or not these institutional arrangements are now fit for purpose is a question that is open for debate.

---

[41] See https://en.wikipedia.org/wiki/Regulatory_technology (last accessed 28 July 2018).

[42] FCA Press Release 20/02/2018. Available at www.fca.org.uk/news/press-releases/fca-launches-call-input-use-technology-achieve-smarter-regulatory-reporting (last accessed 28 July 2018).

[43] Ibid.

[44] The extent to which the courts do, or should, depart from questions of coherence and principle in order to purse questions of policy (in the fashion of legislators and regulators) is a long-standing bone of contention. Seminally, see Ronald Dworkin, *Taking Rights Seriously* (rev. edn.) (London: Duckworth, 1978); and, compare, Compare Albert A. Ehrenzweig, 'Negligence without Fault' (1966) 54 *California Law Review* 1422, at 1476–1477:

> The negligence rule, though phrased in terms of fault, has with regard to tort liabilities for dangerous enterprise, come to exercise a function of loss distribution previously developed mainly within rules of strict liability. This new function of 'fault' liability has transformed its central concept of reprehensible conduct and 'foreseeability' of harm in a way foreign to its language and original rationale and has thus produced in our present 'negligence' language a series of misleading equivocations.

17.4 Two Responses to Smart Contracts and Networks

In this final part of the chapter, I will speak to the debate about networks and contract law and then sketch how I would expect coherentists and regulatory-instrumentalists, respectively, to engage in these debates where smart contracts are now part of the conversation.

17.4.1 *Networks and the Law of Contract*

According to the classical view, a contract comprises a reciprocal exchange between two parties, A and B. Moreover, the frame of reference is given exclusively by the deal between A and B.[45] However, in much modern business practice, the contract between A and B is connected to contracts with C, D, and others – whether by way of hub and spoke organisation (as in franchises), or by way of chains (as in the carriage and distribution of goods), or in clusters (as in construction), and so on. Moreover, we can also see connected contracts in the financing of consumer transactions, in supply chains and after-sale care for consumers, and in the platforms for the supply of goods and services in the share economy. If we stick with the classical view, the law of contract can fall short in meeting the expectations generated by these networked contracts.

Primarily, it has been the expectations created as between those who are parties to a network (i.e. expectations that are internal to a particular network) that have been the focal reference point for critical assessments of the law of contract. However, it should be noted that networked arrangements might also generate (external) expectations on the part of those who, while not network members, deal with parties who are network members. Moreover, where such networked arrangements are represented by the distributed (but connected) nodes of an autonomous organisation, smart contracts might themselves generate significant external expectations (concerning joint and several liability, collective responsibility, and the like).[46] In the present discussion, though, the focus is on the relationships between those who are parties to a network of contracts and the perceived shortcoming of the traditional law of contract in fulfilling the reasonable (internal) expectations of such parties.

In response to this perceived shortcoming, it has been suggested that the law of contract should be more receptive to the idea of 'network contracts' or 'contracts with network effects' – ideas that have been floated in the academic literature but that have not yet been taken up in mainstream contractual thinking.[47] There are many reasons for being

---

[45] As Ian R. Macneil put it in *The New Social Contract* (New Haven: Yale University Press, 1980) at 61: 'A and B had better be the *only* parties; adding C, D, and other such riffraff is bound to create complicated relations outside the transaction.'

[46] For helpful discussion of this possibility, see Dirk A. Zetzsche, Ross P. Buckley, and Douglas W. Arner (note 5).

[47] For 'networks' as a response to the restrictive third-party rules in English law, see, e.g., John N. Adams and Roger Brownsword, 'Privity and the Concept of a Network Contract' (1990) 10 *Legal Studies* 12; John N. Adams and Roger Brownsword, *Key Issues in Contract* (London: Butterworths, 1995) Ch. 5; and John N. Adams, Deryck Beyleveld, and Roger Brownsword, 'Privity of Contract – The Benefits and the Burdens of Law Reform' (1997) 60 *Modern Law Review* 238. For a second tranche of contractual networks literature, see: Fabrizio Cafaggi, 'Contractual Networks and the Small Business Act: Towards European Principles?' (2008) 4 *European Review of Contract Law* 493; Fabrizio Cafaggi (ed.), *Contractual Networks, Inter-Firm Cooperation and Economic Growth* (Cheltenham: Edward Elgar, 2011); Marc Amstutz and Gunther Teubner (note 4); Gunther Teubner, '"And if I by Beelzebub Cast Out Devils, … ": An Essay on the Diabolics of Network Failure' (2009) 10 *German Law Journal* 395; Gunther Teubner (note 4); Roger Brownsword (note 4); and the chapters on networks in Brownsword, van Gestel and Micklitz (note 4).

attracted by the idea that there should be an explicit doctrinal coding for networks – for example, that such a coding would develop the shape of contract thinking in a way that brings it more closely into alignment with networked forms of economic organisation and business practice; that it would present the opportunity to specify distinctive and desired legal effects – particularly effects that tend towards the heightening of cooperative contractual obligations and the recognition of connected third-party interests; that it would facilitate a more appropriate framing of questions concerning the fairness of exclusion and limitation clauses in connected contracts;[48] and that, by releasing courts from the shackles of classical contract thinking, doctrinal recognition of networks would reduce the artificiality (and increase the transparency) of judicial reasoning.

Over the last twenty years, the emergence in the English law of contract of a more 'contextual' approach has given grounds for thinking that an approach that is more sensitised to networks might evolve.[49] However, in a trio of recent decisions, the Supreme Court has drawn back on this approach – notably, in *Marks and Spencer plc v BNP Paribas Services Trust Company (Jersey) Limited*[50] (on implied terms); and *Arnold v Britton*[51] and *Wood v Capita Insurance Services Ltd*[52] (on interpretation) – reacting against expansive implication and interpretation of terms, particularly in carefully drafted commercial contracts. Although these cases are not concerned with networks as such, the push-back against contextualist thinking does not give any encouragement to the view that the law of contract is about to take a more responsive approach.

But, might there be another way of achieving the desired network effects? Imagine that smart contract technologies are able to automate payments to third parties or code in the kind of cooperative responsibilities that network contractors tend to expect. Imagine that, in a case such as *Clarke v Dunraven*,[53] the transactional technologies were such that, once a collision between the competitors' yachts was reported, compensatory payment at the level specified by the competition rules was transferred from one party's account to the other party's account. So far so good, but there might also be cases where network effects that are activated are not so straightforward. For example, what if a network member is able to immobilise a vehicle where the consumer purchaser or lessee has failed to make payment on time? How are coherentists and regulatory-instrumentalists likely to respond to such technological effects where they are not congruent with the outcomes that the law of contract would endorse and the courts would enforce?[54]

---

[48] See, e.g., Roger Brownsword, 'Network Contracts Revisited', in Amstutz and Teubner (note 4) 31.

[49] See, e.g., Roger Brownsword, 'The Law of Contract: Doctrinal Impulses, External Pressures, Future Directions' (2014) 31 *Journal of Contract Law* 73.

[50] [2015] UKSC 72.

[51] [2015] UKSC 36.

[52] [2017] UKSC 24.

[53] [1897] AC 59. In this case, the courts did actually hold that the competitors were bound inter se (as in a network) by the competition rules. However, to square this with classical doctrine, competitors in the yacht race were treated not only as offerors (in relation to fellow competitors) when they had no awareness that they were acting in this role but also (the first entrant apart) as acceptors of offers of which they were unaware.

[54] Compare Wright and De Filippi (note 2) at 26. Here, having raised the question of 'what is legally versus technically binding', and having noted that there might be some divergence between what the law of contract will enforce or invalidate and what smart contracts, operating 'within their own closed technological framework', will enforce or invalidate, the authors conclude that while 'implementing basic contractual safeguards and consumer protection provisions into smart contracts is theoretically possible, it may prove difficult given the formalized and deterministic character of code'. However, beyond the question of technical possibility, there is the question of how the state manages the conflict between the law of contract,

17.4.2 *Networks, Smart Contracts, and Coherentism*

According to Aaron Wright and Primavera De Filippi, the implementation of blockchain-based governance, with 'transparent decision-making procedures and ... decentralized incentives systems for collaboration and cooperation could make it easier for small and large communities to reach consensus and implement innovative forms of self-governance'.[55] If this prospect were to encourage the development and use of smart contract technologies in network settings, then how would it be viewed by coherentists? Let me suggest some questions that contract lawyers, guided by coherentist thoughts, might ask about smart transactional technologies in commercial networks.

First, what might coherentists make of the technological connection between parties to a network where the law of contract would not otherwise recognise a contractual relationship? Might the technological connection be treated as the equivalent of a standard contractual connection? This will be a particular instance of the general question of whether smart contracts are fiat contracts (e.g. in the sense of being an exchange of promises, or an exchange of a promise in return for an act).[56] Of course, if nothing of any practical importance hinges on the answer to this question, it will be purely academic. Where the technology performs as intended or where a practical problem can be remedied either by a technological measure or by a court order (such as an order for restitution[57]) that does not hinge on the existence of a contract or a finding of a breach of contract, there is no need to agonise about the characterisation of smart contracts. Indeed, even if there is pressure to recognise smart contracts as legally binding and enforceable transactions, so long as smart contracts are used as tools to give effect to the payment obligations of a fiat contract, the difficulty of this first coherentist question has surely been overstated.[58] Quite simply, the reference point for the application of the law will be the background fiat contract, not the smart contract tool that has been used. By contrast, where the coherentist question does become difficult, it is probably no longer the right question to be asking. Nevertheless, the coherentist instinct will be to try to force ill-fitting technological facts into the standard legal template.

Second, coherentists might ask whether the intended technological effects should be treated as a signal of the parties' intentions, as an analogue to express terms in a contract. If they are so treated, this would ease many concerns about whether particular technological effects are compatible with or congruent with the law of contract. For example, if the technological effects are treated as equivalent to express terms for cooperation, or for good faith, or for termination or withdrawal, and so on, this will simply neutralise the objection that such effects would not normally be *implied*. In other words, if the effect of a smart contract is viewed as being analogous to provision made by an express term in a traditional

---

consumer and commercial, and the actual operation of smart contracts. In other words, is there an implicit requirement that the latter should be congruent with the former?

[55] Wright and De Filippi (note 2), at 38. See, too, Primavera De Filippi and Aaron Wright, *Blockchain and the Law* (Cambridge, MA: Harvard University Press, 2018).

[56] For example, see the discussion in Kevin Werbach and Nicolas Cornell, 'Contracts *Ex Machina*' (2017) 67 *Duke Law Journal* 313, at 338 et seq.

[57] In English law, the decision of the UK Supreme Court in *Patel v Mirza* [2016] UKSC 42 has significantly raised the profile of a possible restitutionary response to claims arising in connection with illegal contracts.

[58] Roger Brownsword, 'Regulatory Fitness: Fintech, Funny Money, and Smart Contracts' (2019) 20 *European Business Organization Law Review* 5–27. See, too, De Filippi and Wright (note 55), pp. 74 et seq. At p. 78, we read: 'Even where smart contracts entirely replace formal legal agreements, these programs do not operate in a vacuum.'

contract, then the fact that the law of contract would not *imply* a term having such an effect is not problematic – the effect achieved by the technology should be treated as a legitimate expression of the parties' intentions.

Third, following on from the previous point, it should be noted that coherentists will probably operate with different baselines that they take to represent the standard set by the law of contract (i.e. in relation to what courts, applying the law of contract, will be willing to endorse and enforce). In the context of commercial networks, traditional transactionalists will probably take a more restrictive view than that taken by contextualists with regard to the effects that the law of contract would mandate. For example, unlike contextualists, transactionalists will rarely recognise third-party effects or imply terms for cooperation. It follows that the coherentist benchmark for compatibility will be different as between transactionalists and contextualists. However, whether the benchmark is set by transactionalists or by contextualists, there will need to be some jurisprudence on the guiding principles that regulate the need for symmetry or congruence of the technological effects with the law; and, as we have suggested above, one of the key questions will be whether technological effects are recognised as equivalent to express provision by contracting parties.

Fourth, as Kevin Werbach and Nicolas Cornell have remarked, the private law of contract 'contains a penumbra of public law'.[59] Accordingly, a critical question is whether there is any public policy reason for constraining or condemning particular technological effects. Prima facie, where the law of contract treats a rule or a presumption as a default, there is no problem about the contractors switching the default by the use of technology. However, where the rule is mandatory, switching – whether by express provision or by technological effect – is either simply prohibited or merely not to be assisted (by court enforcement). Accordingly, we might find that we have two questions to consider: one question is whether or not some particular aspect of the law of contract is 'mandatory'; and the second question is whether, if this aspect of the law is mandatory, this means that (a) a particular kind of transactional activity, mechanism, or purpose is prohibited or (b) that such activity, mechanism, or purpose is simply not to be encouraged or assisted. For example, the distinctions between valid, voidable, and void transactions that run through much of the law of contract seem to be elided or eliminated in smart contracts.[60] Accordingly, we might ask whether this elision or elimination is permissible, or whether it is permissible but not to be assisted by courts, or whether it is actually prohibited. In this light, coherentists might worry about, say, cases on incapacity, such as someone who 'digitally signs a smart contract while dead drunk, or another person exploits their circumstances to get them [to] do so'.[61] In cases of this kind, does public policy recognise a waiver of a right to avoid a contract as legitimate? Is this dependent on the context? Whatever the answers to these particular questions, it does not seem to follow

---

[59] Werbach and Cornell (note 56) at 373.

[60] Compare Law Commission, *Thirteenth Programme of Law Reform*, Law Com No 377. HC 640, December 13, 2017, at 20, where the Commission, mindful that blockchain transactional records cannot be rectified or reversed, wonders (in an apparently coherentist way) 'how this feature would interact with contract law concepts such as implied terms or contracts which are held to have been void from the outset'. However, the Commission's thinking is actually more complex: its coherentist questions are posed alongside a background regulatory-instrumentalist concern that, if English courts and law are to remain a competitive choice for business contractors, then there 'is a compelling case for reviewing the current English legal and regulatory framework to ensure that it facilitates the use of smart contracts' (ibid., at 20).

[61] Werbach and Cornell (note 56) at 371.

from the differences between transactionalist and contextualist versions of coherentism that they should take a different view on public policy and its implications for congruence. However, viewing public policy questions through the private law lens of contract law seems a strange way of proceeding. Perhaps we need to step outside contract law to form a view about the public policy function and purpose of some of its historic doctrinal features.

Away from commercial networks, against a background of consumer protection laws, coherentists (giving effect to the policies and principles inscribed in those laws) will be moved to protect consumers against any unfair practices. The fact that those practices involve the use of technological measures will only be relevant to the extent that it might be perceived to make an even stronger case for urgent action. If technological force is used disproportionately or unfairly to immobilise vehicles, or disable services, or the like, coherentists will argue for intervention in line with background laws (which, it should be said, are likely already to express a 'regulatory' view).

Finally, even if the technological effects satisfy the requirement of congruence, coherentists will want to take a hard look at the anchoring arrangement (whether constituted as a traditional contract, or expressed as a condition for using, say, a permissioned blockchain) that authorises the use of the smart technologies with these effects. If there is any suggestion that parties, particularly small businesses or consumers, who have joined the network have not done so on a reasonably free and informed basis, then there might be reservations. After all, if the network were a self-regulatory arrangement, such as a club, with its own rules (rather than technological measures), coherentists of any kind will want to be satisfied that membership is reasonably free and informed. Just because technologies give effect to, or are applied in line with, the house rules, this should not be different.

17.4.3 Networks, Smart Contracts, and Regulatory-Instrumentalism

Regulatory-instrumentalists will not be greatly concerned with the kind of questions that engage coherentists – for example, with the question of whether smart contracts fit with the transactional template adopted by the law of contract, or whether technological effects should be treated as analogous to express terms, or whether there should be symmetry between the effects produced by application of the law of contract and those achieved by the transactional technologies. If there is any doubt about such questions, and if such doubts need to be removed, then regulatory-instrumentalists will simply recommend legislation that does that particular job. Such was the regulatory-instrumentalist response to the embryonic development of e-commerce (for the avoidance of doubt, the law declared that, in principle, online transactions should be treated as legally binding, that there should be an equivalence between the law for offline transactions and the law for online transactions);[62] and, indeed, there are already regulatory-instrumentalist moves to ensure that, in principle, smart contracts should be recognised as legally valid and that blockchain records should be treated as legally admissible.[63]

---

[62] See, Roger Brownsword, 'The E-Commerce Directive, Consumer Transactions, and the Digital Single Market: Questions of Regulatory Fitness, Regulatory Disconnection and Rule Redirection' in Stefan Grundmann (ed.), *European Contract Law in the Digital Age* (Antwerp: Intersentia, 2017) 165.

[63] As to the former, a legislative amendment (HB 2417) to the Arizona Electronic Transactions Act provides that a contract relating to a transaction may not be denied legal effect, validity or enforceability solely

Assuming that a community sees benefits (such as reducing court enforcement costs or designing in compensatory arrangements that are a workaround relative to restrictions in the law of contract [such as third-party claims]) in entrusting transactions to smart technologies, then regulatory-instrumentalists will view smart contracts and networks as an exercise in putting in place proportionate and acceptable measures of risk management.

Of course, the extent of such entrustment as well as the scale of the risks associated with the use of smart contracts will vary from one kind of transaction to another. We can place some transactions, such as the one-off exchange between one-time contractors, at one end of the spectrum of duration and complexity and other transactions, such as major construction contracts, at the opposite end of the spectrum. Once smart machines run the simple exchange at one end of the relational spectrum, they will take over relatively simple formation and performance functions – executing payments is the paradigmatic example; and, to this extent, not only will the interested/connected humans be taken out of the loop, the transaction will be isolated from the web of background social relationships and expectations that Ian Macneil rightly insists give context to human contracting.[64] At the other end of the spectrum, there will be a range of in-contract decisions to be made, for example, involving variation, renegotiation, exercises of discretion, serving notices, and so on. Here, the problem is not that the technologies are unlikely to be up to the task (although we might be surprised in this respect) but that some contractors might be reluctant to entrust such decisions to the machines or, at any rate, they might want to retain control.

In general, where smart transactional technologies are employed, there are at least five kinds of risks that might be anticipated as follows:

(i)   there might be a malfunction in the technology; this means that the regulatory framework must provide for the correction of the malfunction (e.g. completion of performance or setting aside a transaction that should not have been formed); the required corrective measures might include rescission or rectification of transactions on which the malfunction has impacted (which, if smart contracts run on blockchain, could be problematic) as well as arrangements for compensation and insurance;

(ii) the integrity of the technology might be compromised by unauthorised third-party acts; these acts will need to be covered by the criminal law or tort law or both, and there will need to be provision for the adjustment of losses so occasioned;[65]

(iii) the way that the technology functions (not malfunctions) might mean that some decisions are made that do not align with the preferences or interests of a party who is relevantly connected to the transaction – for example, as when Knight Capital Group's automated programme 'flooded exchanges with unauthorised and irrational orders, trading $2.6 million worth of stocks every second';[66] this suggests that regulators need

---

because that contract contains 'a smart contract term': see, e.g., https://newmedialaw.proskauer.com/2017/04/20/arizona-passes-groundbreaking-blockchain-and-smart-contract-law-state-blockchain-laws-on-the-rise/ (last accessed July 7, 2018); and, as to the latter, see, e.g., the initiative in Vermont: https://law.justia.com/codes/vermont/2016/title-12/chapter-81/section-1913 (last accessed 24 March 2018).

[64] See note 45.

[65] See discussion in Kelvin F. Low and Ernie G.S. Teo, 'Bitcoins and other Cryptocurrencies as Property?' (2017) 9 *Law, Innovation and Technology* 235 (concerning the responses to famous hacks at Mt Gox and of the DAO).

[66] Nicholas Carr (note 3) at 156. In all, there were some $7billion in errant trades and the company lost almost half a billion dollars.

to find ways of bringing humans back into the loop for critical decisions, or capping the financial loss that can be generated by the machine, or putting humans in control (just like principals) of the terms and conditions of the machine's authorisation;

(iv) as the famous flash crash of 6 May 2010, reminds us, fully automated algorithmic trading can involve systemic risks to whole markets and not just to individual contractors;[67] which implies that the regulatory framework needs to make provision for 'an "emergency stop" function'[68] – that is, more generally, provision for human oversight of markets along with powers to intervene and suspend trading and transactions; and

(v) although smart technologies might seem to comply with general legal requirements, the fact that some have 'black-box' elements might seem unduly risky[69] – particularly, for example, if there is a concern that they might be operating in unlawful discriminatory ways;[70] this implies that regulators either have to grant a degree of immunity to these technologies (reflecting how far the risk of unlawful practice can be tolerated) or introduce measures to constrain such practices. Taking a stand on a question of this kind, the House of Lords Select Committee on Artificial Intelligence has recently recommended that where, as with deep neural networks, 'it is not yet possible to generate thorough explanations for the decisions that are made, this may mean delaying their deployment for particular uses until alternative solutions are found'.[71]

If, beyond the consumer marketplace and possibly the share economy, the state is content largely to leave commercial contractors to self-regulate, then the adoption of smart contracts is likely to be at the initiative of business contractors themselves. Notwithstanding various coherentist concerns as sketched already, the questions for regulatory-instrumentalists will largely be about bringing the law into line with regulatory objectives (such as supporting innovation, promoting competition, growing the economy, mitigating unacceptable financial risks, and so on) and there is no reason to think that smart contracts – whether or not in networked business settings – will be seen as problematic in this light. If, however, some technological effects are judged to be unacceptable (contrary to public policy in a regulatory rather than a coherentist sense), then bespoke provision can be made to prohibit such effects, and to do so in networks of any kind.

17.5 Conclusion

In this chapter, I have suggested that, when lawyers begin to ask how emerging technologies (such as blockchain) or particular technological applications (such as smart contracts) relate to the existing body of law, we can expect this to develop into two kinds of conversation, one coherentist and the other regulatory-instrumentalist.

Given our current institutional arrangements and conventions, we will expect that, in courtrooms and in litigation settings, lawyers will reason like coherentists. As coherentists,

---

[67] See Frank Pasquale and Glyn Cashwell, 'Four Futures of Legal Automation' (2015) 63 *UCLA Review Discourse* 26, at 38–39.

[68] Phillip Paech, 'The Governance of Blockchain Financial Networks', LSE Law, Society and Economy Working Papers 16/2017 (available at www.lse.ac.uk/collection/law/wps/wps.htm) (last accessed 4 July 2017) at 18.

[69] Generally, see Frank Pasquale, *The Black Box Society* (Cambridge, MA: Harvard University Press, 2015).

[70] See, e.g., Cathy O'Neil, *Weapons of Math Destruction* (London: Allen Lane, 2016).

[71] Report on *AI in the UK; ready, willing and able?* (Report of Session 2017–19, published 16 April 2017, HL Paper 100) at para 105: available at https://publications.parliament.uk/pa/ld201719/ldselect/ldai/100/10007.htm#_idTextAnchor025 (last accessed 28 July 2018).

they will ask how the new transactional phenomena fit with existing thinking in contract law. However, away from courtrooms, in settings that are more obviously policy-orientated, lawyers are likely to reason like regulatory-instrumentalists.

From a state perspective, the use of smart contracts in the consumer marketplace is likely to be one of the hot spots for regulatory debate and, possibly, the share economy will give rise to some questions about an acceptable balance of interests (particularly between innovation and economic risks). However, from the perspective of self-regulating businesses, the use of smart contracts might prompt both coherentist and, for that matter, regulatory-instrumentalist voices in defence of smaller business parties and coherentists might question how far it is permissible to use smart contracts in ways that do not mirror traditional contracts and contract law (or align with public policy considerations that are mediated via contract law).

Applying this analysis to networks, I have suggested that coherentists might have some problems where the effect of using technological measures is not congruent or symmetrical with traditionally restrictive rules of contract law. However, for regulatory instrumentalists, unless these measures and effects are incompatible with pubic policy or particular regulatory objectives, there is no problem. Indeed, the reference points for congruence are quite different as between coherentists and regulatory instrumentalists. Whereas the former refer to legal doctrine, the latter refer to the purposes to be served by the law. To the extent that the fundamental questions are ones of public policy, the regulatory-instrumentalist approach seems to be more direct and pertinent.

This leaves many questions unanswered, questions that I am sure will surface in the debates about smart contracts. For example, even if we concede that, in general, automation is fine, we might question whether a community can afford to lose the skill of contracting. It is one thing to map the different ways in which lawyers are likely to relate to smart contracts but how *should* they relate? Should we, as Holmes apparently thought, follow the regulatory-instrumentalist path (because coherentism does not necessarily address the right questions)?[72] Even if transactions are largely automated, are there not still Rule of Law concerns implying that there will be some limits on the permitted use and characteristics of smart contracts?[73]

My tentative conclusions, each of which is an action point for future work, are as follows. First, if smart contracts are the answer to some problems in business and consumer networks but there are traditional coherentist questions about this, then it is likely to be a regulatory-instrumentalist intervention rather than a coherentist accommodation that properly clears the way. Second, if reservations about smart contracts raise questions that go to matters of public policy, then they should be addressed in a regulatory-instrumentalist way. Third, although regulatory-instrumentalism (with a technocratic adjunct) might be a smarter way of responding to new transactional technologies, it suffers from some potentially serious shortcomings. In particular, there is a risk that by focusing on the most effective way of serving particular policy objectives, regulators will neglect the deepest needs and the distinctive values of their community.

Picking up on this last point, we need to act on two fronts. On one front, we need to articulate a renewed form of coherentist thinking in which the compatibility of new

---

[72] See David Rosenberg, 'The Path Not Taken' (1997) 110 *Harvard Law Review* 1044.
[73] See Roger Brownsword, 'Technological Management and the Rule of Law' (2016) 8 *Law, Innovation and Technology* 100.

technologies (whether for transactions or interactions) are explicitly assessed for their compatibility with a community's fundamental values as well as (even more importantly) with the essential preconditions for any form of human social existence. To be sure, smart contracts might not be a threat in relation to the latter, but the revolutionary potential of blockchain – not to mention AI – invites reflection on the kind of community (local as well as national) that we want to be, including the extent to which we value regulation by rule rather than by technological management.[74] This leads us to a second front for action: namely, taking steps to reform our legal and regulatory institutions, internationally and nationally, so that the new coherentist mission is firmly embedded.[75] Arguably, we need regulatory stewards to operationalise the new coherentist approach assisted by technology foresight commissions to develop standard procedures and best practice in engaging with emerging technologies.

17.6 Coda

Eventually, our fictitious bookshop took the advice of its external consultant and adopted a new classificatory scheme that recognised the existence of, and divisions within, the technological literature. However, the consultant had also advised the bookshop proprietors to think hard about both their business objectives and whether the classification scheme best served those purposes. In a difficult market, the bookshop proprietors agreed that their priorities were to sell books and to maximise their profits. Given these purposes, they took further advice from their consultant. The consultant advised that the bookshop should close its bricks and mortar store and move its business online. Reluctantly, the proprietors heeded this advice and closed their store. The thriving street in which the bookstore once opened its doors is now largely deserted. Blockchain and bookshops have this in common: when traditional coherentism gives way to more focused regulatory-instrumentalism which then yields to efficient technocracy, community life is not necessarily improved.

---

[74] Compare De Filippi and Wright (note 55), at p. 210:

> If blockchain technology matures, we may need to ask ourselves whether we would rather live in a world where most of our economic transactions and social interactions are constrained by rules of law – which are universal but also more flexible and ambiguous, and therefore not perfectly enforceable – or whether we would rather surrender ourselves to the rules of code.

[75] For a fuller account of 'new coherentism', see Roger Brownsword, *Law, Technology and Society: Reimagining the Regulatory Environment* (Abingdon: Routledge, 2019) Ch 4.

18 Observations on the Impact of Technology on Contract Law

Barbara Pasa and Larry A. DiMatteo

18.1 Introduction

Contract automation has started to transform the existing legal landscape. It brings about many exciting opportunities and benefits, but at the same time creates new problems and challenges for the existing legal framework. This chapter will discuss some of the many issues relating to the development of smart contracts based on blockchain technology. It constructs a future research agenda related to the regulation of smart contracts both by targeted government regulation and through the judicial application of contract law.

Multidisciplinary research creates synergistic opportunities by increasing understanding across disciplines often leading to new theories and innovations. The area of smart contracts provides an invaluable platform for computer scientists, legal experts and entrepreneurs to explore the impact of blockchain technology on the legal system from an interdisciplinary perspective. The consensus view among computer scientists, engineers, start-ups, lawyers, judges, and legal scholars is that smart transactional technologies (STTs) will continue to proliferate and their uses will multiple in the global marketplace. From a legal perspective, SSTs will present disruptive challenges to traditional legal taxonomies, and the legal order will need to adjust to meet these challenges.[1]

What forms or types of adjustments inside and outside of contract law is the issue to be discussed in this chapter. At a more profound level is the interaction and tension between the "rule of law" and the "rule of technology," or what is often referred to as "code as law."[2] This tension is found in numerous areas of private law, such as in the data economy

---

[1] Brownsword, "Smart Transactional Technologies, Legal Disruption, and the Case of Network Contracts," Chapter 17; see also, Aaron Wright, Primavera De Filippi, "Decentralized Blockchain Technology and the Rise of Lex Cryptographia," available at http://dx.doi.org/10.2139/ssrn.2580664 (accessed September 10, 2018); a deeper analysis by the same authors is now in *Blockchain and the Law: The Rule of Code*, (Cambridge, MA: Harvard University Press, 2018); see also Linn William Cong & Zhiguo He, "Blockchain Disruption and Smart Contracts," p. 11, http://dx.doi.org/10.2139/ssrn.2985764, available at www.zhiguohe.com/uploads/1/0/6/9/106923057/bdsc.pdf (accessed September 10, 2018); Robert Herian, *Regulating Blockchain Critical Perspectives in Law and Technology*, (Oxford: Routledge, 2018); a special issue of *Law and Critique* on blockchain and law, (2018) 29(2) *Law and Critique* 129–264.

[2] William J. Mitchell, *City of Bits: Space, Place, and the Infobahn* (Cambridge, Mass: MIT Press, 1995), p. 111; R. Polk Wagner, "On Software Regulation" (2005) 78 *Southern California Law Review* 457–496, at 470–71; Lawrence Lessig, *Code 2.0* (New York: Basic Books, 2006; 1st edn., 1999), Chapter 1, p. 1; Roger Brownsword, *Rights, Regulation, and the Technological Revolution* (New York: Oxford University Press, 2013); Frank Pasquale, "Technology, Competition and Values" (2007) 8 *Minn. J.L. Sci. & Tech.* 607–614; Lukas Abegg, "Code Is Law? Not Quite Yet," 2016, available at: www.coindesk.com/code-is-law-not-quite-yet/. (accessed: September 1, 2018); Rolf H. Weber, "'Rose Is a Rose Is a Rose Is a Rose' – What about Code and Law?" (2018) 34 *Computer Law & Security Review* 701–706; Karen Yeung, "Regulation by Blockchain: The Emerging Battle for Supremacy between the Code of Law and Code as Law" (2018, (2019) 82) *Modern Law Review*, 207–396, also available at https://papers.ssrn.com/sol3/papers.cfm?abstract_id=3206546.

in relation to the notions of ownership and possession;[3] smart contract in relation to traditional contract law requirements;[4] and 3D printing in relation to contract and tort law.[5]

The focus here is on the role of private law and its application to STTs, and not the area of the public regulation of new technologies. A large part of the analysis aims to clarify the intersection between traditional contract law and smart contracts. For example, how does traditional contract doctrine relating to contract formation, breach and performance,

[3] Herbert Zech, "Information as Property" (2015) 6 JIPITEC 192, para. 1; Josef Drexl et al., "Data Ownership and Access to Data – Position Statement of the Max Planck Institute for Innovation and Competition of 16 August 2016 on the Current European Debate" (2016), available at http://10.2139/ssrn.2833165 (accessed September 1, 2018); Sebastian Lohsse, Reiner Schulze, Dirk Staudenmayer (eds.), *Trading Data in the Digital Economy: Legal Concepts and Tools. Münster Colloquia on EU Law and the Digital Economy III* (Baden-Baden: Nomos, 2017); Christiane Wendehorst, "Elephants in the Room and Paper Tigers: How to Reconcile Data Protection and the Data Economy" in: Sebastian Lohsse, Reiner Schulze, Dirk Staudenmayer (eds.), *Trading Data in the Digital Economy: Legal Concepts and Tools*, cit., pp. 327–356; Sjef van Erp, "Ownership of Data: The Numerus Clausus of Legal Objects" (2017) 6 *Property Rights Conference Journal* 235–257; Georgy Ishmaev, "Blockchain Technology as an Institution of Property" (2017) 48(5) *Metaphilosophy* 666–686.

[4] Eliza Mik, "Problems of Intention and Consideration in Online Transactions," in Michael Furmston and Gregory Tolhurst (eds.), *Contract Formation: Law and Practice* (2nd edn., Oxford University Press, 2016), chapter 6; Friedrich Graf von Westphalen, "Contracts with Big Data: The End of the Traditional Contract Concept?" in: Sebastian Lohsse, Reiner Schulze, and Dirk Staudenmayer (eds.), *Trading Data in the Digital Economy: Legal Concepts and Tools*, cit., pp. 245–270; Jakub Szczerbowski, "Place of Smart Contracts in Civil Law. A Few Comments on Form and Interpretation," Proceedings of the 12th Annual International Scientific Conference NEW TRENDS (Private College of Economic Studies: Znojmo, 2017), available at https://ssrn.com/abstract=3095933 (accessed September 1, 2018); Gabriel Jaccard, "Smart Contracts and the Role of Law" (January 10, 2018) available at https://ssrn.com/abstract=3099885 or http://dx.doi.org/10.2139/ssrn.3099885 (accessed September 1, 2018); Eric Tjong Tjin Tai, "Formalizing Contract Law for Smart Contracts" (September 18, 2017), Tilburg Private Law Working Paper Series No. 6/ 2017 available at https://ssrn.com/abstract=3038800 or http://dx.doi.org/10.2139/ssrn.3038800 (accessed September 1, 2018); Paul Catchlove, "Smart Contracts: A New Era of Contract Use" (December 1, 2017) available at https://ssrn.com/abstract=3090226 or http://dx.doi.org/10.2139/ssrn.3090226 (accessed September 1, 2018); Reggie O'Shields, "Smart Contracts: Legal Agreements for the Blockchain" (2017) 21 N.C. *Banking Inst.* 177–194, Sally Wheeler, 'Visions of Contract' (2017) 44(1) *Journal of Law and Society* 74–92; Alexander Savelyev, "Contract Law 2.0: 'Smart' Contracts as the Beginning of the End of Classic Contract Law" (2017) 26(2) *Information & Communication Technology Law* 550–561; Jake Godenfein and Andrea Leiter, "Legal Engineering on the Blockchain: 'Smart Contracts' as Legal Conduct" (2018) 29(2) *Law and Critique* 141–149.

[5] Nora Freeman Engstrom, "3-D Printing and Product Liability: Identifying the Obstacles" (2013) 162 *U. Pa. L. Rev.* 35–41, available at www.pennlawreview.com/online/162-U-Pa-L-Rev-Online35.pdf; Nicole D. Berkowitz, "Strict Liability for Individuals? The Impact of 3-D Printing on Products Liability Law" (2015) 92 *Wash. U. L. Rev.* 1019–1053, available at http://openscholarship.wustl.edu/law_lawreview/vol92/ iss4/8 (accessed September 1, 2018); Eric Lindenfeld, Jasper Tran, "Strict Liability and 3D-Printed Medical Devices," *Yale Journal of Law and Technology* (December 11, 2015), available at http://10.31228/osf.io /k2h4z (accessed September 1, 2018); Christian Twigg-Flesner, "Conformity of 3d Prints – Can Current Sales Law Cope?" in Reiner Schulze, Dirk Staudenmayer (eds.), *Digital Revolution: Challenges for Contract Law in Practice* (Baden Baden/Oxford: Nomos/Hart, 2016) pp. 35–66; Geraint Howells, Chris Willett, "3D Printing: The Limits of Contract and Challenges for Tort," in Reiner Schulze, Dirk Staudenmayer (eds.), *Digital Revolution: Challenges for Contract Law in Practice* cit., pp. 67–87; James M. Beck & Matthew D. Jacobson, "3D Printing: What Could Happen to Products Liability When Users (and Everyone Else in Between) Become Manufacturers" (2017) 18 *Minn. J.L. Sci. & Tech.* 143–205 available at: https://scholarship.law.umn.edu/mjlst/vol18/iss1/3 (accessed September 1, 2018), Dirk A. Zetzsche, Ross P. Buckley & Douglas W. Arner, "The Distributed Liability of Distributed Ledgers: Legal Risks of Blockchain" (2017), available at www5.austlii.edu.au/au/journals/UNSWLRS/2017/52.pdf. (accessed September 1, 2018)

remedies, and excuse apply to self-enforcing smart contracts? Associated areas will also be discussed, including electronic platforms and networks, privacy, data protection, and consumer protection. A special focus will be devoted to the Chinese regulation and robust application of blockchain technology and smart contracts in numerous sectors of its economy. Finally, the reflections from professionals on the ground – practicing lawyers and judges – at the forefront of law and quickly evolving nature STTs will be examined.

18.2 Smart Contracts: Old Legal Constructs or New Regulations?

The most difficult issue for lawyers is gaining a working understanding of the technology behind smart contracts and how SSTs relate to contract law and the legal system. So, the best starting point for lawyers is to obtain necessary background knowledge on the blockchain in order to understand the general technological framework behind smart contracts and determine the relevant legal issues presented by that technology. This knowledge base begins with an understanding of the relevant technical terms such as distributed ledger technology ('DLT'); also called shared ledger,[6] blockchain,[7] permissioned (Hyperledger Fabric)/permissionless (Bitcoin and Ethereum) blockchains,[8] network nodes,[9] cryptography rules,[10]

---

[6] "A collection of records (making up a database), where identical copies of each record are held on numerous computers across an organization, a country, multiple countries, or the entire world, either jointly or partitioned by the parties to which each record relates. A blockchain is a form of distributed ledger, but not all distributed ledgers are blockchains": Sean Murphy and Charley Cooper, "Can Smart Contracts Be Legally Binding Contracts?", White Paper R3cev and Norton Rose Fulbright 2016 at 46, available at www.nortonrosefulbright.com/knowledge/publications/144559/can-smart-contracts-be-legally-binding-contracts, at 46 (accessed September 9, 2018). See also, (2016), available at https://assets.publishing.service.gov.uk/government/uploads/system/uploads/attachment_data/file/492972/gs-16-1-distributed-ledger-technology.pdf (accessed September 9, 2018).

[7] The idea of a "chain-of-blocks" was first introduced by a researcher under the name of Satoshi Nakamoto, *Bitcoin: A Peer-to-Peer Electronic Cash System* (2008), available at https://bitcoin.org/bitcoin.pdf. A blockchain is "a distributed ledger taking the form of an electronic database that is replicated on numerous nodes spread across an organization, a country, multiple countries, or the entire world. Records in a blockchain are stored sequentially in time in the form of blocks. Each hash for a block depends on the block header for that block. The block header for that block contains a reference to the previous block in the chain. Accordingly, there is a continuous chain back in time. In order to change one block in the chain it would be necessary to change every block that came after it." Murphy & Cooper, cit, 46. As known, the blockchain was set up to deal with the cryptocurrency sector, but in order to become platforms enabling different types of transactions, the blockchain's functionalities must be extended adding protocol layers on top of it (i.e., smart contracts). Cf Andreas M. Antonopoulos, *Mastering Bitcoin* (Sebastopol: O'Reilly, 2015); Chris Reade, *Elements of Functional Programming* (Boston, MA 1989).

[8] Permissionless blockchains are open, do not have access controls, and reach decentralized consensus through costly proof-of-work calculations; permissioned blockchains have identity systems to limit participation and do not depend on proofs-of-work. See David Cerezo Sánchez, "Raziel: Private and Verifiable Smart Contracts on Blockchains" (July 25, 2018), available at https://arxiv.org/pdf/1807.09484.pdf (accessed September 12, 2018).
   Blockchain can also be private, which means it is only accessible for the selected participants, or public, as the bitcoin system where any curious party is able to inspect the input parameters and detailed execution of any on-chain smart contract. But quite often in the literature "permissionless" becomes synonymous of "public," as well as "permissioned" synonymous of "private."

[9] "A node is a single computer involved in processing a message in order to reach consensus. Nodes are connected to each other via the Internet." Every transaction is broadcast across the network to all nodes, which then add valid blocks to the blockchain on a regular basis. See Murphy & Cooper cit, 47.

[10] "Transactions rely on public key cryptography, which involves the use of a public and a private key. The keys are generated together by a complex algorithm, which guarantees that it is impossible to derive the

wallet,[11] majority consensus rule,[12] address,[13] hash,[14] mining process,[15] proof-of-work,[16] proof-of-stake,[17] and oracles.[18] The next step is to consider the potential uses of smart contracts in such areas as the financial industry, medical applications, processing of insurance compensation, and so forth.[19]

private key from the public key. To give a practical example: a payment transaction contains a script that states that the token(s) are payable to whoever presents the private key corresponding to the account (public key) associated with the payee. On a technical level, scripts 'lock' tokens to a specific public address and to unlock (i.e. spend) them it is necessary to provide the private key." See Antonopoulos, cit, 117.

[11] It is a software program that allows users to buy, sell, and check balance for their digital currency (or assets). See Murphy & Cooper cit, 46.

[12] "More than 50% of nodes conclude that a proposed block message is authenticated and verified, so that the block can be appended to the chain." Murphy & Cooper cit, 46.

[13] "An identifier (typically seen in alphanumeric string form) constitutes a hash over the participant's public key for the authentication of messages from that participant." Murphy & Cooper, cit, 46

[14] "Hash/Hashing is the process by which a grouping of digital data is converted into a single number, called a hash. The number is unique (effectively a 'digital fingerprint' of the source data) and the source data cannot be reverse engineered and recovered from it" Murphy & Cooper, cit, 47.

[15] A blockchain is made of interconnected blocks. Each block contains a list of all prior transactions. The creation of each block requires a significant amount of computation ("mining"). Miners are incentivized to add new blocks by obtaining Bitcoins (when their block is added to the blockchain) and transaction fees (when they include a particular transaction in their block); a proof-of-work-based consensus is only indispensable in permissionless ledgers, where the parties cannot trust each other. See Eliza, Smart Contracts: Terminology, Technical Limitations and Real World Complexity' (2017) 9 *Law, Innovation and Technology* 269–300, For an overview of different types of consensus see: Hyperledger Architecture Working Group (WG), *Introduction to Hyperledger Business Blockchain Design Philosophy and Consensus* (2016) "Hyperledger Architecture," Volume 1, at 3–4, available at www.hyperledger.org/wp-content /uploads/2017/08/Hyperledger_Arch_WG_Paper_1_ Consensus.pdf (accessed September 13, 2018).

[16] To create a block and append it to the blockchain, each mining node (i.e., participant in the network) must provide a "proof-of-work": a piece of data, which is computationally difficult to produce but easy for other nodes to verify. As these computations are extremely expensive in terms of electricity costs, it is more economical to produce new valid blocks (i.e., those that follow the rules) than to commit resources to corrupting the blockchain by changing old blocks. Given the cost and difficulty of retrospectively changing the existing blockchain, the possibility of a transaction being altered or reversed is infinitesimal. See Antonopoulos, cit 162.

[17] The whole mining process described above as "proof-of-work" is inefficient as the time required for validation and as the energy consumption by nodes. So, researchers are working on a different validation mechanisms, for example one is called "proof-of-stake": it is still an algorithm but, unlike the proof-of-work, it delegates the validation to a selected portion of nodes; furthermore, any creator of a new block is chosen in a deterministic way, depending on its wealth (also defined as "stake"), so there is no block reward; the miners are called forgers, indeed, and they are always those who own the coins minted. See Antonopoulos, cit 162ff.

[18] The word is suggestive: in ordinary language, oracles are "Mediums through whom advice or prophecy was sought from the gods in classical antiquity" (*Merriam-Webster* and *Cambridge English Dictionaries*). Thus, oracles are "agents" who connect the real world to the "smart" one: smart contract may indeed need to refer to facts in the real world, such as when a contract pays out if a stock exceeds a certain price on a certain date. For instance, the bitcoin blockchain knows nothing about stock prices; that information must be provided through an external data feed. The contractual parties must trust the oracle and the authenticity of the data feed, but the oracle could inject wrong information into the blockchain, thus compromising the "smart-ness" of contracts. See Stefan Thomas and Evan Schwartz, 'Smart Oracles: A Simple, Powerful Approach to Smart Contracts' (White Paper July 17, 2014), available at https://github.com/codius/codius/wiki/Smart-Oracles:-A-Simple,-Powerful-Approach-to-SmartContracts (accessed September 13, 2018).

[19] There are many examples on the potential uses of smart contracts and blockchains to be found in various types of resources, such as blogs and White Papers, which are regarded as authoritative by the tech community, although researchers in this area face the challenges of finding reliable information and reconciling inconsistent terminology. Cf Alyssa Jarrett, "Ripple and R3 Team up with 12 Banks to Trial XRP for Cross-Border Payments," 2016, available at https://ripple.com/insights/ripple-and-r3-team-up-with-12-banks-to-trial-xrp-for-cross-border-payments/ (accessed September 1, 2018); Shanna Leonard 'Do Corporate Giants Need Banks?'

After gaining a basic understanding of the technological aspects of the blockchain, the further step is defining what a smart contract is and how it compares to traditional contracts. In this way, legal issues can be determined by analyzing the divergence between smart and traditional contracts.[20] The novelty of smart contracting has led to some initial regulations in a few jurisdictions,[21] but generally regulations of smart contracts (blockchain technology) remains lacking or inadequate in most jurisdictions. In fact, much like franchising in its early development, or the continuing evolution of the sharing economy, "smart" contracts have unclear legal status in most countries and are not yet specifically regulated.

Without specific regulations, a first option is to apply existing legal categories or constructs such as contract and agency law. De Caria, like Werbach and Cornell, and Catchlove,[22] argues that the requirements for a traditional contract are satisfied by smart contracts: "smart contracts are just technological manifestations of familiar contractual processes."[23] They are instruments of agreement between parties with the intentions to be bound by the obligations embedded in that agreement. In more general terms, they are contracts as long as they are meant to alter concretely the normative relation between the parties.[24] Smart contracts, however, give rise to new challenges to existing law, in particular on the determination of applicable law in international trade.[25] If the applicable law and the jurisdiction are not determined in the agreement, smart contracts

---

(2017), available at https://ripple.com/zh/insights/corporate-giants-need-banks/ (accessed September 13, 2018). Devine, Beyond Bitcoin: Using Blockchain Technology to Provide Assurance in the Commercial World" (2017), 5 *Computer Fraud & Security* 14–18; Deloitte Center for Financial Services, "Blockchain in Commercial Real Estate: The Future Is Here!," (2017) available at www2.deloitte.com/content /dam/Deloitte/us/Documents/financial-services/us-fsi-rec-blockchain-in-commercial-real-estate.pdf. (accessed March 8, 2018); Roman Beck, Christian Becker, Juho Lindman, and Matti Rossi, "Opportunities and Risks of Blockchain Technologies (Dagstuhl Seminar 17132)," (2017) 7 *Dagstuhl Reports* n. 3,available at http://10 .4230/DagRep.7.3.99; Huang Xiaohong et al., "LNSC: A Security Model for Electric Vehicle and Charing Pile Management Based on Blockchain Ecosystem," (2018) IEEE Access, available at http://10.1109 /ACCESS.2018.2812176; Jane Thomason, "Blockchain: An Accelerator for Women and Children's Health?" (2017) 1 *Global Health Journal* 3–10; Antoinette O'Gorman, "Banning Cryptocurrency Would be as Sensible as Banning the Internet" (2018), available at https://ripple.com/zh/insights/banning-cryptocurrency -would-be-as-sensible-as-banning-the-internet (accessed September 1, 2018). See also Valentina Gatteschi, Chapter 3.

20 Alexander Savelyev, "Contract Law 2.0: 'Smart' Contracts As the Beginning of the End of Classic Contract Law," (2017) 26 *Information & Communications Technology Law* 116–134, available at Higher School of Economics Research Paper No. WP BRP 71/LAW/2016, available at https://ssrn.com/abstract=2885241.

21 Arizona House Bill 2417, available at www.azleg.gov/legtext/53leg/1R/laws/0097.htm and at https://legis can.com/AZ/text/HB2417/2017; and Vermont: Sec. I.1. 12 V.S.A. § 1913 available at https://legislature .vermont.gov/assets/Documents/2016/Docs/ACTS/ACT157/ACT157%20As%20Enacted.pdf. Blockchain legislation trend seems to be accelerating. A search for "blockchain" in the legislation-tracking database LegiScan Shows five bills that were acted on in 2017 and 2019. Currently, Hawaii, New York, Colorado, Nebraska, Vermont, Virginia, Florida, Maryland, and North Dakota are among the states considering laws relating to the blockchain or cryptocurrencies: see Adrianne Jeffries, "Blockchain laws tend to be hasty, unnecessary, and extremely thirsty" (March 29, 2018), available atwww.theverge.com/2018/3/29/ 17176596/blockchain-bitcoin-cryptocurrency-state-law-legislation (accessed: September 7, 2018).

22 See Riccardo De Caria, Chapter 2; Kevin Werbach and Nicolas Cornell, "Contracts Ex Machina" (2017) 67 *Duke Law Journal* 313–370; Paul Catchlove, "Smart Contracts: A New Era of Contract Use," (2017), available at http://10.2139/ssrn.3090226.

23 Werbach & Cornell, cit, at 324.

24 Ibid., at 321.

25 Riccardo De Caria, "Law and Autonomous Systems Series: Defining Smart Contracts – The Search for Workable Legal Categories" (May 25, 2018), available at www.law.ox.ac.uk/business-law-blog/blog/2018/ 05/law-and-autonomous-systems-series-defining-smart-contracts-search (accessed September 7, 2018), for the analysis of challenges caused by smart contracts to international financial transactions, see

became "less smart"; they become even less smart if there is an international dispute between contracting parties and conflict of laws rules apply to determine applicable law. A similar problem would arise with regard to jurisdiction. As observed, in commercial practice an *ad hoc* provision on judicial enforcement is needed, but smart contracts are not built with the aim of depending on a third-party judicial enforcement.[26]

A second option is to consider smart contracts (and the blockchain) as licensed goods protected by intellectual property laws,[27] either through copyright law, as they are pieces of software, or through patents at least in those legal systems where the patentability of software is allowed and in those which recognize the patentability of inventions assisted by software, assuming they are new, involve an inventive step, and are capable of industrial application.[28] "Each smart contract by its legal nature is also a computer program within the meaning of IP law."[29] If the blockchain at the core of the online platform which contains the creation and management of smart contracts and is patented (or if the software which runs the platform itself is protected by copyright), it is possible (and profitable) that the access to such a platform is sold as a service to customers willing to pay a subscription fee. What will be then the relation between the owner of the platform where smart contracts are managed and its users? differences that come with the use of technological tools in the formation and performance of smart contracts.

18.2.1 *Smart Contracts as Traditional Contracts*

Assuming smart contracts are recognized as traditional contracts, legal issues nonetheless arise due to their technological components that relate to the formation and enforcement of contracts.

18.2.1.1 Formation

The formation of contracts through blockchain technology questions the applicability of legal rules and doctrines relating to that area of contract law. The ability of smart contracts to meet the traditional requirements, such as capacity, mutual assent, and legality, calls for more interdisciplinary collaborations between lawyers and scientists.[30]

A first issue relates to the common law point of view: Do smart contracts involve promises in a strict legal meaning? Probably not, because a smart contract does not say:

Philipp Paech, "The Governance of Blockchain Financial Networks" (2017) 80(6) *Modern Law Review* 1073–1110.

[26] Sarah Manski and Ben Manski, "No Gods, No Masters, No Coders? The Future of Sovereignty in a Blockchain World" (2018) 29(2) *Law and Critique* 151–162.

[27] For the analysis of the US law, see, Craig A. De Ridder, Mercedes K. Tunstall and Nathalie Prescott, "Recognition of Smart Contracts in the United States" (2017) 29(11) *Intellectual Property & Technology Law Journal* 17–19.

[28] The protection under rights granted by the Directive 96/9/EC on the legal protection of databases does not work: see De Caria, Chapter 2 in this book; Birgit Clark, "Blockchain and IP Law: A Match Made in Crypto Heaven?" (February 2018), available at www.wipo.int/wipo_magazine/en/2018/01/article_0005.html (accessed September 12, 2018).

[29] Savelyev, cit., at 120.

[30] Mateja Durovic & André Janssen, Chapter 4 in this book.

"I will pay you one bitcoin if such-and-such happens," but rather declares or attests: *"You will be paid one bitcoin if such-and-such happens."*[31] In this regard, Werbach and Cornell compare a smart contract to a traditional contract, such as a conveyance (title transfer), a written contract between the buyer and seller for the purchase and sale of real property. After the conveyance there is no promises left to be performed. Unlike a physical conveyance, however, the smart contract does not transfer property at the time. As such, it is neither executory, to offer (insofar as there is no action left to be performed). This ambiguity between contract offer, execution of a contract, and the performance of the contract (executed) is what causes conceptual difficulties from the perspective of contract law.[32]

A second conceptual difficulty is that smart contracts on Ethereum for instance, are, by default, "unilateral" in the sense that only one party places them on the blockchain.[33] For these reasons, smart contracts are presently best suited to execute automatically two types of transactions: ensuring the payment of funds upon certain triggering events, and imposing financial penalties if certain objective conditions are not satisfied.[34] One could approximate a bilateral (or multilateral) contract through the creation of two (or more) interrelated unilateral contracts, but two unilateral contracts are not precisely the same as a bilateral contract.[35]

A third issue is raised from a traditional civil law perspective: Do some blockchain platforms, such as Insurwave,[36] used to support marine hull insurance, contain a shared understanding of the agreement by the parties and a shared intent to be bound by its terms? Can smart contracts – "a chunk of code in a blockchain" – constitute a shared expression?[37] Is the contractual requirement of the "meeting of the minds" or mutual consent, either through words or conduct, fulfilled by entering code into a blockchain? At first glance, an agreement can be expressed in computer code: "at a minimum, contract laws do not explicitly prohibit expressing contractual obligations in terms of data."[38] However, smart contracts, especially those involving a complex transaction, are unlikely to capture the full intentions of the parties in code form. The meaning of intentional ambiguity and the halo of the implicit meaning surrounding terms remain untranslatable into "dry code."

18.2.1.2 Enforcement

The distinctive characteristics of smart contracts, such as self-enforceability, automatic execution, and immutability pose challenges to traditional contract law.[39] One issue is

---

[31] Similarly, see Werbach & Cornell, cit, at 21–22.

[32] The smart contract breaks down the traditional line between executory and executed contracts. Ibid. 22ff.

[33] See http://coda.caseykuhlman.com/entries/2014/notes-from-my-ethereum-talk.html

[34] Stuart Levi and Alex Lipton, "An Introduction to Smart Contracts and Their Potential and Inherent Limitations," May 26, 2018, available at Harvard Law School Forum on Corporate Governance and Financial Regulation, at https://corpgov.law.harvard.edu/ (accessed September 12, 2018).

[35] Werbach & Cornell, cit. 24

[36] "World's First Blockchain Platform for Marine Insurance Now in Commercial Use" (May 24, 2018), available at www.acord.org/research-education/news/2018/05/24/world's-first-blockchain-platform-for-marine-insurance-now-in-commercial-us (accessed September 12, 2018).

[37] Werbach & Cornell, cit, 23

[38] Harry Surden, "Computable Contracts," (2012) 46 *U.C. Davis L. Rev.* 629–700.

[39] Perfect enforcement may not be desirable: cf Lisa Shay et al., "Confronting Automated Law Enforcement," in Ryan Calo, Michael Froomkin, and Ian Kerr (eds.), *Robot Law* (Edward Elgar 2016) 258; Christina M. Mulligan, "Perfect Enforcement of Law: When to Limit and When to Use Technology"

whether smart contracts are theoretically equipped to replace the role of courts in contract law. The centrality of self-enforcement to smart contracts means that smart contracts are not intended to be legally enforced. Therefore, legal enforcement related to smart contract is a moot point since enforcement is achieved by technological means.[40] With a smart contract, performance is guaranteed by their immutability. The transaction is irreversibly encoded on a distributed blockchain. Computers in the blockchain network ensure performance. The blockchain's distributed (trust or trustless) character is what allows smart contracts to self-perform through unknown or untrusted counterparties. The parties do not have the option to turn to the court to prevent or compel performance. However, it is possible to incorporate into a smart contract various exceptions or conditions to the insularity of the blockchain from the legal system. For example, enforcement could, in theory, be structured to allow for arbitration.[41] Such flexibility, however, has to be coded into the smart contract from the outset, and is contrary to the decentralization and the tamper-proof quality that are the core features of smart contracts.[42]

Max Raskin characterizes smart contracts as a form of self-help: "[a]utomated execution of a contract is a preemptive form of self-help because no recourse to a court is needed for the machine to execute the agreement."[43] Viewing smart contracts as self-help mechanisms make their enforcement not only easier, but unavoidable.[44] But in order to do so, smart contracts change the nature of traditional contracts[45] in that party autonomy is diminished since the parties no longer have the ability to adjust the contract

The fact that smart contracts can never be voided in cases of mistake or lack of capacity, because the blockchain (on the top of which a smart contract is inserted) is immutable, means traditional contract law cannot be applied (at least not in the preperformance of nonperformance phase) to reverse the transaction. Some commentators have categorized contracts as "smart," "quasi-smart," and "dull" contracts.[46] According to them, even though the formation phase may differ (being on paper, for example in the case of "dull" contract), the execution phase will always be "smart," that is, in both cases there will be an automated performance. In practice the market of smart products and services will be populated by quasi-smart contracts in which only the execution is automated and purely smart contracts, such as the transfer of cryptocurrencies. Thus, one of the main issues for the legal system is

---

(2008) 14 *Richmond Journal of Law & Technology* 1–49, at note 13 (explains the dangers of perfect enforcement); see also Eliza Mik, "Smart Contracts" cit., at 13; Gavin Wood, 'Ethereum: A Secure Decentralised Generalised Transaction Ledger' (2015), available at https://pdfs.semanticscholar.org /ac15/ea808ef3b17ad754f91d3a00fedc8f96b929.pdf (accessed September 12, 2018) (he proclaims the impartiality of autonomous enforcement by code).

[40] Werbach & Cornell, cit., at 20ff.

[41] Pamela Morgan, "At Bitcoin South: Innovating Legal Systems through Blockchain Technology," Brave New Coin (December 17, 2014), available at http://bravenewcoin.com/news/pamela-morgan-at-bitcoin-southinnovating-legal-systems-through-blockchain-technology/ (accessed September 12, 2018).

[42] Sklaorff argues that rather than improving efficiency the inflexibility of smart contracting leads to inefficiency in the contracting process. Jeremy Sklaroff, "Smart Contracts and the Cost of Inflexibility," (2017) 166 *U. Pa. L. Rev.* 263–303.

[43] Max Raskin, "The Law and Legality of Smart Contracts" (2017) 1 *Geo. L. Tech. Rev.* 304–341 available at https://www.georgetownlawtechreview.org/the-law-and-legality-of-smart-contracts/GLTR-04-2017/ (accessed September 10, 2018). He draws an analogy to starter interrupters, which are remote-controlled devices that can be installed in cars to prevent them from operating, when payments on the car are in arrears.

[44] Cf. Zoe Sinel, "De-Ciphering Self-Help" (2017) 67 *U. Toronto L.J.* 31-67, at 55ff.

[45] Werbach & Cornell, cit, 28.

[46] See Mateja Durovic & André Janssen, Chapter 4.

how to deal with the immutability of smart contracts in cases of mistake, lack of capacity, or change of circumstances. Durovic and Janssen conclude that "code" is not law, although the law may be adjusted and applied to smart contracts *post hoc*.[47]

18.2.2 *Impossibility of Performance and Self-Sufficiency*

The more difficult legal issues presented by smart contracts are in the areas of performance, force majeure, and other excuses. Tjong Tjin Tai meticulously discusses, as a lawyer, the differences between the common law and civil law systems in relation to the causes of breach of contract.[48] The issues that need thorough examination are the problems of vague terms, general principles and doctrines, such as impossibility of performance, frustration of purpose, supervening illegality, public policy, good faith and hardship. In particular, a list of possible causes of nonperformance includes: (1) the inability to determine identifiable oracles; (2) the inability of adequately coding the use of automatic oracles in algorithmic language; (3) the difficulty of identifying future events that would trigger an excuse from performance (force majeure events need to be identified through TTP or expert oracles); and (4) if identifiable, then the triggering events need to be embedded in algorithmic standard contracts, anchored in contract law rules, but relying on experts or TTP oracles for their application.

Tjong Tjin Tai concludes that *ex ante* programming can theoretically substitute for the *post hoc* application of contract law, but it is not feasible at the current level of technological advancement.[49] In the future, best practices could be standardized and implemented by smart contract platforms; the above-mentioned lists of possible causes of nonperformance could be "translated" in coded language and embedded in algorithmic standard contracts. At this time, however, the nature of majority of contracts, often complex, relational, and long term, allows the use of smart contracts for only limited and specific applications, such as fund transfers.

As mentioned above st § 18.2.1., in the area of remedies the self-enforcement feature of a smart contract poses the question of whether traditional contract remedies will matter anymore. Self-enforcement suggests that breach of contract is impossible and thereby there is no need for legal remedies such as damages for non-performance or specific performance. The "self-sufficiency" of a smart contract is premised on its completeness. If the smart contract is incomplete, then some form of legal redress may be needed.

In sum, proponents of smart contracts and blockchain technology assert that any problems, technical, legal, or otherwise, can be solved by the application of the majority consensus rule. This assertion is counterintuitive since contracts are hopelessly incomplete; words that are coded to form a contract will also result in incomplete contracts. Poncibò and DiMatteo suggest that the theory of contract incompleteness would be a good theoretical rationale to search for better solutions, such as incorporating a remedial scheme within the smart contract.[50] Under such an approach, smart contracts become smarter and some transactions are more amenable to smart contracting than

---

[47] See also Riccardo de Caria, "Smart Contracts: the Search for Workable Legal Categories," *Oxford Business Law Blog* (May 25, 2018), available at www.law.ox.ac.uk/business-law-blog/blog/2018/05/law-and-autonomous-systems-series-defining-smart-contracts-search (accessed September 10, 2018).
[48] Eric Tjong Tjin Tai, Chapter 5.
[49] Ibid.
[50] See Larry DiMatteo & Cristina Poncibò, Chapter 7.

others. This approach rests on a contextual vision of "smartness" – is the smart contract embedded within a relational context? Can parties' expectations be captured within a smart contract?

The desirability of smart contracts and their independence from the legal system may hinge on their ability to code "self-help remedies." Assuming that smart contracts are an ideologically driven technology, decentralized and designed for guaranteeing the "anonymity" (public blockchain) of the parties, remedies will need to be implanted within the code itself. Self-adjusting remedies can be divided into "proactive" (security and data protection) and "reactive" measures (reputation, computer and social repudiation).[51] In sum, the code needs to be a facilitative and a regulatory instrument.

The promise of smart contracts may be realized in the future through the advancement of robotics and artificial intelligence (AI), where the main issue at stake will be the liability for harm caused by the "superintelligence misalignment problem."[52] This problem occurs when AI makes a value judgment that is not aligned with the values or expectations of the contracting parties. This is akin to the agency problem found in corporate law where director-officer-employee interests may diverge with the interests of the corporation and its shareholders.[53] The conclusion at this point of time is that smart contracts cannot avoid contract law, because the latter provides flexible standards and doctrines (duty of good faith, change of circumstances) essential to long-term, relational, complex business networks that are a part of the global market.[54] The smart contract is best applied to simple, highly standardized transaction, such as is found in finance and banking. But, even non-customized contracts are vulnerable to *post hoc* judicial intervention premised on issues of illegality, incapacity, mistake (coding errors), unfairness (unconscionability), and the interpretation of coded words.

18.2.3 *Interpretation*

Another shortcoming of smart contracts concerns the interpretation of coded language. Put simply, computer language is different from natural language in many important ways, and the existing legal rules on contract interpretation are not tailored to interpret smart contracts.[55] Michel Cannarsa poses the question of whether legal interpretation of

---

[51] Larry DiMatteo & Cristina Poncibò, Chapter 7, see Raskin, cit. 304; compare O'Shields, cit., at 177.
[52] Peter McBurney and Simon Parsons, "Talking about Doing" in Katie Atkinson, Henry Prakken, and Adam Wyner (eds.), *From Knowledge Representation to Argumentation in AI. Law and Policy Making* (London, UK: College Publications, 2013) 151–166. Philosophers of language realized that for utterances about actions, such as promises, the rules of pragmatics (or norms of usage) are as important as the meaning. Under what conditions, for example, does a promise take effect? These notions have been explored in the law and more recently in automated communications between machines. See Alessandro Capone, Francesca Poggi, (eds.), *Pragmatics and Law, Philosophical Perspectives* (Switzerland: Springer International Publishing, 2016); cf see also Daniele Magazzeni, Peter McBurney, William Nash, "Validation and Verification of Smart Contracts: A Research Agenda" (2017) 50 *Computer* 50–57, available at 10.1109/MC.2017.3571045.
[53] See Patrick McColgan, "Agency Theory and Corporate Governance: A Review of the Literature from a UK Perspective" (May 22, 2001), available at https://pdfs.semanticscholar.org/79c5/2954af851c95a27cb1fb702c23feaae86ca1.pdf (accessed September 13, 2018).
[54] See Werbach & Cornell.
[55] Sarah Green, "Smart Contracts, Interpretation and Rectification" (2018) *Lloyds Maritime and Commercial Law Quarterly* 234–251.

computer codes is even possible.[56] He analyzes the differences between smart and regular contracts, based on the difference between human or natural language and computer language.[57] Word contracts are inherently flexible especially when they incorporate general principles and standards-like provisions, such as duty of good faith, duty to cooperate, readjustment and renegotiation, satisfaction, force majeure, and best effort clauses. In contrast, coded contracts are inherently inflexible, unable to adapt to circumstances by means of general clauses or vague concepts, such as good faith or reasonableness. Cannarsa concludes that smart contracts are complete and unambiguous only in theory. Moreover, smart contracts, especially those dealing with complex transactions, will not lower transaction costs, given the costs of coding, and will not prevent litigation or arbitration costs, and may add the costs of the translation of code into legal language.[58] In sum, the "perverse fascination" with the indiscriminate promotion of the blockchain is often based on a misunderstanding of the tech itself.[59]

18.2.4 Transmission of Real Estate and Smart Property

Sjef van Erp and Louis-Daniel Muka Tshibende address the issues of smart contracts in the areas of property and warranty law.[60] The creation of "smart property" from a theoretical point of view is explored. How is possible to redefine traditional property rights to fit the digital world? Can data be an object of property law and what are the drawbacks? Can AI be a subject of property law? Is still there a "numerus clausus" of legal objects?

In the area of property conveyance, the blockchain could play a fundamental role in the transmission of real estate where the form is *ad validitatem* (notarial authentication requirement in civil law countries) and for warranties. Actually, a "blockchain mortgage" for home loans in common law countries may become ordinary. In this case, property records could be stored on a blockchain, and the public could trace the home's

---

[56] Compare also Eliza Mik, 'cit., at § 3.2.1: Terminology, Technical Limitations and Real World Complexity' (2017) 9 *Law, Innovation and Technology* 269–300: "Developers fail to recognize that in contract law, ambiguity is a feature not a bug. Apart from the natural ambiguity accompanying all human languages and the ambiguity that results from sloppy drafting, many contractual provisions are deliberately written in a broad, slightly imprecise manner to ensure a certain degree of leeway. The ambiguity of certain provisions may also reflect the stronger bargaining position of one party, who drafts the contract in a manner enabling it to deliver the absolute minimum without being accused of breach. Terms may also be left vague because of an unwillingness to invest resources in extended negotiations or drafting ... ".

[57] The works that consider the issue of authoring smart contracts from the subject-matter expert's perspective are those proposed by Frantz, Nowostawski, and Clack et al.: Christopher Frantz and Mariusz Nowostawski, "From Institutions to Code: Towards Automated Generation of Smart Contracts" (2016) *iEEE* 1st International Workshops on Foundations and Applications of Self* Systems (fAS*W), 210–215; Christopher Clack, Vikram Bakshi, and Lee Braine, *Smart Contract Templates: Essential Requirements and Design Options* (ArXiv eprints, December 2016).

The involvement of a lawyer in the authoring of smart contracts is paramount. See Firas Al Khalil et al., "A Solution for the Problems of Translation and Transparency in Smart Contracts" (White Paper, 2017) available at http://www.grctc.com/wp-content/uploads/2017/06/GRCTC-Smart-Contracts-White-Paper -2017.pdf, 8ff (accessed September 10, 2018).

[58] Scott Farrell, Heidi Machin, and Roslyn Hinchliffe, "Lost and Found in Smart Contract Translation – Considerations in Transitioning to Automation in Legal Architecture" in *Proceedings of the Congress of the United Nations Commission on International Trade Law*, (Wien, Uncitral, Ebook 2017), pp. 95–104.

[59] Mik, "Smart contracts" cit., at 269ff

[60] Sjef van Erp, Chapter 12; Luis-Daniel Muka Tshibende, Chapter 13.

ownership. Anyone can view liens against the property in chronological order, which is important because liens are paid on the basis of priority.[61]

18.3 Shortcomings of Blockchain and Regulation of Smart Contracts

The evolution of smart contracts and the uses for blockchain technology is in its early stages. Scientist Stuart Kauffmann coined the term "adjacent possible" as a way of foreshadowing the future by analyzing the edges of the present states of things, where the number of potential first-order reactions is a finite number and only certain innovations are possible.[62]

For smart contracts, the "adjacent possible" that is the related paths to be explored include electronic platforms and networks, and other issues such as privacy, data, and consumer protection. These issues need to be addressed in order to better understand the impact of the blockchain and its applications. They form the ecosystem that will encourage the reinvention of smart contracts by unlocking new doors for their application. This new ecosystem raises numerous liability and regulatory issues.[63]

18.3.1 E-Platforms and Networks

Piotr Tereszkiewicz sketches the economic notion of electronic platforms as digital environments grounded on a membership agreement.[64] Such a framework creates a fragmented legal system of business and informational connections. EU law is based on a binary model of the relationship between service provider and intermediaries. Safe harbor or nonliability provisions are provided for digital platforms, such as the "mere hosting" liability exemption.[65] The European Court of Justice limited the scope of the exemption reasoning that some electronic platform-based models, such as Uber, are not "normal service providers."[66] As a result, the EU adopted a proposal that provides a framework for regulating intermediation services.[67] It aims at regulating platform-business relationships (P2B) by promoting fairness through the use of clear terms and simple language, recognizing a duty of due care during the precontractual stage, and extending the responsibility of intermediaries. The proposal focuses on the "three-party relationship" (platform operator + supplier of good/services + consumer) and relies on a reputational feedback system to enhance the due diligence of operators and suppliers.

Eliza Mik defines e-platforms simply as Internet-based intermediaries, essential entities without which the Internet would not have evolved.[68] This is in line with the parlance of modern programmers who imagine the Web as a kind of archeological site, which evolves

---

[61] Kannice Käll, "Blockchain Control," (2018) 29(2) *Law and Critique* 133–140.
[62] For a discussion of this theory see Stuart Kauffmann, *At Home in the Universe: The Search for the Laws of Self-Organization and Complexity* (New York: Oxford University Press, 1995).
[63] Robert Herian, "Taking Blockchain Seriously" (2018) 29(2) *Law and Critique* 163–171.
[64] Piotr Tereszkiewicz, Chapter 8.
[65] Art. 14 Directive 2000/31 of the European Parliament and of the Council of June 8, 2000 on certain legal aspects of information society services, in particular electronic commerce, in the Internal Market ("Directive on electronic commerce") OJ L 178, 17.07.2000, 1–16
[66] *Asociación Profesional élite Taxi v. Uber Systems Spain SL*, Case C-434/15 (December 20, 2017), para 37.
[67] Proposal of Regulation on promoting fairness and transparency for business users of online intermediation services of April 2018 (COM (2018) 238 final).
[68] See Eliza Mik, Chapter 9.

via stacked platforms, building upon layers of platforms buried beneath every page. The functioning of platforms is very centralized,[69] and it is conflictive with the three features of blockchain technology: decentralization, transparency (provenance tracking), and immutability (recordkeeping).[70]

The power of the blockchain, in the public's eye, is based on a number of assumptions including people's preferences for decentralization and for anonymity. These assumptions are more rhetorical than factual. A party may want to remain anonymous but would like to know identity of the the person or entity that is on the other side of the transaction. Of course, one-sided transparency is antithetical to the blockchain whose major feature is its nontransparency (public blockchains) or selective transparency (private blockchain). The confidence that is associated with knowing the identity of the other party to a transaction is lost on the blockchain. The other illusion associated with smart contracts is the immutability of the blockchain, which prevents any amendments to correct coding errors or shortcomings that become apparent before or during the performance of the smart contract. In fact, smart contracts usually "sit on the top" of and remain independent from the underlying blockchain.[71] This detachment means that the blockchain is unable to detect or correct coding errors. The correctness of the coding of smart contracts is not verified or validated by the consensus algorithm. Expert coders or amateur coders can create smart contracts. For example, Solidity advertises training that will allow people to learn to "code [their] own smart contract in less than a day!"[72] Thus, the quality of coding can vary across a broad spectrum.

The alleged neutrality of code is also an illusion. In given circumstances, a coder can create a smart contract with accidental and intentional errors and coding can incorrectly express the parties' agreement and thus fail to properly translate the contract clauses into algorithmic form.

Finally, errors can also occur when a smart contract allows for reaching outside of the blockchain to verify information (oracles) in order to adjust terms or fill in terms in the contract. The ability to "communicate" to off-chain assets or sources of information related to events subsequent to the formation of the smart contract also has its shortcomings. Even though the blockchain is given the responsibility to track or record transfers recorded in the smart contract, it cannot guarantee their actual physical location. The blockchain can only record the party who in theory should own the objects or assets. Verification of actual transfer would need to be provided by intermediaries, such as oracles that feed basic information into the blockchain.

---

[69] See, e.g., eBay, Amazon, Facebook, Amazon (GAFA); Franklin Foer, *World without Mind: The Existential Threat of Big Tech* (New York: Penguin Press, 2017); Matt Word, *Gods of the Valley: How Today's Tech Giants Monopolize the Future* (Independently Published 2018).

[70] Trevor Kiviat, "Beyond Bitcoin: Issues In Regulating Blockchain Transactions" (2015) 65 *Duke Law Journal* 569–575; Jeanne Schroeder, "Bitcoin and the Uniform Commercial Code" (2016) 24 *University of Miami Business Law Review* 1–65; Joshua Fairfield, "Bitproperty" (2015) 88 *South California Law Review* 805–74.

[71] See Mik, Chapter 9; with the exception of the bitcoin blockchain, which effectively equates smart contracts with transactions: see Antonopoulos cit., at 128, 129, 137.

[72] Solidity it is a Turing-complete language (a Turing-complete means it can be proven mathematically to be capable of performing any possible calculation) and it has been developed within the Ethereum system.

18.3.2 Data and Privacy Protection

The blockchain and smart contracts pose serious concerns in a variety of areas including privacy. Lauren Henry Scholz reflects on smart contracts and consumer privacy in drawing from the work of Kar and Radin.[73] For her, the term "algorithmic contract" has greater descriptive value than the term "smart contracts" because it better captures the essence of blockchain technologies. Algorithm can be perceived as a constructive "agent" for the company using it, which means its acts are indicative of the company's intent. Thus, it is possible to contract with a company using an algorithmic agent. The algorithmic contracts that present the most significant problems for contract law are those that involve "black box" algorithmic agents. The algorithm can be seen as a type of invisible standard form contract, where the party with superior bargaining power unilaterally decides its terms. Scholz argues that these coded terms are "pseudo-contracts" that represent a new form of "personalized law," which mostly ignores issues involving private privacy and consumer protection. These contracts actually can diminish freedom of contract by undermining the objective manifestation of mutual assent, which lies at the heart of contract law.

A partial solution to the lack of real consent is requiring that privacy protections be coded into smart contracts. However, privacy issues are much broader than merely contracting for privacy. Privacy clauses contained in clickwrap and browsewrap agreements have not provided the level of privacy that many parties (consumers) may expect. Privacy, besides its constitutional dimension,[74] has more in common to property rights, than to contract rights.[75] Scholz argues that the law should force individuals to maintain privacy rights (based upon the presumption of the inalienability of the right to privacy),[76] which requires strong regulations guarding against or limiting the sale of privacy interests via contract.[77]

The core question then becomes: What regulatory strategies should be used to protect privacy rights in smart contracts? For example, should a party's personal information, religious faith, race, and political view be nonwaiveable in certain transactions?[78] Should regulatory authorities, especially in consumer contracts, be given access to distributed

---

[73] Lauren Henry Scholz, "Algorithmic Contracts" (2017) 20 *Stanford Technology Law Review* 128–169; see also Robin Bradley Kar and Margaret Jane Radin, "Pseudo-Contract and Shared Meaning Analysis" (2019) 132 *Harvard Law Review*, available at https://ssrn.com/abstract=3124018 (accessed 12 September 2018).

[74] The U.S. Supreme Court recognized a constitutional right to privacy in the landmark decision *Roe v. Wade*, 410 U.S. 113 (1973), but U.S. privacy legislation was originally introduced as a response to the invention of the portable camera: see Samuel D. Warren and Louis D. Brandeis, "The Right to Privacy" (1890) 4 *Harvard Law Review* 193–220 available at www.cs.cornell.edu/~shmat/courses/cs5436/warren-brandeis.pdf.

[75] See Anita Allen, *Unpopular Privacy: What Must We Hide* (New York: Oxford University Press, 2011).

[76] Pamela Samuelson, "Privacy as Intellectual Property?" (2000) 52 *Stan. L. Rev.* 1125–1174; for a skeptical perspective on privacy as property see Jessica Litman, "Information Privacy/Information Property" (2000) 52 *Stan. L. Rev.* 1283, 1284–85.

[77] For an overview, see Cécile de Terwangne, Elise Degrave, Séverine Dusollier and Robert Queck (eds.), *Law, Norms and Freedoms in Cyberspace / Droit, normes et libertés dans le cybermonde: Liber Amicorum Yves Poullet* (Louvain la neuve: Larcier, 2018). Compare civil law and common law perspective in: Huw Beverley-Smith, Ansgar Ohly, and Agnes Lucas-Schloetter, *Privacy, Property and Personality: Civil Law Perspectives on Commercial Appropriation* (Cambridge University Press, 2006); Paul M. Schwartz, "Property, Privacy, and Personal Data," (2004) 117 *Harv. L. Rev.* 2055–2129; Edward J. Janger, "Privacy Property, Information Costs, and the Anticommons" (2003) 54 *Hastings L. J.* 899–925.

[78] The regime for special categories of personal data (health data, criminal data, religion, race and ethnic background, etc.; see Articles 9-10 GDPR) is no longer meaningful according to some commentators,

ledgers (storage of private information)? Would such access stunt the growth of smart contracts and blockchain technology? As in other contexts, a proper balance needs to be struck between paternalism and private autonomy.

Lokke Moerel describes the development of smart contracts as happening in two phases. The first phase was grounded on a decentralized identity management system, which shared data with trusted third parties. This "decentralized system" evolved to include a vast set of data collected, stored, and managed by a "centralized data collector" in that the controller (entity which determines the purposes and means of the processing of personal data) is quite often also the processor (entity which processes data on behalf of the controller and maintains detailed records of the data), according to the definition of Article 4 of the European General Data Protection Regulation (GDPR).[79] Businesses, indeed, can be either data controllers and processors, such as a cloud service provider which control and process personal data or as any payroll company, which is controller of data about its own staff, but acts as a processor when it comes to its clients. But, this centralized model provided by the GDPR is ineffective in the decentralized ecosystem of blockchains[80] (also called distributed ledger technology or DLT) where in fact there is no central controller since it is based on a grouping of nodes.[81] Moerel predicts that a new ecosystem is increasingly gaining ground, in which every node would be responsible to be GDPR-compliant, which is grounded on the principles of fairness and transparency, data minimization, accuracy, right to be forgotten, and confidentiality (Article 5). In such a legal order, each individual customer would be, at the same time, both a data subject and a data controller/processor. In such a new ecosystem, it would be best to have tailored regulation balancing the various interests at stake, including the commercial interests and the interests of the individuals involved, as well as those of society in general.

At this time, the (new) ecosystem must comply with an (old) invasive strategy grounded on the intricate privacy policies that are not comprehensible to the average citizen, because of both their content and excessive length. The new system must also follow the "mechanical proceduralism," whereby data controllers notify individuals and ask for their consent in a mechanical manner. Thus, individuals are becoming more and more transparent to everyone except for themselves.[82] Notwithstanding the GDPR's core principle according to which "natural persons should have control of their own personal data" (recital 7, GDPR), the current information and consent requirements are quite ineffective. The controllers and processors privacy policies are not based on true consent

---

because businesses (and also governments) use potentially "innocent" data, some of which are freely available in the public domain. See Lokke Moerel and Corien Prins, "Privacy for the homo digitalis. Proposal for a new regulatory framework for data protection in the light of Big Data and the Internet of Things," (May 25, 2016) available at https://ssrn.com/abstract=2784123 or http://dx.doi.org/10.2139/ssrn .2784123 (accessed September 12, 2018) at 11: they suggest the "legitimacy test" for the reuse of data, that is for the "further processing of data," which is essential for Big Data and the Internet of Things (IoT), the latter designed to generate new correlations on the ground of identified patterns and on the basis of the reuse of information.

[79] Regulation (Eu) 2016/679 of the European Parliament and of the Council of April 27, 2016 on the protection of natural persons with regard to the processing of personal data and on the free movement of such data, and repealing Directive 95/46/EC (General Data Protection Regulation), OJ L 119/1, 4.5.2016, pp. 1–88.

[80] WEF Report on Blockchain 2017 identifies fifty-two global solution networks. DLT just disrupted what Moerel called the "existing middleman" model (bank, social net, governments).

[81] Ibid.

[82] Moerel & Prins, cit., at 8.

(not freely given) when the waiver of privacy rights is required to get something in return[83] on the ground of preemptive predictions. This means that the actions of customers are influenced by means of denying options (such as excluding them from insurance schemes or rejecting their application for a loan) and this often occurs without the person's knowledge. Until now, predictions were based on individual past preferences: the customer's freedom to accept or not to accept an offer. But preemptive predictions can result in a violation of fundamental rights and values, because they lower the degree of individual self-determination with regard to how personal data is used, thus affecting the right to privacy, protection of personal autonomy, freedom of choice, and self-identity, rights, and freedoms which are fundamental for the proper functioning of democratic societies.[84]

Within this perimeter, Moerel suggests to data controllers who have a commercial interest in the collection and processing of data and to suppliers of technical infrastructures and infrastructure components (such as software) to implement their data-processing systems on the basis of "privacy by design."[85] "Privacy by design" minimizes the impact of the process of processing data and complies with the GDPR if it is user-centered (focus is on who uses it, not on who provides the software and infrastructures). Moerel suggests that "privacy by design" can act as a meta-regulation by which producers of smart goods and services are encouraged to design their products and services according to data protection standards, thus mitigating the privacy impact on individuals from the outset.[86]

18.3.3 Blockchain and Consumers

The issue of the effectiveness of consumer protection over transactions conducted over the blockchain is one in which government intervention is warranted. But do consumers need such protection? The answer is a definite "probably" since any relationship consisting of bargaining power and informational asymmetries is likely to result in some form of abuse of the weaker party. The most pro-protection avenue would allow government authorities access to the distributed ledger in order to police any such abuse. Oscar Borgogno is a proponent of such a paternalistic regulatory approach.[87] He questions whether smart contracts are a smart choice in commercial (B2B) and consumer (B2C)

---

[83] For example, a lower premium under insurance schemes based on pay-how-you-drive allows citizens who are found to have a better driving style to pay less for their insurance than those who drive less carefully. Using sensor devices fitted into cars, driving style (including a large number of variables that were never previously monitored, such as acceleration, speed, and cornering) can now be monitored in real time at the individual level.

[84] See Lokke Moerel & Corien Prins, cit., at 20. The U.S. government took seriously these risks and initiated a public consultation in the summer of 2014 entitled "Big Data and Consumer Privacy in the Internet Economy," 79 *Federal Register* 32714 (June 6, 2014). For more information about the debate in the United States and opinions based on science and policy, see Seeta Peña Gangadharan, "The Downside of Digital Inclusion: Expectations and Experiences of Privacy and Surveillance among Marginal Internet Users" (2017), 19 *New Media & Society* 597–615.

[85] See also article 25 GDPR.

[86] Lokke Moerel & Corien Prins, cit., at 82ff. Privacy by design means to build into the technology limits and requirements applicable to data processing. Examples include software that can block access to certain data for certain categories of employees; technologically facilitated protocols under which data are automatically deleted after a certain period of time has elapsed; or the automatic encryption or pseudonymization of data.

[87] See Oscar Borgogno, Chapter 16.

transactions alike. On the pro-consumer side, the blockchain could be used to benefit consumers by lowering enforcement costs by providing automated relief. For example, blockchain technologies can be used to enforce the rights of train and airline passengers. The application of a blockchain to automatize the reimbursement procedure would be a good testing ground for the functionality of smart contracts to advance consumer protection. This can be accomplished without the use of oracles because the rail and air industries sectors are already highly digitalized and coordinated via open platforms.

Then he addresses the regulatory issues of whether the regulation of smart contracts in B2B and B2C sectors should be left to public policy decisions or left to the advancement of technology to decide? Just as governments regulate automobile safety, it will have to at some point regulate the blockchain and smart contracts even if it is restricted to the level of consumer protection. But, potential regulations should also look to relational contract theory to protect long-term commercial relations against the rigidity of the blockchain. Moreover, as in traditional consumer contracts, procedural fairness that allows for cost effective ways for consumers to seek redress is necessary. In addition, class actions at least at the EU level should also be deployed as a device of legal enforcement.

Borgogno concludes that regulation of B2B smart contracts should be based on sector specific policies. This could entail the use of "regulatory sandboxes"[88] to establish a legal framework that will allow businesses to test STTs in their specific industries. In B2C smart contracts, general regulations should be implemented to prevent consumers from relinquishing all their personal data rights.

18.4 Intersection of Law and Technology: A View from the Balcony

Roger Brownsword provides a meta-appraisal of the interaction between legal development and technological innovation.[89] This interrelationship began in earnest with the creation of the Internet and proceeded though various forms of electronic or digital contracting. The smart contract is merely another step in the evolving nature of technology. He proposes a classificatory scheme that will allow lawyers and others to better understand new innovations in technology and if and how the law should respond to these developments. Drawing on network theory,[90] he works on the premise that technology change often leads to both economic and legal disruptions.[91] The widespread use of the concept of disruption implies that there is a need for a new theoretical framework to guide legal discourse. Lawyers and judges deal with technological change by prioritizing the need for legal coherency and integration to existing legal constructs (contract, agency, fiduciary, duty and so forth) over pragmatic values. Law and business, it has been said,

---

[88] Ibid.

[89] See Roger Brownsword, Rob van Gestel, & Hans W. Micklitz, "Introduction: Contract and Regulation: Changing Paradigms" in Roger Brownsword, Rob A. J. van Gestel, & Hans W. Micklitz (eds.), *Contract and Regulation: A Handbook on New Methods of Law Making in Private Law* (Edward Elgar: Chelthenam, Northampton, 2017), 1–38. See also, Brownsword, Chapter 17.

[90] For a brief sketch of the concept of networks in contract law, see Eric Tjong Tjin Tai, "Networks and Informal Contract Law" in Roger Brownsword, Rob van Gestel & Hans-Wolfgang Micklitz, above at 235–258; see also Catherine Mitchell, "Network Commercial Relationships: What Role for Contract Law?" Ibid. at 198–234; Gunter Teubner, *Networks as connected contracts*, International Studies in the Theory of Private Law (Hart Publishing: Oxford, 2011); Fabrizio Cafaggi, "Contractual Network and the Small Business Act: Towards European Principles?" (2008) 4 *European Review of Contract Law* 493–539.

[91] See in general terms, Peter F. Cowhey & Jonathan D. Aronson, *Digital DNA: Disruption and the Challenges for Global Governance* (New York: Oxford University Press, 2017).

prefer incremental legal change to radical legal reforms.[92] Businesses are averse to unexpected risks and, thus, like law that is certain and predictable. The approach advanced by Brownsword applies to all types of technological disruptions, and not merely to the impact of disruption on contract law issues stemming from the diffusion of STTs.

Brownsword thesis is that new economically disruptive technologies inevitability led to some degree of "legal disruption." This is because technology is changing both the idea of existing law as a system of legal rules and standards and the way that lawyers, judges, and legislators think of the law's role. Traditionally, law, through its surrogates (judges and legislators), aimed at coherency of statutes, integrity of doctrines, and certainty in the system of precedents. Traditionalists, or what Brownsword calls "coherentists," are still reluctant to co-opt new technologies to achieve new regulatory effects. He asserts that a new regulatory mind-set should focus on the risk to be managed (privacy, protection of personal data) and also on how best to manage that risk by using new technologies.[93] The traditional classificatory scheme of contract law, therefore needs to be revised, to accommodate novel forms of agreement formed by way of hubs, chains, clusters, and platforms (such as franchise, carriage of goods, construction, share economy) to find a place for "network contracts" or "contracts with network effects"[94] in the old legal classification scheme.[95] As it happened with the development of software, a "coherentist" assessment of new technologies based upon preserving the integrity of law remains the prevailing mind-set of legal scholars and policymakers. In the case of the blockchain, the need for legal coherence is overwhelming lawyers and judges' views of how to treat the new technology. Thus, Brownsword advocates a new kind of theoretical discourse for the regulation of smart contracts. His approach is premised on three questions: (1) What are the regulatory goals? (2) What are the interests which should be taken into consideration? (3) How should a balance of competing interests be struck?

Instead of top-down regulation, Brownsword's framework sees the new technologies themselves being used as regulatory tools. Technology has a regulatory effect and policymakers must begin to think that they can reach the same effect formerly provided by traditional or existing legal rules by designing regulatory features (such as "privacy by design") directly into tech products and services. Instead of immutability of law, technology that regulates itself mimics a risk management approach to law.

Although the regulatory-instrumental approach seems inviting, difficulty lies in the nonalignment of blockchain technology with the law of contract. This occurs when parties use the blockchain and smart contracts to achieve something prohibited by the law, because contract law's policing doctrines are not waivable and, therefore, possess a "penumbra of public law."[96] Philosophically, new technologies cannot be seen as purely exercises of freedom, or creative spirit, but as quests for greater efficiency. These benefits must be weighed against the technologies' compatibility with a community's fundamental values.[97] Just as the economic analysis of law has failed to provide a full understanding of the descriptive and normative

[92] Roger Brownsword, Chapter 17.
[93] Lawrence Lessig, cit. ft. 2.
[94] Roger Brownsword, Chapter 17.
[95] Ibid.
[96] Werbach & Cornell, cit., 50. Mandatory rules in consumer law standard contracts cannot be avoided through the use of smart contracts in consumer transactions.
[97] Cf Pasquale, cit. ft. 2.

dimensions of contract law,[98] smart contracts cannot replace the broader, contextualized view provided by contract law. In sum, efficient technocracy does not necessarily improve community life and, in some cases, may have negative impacts on societal values.

18.4.1 *A Perspective from China*

Angelia Wang and Chen Lei provide a case study on the use of smart contracts and regulation of blockchains technologies in China. The use of blockchain technologies in China has experienced a rapid expansion since 2016. It has been used in a wide range of industries and sectors, such as digital storage of DNA in medicine, logistics such as *VeChain* in transportation, and automated contract drafting in legal services.[99]

They provide a taxonomy of types of smart contracts based on a number of variables including: (1) the types of functions that smart contracts offer ("smart-smart" contracts and "not so smart" contracts and other e-tools, such as intelligent contract drafting by scanning contracts to find unrecognized risks and other uncertainties; copyright e-registration at low costs; and so forth), (2) the types of user (private companies, like Alibaba, and public authorities, like the Ministry of Industry responsible for the standardization of the industrial sector; as in most services, there are often public-private hybrids).

An optimistic assessment sees technology as providing legal solutions. At the same time, the rigidity that characterizes blockchain gives rise to many difficult problems in practice. For example, a void contract or an illegal contract would remain permanently on the blockchain. Wang and Chen conclude that a purely technological approach (self-regulation), such as application programming interface (API), will not be sufficient and would have to be supplemented by a constant precautionary monitoring,[100] as a crucial element in preserving legality.

18.5 Blockchain from the Front Lines

Legal professionals, lawyers, barristers, judges, and arbitrators are currently confronted by the newness of smart contracts and the uncertainty of the application of existing law to new technologies.[101] Lawyers remain an essential element to the drafting and interpreting of smart contracts, while judges are being challenged to interpret such contracts and to determine if legal redress is needed, and, if needed, whether it is sufficient. Judge Marc Clément of the Lyon Administrative Appeal Court, an engineer and jurist by training, discusses the role of courts in the era of smart contracts.[102] In contrast with the scientific proposition that blockchains are fully functional without the need for legal intervention, Clément asserts that this is true only in the virtual world (e.g., with cryptocurrencies and in videogames), but as a general matter the proposition proves false when the virtual world interfaces with the real world. In many cases, the law is needed to regulate that

---

[98] See Eric Posner, *Economic Analysis of Contract Law after Three Decades: Success or Failure?*, (2002) 112 *Yale L.J.* 829.
[99] See Jia Wang & Lei Chen, Chapter 10.
[100] Rather than by a "regulatory approach" in Brownsword's terms.
[101] Dena Givari, "How Does Arbitration Intersect with the Blockchain Technology That Underlies Cryptocurrencies?" (May 5, 2018) available at http://arbitrationblog.kluwerarbitration.com/2018/05/05/scheduled-blockchain-arbitration-april-17-2018/ (accessed September 13, 2018).
[102] See Marc Clément, Chapter 15.

interface. For example, the virtual world's retrieval of personal data from the real world requires that it respects the rights of the users of the applicable technology.

Smart interfaces possess certain characteristics and each characteristic requires a specific legal assessment. Courts will need to assess whether they should intervene to ensure the accuracy of information; security in communication and liability for fraud; guarantee results due to inadequate performance; whether the performance or transaction is legal; whether the smart contract is actually a legal contract (incapacity, illegality); and so forth. Given the speed of technological advancement, Clément argues that there will be more for judges to do including gaining technical expertise, evaluating the burden of proof, assessing power and informational asymmetries, among other things. He concludes that more educational resources will have to be assigned to the relationship of law and technology.[103] Practicing lawyer supportive of Judge Clément's assessment assert that smart contracts represent a great challenge for lawyers with no technological training.[104] Most lawyers are unable to draft and code a smart contract. The solution will require lawyers to gain proficient knowledge of basic programming (in law schools or continuing education). From the technological world, software is needed to assist sparsely trained lawyers in fulfilling their traditional legal tasks.[105]

18.6 Assessing the Present and Fearing the Future

18.6.1 Terminology and Lawyers as Coders

The common understanding is that a blockchain is a shared ledger, stored and maintained in network nodes, which records transactions in the form of messages sent from one node to another. Information stored on the blockchain can be inspected by all members of the blockchain and are nonmodifiable.[106] The UK Government Chief Scientific Adviser defines blockchain as "a type of database that takes a number of records and puts them in a block. Each block is then 'chained' to the next block, using cryptographic signatures. This allows blockchains to be used like a ledger, which can be shared and corroborated by anyone with the appropriate permission."[107]

---

[103] An example would be new student exercises in "experimental law." This would include new courses and moot courts connecting legal education and research with new technologies.

[104] See "Smart Contracts: The Blockchain Technology That Will Replace Lawyers," available at https://block geeks.com/guides/smart-contracts/ (accessed September 10, 2018); Andrea Tinianow, "Blockchain for Lawyers," *ABA Business Law Section* (2018), available at www.americanbar.org/content/dam/aba/administra tive/business_law/newsletters/CL930000/full-issue-201804.authcheckdam.pdf. (accessed September 10, 2018); cf also "Techup Law 2017," available at www.monash.edu/__data/assets/pdf_file/0006/973023/ TechUp-Law-Publication-Final-1.pdf (accessed September 10, 2018).

[105] See the online training programs of the Blockchain academy at www.theblockchainacademy.com/store/ VKNrZAnA; or the university program "DU Juriste Digital et Data Protection Certified Education" at the Lyon Law Department; cf as an example the prototype of a self-enforcing smart contract that can be used in software escrow agreements: "Frost Brown Todd Creates Smart Contract App for Software Escrow Agreements" (May 22, 2017) available at www.frostbrowntodd.com/newsroom-press-frost-brown-todd-creates-smart-contract-app-for-software-escrow-agreements.html (accessed September 10, 2018).

[106] See Melanie Swan, *Blockchain: Blueprint for a New Economy* (O'Reilly Media: Sebastopol, 2015) 9; previously, Szabo in his seminal work: Nik Szabo, "Smart Contracts: Building Blocks for Digital Markets," (1996) Extropy, available at www.fon.hum.uva.nl/rob/Courses/InformationInSpeech/CDROM/Literature/ LOTwinterschool2006/szabo.best.vwh.net/smart_contracts_2.html and Nick Szabo, "Smart Contracts: Formalizing and Securing Relationships on Public Networks" (accessed September 12, 2018) 2 (9) *First Monday* 2.

[107] Cit. ft. 6.

In contrast, the interdisciplinary world has produced inconsistent notions of smart contracts. In sum, there are persisting differences in the definitions of smart contracts adopted by scholars, where sometimes the emphasis is on decentralization, sometimes on immutability; in other cases, the focus is placed on the fact that they are self-executing, provide self-help remedies, or are self-sufficient tools.

For lawyers, the term "smart contract" ought to be used with caution. It is misleading to treat a smart contract as a contract in a strictly legal sense. A contract is defined in law as a legally enforceable agreement, which creates legal rights and reciprocal duties. Smart contracts implement a default computing programme, which can be used to form and execute agreed to performances. It is more appropriate to call this new form of technology as contract automation with three distinctive features: automatic execution, immutability, and inclusiveness.

18.6.2 Detachment of Human Element from Contracting

The formation of a contract normally requires parties to negotiate terms, to give consent, and, more importantly, to perform their contractual obligations. The high degree of human involvement in the life cycle of a contract is inevitable. Although the performance of a contract may be delegated to a third-party electronic agent, the contract is still directly formed and performed by human beings. A contract formed by blockchain technologies needs only a minimum level of direct interactions between the contracting parties. The blockchain can make and perform a contract. One party creates a blockchain and stores its terms and conditions in a node. Anybody who is willing to make the contract just follows the instructions and accomplishes the required tasks on the blockchain. The stage of negotiation and formal grant of consent are ostensibly missing.

Contract automation also reduces human involvement in performance of a contract. For example, the use of contract automation allows for the processing of insurance claims. An insurance company can design a compensation claim programme on a blockchain, setting up the conditions for a claim, the documents to be submitted, and other requirements. The policyholder uploads all of the needed documents and satisfies the requirements; the programme then automatically calculates the amount of compensation payable and transfers the money directly to the policyholder's bank account. The contract is automatically executed.

The second feature of contract automation is immutability. A smart contract is simply a computer program. Once the required conditions have been created, nobody, even the party writing the programme can make modification by adding new conditions or by amending and deleting the existing conditions. A contract concluded via blockchain technology cannot be modified either unilaterally or bilaterally. In cases of systematic failure, such as hacking, a blockchain can be changed by agreement of the majority of participants (the so called hard fork). This is only be necessary in the rare cases where the integrity of the blockchain has been breached.

A more contract compatible approach would incorporate the characteristic of flexible immutability in the coding of a smart contract. This is accomplished by creating communication channels to information made available subsequent to the formation of the contract. The code would allow the blockchain to communicate with oracles, which could include input/output devices, sensors, connections to websites, or "Trusted

Intermediariesed Third Parties" (TTPs). Human oracles could also be used, such as an arbiter or a judge for the purpose of assessing damages. This essentially creates a modified blockchain in which a degree of decentralization is lost in order to break out of a completely immutable system through the use of oracles, which are centralized entities.

The third feature of the blockchain is inclusiveness. A conventional contract is exclusive in a legal sense that the contracting parties are normally identified prior to the formation of the contract, and the contract is only binding on those parties. In contrast, smart contracts are inclusive since the party creating the blockchain does not know the identity of the other party or parties. From a legal perspective, a smart contract can be viewed as a unilateral contract.[108] One party makes a unilateral offer, and an acceptance is effective when someone accomplishes the required tasks, thus creating a legally binding contract.

18.7 Observations

Technology is a transformative and disruptive force that brings both benefits and costs. From an economic perspective, new technologies can make old models of business obsolete. There are clearly winners and losers, but that is the essence of capitalism. If new technologies result in overall growth, then there is little society can or should do to prevent such innovation. From a legal perspective, law also serves as a cornerstone of the free market system. Contract law is the engine that allows or facilitates entrepreneurial enterprise. So, contract law and regulatory law will continue to facilitate the creation of wealth through technological innovation, but must also intervene when necessary to police the use of such technology, especially when it is used to commit crimes, fraud, or to take advantage of weaker parties. Smart contracts are here to stay because they provide greater efficiency to business transactions and offer potential solutions to existing legal and business problems. For example, smart contracts in funding significantly reduces transaction costs in matching entrepreneurs and investors.[109]

Smart contracts can make the law more efficient. For example, it has always been a thorny issue in common law jurisdictions whether the offeror to a unilateral contract can revoke the offer after the offeree has started to perform but before the completion of the performance. There is no clear answer to this question. The policy dilemma is obvious. If the law allows the offeror to withdraw the offer, the offeree's reliance interests are not properly protected. How should the law prevent the promisor from withdrawing a unilateral offer opportunistically? French courts and other civil law jurisdictions solve the problem under tort law, recognizing that a revocation is abusive if it frustrates the legitimate expectations of the offeree; thus, the offeror must compensate for damages

---

[108] Both in Acquis Communautaire and Acquis International the prevailing approach for understanding of contracts has been to place emphasis on exchange and reciprocity, leaving little space for unilateralism. See Bénédicte Fauvarque-Cosson & Denis Mazeaud (eds.), *European contract Law. Materials for a Common Frame of Reference: Terminology, Guiding Principles, Model Rules* (Munich: Sellier, 2008) at 5–11. The issue is probably more theoretical than practical. It is about knowing if an offeror is bound even without the acceptance of the offeror, for instance in case of an advertisement for a reward: *cf* for a discussion of the differences between the French and Dutch versus the English and German approaches see Jan M. Smits, *Contract Law. A Comparative Introduction* (Edward Elgar: Cheltenham/Northampton, 2014), 44–50. Compare also Samuel J. Stoljar, "The False Distinction between Bilateral and Unilateral Contracts" (1955) 64 *The Yale Law Journal* 515–36.

[109] See Jia Wang & Lei Chen, Chapter 10.

(costs and lost profits on foregone opportunities). This problem is solved by a smart contract in which revocation of an offer is impossible, at least in the short-term. If I make a promise through a smart contract, the promise will be embedded in the blockchain. The offeree would simply upload evidence to prove its completion of performance, thus triggering payment. The immutability feature of a smart contract can solve numerous issues such as opportunistic modification of a contract, the risk of payment, and the risk of breach of less complex contracts.

On the negative side, smart contracts pose many challenges. These challenges can be divided into two categories. The first category is the problem of unfitness in the existing legal framework – smart contracts do not fit nicely into the existing legal regime, or existing legal rules cannot provide satisfactory answers to the questions posed by this new use of technology. As mentioned above, in the area of contract interpretation, a smart contract is written in computer codes. How should these codes be interpreted? Do the traditional rules of interpretation (often used together or used in different types of contracts) – four-corner rule, contextual construction, purposive interpretation, and literal interpretation apply? Clearly, a formalistic interpretative approach is the best fit. This explains why smart contracts have so far been mainly used in formalistic types of transactions, such as funds or title transfers. But formalism is not a good fit in many types of transactions where meaning is relational or contextual in nature. Also, coded language is a technical language. Issues of errors in coding (input), improper translation of code to human language, and the problem of coding conceptual and vague contract terms present challenging issues for the drafting and interpretation of smart contracts. These issues may require the creation of new specialized rules in contract law.

The second category of challenges that smart contracts present relate to an assortment of risks. The first risk, as in the case of standard form contracts or contracts of adhesion, is the abuse of bargaining position. Smart contracts, whether in B2B or B2C transactions, are prone to one-sidedness when they are written by one party, who dictates the terms and conditions, without the need for negotiations and, therefore, no advanced agreement is then coded. The threat of gross one-sidedness, as in traditional form of contracting, is most acute in B2C smart contracts. The other party or parties only have the option of accepting on a take-it-or-leave-it basis. There is little chance for negotiation. This type of abuse is replicated in B2B contracts involving a large entity and a small or medium size enterprise (SME), where bargaining power and informational asymmetries are as severe as in B2C contracts.[110] Also smart contracts are often based on the use of big data,[111] where there is considerable risk of misuse.

Diana Wallis notes that in the near future policymakers will need to engage in a democratic debate on the role of technology in society and the dangers it presents to democratic institutions.[112] In essence, society is entering a paradigm shift and will need to be aware that technocracy can have negative societal effects. She concludes that a totally self-driving or self-sufficient private ordering will need to be safeguarded against

---

[110] See the EU recognition of B2SME status in the Proposal for a Regulation of the European Parliament and of the Council on a Common European Sales Law (CESL), COM/2011/0635 final 2011/0284 (COD). See also Amelia Fletcher, Antony Karatzas and Antje Kreutzmann-Gallasch, "Small Businesses as Consumers: Are They Sufficiently Well Protected?" (January 2014), available at http://competitionpolicy .ac.uk/documents/8158338/8264594/fsb+project_small_businesses_as-consumers.pdf/f1ed4da5-14cf-4b80-a1d8-ff76a0781def (accessed September 10, 2018).

[111] See above § 18.3.2.

[112] See Diana Wallis, Chapter 19.

for purposes of retaining the rule of law as societally determined. A private law outside the legal system based on automated performance and immutability may be a precursor of "dictatorial rule" and an extinguishment of the "rule of law" as currently understood.

18.8 Conclusion

Code is not law. It is used to program the architecture of new (social) objects, such as smart contracts placed on a blockchain. On the other hand, law is not *the* code. Both can be conceived as regulatory tools; however, law and codes operate through different modalities. Law will continue to reign supreme, but it should also use its force to require technology to self-regulate based upon fundamental principles. Smart Transactional Technologies (STTs) may have regulatory effects by design, which can modify human behavior. For example, as suggested by some scholars, a risk management approach to law would mandate "privacy by design"[113] to control the use and access to personal data; producers should be required to design their smart products and services according to privacy standards.

In more general terms, "law by design"[114] can allow a better allocation of risks, improve legal services delivery, through data analysis, smart assistance, and interactive customization; it can also incentivize access to justice by engaging and educating people about the law and to foster a culture of innovation inside legal service organizations. Law by design needs to be user-centeredness, which concerns the means of doing things, but also with how people use things and deal with systems. Human-centered design, using creative, collaborative methods to improve human experiences with technology can be as much a driver of innovation as technology. It can be a dynamic regulatory tool in the service of law. Regulators can learn from the best practices of producers and use design mind-sets and processes to better regulate and harness the technological revolution for the benefit of users and society in general.

Borrowing the metaphor from evolutionary biology, society, law, design, and technology are currently experiencing a period of exaptation,[115] where there is frequent borrowing of technology developed in one field and applied to a different field, or to solve an unrelated problem. Sometimes the initial transformation is accidental, but unexpectedly becomes extremely useful in solving problems in the borrowing field. Interdisciplinary research projects, in this case technology, design, and law, provide unique opportunities for generating new ideas that a single discipline is unlikely to produce. This type of synergy is needed to better understand the relationship between contract law and smart contracts, within the international legal environment. The high complexity of the issues involved cut across the fields of law, computer science, ethics, and technology. It manifests the urgency to turn future conversations on these questions into a "liquid

---

[113] See above § 18.3.2.
[114] On the expression "law by design" see Margaret Hagan, *Law by Design* (2017), e-book available at www .lawbydesign.co/en/home/. She wrote the book "to counteract the trend of talking about legal innovation *only* in terms of technology" (…) "It does not means design-driven approach is anti-technology." She advocates for a design-driven approach to legal innovation, with practical, agile, and user-centered methods to make the legal system clearer, more efficient, more usable. "A design-driven approach to innovation can center our work on real, lived human problems."
[115] See Stephen Gould and Elisabeth Vrba, "Exaptation: A Missing Term in the Science of Form," (1982) 8 *Paleobiology* 4–15; Steven Johnson, *Where Good Ideas Come From?* (Penguin Group: New York, 2010) at 153.

network,"[116] an interdisciplinary space expanding and generating a reliable flow of knowledge.

This randomizing environment where the above fields come into conflict requires balancing the benefits and costs of too much order and too much anarchy. The outcome of this conflict is likely to result in new forms of collaboration between private/public, soft/hard law, and theory/practice with attendant spillover effects.[117] Computer scientist Christopher Langton argues that technology produces an "edge of chaos"[118] that may help policymakers to address known and currently unknown issues related to blockchain and smart contracts. The most obvious issues to be dealt with include privacy and data protection, as well as consumer protection. Probably in the end, as technology advances and the use of oracles expands, the distinction between traditional and smart contracts will become less meaningful. There will be levels of smartness depending on the ability to code more complex contracts and the ability to align coding with real world contracts.

---

[116] Steven Johnson, cit. at 45.

[117] The term "spillover" captures the essential tendency to flow of information (from mind to mind) in a dense settlement (in a globalized world, with thousands of people who share a common civil culture). In dense networks, indeed, ideas have a natural propensity to get into circulation they spill over (with Internet the transmission costs of sharing ideas are radically reduce), and generate good ideas that make it easier to have other good ideas. Steven Johnson, cit., at 242–243.

[118] New configurations emerge from random connections: see Christopher Langton et al., "Life at the Edge of Chaos" (1992) 10 *Artificial Life II*, 41–91; Steven Johnson, cit., at 52.

19 Visions of Future

Smart Contracts, Blockchain, and Artificial Intelligence

Diana Wallis

19.1 Introduction

This concluding chapter examines the challenge of future technologies, like advanced Artificial Intelligence (AI) to the way society is structured and the role of democratic government as both legislator and as the guardian of the rule of law. The following sections place the development of the blockchain and advanced AI in the context of democratic institutions. It concludes that as important as the technologists are in developing self-enforcing, self-learning, and self-thinking technologies, equally important are the roles of elected lawmakers who will be required to manage the impact of these developments' on the process of democratic law-making.

19.2 Legislation and the Legislator

The most crucial perspective on the future of technology is that of the legislator tasked in a democracy with advancing the interests of citizens and society. This view sees law as legislation focused on issues relating to smart contracts, blockchain, and AI. Our governments through a democratic process will determine the future use of technology. Legislative law will be used in ordering our contractual dealings and determining the procedures applied to them in resolving our resultant disputes in state courts, which will then in turn continue the evolution of law. How governments choose, or perhaps do not choose to legislate around these issues will have profound consequences for future generations.

A foretaste of the consequences of not regulating appropriately is seen in the recent case of Facebook's misuse of personal data. This should be a warning that legislators and regulators need to possess foresight in anticipating problems when new technologies are created and applied. The acceleration of technology – blockchain, smart contracts, and AI – has made the stakes much higher. They represent a societal shift; how existing law applies to new technologies and whether new laws will be required will be the key to producing the most benefits to society, while diminishing the risks of harm. The possibility of real AI-driven robots in Westminster and other legislatures may be seen as a welcome relief from dysfunctional politicians. However, the reality is rather more complex perhaps offering exciting opportunities for improvement but also posing deep questions about the future functioning of democratic law-making. The sooner we start as a society discussing the issues now presented by advanced technologies, such as AI and superintelligence, the more it is likely that national and international legal systems can develop a holistic approach to the appropriate use and ethical safeguards related to such technologies.

Currently, it is unnerving to see the seeming insouciance about who should be regulating blockchain and similar developments. For example, the idea that we could somehow simply delegate this task to some or another international standards body is neither plausible nor appropriate. However appealing such a self-regulatory approach may be, especially given the current lack of trust in political decision-making, the enormous disruptive effect of these technologies require government led study and action. There is sometimes a tendency to refer to key actors interchangeably as politicians, policy-makers, regulators, or legislators, but these roles are different, and elected politicians as legislators sit at the very heart of our law-making and democratic processes. Thus, the future of how new technologies are used and integrated should ultimately be dependent on the decisions of these elected law-makers. It is important that governments fully and carefully articulate their policies for the new technologies that currently exist and those that are likely to exist in the future, such as advanced AI. It is the government's role to facilitate the development of advanced technologies and also to prohibit impermissible uses of those technologies.

19.2.1 Limits of Jurisdiction

It is perhaps instructive to start by considering the nature of the legislative process, which is most likely to impinge on blockchain activities and the development of AI. The first thing to be appreciated is that blockchain activities and many aspects of AI will occur via the borderless medium of the web. That is part of their attraction; they cross and transcend national boundaries. Of course at the same time this provides challenges to national legislators and regulators. An immediate issue to be determined is the jurisdictional location of the various actors or parties in relation to the transactions they are undertaking. This issue might normally be dealt with by rules of private international law; other aspects may not be so easily solvable and may require some form of international or transnational regulation. Any national or state legislation acting alone is likely to face challenges in bringing forward effective answers. Any effective solution will likely be found in new international conventions, and in the European Union (EU) through new EU legislation.

19.3 Law as Reactive

In addition to the transnational nature of legislation is the phenomenon that lawmakers and law are nearly always running behind the curve of real-world developments, playing catch-up after the advent of new technology. Nowhere is this more obvious than in the area of the use of new media in communications and advertising or propaganda, especially if we trace the growth of the advertising and marketing industries and how these now combined with the tech giants are able to use our data. The legislator has never really had the upper hand running after those who have been manipulating an unsuspecting public since the days of the original snake oil sales man Clark Stanley and his outrageous but believed claims for his liniment. This game of running behind developments continued through the early use of newspaper advertising and into radio and TV and now in alarmingly ways into the Internet and e-commerce. This history is well and frighteningly documented by Tim Wu in his book *The Attention Merchants*.[1] Recent examples include the use of personal data by Facebook and Cambridge Analytica, which shows the need to be better prepared and more aware of the interface between these actors, their methods, and the integrity of our political and democratic institutions.

19.4 Flight from Law

Another part of the legislative challenge, which now confronts us, is 'the flight from the law'; that is 'law' as represented by national or EU made black letter legislation and regulation. The blockchain has the potential (to some extent) to take those who use it beyond and outside of the traditional state legal systems and their 'real-world' regulation and enforcement of contracts. This 'flight from law' maybe an active and purposeful choice by some. The same philosophy attended the early days of the Internet and e-commerce; seeing it as a place to exercise freedom without regulation. This phenomenon can be viewed as an odd alignment between freedom-seeking individuals or movements, recently referred to as 'crypto-anarchists'[2] and ultra-capitalists, which include big tech companies wishing to escape regulation. These groups are a mixture of strange ideological bedfellows, with a compelling and outsized influence on many legislatures.

19.4.1 *Lessons from History: E-Commerce Directive, Brussels I, and Rome II*

As an elected member of the European Parliament and sitting on the JURI[3] committee during the years 1999–2012, I saw first-hand the legislative problems as the EU Parliament tried to grapple with various legislative proposals which impinged on or tried to regulate the Internet and e-commerce. Amongst some there was the view that the Internet was like the Wild West, where eventually the sheriffs would to turn up; however, in the early days there was a reticence to intervene.

A number of examples show the difficult relationship between the creation of new technologies and the regulatory response. First, around 2000 two pieces of legislation were making their way through the EU legislative process; the ground-breaking E-commerce Directive and the Brussels I Regulation on Jurisdiction and Judgements.[4] This latter was considered to be a 'europeanisation' of the old Brussels Convention,[5] which had been successfully in operation for some years. The problem was that the new directive worked on the so-called COP, or 'country of origin' principle, which put simply meant that Internet traders and businesses should expect to be 'regulated' only in their 'country of origin'. This type of certainty was though to be needed to obtain the full

---

[1] Tim, Wu, 'The Attention Merchants: The Epic Struggle to get Inside our Heads' (2016) *Atlantic Magazine*.
[2] Jamie, Bartlett *The People Vs Tech: How the Internet Is Killing Democracy*.
[3] JURI is the shortened name used to refer to the European Parliament Committee on Legal Affairs, up until 2004, the Committee on Legal Affairs and the Internal Market.
[4] Regulation (EC) 44/2001 on jurisdiction and the recognition and enforcement of judgements in civil and commercial matters (Brussels 1 Regulation), which was essentially the 'europeanisation' of the old Brussels Convention, which had been successfully in operation for years (Brussels I Brussels Convention on Jurisdiction and the Enforcement of Judgements in Civil and Commercial Matters 1968).
[5] Brussels Convention on Jurisdiction and the Enforcement of Judgements in Civil and Commercial Matters of 1968.

benefits of the Internet, which would otherwise be endangered if they were subject to a plethora of potentially differing national laws as their activities inevitably crossed national boundaries. However, to some interest groups (free marketeers, small 'l' liberals and Internet libertarians) these new laws were seen as setting a collision course with the traditional rules of private international law contained in the original Brussels Convention. The Convention, now the Regulation, provides rules for determining which courts should have jurisdiction in the event of a dispute with 'international' elements. The battle lines were drawn most starkly in the area of consumer rights. The key question was whether a consumer buying from 'a foreign' website is obliged to file suit in the business's home courts? The ECJ in *Oceano Grupo Editorial SA v Quintero*[6] answered the question in the 'real'-world context, determining that consumers have the right to seek protection in their own courts if sued and by inference have the option to sue in their home courts.

Conversely, the e-commerce lobby advocated turning the country of origin rule into a rule of private international law. The final passage of the Brussels I Regulation resulted only after many contentious debates among different factions. Those who wanted to 'liberate' the Internet were all too often unwilling to balance this liberty with the rights of weaker parties such as consumers, by taking a very dogmatic and ultra-libertarian view. In the end however, the consumer friendly rules were adopted.

The Brussels I process was merely a foretaste of what was to follow with the Rome II Regulation.[7] Rome II represented a completely new private international law regulation dealing with the law applicable to non-contractual relations or tort. Amongst such torts is defamation or violation of personality rights. Here the Internet community and publishers were in full attack mode, some seeing such proposals as a threat to their new free space, where absolute freedom of expression had finally been realised. Traditional publishers who had moved online saw themselves potentially being exposed to all types of 'privacy' litigation, which they alleged would have a 'chilling effect' on publishing and undermine fair commentary on matters of public interest. Tech companies and Internet providers were unwilling to undertake editorial responsibility for the content placed on their systems. Again in balancing rights the cases of ordinary individuals that are, defamed, trolled, and hunted on the Internet were obscured and lost. The furore was such that eventually in an unprecedented move the European Commission completely withdrew the part of the proposal dealing with provider and services companies' responsibility from the regulation. However, now due to recent cases of misuse, Facebook and Twitter have gradually been forced to take responsibility for the content they carry.

These earlier examples demonstrate the slowness of enacting it takes for traditional legislation in response to the development of new technologies. Another example is found in the reticence of the EU to regulate the platform economy on the basis of not wanting to stifle innovation and growth. This may be the correct approach, but the development of the blockchain and AI offers greater opportunities to those who prefer a 'flight from the law'. They represent real challenges for the rule of law and the concept of the democratic state, as we know it.

---

[6] *Oceano Grupo Editorial SA v Quintero* (C-240/98).
[7] Regulation (EC) 864/2007 on the law applicable to non-contractual obligations (Rome II).

19.5 Digital Paradigms

David Harvey has analysed the challenge that the new digital paradigm poses to law and rule-making.[8] Whilst recognising the flight from the law or what he and others describe in various contexts as 'Internet exceptionalism', he describes a clash of paradigms, one pre-digital and one digital. He urges as a starting point the greater concentration on the medium of communication rather than the communication itself. He equates this with the shift from a 'scribal' or manuscript-based culture to one driven by the invention of the printing press in early modern times.[9] By highlighting the method of communication, he demonstrates that reliance on previous forms of reasoning to arrive at legislative outcomes may not be appropriate in the digital age. For example, the use of such tools as 'functional equivalence' or 'analogy' between pre-digital and digital is not as helpful as it may seem. Likewise, he predicts a difficult future for the common law's reliance on precedent, which is perhaps more likely to be overtaken by data analytics.

Harvey's thought-provoking analysis should make legislators and scholars consider the very basics, such as what is a contract in the world of the blockchain, robots, and AI; put simply, the old paradigm of using lawyers to write documents to provide evidence in writing, 'signed' by the parties, is no longer sufficient. E-signature and attribution have already made the written form and traditional signature less important.

The other aspect of the digital paradigm relates to the use of information, information persistence, information overload, and the democratic erosion caused by the idea of fake news (reducing discourse to everyone being entitled to their own facts). The quantity of information we now have to deal with as human beings induces both psychological and societal effects, the results of which we are still working through. One result of immediate access to almost unlimited amounts of information, not all that are fact based is a decline in trust for traditional institutions and news sources. Nowhere has this problem been more acute than in relation to politics, where this phenomenon threatens to undermine the democratic process such that our trust in the work of democratically elected politicians as legislators is called into question. Everyone's motives are subject to examination and question, but none more than those of the politician. In this atmosphere, there is a danger not only of 'flight from the law' but also to look for answers not through the political process but, instead, to seek a technocratic answer or deferring to AI to provide an answer. There is a growing inclination to seek trust in something completely neutral and immutable. It is interesting to see that when the French government recently decided to update the Civil Code, a code having such a central place, indeed almost constitutional standing in French law, a conscious decision was made to keep the technical aspects of issues away from the French Parliament.[10] This can be seen as an abdication to external 'neutral' legal mechanisms. If so, care should be taken that it does not mark the start of a slippery slope away from democratic input. By contrast, any such removal of a technical legal subject area like that of a European contract law would have met with strong resistance from democratically elected politicians and

---

[8] David, Harvey. *Collisions in the Digital Paradigm Law and Rule Making in the Internet Age* (Oxford: Hart Publishing 2017).

[9] See also, Elizabeth Eisenstein, *The Printing Press as an Agent of Change* (New York: Cambridge University Press 1979).

[10] Bénédicte Fauvarque-Co sson, *The French Contract Law Reform and the Political Process*, 13 (4) *European Review of Contract Law*(2017).

legislators in the European Parliament. It is important that parliamentarians and voters keep their eyes wide open to the increased use of digital technology or AI in the legislative process.

Into this context of distrust – distrust of politicians, distrust of institutions, and the distrust and denigration of experts[11] – comes the discussion of a depoliticised, unbiased, 'self- driving law'. A world where AI replaces adjudicators by 'self-driving law' is one also free of the reach of regulators and legislators. This is the prospect raised in Anthony J. Casey and Anthony Niblett's 2017 article *The Death of Rules and Standards*.[12] The future scenarios which they describe follow the analysis of David Harvey, discussed above, that society is facing a paradigm shift that presents a challenge to law and its legal and political structures. This challenge should focus the nature of legislation and the goals of law-making as we know it. Self-driving law merits closer examination in relation to the paths we might take as a society.

The continued development and refinement of deep-learning AI needs to be guided by a deliberative political process, to determine how fast and how far such technology should go. If we wish to be able to use AI for law-making, the 'law-maker' (through AI) will need data, lots of data about how we behave and react. To achieve the full usefulness of AI – to make a medical prognosis or to operate driverless cars – it needs to be able to learn. To attain the best legislative results will necessitate data collection on a gargantuan scale about how we behave in many and various scenarios. In the consumer sector, consumers have perhaps been too relaxed about giving over their data in return for goods and services. Should we be relaxed about such information being collected by the state for the purposes of legislative activity? Many of the main developments in this field currently come from the private commercial sector; are we sure we have sufficient safeguards in place? One plausible outcome is where legislators not only 'make' the law by using AI but they can also automatically enforce the law through the use of advanced predictive and communication technologies. Notice needs to be taken of the accelerated pace of technological development; we need to consider how traffic light phasing can already be remotely controlled by AI to reduce congestion caused by traffic flows, to appreciate that we are not so far away from many other such developments.

The core questions relating to technological advancement revolve on proper governance of the numerous issues presented here. Some argue that in this borderless virtual new world there is inspiration to be gained from 'internet' governance; however, given that this does not seem to have been unproblematic, especially in terms of foresight as to how things might evolve and that arguably the challenge this time around is even greater, something more robust is needed. To be fair, the EU in its various institutions, but especially the Parliament, has begun to rise to the challenge. As early as 2015, the Parliament's Legal Affairs Committee (JURI) produced a detailed 'own initiative' Report on Robotics.[13] The committee can also no doubt take credit for finally pushing

---

[11] See for example, Helen Jackson, Paul Ormerod, *Was Michael Gove right? Have We Had Enough of Experts?*, Prospect Magazine (August 2017).

[12] Anthony J. Casey; Anthony Niblett, *The Death of Rules and Standards*, 92 Ind. L.J. 1401 (2017).

[13] REPORT with recommendations to the Commission on Civil Law Rules on Robotics (2015/2103(INL)) Committee on Legal Affairs Rapporteur: Mady Delvaux

the European Commission to establish a 'High Level Expert Group on AI' announced in June 2018.[14]

The dangers presented by evolving technology require the conclusion that we need some sort of framework for the future, above all perhaps an ethical framework for how law-making and legislative activity might proceed in this new age to ensure societal values are preserved. We need to envision how the rule of law will fit into the new robotic age and implement checks and balances on technological development to ensure the 'constitutionality' of borderless and stateless law and governance.

There are two ways things might generally progress and two alternative sets of implications. On the one hand, taken to the extreme are science fiction scenarios, like those presented in the Westworld TV series where robots take over the world. If we travel along that road, there are perhaps various possibilities that might arrest such a bad outcome. Decisions made by AI through algorithmic decision-making undermine individual autonomy. It is this autonomy that has been central to contract law in modern liberal democracies; party autonomy, for better or worse, is highly prized in the English common law system. Therefore, there needs to be a democratic debate on whether automated contracting and enforcement should be regulated through a risk-controlled approach.

If automation and self-enforcing contracts eliminate the need to think about right or wrong ways to proceed in our relations, human beings will suffer psychologically from a form of moral atrophy, bereft of our sense of what is appropriate conduct. This problem has been referred to as the law becoming 'command' rather than 'counsel'. Alternatively, there are virtues in certainty (automation) and flexibility (adjustability). In the drafting of the Rome II Regulation, the Commission and many civilian scholars and lawyers argued in favour of general rule, along with a catalogue of exceptions. The common law representatives argued for a flexible general rule but with few exceptions. Symeon Symeonides pointed to the experience in the United States, where flexible rules allowed judges to look at individual circumstances in order to do justice, resulting in a lower appeal rate.[15] AI might inform or predict trial outcomes; nonetheless, there remains a very human need to tell one's story in court, rightly reflected in the procedural right to be heard. A fast-and-cheap AI-determined outcome may be the right approach in certain cases; however, a more human approach is needed in other types of cases. In brief, society and law will need to decide when to use and how to regulate the new technological tools at its disposal.

The task of the law-maker is to determine when technological change can be used within the law-making system to positive effect. This would entail the adoption of a body of law that is precise, consisting of tailored rules directed at achieving the wished for legislative outcomes. In order to bring greater clarity and legal certainty, the law-making process (legislative and judicial) should become more transparent so that 'good robots' remain tools in human hands to enhance justice delivered by the law. To this end, instead of simply guarding against unwanted outcomes, a more proactive approach is needed in anticipation of technological development such as advanced AI. The debate needs to

---

[14] More details at https://ec.europa.eu/digital-single-market/en/high-level-expert-group-artificial-intelligence (accessed June 12, 2019).

[15] Whilst published subsequently, some of these ideas are set out at Chapter 4 of Symeon Symeonides, *Codifying Choice of Law around the World* (New York: Oxford University Press 2014).

begin now in order to have a plan in place. The EU has taken preliminary steps in this direction. However, a wider public discussion is needed about the future of these technological developments and their impact on our law-making process in order to preserve the integrity of democracy and the political-legal system, and the values they reflect.

For EU product safety concerns, contact us at Calle de José Abascal, 56–1°,
28003 Madrid, Spain or eugpsr@cambridge.org.

www.ingramcontent.com/pod-product-compliance
Ingram Content Group UK Ltd.
Pitfield, Milton Keynes, MK11 3LW, UK
UKHW030903150625
459647UK00022B/2841